ALSO BY DONALD RAYFIELD

Chekhov:
The Evolution of His Art (1975)

The Dream of Lhasa:
The Life of Nikolay Przhevalsky,
Explorer of Central Asia (1976)

INTRODUCTION AND TRANSLATIONS:
Vaza Psavela, *Three Poems* (1981)

TRANSLATED AND EDITED:
Anon., *The Confessions of Victor X* (1984)

The Cherry Orchard:
Catastrophe and Comedy (1994)

The Literature of Georgia—A History (1994)

The Chekhov Omnibus:
Selected Stories (1994)

Chekhov's Uncle Vanya *and*
the Wood Demon: *Critical Study* (1995)

ANTON CHEKHOV

ANTON CHEKHOV

A Life

DONALD RAYFIELD

HENRY HOLT AND COMPANY
NEW YORK

Henry Holt and Company, Inc.
Publishers since 1866
115 West 18th Street
New York, New York 10011

Henry Holt® is a registered trademark of
Henry Holt and Company, Inc.

LIBRARY OF CONGRESS CATALOGING-IN-PUBLICATION DATA
Rayfield, Donald, date.
Anton Chekhov: a life / Donald Rayfield.
p.   cm.
Includes bibliographical references and index.
ISBN 0-8050-5747-1 (hardbound: alk. paper)
1. Chekhov, Anton Pavlovich, 1860–1904—Biography.   2. Authors,
Russian—19th century—Biography. I. Title.
PG3458.R35   1998   97-28888
891.72'3—dc21   CIP
[B]

First published in Great Britain in 1997 by
HarperCollins*Publishers*

First American Edition 1998

Printed in the United States of America
All first editions are printed on acid-free paper. ∞

1 3 5 7 9 10 8 6 4 2

For Alia, Galia, Maia and Tolia

CONTENTS

PART III
My Brothers' Keeper:
1886–9

PART IV
Années de Pèlerinage:
1889–92

PART V
Cincinnatus:
1892–4

PART IX

Three Triumphs:
1898–1901

PART X

Love and Death:
1901–4

ILLUSTRATIONS

PREFACE

Anton once told me, 'In time all my things must see the light of day and I have no reason to be ashamed of them.'
Bykov to Maria Chekhova, 7 April 1910 (*LN87*, 356)

We recognize Anton Chekhov today as a founding father of the modern theatre, where the author, not the actor, is king. We acknowledge him as the author who gave Europe's narrative fiction a new ambiguity, density and subtle poetry. Of all the Russian 'classics' he is, to non-Russians especially, the most approachable and the least alien, whether on the stage or the printed page. He lets his reader and spectator react as they wish, draw their own conclusions. He imposes no philosophy. Chekhov's approachability is inseparable from his elusiveness. It is very hard to say what he 'meant', when he so rarely judges or expounds. From Tolstoy's or Dostoevsky's fiction we can reconstruct a philosophy and a life. From Chekhov's work, and from his many letters, we get only fleeting and contradictory glimpses of his inner world and experience. His many biographers have tried to build out of the evidence a consensual life of a saint – a man who in a life shortened by chronic illness pulled himself from poverty to gentility, became a doctor and tended to the oppressed, won fame as the leading prose-writer and dramatist of his time in Europe, was supported all his life by an adoring sister and, though too late, found happiness in marriage with the actress who interpreted him best.

All biography is fiction, but fiction that has to fit the documented facts. This life of Chekhov tries to encompass rather more than has been documented before. The picture of Chekhov is now more complex. If, however, the man that emerges is less of a saint, less in command of his fate than we have hitherto seen him, he is as much a genius and no less admirable. His life should not be seen as an adjunct to his writing: it was a source of experience that fed his fiction. It is, above all, a life enthralling for its own sake. Anton Chekhov suffered the irreconcilable demands of an artist with responsibilities to his art as well as to his family and friends. His life has many meanings: we read into it the story of a disease, a modern version of the Biblical 'Joseph and his Brothers', or even the tragedy of Don Juan. Chekhov's life could be a novel by Thomas Mann about the unbridgeable gap between being an artist and a citizen. It also exemplifies the predicaments of a sensitive and talented Russian intellectual at the end of the nineteenth century – one of the richest and most contradictory periods in Russia's political and cultural history.

Few writers guarded their privacy from the public eye as assiduously as Chekhov. Yet no writer so carefully preserved and filed every scrap of paper – letters, bills, certificates – connected with him and his family. Nor did his proclaimed 'autobiographophobia' prevent him from sorting out the year's letters into cartons every Christmas.

There are many biographies available – some comprehensive, such as E. J. Simmons's or Ronald Hingley's, some flamboyant, such as Henri Troyat's, some finely judged, such as Mikhail Gromov's or V. S. Pritchett's. Russian or not, they all use the same range of printed sources. Nearly five thousand letters written by Anton Chekhov have been published, but several have been severely bowdlerized. (The import of another fifteen hundred letters, now lost, can be inferred from the replies.) These sources, notably the complete works and letters in thirty-one volumes published in Moscow between 1973 and 1983, have a remarkably full and intelligent scholarly apparatus, all of which provides biographers with an enormous range and quantity of material.

The untapped sources are just as vast. In the archives, principally the Manuscript Department of the Russian State Library (once the Rumiantsev Museum, then the Lenin Library), there are some seven thousand letters addressed to Anton Chekhov. Perhaps half of the letters in the archive have never been referred to in print, primarily letters that reflect Chekhov's private life. Moreover, in various archives (notably the Russian (formerly Central) State Archives for Literature and Art, the theatrical museum archives in Petersburg and Moscow, the Chekhov museums in Taganrog, Melikhovo and Sumy) there is a mass of documentary and pictorial material, letters of contemporaries which shed light on Chekhov's life as a writer and a man. Archival records show that a small circle of Russian scholars have over the last thirty years combed these sources thoroughly, yet their published work, detailed in the bibliography of this book, uses only a fraction of these sources. A Russian and Soviet tradition of not 'discrediting or vulgarizing' (the phrase comes from a 1968 Central Committee resolution forbidding publication of certain passages) has even today made Russian scholars hesitant about bringing the full range and depth of the Chekhov archives into the public domain. Three years' work systematically searching, transcribing and mulling over the documentation has convinced me that nothing in these archives either discredits or vulgarizes Chekhov. Quite the opposite: the complexity, selflessness and depth of the man become even clearer when we fully account for his human strengths and failings.

Chekhov's life was short, but neither sweet nor simple. He had an extraordinary number of acquaintances and liaisons (though few true friends and lovers). He moved in many orbits – he had dealings with teachers, doctors, tycoons, merchants, peasants, bohemians, hacks, intellectuals, artists, academics, landowners, officials, actresses and actors, priests, monks, with officers, convicts, whores, foreigners and landowners. He got on well with people of every class and condition, except the nobility and court. He lived for virtually all his life with his parents and sister, and much of the time with one or more of his brothers as well, not to mention a network of aunts and cousins. He was restless: he had countless addresses and travelled widely from Hong Kong to Biarritz, from Sakhalin to Odessa. To write a full biography would take a lifetime longer than Chekhov's own. I have concentrated on his relationships with family and friends, but there is a sense in which his life is also a *historia morbi*. Tuberculosis shapes it and ends it: his efforts to ignore and to cope with disease form the weft of any biography. There are many works in English offering a critical study of his work. If we read about Chekhov, it is primarily because he is a writer of very great importance. Any good bookshop or library offers a number of critical studies to enrich the reader's understanding of Chekhov's work. In this biography, however, his stories and plays are discussed inasmuch as they emerge from his life and as they affect it, but less as material for critical analysis. Biography is not criticism.

Not all the mysteries in Chekhov's life can be solved, and much evidence is missing: Chekhov's letters to his fiancée Dunia Efros, to Elena Pleshcheeva, to Emilie Bijon almost certainly exist in private hands in the West. It is equally possible that the hundreds of letters that Suvorin wrote to Chekhov are mouldering in an archive in Belgrade: their discovery would force Chekhov's life, and (because of what Suvorin knew and confided to Anton) Russian history, to be rewritten. A few archival items have also proved difficult to trace, for example most of Chekhov's student exercises in medicine. Nevertheless, the material that is now available enables a much fuller portrait of Chekhov and his times than ever before.

D. R.
Queen Mary & Westfield College, London
February 1997

ACKNOWLEDGEMENTS

My warmest thanks go to Alevtina Kuzicheva. Without her assistance my work in the Otdel rukopisei (The Manuscript Department) of the Russian State Library and RGALI (Russian State Archives for Literature and Art) would have been more trammelled, and through her I had introductions to every major Chekhovian scholar and museum in Russia and the Ukraine. I want to thank the staff at the Russian State Library and the Manuscript Department who, despite the demoralizing conditions, a dilapidated building and grim prospects, managed to deliver most of what I sought; the same applies to the staff at RGALI. I am grateful to Galina Shchiobeleva of the Moscow Chekhov Museum, and to Igor Skvortsov of the Sumy Chekhov Museum for allowing me so much access. To Liza Shapochka and her husband Vladimir Protasov of Taganrog I owe a special debt for their hospitality and consultations. Olga Makarova of Voronezh University Press has been very helpful in providing local material. Among my Western colleagues, Professor Rolf-Dieter Kluge, the energetic organizer of the Badenweiler conferences of 1985 and 1995, has been a great stimulus. I want to thank Dmitri Konovalov of Ufa for lending me his manuscript notes on the Andreev sanatorium, as well as for his hospitality. (None of these experts, or anybody else I have consulted, bears any responsibility for my judgments or approach.)

I also thank the doctor in charge of the hospital that was once Bogimovo and the staff at the Andreev sanatorium at Aksionovo. Apart from Siberia, Sakhalin and Hong Kong, I feel I have stood and sat, and have been a minor or major nuisance, in almost every place that bears Chekhov's imprint. Descendants of Chekhov's friends, for instance M. Patrice Bijon, have been most tolerant of my search for material. Countless people will be grateful that the work is finished. Thanks and acknowledgements for illustrations to the Bakhrushin Theatre Museum (Moscow), to the Chekhov Museums in Melikhovo, Moscow, Sumy, Taganrog and Yalta, to the Pushkinski Dom (St Petersburg), and to the Russian State Library.

This book owes much to British Academy support: notably a three-month humanities research fellowship, which extended my sabbatical leave long enough to make headway. To my colleagues at Queen Mary and Westfield College, who had to put up with frequent dereliction of duty, I proffer my apologies.

ABBREVIATIONS AND REFERENCES

This book is meant for the general reader, but for specialists I have given sources for quotations and new information. References are given to archive sources and less accessible publications: Chekhov's letters and the best-known memoirs (see Select Bibliography) are well indexed, and the reader can check these sources without additional reference. All translations into English are my own. In footnotes I have used a few abbreviations (the place of publication is Moscow, unless otherwise indicated):

MXaT	Moscow Arts Theatre Museum Archive
OR	Manuscript Department of Russian State Library (*otdel rukopisei*)
RGALI	Russian State Archives for Literature and Art
PSSP	A. P. Chekhov *Polnoe sobranie sochinenii i pisem:* 1–18, works (referred to as *I–XVIII*); 1–12 (+ indices), letters (referred to as *1–12*), 1973–83.
Gitovich *Letopis'*	N. I. Gitovich *Letopis' zhizni i tvorchestva A. P. Chekhova*, 1955
Pis'ma 1939	I. S. Ezhov *Pis'ma A. P. Chekhovu ego brata Aleksandra Pavlovicha*, 1939
Pis'ma 1954	M. P. Chekhova *Pis'ma k bratu A. P. Chekhovu*, 1954
Perepiska 1934, 1936	A. P. Derman, *Perepiska A. P. Chekhova i O. L. Knipper*, 1934, 1936
Knipper-Chekhova 1972	V. Ia. Vilenkin, *Olga Leonardovna Knipper-Chekhova*, 1972
Levitan *Pis'ma* 1956	A. Fiodorov-Davydov, A. Shapiro *I. I. Levitan: Pis'ma, dokumenty, vospominaniia*, 1956

Perepiska I, II, 1984	M. P. Gromova et al. *Perepiska A. P. Chekhova*, 1984, 2 vols. (Expanded 1996, 3 vols.)
Letopisets	A. P. Kuzicheva, E. M. Sakharova *Melikhovskii letopisets: Dnevnik P. E. Chekhova*, 1995
O semie 1970	Sergei Mikhailovich Chekhov, *O semie* Iaroslavl, 1970
Vokrug Chekhova	*Vokrug Chekhova* (comp. E. M. Sakharova), 1990
V vospominaniiakh	*Chekhov v vospominaniiakh sovremennikov* (comp. N. I. Gitovich), 1986
LN68	*Literaturnoe nasledstvo 68: Chekhov* (ed. V. V. Vinogradov), 1960
LN87	*Literaturnoe nasledstvo 87: Iz istorii russkoi literatury* . . . (ed V. R. Shcherbina), 1977

A NOTE ON TRANSLITERATION

Transliteration from Russian is standard British, except that I use *i* for both и and й. I also transcribe Russian *e* as *e*, although initially and after a vowel it is pronounced *ye*. Russian surnames of transparently French or German origin are given in more familiar forms, thus Бонье, Шехтепь are rendered *Beaunier, Schechtel*, not *Bonie, Shekhtel'*. Tchaikovsky is spelt traditionally; so is Chaliapin. Russian female names are given feminine form: Chekhova, Ternovskaia. Crimean Tatar names are given Turkish spellings. I have taken liberties with Russian first names. Patronymics (the middle names ending in *-ovich, -ovna*, etc.) have been omitted except where needed; I have reduced the varied forms of Christian names, whose choice depends on degree of acquaintance, intimacy, mood, to the minimum: for example, it may not be clear to an English reader that Maria, Mariushka, Marusia, Mania, Mosia and Masha are all the same person. In the case of Chekhov's siblings, I hope I may be forgiven for referring to Maria Pavlovna Chekhova as Masha, Nikolai Pavlovich as Kolia, Ivan Pavlovich as Vania, Mikhail Pavlovich as Misha; as there are other Sashas in Chekhov's life, Aleksandr Pavlovich Chekhov remains Aleksandr. In the interests of clarity, I use the better known pseudonyms of some persons (Gruzinsky for Lazarev, Andreeva for Andreeva-Zheliabuzhskaia, etc.). The index should resolve any ambiguities. Dates are given by the Russian (Julian) calendar, twelve days behind Europe until 12 March 1900, then thirteen days behind. All dates are Russian, except when the action takes place abroad when both dates are given. Russian temperatures in Réaumur have been converted to centigrade.

EGOR Chekhov = **EFROSINIA** Shimko
1798–1879 | 1798–1878

Mikhail (Chokhov) = Elizaveta
1821–75 | 1826–86

Aleksandra = Vasili Kozhevnikov
1831–1908 | 1819–1904

Anastasia Natalia Vasili Vera Maria Grigori Olga Mikhail
1849– 1855– 1859– ? ? ? ? –before 18

Ekaterina Mikhail Aleksandra Grigori Elizaveta Klavdia
1846–1930 1851–1909 1853–1935 1857–1934 1858–84 1863–1920

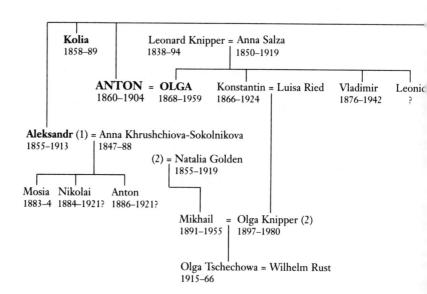

Kolia
1858–89

Leonard Knipper = Anna Salza
1838–94 | 1850–1919

ANTON = **OLGA** Konstantin = Luisa Ried Vladimir Leonid
1860–1904 1868–1959 1866–1924 1876–1942 ?

Aleksandr (1) = Anna Khrushchiova-Sokolnikova
1855–1913 | 1847–88

(2) = Natalia Golden
1855–1919

Mosia Nikolai Anton
1883–4 1884–1921? 1886–1921?

Mikhail = Olga Knipper (2)
1891–1955 | 1897–1980

Olga Tschechowa = Wilhelm Rust
1915–66

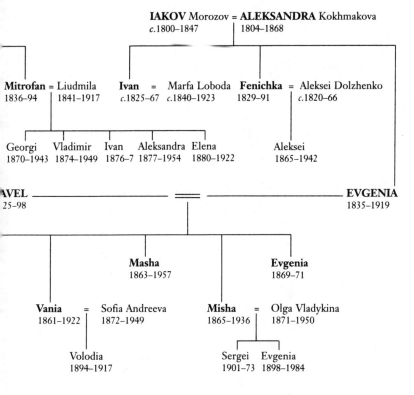

IAKOV Morozov = **ALEKSANDRA** Kokhmakova
*c.*1800–1847 | 1804–1868

Mitrofan = Liudmila   **Ivan** = Marfa Loboda   **Fenichka** = Aleksei Dolzhenko
1836–94 | 1841–1917   *c.*1825–67   *c.*1840–1923   1829–91 | *c.*1820–66

Georgi   Vladimir   Ivan   Aleksandra   Elena   Aleksei
1870–1943   1874–1949   1876–7   1877–1954   1880–1922   1865–1942

AVEL ————————————— ⚌ ————————————— **EVGENIA**
25–98   1835–1919

Masha   **Evgenia**
1863–1957   1869–71

Vania = Sofia Andreeva   **Misha** = Olga Vladykina
1861–1922 | 1872–1949   1865–1936 | 1871–1950

Volodia   Sergei   Evgenia
1894–1917   1901–73   1898–1984

The Chekhov Family Tree

Chekhov's Russia

Chekhov's Moscow
& its Surroundings

IAROSLAVL

To Tver and
Petersburg

Klin

St Sergei
Monastery

Babkino 1883-7
Voskresensk
New Jerusalem
Zvenigorod

Liubimovka 1902

MOSCOW

1883-5
PODOLSK
Nara 1903

Tsaritsyno

R Moscow

Meshcherskoe

Ugriumovo
Lopasnia   Vaskino
Melikhovo 1892-9
Talezh
SERPUKHOV   Kriukovo

R Oka

Bogimovo
1891
KALUGA
Aleksin

R Oka

TULA

Iasnaia
Poliana

To Kharkov, Crimea
and Taganrog

0   25   50   100 km

0   25   50 miles

I

Father to the Man

We could hear screams coming from the dining room ... and knew that poor Ernest was being beaten.

'I have sent him up to bed,' said Theobald, as he returned to the drawing room, 'and now, Christina, I think we will have the servants in to prayers."

Samuel Butler, *The Way of All Flesh*

ONE

Forefathers
1762–1860

Who would have thought that such genius could come from an earth closet!

ANTON CHEKHOV and his eldest brother Aleksandr were bewildered: in two generations the Chekhovs had risen from peasantry to metropolitan intelligentsia. Little in Anton Chekhov's forebears hints at his gifts for language, or foretells the artistic talents of his brother Nikolai or the polymath versatility of his eldest brother Aleksandr. The key to Chekhov's character, his gentleness and his toughness, his eloquence and his laconicism, his stoical resolution, is hidden in the genes he inherited as well as in his upbringing.

Chekhov's great-grandfather, Mikhail Chekhov (1762–1849), was a serf all his life. He ruled five sons sternly: even as adults, they called him *Panochi*, Lord Father. The first Chekhov of whom we know more is Mikhail's second son and Anton Chekhov's paternal grandfather, Egor Mikhailovich Chekhov. As a child Chekhov met him on a few summer holidays. There was no affection between them.[1] Grandfather Egor fought his way out of bondage. He was born in 1798, a serf of Count Chertkov at Olkhovatka in Voronezh province, the heart of Russia, where forests meet steppes, half way between Moscow and the Black Sea. (Chekhovs are traceable in this region to the sixteenth century.) Egor, alone of his kin, could read and write.

Egor made sugar from beet and fattened cattle on the pulp. Driving Count Chertkov's cattle to market, he shared the profits. Through luck, ruthlessness and thirty years' hard work, Egor accumulated 875 roubles.[2] In 1841 he offered his money to Chertkov to buy himself, his wife and his three sons out of serfdom into the next class of Russian citizens, the petit-bourgeoisie (*meshchane*). Chertkov was generous; he freed Egor's daughter Aleksandra too. Egor's parents and brothers remained serfs.

3

Egor took his family 300 miles south to the new steppe lands, tamed after centuries of occupation by nomadic Turkic tribes. Land was being sold to veterans of the Napoleonic wars and to German immigrants. Here Egor became estate manager to Count Platov at Krepkaia (Strong-point), forty miles north of Taganrog on the Sea of Azov. He pushed his three sons onto the next rung in Russia's social ladder, the merchant class, by apprenticing them. The eldest, Mikhail (born 1821) went to Kaluga, 150 miles southwest of Moscow, to be a bookbinder. The second, Anton Chekhov's father, Pavel, born 1825 and now sixteen, worked in a sugar-beet factory, then for a cattle drover, and finally as a merchant's shop boy in Taganrog. The youngest son, Mitrofan, became a shop boy to another merchant in Rostov on the Don. Egor's daughter Aleksandra, her father's favourite child, married a Vasili Kozhevnikov at Tverdokhliobovo near the steppe town of Boguchar.[3]

Egor remained on the Platov estates until he died, aged eighty-one. He was ruthless and eccentric. Like many managers of peasant stock, he was cruel to the peasantry: they called him the 'viper'. He also earned the dislike of his employers: Countess Platov banished him six miles away to a ranch. Egor could have lived there in a manorial house, but preferred a peasant's wooden cottage.

Chekhov's paternal grandmother Efrosinia Emelianovna, whom her grandchildren saw even less, for she rarely left the farm, was Ukrainian.[4] All the loud laughter and singing, the fury and joy that Chekhov associated with Ukrainians, had been beaten out of her. She was as surly as her husband, with whom she lived fifty-eight years before her death in 1878.

Egor emerged once or twice a year to escort a consignment of the Countess's wheat to Taganrog, the nearest port, and to buy supplies or spare parts in the town. His eccentricity was notorious: he devised dungarees as formal dress and moved 'like a bronze statue'. He flogged his sons for any misdemeanour – picking apples, or falling off a roof they were mending. Pavel Chekhov developed a hernia after one punishment, and had to wear a truss for it throughout his adult life.

Late in life Chekhov admitted:

I am short-tempered etc., etc., but I have become accustomed to

holding back, for it ill behoves a decent person to let himself go . . .
After all, my grandfather was an unrepentant slave-driver.[5]

Egor wrote well. He is reported as saying: 'I deeply envied the gentry
not just their freedom, but that they could read.' He apparently left
Olkhovatka with two trunks of books, unusual for a Russian peasant
in 1841. (Not a book was seen, however, when his grandsons visited
him at the Platov estate thirty-five years later.)

His efforts for his children were not matched by much affection.
A bully in life, on paper he could be rhetorical, obfuscating, or sentimental. A letter of Egor's to his son and daughter-in-law runs:

> Dear, quiet Pavel Egorych, I have no time, my dearest children, to
> continue my conversation on this dead paper because of my lack of
> leisure. I am busy gathering in the grain which because of the sun's
> heat is all dried up and baked. Old man Chekhov is pouring sweat,
> enduring the blessed boiling sultry sun, though he does sleep soundly
> at night. I go to bed at 1 in the morning, but up you get, Egorushka,
> before sunrise, and whether things need doing or not, I want to
> sleep. Your well-wishing parents Georgi and Efrosinia Chekhov.[6]

Like all the Chekhovs, Egor observed name days and the great Church
feasts, but he was laconic. Pavel on his name day (25 June) in 1859
received a missive which read: 'Dear Quiet Pavel Egorych, Long live
you and your dear Family for ever, goodbye dear sons, daughters and
fine grandchildren.'

Anton's maternal line was similar, and Tambov province, where
the family came from, was as archetypically Russian as neighbouring
Voronezh. Again, a peasant family of thrust and talent had bought its
way into the merchant classes. Anton's mother, Evgenia Iakovlevna
Morozova, had a grandfather, Gerasim Morozov, who sent barges
laden with corn and timber up the Volga and Oka to market. In 1817,
aged fifty-three, he bought for himself and his son, Iakov, freedom
from the annual tax which serfs paid their owners. On 4 July 1820
Iakov married Aleksandra Ivanovna Kokhmakova. The Kokhmakovs
were wealthy craftsmen: their fine woodwork and iconography were
in civil and ecclesiastic demand. The Morozov blood had, however,
a sinister side. Some of Gerasim Morozov's grandchildren – a maternal
uncle and an aunt of Anton and his brothers – died of TB.

Iakov Morozov lacked the stamina of Egor Chekhov: in 1833 he went bankrupt, then found protection (like Egor Chekhov), from a General Papkov in Taganrog, while Aleksandra lived with her two daughters in Shuia. (Their son Ivan was placed with a merchant in Rostov-on-the-Don.) On 11 August 1847 a fire burned down eighty-eight houses in Shuia: the family property was lost. Then, in Novocherkassk, Iakov died of cholera. Aleksandra loaded her belongings and her two daughters, Feodosia (Fenichka) and Evgenia, into a cart and, camping on the steppes, trekked 300 miles to Novocherkassk. She found neither her husband's grave nor his stock in trade. She travelled 100 miles west to Taganrog and threw herself on General Papkov's mercy. He took her in to his house and provided Evgenia and Fenichka with a rudimentary education.

Anton's maternal uncle Ivan Morozov, forty-five miles away in Rostov-on-the-Don, served under a senior shop boy: Mitrofan Chekhov.[7] Either Mitrofan or Ivan introduced Pavel Chekhov to Evgenia Morozova. In his twenties Pavel had a signet ring made. He inscribed on it three Russian words meaning 'Everywhere is a desert to the lonely man'. (Egor read the inscription and declared, 'We must get Pavel a wife.') The autobiographical record that Pavel compiled for his family in his old age has a laconic melancholy that surfaces at the rare moments of frankness in Anton's letters and frequently in the heroes of his mature prose:

> 1830 [*he was then 5 years old*] I remember my mother came from Kiev and I saw her
> 1831 I remember the powerful cholera, they made me drink tar
> 1832 I learnt to read and write in the priest's school, they taught the lay ABC
> 1833 I remember the grain harvest failing, famine, we ate grass and oak bark.[8]

A church cantor taught Pavel to read music and to play the violin, folk-style. Apart from this, and the ABC, he had no formal education. His passion for church music was the salve for his unhappiness, and he also had artistic ability, but his creativity drained away in compilations of ecclesiastical facts and what casual visitors called his 'superfluous words'. In 1854 Pavel and Evgenia were married. Evgenia had beauty but no dowry; while Pavel's appeal as a future merchant compensated for his equine looks.

Ivan Morozov, sensitive and generous, refused to sell suspect caviar, and was dismissed from Rostov-on-the-Don. He returned to Taganrog where Marfa Ivanovna Loboda, the daughter of a rich city merchant, fell for him. The youngest of the three Morozov children, Fenichka, married a Taganrog official, Aleksei Dolzhenko. She had a son, Aleksei, and was soon widowed.

Anton's mother, Evgenia, survived seven live births, financial disaster, the deaths of three of her children and her husband Pavel's tyranny. She had a shell of self-pity to retreat into, but she had few resources beyond the love of her offspring: she read and wrote with reluctance. Of the three Morozov children only Ivan had talent: he spoke several languages, played the violin, trumpet, flute and drum, drew and painted, repaired watches, made halva, baked pies from which live birds flew out, constructed model ships and tableaux, and invented a fishing rod which automatically landed fish. His *tour de force* was a screen painted with a mythological battle scene: it divided his shop from his living quarters, where he gave his visitors tea.

Anton loved and pitied his mother. He deferred to and detested his father, but from the son's birth to the father's death father and son never permanently separated. Pavel, like his own father Egor, could behave like a heartless monster or callous humbug, and portray himself as an affectionate self-sacrificing patriarch. He inspired loathing in his eldest son Aleksandr and saccharine affection in his youngest, Misha. Few outside the family could regard him without amusement or irritation. Apart from the Lord God, with whom he constantly communed, his closest friend was his brother Mitrofan.

Mitrofan was a modestly successful merchant, liked in Taganrog. Constantly gathering and disseminating family news, he was the chief link in the family, a willing host and an effusive, if calculating correspondent. Mitrofan Chekhov and his brothers, Mikhail in Kaluga and Pavel a few hundred yards away, shared a fanatical piety and, sometimes, humbug. They were all founder members of a Brotherhood attached to the Cathedral in Taganrog. It collected money to support the Russian monastery on Mount Athos and to provide charity to Taganrog's poor. Pavel writes to Mitrofan in summer 1859 (the brothers addressed each other with the formal *Vy*, never the intimate *Ty*), giving the first hint of TB in the family:

go to the trouble in Moscow of asking the Medical men regarding the illness of Evgenia Iakovlevna, the sort of illness is very well known, she spits every moment, this dries her out extremely, she is very fussy, the slightest thing becomes unpleasant to her, she loses her appetite and there is no way now of putting her right, would there be a means or a medicine to give her peace of mind and settle it?[9]

Family reunions were melancholy, quarrelsome occasions: from Kharkov in May 1860 Mitrofan writes to his brother:

this was a heavy day for me, from morning until dinner, I could in no way distract my heart, just the recollection that I am alone depressed me to the point of exhaustion ... I was taken to dine at Nikolai Antonovich's ... where I was received with affection and well, which rarely happens with us.

All three of Egor Chekhov's sons were life-affirmers in one respect: as patriarchs. Mikhail had four daughters and two sons, Mitrofan three sons and two daughters. Pavel and Evgenia had seven children. They married on 29 November 1854; two more years elapsed before Pavel scraped together 2500 roubles to join the Third Guild of Merchants. Their first child, Aleksandr, was born on 10 August 1855, as the Crimean War ended. Two English ships bombarded Taganrog, demolishing the dome of the cathedral, the port and many houses. Evgenia and her sister-in-law Liudmila abandoned their homes, leaving a chicken still cooking, and fled to the steppes, to stay with Egor Chekhov. Here Evgenia gave birth in the priest's house. She returned to a tiny house belonging to Efrosinia, Pavel's mother, which Egor had divided between Pavel and Mitrofan. When Mitrofan married Pavel moved a few streets away to a rented two-room mud-brick house on Politseiskaia Street. In 1857 he began trading; on 9 May 1858 a second son, Nikolai [Kolia], was born. In 1859 the Third Guild was abolished; raising more capital, Pavel became a Second Guild merchant. Evgenia was pregnant again. Pavel was a conformist: he became alderman on the Taganrog Police Authority. In January 1860 he wrote to brother Mitrofan: 'last Saturday the Church of St Michael was struck by lightning and caught fire right in the dome.' This seemed to him a portent before Anton's birth on 16 January 1860.[10]

TWO

❦

Taganrog
1860–8

TAGANROG HAD imperial status and a cosmopolitan population that made it more of a colonial capital than a provincial city. Visually, it was striking: a decrepit military harbour and a thriving civil port at the foot of a promontory jutting into the shallow Sea of Azov; half a dozen avenues, lined with Greek merchants' houses, punctuated with Russian government buildings, radiating northeast from the tip of land towards the steppes. You might have thought you were in a dusty city of Thrace, until you reached the wooden shanty town of the Russian suburbs.

Founded by Peter the Great to establish a foothold on the Sea of Azov and challenge Ottoman suzerainty, Taganrog was, like Petersburg, built without consideration for its inhabitants. Its sandy soil made poor foundations; fresh water was hard to find; it was hot in summer and cold in winter; the sea was so shallow that steam boats had to be unloaded a mile offshore. In 1720 Turks forced the Russians to demolish and abandon Taganrog. It was refounded by Catherine the Great in the 1770s and populated by Greek colonists who, like the Greeks of classical times, took refuge from poverty or tyranny in townships around the northern Black Sea and the Sea of Azov. Some Greeks had been Mediterranean pirates and were now tycoons; many lived by cheating Russian farmers and bribing Russian customs officials. They spread wealth, not only by conspicuous consumption, but by generous civic arts, founding orchestras, clubs, schools and churches, bringing in French chefs to cook Lucullian dinners and importing Italian sculptors to carve their tombs in the cemetery. In Chekhov's boyhood, they were followed by Italian and Russian merchants, and by dealers of all nations, exploiting the wealth of Taganrog's awakening hinterland. The city developed feverishly.

Tsar Alexander I also left his mark on the city. He came to Taganrog

9

for spiritual solace at the end of his reign, and settled in a modest single-storeyed 'palace' where he died three months later; Taganrog was briefly a shadow capital of the empire. Anton was born when Taganrog's future still looked bright. The building of railways to the south of Russia still awaited imperial consent. Cartloads of wheat and meat from the steppes – the nearest large town, Kharkov, was three hundred miles north over trackless steppes – descended on Taganrog to be shipped.

At Anton's christening in the Russian cathedral the godparents were Greek customers of Pavel and Mitrofan. A Russian nurse was hired, a serf who had been sold by her owners for helping the daughter of the family to elope. The Chekhov family expanded, moving house, sometimes living with members of Mitrofan's family. They were in the house of Pavel Evtushevsky, Mitrofan's father-in-law, when, on 18 April 1861, a fourth son, Ivan [Vania], was born. A daughter Maria [Masha] was born on 31 July 1863. The family moved in 1864 to a larger house on a more prestigious street. There a sixth child, Mikhail [Misha], was born on 6 October 1865.

Memories of Anton in infancy come from his elder brothers. As Kolia, barely thirty years old, lay dying in 1889 he set down childhood memories.[11] He recalled the house when Anton was still a baby, and the weeds and the fence which recur in Anton's late stories:

> I lived in a little one-storey house with a red wooden roof, a cottage ornamented with burdock, nettles, buttercups and such a mass of pleasant flowers as honoured the grey palisade that surrounded these dear creatures on all sides ... In this cottage there are five rooms and then three steps lead through the kitchen to the shrine where the great men [*the three eldest Chekhov sons*] lie, although the eldest of them is only just three feet high.

Kolia's memory then leapt to a time when Anton was eight. Uncle Ivan Morozov had carved a toy horseman, 'Vaska', out of cane for the four-year old Vania: the four boys slept in one bed and a sunbeam moved across their faces:

> at first Aleksandr waved the sunbeam off as if it were flies, then uttered something like 'Thrash me? What for?', stretched out and sat up ... Anton dragged from under a pillow a wooden toy ... first of all Vaska leapt over his knees and then he and Anton crawled

over the marbled wall. Aleksandr and I watched all Vaska's adventures with great enjoyment until Anton looked round and hid it very quickly under the pillow again. Vania had woken up. 'Where's my stick-toy, give me my stick-toy,' he squealed.

Kolia also recorded his last sight of Uncle Ivan, who could not bear the rough merchant world:

> We rarely saw uncle Vania's red beard, he didn't like to visit us, as he disliked my father who ascribed Uncle's lack of trade to his incompetence. 'If Ivan Iakovlevich were given a good thrashing,' my father used to say, 'then he'd know how to set up in business.' Uncle Vania had married for love, but was unhappy. He lived with his wife's family and heard the accursed 'a good thrashing' there as well. Instead of supporting the man, everyone thought up threats, more and more absurd, and finally deranged him and ruined his health. The family hearth he had dreamed of no longer existed for him. Sometimes, to avoid undeserved reproaches, he would shut up shop, not go to his room and spend the night under the fence of his house in the dew, trying to forget the insistent 'a good thrashing', 'a good thrashing'.
>
> I remember him once running in to see my aunt asking for some vinegar to rub himself with and when she asked questions, he flapped his arms at her, tears in his eyes and quickly ran aw . . .

Kolia died of TB before he could write any more. Uncle Vania died of TB shortly after the vinegar incident.

Aleksandr also recalled the toy Vaska and the shared bed. Aleksandr had often been left in charge of Anton: he remembered the infant Anton straining on his pot, shouting to Aleksandr to 'get a stick, get a stick' to help him:

> But sensing my inability to help you, I got nastier and nastier and finally pinched you as painfully and viciously as I could. You 'let rip' and I reported to mama when she came to your yelling, as if butter wouldn't melt in my mouth, that it was all your fault, not mine.[12]

When Anton was aged about ten, the scales of dominance swung the other way. For a decade he and his eldest brother jostled for power until Anton became the effective head of the family. Aleksandr recalls his first defeat when they were left minding the stall by the railway station:

You were chanting 'Bang your head, bang your head, drop dead!'
... I banged you on the head with a piece of corrugated iron. You
left the shop and went to see father. I expected a severe thrashing,
but a few hours later you majestically walked past the door of my
stall, accompanied by the shop-boy Gavriusha, on some mission for
father and purposely did not look at me. I watched you walking off
for a long time and, I don't know why, burst into tears.

Anton's earliest years were spent more with the clan than the family.
When he was six, the family moved in with Mitrofan and Liudmila,
while Aleksandr spent two or three years living with Fenichka. The
Chekhov and Morozov marriages tied Pavel and Evgenia to several
Taganrog families, both rich and poor. A number of Russified Greek
families were related to the Chekhov clan: godparents, and the Kam-
burovs, close neighbours on Politseiskaia street, rich merchants whose
Russian bourgeois veneer was skin-deep, for old man Kamburov would
curse the children, 'Fuck your mother', in a thick Greek accent. They
combined Mediterranean temperament with liberal Russian mores:
their daughters Liubov and Liudmila Kamburova were much in
demand. In such milieus Aleksandr's and Kolia's schoolboy romances
began – hence the command of demotic Greek that Aleksandr
retained, and the Taganrog urban jargon which he used in his letters.
Taganrog's Greeks called Aleksandr 'lucky Sasa' for his fluency.[13]

The first eight years of Anton's life were punctuated by family name
days and Church feasts, particularly Easter, which Pavel observed with
zeal. Everyday life was freer: in school holidays he and Kolia could
follow Aleksandr around Taganrog, catching fish in the smuggler's
bay of Bogudonie, trapping finches in wasteland to sell for kopecks,
watching convict gangs catching stray dogs with hooks and clubbing
them to death, coming home in the evenings covered with lime and
dust or mud.

THREE

Shop, Church and School
1868–9

PAVEL CHEKHOV was a bad merchant, taking too much pleasure in
calligraphy, copying out price lists, inventories and lists of creditors.
He turned his shop into a forum for endless moralizing with customers, a club where they could gossip over a glass of wine or tea.
Church music was his opening into Taganrog society. Pavel had an
unbounded passion for sung services. Despite limited training and
ability, he became the *regent* (kapellmeister) of the cathedral choir in
1864, after years as an amateur. He refused to omit a bar of music or
a word of the liturgy; cathedral services became interminable. Par-
ishioners and clergy asked Evgenia to persuade him to shorten them,
but Pavel never compromised over his favourite quality 'splendour'.
In 1867 he was dismissed.

Pavel moved to the Greek monastery, which, to broaden its congregation, now held services in Russian. The Greek clergy had little
Russian and needed a Russian cantor. Pavel formed a choir of blacksmiths, whose powerful bellows-lungs made them strong, rough,
basses and baritones. Pavel's choir lacked altos and sopranos. He
rehearsed with two young Taganrog ladies, but their nerves led to a
calamity, and the blacksmiths had to take over. Pavel renounced female
singers and recruited his three eldest sons. Aleksandr recalled 'the
doctor who treated our family protested at this premature violence
to my infant chest and vocal cords'.[14] For years church singing became
torture, especially at Easter, when the boys were hauled out of bed
on a freezing morning for early matins. They would sing at two more
long services in the day, before rehearsing all evening in the shop,
under a choirmaster who thrashed them. During his adult life, right
up until his death, Anton would rarely spend an Easter night in bed;
instead he would wander the streets, listening to the church bells.
The congregation's wonderment at the sight of Aleksandr, Kolia and

13

Anton, on their knees on the freezing stones, singing the three-part Motet of the Robber on the Cross, was not shared by the singers. Anton Chekhov recalled that they 'felt like little convicts', kneeling, worrying that the holes in their shoes were visible. Joys were few: watching merlins nesting in the bell-tower, an uncalled-for crescendo or peel of bells as their mother entered. The music, but not the doctrines of the Christian church, entered Anton's blood: 'The Church bells of Easter Sunday are all that I have left of religion,' he was to tell his schoolfriend, later the actor, Aleksandr Vishnevsky. To another writer, Shcheglov, he confessed in 1892: 'In my childhood I had a religious education and a religious upbringing ... And the result? When I recall my childhood I now find it rather gloomy; I now have no religion.'

In 1872 the Greek monastery church had a new priest who had no command of Russian, and Pavel's Russian choir was dismissed. The church that stood in the new Taganrog market, where Pavel, his blacksmiths and his fellow merchants worshipped and sang, had a paid professional choir. Only in the chapel of Tsar Alexander's 'palace' could Pavel display his family 'trio'.

The doctor may well have been right to blame the ill health of the three eldest Chekhov boys on those early services and late rehearsals. The positive side was that Anton's mind was saturated with the Church Slavonic language of the psalms, of the Orthodox free-verse psalmodic variations known as *akafisty*. His love of Russian church music long outlasted his faith in God, though he could only sing, or pick out a tune on a piano with one finger. Kolia, on the other hand, played the violin and piano, the latter with what a professional witness called virtuosity. In his brief prosperity in the late 1860s and early 1870s Pavel hired both a music teacher and a French teacher for his children. Both Aleksandr and Kolia acquired fluent French, whereas Anton's foreign languages, like his musical talents, remained undeveloped.

Aleksandr was a star pupil at Taganrog *gimnazia* [grammar school]. Pavel wavered about Kolia and Anton. Greek customers persuaded him that prosperity lay with a job as a broker in a Greek trading firm. This future 1500 roubles a year salary required a command of demotic Greek. When a debt of 100 roubles was unexpectedly paid, Pavel invested in Kolia's and Anton's education. For modern Greek, a child had to attend the parish school attached to the Greek Church of

St Constantine and St Helen. (Aleksandr had two or three years earlier picked up Greek at this school.) The school, where 'Nikolaos and Antonos Tsechoph' were enrolled in September 1867, was a Dotheboys Hall. In one large room with five long wooden benches one teacher, Nikolaos Voutzinas, took five classes simultaneously, starting with the alphabet and ending with syntax and history. In each corner of the schoolroom was an iron semicircle where an older pupil would test and punish pupils of a lower form, who were each sold a tatty primer. Aleksandr and Anton never forgot Voutzinas' catch phrase: 'Their parents will pay for everything.' Voutzinas would periodically disappear to his private quarters, where a Ukrainian housekeeper met his needs. (It is said he also raped a Greek boy there.) His red beard, loud voice and metal ruler restored order when he reappeared. Voutzinas devised a number of tortures, including strapping a boy to a stepladder to be spat at by the class. The fees, however, were modest, and the boys needed no uniform.

The school year ended: Pavel decided to demonstrate his sons' command of Greek to his customers. Despite stickers for 'diligence' and 'exquisite work' which Voutzinas awarded his pupils, neither Kolia nor Anton had more than the alphabet. In the row that ensued, the boys, not Voutzinas, were punished. In August 1868 they were enrolled into the *gimnazia*, Anton entering the preparatory class.

Taganrog school has been portrayed both as the prototype demesne of Chekhov's degraded fictional schoolteachers and as the Eton of the Pontus Euxine. It was hell and heaven – like a good English 'public' school, minus sport, sodomy and the cane. During Anton's eleven years there it flourished. A survey of its teachers and its pupils shows it evolving into a hotbed of talent. School formed Anton Chekhov as strongly as home, and liberated him from home.

In September 1809 the city's leading citizens had founded a *gimnazia* for their city. In 1843 the school was moved to a light and airy two-storey classical building, situated at Taganrog's highest point. It began to produce famous alumni – for instance, the poet Shcherbina, translator of Homer into Russian. When the era of reforms began in 1856, the school entered two decades of turbulence. The expansion of cities in southern Russia led to a turnover of staff; the heady atmosphere of Alexander II's reign brought in radicals who conflicted with authority.

In 1863, the headmaster was sacked and wandered Taganrog as a mad tramp. The new head, Parunov, gave him a burial in 1865. In 1867 the Minister for Education, Count Dimitri Tolstoy, visited the school, to make it an example of a new conservative, classical *gimnazia*: dubious subjects were replaced with double and compulsory Greek and Latin; Russian literature, as a ferment of rebellion, was severely restricted. Subversive teachers were squeezed out. Country pupils who boarded with Taganrog families found their quarters under surveillance. Dmitri Tolstoy felt that the education system and the church should shadow the gendarmerie which he had established. His reforms made many teachers into policemen and much teaching into parrot-learning, but created a framework within which canny teachers and able pupils flourished. The school was an avenue for Jews, merchants, petit-bourgeoisie, sons of priests into the new professional classes, the intelligentsia. They became doctors, lawyers, actors, writers – which worried a government, rightly afraid of under-employed intelligentsia as a force for revolution.

In a Russian *gimnazia* all pupils were treated as members of the gentry. The only discipline was detention in a whitewashed cell under the school's vaulted staircase. Physical punishment was forbidden: a teacher who struck a pupil would be dismissed. After the Voutzinas regime of thrashed palms and crucifixion, not to speak of the floggings in Pavel Chekhov's household, the preparatory class was paradise to Anton. He discovered that few fellow-pupils were beaten even at home. That quiet resistance to all authority, the core of Anton's adult personality, was fomented in the classroom. The *gimnazia* was a great leveller – upwards, rather than downwards. It gave pupils from poor, clerical, Jewish or merchant households the rights and aspirations of the ruling class. Some parents, however, could no longer afford the fees and uniform, and transferred their sons to technical school, to become tailors or carpenters. Efim Efimiev, who left school at 12 in 1872, eventually to become a watchmaker and fine joiner, recalls:

> We were considered people of plebeian origin . . . by the cheap cloth uniform . . . I took a lunch of a small piece of bread and dripping which I often shared with Anton, because he had no nourishment apart from bread, a baked potato and a gherkin.[15]

Pavel's fondness for the rod, exceptional even for the unenlightened merchant class, was an aspect of his personal cruelty. The younger children, especially Misha, were brought up in Moscow, where Pavel was restrained by the urbane prejudices of his landlords from exercising full paternal rights. Masha, the only surviving girl, was treated as a doll: she was remembered as the 'blushing Murochka' in her starched pink dress. The elder sons were thrashed mercilessly. While the Chekhovs' rich in-laws, the Loboda family, were notorious for flogging servants and children, Pavel's children envied Mitrofan's family, where the children were preached at, not flogged. Aleksandr was traumatized by floggings – both he and Kolia wetted their beds well into their teens. Efim Efimiev, Anton's schoolmate from 1869 to 1872, recalls: 'in the Chekhov household ... as soon as his father appeared we went quiet and ran home. He had a heavy hand. He punished children for the most innocent naughtiness. Thrashings.' In the mature work 'Three Years', Chekhov gives a graphic account of a young intellectual alienated from his merchant background, with many details that tally with what we glean from Anton's correspondence about his own childhood anguish.

> My father began to 'teach' me, or, to put it simply, to beat me, when I was less than five years old. He thrashed me with a cane, he boxed my ears, he punched my head and every morning, as I woke up, I wondered, first of all, would I be beaten today?

In his late twenties Anton recalled to Aleksandr:

> Tyranny and lies crippled our childhood so much that it makes me sick and afraid to remember. Remember the horror and revulsion we felt in those days when father would flare up because the soup was over-salted, or would curse mother for a fool.

At the end of the century Aleksandr told his sister:

> It was a sheer Tatar Yoke, without a glimmer of light ... I look back on my childhood with crushing anguish.[16]

The journalist Nikolai Ezhov's memoir of 1909 confirms the horror:

> After thrashing his children, Pavel Egorovich went to church and told the victims to sit and read so many pages of the psalter. Chekhov ... told a fellow-writer: 'You know, my father thrashed me so much

when I was a child that I still cannot forget it.' And the writer's voice quivered.

The teacher of Religious Knowledge at the school was Father Fiodor Pokrovsky, then in his early thirties. He preferred to visit Mitrofan Chekhov's house rather than Pavel's: in Mitrofan's family the hospitality was not punctuated by children being beaten or by Pavel's ranting. Pokrovsky misjudged the Chekhov boys, telling Evgenia: 'Something may come of your eldest [Aleksandr], but absolutely nothing can come of the two younger ones.' Pavel Filevsky, an ex-pupil and a fellow-teacher, described Pokrovsky as follows: 'Appearance, stance, musical voice, inventiveness, the gift of the gab – everything was attractive. But he was insincere ... he had little erudition, his theology was "from the gut".'[17] The children, however, saw Pokrovsky as their defender. He often overrode the headmaster Parunov at meetings. He argued with the deputy-head, the *inspektor*, a key figure in a Russian *gimnazia*, on behalf of pupils whose parents could not pay the fees (from ten to twenty roubles a year). He lobbied for the Chekhov brothers, too. In class he would forget the catechism and talk of his war exploits or of Goethe, Shakespeare and Pushkin. Chekhov kept in touch with the priest until he died in 1898, and Pokrovsky eagerly read what his ex-pupil wrote. Years later Mitrofan was to report to Pavel: 'Antosha told me in his letter that he owes the Priest not just his knowledge of scripture but literature, the ability to understand the living word and to clothe it in elegant form.'

The preparatory class of 1868–9 was taken by kindly men: the elderly but lively Swiss Montagnerouge, who had been the boarding housemaster, was affectionately known as Stakan (*wineglass*) Ivanych.

The Latin teacher, Vladimir Starov, left the deepest impression: a gentle, much liked man, he fell in love with the stepdaughter of his colleague Andrei Maltsev, Ariadna Cherets, a wanton beauty known as Rurochka. She married and ruined him. In the late 1880s, when the school's self-appointed secret policeman, a Czech called Urban, denounced him, Starov was removed to a remote school in the steppe: Ariadna abandoned him and eloped with an actor well-known all over Russia, Solovtsov, and began to act herself. Starov died of alcoholism in hospital. Not just Chekhov's stories ('Ariadna', 'My Life') but also the story 'My Marriage' by his geography teacher Fiodor Stulli, were based on Starov and his Ariadna. Another of Chekhov's teachers, Belovin, a radical historian, died of alcoholism. Ippolit Ostrovsky, a mathematics and physics teacher, died in service of TB.

The teacher who determined the fate of most pupils was the *inspektor*: in Taganrog *gimnazia* this was the 'Centipede' A. F. Diakonov, whose sayings were a compendium of moral clichés that pupils memorized and derided: 'If a law exists, it is not for the amusement of the lawmakers and must be observed.' Diakonov is one source for Chekhov's automaton of a Greek teacher, *The Man in a Case*, but in life his unbending principles, his lack of animosity, even his loneliness and taciturnity, won him grudging respect.

Greek caused the school and Anton Chekhov most problems. Aleksandr and Kolia were good Greek scholars, but Anton did not always manage to achieve the '3' mark necessary to pass into the next form. There were too few classical Greek teachers; finally the authorities recruited Zikos from Athens. A fine teacher, Zikos was, nevertheless, as Filevsky puts it, 'not too fastidious about seeking enrichment'. He took bribes, muttering to pupils with '2' marks '*chremata* [money]!' Corruption was endemic in Russian schools. Teachers took laggards as boarders and then charged 350 roubles a year, feeding the boys, as Anton later put it 'like dogs, on the gravy from the roast'. Zikos was so blatantly exploitative that he 'compromised' the school and in the early 1880s was repatriated.

Another recruit was a Czech called Jan Urban. The school bogey, he had worked in Kiev (where somebody broke his leg), and in Simferopol (where his windows were smashed).[18] Each town he left after denouncing pupils and staff to the authorities. Taganrog was his last chance, but his denunciations continued. One of the pupils he harassed killed himself. In Anton's last years at the *gimnazia* boys packed a sardine can with explosives and hurled it at Urban's house. The bang was heard ten blocks away. Urban demanded that the police arrest the anarchists responsible, but the headmaster and police did nothing. Urban had difficulty finding a new landlord. Such was his standing that even the city gendarme forbad his daughter to marry Urban's son. In the 1905 disturbances schoolboys stoned Urban: he picked up the stones and carried them in his pocket until his death.

Some teachers were never recalled by Anton. Yet one wonders how he could forget Edmund-Rufin Dzerzhinsky, 'a pathologically irritable man' says Filevsky. Until 1875 Edmund-Rufin taught mathematics and later fathered the murderous head of Lenin's secret police, Felix Dzerzhinsky. Anton remembered best the teachers who stayed throughout his years there, and those who met grotesque ends.[19] In later life he dismissed them as *chinodraly* (careerists) and used their eccentricities and tragedies for fiction.

In his first years Anton was academically mediocre and not very docile. Only Pavel Vukov, responsible for discipline, when asked after Chekhov's death, spoke out: 'He got on our nerves for nine years.' (Later Vukov put it more tactfully: 'His ideas and witty phrases were taken up by his schoolmates and this became a source of merriment and laughter.') As for Anton's fellow-pupils, friendships were not formed until later. The Chekhov family was still too clannish.

From 1868 Pavel's income grew and provided an education for all of his children. The death of their grandmother, Aleksandra Kokhmakova in 1868, was barely noticed: paralysed, she had been unaware of the world for four years.

Anton's life of a schoolboy and a chorister was made tougher when, early in 1869, the Chekhovs moved into a rented two-storey brick house on a corner site, at the edge of town, on the route taken by the carters and drovers on their way to and from the port and the steppes. On the upper storey they had a drawing room, with a piano; the lower storey was a shop, its side rooms crammed with tenants and stores. Outside, where one of the shop boys or Chekhov children would stand to solicit customers, hung a sign: TEA, COFFEE, SUGAR, AND OTHER COLONIAL GOODS. In addition to the family (although Aleksandr often lived elsewhere), two shop boys, the young Kharchenko brothers, Andriusha and Gavriusha, about 11 and 12 years old, were taken in, receiving no salary for their first five years, not even allowed pockets in their clothes, lest they be tempted to steal, and thrashed even more often than the children of the house. They were trained to give short change and short weight and to pass off rotten goods as sound.[20]

Here, on 12 October 1869, Evgenia, the last of the Chekhov children, was born. Somehow the Chekhovs found room for tenants – Jewish traders, monks, schoolteachers. One tenant played a key role in the family's last Taganrog years. The Chekhovs never forgot Gavriil Parfentievich Selivanov, who worked in the civil courts by day and at night went to the club where he earned another living as a gambler. An elegant bachelor, he fought to keep his straw hat clear of the sunflower seed husks and other debris that blew in the wind around the Chekhov shop. Selivanov soon became a member of the family, even calling Evgenia 'mama'. Another tenant was a pupil in the senior classes of the *gimnazia*, Ivan Pavlovsky, later to be a journalist-colleague of Chekhov's. Pavlovsky left an indelible mark on the memory of his schoolmates. In 1873 he left to study in Petersburg, but was arrested as a revolutionary and sent to Siberia.

From the upper storey of the Moiseev house the family could see Taganrog's new market square. To this square convicted criminals, their hands tied behind their back, a placard naming their crime round their necks, would be brought on a black tumbril to a scaffold. The drums rolled, the convict was lashed to a pillar, and the sentence was read out, before they were led off to prison or exile. Evgenia and uncle Mitrofan, like many citizens in provincial Russian cities, visited the prison on name days or on feast days.

Pavel's charity was limited: he merely allowed two monk-priests, ostensibly collecting alms for Mount Athos, to shelter in his yard and turned a blind eye to their drinking. Pavel was not so indulgent to his sons. Regardless of school, they were given the duties and punishments that he had endured. Latin homework could be done while keeping an eye on the shop, which was open from before dawn until well into the night. The paternal phrases which Aleksandr remembered ran: 'I had no childhood in my own childhood. Only street urchins play in the street. One beaten boy is worth two unbeaten.'

With a properly equipped shop, scales, a table and chairs for customers, shelves and cupboards everywhere, sheds and attics, Pavel tried to deal in everything. He was, surprisingly, a gourmet, who would dine with the devil if the food was good, and he made his own mustard. In his shop he kept the finest coffee and olive oil. Aleksandr tried to reconstruct the inventory forty years later:

> tea by the pound or ounce, face-cream, pen-knives, phials of castor oil, waistcoat buckles, lamp-wicks, medicinal rhubarb, vodka or Santurini wine by the glass, olive oil, 'S' Bouquet perfume, olives, grapes, marbled backing paper for books, paraffin, macaroni, laxatives, rice, Mocha coffee, tallow candles, used tea-leaves, dried and re-coloured

[*bought from hotels, for servants*], honey sweets and fruit-gums – next to floor polish, sardines, sandalwood, herrings, canisters for paraffin or cannabis oil, flour, soap, buckwheat, home-grown tobacco, ammonia, wire mouse-traps, camphor, bay leaves, 'Leo Wissor' Riga cigars, birch brooms, sulphur matches, raisins, strychnine . . . cardamom, cloves, Crimean sea salt in the same niche as lemons, smoked fish and leather belts.

Pavel also sold a number of medicines. One of them, called 'bird's nest', contained among other ingredients mineral oil, mercury, nitric acid, 'seven brothers blood', strychnine, and corrosive sublimate. Bought by customers for their wives, it was an abortifacient. 'That "birds nest" probably despatched many people to the next world,' Anton remarked after finishing medical training. Serving customers vodka and sweet red Santurini wine,[21] Pavel still traded unprofitably. The intense labour involved in drying out and repackaging used tea leaves was unrewarding. To important customers Pavel was servile, but when anyone complained that the tea stank of fish or the coffee of candle wax, he would publicly punch and kick the shop boys, Andriusha and Gavriusha Kharchenko. (Pavel was summoned to the Taganrog magistrate for excessive beating.) Pavel's ideas of hygiene and safety did not meet even the lax standards of the time: he assured his youngest son that flies cleared the air. When Pavel found a rat in a barrel of his olive oil, he was too honest to say nothing, too mean to pour the oil away, too lazy to boil and re-filter it. He chose consecration: Father Pokrovsky conducted a service in the shop. The incident of the drowned rat was enough to drive away the least fastidious customer, and heralded the collapse of Pavel Chekhov's Colonial Store.

FOUR

The Theatres of Life and Art
1870–3

A WELL-FITTED SHOP and a bourgeois drawing room overlooking two tree-lined avenues, soon to be lit by gas, formed the European façade of the Moiseev house. The crowded bedrooms, the sheds in the yard, the kitchen without running water, the absence of a bath, represented the Asiatic reality behind the façade. The image of a provincial home with stinking, cockroach-infested back rooms and a magnificent façade would haunt Anton's prose to his last story. The prosperous European façade was fragile, for Pavel lacked financial acumen. Within a year he had competition just across the road; he bought unsaleable wine on credit. Debts mounted, and the family fortunes turned. In September 1871 Anton's baby sister Evgenia died. Evgenia was far more deeply affected by this than by the later deaths of three adult sons. Even sixteen years later Aleksandr remarked that his mother remembered that death 'as if it were today'.

Pavel extended his opening hours and rented a stall on the square by the new railway station. When the stall failed to cover even the costs of its paraffin lamp, he rented a stall in the new market. Worst of all, in the summer holidays he forced his sons – including the twelve-year-old Anton – to run these outposts, opening a stall at 5 a.m. and staying until midnight to return with pitiful takings.

The summer holidays gave relief in Anton's childhood: fishing the rivers and roaming the countryside were to be prerequisites of happiness in his adult life and his fiction. On Anton the sea left a mark even stronger than the countryside. Taganrog boys fished from the piles driven into the shallow bed of the unfinished port, or went west, to the stony beach of Bogudonie, known as Smuggler's Bay. Diving into the water one day, Anton cut open his head, acquiring the scar listed on his identity papers. Here he sat with his eldest brother, often next to the school *inspektor* Diakonov, like prey and predator visiting the same watering hole. They angled for the tiny, edible Gobius fish. A thread was passed through the gills of each one; the chain of trans-fixed fish was left writhing in the water, to keep them fresh until they were taken to market. There were diversions on the way back: schoolboys would slash the sacks of clementines or walnuts in the carts that climbed slowly from the port to the town. If the driver caught the thieves, he would lash out with his knout.[22] Fishing gave Anton the stillness he desperately missed at home. More exciting sport was found on wasteland, with a school friend, Aleksandr Drossi, catching finches. (Some of the Chekhov brothers were to keep finches and songbirds, flying around their living rooms, in adult life.) The other sport was in the cemetery, whose mixture of Orthodox austerity, flamboyant Italian statuary and permanent decrepitude haunts much of Chekhov's prose. Here Anton caught tarantula spiders with a ball of wax.[23]

Even in boyhood the sea and the river Mius had a primarily melan-cholic effect on Anton, becoming *memento mori* in his mature stories. Writing to his patron, the novelist Grigorovich, in 1886, Chekhov would recall:

> When my blanket falls off me at night, I begin to dream of enormous slippery rocks, the cold autumn water, the bare shores – all this is vague, in a mist, with not a fragment of blue sky ... When I run away from the river, I pass the tumbledown cemetery gates, the funerals of my schoolteachers.

Anton's life broadened in the early 1870s. He explored the sur-roundings of the town and visited school friends and their parents. Aunt Fenichka's *laissez-faire* household allowed pillow fights, while the families of Taganrog's officials and merchants gave still greater relief from a grim home life. Anton now had intimations of future torments: migraine, and abdominal illness, then called 'catarrh of the stomach' or 'peritonitis', and attributed to bathing in cold water. Summer brought malarial fevers. Anton thought of diarrhœa and a constant cough as normal. Although Evgenia had shown symptoms – spitting blood, fever – Uncle Vania Morozov had already died of TB, and Aunt Fenichka suffered fits of coughing and debilitation, nobody suggested that tuberculosis might have struck Anton. For the time being, Anton's vitality fought off recurrent infection. The boy looked very different from the man. We know a face honed by suffering, a chest hollowed by coughing: the broad-shouldered, wide-cheeked peasant boy before the mid 1880s is a shocking contrast to the later stereotype. He was known as 'bomba' at school for his large head.

In July 1871, when Anton was eleven, an ox cart stopped at the shop: it was the engineer from Krepkaia, where grandfather Egor was employed. He had come to Taganrog to buy a piece of farm machinery. Aleksandr and Anton begged their parents to allow them to ride the ox cart and stay with their grandparents. They left in such haste that they had no protection from the rainstorms that struck the cart as it trundled over the steppe: it took two days to cover forty-five miles. Being soaked in the storm, getting lost in the reeds of a steppe lake, being berated by the drunken carter, meeting a Jewish innkeeper (whom the carter and engineer cheated) – all these incidents were transmuted sixteen years later into Chekhov's masterpiece 'Steppe'. And just as 'Steppe' climaxes in a great disillusionment when the mysterious old man who is the object of the first part of the journey turns out to be of little interest, so Aleksandr and Anton finally reached their grandfather's estate to find that he had long been posted to an outlying village, Kniazhaia, where he was hated as 'the viper'. Egor himself expressed no animation when he finally saw his grandchildren. Worse, as soon as the peasants realized that these boys were the grandchildren of the manager, they turned away and cursed them as the 'viper's' offspring. Egor and Efrosinia lived like peasants. The boys camped among the dustsheets in the house of the absentee young countess. After nearly a week, Aleksandr and Anton struck up a relationship with the blacksmith and purloined a sheet to trawl the millpond for fish. Old Egor did not back up his reputation as a self-taught man of books: he dismissed his grandsons' grammar-school education as a hotbed for 'learned fools'. Anton was shocked by his grandmother's revelations: privation and thrashings from Egor, in an outpost surrounded by resentful peasants, had broken her. For the first time the boys understood how their father had been formed, and that his childhood had been even worse than theirs.

A week with their grandparents was enough for Aleksandr and Anton. Aleksandr insisted on walking six miles back to the main village, Krepkaia, and asked Countess Platova to arrange for them to be taken home. A few days later the two boys were loaded onto a cart returning to Taganrog.

In May 1872, Anton (like a quarter of the pupils) failed to pass the third-year examinations – he did not reach the minimum '3' mark required in all subjects, Greek being his Achilles heel. He faced exile in 'Kamchatka', the back row in the third year, for 1872/3. That summer, for a while, Anton could forget this humiliation: the Chekhov children were, to their joy, left behind by their parents. Pavel and Evgenia set off on a pilgrimage around Russia, to visit the great monasteries and Holy Relics, Mikhail Chekhov (fatally ill with TB) in Kaluga, the Polytechnical Exhibition in Moscow, and then, on the way home, Evgenia's rich cousins and in-laws in Shuia. It was this summer which gave Masha, then nine, her first memories: she would try not to harbour grudges, and see the best of the Chekhovs' childhood. She remembered only peaceful pursuits – Aleksandr making electric batteries, Kolia painting, Vania binding books.

In 1873 the sons' horizons broadened, while Pavel's contracted. Anton had a social life: both older brothers, Aleksandr and Kolia had romances, perhaps love-affairs, with girls from the *gimnazia* that often collaborated with the boy's school and was only a few blocks away. Aleksandr was in love and virtually engaged to Maria, the daughter of Franz Faist, the Taganrog watchmaker. Kolia, who was highly attractive, despite his Mongoloid looks and his short stature, was much pursued, particularly by Liubov ('Love') Kamburova, a cousin of the Chekhov family. To judge by the letters from the girls of Taganrog to Moscow, when the brothers left town, these were only a few of the daughters of Greek and Russian merchants who found the Chekhov brothers attractive. Aleksandr was clever and articulate; Kolia could clown, act and play music; Anton had wit and exquisite manners. Taganrog families long remembered his considerateness to everyone – a concern that seemed at odds with his mocking mimicry of hosts and guests. Even those to whom his literary fame was irrelevant, such as Irinushka, the nanny in Mitrofan's household, remained bewitched by Anton. The secret of his appeal not just to women and girls, but to hotel servants and council officials, publishers and tycoons, lay in the tact and restraint which he cultivated even on his deathbed. Charm led Anton into the houses of the rich: he valued not so much their governesses, amateur dramatics, concerts, fluency in French, tea served in china cups, as the respect they seemed to have for others' dignity and privacy.

Anton's tastes and mind were also stimulated by the Taganrog theatre. For decades (it was founded in 1827) it had been regarded by the school as a threat to the morals of the pupils. Pupils were only allowed to visit the theatre after the *inspektor* had approved the play and was satisfied that the boy would not be distracted from his homework. Teachers patrolled the theatre to spot any unauthorized schoolboys – they might cover the heads with scarves, abandon school uniform, or bribe the doorman to let them in when the auditorium was plunged in darkness. The semiforbidden nature of the theatre allured them. A rich cosmopolitan clientele allowed Taganrog to maintain a theatre and a repertoire out of all proportion to the city's size or appeal, with singers from Italy and actors from Moscow to challenge local performers.

Pavel regarded the theatre as the gateway to hell (he is not known to have seen even his son's plays), though his brother Mitrofan was a keen member of the audience. In 1873 the school's hostility to the theatre was temporarily neutralized by the appointment of a young *inspektor*, the appropriately named Aleksandr Voskresensky-Brilliantov, who liked to clown in the classroom, constantly took out a pocket mirror to check on his magnificent red beard and was conspicuous in the theatre, where he would crush nuts with his boot and chew loudly at the most pathetic points. This Narcissus was dismissed within the year, but by then Anton was hooked on the theatre. The first performance he saw from a 15 kopeck seat in the gallery, Vania testifies, was Offenbach's *La Belle Hélène*. Offenbach's Helen of Troy, torn between an ineffectual Menelaus and a trouble-making Paris, was to become the model for Chekhov's own dramatic heroines.

In the 1870s, Taganrog's repertoire had 324 different productions.[24] Much was French farce and vaudeville, adapted or merely translated, and operetta. Shakespeare too was performed: *Hamlet, King Lear, The Merchant of Venice.* Anton's fascination with, and variations on, *Hamlet* were spawned by the Taganrog theatre. Its range of mainstream Russian drama, particularly of Ostrovsky's beautifully constructed 'realist' studies of the horrors of merchant life – *Poverty Is No Vice, The Thunderstorm, Wolves and Ewes, The Forest* – left Anton an admirer of Ostrovsky. Romantic drama, however – Victor Hugo and Friedrich

Schiller – aroused his mockery. The great European operas – Bellini, Donizetti and Verdi, especially *Rigoletto, Il trovatore, Un ballo in maschera* were also performed – evoked in Anton an ambivalent response.

The Taganrog public was demanding and rowdy. Bad singers were whistled off the stage. The provincial reviewers were well-informed. Schoolboys wore special ties to mark their support for one soprano or another. Close underground bonds linked the school and the theatre: one technician spread information on the programmes to come, another sneaked boys in out of sight of the school's police. One of the actors, Iakovlev, had a son studying in the *gimnazia*. Anton and his friends, including the future actor-manager (and rake) Solovtsov, met him and other actors offstage.

Apart from symphonic concerts in the theatre, there was music elsewhere in Taganrog: the town's park had a symphony orchestra and for many years entry was free. The repertoire was checked by Diakonov and the headmaster before boys were allowed to attend. Music was the only force that could bring Anton to the verge of tears, while Kolia could replay by ear pieces he had heard just once. What she saw as the pernicious influence of the theatre and the concert hall dismayed Evgenia.

Amateur dramatics were inspired by the Taganrog professionals. Until illness weakened his voice, Anton took on several parts, notably the mayor in Gogol's *Government Inspector*, with Vania playing the antihero Khlestakov, Kolia the servant Osip, and Maria, embarrassed at being publicly kissed, the eligible daughter.

In 1873 Parunov was replaced as headmaster by the statuesque and stentorian Edmund Rudolfovich Reutlinger. He was related by marriage to the new *inspektor* Diakonov and, although they avoided each other outside school, they made a triumvirate with Father Pokrovsky. Reutlinger could reassure the ministry of his solid conservatism, while running a school that was innovative and tolerant. Under Reutlinger joint concerts and performances were held with the girls' *gimnazia*. The two schools had teachers in common, although male teachers were mercilessly teased in the girls' school. The French teacher Boussard was entrusted with joint social events: a fine cellist, a well-known Taganrog host, he was loved by both schools. His death in service and his tomb in Taganrog cemetery haunted Chekhov's adult nightmares.

Like many successful headmasters, Reutlinger had more style than substance. He may not have been particularly intelligent, but he was fond of his pupils. To the Chekhovs he was a godsend. Like Parunov, he recognized the brilliance of Aleksandr, and made him a proposition. In return for board and lodging, Aleksandr went to live with Reutlinger, where he could study peacefully and repay his host by tutoring one of the headmaster's boarders. (This gave Aleksandr, like Pavel as alderman on the Police Authority, the reputation of being an informer.) Aleksandr's pupil was Aleksandr Vishnevetsky, later (as Vishnevsky) to be the handsomest, and stupidest, star in the Moscow Arts Theatre firmament. It was not Reutlinger, however, but an outsider in the school, a law specialist called Ivan Stefanovsky, who drew the attention of the school's examining council to the exceptional literary qualities of Chekhov's otherwise 'mediocre' compositions.

When Anton passed into the fourth class, he was threatened with losing his new foothold in educated society. Pavel decided to insure against failure. (Anton had already failed one end-of-year exam, while Kolia had failed two.) Kolia, Anton and Vania were made to write to the headmaster:

> Desiring to learn in the trade class of the Taganrog District College the following crafts: Ivan, bookbinding; and Nikolai and Anton, cobbling and tailoring, we have the honour of most humbly asking your excellence to permit us to study the above-mentioned trades.
> 20 October 1873

Kolia and Vania were probably expelled from Technical College, although Vania became a competent bookbinder. Anton persisted for nearly two academic years. Records show Anton making a pair of fashionable stovepipe trousers, which Kolia wore, and early in 1874 a tricot waistcoat and trousers for himself. But never again was Chekhov seen to pick up a needle and thread – except for medical purposes.

Before his first year of double schooling, Chekhov had a holiday with his mother and all his siblings. Leaving Pavel in charge of the shop, they set off slowly by lumbering ox cart, past the Jewish cemetery, up the Mius river valley and northwards to the spring of Krinichka; they camped under the stars in the settlement of Sambek, where the marmots whistled from their burrows in the steppe. Another day took them twenty-five miles to Kniazhaia, where Egor and Efrosinia received – welcomed is too strong a word – their family and housed them in the deserted manor house. Watching Ukrainians threshing corn fifteen years later, Anton recalled how, at harvest time, Egor put him to work:

> For whole days from dawn to dusk I had to sit by the steam-engine and write down the bushels and pounds of grain that had been threshed; the whistles, the hissing and the bass wolf-cub sound which the steam-engine utters when working at full tilt, the screech of wheels, the slow gait of the oxen, the clouds of dust, the black sweaty faces of fifty or so men are all etched into my memory like 'Our Father'.

FIVE

Disintegration
1874–6

In 1874 Pavel Chekhov borrowed to buy stock. As security he used the little brick fortress of a house he had built in 1873 (also on credit) on a plot of land half a mile away. The house had been built to let, but trade in Taganrog was in the doldrums, and the house was empty. The contractor, Mironov, had cheated Pavel by building the walls far too thick: the extra debt to Mironov for the unnecessary materials he had used was to prove ruinous. Others who lent Pavel 200 or 1000 roubles were themselves pressed; they offered his bills of exchange to the banks as security for their own debts, but times were abnormal. Ruin loomed. Taganrog's commercial life was turned upside down by the railway. While the engineers were not sufficiently well bribed to place the station in the centre of town, they did bring the rails down to the port. The rich now became very rich, for wagons of coal from the newly mined steppes and the wheat and wool that was now coming from the mechanized ranches of the Black Earth earned the Greek and Russian commodity dealers millions. (Pavel's in-laws, the Lobodas, flourished, importing cheap haberdashery by rail from Moscow.) But the small traders who lived by supplying steppe farmers and carters were now going bankrupt. The railway that brought the wheat to Taganrog also delivered to the steppes cheap goods from Moscow. Taganrog was no longer a source of haberdashery, ironmongery or colonial goods. Few carters now passed Pavel's shop.

In summer 1874 Pavel surrendered the tenancy of his 'Colonial' shop and moved his family and his tenants, including the canny Gavriil Selivanov, into his new, but mortgaged, house. The shop boys Andriusha and Gavriusha Kharchenko lost their jobs; poor Andriusha was conscripted into the army and died in training the following year. Pavel continued trading from market stalls, but the writing on the wall was clear to all but himself. He had more dependants. Aleksandr had moved out to live with the headmaster, but Aunt Fenichka, widowed and destitute, with her nine-year-old son Aleksei, had moved in with the Chekhovs. The new house was crowded, but it had a view of the sea from the upper window.

In 1874 Anton began to write: a satirical quatrain, apparently about the *inspektor* Diakonov, for a class magazine. His youngest brother Misha remembered another quatrain written by Anton on the garden fence. A schoolgirl who lived next door to the Chekhovs chalked up a sentimental poem on the fence. Anton's response ran:

> Why don't you wipe the milk off your lips,
> Fence-writing poetess in skirts?
> You should be playing with your dolls
> Rather than trying rhyme and verse.

When the heat was unbearable Anton slept outside with the two black yard dogs under a vine, calling himself 'Job beneath the fig-tree'. Once Anton insisted on bringing home from market a live duck and tormenting the bird so that it would let the neighbours know that the Chekhovs could still afford meat. Anton's other activities were those of the town's urchins: he went to the old Quarantine graveyard, where victims of the 1830 cholera epidemic were buried, to search for human skulls; he looked after pigeons in a dovecote; he trapped goldfinches or shot at starlings, steeling himself to the screeches of wounded birds in their cages at night. He never forgot those tormented starlings.

By now the eldest Chekhov fledgling was also ready to fly. In July 1874 Aleksandr, with a few roubles in his pocket, set off by boat to Sevastopol. Dressing up and being taken for a member of the gentry were addictive pleasures. At the first port in the Crimea, Feodosia, he visited the one-kopeck baths:

> They gave me a sheet and pitcherful of water for my feet. When I came out of the water, it was like being a Lord. Naturally I didn't miss the opportunity to put on airs and strut for a kopeck. Then the ladies took hold of me, put me in a phaeton ... and drove me around town.[25]

On his return, Aleksandr continued to live in gentility with Reutlinger and contrived to keep his petit-bourgeois family at a distance. At Easter 1875 Pavel reproached him: 'Aleksandr, I can see that you don't need us, that we have given you a freedom to live and to manage so young ... you cannot see yourself and a spirit of arrogance lives in you.'

Kolia and Anton also stretched their wings. Anton had passed his examinations in May 1874 and in August joined the fifth year. He became a frequent visitor to the household of a schoolmate Andrei Drossi and his sister Maria.[26] Maria was particularly fond of Anton (both were taught by Father Pokrovsky) and allowed him into her bedroom on payment of 20 kopecks' worth of sweets. The Drossis were rich corn merchants, and liberal parents. Visitors took part in charades and amateur dramatics, and the Drossi family governess arranged tea parties. Anton composed and acted in vaudevilles, but destroyed the scripts afterwards. Here Anton befriended a Jewish schoolmate; here too he expanded his acting to parts from Ostrovsky as well as Gogol. Uncle Mitrofan occasionally called to express benign approval, but Pavel never appeared. The dislike between Pavel Chekhov and the Drossis was mutual. Maria Drossi to her dying day remembered her one purchase at Pavel's shop: she had handed over 3 kopecks for an exercise book and walked out, by mistake, with a 5-kopeck book: Pavel rushed out after her and in silent fury snatched the book out of her hands. It was Maria Drossi who first noticed that Anton referred to Pavel as 'my father', never 'Papa' or 'Dad'.

Pavel had cause to be irritable. In spring 1875 he could not pay his dues for the Second Guild of Merchants and was expelled from the guild and demoted to a simple *meshchanin*. This entailed loss of privileges for himself and, worse, for his male offspring (if they failed to become university graduates) – as *meshchane* they became liable to corporal punishment and six years' military service. That spring Anton failed his Greek examinations and had to repeat the fifth year.

The summer holidays of 1875 were the last that the Chekhov brothers were to spend all together, fishing with a special moving cork float that Anton had devised. The boys took with them a frying pan and, if Pavel was out of the way, a bottle of Santurini wine, and cooked their catch on the shore.

In the summer of 1875 Anton was first invited by the family tenant, Gavriil Selivanov, to stay with one of his brothers, Ivan Selivanov (a notorious gambler) and the latter's new wife, a rich widow. It was the first of four or five unforgettable occasions on which Anton went to live on a semisavage Cossack ranch, where the livestock and the

Ukrainian peasants were terrorized by the incessant carousing and gun shots from the house. In 1875, on his first visit, after bathing in a cold river, Anton became for the first time so ill that Ivan Selivanov panicked in fear for the boy's life, and drove him to Moisei Moiseich, a Jewish innkeeper. The innkeeper sat up all night applying mustard poultices and compresses to the sick boy, and over the next few days the innkeeper's wife nursed Anton to a state fit for the cart-ride back to Taganrog. (Moisei Moiseich and his wife inspired the Jewish innkeepers in the story 'Steppe' written twelve years later.) In Taganrog Anton's 'peritonitis' was treated by the school doctor, Doctor Schrempf from Dorpat in Estonia, who inspired Anton to take up medicine as a career. After this illness, Anton took an interest in German, the language of instruction at Dorpat, and showed unsuspected motivation.

That summer of 1875 Aleksandr had matriculated with a silver medal. Despite their poverty, the family decided to send both Aleksandr and Kolia to Moscow, Aleksandr to study mathematics and science in Moscow University, and Kolia to enrol at the Moscow College of Art and Architecture, which willingly accepted students, even if they had only completed half their secondary education, on a portfolio of work. As Tsar Alexander II and his ministers planned more wars, military conscription (for six years) was in 1874 extended: not just the peasantry, but also sons of any class who failed to secure exemption, were liable. If they enrolled in university, the spectre of military service receded; if they graduated it melted away for ever. On 7 August 1875, their luggage packed by uncle Mitrofan, Pavel's two eldest sons took the train to Moscow. They were not friendless there. They would soon be joined by a fellow student from Taganrog, Gauzenbaum; the wealthy Ivan Loboda, a frequent traveller, would check up on them. Apart from fellow students from Taganrog they would find in Moscow their twenty-four-year old cousin from Kaluga, Mikhail [Misha] Chekhov (or Chokhov as many pronounced his surname). Misha was a clerk in Gavrilov's wholesale haberdashery firm of Gavrilov, agent for Coats & Paisley's threads. Gavrilov supplied many Taganrog merchants, notably the Lobodas, and had even dealt with Pavel Chekhov. Mikhail, however different in his shop boy's background from his educated provincial cousins, was a sharp 'likely lad' who could find them cheap lodgings.

The shock of the big city was considerable, particularly for Kolia who was less resourceful and who had to prove himself to the College of Art. Aleksandr, however, wrote a blasé letter on his twentieth birthday:[27]

> We arrived safely. We met Misha. When we talk to him we use the polite *Vy* just like papa and uncle. I think we are going to get on with him. . . . The hotel is real rubbish. The table somehow dances and limps on one leg. The samovar is like a drunk . . . My respects to his Excellence Anton as the oldest child in the house . . . If Vania knew how plump the women are in Moscow. But don't tell him or he'll be seduced . . . Kolia is spitting in all the corners and under the table. He kept crossing himself on the journey. We are quarrelling over that . . . Misha is very kind. We haven't found a flat yet. When someone is coming to Moscow, send the violin, a balaclava, my galoshes and my pen . . .

That same day Kolia explained why he spat and crossed himself against the evil eye:

> . . . the rail journey was shaky to Kursk and at one place our train nearly crashed into a goods train, if it hadn't been for a circle blocking the track. All the passengers were very scared . . . after tea we went in search of cousin Misha. We asked for him [at the warehouse] and he appeared. A real dandy, quite unrecognizable from his photograph . . . we answer, 'don't you recognize us?' 'Yes, judging by what Ivan Loboda tells me, if I'm not mistaken.' 'We're your cousins', says Aleksandr.[28]

Two days later, the brothers were installed in the first of many lodgings, 'Furnished Rooms over the Smyrna Dining Rooms', two minutes from the Art College and twenty from the university. Moscow landladies disliked students, but the brothers' charm worked. Their landlady told them, said Kolia: 'No rows: play, sing, dance, the only thing that frightens me is rows. Of course you're young men and I have no right to forbid you anything.'

Aleksandr was enrolled, but Kolia was embroiled in misunderstandings that sapped his will power. On 13 August Aleksandr (who had his father's obsession with accounts) broached the subject of money:

> Enrolling in the University cost me 1 rouble. If [Kolia] passes his examination he won't be able to pay the whole fee: he has to pay

30 silver roubles by 19 August . . . The flat costs us [*each*] per month 5.33, board 6.50, bread and tea 1.50, laundry 1, lighting 1.50, total 15 roubles. We can't live on less . . . Kolia doesn't know about this letter. He has gone completely dozy, just crosses himself all the time and touches the icon with his forehead.

Four days later Aleksandr was still complaining: 'Damn Kolia's pomade. He's been carefully greasing his hair and combing it in with both combs, so that I have got my hair terribly greasy.' Pavel was not interested in his sons' hair. He planned to get Aleksandr to buy goods wholesale on credit and send them to Taganrog. Aleksandr was set against this and, using cousin Misha as a commercial authority, told his father why:

Firstly, when Loboda finds out, he'll undercut you in Taganrog . . . secondly, you can only buy for cash in Moscow . . . , thirdly, buying on credit costs three times more . . . , fourthly, Moscow will ask Loboda what sort of person you are, and Loboda will naturally say as suits him: fifthly, Loboda is an expert . . . sixthly, Loboda is in place and has customers; seventhly, Loboda will squash us with his prices; eighthly, you will inevitably quarrel with him. And now consider Misha's position . . . he will lose his reputation and his boss will look askance . . . Keep struggling with the grocery.

For the first time, the tables had turned. Pavel had lost his authority and his sons were finding independence. Aleksandr could as a silver medallist always find private pupils in Moscow. Acrimony between him and his father poisoned their relations, though Aleksandr sympathized with Pavel as Taganrog's merchants squeezed him: 'because of some bastard who is only concerned about his ugly mug you and I have to suffer, the thought makes me spit blood.'

Kolia was paralysed by the financial obstacles: he wanted to move on to Petersburg, where entry to art college was free, but had no money for the fare. Pavel, after repeated pleas, petitioned Liubov Alferaki, the wife of Taganrog's richest merchant, asking her to pay for Kolia's transfer to the Petersburg Academy of the Arts:

Give him an education in the arts, which bounty you have bestowed on many . . . for twelve years my son and I have read and sung in the Palace church when you pronounced your prayers to the Almighty God with great ardour.

36

The Alferakis did not help. Kolia felt abandoned, and sank in despair at the prospect of joining Misha Chokhov in Gavrilov's warehouse. Aleksandr was hurt by his parents' apathy. They offered reproaches, not support. Evgenia suspected him of hating his brother; Pavel ordered him to church. Aleksandr begged them: 'And for God's sake I ask you to write more warmly to us, from the heart: daddy, you just give lectures which we have learnt by heart since we were children . . .'

Evgenia was distressed by Aleksandr's closing remark: 'I've been to the catholic church. Wonderful music.' 'Aleksandr, pray properly, you've no business going round catholic churches,' she replied. She sent Aleksandr two roubles and a torrent of complaints for his name day, and begged Aleksandr to apply to the railway millionaire Poliakov for a free ticket, so that she could come and settle Kolia in. She was desperate enough finding money and space in Taganrog, and persuading the two *gimnazia* to keep Maria, Anton and Vania on, when the fees could not be paid. As soon as her two eldest sons had left, she took on Selivanov's niece Sasha as a paying guest. Anton was in the country, too ill to write. Evgenia poured her heart out to Aleksandr:

> Kolia must be ill, my heart can sense it. We've let the annexe to tenants and we are living like sardines in a can, I'm worn out with running from living room to kitchen and I expect the people in the rooms are finding it very tight . . .

The younger brothers in Taganrog were still full of the joys of their summer holidays: on 16 August 1875 Vania wrote to Aleksandr and Kolia:

> It was good, I rode a horse yesterday was Mama's birthday and I spent the whole day in the shop and the day before was a dinner at uncle Mitrofan's where our cousins had dinner and there were a lot of priests . . . I had the first letter from you and took it especially it interested the Kamburovs when I read out that Kolia was crossing himself at every step. I'm well Anton is not very well . . .

By September 1875 the two brothers were living in conditions that Aleksandr recalled as 'a cloaca with fish floating up from beneath the floorboards'. Aleksandr wanted to send Kolia home for Christmas alone. 'I've no reason to go to Taganrog, I find it repulsive now.'

Evgenia's sons had done what she had asked them not to: they had asked a Jew for help. Kolia described his visit to Rubinstein, a member of the distinguished composer's family, well known for philanthropy to provincial students: 'I already know half Moscow. I've been to see Rubinstein. He is a tiny little yid, about the height of our Misha, he received us rather coolly, he hardly speaks any Russian and so I talked through a Jewish interpreter . . .' Kolia wanted private pupils. Rubinstein promised to help. Kolia explained to his mother, at great length, that as a stranger in Moscow he had only expenses and no prospects of earnings. Anton still had Kolia's paints in Taganrog. 'I sit alone at home, I'm fed up with sloping around Moscow.' Finally on 4 September he passed a mathematics exam, was enrolled at the Art College and began to draw. Even though he could now only afford half a roll for breakfast and his shoes let in the rain, Kolia's mood swung violently from depression to euphoria. Ivan Loboda brought him a violin from Taganrog. Kolia reassured his mother in a tone that must have aroused Anton's envy:

> a life outside the parental home, independent! And in an independent life you have to keep your ears sharp and your eyes open, because you're dealing not with boys but with mature people . . . Today I had for dinner: borshch and fried eggs, yesterday I had borshch and chops . . .

Kolia's high spirits lasted all autumn. He found pupils among his fellow students for calligraphy and drawing, but he still had to complete his secondary education while studying Art and Architecture: Anton sent him his Ovid and a crib. By now Kolia was known to a circle of students as 'The Artist', trawling Moscow's drinking dens. The trickle of money from Taganrog dried up. While attending university only on Tuesdays, in return for board and lodging for himself and Kolia, Aleksandr worked in a crammer run by two Scandinavians, Brukker and Groening. Kolia's eccentricities made life intolerable: he worked spasmodically, rarely washed and often wet his bed. In October 1875 Aleksandr complained to Anton:

> I'm writing on my bed, half-asleep, for it is past one in the morning. Kolia has been snoring for some time after his constant 'I can't spare the time'. The poor boy is wiped out. He's stunk the whole room out. He has an odd way of sleeping. He covers himself so that his head and back are covered up, but a yard of his legs are uncovered.

He's trouble, he slops about bare-foot in the evening, wears no socks, there's mud in his boots ... his feet are filthy. He went to the baths on Saturday and by Sunday his feet are like an Ethiopian's ... We have floods almost every night and all his rotten stuff is drying in my room. I swear to you by God that I'll lose my job because of his arsehole ... Mama is afraid I'm treating him badly, but she's the one, because she doesn't bother to do anything about acquiring an overcoat for him, while Papa tries for miracles and writes to tell us to borrow money ...

Although his pupils were charged 700 roubles a year, Brukker had stopped feeding, let alone paying, his student-teacher. In a freezing November the school was no longer heated, the boys fell ill and their parents retrieved them. Groening and Aleksandr fled. Despite a libellous letter from Brukker's wife, a Prince Vorontsov paid Aleksandr board and lodging to teach his sons for a few months. Kolia plunged into destitution, and complained to his parents:

Aleksandr has left and I wandered all day around town looking for somewhere to live and came back hungry at night, I hadn't eaten since breakfast and when I got back I asked for food and they told me there wasn't any. Aleksandr's at Vorontsov's, I'm sitting in a little room and there's revolution in the building, they're saying Aleksandr has poached all the pupils that the parents have removed because of the bad state of things. In the next room Brukker is raging and I'm sitting and waiting for him to say, 'Clear out.'

Ten roubles from Loboda got Kolia lodgings in December, but he was desperate: 'I shall be spending the night in 30 degrees of frost by Sukharevka tower and I shall die of starvation if nobody lends me anything ...' The noose tightened in Taganrog. Evgenia told Aleksandr that she could not cope, let alone find the fare to come and comfort her sons:

Antosha and Vania have spent all week at home, the school is demanding payment and we have no money. Yesterday, 9 October, Pavel went and asked the headmaster to let Vania off, but Antosha is still at home, in all 42 roubles have to be paid for him and Masha. Now tell me not to moan. I'm so weak with worry that I can hardly walk, if I had my health I might earn some money, but I can't, yesterday I spent all day in bed ... I asked Selivanov for 30 roubles to pay back at 10 roubles a year. He wouldn't ... what are we to do with Kolia, he mustn't drink tea before bedtime. Please see to his underwear, don't let him drop it about and let it rot. I'm even crying because we haven't sent you any money. . . . Daddy isn't sending you money, but not because he's mean, God sees that he has nothing. This month we have to pay 50 roubles interest on the house to the bank . . . Vania's been sent back from school. Diakonov just threw him out. Pokrovsky spoke up for us, but Diakonov wouldn't hear of it . . .

December 1875 in Taganrog was severe: Evgenia had frostbite on both hands. She had thanked Ivan Loboda for keeping an eye on her sons and Loboda lent her enough money for Kolia to come home for Christmas and the New Year. So severe were the snows, however, that the railway from Taganrog was blocked. Kolia had to leave the train south at a halt by a Scythian barrow, Matveev Kurgan: on 23 December Anton was sent by sledge with fur coats to carry him back, hungry and ill, over the last forty miles. Kolia stayed with his family until February, when the lines were kept clear, and he could beg his fare back to Moscow from a family friend.

Kolia was busy in Taganrog contacting old flames. He wrote in dog-French, German and Russian reassuring Aleksandr that Maria Faist, his fiancée, loved him:

Quand je disais que tu are putting on weight elle disait toujours: Good boy! . . . I don't know how I shall leave here; Vater refuses to send any money. I told him if I'm not sent off by the 15th I'll steal it and go. Vater envoyé pour moi de tabac, deja 2 fois Vania is such a little bastard that nobody gets any peace.[29]

Anton too reported to Aleksandr on Maria Faist – in dog-German. On 3 March 1876 he wrote his first surviving letter:

Ich war gestern im Hause Alferakis auf einen Konzert, und sah dort deine Marie Faist und ihre Schwester Luise. Ich habe eine discovery gemacht: Luise is jealous of dich and Marie und the other way round. Sie fragten mich von dir separately, secretly. But was ist das? Du bist ein lady's man . . .

Evgenia and Pavel were busy salvaging every penny owed to them. Selivanov's niece Sasha owed rent, but Selivanov had left for warmer premises and taken her with him. Evgenia could not afford a rouble a day to heat the house for her remaining tenants: they piled into the kitchen for warmth. Somehow in these conditions Anton gained '5's for Religious Knowledge and German. When Kolia left, his younger brothers and sister cried 'Take us too!', but it was not the children who were off to Moscow. At Easter, early in April 1876, a family council was held: Egor came from Krepkaia, leaving the blind Efrosinia. He read his grandsons' letters from Moscow and agreed that Pavel had to seek his fortune there. Loboda saw no way out: bills of exchange were falling due. In Russia debtors' prisons existed until 1879 and, despite Pavel's status as police alderman, he risked confinement in the 'pit'. Evgenia told her father-in-law that there wasn't even money for the fare to Moscow. To her amazement, she told Aleksandr, 'he pitied us and gave money . . . I don't know how to thank him for all his benefactions, he's old and works hard for all his children, for God's sake write to him and thank him, he's already given Kolia 10 roubles.' Egor was dismayed by his sons. In Kaluga Mikhail had died; in Taganrog Mitrofan was just keeping his head above water; Pavel was about to flee in disgrace.

Plans were made to abandon ship. Loboda would not buy the stock. The family hid their unsold wares in the stable. Evgenia hovered between despair and wild hope. She wrote to Aleksandr and Kolia on 8 April: 'Anyone who meets me will be amazed, I've aged all at once, could you give Papa any more, or might we find a little shop in Moscow to rent . . .'[30]

Evgenia scraped together 11 roubles for Kolia's fees at College and handed the money, with Easter eggs and cake, to a Taganrog merchant leaving for Moscow. She packed Pavel's bags. The market stall was locked up and the keys entrusted to Ivan Loboda's younger brother, Onufri. The deadline for Pavel's payment of 500 roubles to the Mutual Credit Society passed. The guarantor, a merchant called Kostenko, paid the 500 roubles and counter-sued Pavel. The builder, Mironov, was suing for the 1000 roubles owed to him.

On 23 April 1876, before dawn, Pavel left Taganrog by cart, so as to evade his creditors' spies at the railway station. He went to the first country halt in the open steppe where the Moscow-bound train would stop. At 2.00 p.m. on 25 April he was in Moscow. In Taganrog Anton took over his father's battle for survival.

SIX

Destitution
1876

THE YEARS FROM 1876 TO 1879 were traumatic in Anton Chekhov's life. His letters to his father and brothers in Moscow have mostly been lost, but their letters to him, as well as his mother's and his Uncle Mitrofan's letters, show unremitting hardship and fear of worse.

At sixteen Anton became the head of the household, dealing with creditors, debtors, relatives and friends of the family whose sympathy was limited, coping with his mother's misery and his younger siblings' dismay. Gavriil Selivanov showed himself a hard-headed businessman as well a family friend: the grim comedy of *The Cherry Orchard* with the auction, the transformation of Lopakhin from friend into predator and the dispersal of the household to the four winds originated in Chekhov's adolescent years in Taganrog. Gavriil Selivanov played Lopakhin to the improvident Chekhovs. Anton, distress forging both his willpower and his reserve, grew strong.

In this debtor's hell, surprisingly, Anton's marks at school improved. The theatre and private concerts continued to occupy him, and he also went to classes with Taganrog's dancing teacher, Vrondy.[31]

Anton had already started a handwritten class-magazine, *The Hiccup*. Aleksandr, when sent an issue in September 1875 and two issues early in 1876, was encouraging, and he showed them to cousin Misha Chokhov. Everyone in the Gavrilov warehouse, including its owner, Ivan Gavrilov, found them amusing. In 1876 a wider window on the world, in the form of the Taganrog Public Library, opened for Anton. The school authorities were reluctant for pupils to use it: the school library had a restricted range of books, cutting pupils off from radical works, or anything seditious, such as the new satirical weeklies and monthly journals – the staple diet of the Russian intellectual. (In school only Father Pokrovsky subscribed to such 'subversive' journals

42

as *Notes of the Fatherland*.) Anton joined the library in January 1877, sometimes retrieving his two-rouble deposit to buy food.

The Moscow and Petersburg satirical weeklies influenced all of Taganrog's youth. Destined for the newly literate of the metropolis, for uninhibited students and new professionals, these journals showed irreverence to received ideas and prominent personalities. They encouraged their readers to submit their own pieces – comic sketches, caricatures, polemical articles – for publication and payment. Anton began to submit his own anecdotes for Aleksandr to edit and market through his university contacts.

Pavel's first letters from Moscow are full of pathos. Penniless, dependent on his student sons, he was apparently blind to the irony of the situation. From the day after his arrival he continued to dictate:

> Dear beloved Evochka, Antosha, Vania, Masha and Misha, I arrived safely yesterday in Moscow at 2 in the afternoon. Kolia met me at the station and we got a cab and went to the Flat, where Aleksandr was waiting for us. They were very pleased that I had come. After a talk, we went round Moscow and then to the Dining Rooms for a good dinner. Three dinners cost 60 kopecks and one bottle of kvas 7 kopecks. I saw the college where Kolia is studying, the university, the Post Office, the Telegraph, the 'Saviour in the Pine Grove'. When we went up there to pray, we were shown the most Sacred relics of St Stefan of Perm . . . The flat is suitable for three, the landlady is kind, I was only astonished that they never lock their room when they leave, they say there's no need, but a hired servant does the cleaning and might take something, God grant that it is safe. . . . Moscow is not like our Taganrog, there's endless noise, people bustling, the people live the lives they should, there is order in everything, everyone knows their business. . . . I ask you children to listen to Mama, do not upset her, don't argue with each other, do your homework properly. Vania, see you make an effort. The exams are soon. Farewell, my dear ones. I am always with you. P. Chekhov.[32]

Pavel and his two elder sons now lodged in one room in a house belonging to a Karolina Schwarzkopf and her family, the Polevaevs. The house was on the sleazy Grachiovka ('Rookery', also known as the Drachiovka, 'Rip-off, or Brawl Alley', but now Trubnaia street);

the Polevaevs were considered 'fast' and Masha Chekhova later accused them of corrupting both Aleksandr and Kolia.

Pavel did not yet detect Bohemian influence. He was obsessed with religious pilgrimage: he spent a day and a night at the St Sergei monastery thirty miles north of Moscow and wrote sermons to his wife. He did not hurry to find work: Kolia, he told Evgenia, was copying paintings in the Museum and a shop had offered 25 roubles for one painting. Pavel told Anton to hide furniture from creditors and stave off bailiffs; he was to sell furniture to pay fares to Moscow for other family members. Pavel had signed his goods over to Aunt Fenichka to deflect his creditors. Complacent Father Chekhov told his younger children on 6 May 1876:

> Dear Children . . . If you go on living a good life, I shall bring you to Moscow. Here there are many Institutions for study, *Gimnazias* . . . stay quiet, don't spread it to anybody, try to take your exams as well as you can and get matriculation, don't talk to anybody about this.
>
> Thank you Antosha that you are running the household and collecting what is owed to us . . . Vania, the rains have started, I'm very glad you have put the barrel under the drainpipe. Misha is a good boy, he will try to write and tell me how he is progressing. And Masha probably hasn't forgotten what I ordered her to do, when I left for Moscow, to study well in the *gimnazia* and to play the piano three times a day, according to my method, not hurrying, looking at the music and not leaving a single note out. If she plays well, then I shall bring you to Moscow and buy a good piano and music then she will be a complete Artist and perform in Public.

To his wife, a week later, Pavel was less sanguine about salvaging anything: he trusted neither his creditors, nor his 'well-wishers'.

Pavel still believed that, if need be, he could sell his house for more than he owed. In Taganrog that same day, appropriately the Assumption of the Cross, Evgenia tried to shake Pavel into a sense of reality:

> My darling Pavel Egorych, We received the letter where you write that we must sell the house. I wanted to sell it a long time ago only to get rid of the debts but there are no buyers . . . I said, Antosha go to Tochilovsky, he lends money against security, so Antosha went yesterday . . . Tochilovsky just shouted, 'That's a bog, God forbid,

no question, I want nothing to do with Taganrog,' so Antosha came home and now I don't know who to turn to ... yesterday, the 13th, we were sitting having tea, we hear the bell, we opened the door, there was Grokholsky with papers, the first question was, is Pavel Egorych at home. We say no ... I asked Grokholsky whether he would bother Pavel in Moscow and he says, 'You just warn your husband.' This is what I advise you to do, my dear, you write an open letter to all of us saying you are leaving for Tambov, write in it 'I am leaving for Tambov now' or wherever you like, but write it ... Anxiety and worry have finished me and now our old nanny came last Wednesday started crying ... I pulled myself together and told her, 'Nanny I can't keep you, I haven't got even a kitchen-maid, I'm alone.' ... fetch us quickly or I could soon go mad. Aleksandr is already listed for military service, I don't know why, it's posted on all the fences ... I hoped we'd mortgage the house and just be in debt to Kostenko, and now I can't think what to do. Answer quickly. E Chekhova.[33]

A tenant in Moscow had to register with the police. Fortunately, the Polevaevs were not law-observing: Pavel escaped arrest, but could offer no counsel to his stranded family. Anton, a mere boy, could not dun debtors or fight off creditors, even if some, like Grokholsky, were the fathers of school friends. Mironov and Kostenko, who held the house as security, would not waive the 1000 roubles they were owed. Pavel's illusions about the Cathedral Brotherhood that he and Mitrofan belonged to were shattered. On 9 June 1876 he complained:

I've lost any desire to even discuss our foul affairs. In my letter I asked you to give 300 roubles' worth of receipts as payment to Kostenko. Mironov has damaged everything, he called in the loan in a very unChristian way, even a wicked Tatar wouldn't do that ... Evochka, about mortgaging the silver setting of the icon, how can you? ...[34]

For once, Pavel felt abashed by the distress he had caused and praised his wife and son for coping so well. But he also felt betrayed. Gavriil Selivanov had promised Evgenia: 'For you, Mama, I'll do anything.' He had brought his niece Sasha, as a paying guest, back to the Chekhov house to share Masha's room. Selivanov knew everything that happened in the civil courts and chose his moment. Before the Chekhov home could be auctioned, he made a deal with Mironov, Kostenko and the court. He paid a mere 500 roubles, and promised Kostenko that the furniture could be sold to meet the interest payments that Pavel had defaulted on. In July, Selivanov, Masha claimed years later, announced to Evgenia: 'I've paid off the bill of exchange and forgive me, Mama, but now this is my house.' Evgenia's letter to Anton of 12 March 1877 confirms that rather than an act of betrayal, Selivanov's purchase was a favour which Anton had asked of him, to protect the family from more predatory creditors.

For the next eighteen months Selivanov offered to sell back the house to the family at the price he had paid – thus saving them, not robbing them of, 500 roubles. His attitude hardened only after losing patience with his improvident former landlords. He repaired the property and contemplated marrying and living in it. The Chekhovs hoped against hope that he was genuinely their nominee purchaser in a stratagem to save their home. On 1 October 1876, when only Anton and Vania were left in Taganrog, Pavel still showed trust, writing to Selivanov and giving him powers of attorney to rent the house on his behalf.

Pavel and his family were not cheated: they never did offer Selivanov the price for which he had redeemed their house. Kolia and Antosha sought out Selivanov's advice and trusted him as much as they did Uncle Mitrofan. Good relations persisted between the Chekhovs and Selivanovs. The friendly correspondence between the Chekhovs and Selivanov's niece Sasha and brother-in-law and nephews, the Kravtsovs, suggests that Selivanov, though hard-nosed, was no rogue.

Mitrofan's lukewarm sympathy hurt Pavel and Evgenia more. Mitrofan wrote effusive sermons (Aleksandr called him and his wife 'the Holy Fathers'), assuring Pavel that their trials were from God.[35] When Pavel asked for money, Mitrofan pleaded poverty (although he had no debts) and limited his support to feeding Anton, hiding Evgenia's treasures and sending two or three roubles to Pavel in Moscow. Pavel's fraternal love faltered: in September 1876 Aleksandr reported to Anton:

> He used not to let anyone say anything bad about his brother and his spouse, but now he never misses a chance to besmirch them, which by the way they thoroughly deserve. Once he even went so far as to say about them: 'Pharisees, sons of bitches.' . . . Selivanov in my view is a thousand times right when he warns mother against the Holy Fathers.

On 3 June 1876, after a grim family conference with Egor and his blind wife, Mitrofan wrote to his brother:

> We can see Evgenia is very unhappy; she has lost weight, and so has Anton, only we do not know how you are living in Moscow, what you are doing, how you are feeding yourself. A great Divine Visitation is upon you ... Evgenia was with us today to see Papa off and drank a glass of fine wine. She said, 'For grief.' We said, 'For future joy.' Mironov hopes you can be saved, but you must pray for him.

Pavel did not remonstrate with Mitrofan, but with Anton for showing his anxiety.

> Antosha! I'm told that you and Mama have supposedly lost weight. How can this be? You write to me, 'Daddy, be brave and strong, be cheerful and pray.' ... So you are as big a coward and as poor in spirit as your elder Brother ... Antosha, take care of Mama, if anything happens, you will have to answer. She could come and join us, perhaps you can gather say 100 roubles for her fare. Life is no bowl of cherries here either ...

Pavel saw his whole life as a great sacrifice; he lectured Anton: 'we have not had a single peaceful day in our lives, have cared, have laboured, have endured everything, suffered, pleaded, so as to educate you as best we could, to make you cleverer, to make your life easier.' The other children were told to clean the barrels in the cellar, asked about the latest trials of corrupt merchants in Taganrog, reproached for poor marks at school. Pavel, Aleksandr and Kolia had moved, in the same house, from a 13-rouble room to a 7-rouble room. In the holidays Aleksandr and Kolia went to the country with Mrs Polevaeva, leaving Pavel alone in Moscow. He vented his discontent to Anton:

> Here we don't know the taste of beef or potatoes or fish or vinegar ... Tell Mama not to let anyone into the House and not to let the Creditors see her, say that she's not at Home ... Sell the furniture, the Mirrors and the beds, get the money together and send Mama to Moscow ...

Anton was unhappy at being left behind in Taganrog to fend for himself and his indigent parents. Pavel brushed aside his protests:

47

Antosha . . . I'm amazed that you and Masha want so much to come to Moscow and not to live in Taganrog. The bedbugs in Moscow would eat you in one night, I've never seen such enormous insects in my life. Worse than Taganrog creditors, I literally scrape them by hand off my pillow at night. You write that whether I find a job or not, you still have to come, but you don't consider that it's impossible to live in Moscow without money . . . I am definitely going mad with nothing to do, I am weak with idleness, never in my life have I experienced such an agonising situation . . . Mama writes that she won't be allowed to leave Taganrog, and that she has debts. I am astounded by such an opinion . . .

Kolia desperately wanted his mother to come, together with the youngest children, Masha and Misha. But he agreed with Pavel that Anton and Vania should stay. He took his father's side and said that it was not worth Pavel working for less than 50 roubles a month. Nobody in Moscow would employ a bankrupt merchant in his fifties for even half that wage. Gavrilov, cousin Misha's employer, turned Pavel away: 'Why did you come here?' Pavel, a debtor on the run, had no permit to settle in Moscow; any creditors who were not staved off by Selivanov or the Taganrog Brotherhood could extradite him to Taganrog. Aleksandr and Kolia had seen fugitive debtors escorted by soldiers to the station; they urged Pavel to face the music, declare himself bankrupt and only then to return to Moscow openly, with a valid passport. A Taganrog police official, Anisim Petrov, much feared as an informer, but a friend of the Chekhovs, assuaged Pavel's fears. Kolia asked Anton to find out from Selivanov whether the Taganrog authorities were trying to have Pavel extradited. To Kolia's anxious letter of 9 June, Pavel added an angry note: 'What's the point of looking for me when there's nothing to be got out of me? I escaped empty-handed and Glory to God for that!'

Glimmers of hope soon eclipsed. In mid June Gavrilov lent Pavel 115 roubles to buy 90 pounds of tea to pack into one-pound bags for 9 roubles profit. Gavrilov even let Pavel take home the tea samples. The Micawber in Pavel came to life. By late June he was painting a rosy future to Evgenia:

Come to Moscow, bring Masha. Just get 50 roubles together and come. We'll find a flat or a country cottage. The Moscow air is good, my health is restored. I don't miss Taganrog any more and don't want to go there. Who'll be in the house – just Antosha. Leave him to Fenichka . . . bring the valuables, the silver frames. Here you can pawn them and get good money, the interest is small, 1½% a month. When we earn some money, we'll redeem them again. If you can't let Mitrofan have my fox-fur coat for 50 roubles, bring it with you, we'll pawn it here and get whatever money we need. Where you are you're likely to starve to death, but here we have credit. [*Ivan*] Loboda is here and is nice and respectful to me. He says he's seen you at his family's house. I suppose the children's clothes must be worn out, but here we have everything, we live like Lords . . .

Mitrofan now claimed that he was rallying support for his brother:

All the others sympathize and commiserate and nobody thinks that you did anything on purpose. Grigori Bokos . . . said, 'Write and tell your brother that I have mortgaged my last property and re-deemed the bill, which I shall not call in, but I would like Pavel to renew it . . .'

On 29 June 1876 the blind Efrosinia, Pavel and Mitrofan's mother, broke her leg. She never rose from her bed again. (The bearer of these tidings took Vania and Misha to stay with Egor for a month.) On 11 July Mitrofan's infant son Ivan died.

Using Anton's earnings from selling the household goods and tutoring fellow pupils, Evgenia paid for three fares to Moscow. Vania and Misha returned from their grandparents' house. On 23 July 1876 Evgenia, taking Masha and Misha with her, caught the train to Moscow. The Chekhov house stood empty.

Vania moved in with his widowed aunt Marfa Morozova, who, in spite of her Loboda resources, did not pay his school fees. Anton spent a month with Selivanov's relatives in the country: there he lay ill for a fortnight, apparently with a hernia. In Taganrog he was taken in by Gavriil Selivanov, agreeing, for board, lodging and fees, to coach Selivanov's Cossack nephew Petia Kravtsov for cadet college, and his lively niece, Sasha Selivanova, for grammar school. Sasha Selivanova wore a red dress with black spots: Anton called her 'ladybird' and developed a flirtation with her that endured for decades. On one occasion they were spotted 'cooing like doves' on a bench overlooking Taganrog's great flight of steps to the seashore; when disturbed they slipped away to the nearest courtyard.[37]

Judging by the letters the young Kravtsov wrote and by Sasha's later career as a schoolteacher, this first love did not stop Anton from being an effective tutor. He and Selivanov established a *modus vivendi.* Four years later Selivanov would write to Anton: 'When I invited you to my quarters, we understood each other the moment we spoke and we recognized in our hearts that I needed you just as much as you needed me.'[38]

Pavel and Evgenia had left Anton and Vania to fend for themselves.

SEVEN

Brothers Abandoned
1876–7

ONCE HIS MOTHER had left for Moscow Anton was pressed even harder to raise money by selling furniture, finding tenants and collecting debts, but the worst had happened: Pavel's creditors did not hope to recover their money from two schoolboys. Living with Selivanov, dining with aunts and uncles, Pavel's sons did not fear the bailiff's knock. Four heady summer holidays, from 1876 to 1879, were spent on ranches belonging to Gavriil Selivanov's brother Ivan or his sister Natalia Kravtsova. As guests of the Kravtsovs (another Gavriil, Natalia, and their four children), on a ranch where even chickens and pigs ran wild, Anton and Petia went out with a shotgun to get the dinner. Here Anton rode stallions bareback and, as he confessed years later,[39] spied on peasant girls bathing naked. He kissed one of them, without a word, by a well.

On 16 August 1876 school started again and Anton reigned himself in. Public Library chits show that he was reading classics – from Cervantes to Turgenev. He was now in the 6th class, where the brightest boys were looking forward to freedom and wealth as doctors or lawyers. Anton's best marks were for Religious Knowledge; his father and uncle, after all, were members of the Cathedral Brotherhood. It was assumed that Anton would join the clergy, and Anton was teased as 'Pious Antosha'. Few pupils from Taganrog became priests, but the matriculating classes of its *gimnazia* in the late 1870s produced a great number of professionals: there were to be at least eleven doctors.[40] Outside school the schoolboys led a wild social life. They would meet in a den, play cards, drink, smoke and indulge in amateur dramatics. The landlord tolerated this youth club. Precocious *gimnazia* boys also frequented Taganrog's notorious brothel. (Chekhov later admitted[41] that he lost his virginity at the age of thirteen – probably at this establishment.)

51

Vania, eighteen months younger, left the childless house of Marfa Morozova – where the sounds of thrashings still resounded – and moved in with his gentle Aunt Fenichka and her son Aleksei, calling in on the Loboda household for meals. On 1 November 1876 Mitrofan reported to Pavel: 'Vania . . . is living with Fenichka, he's only been going to school for the last week; he has some money from book-binding; he asks you not to miss him or worry about him.' A fortnight later, Mitrofan clarified: 'Vania hasn't been going to school, but in late October there was a concert in the school hall for the benefit of poor pupils and it was a success. The next day Vania started attending and is getting good marks.'

Anton, on the other hand, Mitrofan saw only when the boy came to beg for a postage stamp or a glass of tea. All winter 1876–7 Pavel nagged his son: 'I told you to give the wall clock to Mitrofan and you sold it . . . Mama was expecting 20 roubles from you. When she heard that only 12 had been sent, she burst into floods of bitter tears.' The three roubles a week Antosha earned coaching barely paid his own costs, and he was sharing his income with a Jewish friend, Srulev. Although Selivanov owned the house, he was willing to let Pavel have the income from any tenants. This was Pavel's only hope. Anton persuaded the widow Savich, who lived next door with her daughter Iraida, to take a room in the Chekhov house. A rabbi was willing to take the house for 225 roubles a year; Pavel and Selivanov both held out for 300. Pavel was being unrealistic; Selivanov was perhaps now prevaricating, for he had no interest in Pavel earning enough to redeem his house. In mid December Selivanov made a surprise visit to Moscow, on his way to see his brother in Petersburg, and visited Pavel for just half an hour. They talked mainly about Pavel's debts; Pavel still trusted his former tenant. He wrote to Anton: 'We were very glad to see him.'

Pavel felt the house was morally his. On 21 December 1876 he sent a new power of attorney to Evgenia's bachelor brother-in-law, Onufri Loboda: 'To rent out as living accommodation the brick house with iron roof and all outbuildings, a brick annexe and a carriage-house that is mine personally, at a price that you consider right for not less than one year . . .'

Pavel even three months later had no doubt that a tenant would be found. Evgenia, however, was alarmed by Selivanov's vagueness about the ownership of their house. In Spring 1877 she wrote anguished notes to Selivanov and to Anton: she was searching for another saviour. Her rich relatives, the Zakoriukins from Shuia, visited Moscow on their way back from a pilgrimage: they gave Masha 10 roubles for a new dress and offered Evgenia and her younger children hospitality in Shuia:

> I shall ask them to buy back the house and then we shall sell it to Gavriil Selivanov for 3400 roubles . . . ask him personally for Christ's sake to keep his promise to me, to let us buy it back and not to charge too much for the rebuilding, while we have a chance of asking the Zakoriukins. For God's sake, Antosha, talk to Mr Selivanov . . . our only hope is that God the King of Heaven will inspire Selivanov to do the good deed he promised [*giving back the house D.R.*]. Our life is very short and if he does a good deed for us, then he will live long, and if he does not, he will die before the year is out, I have entrusted this to St John the Divine . . . If Selivanov agrees and doesn't charge much for the house, then I shall come at the end of June and you and I will go to Moscow together.

Anton read the letter to Selivanov, who snorted, 'I thought Evgenia was cleverer than that.' Evgenia intended, as soon as the weather was warm, to walk the thirty miles to the St Sergei monastery to pray for Selivanov's soul. Pavel merely asked Selivanov to get the family a 300-rouble grant from the Brotherhood.

The Shuia relations understood Evgenia's plight, but would not buy out Selivanov. Day-to-day living in Moscow was fraught and Pavel still had no work. In February 1877 he found a job as a builder's clerk on a church site. He was dismissed in two days. All that autumn and winter he had sat, idly pontificating. Infuriated, Aleksandr (who was then living with Kolia in a school) described to Anton Pavel's life in Moscow:

> We've borrowed 10 roubles from Misha Chokhov and they've been squandered and we sit weeping. Worst of all, we've lost all hope of finding a job. Every, every day we go to church and invariably, like an ex-businessman at the Exchange, we listen to talk about the Serbian war and usually come home empty-handed, for which we are met with tears of joy and the phrase: 'My bitter judgement', after which we disrobe, take a printed sermon out of our pocket, bought from the church elder, and begin to read aloud. Everyone

listens to us and only occasionally does the Artist [*Kolia*] slap his model's head and shout, 'Good Lord, Misha, when are you going to pose properly? Turn three-quarters-face.' Then after the injunction, 'Quieter you Antichrists,' order is restored. When the reading is over, the sermon is hung on a nail, with its number and the words 'Price one silver kopeck. Glory to Thee, Lord,' written on it.'[42]

Misha Chokhov could cheer up his destitute uncle and aunt, and even lend them 10 roubles, but he was busy at Gavrilov's and in his social life, and in no position to offer charity. A bleak winter followed. Evgenia felt bereft not only of food, clothes and hope, but also of Anton's concern:

We've had two letters from you full of jokes while we had only 4 kopecks for bread and dripping and waited for you to send money, it was very bitter, obviously you don't believe us, and Masha has no fur coat. I have no warm shoes, we stay at home, I have no sewing machine to earn money with . . . For God's sake send money quickly . . . please don't let me die of misery, you have plenty to eat and the sated can't understand the hungry. Tear this letter up. E. Chekhova. We sleep on the floor in a cold room . . . and tomorrow . . . we have to find 13 roubles for the flat.[43]

Anton showed little compassion. In a letter to Aleksandr he enclosed an iron hinge, a bread roll, a crochet hook and a picture of Filaret the Merciful. He teased his mother's lack of punctuation: when she instructed him 'Antosha in the pantry on the shelf' he replied that there was no 'Antosha on the shelf in the pantry'.

When Mitrofan sent money, it was for Pavel to buy and send him a Church elder's uniform. He expected other services from Pavel, such as distributing his spiritual adviser's sermons in Moscow. Mitrofan would have sent with Ivan Loboda the coffee and halva that Evgenia loved, but 'Loboda refuses to take anything crumbly'. Neither did Mitrofan send the sewing machine, because the railways were refusing freight that winter: the trains were requisitioned for the Russo-Turkish war, soon to rage in the Balkans and the Caucasus. Kolia's paintings, which he offered to his Taganrog relatives, were stranded at the station in Moscow for the same reason. Mitrofan wrote to Pavel and Evgenia: 'Without your sewing machine you have time to pick up a pen and tell Taganrogians about your life . . . have you got into debt there, or not? You write, my unforgettable brother, that you have no money . . . God will never abandon you.'

As November ended, Pavel's father Egor came to the rescue. Mitrofan announced: '. . . the old man, our kind parent, grieving and commiserating, cordially deigns from his own small earnings to send you, his beloved offspring, to feed your family, one hundred roubles. Let us give thanks to the Lord.' That Christmas saw another family conference in Taganrog. Old Egor summoned Selivanov to Mitrofan's house. Selivanov offered to sell Pavel's house to Mitrofan or Egor for the 500 roubles he had paid the bank. Neither Egor nor Mitrofan took up the offer. Selivanov felt his obligations to the older Chekhovs were now over. Within a year, after he had made repairs, he moved in, taking with him his nephew Petia Kravtsov, niece Sasha and Anton. Anton seemed happy as Selivanov's lodger. He was treated well by everyone except the cook Iavdokha, the only servant in Chekhov's life to mistreat him. She saw Anton as a hanger-on to be bullied, not a master to be obeyed. Anton and Petia greeted the New Year of 1877 raucously, firing a shotgun at the fence. He wrote to cousin Misha in Moscow: 'The room stinks of gunpowder and gun smoke covers the bed like fog; a terrible stench, for my pupil is firing rockets off in the room and at the same time is letting off his natural Cossack, rye-bread, home-grown explosive from a certain part of the body that is not called artillery.'

New Year in Moscow was grim, although the Taganrog authorities now allowed Mitrofan to buy Pavel and Evgenia a year's passport, so that they could live openly in Moscow. The eleven-year-old Misha showed enterprise. When threatened with joining the Gavrilov warehouse as a shop boy, he roamed all over Moscow, until he persuaded one headmaster to take him until a benefactor was found to pay the fees. In the severe cold of the winter of 1876-7 the eleven-year-old Misha ran to school without a coat. Egor's 100 roubles had soon gone. Anton was told to sell the family piano. Anton's earnings from his three pupils also went to Moscow. Kolia sold a painting, Aleksandr an anecdote, but both dressed fashionably and drank, and for much of the time lived apart from their parents or from each other. When Anton stopped sending cheap tobacco from Taganrog, Aleksandr spent his money on sweet, oval Saatchi and Mangoubi cigarettes.

Money trickled in both directions. Aleksandr sent Anton 15 roubles for the journey to Moscow in the Easter holidays. On 17 March 1877 Anton took the train for his first visit to Moscow, though nobody knew how they would pay his return fare. Aleksandr urged him to stay with him in the sordid Grachiovka, rather than in the crowded family flat:

> Firstly, because I live alone and therefore you won't be in my way, but will be a welcome guest; secondly, because our parents have just two rooms with a population of five human beings (the cur that lives there doesn't count); thirdly, my place is far more convenient than theirs and there are no Paul de Koks [*Pavel*], no Ma [*Mama*], nor 2 Ma [*Masha*] constantly weeping for any conceivable reason. Fourthly, I don't have the hideous drunken Gavrilov crowd; and fifthly, living with me you'll be free to do and go as you like.

Rows were shaking the main family home. Kolia swore five times a day that he was leaving. Pavel and Evgenia were, half way through the academic year, despondently looking for a school for Masha and loudly complaining. Aleksandr was summoned to mediate by Masha. He found Evgenia shivering in a soot-covered overcoat in the kitchen, while Pavel sat in the living room mending his fur-coat, oblivious to the tears he had caused by swearing at his wife. Kolia would try to paint members of his family – his habit of screwing up one eye as he studied his model had earned him the nickname 'Cross-eye' – but Pavel would drive him and his 'stinking paints' into the kitchen. Pavel would then declare that he would no longer support his ungrateful family, muttering 'Blessed is the man that goes not to the council of the ungodly'. Evgenia felt insulted that Aleksandr lived apart. Aleksandr told Anton:

> I have a nice comfortable room, decent healthy board and clean linen, and above all peace and quiet, where you don't hear the voices of the beaten and the voice of the beater, where nobody fumes, bothers or gets in the way . . . None has ever asked me if I have any money, where I get it, how I earn it and if I have enough. They don't care. They only know that every month they get at the same date 5 roubles from me and about eight times a month, outside the due time, they send for a loan from me (repaid in the next world in burning coals). They can see I'm dressed decently, my linen is shining clean, gloves, top hat, and they're sure I'm a millionaire.

Aleksandr still dreamed of Marie Faist, even though there was now a Moscow woman whom Aleksandr called his wife. Aleksandr's sexual drive was strong. 'Fuck while the iron's hot,' was his motto. The 'wife' was, perhaps, Maria Polevaeva, his landlady. In summer 1878 Masha spent a week in the country with Maria Polevaeva. She and her sister Karolina Schwarzkopf (known as Kshi-Pshi) were the only women in her brothers' lives about whom Masha publicly said a bad word. Ten years later Aleksandr declared not marrying Marie Faist had wrecked his life. After two years apart, in early 1877, he still wanted her to be his bride:

> Could I stop loving her or forget her? Daddy and Mummy can set their minds at rest! No devil will make me get married. Let it be known to them that only she will be the wife in my home. But this will not happen before I am completely secure and have stuffed our parents' throats.

Anton stayed with Aleksandr in Maria Polevaeva's house for two weeks among the thieves' dens and brothels of the Grachiovka. The most memorable aspects of his stay were visits to the theatre and the cementing of his friendship with his worldly twenty-five-year-old cousin, Misha Chokhov. Misha made the first move; in December 1876 Anton clasped the hand of friendship in tones that recall his father or uncle:

> Why should I hang back and not take up the blessed chance of getting to know a person like you and moreover I consider, and always have considered, it my obligation to respect the oldest of my cousins and respect a man whom our family regards so warmly.

Misha Chokhov and his fellow shop-workers would visit the Chekhov household, down innumerable bottles and sing both church and folk songs at the top of their voices, Pavel rising to conduct the singers as he used to in the Palace chapel at Taganrog. The womenfolk – Evgenia, Masha and Misha Chokhov's sister Liza – would cover up the men when they fell asleep.

After the Easter holidays of 1877 the family scraped the money together to send Anton back to Taganrog and fabricated a medical certificate to explain the delay to the school *inspecktor*. Anton begged Misha to look after Evgenia: 'she is shattered, physically and morally

... My mother has a character on which an outsider's moral support acts strongly and beneficially...'.

Moscow stimulated Anton. On his return he contributed to a new school magazine, *Leisure*, a sketch based on Taganrog scenes. That May examinations distracted him – 'I nearly went mad', he told Misha Chokhov. In the summer Anton resumed his effusive letters, begging his cousin once again to keep an eye on his mother. He expressed an affection that seemed to have survived beatings and tribulations:

> My father and mother are the only people in the whole wide world for whom I shall never ever grudge anything. If I ever stand high, it is their doing, they are glorious people, and their unbounded love of their children puts them above all praise, compensates for any faults of theirs.

Anton missed Pavel and Evgenia badly. On 18 June 1877 Vania left Taganrog to join them in Moscow. Anton was invited to the wedding of Misha Chokhov's sister to a linen pedlar in Kaluga on 13 July, a merchant's extravaganza which Aleksandr, Kolia and Masha all attended (though Aleksandr thought the bride and groom the 'stupidest asses I ever met'). Nobody offered to pay Anton's fare from Taganrog, so he could not go.

EIGHT

❦

Alone

1877–9

ANTON STARTED the seventh and penultimate class in August 1877, after a month with the Kravtsovs in the steppes at Ragozina Gully and some weeks with Ivan Selivanov, riding to outlying farms. Back in Taganrog, Anton lived in the old family house with Gavriil Selivanov and the Selivanov-Kravtsov offspring, Petia and Sasha. He wrote. He sent sketches and verses via Aleksandr to journals such as *The Alarm Clock*, signing himself 'Nettles'. Some were rejected, all were lost.

In late 1877 and early 1878 Anton tried his hand at drama. (Even at fourteen he is reported dramatizing Gogol's historical tale *Taras Bulba*.) At eighteen, he composed a farce *The Scythe Strikes the Stone* and a full-length drama, *Fatherlessness*. *Fatherlessness* is an appropriate title for his last years in Taganrog, but what the play was about we do not know.[44] In October 1878 Aleksandr delivered his judgement on his brother's work:

> Two scenes in *Fatherlessness* are handled with genius, even, but on the whole it's an unforgivable, if innocent lie ... *The Scythe Strikes the Stone* is written in excellent language which is very typical for each character developed, but your plot is very shallow. The latter I said (for convenience) was mine and read it to friends ... the answer was: 'The writing is fine, it has skill, but little observation and no experience of life.'

What Anton read and saw in the 1870s we know from Taganrog's library and theatre. Presumably, Pavel took to Moscow in 1876 his substantial collection of religious books. Anton's own books give us few hints. Perhaps his books from the 1860s and 1870s were bought later; as a schoolboy he could afford little. Translations of *Hamlet* and *Macbeth* (1861–2) may be the first books Anton acquired. *Hamlet* looks

59

like a schoolboy's possession: the owner's name is written five times, and it has pencil marks in the margins. A few books are numbered: a prayer book of 1855 is No. 63, *Hamlet* is No. 82; *Macbeth* No. 8 – No. 85, however, is a medical textbook published in 1881. Anton may as a boy have owned from youth Goethe's *Faust* in a Russian version of 1871 and an 1803 Russian translation of Beccaria's pioneering *On Crimes and Punishments*.[45]

Medicine, not literature, was the career he contemplated, and he wanted to go straight from Taganrog to Zürich university – the Mecca for Russian medical students. Aleksandr argued against this plan and gave Anton a guide to the universities of Russia, from the distinguished German university of Dorpat to the Armenian academy in Nakhichevan where they taught 'hairdressing, shaving and cutting corns'. Aleksandr himself was happy in the science and mathematics faculty of Moscow university. He focused Anton's ambitions on Moscow.

Anton was set on university; he announced to Aleksandr in June 1877 that he 'sent all young ladies packing'. Aleksandr responded: 'You shouldn't be a skirt-chaser, but there's no need to avoid women.' The Taganrog theatre too lost its appeal, after the excitement of Moscow. *Uncle Tom's Cabin*, one of its most successful stagings, seemed just a 'tear-jerker'. Although the authorities removed some 300 'seditious' books and journals in 1878, the Public Library was Anton's lifeline, and his reading was now serious. He even advised his elder brothers to read Turgenev's essay *Don Quixote and Hamlet*, a study of the Russian antihero which has a bearing on Chekhov's own fictional heroes who would be, like Turgenev's, either Quixotic men of action who do not think, or cerebral Hamlets who cannot act.

The pressure to send money to his family – and tobacco and cigarette paper to Aleksandr – did not relent. In return Anton asked for drawing instruments, but Aleksandr claimed that they were too expensive to send. He asked for Aleksandr's chemistry notes, but Aleksandr said that they were beyond his understanding. He asked for logarithm tables, but Pavel could not afford a set.

Hope dawned in Moscow. Konstantin Makarov, a drawing teacher who had taken a liking to Anton in Easter 1877, invited Masha to a ball at the Moscow cadet school where he taught. There she met a pupil of the episcopal Filaret girls' *gimnazia*. Masha followed her young brother Misha's example. She went to ask the Bishop of

Moscow for a free place, but the Bishop told her, 'I'm not a millionaire' and refused. A Taganrog colleague of Pavel's, the merchant Sabinin, then took pity and offered to pay. She was quickly tutored for entry into the second year, and in August 1877 was accepted into the Filaret school. Misha, too, had found a benefactor: old Gavrilov paid his fees. Evgenia pawned her gold bracelets to pay the rent, but Pavel now had hopes of returning south. Another bankrupt merchant had returned to Taganrog, Mitrofan reported, and would start afresh; perhaps Pavel might do the same. Alms arrived: Pavel's sister Aleksandra sent three roubles through Mitrofan; Father Filaret, treasurer of the Brotherhood, sent a rouble; an old colleague sent two. Finally, a member of the Taganrog administration hinted that if Pavel returned, he might have a clerical job at 600 roubles a year. In June 1877 Mitrofan was encouraging: 'have faith that the Lord will not abandon you. Many people are suffering, but not Ivan Loboda and Gavriil Selivanov: those two will probably never be touched by poverty.'

Pavel was offered a clerical job by a church charity. Although he could compose a lament or a sermon, he could not write a memorandum and was dismissed. In their Moscow flat, at the end of September, he posted up a family roster:

> *Timetable of jobs and household obligations to be carried out in the family house of Pavel Chekhov, resident of Moscow.* Where it is stated who is to get up, go to bed, dine, go to church and when, and what jobs to do *in their free time, namely* . . . Mikhail Chekhov, aged 11; Maria Chekhova, aged 14: Going to church without delay for all night Vigil at 7 p.m. and early Matins at 6.30 and late Matins at 9.30 on Sundays.

Misha had to 'clean boots with a rag', Masha 'to comb her hair carefully'.

> Those who do not obey this roster are liable first to a severe reprimand and then to punishment, during which crying out is forbidden. Father of the Family Pavel Chekhov.

Misha was beaten for oversleeping by eight minutes and not looking at the timetable. He was then instructed: 'Get up and look at the timetable to see if it is time to get up and if it is too early, then go back to bed.' A row blew up between Vania and Pavel over a pair of trousers: Aleksandr described it to Anton (1 November 1877):

The father of the family followed him and, in the Taganrog custom, started hitting him round the face. Offended by such cruel treatment, Member of the Family Ivan Chekhov, aged 17, opened his throat wide and called out as loud as he could. The landlord and landlady and the family members who ran towards the row shamed the Father of the Family and made him release the Member. Then the landlord and landlady made things very clear, pointing to the gate, while the Father of the Family smiled in the most innocent way . . .

Salvation came from old Gavrilov: on 10 November 1877, after seventeen months' idleness, Pavel Chekhov was hired as a clerk. For 30 roubles a month, with free board and lodging, this ex-merchant, aged fifty-two, had to live like the shop boys, working from before dawn well into the night, with the 'right' to board and lodging on the premises (of which he usually availed himself). He could bring home sugar, which the family fed to Misha's puppy, now Korbo the family dog. The roster was taken off the wall. Work in the warehouse stopped the quarrels at home; now the shop boys bore the brunt of Pavel's lectures on how to trade and live. These earned him the name of 'Teacher of Morals'. Pavel was no longer head of the household but a visiting relative, though he never accepted demotion. Evgenia wept less. Kolia worked at home for his gold medal; his best friend, a mortally consumptive artist Khelius (known as Nautilus), came to live with them. Kolia's fame grew: he was now painting theatre sets for a wealthy patron.

In August Anton had written to Misha Chokhov asking him to lobby Gavrilov for Aleksei Dolzhenko. Old Gavrilov not only took on Pavel, but also subsidized Mikhail Chekhov's schooling and promised Pavel's nephew, Aleksei Dolzhenko, a place from February 1878. What had driven Gavrilov to relent towards the Chekhovs? Undoubtedly Misha Chokhov had pleaded Pavel's case. For all the Chokhov hedonism – 'If you drink, you die, if you don't drink, you die, so better drink' – Misha and his siblings were amiable.

Pavel made decisions and paid off minor creditors, such as the old family nurse. He fantasized about becoming rich. At the end of 1877 he had decided: 'Antosha! When you finish studying at the Taganrog *gimnazia*, you must join the Medical faculty, for which you have our blessing. Aleksandr's choice was frivolous against our wishes and so quite unsuccessful.' In fact Aleksandr excelled in everything from

Scripture to Physics, but no longer propitiated a father on whom he did not depend. Now that Pavel spent all day and most nights at Gavrilov's, Aleksandr rejoined his mother, his siblings and the dog. Anton, unlike Aleksandr, went through the motions of consultation. Even Kolia's art won Pavel's approval. In January 1878 he told Anton: 'We desire you to have the character of your brother Kolia! ... by his behaviour he has won good comrades ... Nothing in the world cheers us now, we have just one consolation, *our children*, if they are good.'[46]

Pavel fought any wilfulness in his offspring. Anton had written about his 'convictions' and at the end of January Pavel responded with irony: 'Our own convictions feed us no bread, which is why I work for Mr Gavrilov according to his convictions.' Pavel embarrassed Anton by asking Father Pokrovsky to protect the boy. He devised ploys for buying back the family house. He conceded that Selivanov might never let the house revert, but perhaps he could retrieve his lost capital. To Mitrofan and Liudmila Pavel wrote:

> So, my dear Brother, if I can buy back our house perhaps with the money collected for Mt Athos monastery and the income from the house can be the interest for the loan, when business in Taganrog improves and a starting price can be named, then ask permission to sell it.[47]

Mitrofan quashed the idea almost by return of post:

> the Athos fathers' money kept in the Taganrog branch of the State bank is held solely by Father Filaret to be sent to Odessa ... But Father Filaret, for all his kindness, finds joy in the miseries of those who do not live as he does ... I shall tell him frankly that I am trading badly, not covering my expenses, so that he does not reproach me for not helping you ...

Egor's 1878 New Year letter to Pavel is gruesome:

> Your mother, Pavel, has been suffering for nearly two years with an untreatable illness, neither her arms nor her legs work, not only was her body withered, but her bones are like splinters, she lies in bed not moving, moreover recently she has a disease of the head, the tumour on her face is like a pillow and there are water blisters and now she cannot see the light of heaven. She is suffering and I am struck down by exhaustion of spirit and strength, she repeatedly asks

God for death, but the hour for her soul to depart has not come, she is fed and watered by strangers, when there is no kin, in this grief she often calls on the Lord, she rails, groans day and night, like a fish against the ice, she recalls past happiness, and the present is not happy, she says 'I gave birth to children and saw them, but they are no more, they have scattered over the face of the earth, now they would help me and pity me in my great need.'

On 26 February 1878, nearly eighty years old, Efrosinia died – of smallpox, it is reported. Efrosinia's death broke Egor. That summer, at the age of eighty, he left Countess Platova and visited each of his surviving children and grandchildren in turn: first in Taganrog, then in Kaluga, and in Moscow. In December Egor wrote to Pavel and Evgenia and their children, whose names he confused:

I speak to you perhaps for the last time . . . as the first cause of your existence on the earth . . . I have eaten our daily bread from the table of kind, giving gentlemen, my kind children . . . forget not the sinful Egor in your prayers . . . console me with your letters while I am here on earth and when I am in the next world and if by God's mercy I shall be free from deepest hell, I shall write to you from there how sinners live and how the righteous rejoice with the holy angels . . . now lettest thou thy servant depart in peace.

In early 1879 the 'mobile bronze statue' went to stay with his daughter in Tverdokhliobovo and died there of a heart attack on 12 March 1879. At nineteen Anton had lost all his grandparents and three of his uncles. Little wonder that cemeteries haunted his dreams and his waking hours.

Others close to him in Taganrog were disappearing. In early May 1878 his cousin Aleksei Dolzhenko left for Moscow to begin, at the age of thirteen, a life of drudgery at Gavrilov's. After two weeks Aleksei took to Moscow life, while his mother, Fenichka, grieved, for two months alone and chronically ill, in Taganrog. On 31 July, her bags packed by Anton, with presents from Mitrofan and old Egor, Fenichka arrived in Moscow to live with Evgenia. Her sister hesitated, for Fenichka was a 'grumbler' and a drain on the house, but when the widow arrived Evgenia was ecstatic: 'I talk and I cry when I have to tell her about past grief.' For the next thirteen years the two sisters were almost inseparable, nursing each other, visiting holy relics, cooking and sewing. Pavel was far cooler. He wrote to Anton: 'Mrs Dolzhenko arrived . . . let her not yearn and may she live better than with Aleksei in Taganrog, she has already seen him and upset herself . . .'

Selivanov and the Kravtsovs had by this time become more of a family to Anton than his own. He was now eighteen. He even contemplated taking Sasha Selivanova with him when he went to Moscow and enquired about the curriculum in the girls' school which Masha was attending. (The Filaret school had compulsory German, strict Religious Knowledge, and no dancing – to the dismay of a vivacious Cossack girl like Sasha Selivanova.) Despite all his extra-curricular work, Anton's marks in May 1878 were excellent. He rejected his mother's pleas to join the family that summer. He roamed the steppes around Ragozina Gully with Petia Kravtsov and gun dogs.

Life in Moscow was less harrowing now that Pavel had found work. Aleksandr and Kolia socialized with the *demi-monde* of Moscow. By March 1878 Aleksandr had left his 'ungodly' wife. Pavel was overjoyed and called him Sashenka again, but Aleksandr's 'room' was occupied by a tenant. Despite Pavel's long absences, the family found a new subject for quarrelling. On 17 March 1878 Aleksandr told Anton:

> Vania simply rages. Yesterday he virtually thrashed mother and when father is there he turned out to be such an angel that I still can't get over my astonishment. He really is a nasty piece of work, brother! . . . He answered that he doesn't *have* to work, that his affairs are none of his mother's business and that he has to be fed, cared for and nurtured because he was summoned from Taganrog to Moscow!!! . . .

Vania, now seventeen, gravitated away from school to his elder brothers' bohemian life. He went carriage-riding; he serenaded girls. In April 1879 he failed his examinations. Masha also had to retake a year, Misha only just scraped through, and even Kolia failed History of the Christian Church. Kolia was on the road to fame; Aleksandr had returned to the fold, but Vania, Kolia complained to Anton,

> is trouble. He can't walk past without punching Masha or Misha in the neck . . . You can't get through to Vania with preaching, he just does nothing, despite the unbearable family quarrels which he is the only reason for . . . we have rows, violence . . . I get myself a room which I obviously pay for, and now Vania has moved in with me . . .

He was in real danger of servitude, for Pavel now proposed to put him in a factory. Mimicking the parental tone, Kolia copied out an interminable letter to their father:

> What's the point of him working two years at a factory and then being recruited for six years as a soldier? . . . if he is a workman, this reflects badly on you . . . what will he do with his limited pay? . . . No, Papa![48]

Vania was too big to thrash. In May Pavel reprimanded his errant son:

> Recently you have become useless, idle and disobedient . . . How many times have I asked you . . . your conscience is asleep . . . you come home at midnight, you sleep the sleep of the dead until noon . . . With God's help and blessing try to find yourself a job in Moscow in a Factory or in a Shop . . . the Iron foundry or a Technical Institute.[49]

Vania was saved in 1879 by being examined and passed, thanks to Mikhail Diukovsky, a teacher and close friend of Aleksandr and Kolia. Vania was transformed from lout into student-teacher. Pavel was delighted.

Kolia was to be in more serious trouble. He was only interested in finding a studio where his models could pose for him. He never bothered to register with the military for exemption. He asked Anton to send the necessary papers from Taganrog to Rostov-on-the-Don, but Anton replied only with jokes about him being conscripted. The worse the rows, the more the family longed for Anton, the one member of the family never to shout, hit out or weep. Kolia promised his father: 'You and Mama will be considerate to each other, our *submissive* brother Anton will come and we shall live, thank God, a glorious life.'

The women of the household had respite from Kolia and Vania in September 1878: their rich relatives, the Zakoriukins and Liadovs, invited them to Shuia, where Evgenia had spent her childhood. Showered with presents and friendship, they returned in early October, and the Chekhov family moved to a more spacious apartment. Still on the notorious Grachiovka attached to the church of St Nicolas, it was a dank basement: all that the inmates could see from the window were the ankles of passers-by. Here the Chekhovs took a lodger: an art student who paid 20 roubles to be fed by Evgenia and taught by Kolia.

Evgenia longed to reunite her family. On New Year's day 1879, after the older Chekhovs had returned at 4 a.m. from the Polevaevs, Evgenia wrote to Anton:

> I want you to finish your course in Taganrog safely and come to us as quickly as you can. I have never been at peace it's soon two years since we saw each other . . . I have a lot to tell you, but I can't see well and I don't even want to write . . . Aleksandr took us to the Artistic Circle Christmas party. Masha danced a lot, tell everybody.

On Anton's nineteenth birthday the message was reinforced by Pavel: 'Use every means to lighten Mama's burdensome fate, she is your *Only One*. Nobody loves you like your *Mother*.'[50] Feeding and clothing her children and a tenant left Evgenia exhausted. By the standards of her class she was living in disgraceful poverty, for she had no servant and stoked the stoves and swept the rooms herself.

Fenichka was bedridden – terrified of fire, she would lie down clothed in all her garments, including her galoshes. She added to the burdens by adopting a stray bitch. When Pavel came home, he offered to help, but complained of giddiness and exhaustion from his labours at Gavrilov's. 'At least come quickly, Fenichka says you're hard-working,' Evgenia begged Anton on 1 March:

> Every hour I ask God to bring you quickly, but Papa says when Antosha comes he will just go visiting and won't do anything, but Fenichka argues that you are a homebody and a hard worker. I don't know whom to believe . . . I have no time to sleep. Antosha, on Easter Sunday go to Matins at the St Michael church and then be shriven . . .

Evgenia's eldest sons led unshriven lives. Aleksandr caroused at weddings. Kolia wallowed in misery: his beloved had left him to marry the manager of a hospital; Khelius, his closest friend, died of TB. Rather than come home, Kolia would spend the night at the school where Diukovsky taught. Easily led, he began a dissolute life. He and Aleksandr frequented the notorious pleasure gardens of Strelna that winter. Aleksandr warned Anton in February: 'Kolia is starting new pictures and not finishing them. He's in love again, not that this stops him from visiting the Salon des Variétés, doing the cancan there and taking ladies off for all-night vigils.' This Bohemianism eclipsed in Evgenia's eyes the prestige of paintings that were used as cover pictures for a satirical weekly. She wanted Anton's support: 'Quickly finish your studies in Taganrog and come as fast as you can, please . . . I need you to start on the medical faculty . . . We don't like Aleksandr's occupation, send us our icons a few at a time . . .'

Kolia too put store on Anton's arrival, promising that with Misha they would walk to St Sergei monastery as soon as he reached Moscow. Perhaps he felt penitent. Now Aleksandr frequented the editorial offices of the weekly magazine *Chiaroscuro*, where he also published sketches and stories. A new family entered the Chekhovs' lives: the wife of the publisher Nikolai Pushkariov was Anastasia Putiata-Golden. Her two sisters were to play a fateful part in the lives of Aleksandr, Kolia and Anton. The second sister, the Valkyrian Anna Ipatieva-Golden, was already Kolia's mistress.

Anton sent a description of his grandfather's funeral, then faced the examinations on which everything hung. He knew what awaited those who did not qualify for tertiary education: on 1 March he had registered at a Taganrog recruiting centre. Every examination had to be passed. On 15 May he took the Russian essay: set by the Chief Education Officer in Odessa, the topic reflected the convictions of the Tsar's government: 'There is no greater evil than anarchy'. The examination started at 10.20 a.m. and Anton was the last to finish, at 4.55 p.m. The longest philosophical discourse that Chekhov ever wrote, his essay earned a commendation for its literary finish. The next day Anton took Scripture and gained a '5'; successive days brought History Oral ('4'), Latin ('3') and Latin Oral ('4'). After a fortnight came Greek ('4'), Greek Oral ('4') and Mathematics ('3'). On 11 June disaster nearly struck: in Mathematics Oral Anton failed to multiply fractions correctly, and only after a vote was he conceded the vital '3'. On 15 June 1879, he received a matriculation certificate, signed by Actual State Councillor and Chevalier Edmund Reutlinger, Diakonov, Father Pokrovsky and seven other teachers. Chekhov had been awarded '5's in Religious Knowledge (both examination and course work), Geography, French and German (course work). In Latin, mathematics, physics and natural sciences – the relevant subjects for medicine – he had scored only '3's. He had a '4' for Russian language and literature. His behaviour was 'excellent', his attendance and effort 'very good'.

In August Taganrog's administration for the *meshchane* (petit bourgeoisie) issued Anton with a 'ticket of leave' for study in Moscow. This includes a physical description: height 6′ 1″ (2 arshins, 9 vershki, i.e. 1.84 m.), dark auburn hair and eyebrows, black eyes, moderate nose, mouth and chin, long unmarked face, special marks: scar on forehead under hairline.

He left for Moscow at the last possible moment. Pavel and Evgenia begged him to sell the kitchen table and the shop scales. Anton was to bring with him Pavel's iconostasis, ledger books and shop drawers, Misha's bedstead, and buckets and baskets filled with Fenichka's belongings. Evgenia asked him to shame Selivanov into returning the house. Pavel issued him with a sermon:

> Fight your bad tendencies ... I give you good advice and so does Mama: never do anything according to your own will, always act as we desire; live as God commanded, Your friends, your true friends are Papa and Mama.

Anton lingered in Taganrog – he planned to stay the summer at Ragozina Gully and at Kotlomino, twenty miles from the city, with a school friend, Vasili Zembulatov. Pavel wrote to him that 'we shall just be looking forward to you and withering'.

In late July Anton prepared to leave for Moscow. On 2 August Taganrog gave Anton his 'ticket of absence'; on the 4th he had his permit to study at Moscow university signed by the city elder for the *meshchane*. He was also awarded what he had lobbied for all summer: one of ten new bursaries of 25 silver roubles a month that Taganrog city council awarded its best school-leavers. Anton recruited two tenants: his school friends Dmitri Saveliev and Vasili Zembulatov, two years older than Anton, who were also starting medicine at Moscow University. They each offered 20 roubles a month to the household on the Grachiovka. On 6 August, laden with baggage, Anton boarded the train to a new life.

II

Doctor Chekhov

I was frequently more proud of a skilful amputation,
of the successful cure of a rash, of progress in riding,
or of conquering a woman, than of the praise I
heard for my first ventures in literature.

Konstantin Leontiev, *My Literary Fate*

NINE

Initiation
1879–80

ON 10 AUGUST 1879, in the basement flat on the Grachiovka, after two years away from them, Anton Chekhov was reunited with his family.[1] Misha, now eleven, sunning himself at the yard gates, took time to recognize his brother; Pavel was sent a telegram at Gavrilov's across the river. Misha took Anton and his two friends on a walk around Moscow, before the family's first celebratory supper in five years. The next day brought a gentleman from the northern city of Viatka. He asked the Chekhovs to take in his son, Nikolai Korobov, another medical student. Korobov was a virginal, gentle person, unlike the extrovert southerners, Anton's companions from Taganrog, Seveliev and Zembulatov, but gruelling studies and the Grachiovka made the four medical students friends for life. The Chekhovs' poverty had been alleviated. Never again would Evgenia take in washing, or Masha cook in neighbours' houses. Evgenia fed her household to satiety, and almost made ends meet. Aleksandr and Kolia rarely came to stay; soon Vania, too, would cut loose. Evgenia and Fenichka had a servant girl. After a month in the basement, the family moved down the Grachiovka to more salubrious quarters. Here they slept two to a room, with a room for dining and entertaining.

Anton and his friends went to register at the University. Medical students had their classes in spacious clinics on the Rozhdestvenka (near the Grachiovka). Moscow University's medical school was in its prime, with professors of world renown, and 200 students graduating annually from a demanding five-year course. The first generation of purely Russian specialists was ousting the Germans who had dominated Russian medicine until now. First-year students, however, did not attend the lectures of the great professors Zakharin, Sklifosovsky and Ostroumov. They were taught by junior assistants. Anton had to study inorganic chemistry, physics, mineralogy, botany and zoology, not to mention theology. He studied the 'anatomy of the healthy human being'. The modern student gets a pickled limb, dissected by dozens before him; in nineteenth century Moscow, as in London and Paris, each student had a corpse from Moscow's poor who had been hanged or drowned, died of alcohol poisoning, cold, typhoid, TB or starvation, been murdered or crushed by machinery. Anatomy was a testing ground for new students; even those taking philosophy and literature came to the anatomy theatre to steel their nerves. Chekhov was not the first Russian writer whose powers of observation and analysis were trained by the dissection of corpses.

There were mundane reasons for choosing medicine: it was a secure and prestigious profession. Anton was a student who never failed an exam, but not an academic high flyer. In therapeutic medicine he was unadventurous. His bent – for diagnosis and forensics – was apt for a writer too. All his life his eye for a fatal disease and a victim's life expectancy was feared, and his autopsies admired. In psychiatry, then in its infancy, Anton also showed prowess. He lacked, however, a surgeon's callousness and dexterity. Some had reservations about his choice of career. Selivanov wrote:

> I read the letter of a doctor-to-be who in the not too distant future will in the course of his profession be despatching several dozen people into eternity ... I would not like to see you become a bad or mediocre doctor, but to meet you as a sensational Professor of Medicine.[2]

Anton did not cut the cord tying him to Taganrog. He wrote to Petia Kravtsov, who, after Chekhov's tutoring, was in cadet college (much to Selivanov's gratitude) and also to Uncle Mitrofan. Anton needed friends in Taganrog, and had to grovel to the city fathers, who disliked disbursing their ten scholarships.

Anton now took up with friends he had made in Easter 1877, who were part of Kolia's social circle. Their friend the drawing-teacher Konstantin Makarov died of typhoid in 1879, but another teacher, Mikhail Diukovsky, fanatically admired Kolia, Anton and Masha. Through Diukovsky and Kolia, Anton was befriended by art students who were to shape his future – Franz Schechtel, the future architect who would design the cover for his first collection of stories, and Isaak Levitan, soon to become Russia's leading landscape painter.

Aleksandr was for Anton a link to literature, through the Moscow weeklies, where Aleksandr was both a contributor and an editorial hanger-on. Aleksandr, still studying chemistry and mathematics, was at first little help: he was drifting to the gentry with his friends, the rich, sick and dissipated orphans, Leonid and Ivan Tretiakov. Their guardian, Malyshev, was chief inspector of Village Schools for Moscow province and helped to find work for Vania. He sent the lad forty miles west of Moscow to Voskresensk, where there was a school attached to a cloth mill owned by a magnate named Tsurikov. Tsurikov allotted Vania an adequate salary, and a house substantial enough to accommodate all the Chekhovs when, from May to August, Anton, Masha and Misha were free from study. Vania, at eighteen, was transformed from an undesirable lodger into a giver of sanctuary. Pavel was exultant: Voskresensk stood by the famous monastery of New Jerusalem. Mitrofan congratulated the Moscow Chekhovs: 'How pleasant that you have an occasion to visit New Jerusalem often . . . I live badly, I sin much, pray for me.'

Anton tried to break into the weekly journals, but destroyed the manuscript of *Fatherlessness*, the play he had sent for Aleksandr's verdict. In October, as 'Chekhonte', a nickname that Father Pokrovsky had given him, he despatched a story, 'Bored Philanthropists', to *The Alarm Clock*, where Aleksandr was a familiar. He waited for one of *The Alarm Clock*'s acerbic responses, but the rejection, when it came, was polite. On Evgenia's name-day, 24 December 1879, there was no money for a cake. Anton sat down and wrote a parody of his father's and grandfather's ignorant and menacing pomposity, 'A Don Landowner's Letter to a Learned Neighbour' for *The Dragonfly*. On 13 January he received his first acceptance.

The Dragonfly was a breakthrough, but only for a year. Its editor, Ippolit Vasilevsky, had a poor eye for new talent.[3] Two years passed before *The Alarm Clock* and then *The Spectator* published Anton, though these journals were a second home for Aleksandr and Kolia. The 5 kopecks a line that Vasilevsky paid his contributors was a pittance: six stories published in the second half of 1880 brought Anton a total of 32 roubles 25 kopecks. Such journals sold to 2000 subscribers and twice as many casual buyers at 10 to 20 kopecks a copy; no editor could offer even regular contributors a living wage. The trap into which Chekhov was falling forced writers to compose weekly stories, each under a different pseudonym, for several journals, to earn no more than Pavel Chekhov's wages in a warehouse.

The Dragonfly rejected as many as it accepted of Anton's first sketches. His contributions were as good as any, but he restricted himself to parody. Another piece, 'What do we find most often in novels, stories etc.', printed in March 1880, mocked the clichés of Russian authors and predicted what the mature Chekhov would shun:

> A count, a countess with traces of long lost beauty, a neighbour (a baron), a liberal writer, an impoverished gentleman, a foreign musician, dim footmen, nurses, a governess, a German estate manager, an esquire and an heir from America . . . Seven deadly sins and a marriage in the end.

That year Anton made no impact on his readers, nor on the family finances. Kolia earned far more and, when he painted stage sets or portraits of the Tsar, could subsidize the family as well as pay for his own dissipation. The Chekhovs still looked on their rich relatives in Shuia with envy, and Mitrofan, impressed when he saw his nephews in print, still saw the Moscow Chekhovs as pitiably poor relations. The Moscow Chekhovs did not put down roots: they had nearly a dozen addresses in Moscow in Anton's student years. Spring 1880 found them in another house on the Grachiovka belonging to a priest, Father Ivan Priklonsky. Even with the lodgers' income and Vania's new career, the Chekhov household sank back into debt. In April 1880, Pavel reproached Anton for

> our house [*in Taganrog*] which still has no tenant after two years, and the goods taken on tick from the Grocer's Shop. I am shaken by any unjust action and my health is harmed. I am pleased and content when modesty, moderation and punctuality in life are observed by my children . . . I'm sorry that Kolia . . . has abandoned art and is busy with things that bring him neither money nor a profession. It is very disagreeable to me that I and your Mother have made efforts to set him straight, but he has gone by his own will and desire, has lost his path and become stuck in a bog . . . Aleksandr has shortened my life by half and has ruined my health. Antosha, my friend, note what I have written and treasure these words and pass them on to your brothers. P. Chekhov.

In the April examinations, Anton had a mere '3' for anatomy. (Aleksandr, who as a natural scientist also took anatomy, had a '5'.) He consoled himself with Aleksandr and other students in the bars of Sokolniki park, drinking punch and Russian 'cognac'. Anton and Aleksandr composed a drunken letter to the 'cross-eyed' Kolia, after rounding off the night with the whores of the Salon des Variétés: 'I salted the dives and hammered the lamp into the crème tartare of chastity,' Anton ended cryptically.

Uncle Mitrofan knew nothing of this. He dined out on Anton's selective accounts of Moscow life, and read them out to neighbours, priests and relatives. He invited Anton to Taganrog for the summer holidays. Anton was only too pleased to accept. By early June Korobov had returned to the Urals, and Zembulatov to Kotlomino; Taganrog town hall hinted that Anton had to fetch his bursary in person. Pavel's behaviour drove his sons south. One evening, fuelled by vodka, he raged at their guests. His apologies to his sons did not undo the damage:

> [Saveliev] is worse than any old woman. He had 3 glasses while I was there, and he got carried away, well, nobody suited him, I very much regret that I had a conversation with him, thanks to a sip of vodka he has twisted my words in the worst sense, has turned everything inside out. To Hell with him! I excuse him, but I'm embarrassed with regard to Maria Egorovna [Polevaeva] and Karolina Egorovna [Schwarzkopf].[4]

In July Anton and Kolia took the train south. Anton stayed a month with Vasili Zembulatov. They dissected rats and frogs. He lingered in the steppes with the Zembulatovs, before visiting Taganrog, where he collected 75 roubles from the town hall and sent his father 15. Nevertheless, leaving for Moscow on 26 August, Anton had to beg Zembulatov to advance him the rent. August in Taganrog was expensive. Evgenia and the younger children were with Vania in Voskresensk. Pavel, alone in Moscow, told Anton and Kolia to visit Father Bandakov, to get news of their old nanny, to visit their grandfather's grave at Tverdokhliobovo 400 miles away, and to list outstanding debts in Taganrog. Most precise was his order for 'a gallon of Santurini wine from Titov or Iani at the Old Market at 4 roubles the two gallons.'[5]

The girls of Taganrog in the 1880s were in a predicament that preoccupied Anton Chekhov's mature prose. Every enterprising, intelligent male school-leaver left for university in Moscow, Petersburg or Kharkov; the girls were left with their impatient parents, playing the piano, embroidering pillow cases, their only potential grooms the sons of merchants and officials, too complacent to leave. Work as schoolteacher or midwife meant poverty and exploitation. Their third choice was to elope with an actor or musician, and blot the family escutcheon. Their predicament was to be lamented in many of Chekhov's stories of provincial incarceration. In Moscow, among more calculating beauties, Anton had missed the impetuosity of Taganrog's Greek girls. Now he and Kolia had romantic hopes. Kolia addressed Liubochka Kamburova as 'Empress of my Soul, Diphtheria of my Thoughts, Carbuncle of my Heart', though he had been pursuing her friend Kotik ('Kitten'). Of the Taganrog girls, the boldest on paper was, however, the half Greek Lipochka Agali. In October she wrote: 'None of your young ladies dares write to you, for fear you will criticize their spelling. But I'm not afraid since I'm sure that you won't laugh at me, you're my defender, aren't you . . .'[6] Selivanov cynically congratulated Kolia on his luck: 'You've had payment in kind which you enjoy, if I'm not mistaken, right left and centre, I mean on canvas and between the sheets – and she's not bad-looking – I've seen her portrait; your adolescent fancy "Kitten . . ."'

Anton brought back a human skull from Taganrog: it had pride of place in his room, this time in yet another house on the Grachiovka.

TEN

The Wedding Season
1880–1

THE CHEKHOV FAMILY moved again in November 1880, a quarter
of a mile uphill from the Grachiovka, to more reputable, long-term
quarters; the landlady, Mrs Golub, had a weakness for Anton. Their
lodgers did not follow: Korobov, Saveliev and Zembulatov sought a
less turbulent host than Pavel.

Anton's second year of medicine was demanding: students dissected
corpses by day, and studied pharmacology by night. Medicine
absorbed Anton more than literature in early 1881. The weekly journals were lukewarm to Anton. *The Dragonfly*'s rejections became ruder:
in December, Vasilevsky printed an opinion, 'You are fading before
you blossom. Great pity.' It took six months to find an outlet for his
work. Politics was stifling the popular press. Censorship in 1881
became so harsh as to endanger the journals in which Anton made
his début. *The Talk of the World* had an issue confiscated for its cover
picture – pens and inkwell in the shape of a gallows with the caption:
'Our instrument for deciding vital questions.'

The public mood was no longer inclined towards humour. That
spring the atmosphere had become oppressive. On 1 March terrorists
blew up Tsar Alexander II in Petersburg. Petersburg was shaken by
the wave of arrests, and the barbarous spectacle of a multiple hanging
by a drunken hangman, before the world's ambassadors. In Moscow,
professors who called on Alexander III to reprieve his father's murderers were dismissed. The Tsar's family believed that God had killed
Alexander II for adultery and for undermining autocracy, but would
not spare his killers. Alexander III, a bluff military man with a love
of the bottle, left ideology to his tutor, the Procuror of the Holy
Synod, Konstantin Pobedonostsev. The Procuror was an intellectual
– he had presumed to advise Dostoevsky on the composition of *The
Brothers Karamazov*. His views were that the State should only prepare

79

souls for the afterlife. 'The existence of unbridled newspapers,' he said, had no part in the salvation of the populace. Police spies were everywhere: Anisim Petrov came from Taganrog to stay with the Chekhovs for a month, almost certainly on official instructions.[7] The student body was in turmoil. In student meetings held at the university during March, as far as Nikolai Korobov recalled, Anton was present but silent, 'neither indifferent nor active'. On anti-Semitism, however, Anton spoke his mind. When his school friend, Solomon Kramariov, bemoaned his hardships as a Jew studying law in Kharkov: 'The Jews are being beaten everywhere and all over, which won't gladden the heart of Christians like you, for example.'[8] Anton offered vigorous support: 'Come and study and teach in Moscow: things look good for Taganrog men in Moscow ... Disraelis, Rothschilds and Kramariovs don't and won't get beaten up ... If you are beaten in Kharkov, write and tell me: I'll come. I like beating up those exploiters ...'

In this unhappy spring 1881 Anton asserted his authority in the family: he quarrelled with Aleksandr for turning up drunk and sparking off a family row: 'I don't let my mother, sister or any woman say a word out of place to me ... "being drunk" doesn't give you a right to shit on anyone's head ...'

Anton published nothing in spring 1881: perhaps he was writing his first surviving play, a monstrous melodrama usually known by the name of its main protagonist, *Platonov*. Misha recalled copying out the whole text twice, and handing it to the actress Ermolova. She rejected it, and Anton never took up the manuscript again. (It was published nearly twenty years after his death.) To perform it would take five hours; it is full of clichés and provincialisms. Yet *Platonov* is a blueprint for Chekhovian drama: a decaying estate is to be auctioned, and nobody can save it. Even the mine shafts making ominous noises under the steppe anticipate *The Cherry Orchard*. The hero, like Uncle Vania, believes he could have been Hamlet or Christopher Columbus and spends his energy on pointless love affairs. The doctor fails to forestall a suicide. The play lacks stagecraft, brevity and wit, but its absurdities and its mood of doom, its allusions to other writers from Shakespeare to Sacher-Masoch make it recognizable as Chekhov's work. It also proved that Chekhov could write seriously and at length.

In June 1881 *The Alarm Clock* printed one sketch by Anton. Months passed before Chekhov was a regular, but their office gave him an insight into Moscow's 'Grub Street'. *The Alarm Clock*'s owner was a crooked nonentity. One editor, Piotr Kicheev, was notorious for having murdered a student.

Summer offered relief from oppression. Only Vania had to stay at his post, in his school house at Voskresensk all summer, so that Pavel ordered him: 'Don't be absent . . . prepare to receive your family with the appropriate honours: Mama, your brother [*Misha*] and your sister.'

While Aleksandr went to the country to stay with his rich friend Leonid Tretiakov, Kolia and Anton decided to represent the Moscow Chekhovs with Gavriil Selivanov and Uncle Mitrofan at Taganrog's most resplendent social occasion that summer – the wedding of their cousin Onufri Loboda. Anton arrived in a magnificent *chapeau-claque*, a folding top hat, which kept blowing away on the journey to the church. Kolia drew a caricature, and Anton wrote facetious captions. Taganrog never forgot that wedding, nor the caricature, when it was published in autumn.

Wisely, neither Anton nor Kolia stayed long after the wedding. Anton was not to see his native city again for nearly six years. By late July he had joined his mother and younger siblings in Voskresensk. Here, to judge by a letter to his rich cousin in Shuia, the 'peritonitis' that had nearly killed him as a boy recurred. When he recovered he got to know the hospital at Chikino, a mile north of Voskresensk. The Chikino doctors, particularly Piotr Arkhangelsky, reinforced Anton's vocation. Throughout August 1881 Anton nervously helped Arkhangelsky treat the ill-nourished and diseased peasantry who flocked to the hospital for free relief. Doctor Chekhov found himself dealing with rickets, worms, dysentery, tuberculosis and syphilis, all of them endemic among the Russian peasantry.

ELEVEN

The Spectator

1881–2

IN SEPTEMBER 1881 the third-year medical students were introduced to new subjects: diagnostics, obstetrics and gynaecology. They became familiar with live bodies. Venereal diseases, then under the aegis of 'skin diseases', were central to the course, as a primary source of income for many practitioners. In Russian cities, as in France, prostitution was regulated with compulsory inspections and treatment. In Moscow hordes of prostitutes were inspected at police stations, twice weekly if in brothels, once a week if free-lance. A junior doctor could earn a good living. To stop syphilis becoming as endemic in cities as it was in the countryside, this demeaning procedure continued, despite the protests of enlightened doctors. A doctor became, as Anton later put it, 'a specialist in that department'. If Anton had 'difficulties with women', in the sense that his sexual encounters had to be light-hearted, even anonymous, and certainly without emotional involvement, these difficulties may stem from, or have encouraged, his familiarity with the whores of Sobolev lane, the Malaia Bronnaia and the Salon des Variétés, whom he met not only professionally. He never disowned them: even when his women friends were more reputable, he nostalgically recalled the 'smell of horse sweat' of the 'ballerina' he knew when a second-year student. For his first three years in Moscow, his girlfriends were nameless denizens of the red-light districts.

Literature also took Chekhov into new worlds. He was invited to become a contributor to a new Moscow magazine that came out sometimes weekly, sometimes more often, *The Spectator*. This journal became the workplace of four Chekhov brothers. On the Strastnoi boulevard, little over a mile from the Chekhov apartment, *The Spectator* became the brothers' club: Aleksandr worked on it as an editorial secretary, Kolia as an artist, Anton as a regular humorist, and Misha, who called after school, as an occasional translator and tea boy. The founder editor, Vsevolod Davydov, was saner than Kicheev on *The Alarm Clock* and kinder than Vasilevsky of *The Dragonfly*.

Kolia's best artwork was done for *The Spectator*, where he felt loved – not just by his colleagues, but also by *The Spectator*'s secretary, Anna Aleksandrovna Ipatieva-Golden, a divorcee who became his common-law wife for seven years. The 'three sisters' motif entered Anton's life: over the next ten years Anton and his brothers were to be involved with at least five trios of sisters. The first of these trios – Anna, Anastasia and Natalia Golden – left a deep mark on the Chekhovs. Anastasia Putiata-Golden was, like her sister Anna, an editorial secretary, and lived with the genius Nikolai Pushkariov, editor of *Chiaroscuro* and *Talk of the World*.[9] Only the youngest, Natalia Golden, was unmarried: she fell in love with Anton for life, a love that he reciprocated for two years. Anna and Anastasia were magnificent blond Valkyries – dubbed by their disparagers as *kuvalda* ('sledgehammer' or 'big slag') No. 1 and *kuvalda* No. 2. Natalia Golden looked utterly different, a thin, obviously Jewish girl with wavy black hair and an aquiline nose. Of the Golden sisters' origins almost nothing is known except that they were Jews who had converted to orthodoxy, but in the early 1880s, with their notorious appetites for eating and making love, they were at the centre of the lives of Anton and Kolia.[10]

Aleksandr's affections were focused elsewhere. His story 'Karl and Emilia' made an impact at *The Alarm Clock* and he won the heart of the editorial secretary there, Anna Ivanovna Khrushchiova-Sokolnikova.[11] Anna Sokolnikova ousted the Polevaeva sisters from Aleksandr's heart: she was to be his common-law wife until her death, and bear him three children. Born in 1847, greying and stout, Anna was eight years older than Aleksandr, and she had tuberculosis. Worse, she already had three children and, as the guilty party in a divorce, she was forbidden by a Russian ecclesiastical court to remarry.[12] Pavel – with the assent not just of Evgenia but also of Anton – refused to treat Anna or her eventual offspring, his first grandchildren, as family.

Pavel respected Jews: in his diaries he marked off the Jewish Passover as assiduously as the Christian Easter. Natalia Golden, unmarried, was acceptable to Pavel, who raised no objections when Anton stayed the night at her more spacious house. Anton's pretext was studying for exams; in any case he wanted greater privacy than a room shared with Misha. Soon Anton and Natalia were calling each other Natash-chez-vous and Antosh-chez-vous (i.e. Natasha at your place), Russified as Natashevu and Antoshevu.

Love and literature brought Kolia and Anton to *The Spectator* and tied Aleksandr to *The Alarm Clock*. Through Anna Sokolnikova, Anton, too, within the year, became a contributor to *The Alarm Clock*, and through Anastasia Putiata-Golden, Anton met the editor and owner of *Chiaroscuro* and *Talk of the World*, and became a contributor to both.

The sleazy world of the Moscow weeklies and the nightclubs, such as the Salon des Variétés where the contributors congregated, gave Anton material both for personal enjoyment and literary indignation. On one occasion, he exploited a visit he made to the Salon des Variétés at the end of September 1881 with two rich cousins from Shuia, Ivan Ivanovich Liadov and his brother-in-law Gundobin, whom Chekhov nicknamed Mukhtar after the Turkish general who fought the Russians in the Caucasus. Had Anton signed his article with his real name, the doors of the Salon would have closed to all Chekhovs. In it he describes the 'hostesses' – the Blanches, Mimis, Fannis, Emmas – whose fortune-seeking in Russia ended in this sordid nightclub – while the customers, named as Kolia, Ivan Ivanovich and Mukhtar, drink and disappear into private rooms. The thrust of the article is in the end: 'Antosha C.' advises the management that they would make more money by charging to leave, not to enter. Chekhov wrote many sallies against the Salon: perhaps he was responsible for it closing and reopening as the Theatre Bouffe in 1883. The distaste in Anton's article is at odds with Kolia's illustration, a centrefold, crowded with flirtatious hostesses, daring cancan dancers and happy punters.

In September 1881, euphoric after the family wedding, Aunt Marfa Loboda wrote to congratulate Anton on his achievements. Aunt Marfa could not have been more cruelly deceived. Taganrog did not admire Anton long. The issue of *The Spectator* (No. 9, 4 October 1881) that printed the Salon des Variétés, carried a double-page spread of Kolia's wicked caricatures and Anton's disrespectful text, 'The Wedding Season'. The Lobodas, the Chekhovs and Gavriil Selivanov could see their faces drawn as the various wedding guests: a noisy drunken Mitrofan; the bridegroom, Onufri Loboda, captioned 'As stupid as a cork . . . marrying for the dowry'; Gavriil Selivanov as 'a lady-killer . . .'

The scandal broke when Aleksandr moved to Taganrog. He advised Kolia and Anton:

> If you two value your backs, I advise you not to go to Taganrog. The Lobodas, Selivanov, their kith and kin are all seriously furious with you for 'The Wedding' in *The Spectator*. Here that cartoon is seen as an expression of the blackest ingratitude for hospitality.
>
> Yesterday Selivanov came ... with the following speech:
>
> 'I'll tell you that Anton and Nikolai's behaviour was caddish and in bad faith, taking material for their cartoons from houses where they were received as family ... I don't know what I did to deserve this insult.'

Anton was unperturbed: he replied that he disliked all issues of the Lobodas as much as they disliked issue No. 18 of *The Spectator*. Chekhov had a lifelong blind spot: despite his powers of empathy, he never understood the hurt of people whose private lives he had turned into comedy. Mitrofan had probably never been drunk in his life; he read *The Spectator* and felt betrayed: how did this barb tally with Anton's protestations of love four months before? Years passed before Aunt Marfa wrote again. Gavriil Selivanov left Anton's letters unanswered. The affectionate Lipochka Agali, probably the Hellenic beauty portrayed as 'the Queen of the Ball', also fell silent. Not for the last time were those most sure of Anton's affection embarrassed and humiliated in his fiction, and never would Anton admit, let alone repent, his exploitation.

Anton was now attacking more formidable targets. On 26 November 1881 France's most renowned actress, Sarah Bernhardt, came to Moscow, fresh from America and Vienna, and began twelve nights at the Bolshoi theatre in Dumas-fils' *La Dame aux camélias*. Sarah Bernhardt had a poor press from Moscow's reviewers, but nobody panned her like Anton Chekhonte in *The Spectator* in November and December 1881.[13] Despite Bernhardt's histrionic skills, he declared her so soulless, so tedious that 'if the editor paid me 50 kopecks a line I would not write about her again'. The crux of Chekhov's reaction was: 'She has no spark, the only thing to make us cry hot tears and swoon. Every sigh of Sarah Bernhardt, her tears, her dying convulsions, all her acting is nothing but a faultlessly and cleverly learnt lesson ...'

The actress in Chekhov's drama – Arkadina in *The Seagull* – is likewise an egocentric exhibitionist who has to be curbed. This review of Bernhardt is the first shot in a war that Chekhov as dramatist and later Stanislavsky as director were to wage against the stars of the stage and their pretensions. Like the Salon des Variétés, actresses were frequented by Anton in private and denounced in public.

Chekhov was becoming a journalist. Frequenting *The Alarm Clock* he got to know Moscow's most fearless reporter, Giliarovsky ('Uncle Giliai'), the linchpin of Moscow's best newspaper, the *Moscow Gazette*. Kolia and Anton had been invited to become founder members of Moscow's gymnastic society (in 1882 Anton was muscular and broad-shouldered). Their first sight in the gym was Russia's champion boxer, Seletsky sparring with the bear-like Uncle Giliai. Giliai represented for a while Anton's ideal of versatility. True, Anton did not frequent thieves in the slums around the Khitrovo market, drink spirits by the gallon, uproot large trees without a spade, stop a speeding cab by grabbing hold of the rear of the carriage, break the test-your-strength machine at the *Ermitage*, tame a horse so vicious that it had been expelled from the cavalry, lift friends bodily off the platform onto a departing train, nor perform any other of Giliarovsky's legendary feats, but in his later determination to be a journalist, an explorer and a farmer, as well as a doctor and writer, Anton was to emulate Uncle Giliai.

As much as a nervous censorship allowed, Chekhov wrote of crime. In 1881–2 three scandals rocked Russia: a railway crash at Kukuevka on 30 June 1882, on the line to Moscow from Kursk (and Taganrog), where an embankment collapsed and entombed hundreds of passengers; the Rykov affair (which lasted until 1884), the embezzlement by a bank's directors of millions of roubles; and the arrests of Taganrog merchants and customs officials, for smuggling. In all cases the accused were punished so leniently, that the stench of corruption hung in the air. After the Kukuevka affair everyone feared for their lives on Russia's jerry-built railways: the government forbad further discussion of accidents. Kukuevka injected into Chekhov's stories the same morbid distrust of railways that we find in Tolstoy's *Anna Karenina* or Dostoevsky's *The Idiot*.

The Taganrog customs scandal affected the Chekhovs most. In June 1882 Aleksandr graduated from Moscow university. He wanted to set up house with Anna Sokolnikova and escape Pavel's strictures, so he applied for one of the posts vacated by Taganrog's imprisoned officials.

By mid 1882, Anton had enough published in *The Spectator* and *The Alarm Clock* to swell the family income. (Nevertheless, he accepted an Easter job tutoring the seven-year-old son of a senator, Anatoli Iakovlev.) He was invited to write for a serious weekly illustrated magazine, *Moscow*, and he collaborated with Kolia on a miniature novel *The Green Spit of Land*, about a country house on the Black Sea. Again, the characters bear the names of real people: the artist Chekhov, Maria Egorovna (presumably Polevaeva), while the narrator, unnamed, resembles Anton, for he teaches the heroine's daughter German and goldfinch trapping. *The Green Spit of Land* showed that Chekhov could parody the pseudo-aristocratic pap – the 'boulevard novel' – which was then in demand; now he was challenged by Kurepin to give *The Alarm Clock* a pastiche that the reader might take for the real thing. The result, 'The Unnecessary Victory', was serialized from June until September 1882 and earned 'Antosha Chekhonte' several hundred roubles. This pastiche, too, apes the boulevard novel – a singer, exploited and then triumphant, a desperate aristocratic lover. Readers took it to be a translation of a novel by the Hungarian Mór Jókai.[14] It stretched Chekhov's narrative ambitions.

In summer 1882, after the exams, Chekhov published in *Moscow* his first bid for literary renown. Called 'The Lady', the story is full of modish clichés: a selfish lustful widow, a villainous Polish manager, a noble peasant, a violent dénouement, and the narrator's radical indignation. It is, nevertheless, a harbinger of better things. Anton's later stories of oppressed peasantry, and his fiction of the mid 1880s, where sexuality leads to violence, grow out of 'The Lady'.

So encouraged was Chekhov by success, that he devised more pseudonyms – Chekhonte spawned 'the Man without a Spleen' and 'Mr Baldastov'. With Kolia as illustrator, Anton compiled 160 pages of his best work to print and bind on credit. He himself would market the book (which had several titles – *At Leisure, Idlers and Easygoers, Naughty Tricks*). On 19 June 1882 the censor rejected the application. When a second request was submitted, pointing out that these stories had already passed the censor once, the argument was accepted, but, in an ever more repressive atmosphere, the book was banned in page proof.

If Anton was to support the family, he would have to write a hundred stories a year for Moscow's weekly magazines. Vania was independent now and Aleksandr, as a customs officer, would receive a regular salary, but Masha and Misha were still students, while neither Kolia nor Pavel brought much to the household. There were other dependants too: Aunt Fenichka, Korbo the whippet, and Fiodor Timofeich the tomcat. Aleksandr had brought home Fiodor as a kitten who had been abandoned in a freezing latrine. Anton was much comforted when Fiodor stretched out on his lap and to this cat he first addressed an expression he applied to himself and his brothers: 'Who would have thought that such genius would come out of an earth closet?'

TWELVE

Fragmentation
1882–3

ON 25 JULY 1882, in bad debt, and not telling the Chekhovs that Anna was two months pregnant, Aleksandr, his common-law wife and her teenage son Shura left their dog with Aunt Fenichka and Korbo and caught the train south for Tula. There they stayed for a day, entrusting Shura to Anna's relatives, before travelling to Taganrog. Aleksandr saw familiar faces: 'In Tula, Antosha, I saw at the station your bride, she who is on the Grachiovka, and her mama. They say of this mama that when she got in the saddle, she broke a horse's back.' Aleksandr did not like his wife's home town, and sent Anton an anti-ode to Tula. It is similar in tone to Betjeman's poem 'Slough':[15]

> I entered Tula with distress,
> My greying girlfriend would insist
> On dragging me, she could not see.
> Alas, I could not overrule her,
> I suffered and I went to Tula . . .

In Taganrog, at first, all went well: Aleksandr had returned to his native town in glory – a graduate, a civil servant, and apparently married to a gentlewoman. Stopping at the Hotel Europa, Aleksandr entered Mitrofan's shop as customer, to be swamped by avuncular embraces and hospitality. Mitrofan and Liudmila (who now had four children) removed Aleksandr and his partner from the hotel, in exchange for teaching their twelve-year-old son Georgi grammar. Then they stayed with old friends, the Agalis, as paying guests. Very soon, however, Taganrog had read Anton and Kolia's skit of the Loboda wedding, and only the Chekhovs' nanny Agafia was still pleased to see Aleksandr.

Taganrog was not on Anton's mind. All July 1882 he had to earn money in Moscow, while his mother and the younger Chekhovs were in Voskresensk with Vania. Pavel stayed overnight at the Moscow apartment every other day, so Kolia and Anton moved to a dacha with Pushkariov and his consort Anastasia. Deserted, Pavel called his wife and younger children back from Voskresensk and then threatened to join his sons at Pushkariov's. While the friendship with Pushkariov lasted, Chekhov contributed to his journals. *Talk of the World* aimed high: Anton printed a story, 'Livestock', that recalls the perpetual triangle in Dostoevsky's *Eternal Husband*. In 'Livestock' too the lover is saddled forever with the husband of the woman he has seduced.

After the holidays, Pushkariov printed Chekhov's longest piece in a Moscow weekly: four issues of *Talk of the World* carried 'Belated Flowers'. (This story was dedicated to Anton's former lodger, the medical student Nikolai Korobov.) The 'belated flowers' are a patrician family fallen on hard times. The story line, though crude, is strong. The central hero shows the author's wishful thinking: a doctor of humble origins flourishes as the 'belated flowers' wilt. Chekhov re-used the story line less crassly in 'Ionych' of 1899, where a plebeian doctor likewise turns the tables on the town's patrician family.

'Livestock' and 'Belated Flowers' like 'The Lady', were impressive: they brought respect, demand and money. That year, 1882–3, was strenuous for Anton. Fourth-year medics were taught by the luminaries of Russian surgery and internal medicine. Chekhov's practicals were in pædiatrics. Here he wrote up the case of Ekaterina Kurnukova, a doomed infant, paralysed and pustulent with neonatal syphilis, whom he tended for twelve weeks.[16] To mix harrowing study with a social life and some hundred literary pieces needed superhuman determination and energy.

To make a name, however, a writer had to be printed in Petersburg, where periodicals printed what was considered to be serious literature. Chekhov owed his breakthrough to the poet Liodor Palmin, who wrote for both Moscow's and St Petersburg's press. When Chekhov first saw him at *The Alarm Clock* Palmin, at forty-one, looked like a tramp: hunched, pockmarked and dirty. A few lyrics of noble civic sentiment, some elegant translations of the classics and a talent for improvisation made him popular. He was an unusually compassionate soul in the literary world. Flitting from one tenement to another, in dingy parts of Moscow where visitors risked their lives at night, with his servant Pelageia, who became consort and eventually wife, Palmin took in stray dogs, cats, ducks and hens, the crippled, the blind and the mangy. He and Pelageia drank heavily.[17] Chekhov was as fascinated by Palmin as by Uncle Giliai; the fascination was mutual.

In October 1882 Nikolai Leikin, editor of the St Petersburg weekly journal *Fragments*, came to see Palmin. They dined at Moscow's best restaurant, Testov's. As they drove away, Palmin spotted Kolia and Anton Chekhov on the pavement. He recommended them to Leikin, always in search of talent, as contributors. By 14 November Leikin had accepted three of Anton's pieces (and rejected two). He paid 8 kopecks a line, he wanted weekly contributions and he allotted Anton up to a quarter of each issue of 1000 lines. (In Russia even writers as famous as Tolstoy were paid by the line for short works and by the printer's sheet of 24 pages for longer works.) Kolia provided centrefold and cover pictures. Leikin was Russia's most prolific writer of comic sketches: every Taganrog schoolboy knew his work. As an editor he was ruthless (he rewrote without consulting his authors), but he won respect for his tenacity against the censors and drew major writers, notably the novelist Nikolai Leskov, to *Fragments*.

Despite a weekly correspondence, which became frank,[18] Anton found Leikin's boasting and pedantry tiresome. A *nouveau riche* eccentric, Leikin nevertheless commanded admiration for his love of animals and children. In 1882 he adopted a baby left on his doorstep. For his two hounds, Apel and Rogulka, he hung his Christmas tree with raw meat. Anton's physical distaste for Leikin, 'the lame devil', a squat, hirsute man with tiny eyes, and his irritation with Leikin's manipulative ploys were tempered by gratitude for spotting his talent. Leikin wanted exclusivity, and Anton had to write less for the Moscow journals. This jealousy became paranoiac at the end of the year, when subscribers were deciding which magazines to take for the new year. Leikin needed to show that anyone who wanted to read Antosha Chekhonte had to buy *Fragments*. Leikin's motives were economic, and agreed with Anton's artistic principles on one point only: the need for precision, speed and brevity. Yet, under Leikin's and the censor's stringent tutelage, Chekhov began to show a telling, ironic turn of phrase, a gift for dialogue, for an impressionistic image.

A new rhythm started: *Fragments* came out every Saturday and various Chekhovs put Anton's contributions on Tuesday's midnight

mail train to Petersburg so that Leikin could set them up, submit
them to the censor and get them out in time. The discipline was
stricter still when Leikin asked Chekhov to provide a weekly column
called 'Fragments of Moscow Life'. This was to parade the corruption
and provinciality of Moscow for the amusement of Petersburg's
readers, who needed to believe that they were in Europe and Moscow
was in Asia. To be exposed as the author would have made life difficult:
Chekhov had a new pseudonym for these articles, 'Ruver', and, when
his hand was suspected after a few months by others in Moscow's
'Grub Street', switched to 'Ulysses'. Writing less for Moscow and
mocking Moscow's writers and editors lost Anton friends in the offices
of *The Alarm Clock*, where he even used editorial conferences as
material for his *Fragments* articles. Eight kopecks a line justified
betrayal. In Moscow Anton published in *The Spectator* where friendly
relations with the Golden sisters helped, and where Davydov also paid
8 kopecks a line. Any Moscow publication, especially at the end of
the year, was to Leikin a dagger in the back. Often Leikin accused
Palmin and Chekhov of losing him subscribers by their promiscuity.

Socially, Anton was moving in more refined circles. His sister
Masha, whom her elder brothers had spurned as the family crybaby,
had grown up to be a friend and confidante. In May 1882 she matriculated from the episcopal *gimnazia* and started university courses (in
Russia, as in Britain, female students were taught extramurally).
Enrolled on the prestigious Guerrier courses, where eminent his-
torians such as Kliuchevsky lectured, Masha had become a *kursistka*
(a female external student). The friends Masha brought home in
autumn 1882 to her brothers were more salubrious than the editorial
secretaries of the weekly magazines, let alone the landladies with
whom her brothers roomed, but only the more daring girls on the
Guerrier courses could breathe the Bohemian atmosphere around
Kolia and Anton. Masha's fellow students rivalled Anna and Natalia
Golden for Kolia's and Anton's affections. To one, Ekaterina Iunosheva, an entomologist, Anton sent a beetle 'which has died of desperate
love', but she favoured Kolia.

Olga Kundasova, known as 'the astronomer', was a *kursistka* who
found work at the Moscow observatory. In 1883 she and Anton became
lovers, a relationship that limped on for two decades. Olga Kundasova
was gawky, strong-boned, highly strung, but even in her most unhappy

and infatuated moments too penetrating and frank for Anton to be comfortable with. More seductive was a temperamental, mordant Jewish student, Dunia Efros. Both Olga Kundasova and Dunia Efros experienced much distress before finding their places on the periphery of Anton's life. Far more complex and less Bohemian than earlier women in the three brothers' lives, they also behaved as equals. They changed Anton's perception of women. If the best stories Chekhov wrote for *Fragments* have psychological depth, we must thank the women whom Masha brought into Anton's life. Masha was hostess, secretary, *éprouveuse* and protector of Anton's private life, and began to share with him the power in the family.

Anton's older brothers were marginalized. Kolia's dissipation, and his tuberculosis, were undermining his reputation as an artist. He now took morphine, initially for the pains in his chest, as well as consuming copious amounts of alcohol. For some time the family tried to ignore him. In Taganrog Aleksandr was half-forgotten, despite regular letters which showed that he too was unhappy. Aleksandr and Anna were hopelessly inept housekeepers and Aleksandr did not present the Customs Office with the graduation certificate necessary to receive a full salary. The salary he did receive did not pay for even food and fuel. At first, the couple were lulled by Uncle Mitrofan and Aunt Liudmila's friendliness. Anna joined a confederacy of women and Aunt Liudmila confided her intimate secrets. Aleksandr tantalized Anton:

> Auntie even told my better half a few things about the general bliss that uncle provides her with. Naturally, I too know these details but I shall conceal them from you, for in fact they are quite unlike the slow motion which you, Antosha, make when you fold your fingers in a certain way.

Anna was clearly pregnant; the couple equivocated about christening the child. Mitrofan and Liudmila were embarrassed. In October 1882 Aleksandr, living on Kontorskaia, the street where he lived when he was a boy, begged Vania to come and stay: 'Write to me, don't let our links die. Anna is pregnant and invites you to the christening . . . I shall hand my offspring over to your school for you to teach, with the right to beat no more than five times a day.'[19] Aleksandr attempted to lure Kolia to Taganrog in the most effective way he knew: 'Liubov Kamburova was there. She is still in love with you. For God's sake come and copulate with her, for she is desperately seeking what in Latin is called *inter pedes . . . figura longa et obscura*. You are besought, come.'[20]

To Anton, as a budding gynæcologist, Aleksandr turned for sexual advice: Anna's pregnancy left him frustrated. Anton replied to Aleksandr (with a gift of money) and told him that 'medicine, while forbidding coitus, does not forbid massage.' The quality of Anton's mercy was a little strained: he was more preoccupied with medical studies by day and writing, to Pavel's fury at the paraffin consumed, by night. He asked Aleksandr and Anna to send material for stories – descriptions of spiritualist seances in Tula, schoolboy rhymes from Taganrog, photographs. Only Pavel, horrified by Anna's pregnancy, was utterly unbending. At first Aleksandr just remonstrated: 'Dear Papa . . . I am saddened only that you won't send your regards to Anna, knowing full well that if we are not married, it is not my fault.' On the eve of New Year 1883 Aleksandr tried emotional blackmail on his parent:

> you have mercilessly poisoned the rest of the holidays for me – there is no doubt about that. All December I've been poorly, I'd begun to recover in the holidays. Your reproach upset, offended, insulted and alarmed me . . . Today I am confirmed in Petersburg as Head of the Imports Desk and Customs Translator. My sufferings are over . . . What a pity your reproach came just when for the first time I breathed freely.

In mid February 1883 Anna gave birth to a daughter. Pavel would not acknowledge his first grandchild or speak to her mother. None of her uncles, even Anton, expressed any joy at the birth of Mosia, as her parents called her. Aleksandr complained that Mitrofan and Liudmila would not be godparents to the baby. Mitrofan could not face neighbours' questions if a priest came to the house. Liudmila told Father Pokrovsky that Aleksandr and Anna had married in St Petersburg. Aleksandr accepted Mitrofan's conditions: the child must go to church daily and observe all fasts. Liudmila then declared that Pavel would not let them condone sin. Aleksandr wept.

Anton sent his brother at the end of February 1883 a harsh ten-page tirade:

> What do you expect of father? He is against tobacco smoking and illicit cohabitation – and you want to be friends with him? You

might manage it with mother or aunt [*Fenichka*], but not with father. He's the same flint as the dissenters, no worse, and you won't budge him ... You carry your cohabitation like a stolen watermelon ... You want to know what I think, what Kolia, or our father thinks?! What business is it of yours?

Anton detected and disliked in both Aleksandr and in Kolia a disparity between high-minded pretensions and sordid actions. Kolia was taking on prestigious commissions – to paint the sets at Lentovsky's theatre in the Ermitage, to illustrate Dostoevsky – and doing nothing except to complain that he was misunderstood. Within a year, Anton predicted, Kolia would be finished. Both brothers, in his view, were destroyed by self-pity. He alone felt in the ascendant and triumphantly told Aleksandr on 3 February 1883:

> I'm becoming popular and have now read a critique of myself. My medicine is going *crescendo*. I know how to treat and I can't believe it. You won't find, old boy, a single disease I wouldn't undertake to treat. Exams are soon. If I get into the 5th class, then *finita la commedia*.

The family appeared to be dissolving. Aleksandr was stuck in Taganrog. Kolia moved out to live in a sordid tenement, Eastern Furnished Rooms. Vania stayed all year in Voskresensk. Masha spent all the time she could at her courses or at girlfriends' houses. Only Misha stayed home, studying for matriculation. Anton felt untrammelled, apart from the times when Pavel spent the night on Golovin lane. Then Anton sheltered at night with the artists, Levitan and Kolia, or with Natasha Golden, to study or write, where Pavel did not moan about the cost of candles. The insolvent bankrupt lectured his sons on finance. A pencilled folio runs:

> Kolia and Antosha, You have left things to the last day and I told you several times that 10 roubles had to be ready to pay the rent, you know that it can't be put off and I like Punctuality. You have put me in an awkward position. To blush when the landlord comes is not right for a man of my age, I am a Person with a positive Character.[21]

95

THIRTEEN

The Death of Mosia
1883–4

ALEKSANDR AND KOLIA sank into maudlin drunkenness while Anton worked frenetically. In March 1883 he was writing a weekly story for *Fragments* and for *The Spectator*. At the same time Anton had a series of examinations to sit: he had a '4' (good) from Sklifosovsky for operative surgery; his gynæcology was outstanding ('5').[22] As Tsar Alexander III was to be crowned in Moscow, a few examinations were postponed until September.

Anton could relax and turn his attention to the arts and to his family. His impatience with the feckless had not abated: he saw in actors the same weakness and lack of professionalism that he deplored in his brothers. The contemporary theatre seemed just Aleksandr and Kolia writ large, and had to be fought with, he told the dramatist Kanaev: 'our actors have everything except good breeding, culture or, if I may say so, gentility . . . I expressed my fears for the future of the modern theatre. The theatre is not a beer garden and not a Tatar restaurant.'

Anton forced a little gentility on his father, and, not altogether disinterestedly, Pavel acknowledged Aleksandr's family:

> Dear son Aleksandr! You must give Masha a briefcase for Easter, she cannot do without. I have no means to order one. Kindly send in good time what you promised. We are well, Mama has toothache. We have no letters from you. Regards to Anna, a kiss for Mosia, a blessing for you. Your loving father, P. Chekhov.[23]

Masha never got her briefcase, but Aleksandr received a little paternal affection. Pavel, after a few drinks, even boasted of Aleksandr's uniform in the Customs Service. Home life prospered on 60 roubles a month from *Fragments*: the Chekhovs kept a piano and a servant. Kolia was paid by Utkina, owner of *The Alarm Clock*, in kind: of Kolia's earnings the Chekhovs kept a desk, a candelabra and a wall clock all their lives.

Anton also helped Aleksandr at Easter 1883. He persuaded Leikin to print Aleksandr's stories; at first Leikin did not know that the author whom Anton was recommending was Aleksandr: 'Who is Agathopod Edinitsyn ("Unit")?' 1300 miles from St Petersburg, Aleksandr needed his brother's help to be a writer again. It was rumoured that civil servants were to be banned from the popular press and, as some of Aleksandr's stories were set in the Customs Service, he needed cover. Anton pointed out the miseries of journalism, mixing with rogues, earning a pittance to be devoured by dependants. Aleksandr ignored the warnings, and felt happier. He had his wife and daughter; he sent for his dog and for Nadia, Anna's daughter by her first husband, Sokolnikov; he even contemplated bringing out Aunt Fenichka to run his household. He wrote to Vania (23 April 1883): 'My little daughter is growing . . . and giving me much joy . . . I strongly resemble my Vater, Anna is becoming so attached to me that she has become inseparable and I am quite content with my fate.'

Now Anton became friendlier and broached his preoccupations with women and with sex in a long letter to Aleksandr in April 1883: Anton invited his brother to participate in a doctoral thesis he would write after qualifying – a *History of Sexual Authority*, modelled on Darwin's *Origin of Species*. Surveying the world from insects to human beings, Anton reckoned that the higher the social development in mammals the more nearly equal the sexes become, but he was convinced of the inferiority of even the educated female human being:

> She is not a thinker . . . We must help nature as man helps nature when he creates heads like Newton's, heads that approach organic perfection. If you've grasped my idea, then 1) the problem, as you see, is very real, not like the fucking-about of our female emancipationist publicists and skull-measurers . . . The history of universities for women. Curious: in all the 30 years they have existed, women medics (excellent medics!) haven't produced a single serious dissertation, which proves that they are *schwach* in the creative line.

Anton had been reading the potentially feminist arguments of Herbert Spencer and Sacher-Masoch, but his thinking is shot through with the misogyny of Schopenhauer's 'Essay on Women'. On a personal level Anton's difficulties with women were beginning to torment him. Not that his sexual drive was monstrous: his promiscuity stemmed from a rapid loss of interest in any one woman. Zoologists might compare Anton's sexuality with that of the cheetah, which can only mate with a stranger. Once intimacy is established, cheetahs cohabit impotently. Anton's impotence had something to do – perhaps as cause, perhaps as consequence – with his transactions with prostitutes. Not aroused by women he liked (and, worse, not liking women who aroused him), Chekhov was troubled, until he was too ill to be aroused at all. He told Aleksandr and Anna:

> There's no way I can tie myself to our woman, though there are a lot of opportunities . . . You screw her once, but the next time you can't get it in. I have all the equipment, but I don't function – my talent is buried in the ground . . . I fancy a Greek girl now . . . forgive me, jealous Anna, for writing to your patient [*the sick Aleksandr*] about Greek girls.[24]

Student pranks gave Chekhov some joy, but they too tended to have sinister outcomes. Anton, Kolia and Levitan, with another art student, bought a stallholder's oranges and sold them so outrageously cheaply to the public that the stallholder had them arrested. After the exams were over, in Voskresensk, Anton, Kolia, Vania and Misha and three young doctors from the hospital at Chikino set out on a sixteen-mile pilgrimage to the monastery of St Savva and walked on to see a colleague, Dr Persidsky, at the hospital in Zvenigorod. At tea in Persidsky's garden they sang the popular, but banned, 'Show me the home, Where the Russian peasant does not suffer'. The local policeman charged them with subversion. Although a newspaper, the *Russian Gazette*, and powerful friends intervened, the Governor of Moscow forced Persidsky out of Zvenigorod. After Anton's first experience of injustice indignation seeps into his prose.

Summer 1883 in Voskresensk gave Anton his first footing in genteel society. If Aleksandr and Kolia dragged him down, Vania raised him up, by introducing him to the officers of the battalion stationed at Voskresensk – Lieutenants Egorov, Rudolf and Eduard Tyshko, and Colonel Maevsky and his three children. Known as Tyshko in the Headgear, Eduard Tyshko, irresistible to women, had been wounded in the Turkish war and was never seen in public without black silk

1. End 1860s: *sitting* Efrosinia and Egor (left and centre, paternal grandparents), and Anton's Aunt Liudmila (right); *standing* Evgenia, Pavel, Mitrofan

2. 1874 family portrait: *standing* Vania, Anton, Kolia, Aleksandr, Uncle Mitrofan; *sitting* Misha, Masha, Pavel, Evgenia, Aunt Liudmila, cousin Georgi

3. TOP Taganrog in the 1870s

4. ABOVE On leaving school,
15 June 1879

5. RIGHT 'The Wedding Season',
a caricature of Taganrog relatives
with text by Anton and pictures
by his brother Kolia, 1881

6. ABOVE LEFT
'He's been drinking',
a portrait of a medical
student (perhaps
Anton) by Kolia
Chekhov, *c.* 1882

7. ABOVE Students
and professors
celebrating Tatiana's
Day, 12 January 1882
in Moscow by Kolia
Chekhov

8. LEFT Anton with Kolia (sitting)

9. ABOVE Anton Chekhov, 1883

10. Evgenia, Pavel, Aleksandr, Vania, Masha and Misha in the early 1880s

12. Franz Schechtel with Kolia
Chekhov in the early 1880s

11. Masha, Anna Golden (Kolia's mistress),
Natalia Golden and Kolia, *c.* 1883

13. LEFT Future doctors
Dmitri Saveliev, Anton
Chekhov, Vasili Zembulatov,
Nikolai Korobov, autumn
1883

14. ABOVE Nikolai Leikin,
c. 1883

15. LEFT Natalia Golden as
'Poverty', painted by Kolia
Chekhov

16. ABOVE Anton Chekhov as
painted by Kolia, 1884

17. BELOW Babkino, the
Kiseliovs' house

18. The Moscow house 'like a chest of drawers', painted by Misha

19. Photograph given to Tchaikovsky inscribed 'To Piotr Ilyich Tchaikovsky, to remind him of a cordially devoted and grateful admirer . . .'

20. At the Lintvariovs'
cottage, May 1889:
on landing Vania,
Misha(?); *sitting on steps*
Evgenia, Masha, Marian
Semashko

21. Kleopatra Karatygina

22. Olga Kundasova, mid 1880s

headgear to disguise his wounds; he became a close friend of the Chekhovs. Anton's friendship with the officers was tested when Lieutenant Egorov asked for Masha's hand in marriage. She referred the proposal to Anton, who warned Egorov off. The lieutenant, not surprisingly, then behaved badly when Evgenia rented a cottage from him for the summer of 1884. She complained to Masha: 'We want to move out of this lousy flat, since Egorov has left us nothing, we'll have to move all the crockery from Moscow ... He's left all the furniture locked and sealed.' Only in 1890 would Lieutenant Egorov make his peace with Anton.

Other Voskresensk friendships extended to Vania's brothers. Once, stranded at a Christmas ball by a blizzard, Vania was offered a lift home in a guest's sledge. The stranger was Aleksei Kiseliov, who owned an estate at Babkino two miles up the river Istra from Voskresensk. Aleksei Kiseliov was a very well-connected, if impoverished, aristocrat, with a nostalgia for his rakish past. His wife Maria was an amateur writer and a prude. The Kiseliovs were charmed by Masha and Anton. These Voskresensk friendships were lifelong. Anton had glimpses of new worlds – the officers' life he was to portray so expertly in *Three Sisters*, and the rundown Arcadia of the landowner. Babkino taught Masha how to be a lady. Anton got to know intellectuals, for instance Pavel Golokhvastov, a magistrate who was a Slavophile activist and his wife, a playwright. The Kiseliovs and Chekhovs fished and played croquet together. Anton flirted with their servants and dairymaids. He joined the Russian intellectual establishment. Nevertheless, unlike Misha and Masha, Anton also had business in Voskresensk. He was useful to Dr Arkhangelsky at the Chikino clinic. The stories of summer 1884, with Vania and the Kiseliovs in Voskresensk, show newly acquired surgical, as well as social, skills.

In Anton's absence Pavel grumbled: 'Nice children you are, you've left Mother ailing, and are having fun. It's lucky that God has saved her, but you have no pity. Pavel the Long-Suffering.'

Evgenia too was soon to leave the Moscow household. Anton persuaded Aleksandr that she would be more use to him in Taganrog than Aunt Fenichka: 'Mother badly wants to visit you. Take her on, if you can. Mother still has spirit and is not as heavy going as Aunt.' Evgenia duly went to Taganrog. It was a mistake. Aleksandr's household was sunk in irremediable filth and chaos. The servants did as they liked, Aleksandr spent each month's salary within a few days, Anna could not do housework. Evgenia, never good at crises, did not even have her refuge of coffee and a clean bed. Mitrofan and his wife Liudmila were no support: a few days after her arrival on 26 June 1883, they went, with two of their children, to Moscow to see Pavel and then to Voskresensk. Before the week was out Evgenia was desperate:

> Antosha for God's sake send me just a rouble and quickly I'm afraid to ask your father I need to buy bread for my tea, not to speak of supper ... When Mitrofan returns, send me money for the fare back. In any case, I can't leave while they're away. I've lent them my wicker trunk, such anguish, I'm afraid I shall fall ill ... Aleksandr is as unhappy as can be, if only at least Kolia came. E. Chekhova. Please, answer and don't mention to anyone that I am complaining.[25]

Nobody could rely on Evgenia: she herself thirsted for protection. After a fortnight she begged her fare back to Moscow from her children.

Anton left Voskresensk for Moscow, from where it was easier to send Leikin a constant stream of prose. Aleksandr, Anna and baby Mosia had, however, followed Evgenia from Taganrog, so that to find peace Anton stayed in 'Natashevu' Golden's house or with Palmin at Bogorodskoe in the suburbs. Here he wrote. Leikin restricted Anton from experimenting with new forms, and was petulant if Chekhov made a début in a Moscow weekly, tolerating only *The Spectator* as a Chekhov family concern. Leikin turned down the only long work Chekhov wrote that year, 'He Understood', a charming piece set in Voskresensk. A peasant shoots a starling, is detained for poaching and wins his release by persuading the angry landowner that his yearning to shoot is as incurable as the latter's alcoholism. At the end of 1883 Chekhov placed the story in *Nature and Field Sports*, under his real name for the first time.[26]

Two pieces written in summer 1883 stand out: one is a melancholy story for *The Alarm Clock*, 'The Dowry': the heroine loses her dowry to a drunken uncle and her fiancé cannot help her. The story's effect lies in the narrator's ineffectual sympathy; the ending 'Where are you, Manechka?' introduces the helpless pathos of the typical Chekhovian 'hero'. The other piece, 'The Daughter of Albion', about an ugly

English governess enduring the barbarity of her employer, was the first piece Chekhov wrote for *Fragments* to win renown. Russians joked about frigid Englishwomen – Chekhov himself had written that 'if the Russian evolved from a magpie and the German from a fox, the English evolved from frozen fish' – but 'The Daughter of Albion' has the nature poetry of a 'fishing' story based on Anton's summer angling at Babkino. Not for the last time, Anton's mockery of his hero and heroine is tempered by a lyrical celebration of the country-side.

Leikin wanted even more from his most popular author: 'Fragments of Moscow Life' came out every week: under two pseudonyms Anton might supply half the material for an issue. Kolia, less reliable, was Leikin's best illustrator; Leikin sent him special *torchon* paper from St Petersburg. As August ended and Anton's final year of medicine approached, he complained to Leikin:

> in the next room a baby is crying (it belongs to my brother who has come to stay), in another room father is reading mother [*Leskov's*] 'Sealed Angel'. Someone has wound up a musical box and I can hear 'La Belle Hélène'. I'd like to run off to the country, but it's 1 in the morning . . . For a writer it would be hard to invent anything fouler than these surroundings. My bed is occupied by my brother who keeps on coming up to me and raising the topic of medicine. 'My daughter must have colic in the belly, that's why she's crying.' I have the great misfortune to be a medic and everyone thinks they have to 'discuss' medicine with me . . . I solemnly promise never to have any children.

The gods took note of that promise.

Peace seemed to be restored when Evgenia came back from the country and Aleksandr and his family returned to Taganrog. In autumn 1883, once university life began, Anton and Kolia mixed with Masha's *kursistki*. Ekaterina Iunosheva received a joking 'Last Fare-well' by Kolia. (Anton had a hand in this poem – all three eldest Chekhov brothers had the stuffed owl for a muse):

> As from a cigar a dreamer smokes,
> You float about in all my dreams,
> Bringing with you love's cruel strokes,
> And on your lips a hot smile gleams . . .[27]

Kolia did not stay in the family home for long. He hid behind the ample skirts of Anna Ipatieva-Golden from his creditors and the authorities, and Anton no longer collaborated with him.

In late November Kolia left Moscow and went to stay with Aleksandr and Anna Sokolnikova in Taganrog. Meanwhile Pavel, horrified to discover that Aleksandr and his consort had stolen something precious from him, asked Kolia to intervene:

> My regards to Aleksandr. I am sorry for the ruined creature and those that live with him. He has stolen my wedding certificate and is living on it and this grieves me. Bring it, be sure to take it off him. Those that live without the law shall perish without the law![28]

Pavel's phrase 'shall perish without the law' became a family saying.

Anton kept out of these quarrels: he was drawn to wider horizons. Leikin had been leaking hints to those in Petersburg who asked about the identity of his contributor, Antosha Chekhonte. On 8 October 1883 Nikolai Leskov, revered for his novel *The Cathedral Folk* and for his powerful stories, such as 'Lady Macbeth of Mtsensk', arrived with Leikin for five days in Moscow. Leikin could not resist introducing Leskov to Chekhov. Leskov (with Ostrovsky, the only living writer whom Pavel Chekhov respected) had surly suspicions of young writers, but took to Chekhov. Anton took Leskov on a tour of the brothels in Sobolev lane. They ended up in the Salon des Variétés. Then, as Anton told Aleksandr, Leskov and he took a cab:

> He turns to me half drunk and asks: 'Do you know what I am?' 'I do.' 'No you don't. I'm a mystic.' 'I know.' He stares at me with his old man's popping eyes and prophesies. 'You will die before your brother.' 'Perhaps.' 'I shall anoint you with oil as Samuel did David ... Write.'

Despite Anton's agnosticism and Leskov's Orthodox faith, the two writers were very close in spirit: no other of Leskov's successors had his gift for narrative voice, for showing environment making character, for maintaining an ironical, but mystical appreciation of nature and fate. However inauspicious the future encounters of Leskov and Chekhov (for Leskov hated doctors and Anton was never to be fully at ease in Petersburg), this meeting settled Chekhov's fate: he was to be Leskov's successor.

More lowly writers also saw Anton as a successor. The hack Popudoglo (who at the age of thirty-seven was mortally ill) marvelled that Anton alone understood his disease and, when he died on 14 October 1883, left him all his books.[29] Liodor Palmin was very attached to Anton, although, like Leskov, he abhorred his profession. Palmin's affection came in doggerel missives:

> I sit in silence like an outcaste.
> Meanwhile Kalashnikov's good beer
> Gives me humoristic cheer,
> Sparkling in my empty glass.
> Forgive this naughty fleeting rhyme,
> Like logarithms for arithmetics,
> I always find one just in time . . .'[30]

Every few months Palmin informed 'Mr Rest-in-peace', as he called Chekhov, of his new address, for instance: 'By the Dormition on the Gravelets (don't think it is Dead Lane, Coffin House, Cross-Kisser's Flat, which is for any doctor, especially a young doctor, a suitable address).'

In his final year Chekhov became well acquainted with morbidity: he took charge of cases from registration to death or cure. He had to write a full case history for his professor in the clinic for nervous diseases, and in the internal medicine clinic for Professor Ostroumov (whose patient he would one day become). The final exams began in the winter and were harrowing: a medical student then had to retake all previous exams in his final year; this made a total of seventy-five examinations, as well as course assessment. Chekhov's conduct of a 'nervous' case shows him conforming to the tenets of the time. A young railway clerk, Bulychiov, was admitted for six weeks with impotence, spermatorrhoea and psychosomatic back pain: Chekhov concluded that they were due to frequent masturbation during adolescence, and prescribed Bulychiov nux vomica, potassium bromide, daily baths, each a degree colder than the previous.[31] A modern mind would ascribe Bulychiov's state to fear of the consequences of onanism, but Chekhov and his professors saw masturbation as a morbid habit for which prostitutes, cold baths and sedatives were the remedy.

The autopsy that Anton carried out at a Moscow police station on

24 January 1884 was more acute. Professor Neuding awarded it only '3+', but the report was the germ for several stories:

> On 20 January 1884 he visited the baths. Returning home he had tea and supper, then went to bed. At 8 a.m. on 21 January he said that he would go, as usual, to town, but at about 9 a.m. he was found dead, hanging by a sash in the latrine of Osipov's house. The corpse was dressed in the deceased's usual clothes. One end of the sash was wound around his neck, the other was tied to a wooden beam 8 feet above the floor . . . to determine Efimov's state of mind at the time he committed the crime of suicide, we have only very few data: the smell of spirits on opening the skull, chest and abdominal cavities entitles us to suppose that at the moment of committing suicide Efim was, very probably, intoxicated.[32]

Forensic exercises had their literary parallel. To Leikin's annoyance, Chekhov earned himself 39 roubles from *The Dragonfly* with a detective story that they printed in their annual 'almanac'. It is highly original, like all Chekhov's experiments in the genre, which was popular at the time in Russia. As in France, the Russian legal system used an independent investigating magistrate, a more plausible hero than the private detectives of English fiction. In 'The Safety Match' Chekhov took his friend Diukovsky's name for a Clouseau-like investigator who follows up the clue of a safety match, and finds the corpse alive and well, hiding with a girlfriend.

In January 1884, just before Anton wrote up his autopsy, telegrams came from Taganrog: baby Mosia stopped feeding, became comatose, then half paralysed. The Taganrog doctors injected her with calomel, pepsin and musk; they gave her cold compresses and potassium bromide. The prescriptions that Anton wired back were useless. In the early hours of 1 February, while Anton and Masha were at a ball in Moscow, Mosia died in convulsions. Aleksandr wrote to Anton:

> I can't bear it. Inside and outside me everything shouts one thing: Mosia! Mosia! Mosia! . . . Anna has gone mad. She doesn't think, isn't aware, but senses the loss. Her whole face is a mirror of suffering.
> The undertaker came. We haggled by the little corpse . . . the discussion was about an oval or an ordinary coffin, brocade or satin lining.

Aleksandr and Anna got no sympathy. 'Those that live without the law shall perish without the law.' Pavel wrote to Anton on 20 February:

> Antosha, Be so kind as to turn your attention to Aleksandr, persuade him to leave Anna, it's time he recovered from his madness, . . . you have more influence over him, persuade him to leave this Burden. It's easy to leave Anna now, the child has died and they're not married. If he values my life and respects me as his own Father, then he can overcome himself . . . He doesn't seem to understand that offending one's Father and Mother is a grave sin. Sooner or later he will have to pay for this before God. It's no laughing matter to pick up such a Cabbage and bring her unasked into our family, to disturb peace and order in the house . . . So God has taken the child he loved, therefore his deeds are wrong, he must follow a decent path, as an enlightened man who understands what is bad and what is good. To act out a Comedy and make a novel out of his life is quite unsuitable. We are insulted by this horrible Crime and Misfortune.

Aleksandr's unpublished diaries *My Daily, Ephemeral and Generally Fleeting Thoughts* show he was thinking on similar lines:

> 25 January 1884: Anna . . . has never understood me and never will.
> 1 February 1884: I cannot live with Anna without Mosia . . .[33]

Pavel swallowed his hostility. In spring Aleksandr was transferred to Moscow 'on the grounds of his father's ill health'. He, Anna – and the Sokolnikov children Shura and Nadia – came to live first in Moscow, then with the Chekhovs in Voskresensk. Aleksandr's diaries augured ill for Anna:

> 25 March 1884: Neither my wife nor her children were with me, i.e. around me, for a whole day. How I celebrated this day! I chattered to my heart's delight with Anton on learned subjects, with Nikolai about art, I argued with Ivan!

But compassion, as he put it, kept Aleksandr with Anna until death. She was now four months pregnant with Aleksandr's second child.

Anton was more affected than he showed. In an album given him a year or two later by a grateful patient Anton kept a photograph of little Mosia.

FOURTEEN

The Qualified Practitioner
June 1884–April 1885

O N 16 J U N E 1884 the University Rector gave Chekhov a certificate of General Practitioner: it released him from military service and poll tax and gave him some of the privileges of a gentleman. Anton wanted to graduate as a writer, too. He chose his best work and, with Leikin's help, ordered 1200 copies of *Tales of Melpomene* from the printers, the 200-rouble costs to be paid four months after publication. The book made Chekhov 500 roubles – ten times what Leikin had paid him in May. It also won critical attention, but to make a mark in St Petersburg Anton needed 100 roubles for his fare and hotel. But Leikin did not consider Chekhov was yet ready for St Petersburg. Instead he invited him to come with Palmin and tour the lakes of Karelia. Anton did not go.

In May Chekhov had seen a lot of Palmin, often with Kolia and the Golden sisters. He had exercised his diagnostic skills studying Palmin, his consort and their appalling cuisine and, on the eve of his last exam, told Leikin that Palmin would soon die of alcoholism. Perverse to the last, Palmin married his Pelageia and lived seven more years.

At Babkino the aristocratic novelist Boleslav Markevich was less lucky. In June 1884 Chekhov lived by the monastery of New Jerusalem, fishing, writing and gathering mushrooms, helping Dr Rozanov at Voskresensk hospital every other day. Markevich occupied a comfortable dacha on the Kiseliov estate nearby. Anton told Leikin in August: 'This Kammerjunker has angina and will probably give you material for an obituary.' In November Markevich compliantly died and the Kiseliovs offered the Chekhovs his dacha.

Shadows darkened the summer at Voskresensk. Kolia, the devil in paradise, cost Vania his job. At Easter, using his Taganrog bell-ringing skills, to the delight of the children at Vania's school, Kolia played a carillon on some musical pots he had bought from a drunken potter. The school's governor passed by and dismissed Vania on the spot for blasphemy. Kolia moved to stay with Pushkariov and two of the Golden sisters, before going on to bedevil Pavel in Moscow. His next prank was in July. With Aleksandr's help, Kolia composed a letter in Pavel's name to their mother:

> Evochka! . . . It's a pity we have started keeping pigs, they are shitting everywhere. Fenichka sends her regards. Kolia has taken all the money that Aliosha has brought her and she can't buy anything or get anything from the shop . . . Glory to God . . . Come home, jam has to be made. P. Chekhov.

Next week Kolia had gone too far, and Pavel did write a letter – to Anton. To meet Kolia's debts the bailiffs were holding an auction of his possessions at the house. Pavel nailed Anton's doctor's plate to the door, but to no avail. He and Aunt Fenichka had to endure public humiliation. Anton paid off the bailiffs and Kolia grovelled to his father:

> Dear, sweet Papa . . . I've only just learnt what vile dishonest people exist in the world. My inexperience and trusting nature is the reason for everything. I very much wanted for the family's sake (especially for Masha's) to furnish the flat as elegantly as possible . . . What did the dishonest Utkina do? For that money she sent me not what I'd chosen but old junk, she didn't give me the blinds or curtains &c. I had bought.[34]

Kolia's last tatters of credibility were gone.

Kolia and Anton had new company to distract them. After the Goldens, three more sisters entered their lives, the Markova sisters, Elena, Elizaveta and Margarita, who were staying with their aunt, Liudmila Gamburtseva, at a dacha near Zvenigorod.[35] To Kolia and Anton they were Nelli, Lily and Rita and a flirtatious relationship built up. Nelli was a rival to Anna Golden for Kolia's affection; Lily, until she became Mrs Sakharova in 1886, was an actress in Korsh's theatre at Moscow but stayed friends with Kolia and Anton for years to come; Rita married and became Baroness Spengler, but she still frequented Masha and Anton. The Markova sisters shook the sway of the Golden sisters. Kolia had a fling with Nelli, before Anna Golden reclaimed him. Anton took Lily's virginity.[36]

Medical duties stopped Anton becoming more entangled with the

Markova sisters. Released from the hospital by Rozanov to earn a little extra by carrying out autopsies, Anton told Leikin:

> I've been driving a fast troika with a decrepit coroner, barely breathing and too ancient to be any use, a kind little grey-haired creature, who's been dreaming for 25 years of becoming a judge. I and the district doctor did the autopsy in the open country under the greenery of a young oak, on a cart track ... The deceased is 'not local' and the peasants on whose land the body was found begged us in the name of Christ and with tears in their eyes not to do the autopsy in their village. 'The women and children won't sleep for fear.' ... The corpse, covered with a sheet, is wearing a red shirt, new trousers. There's a towel and an icon on top. We ask the elder for water ... There is water – a pond nearby, but nobody will provide a bucket: we would pollute it ... The results of the autopsy are 20 breaks in the ribs, œdema in one lung, a smell of spirits in the stomach. Violent death from strangulation. The drunk was crushed in the chest by something heavy, probably a good peasant knee.

A story of 1899, 'On Official Business', was to condense fifteen years of such autopsies.

Rozanov, later the authority on suicide in Russia, was a fine doctor. Two other doctors became long-term friends: Dr Arkhangelsky of Chikino hospital north of Voskresensk and Dr Kurkin at the village clinic in Zvenigorod – not that Anton's skills impressed them. On 22 July a boy with an undescended testicle was brought to the Voskresensk clinic: the child squirmed, Anton lost his nerve and summoned Rozanov, who finished the operation. Anton could laugh at incompetence: in 'Surgery' a story for *Fragments* that August, a student pulls the wrong teeth, while Rozanov calmly advises: 'Keep pulling out healthy ones until you get to the bad one.'

Anton returned to Moscow to write and practise medicine. In Moscow a doctor could earn 10,000 roubles a year, charging 5 roubles a visit, enough to keep the horse and carriage needed for these rounds. Anton earned little when he opened his practice in autumn 1884. His patients, pleading poverty or presuming on friendship, paid him with a picture, a foreign coin or an embroidered cushion. Palmin was typically exploitative: 'The bearer of this letter is my cook's husband, a sickly man whom the advice of an Æsculapius wouldn't hurt. ... Let him have arsenic or, after examining the attached patient, prescribe him something of the kind.' Leikin pestered Chekhov with accounts of insomnia and pains, lists of his medicines. In September Anton asked Leikin, privy to the plans of Petersburg city, to tell him of any vacancy for a council doctor.

In Russia every doctor's address was available at any chemist. Patients found Anton. Coping with typhoid, TB and dysentery, frightened of killing his patients or infecting himself, Anton trembled. Patients became attached, and, unlike the doctors in his fiction, he could not shake them off. A typical patient writes:

> Most kind Dr Chekhov! I ask you very urgently to allow just an hour for a visit to me and to calm my nerves. I need to consult you, I hope you will be so kind as not to refuse my request. My maid is ill, I'm afraid the illness might be catching, I sent her to the clinic, but she is so dim, she didn't ask anything, you know I have children whose lives are dearer than anything in the world to me. I haven't slept for two nights, my thoughts are all 'gloomy'. I expect you this evening, whereby you will greatly oblige Yours Respectfully, Liubov Dankovskaia.[37]

Anton took up social medicine: with two colleagues and a sheaf of questionnaires, he toured the brothels of Sobolev Lane. Other ways of supporting indigent Chekhovs had to be found. Anton urged Vania, still in search of a post, to set up in Moscow, and pool 'your salary, my pittance'. Anton approached the loathsome Lipskerov, editor of Moscow's sleazy *News of the Day*, or, as Chekhov called it, *Screws of the Day*.[38] Even judophiles like Chekhov called Lipskerov a yid for his meanness. Lipskerov agreed to serialize Chekhov's first and last novel, *A Shooting Party* (literally *Drama at the Hunt*), over thirty-two issues from August 1884 to April 1885, at 3 roubles an instalment. The money was rarely paid; Misha, whom Chekhov detailed to dun Lipskerov, was offered instead a theatre ticket or a pair of trousers from Lipskerov's tailors.

A Shooting Party is unjustly ignored. As in 1882, Chekhov stretched himself in a pastiche, even parody, of melodramatic stories, with decadent aristocrats on rotting estates, fatal girls in red, and wicked intriguing Poles. The novel is extraordinary: not only at 170 pages is it Chekhov's longest piece of fiction, but it anticipates Agatha Christie: the investigating magistrate, Kamyshev, is revealed, apparently by the editor of *News of the Day*, to be the murderer, who has framed the main suspect. In the wild exotic garden in a mythical south Russian landscape where all falls apart, the world of 'The Black Monk' or *The Cherry Orchard* is sketched out. The story is poetic, ingenious, and sensational.

Leikin was as worried by such diversions as he was pleased by Anton's reputation. *Tales of Melpomene* had attracted approving reviews. At the end of September Leikin paid a visit to Moscow, meeting, he told the poet Trefolev, 'the pillars of my *Fragments*, Chekhonte and Palmin. I boozed with them, gave them parental lectures on what I need.' Anton had ambitious plans. Abandoning his *History of Sexual Authority*, he assembled a bibliography for a new thesis, *Medicine in Russia*. This too lapsed, when his stories won attention. Anton's satire now bit harder. 'Noli me tangere' (later to be called 'The Mask'), printed in the Moscow weekly *Amusement*, drew Tolstoy's attention: a man at a masked ball misbehaves with impunity when he reveals his powerful identity.

The gentrification of the Chekhovs proceeded. The conductor Shostakovsky befriended Kolia after hearing him play; other musicians became family friends. From November 1884, in true bourgeois style, the Chekhovs assigned each Tuesday evening for guests and concerts. Somehow the old patriarch, or the *tramontano* as Aleksandr and Anton called him, was quelled into good behaviour. Masha was hostess to her brother and her parties assembled Dunia Efros and Lily and Nelli Markova for what she promised would be 'Crazy nights!' Palmin reported to the inquisitive Leikin, 'A few days ago I went to the Chekhovs' Tuesday. They have a *soirée fixe.*'

Leikin was proud of his own recent gentility which hard work and fame had bought: 'we don't blow our noses with our left leg,' he boasted and decided Anton was now fit to invite to Petersburg. Chekhov despatched Natalia Golden to see Leikin; she seemed to herald Anton's imminent move to Petersburg, as writer and doctor. Leikin was torn between a desire to make his protégé famous and an instinct to protect his monopoly. Boasting overrode self-interest, and, although a year would pass before he summoned Anton to Petersburg, Leikin revealed to his own employer, Khudekov, editor of the prestigious daily *Petersburg Newspaper*, the identity of Antosha Chekhonte. Khudekov immediately commissioned from Chekhov a commentary on the Rykov fraud trial that was still dragging on in Moscow.

FIFTEEN

Babkino

January–July 1885

The Petersburg Gazette liked Chekhov's reportage on the Rykov fraud trial. The trial was spectacular not just for the eloquence of Plevako, Russia's most colourful defence lawyer.[39] In the courtroom Anton had an ominous hæmorrhage from the right lung. In May 1885 Khudekov commissioned from Chekhov a regular story for the Monday issue (the day when Leikin did not contribute) of *The Petersburg Newspaper*. Khudekov thought that Chekhov's prose had a salacious 'whiff', and offered only 7 kopecks a line, but *The Petersburg Newspaper* was a major newspaper, exempt from precensorship, and its fiction escaped the mutilations inflicted on 'lower-class' weeklies. With Leikin's 8 kopecks a line and Khudekov's 7, Petersburg gave Anton a living. He had, however, to appear in person if he was to establish himself in literary circles. He still had not given literature priority over medicine. Leikin insisted, in March 1885, that in any case Anton had to come to Petersburg if he sought a post as a doctor.

Anton played along with Palmin's gallows-humour attitude to his profession. He saw its grim side. Why concentrate on a cholera epidemic, when in Moscow alone 100 children died daily of cold and hunger? The sick were dangerous. In March 1887 Nikolai Korobov, also newly qualified, nearly died of typhus. Doctors risked cholera and diphtheria from those they tried to save.[40] The worst hazard was exhaustion. Patients would drag Anton to the outskirts of Moscow on any pretext. Even those who knew him well did not think twice about calling him out. Mikhail Diukovsky wrote on a freezing December day: 'For God's sake, if you can, go and see my brother-in-law Evgraf this evening, I've just had news that he's very ill. Don't decline, I shall be eternally grateful. The address is Krasnoe village, by the Riazan gate.'[41]

Two days later, on New Year's Eve, Chekhov had a note from

Palmin: 'I'm sitting drinking vodka by the window. A young man has a deep wound on his shoulder-blade. A carbuncle or something – deciding is the job of Mr Requiem or Mr Coffin or Mr Rest-in-peace or even Messrs Wormeaten, if not the famous (in the future) Doctor Chekhov.' Palmin might pay Chekhov with a poem, but useful recompense was rare. Banter with patients could turn to horror. In early 1885 the Ianova girls, the third set of three sisters in Anton's life, were flirtatious patients. Not for long were they three sisters: at the end of 1885, typhus struck. Their mother and one of the three sisters (clutching Anton's arm as she died) perished.[42]

Anton's own health worried him. On 7 December 1884, he told Leikin, he had bled again. He insisted that his lungs were sound, that only a vessel in his throat had burst. His denial to a schoolmate, the journalist Sergeenko, 'hæmorrhage (not tubercular)' suggests that he knew the truth. To others he complained fulsomely of overwork. He told Lily Markova that he was in pain. In December 1884 at a spiritualist seance Turgenev's ghost apparently spoke to Anton: 'Your life is approaching its decline.' In a letter of 31 January 1885 to Uncle Mitrofan, congratulating him on election to the town council, Anton's anxiety is ill-disguised: 'In December I had a hæmorrhage and decided to take money from the Literary Fund [43] and go abroad for treatment. I'm a bit better now, but I still think I shall have to make a trip.'

In early 1885 the Chekhov household became quieter, even though Saveliev, not yet qualified, lodged with the Chekhovs again and put up with Pavel's fits of temper. Pavel had expelled Aunt Fenichka from the house into her son's care, and had banished Kolia. Anton did not press Kolia to return and merely urged him to pay his debts. To Uncle Mitrofan, however, he painted a picture of domestic harmony:

> Even Mama, the eternal grumbler, has started to admit that in Moscow we live better than before. Nobody grudges her expenses, there is no illness in the house. It's not luxury, but nobody goes without. Vania is at the theatre at the moment. He has a job in Moscow and is pleased. He is one of the family's most decent, solid members . . . He's hard-working and honest. Kolia is thinking of marrying. Misha finishes school this year.

Aleksandr finally found a posting and, after squeezing payment out of Davydov, editor of the now defunct *Spectator*, left Moscow to become an Excise Officer in Petersburg. To his parents' outrage, on 26 August 1884 Anna had given birth to a boy, named after Kolia. Aleksandr despatched Anna to stay with relatives and friends in Tula. In Petersburg, Aleksandr had a pensionable job, free fuel and housing, a maid, a wet nurse, the much-travelled hound Gershka, and a baby. Leikin accepted his stories and he acted as Anton's agent, but happiness eluded Aleksandr, for he squandered his salary. After Easter 1885 Anna, eaten up with jealousy and TB, conceived again. The wet nurse went down with intermittent fever; her husband moved in; Katka, the maid, stole food. The amœba-ridden waters of the Neva made Aleksandr ill. He told Anton: 'The flatulence is so great that I am writing you this letter by the light of a gas lamp stuck up my anus.'

Kolia faded out from the College of Art and Architecture. With no military exemption or valid identity papers, he went underground. Only through Anna Ipatieva-Golden could he be traced. He defaulted on all undertakings. Leikin was furious. When spring came Anton was forced to intervene. He decided to take Kolia to Babkino, away from Anna Golden: 'I'll take that fraud Kolia, remove his boots and put him under lock and key.'

At Babkino the Chekhov family could live next door to their hosts, the Kiseliovs. The Kiseliovs completely refurbished the dacha that Boleslav Markevich had occupied. (Anton admitted to Leikin that he expected Markevich's ghost at night.) On 6 May 1885 Anton, Masha and their mother – Kolia, Vania and Misha were to follow – set off. The railway had not yet reached Voskresensk: it was a hard day's cart journey from the railhead. They nearly drowned fording the Istra in the dark, Masha and Evgenia screeching with fear. They found the dacha ready, with ashtrays and cigarette boxes. Nightingales sang in the bushes. Leikin disapproved of Anton's flight to the country. On 9 May Anton tried to lure him:

> I feel in the seventh heaven and do idle silly things: I eat, drink, sleep, fish, went shooting once. Today we caught a burbot on a long pike hook, the day before yesterday my fellow-huntsman killed a doe hare. Levitan the artist (not your [*Adolf*] Levitan, but [*Isaak*] the landscape painter) is living with me, he's a passionate shooter. It's he who killed the hare. . . . If you come to Moscow this summer and make a pilgrimage to New Jerusalem I promise you something you've never seen anywhere . . . Luxuriant nature! You could pick it up and eat it.

Although Anton's happiest stories come from summer 1885 at Babkino, he could not escape his new profession. As well as the irrational
Kolia, Anton took charge of Isaak Levitan. Levitan lived across the
river with a potter at the village of Maksimovka. He was a dangerous
patient. When Misha and Anton called on Levitan at night, he leapt
out at them with a revolver. Anton told Leikin (who told all Petersburg): 'Something ominous is happening to the poor man. Psychosis
is beginning . . . I was told that he'd left for the Caucasus. At the end
of April he returned, but not from the Caucasus. He tried to hang
himself. I've taken him with me to the country and now I'm walking
him.'

Kolia, now taking opium, also needed care, but he was elusive. Pavel
wrote to Aleksandr in early June:

> I haven't seen Kolia for a long time since our people went to Babkino.
> They say he's in Moscow . . . A woman came on behalf of Anna
> [*Ipatieva-Golden*] from the cottage at Petrovsko-Razumovskoe to
> fetch his linen . . . This is what being carried away by women does,
> they drive a weak man mad. Thus he is given up to idleness, drunken-
> ness and debauchery, so that our labours and cares over his upbring-
> ing are naught to him. Woe to his mother, she is worn out with
> grief over him.

Kolia turned up in Babkino: all June Anton dared not leave the country
for more than a few hours, lest Kolia vanish back to wine, morphine
and Anna Golden's bed.

Misha, the antithesis of his eldest brothers, had matriculated; his
father was appeased. On 10 May Misha was lured to Babkino by
Anton: 'Before my eyes stretches an extraordinarily warm, gentle landscape: the river, beyond it the forest.' Anton wrote mostly about fish
– ruff, gudgeon, chub, burbot, perch, carp – and sent for more tackle.
Anton's stories, plays and letters show that he was as much *The Com-
pleat Angler* as Izaac Walton. He was not the only obsessive angler
on the Istra: a peasant Nikita was arrested for unbolting railway spikes
to use as sinkers for catching burbot – a single-minded character
whom Chekhov put in a story 'The Evildoer'.

Fishing inspired Anton to write more lyrically: 'The Burbot' makes
poetry out of an angler's obsession. Seeing landscape through Isaak
Levitan's eyes enriched Anton's work: after their long walks in May

1885 with gun, rod, or paints and easel, landscape is as evocative in Chekhov's art as in Levitan's. The Kiseliov family, too, developed Anton: their anecdotes from the arts world and Maria Kiseliova's reading of French magazines and novels provided material for *Fragments*. Aleksei Kiseliov, inhibited by his wife, was animated by the bawdiness of Levitan ('Leviathan'), Anton and Kolia. On 20 September Kiseliov wrote:

> Thank you, dear Anton, for fulfilling my request so punctiliously and for sending an exact representation of your illegitimate children, whose similarity to you is enormous. I immediately took the postcard to Duniasha, the cattle girl, and showed her what you're capable of and what she can expect if she becomes pregnant by you and is abandoned to the mercy of fate.

In January 1886 Kiseliov complained: 'The difference between my letters and yours, dear Anton, is that you can boldly read mine to young ladies, whereas I must throw yours into the stove as soon as I've read them in case my wife catches sight of them.'

Anton worked a few days as a doctor, relieving Arkhangelsky at the Chikino hospital in early June and performing an autopsy on a peasant. In mid July the madmen in Anton's care spoilt the idyll. Kolia bolted. Leikin reported: 'A few days ago your brother Kolia turned up with Aleksandr at my dacha. He pressed me for cartoon topics . . . A good artist, but we can't do magazine business with him for he won't keep his word.'[44] A week later Kolia came, drunk, to Leikin's office in Petersburg, took the topics and an advance of 32 roubles. On 20 July he reappeared in Moscow at *The Alarm Clock* and then vanished. He was not seen by his brothers or their friends until mid October. By the end of June Levitan was also in Moscow, in bed with 'catarrhal fever' (as he called his TB). He sent Anton his gun dog Vesta to look after, and two roubles for his rent. Kolia and Levitan had collaborated in painting sets for the opera; Kolia once painted a figure on Levitan's empty landscape, and Levitan painted a skyscape over Kolia's figures. They complemented each other – Levitan an excitable workaholic, reluctant to paint human beings, and Kolia paralytically idle, with a dislike of painting nature. Reluctant as Kolia to return, Levitan made his excuses to Anton: 'Going to the country now is nonsense: it would be poisoning myself – Moscow would seem a thousand times fouler than now and I've got used to the city . . . in any case I shall soon see the dear inhabitants of Babkino and, among other things, your repulsive face.'

It was very hot at Babkino, and Anton had a hæmorrhage. Nevertheless, in mid July, he went to Moscow to take leave of Aleksandr, who had been appointed Customs Chief at Novorossiisk on the Black Sea, and was passing through Moscow with Anna, baby Kolia and the dog. Vania was travelling with them, to support the ailing Anna on the 1000-mile journey beyond the Don and over the Caucasus. Aleksandr and Anton would not see each other for more than a year.

Babkino had worked its magic. Anton sent to Petersburg a story with a game-keeping background, 'The Huntsman' [Jäger]. Short and unpretentious, it pays homage to Turgenev, who had died a year before and whose technique Chekhov was emulating, but it owes much to Levitan's subtle perception and to Babkino's atmosphere. Its peasant characters set the pattern for Chekhov's later love stories. A Chekhovian couple, an unresponsive male and a frustrated female, fail to communicate, while nature all around lives its own life. 'The Huntsman' came out in *The Petersburg Newspaper* on 18 July 1885. Petersburg took heed.

SIXTEEN

Petersburg Calls
August 1885–January 1886

AUTUMN 1885 brought Chekhov a social whirlwind. Among Masha's friends, the fiery Dunia Efros stood out. In Moscow, where the authorities were increasingly hostile to Jews, she would not convert, and insisted on her Hebrew name, Reve-Khave. Anton had many liaisons – with his former landlady, Mrs Golub, with the landlady of friends, Baroness Aglaida Shepping, and, it is said, Blanche, a hostess at the Ermitage. A more serious love, his Natashevu, Natalia Golden, was now thirty. She left Moscow for Petersburg, from where in spring 1885 she wrote Anton a bawdy farewell:

> Little bastard Antoshevu, I could hardly bear the wait for your much desired letter. I can feel you are having a merry, free-for-all time in Moscow, and I'm glad for you and envious . . . I haven't got married yet, but I probably shall soon and I invite you to my wedding. If you wish, you can bring with you your Countess Shepping, but you will have to bring your own sprung mattress, because here there aren't any women of such awful dimensions, and otherwise you won't have anything to <u>be busy on</u>. Since you have turned into a completely debauched man (since I left), you are unlikely to be able to do without –– [*Natalia's dashes*]. I can't belong to you any more, since I have found myself a suitable tiger-boy.
>
> Today you are having a ball, I can imagine you desperately flirting with Efros and Iunosheva. Who will win, I wonder? Is it true that Efros's nose has got 2 inches longer, that's terrible, a pity, she'll be kissing you and what sort of children will you have, all that worries me frightfully. I have also heard that Iunosheva's bust has got bigger, another inconvenience! . . . Antoshevu, if you are irrevocably lost morally, at least don't ruin your friends, especially not the married ones. You scoundrel!
>
> I advise you not to marry, you're still too young . . . You write rubbish to me, as for the main thing that interests me (more than

anything else), your health, not a word about that. You have two diseases, amorousness and spitting blood. The first is not dangerous, but about the second I ask you to give me the most detailed information ... So, Antoshevu, perhaps you haven't forgotten your <u>little skeleton</u>, but I believe that if you come to Petersburg, you haven't, if you don't come, you have forgotten her ... I shall send you stamps, otherwise I fear that the letters will be lost. Farewell, Antoshevu. Your Natasha. I'm glad medicine is looking up, maybe you'll write less and be healthier.[45]

Natalia was not the last woman to send Anton stamps for a reply, but none survives. The field was clear for Dunia Efros: Anton's business in Petersburg was literary.

Anton was back at Babkino until autumn. Khudekov of *The Petersburg Newspaper* had not paid him, and it was cheaper living with the Kiseliovs. When he finally returned to Moscow, the Chekhovs moved from quarters that were airy, convenient and cheap. On 11 October 1885, after waiting for the landlord to stain the floors, the Chekhov family crossed the river south to the Bolshaia Iakimanka, Mrs Lebedeva's house. After five years in one house – the longest period yet in Anton's life – peregrinations had started again. The new flat was small – too small for *soirées*, but cheap (40 roubles a month), and closer to Gavrilov's warehouse. Doctor A. P. Chekhov's brass plate was mounted, and here he was at home except Tuesdays, Thursday evenings and some Saturdays. A month later, Anton was complaining to Leikin: 'The new flat has turned out to be rubbish: damp and cold. If I don't leave it, I shall certainly have last year's outrage developing in my chest: coughing and spitting blood ... Living with the family is horribly nasty.' There was no money for firewood: *The Petersburg Newspaper* took months to pay Anton. He wrote again for *The Alarm Clock*, and collected his fee in person.

As the family thinned out rows because fewer. Misha, starting Law at Moscow University, received on 11 August, Masha's name day, Pavel's last rocket: 'In Moscow instead of the educated boy who studied so long at the *gimnazia* you have turned out a lout, your character in Moscow has become not modest but impatient and rude, what is your education for?'[44] Pavel seemed to mellow. He sent Masha (who lingered at Babkino) an affectionate letter and a 5-rouble note: he even corresponded with Aleksandr, Anna and their illegitimate child, Kolia, in Novorossiisk. Vania had come back from Novorossiisk. Aleksandr and Vania gave their father good reports about each other. Aleksandr was so touched by paternal forgiveness that he sent a fond letter, giving information, so dear to Pavel, on the price of every product and the liturgy of the church services in Novorossiisk. Anna too felt emboldened: 'I hurry to use the permission you gave me to write a few lines to you . . . Aleksandr is not drinking vodka and on your advice just drinks a little wine. Come and see us next summer.'[47] Aleksandr's letters to his brothers are not so rosy. Inducing Vania to come for a job in the Novorossiisk customs or to open a private school, he painted instead a horrific picture of his life in this newly founded port. In hopeless debt, he lived worse than in Taganrog, where relatives helped in crises. Here he had 'no table, no chairs, just bare walls and Kolka's shitty nappies, which are the towels'. Out of scrap Aleksandr made a bedstead and a chair, which broke. Only the job was undemanding:

> By 8 p.m. I am drunk and asleep . . . I drink so much that even I am ashamed . . . I catch gobius fish in the mornings. I hired a servant and sacked her after three days . . . I have instructed people only to shit in the outside latrine, and I recommend pissing in the open . . . Instead of two young girls I've hired a servant woman, but such a woman that I swear to God one night I shall make a mistake and climb on her instead of Anna. I don't mean to be vulgar, I'm express-ing my amazement at her figure. A real Titian woman from a picture of *Weib, Wein und Gesang.*

Aleksandr told Anton how badly doctors were needed in Novorossiisk, how little land cost, how much people would pay for treatment or accommodation. Yet Aleksandr's description of his squalor was so graphic that it beggars belief that he thought he could attract Anton. Vania and Anton refused their brother's invitations to Novorossiisk. Even their sister was not spared the details. Aleksandr told Masha on 18 December 1885 that he wanted 'to start another life, where one wouldn't be nagged day and night, or harassed by an old man's cough and by torn stockings with dirty toes showing through them'.[48]

Kolia lay low, living on quick caricatures for *The Alarm Clock* and on Leikin's money. (Palmin had vanished from Anton's and Leikin's purview since March.) Anton answered Leikin's protests about Kolia's cheating on 14 September:

It's not a matter of intervention, but *la femme*. Woman! The sexual instinct is a worse obstacle to work than vodka ... A weak man goes to a woman, tumbles into her duvet and lies with her until they get colic in their groins ... Kolia's woman is a fat piece of meat who loves to drink and eat. Before coitus she always drinks and eats, and it's hard for her lover to hold back and not drink and eat pickles (it's always pickles!) The Agathopod [*Aleksandr*] is also twisted round a woman's little finger. When these two women will let go, the devil knows.

The family was now Anton, Evgenia, Masha, Misha, Aunt Fenichka and, when he was not lodging overnight at Gavrilov's warehouse, Pavel. Kolia had left Anna Ipatieva-Golden for a sordid rooming house. By 11 April 1886, in the primary school where he was head teacher, Vania had a flat on the Arbat with five rooms, free fuel and light, a servant and, to Pavel's delight, a tricorn and tunic. Aleksandr was out of sight in Novorossiisk. At the end of November the Moscow Chekhovs moved out of Lebedeva's damp, cold house to spacious quarters on the same Iakimanka: Klimenkov's house opposite the Church of St John the Warrior. For the first time each member of the family had a room of their own. Here the Tuesday soirées resumed. Chekhov's friends, whether the louche Palmin or the flirtatious Markova sisters, liked these hospitable apartments. The drawback was one floor up: Chef Piotr Podporin's dining rooms for weddings, balls and funerals, constant dancing, drinking, and the laughter or weeping of strangers.

By the end of 1885 Leikin felt personally attached to Anton, who became one of his very few confidants. He wanted to show off his palatial house and the estate he had bought outside town where the river Tosna joined the Neva, surrounded by pine forests, and raided by wolves. Leikin's letters to Moscow were a torrent equal to the letters and stories that Anton sent to Petersburg. Leikin gave advice on every subject: he told Anton to treat Kolia's morphine addiction with milk. Finally he pressed Anton to make his first visit to Petersburg.

On 10 December 1885 Anton set off for Petersburg to stay a fortnight with Leikin. Although Leikin introduced Anton to men who would change his life – the elderly novelist Grigorovich, doyen of living Russian writers, the newspaper tycoon and publisher Suvorin and his vitriolic leader-writer, Viktor Burenin – Leikin rarely left his protégé's side. Petersburg's literary circles sneered at Leikin, and Chekhov's reception suffered. On this first visit Suvorin and Grigorovich received him coolly, and he was even stood up by Khudekov of *The Petersburg Newspaper*. The only tangible benefit from this first journey to Petersburg was that Leikin agreed to publish a collection of Chekhov's tales entitled *Motley Stories*.[49]

One friendship came of this fortnight in Petersburg: Viktor Bilibin, a newly qualified barrister and Post Office official, Leikin's editorial secretary and, as 'Ygrec', leader-writer. Bilibin was a year older than Anton, naïve, curious and generous. Trust sprang up between them, though Bilibin had none of Anton's Bohemianism and was too gentle a writer for Chekhov, who in March 1886 criticized his 'cotton-wool-ness': 'As a columnist you are like a lover to whom a woman says "You take me too tenderly . . . You must be rougher!" (By the way, women are just like chickens, they like to be hit at that particular moment.)' However tenderly, Viktor Bilibin played Virgil to Anton's Dante in Petersburg's literary circles. To Bilibin alone Anton confided his doubts about Dunia Efros as a possible consort.

Bilibin had no illusions about his employer, Leikin, and he warned Anton of Leikin's duplicity: Leikin might be happy to show Chekhov off to Petersburg's publishers, but he had no intention of letting him escape. Anton passed on the warning to Aleksandr: 'Living with Leikin, I experienced all the agony about which it is said in Scripture: "I have endured unto the end." . . . Don't rely on Leikin. He is putting every spanner in the works for me and *The Petersburg Newspaper*.'

Anton washed away the flavour of Leikin's hospitality by celebrating Christmas, the New Year, University celebrations on Tatiana's day (12 January) and his name day (17 January), very wildly. At twenty-six he was taking leave, if not of his senses, then of his youth.

Friends' weddings were a pretext for weeks of hedonism. Dr Dmitri Saveliev was tied and Dr Nikolai Korobov soon would be. In the New Year the artist Aleksandr Ianov in Moscow, Dr Rozanov from Voskresensk and Viktor Bilibin in Petersburg all announced their weddings. Dr Rozanov asked Anton to be best man, and Masha bridesmaid. Anton borrowed 25 roubles and a morning coat. On Rozanov's wedding morning he wrote to Leikin: 'Today is Tatiana's day [*Moscow University's day*]. By evening I'll be legless. I'm putting on morning dress, off to be best man: a doctor is marrying a priest's daughter – a combination of killer and undertaker.' On Tatiana's day Kiseliov wrote and prescribed an open-air sexual encounter and an obscene purgative as a cure for the inevitable hangover.[50] Kiseliov was not far off the mark. Chekhov wrote to the groom two days later:

> I still haven't recovered from Tatiana's day. I really stuffed myself at your wedding, showing my belly no mercy. Then I went with Dr Uspensky to the Ermitage, then to Velde's restaurant and then to the Salon des Variétés ... The result: an empty purse, somebody else's galoshes, a heavy head, spots in the eyes and desperate pessimism. No-o-o, I've got to get married.

Kiseliov pretended that he was more shocked by Anton than envious of him: 'There are no limits to your debauchery, after the great mystery of marriage you end up in an unused hotel room and take up fornication.' Before his head cleared, in the early hours of 18 January 1886, after his twenty-sixth name day party Chekhov brought matters to a head.

SEVENTEEN

Getting Engaged
January 1886

MARRIAGE WAS TO PREOCCUPY CHEKHOV for fifteen years before he took the plunge. His behaviour reminds us of Gogol's comedy *Marriage* and its hero Podkolesin ['under the wheels'], who, when finally confronted with the betrothal he seeks, jumps out of the window. Chekhov was a close observer of marriage. He watched his parents' marriage for forty years. He studied well Aleksandr's and Kolia's liaisons. Ever the best man, never the groom, Anton drifted in his friends' wake. He wrote on 14 January 1886 to Dr Rozanov two days after the wedding:

> If Varvara [*Mrs Rozanova*] doesn't find me a bride, I'll certainly shoot myself . . . It's time I was ruled with a rod of iron, as you now are . . . Do you remember? A finch in a cage, a new tap on the samovar and scented glycerine soap are the signs indicating a married man's flat . . . Three of my friends are getting married.

Once Anton's head cleared, he wrote a dramatic monologue *On the Harm of Tobacco* and told Bilibin: 'I've just got to know a very striking French girl, the daughter of poor but decent bourgeois . . . Her name is not quite decent: Mlle Sirout.'[51] Four days later Anton wrote again to Bilibin: 'Seeing a certain young lady home, I made her a proposal . . . I want to get out of the frying pan into the fire . . . Wish me luck for my marriage.'

Only to Bilibin did Anton reveal this engagement. Masha, a close friend of the fiancée, Dunia Efros, only suspected. To Leikin Chekhov dismissed all thought of marriage. Overhead, on 19 January, a wedding party was in full swing: 'Somebody banging their feet like a horse has just run over my head . . . Must be the best man. The band is thundering . . . For the groom who is going to screw the bride this music may be pleasant, but it will stop me, an impotent, getting any sleep.'

The impulse to marry Dunia Efros was not her dowry: her family were not rich. Nor did Anton have a desire for progeny (except for a puppy from Leikin's Apel and Rogulka). Aleksandr described with pride how he witnessed the birth of his second son, whom he named Anton, and then declared that after this spectacle he could never make love to Anna again. Aleksandr's picture of philoprogenitive domesticity in Novorossiisk in January 1886 was a deterrent. Aleksandr advised Anton in his next letter: 'You still aren't married. Don't . . . I've forgotten when I last slept.'

Anton's engagement to Dunia Efros was short and secret. His letters to Bilibin trace stormy ups and downs. On 1 February, Anton, with Kolia and Franz Schechtel, went to a ball at the barracks where Lieutenant Tyshko was now stationed. His fervour for Dunia cooled, and he told Bilibin:

> Thank your fiancée for the mention and the consideration and tell her that my marriage is probably alas and alack! The censor won't pass it . . . My *she* is a Jewess. Does a rich Jewgirl have the bravery to take Orthodoxy and the consequences – all right, she doesn't – and there's no need to . . . And anyway, we've already quarrelled . . . Tomorrow we'll make it up, but in a week we'll quarrel again . . . She's so annoyed that religion gets in the way that she breaks pencils and smashes photographs on my desk – that's typical . . . She's a terrible shrew . . . I shall divorce her 1–2 years after the wedding, that's certain.

Dunia's violent spirit attracted and repelled Anton, and would infiltrate the highly sexed and assertive heroines of his stories that year.

On 16 February 1886 Anton told Bilibin: 'Nothing is certain about my marriage yet', and on 11 March:

> I have split up to *nec* [sic] *plus ultra* with my fiancée. Yesterday we met . . . I complained to her of having no money and she told me that her Jewboy brother drew a 3-rouble note so perfectly that the illusion was complete: the chambermaid picked it up and put it in her pocket. That's all. I shan't write about her to you again.

By early April Bilibin stopped asking about Chekhov's fiancée. Troubled by Anton's licentiousness, Bilibin questioned him on love and sex in literature and reality. As for his own love life, Chekhov would only say that 'he thawed like a Jewboy before a gold rouble'

at the 'flowerbed' of beautiful women surrounding Masha. Dunia
Efros remained a family friend, although she quarrelled with Masha
two years later. In her letter from a North Caucasian spa that summer,
four months after breaking with Anton, her conciliatory tone set the
pattern for Anton's discarded lovers:

> I was thinking of a rich bride for you, Anton, even before I had
> your letter. There's a very loving merchant's daughter here, not
> bad-looking, rather plump (your taste) and fairly daft (also a virtue).
> She is desperate to get away from mummy's supervision which
> oppresses her terribly. Once she even drank 4 gallons of vinegar to
> be pale and scare mummy. She told us that herself. I think you'll
> like her. There's lots of money.[52]

Dunia's Jewishness was certainly instrumental in bringing her and
Anton together and in sundering them. Like many southern Russians,
Anton admired and liked Jews. Always a defender of Jews, he asked
Bilibin why he used the word 'yid' three times in one letter? Yet he
himself used the word 'yid' both neutrally and pejoratively and, like
many southern Russians, Anton felt Jews to be a race apart with
irredeemably unacceptable attitudes. 'Jew' and 'non-Jew' were categories in which he classified every new acquaintance, even though
his utterances and his behaviour make him, by the standards of the
times, a judophile.

We can infer Anton's cynicism about love and marriage from two
items he offered to *Fragments* in January 1886. One was a readers'
competition:

> The writer of *the best love letter* will win: a photograph of a pretty
> woman, a certificate signed by the editor and the judges that he has
> won and a free subscription for this or next year, as he wishes . . .
> Terms: 1) Only males may take part; 2) The letter must be sent to
> the office of *Fragments* no later than 1 March and bear the author's
> address and surname; 3) The author's letter is to be a declaration
> of love, showing that he really is in love and suffering, with parallels
> between infatuation and real love . . . 4) *Conditio sine qua non*: the
> author must be literate, decent, gentle, playful and poetic . . . *Ladies*
> are appointed as judges.

Chekhov's other piece, 'For the Information of Husbands', gave six
methods to seduce wives. It was banned: 'Despite its jocularity, how-

ever, the topic's immorality, the indecently voluptuous scenes and cynical hints lead the censor to forbid it.' Bilibin, engaged to marry, told Chekhov that the skit was an affront (22 January): 'So the censor wouldn't pass "The Attack on Wives"! Eh? . . . You deserved it. And to think that you're about to be married.'[53]

In any case Anton wanted a career more than he wanted Dunia Efros. In 1885 he had written some hundred pieces, as much in bulk as he would write in his ten last and finest years. By 1886, a regular contributor to Khudekov's *Petersburg Newspaper*, he was attracting attention among serious readers and writers. Leikin's *Fragments* was unrewarding, for Leikin had no time for polished work. He wrote his fair copy straight out and thought others should do the same. *Fragments* was so strictly censored in 1885 that its existence, and Anton's income, were threatened. There were practical as well as creative reasons for Anton to move to Khudekov's paper, although Chekhov conceded to Bilibin (who had no illusions) that Leikin had merits: 'Where else would you find such a pedant, such a manic letter-writer, such a runner to the censorship committee?' As a literary mentor, however, Leikin was redundant, although he could charm as well as irritate with his egocentric trivia, writing to Chekhov on 26 February 1886:

> I am still bothered with my stomach. It must be a serious catarrh. And bismuth hasn't helped. I've added a grain of codeine to 10 powders (1/10) . . . Yesterday I bought a cow for 125 roubles. A very fine cow. I meant to send it to my country estate, but I couldn't bear to and placed it until Easter in my town house, all the more since I have a spare stable. Now we are drinking genuine milk.

For the stomach Chekhov advised arsenic. (He prescribed Bilibin arsenic, too; Anton and Leikin mocked Bilibin for being too cowardly to take it.)

A reminder of his schooldays inspired Chekhov to aim higher. Viktor Bilibin drew Anton's attention to a talented short novel, *My Marriage*, in the October and November 1885 issues of the monthly *The Russian Herald*. Using material from Taganrog *gimnazia*, it told of a schoolteacher who loses his idle wife, and then his beloved sister-in-law, to an actor, a fiery radical. Anton recognized the author, Fiodor Stulli, as his old geography teacher. *My Marriage* left an imprint on

Chekhov: he was to use its title and some of its motifs years later. To be overtaken as a writer by one of his teachers spurred his ambition.

A new eye for nature, rich experience in Moscow and Babkino, from fishing to autopsies, the training of the anatomy theatre and the *historia morbi*, made Chekhov stand out in Khudekov's *Petersburg Newspaper*. Stories like 'The Dead Body', where peasants guard a corpse until the authorities come, or 'Sergeant Prishibeev' [Basher], about a maniac who takes the law into his own hands, have a radical outlook, and a subtlety quite uncharacteristic of the Antosha Chekhonte of old. Chekhov could risk pure pathos. 'Grief' (of November 1885), based on an incident at the Chikino hospital, has an old turner, himself crippled by frostbite, delivering his dying wife to hospital. It won Palmin's admiration. 'Anguish' of January 1886 (a cabby, whose son has died, turns to his horse for sympathy) convinced Aleksandr of his brother's genius. Chekhov could now be serious, not yet in his letters, but in his art, where he could be sure of hiding behind a neutral, ironical authorial persona. The most telling of the stories on the eve of his breakthrough is 'Artistry': a drunken peasant erects a cross on the frozen river. Typical of all Chekhov's fiction, it is a seasonally appropriate work, timed to appear on the relevant day – the Feast of the Consecration of the Waters – but this is the first of several stories Anton was to write that show a religious mystery and work of art created by a flawed human being. This depth and range also owes much to Maupassant, widely admired in Russia; Bilibin and Chekhov discussed *Bel-Ami* and *Une Vie* in their letters. The impact of a dozen major stories published across thirty or so Monday issues of *The Petersburg Newspaper* softened the hostility of critics to a writer of lowly provincial origins who had, as yet, no influential patron.

EIGHTEEN

Acclaim
February–April 1886

IN THE NEW YEAR Kurepin of *The Alarm Clock* returned from Petersburg. He told Chekhov that the press baron Aleksei Suvorin wanted Chekhov's stories for the Saturday supplement to *New Times*. Chekhov accepted with alacrity and Kurepin told the magnate. On 15 February *Fragments* published 'In Alien Lands', one of Chekhov's best light pieces: outrageously funny and touchingly sad, it paints the predicament of a Frenchman whose Russian host has confiscated his passport, so as to turn his guest into a slave. Anton's début with 'Requiem' in *New Times* the same day overshadowed even the impact of 'In Alien Lands'. 'Requiem' outgrows the humorous genre to which at first sight it appears to belong: a grieving father insists on having his daughter commemorated as a fornicatrix. Apart from initiating Chekhov's theme of the actress as social outcast, this story builds tragedy out of the comedy of misunderstanding. Suvorin sent Anton a telegram and insisted that he allow his real name to be printed. Chekhov reserved his real name for scientific writing. Only *Nature and Field Sports* had ever printed work under his real name. He consented reluctantly. Anton Chekhov consigned Antosha Chekhonte to extinction.

Leikin gave way to the inevitable loss of his protégé: 'I think that it is in your direct interests to write for Suvorin, because he pays almost twice as much.' (Suvorin started Chekhov at 12 kopecks a line, and allowed him three times the length that Leikin allotted. One story might earn 100 roubles.) Leikin and Chekhov had had tiffs, and not only over his publications in Moscow. To Leikin's boasts of potency as both man and editor, Anton responded: 'A penis that smashes walnuts as a measure of editorial ability could be a fine theme for a dissertation.'[54] From mid April, Khudekov cut Chekhov's allocation of space on *The Petersburg Newspaper* to make room for 'Current

Events'. Anton transferred his loyalty to Aleksei Suvorin: he sent a congratulatory telegram to Suvorin and *New Times* for the paper's tenth jubilee. Leikin was at the celebrations, where Suvorin distributed gold medals to his minions. Leikin tried to make the best of Anton's new connection; he was flattered that Suvorin and Grigorovich were 'infatuated' with his protégé. Dmitri Grigorovich, the first Russian writer graphically to portray the miseries of the Russian peasant, despite four decades of resting on his laurels, was still able to open doors, so infectious was his literary enthusiasm.

Chekhov had divined Suvorin's tastes. *New Times*, like its owner, liked brooding sexuality and graphic naturalism in its reports and its fiction. Two stories Chekhov wrote for *New Times* in February 1886 have a highly sexed woman rebelling against her husband: the heroine of 'Agafia' faces a beating from her husband after a day with her lover, while in 'The Witch' a woman awes her elderly husband by conjuring male visitors out of a blizzard. Suvorin, Bilibin reported, was 'simply in ecstasy'. Chekhov's more prudish friends, the architect Franz Schechtel and Viktor Bilibin, were slightly appalled; even Grigorovich, still a notorious libertine, had reservations. At the end of March Chekhov sent Suvorin a story full of social concern, where the picture of deprivation was free of any 'taint': 'Nightmare' shows a newcomer to a country district, shocked by the poverty of the priest and the doctor. The story struck a chord in Suvorin, for the doctor's wife washes her own linen – Suvorin's favourite recollection of poverty was that his first wife, a teacher, did her own washing.

Chekhov's new departure aroused acclaim on 25 March 1886. Dmitri Grigorovich had the previous summer marvelled at 'The Huntsman'. Now he was sure he had discovered a genius to succeed him. He talked to Aleksei Suvorin and wrote at length to Anton:

> Dear Sir, Dear Mr Chekhov, About a year ago I chanced to read a story by you in *The Petersburg Newspaper*; I can't remember now what it was called; I remember being struck by its features of peculiar originality, and above all by the remarkable fidelity, truthfulness in the presentation of the characters and also in the description of nature. Since then I have read everything signed *Chekhonte*, although inwardly I was angry that a man should so little value himself that he thinks he has to resort to a pseudonym. Reading you, I constantly advised Suvorin and Burenin to follow my example. They obeyed

me and now none of us doubt that you have a *real* talent – a talent that sets you far outside the circle of the new generation of writers. I am not a journalist nor a publisher; I can exploit you only by reading you; if I speak of your talent, I do so out of conviction. I am over 65; but I still have so much love of literature and follow its progress with such enthusiasm that I am always glad when I come across something alive, gifted, so that I couldn't – as you see – hold back and I offer you both my hands. But this is not all; I want to add this: judging by various qualities of your talent, a true feeling for inner analysis, mastery of description (snowstorm, night and locality in 'Agafia' etc.), a feeling of plasticity, where you give a full picture in a few lines: clouds on a dying sunset: *'like ash on dying coals'* . . . and so on, – your vocation is, I am certain, to write several excellent truly artistic works. You will commit a great moral sin if you do not justify these expectations. To do so you must have respect for a talent which is so rarely granted. Stop doing hack work. I don't know how well off you are; if you are not well off, better go hungry as we used to in our time, save up your impressions for work that has been pondered, polished, written at several sittings . . . The basis for your stories is often a motif with a somewhat cynical tinge, why? Truthfulness, realism not only do not exclude refinement, they are enhanced by it. You have such a command of form and such a feeling for the plastic that there is no particular need to talk, for instance, of dirty feet and twisted toenails or the sexton's navel . . . Please forgive me such remarks; I decided to make them only because I truly believe in your talent and with all my heart wish it full development and full expression. Soon, I am told, a book of your stories is coming out; if it is under the pseudonym of *Che-khon-te*, I earnestly ask you to telegraph the publisher to put your real name to it. After the last stories in *New Times* and the success of 'The Huntsman' your name will have more success. I should appreciate confirmation that you are not angry with me for my remarks but take them to heart, just as I write to you not as an authority but in the simplicity of a pure heart. I shake your hand as a friend and wish you all the best. Yours respectfully, D. Grigorovich.

Wary of his own father for twenty years, Anton responded with trusting affection to the father figures of Russian literature. Great writers – Leskov, Grigorovich and, later, Tolstoy – and self-made patriarchs like Suvorin aroused filial devotion in Anton. He might back away from adoring young women, but he seized hold of tributes from Grand Old Men. Anton boasted of Grigorovich's praise to Uncle Mitrofan and to Bilibin and answered Grigorovich by return of post with unprecedented emotion:

> Your letter, my kind, ardently loved bringer of good tidings, struck me like lightning I almost burst into tears, I was profoundly moved and I now feel that it has left a deep trace in my soul. May God calm your old age as you have comforted my youth, but I cannot find words or deeds with which to thank you. You know how ordinary people look on the elect, such as you; you can therefore judge what your letter means for my self-regard. It is greater than any diploma and, for a writer who is a beginner it is a royalty for the present and the future. I am bemused. I haven't the strength to judge, whether I deserve this high reward or not . . . If I have a gift which ought to be respected, then I confess to the purity of your heart, I haven't respected it hitherto. I have felt I had it, but have got used to considering it negligible. An organism needs only external reasons to be unjust, extremely dubious and suspicious about itself. And, as I now recall, I have plenty of such reasons. All those close to me have always been condescending about my writing and have never stopped giving me friendly advice not to change my profession, not to become a scribbler. I have hundreds of acquaintances in Moscow, a couple of dozen writers among them, and I cannot recall a single one who reads me or considers me as an artist. There is a so-called 'literary circle' in Moscow; talents and mediocrities of all ages and sorts gather once a week in a private room in a restaurant and let their tongues wag. If I were to go there and read just a bit of your letter, they would laugh at me to my face. My five years' hanging around the newspapers has been enough to imbue me with this general attitude to my literary hack work, I quickly got accustomed to looking condescendingly at my work – and everything has gone to the dogs! That's the first reason . . . The second is that I am a doctor and am up to my ears in medicine . . . I write all this only to justify my grave sin to you a little bit. Hitherto I have taken an extremely frivolous, careless, pointless view of my literary work. I don't remember a *single* story on which I have spent more than twenty-four hours, while 'The Huntsman', which you liked, was written in a bathing hut! As reporters write their notices about fires, so I've written my stories: automatically, semiconsciously, not caring at all about the reader or myself . . . In writing I have done my utmost not to squander on a story images or pictures which, God knows why, I've been saving up and carefully hiding.

The first thing that drove me to self-criticism was a very kind and, as far as I can see, sincere letter from Suvorin. I had begun to prepare to write something sensible, but I still lacked faith in my own literary sense.

Now, out of the blue, your letter has come. Forgive the comparison, but it acted on me like a governor's order to 'leave town in 24 hours!', i.e. I suddenly felt an overwhelming need to hurry, rather to get out of whatever I was stuck in . . . I shall free myself of hack work, but it will take time. There is no easy way to get out of the rut I have fallen into. I don't mind going hungry, as I have before, but it isn't just a question of me. I give my leisure time to writing, 2–3 hours a day and a bit of the night, i.e. time that can be used for small pieces. In summer, when I have more leisure and fewer expenses, I shall take up serious work.

My only hope is the future. I'm still only 26. Perhaps I shall manage to do something, although time is passing quickly.

Leikin still announced to Anton: 'My house, my table are at your service.' Anton wanted to meet his new patrons in Petersburg independently of Leikin, whose motives, after his last visit when he had been received so frostily by Suvorin and others, he now distrusted. He called Leikin 'the uncle of lies' to Aleksandr. Schechtel, who was drawing the cover of *Motley Stories*, reported: 'There is a supposition that Leikin is undermining your interests'.

For Easter Anton sent Suvorin his finest and most lyrical piece of prose so far, 'On Easter Night': a pilgrim listens to the ferryman monk mourning the death of his friend. Easter joy is tempted with lament. Chekhov's prose is imbued with intense love of the archaic language of the liturgy which only he and Leskov could fuse into literary Russian. 'On Easter Night' transcends the author's own unbelief.

Four things, however, stood between Chekhov and a triumphal visit to Petersburg: Easter, his health, poverty and Kolia's behaviour. Only twice, in 1878 and 1879, had Anton spent an Easter away from his parents. He stayed in Moscow until 14 April, Easter Monday. At Easter Anton's health took on an ominous annual pattern: with spring and the rising of the sap, his lungs spurted blood. On 6 April Anton confessed to Leikin that he was spitting blood, too weak to write, but 'afraid to submit to the soundings of my colleagues'. Family and friends gave him no respite. Giliarovsky wrote a hoax letter, saying he had a broken leg, extensive burns and wounds after a fire: Anton rushed to his bedside to find a case of St Anthony's fire. Vania's diarrhœa and Aunt Fenichka's chronic cough demanded nursing and kept Anton in Moscow. He even lacked money for the fare to Petersburg, although Suvorin, unlike Khudekov, paid his authors on time. On 5 March Anton was ordered by the magistrate to pay 50 roubles of Kolia's debts; apparently Kolia owed another 3000.

Anton's elder brothers were inexcusably irresponsible: they stood in his way. He lectured them both, writing to Aleksandr on 6 April:

> You write that you're 'being burnt, slashed, ground and blood-sucked'. You mean, you're being dunned? My dear brother, you've got to pay your debts! You *must* at any cost, even to Armenians, even at the price of going hungry ... If people with a university education and writers think debts are just forms of suffering, what will everybody else think? ... Look at me, I have a family round my neck far larger than yours and groceries in Moscow cost 10 times more than where you are. Your rent is what I pay for a piano, I don't dress any better than you.

At the same time Anton gave Kolia an ultimatum:

> You are kind to the point of being wet, magnanimous, unselfish, you will share your last penny, you're sincere; you don't know envy or hate, you're simple, you pity people and animals, you're not spiteful or vindictive, you're trusting ... You are gifted from above with what others don't have ... on earth there is only one artist for every 2,000,000 people ... You have just one fault. This is your false excuse, your grief and your catarrh of the gut. It is your extreme lack of good breeding ... The lower-class flesh brought up on thrashings, wine cellars and handouts shows. It's hard, awfully hard to overcome it.
>
> Well bred people in my opinion must satisfy the following conditions:
> 1) They respect human personality and are always considerate, gentle, polite and yielding ...
> 2) ... They go without sleep ... to pay for their student brothers, to buy clothes for their mother ...
> 3) They respect others' property and therefore pay their debts ...

The tirade ended:

> 8) They develop an aesthetic sense. They can't go to bed in their clothes, look at cracks full of bedbugs in the wall, breathe foul air,

walk on floors covered with spittle, eat out of an old paraffin can. They try as far as they can to tame and ennoble the sexual instinct ... They need from a woman not bed, not equine sweat, not the sounds of urination, not a mind expressing itself in the art of deceiving you with fake pregnancy and lying non-stop. They, especially artists, need freshness, elegance, humanity, a capacity to be a mother, not a hole ... They don't knock back vodka, don't sniff cupboards, for they know they are not pigs. They drink only when free to, on the right occasion ... Come home to us, smash the vodka decanter and lie down and read ... if only Turgenev, whom you haven't read ...

You must drop your fucking conceit, because you're not a little boy ... You'll be 30 soon! It's high time!

I'm waiting ... We're all waiting.

Kolia's delinquency affected many. Franz Schechtel had shown trust: he found Kolia work restoring icons for a new church, where, as architect, he was penalized for delays. Kolia took the money and materials. Schechtel appealed to Anton: 'I'm tearing my hair and pulling my teeth with despair: Kolia has vanished and left not a trace: there's no way I can get to him.'[55]

Eventually, on Easter Sunday Kolia was traced, but no materials were recovered.

Anton had done all he could. He was leaving for his second fortnight in Petersburg. *Motley Stories* was launched on 27 April; there were cogent financial reasons for going. If Suvorin paid 87 roubles for one story, why should not Khudekov raise his rates? Leikin encouraged Anton: 'It wouldn't be a bad idea for you to come to Petersburg the week after Easter, and meet Suvorin and Grigorovich [*again*]. I would do that for the sake of literary connections which are essential for a writer.' On 25 April 1886, Anton stepped out of the train in Petersburg: he was to be enthusiastically received by the Great and the Good.

III

My Brothers' Keeper

And Joseph nourished his father, and his brethren, and all his father's household with bread, according to their families.

Genesis XLVII, 12

NINETEEN

The Suvorins
April–August 1886

In April 1886 Anton Chekhov met Suvorin again. A powerful bond, built on misconceptions that would weaken it, was formed. Suvorin saw in Chekhov genius and delicacy; Chekhov saw in Suvorin sensitive authority. Twelve years would pass before Suvorin found the 'flint' in Chekhov's make-up and Chekhov detected the 'lack of character' in the publishing baron. They needed each other: *New Times* had no genius among its talented writers; Chekhov had no other access to Petersburg literary circles. For a decade Chekhov was frank with Suvorin as with nobody else. Suvorin responded to Chekhov with candour; they were soon equals.

A soldier's son, born in the heartland of Russia, Voronezh province, Suvorin had much in common with Chekhov: he had fought his way up as teacher, journalist, critic, playwright. He had made his name as a radical in the 1860s, as a friend of Dostoevsky at the end of 1870s and had burst into politics, making *New Times* a paper that was read, admired and detested – for its closeness to ruling circles, its national-ism and cynicism, its advertisements where unemployed French women 'sought a position'. Suvorin kept independent: he had a nom-inal editor, Fiodorov, who kept a suitcase packed, ready to spend a few months in prison for any offence Suvorin might commit. He was now becoming a major publisher and the proprietor of most of Russia's railway-station bookstalls.

Suvorin was a complex figure – a man of much wit, but little humour, a supporter of autocracy in his leader articles, an anarchist in his diary. His faults were offset by virtues: the anti-Semitic ravings of *New Times* were countered by his private fondness for an elderly Jewish lady, his children's music teacher, who lived in the household. The worst Suvorin's enemies said of him was that he feared 'only death and a rival newspaper'. The theatre critic Kugel wrote of him:

in his fur hat, his fur coat hanging open, carrying a big stick, I almost always saw the figure of Ivan the Terrible ... Something foxy in the lower jaw, in the gape, something sharp in the line of his forehead. A Mephistopheles ... The secret of his influence and his sharp vision was that, like the greatest political and philosophical geniuses, he deeply understood the bad side of human nature ... The way he entertained Chekhov, looked at him, enveloped him with his eyes reminded one somehow of a rich man showing off his new 'kept woman'.

Suvorin's first wife, Anna Ivanovna, died in circumstances that won even his enemies' pity. One summer evening in 1873 Suvorin, entirely unsuspecting, was summoned to a hotel room, where he found her dying of a revolver wound inflicted in a suicide pact with her lover. Three years later, Suvorin married another Anna Ivanovna, twenty-two years younger than he: she, though flirtatious, defended her husband like a tigress; he loved her, he declared, third after his newspaper and his theatre. Suvorin suffered one bereavement after another: in 1880 his daughter Aleksandra died and then his infant son Grisha, of diptheria. Two of his sons and a favourite son-in-law would also die before him. He became a lonely insomniac. Suvorin rarely went to bed before his paper came out, and spent hours alone in his office with just a cup of coffee and a chicken breast for sustenance. He strode the streets and cemeteries of Petersburg. After his bereavements began, he retreated to the country, allowing his son Aleksei, 'the Dauphin', to wrest power from him and, eventually, to undo his empire.

Like Anton Chekhov's, Suvorin's love for his many dependants could give way to irritation. Like Anton, Suvorin would long for company when alone, and for solitude when in company. Suvorin had, however, the warmth of the nepotist. Anton Chekhov was not the first alumnus of the Taganrog *gimnazia* he was to adopt: his legal manager, Aleksei Kolomnin, left Taganrog ten years before Chekhov, and married Suvorin's daughter. Suvorin had taken the entire Kolomnin family under his wing. Now the Chekhovs came under his aegis; Suvorin was to offer employment to Aleksandr, Vania, Masha and Misha Chekhov. Soon Anton would have his flat in the Suvorin house and be offered Suvorin's younger daughter, Nastia, then nine years old, in marriage.

Forty years later Anna Suvorina would recall Anton's visit that spring:

> Our apartment was unusual: the hall was the domain of the children ... In one corner stood an aviary with a pine tree where up to fifty canaries and finches lived and bred. The hall was sunlit, the birds sang loudly, the children, naturally, made a lot of noise and I must add that the dogs also took part ... we sat down together on a little sofa by the aviary. He asked the children the names of all the dogs, said he was very fond of dogs himself and then made us laugh ... We talked for rather a long time ... he was tall, slim, very good-looking, he had dark reddish waving hair, a little greying, he had slightly clouded eyes that laughed subtly, and a fetching smile. His voice was pleasant and soft and, with a barely perceptible smile ... Chekhov and I quickly became friends, we never quarrelled but we argued often, almost to the point of tears – or at least I did. My husband just adored him, as if Anton had bewitched him.[1]

Anton won the hearts of Suvorin's children (even, for a while, of the Dauphin), of his valet Vasili Iulov and the children's governess Emilie Bijon. The philosopher Vasili Rozanov, also rescued from obscurity by Suvorin, contemplated the publisher's love: 'If Chekhov had said "I now need a flat, a desk, shoes, peace and a wife," Suvorin would have told him "Take everything I have." Literally.'[2]

The journalists in Suvorin's entourage were jealous. One, Viktor Burenin, was Suvorin's oldest friend and perhaps his only confidant. Burenin could, with unprintable epigrams and printed barbs, destroy a sensitive writer. Twenty years earlier, when Suvorin sat on a park bench, too poor to hire a midwife for his pregnant wife, Burenin, then a student, had talked to him and insisted on giving him all the money he had. They became inseparable. Burenin's prognosis, as much as Grigorovich's enthusiasm, persuaded Suvorin of Chekhov's importance, but Burenin was allowed to attack Suvorin's favourites with impunity and soon turned on Chekhov: the spiteful *New Times* clique very soon germinated in Petersburg a hostility to Chekhov.

Anton had a happy spring in 1886: he hardly slept. Suppers with Suvorin, being lionized, intoxicated him. He could now write less for more money: Leikin no longer counted on a weekly contribution. That spring Chekhov gave *New Times* just one story of note, 'The Secret Councillor'. A touching portrayal of the disarray brought into a country household by the arrival of a distinguished relative, the story anticipates the pattern of *Uncle Vania*: a great man comes from the city and wrecks the lives of his country relatives. 'The Secret Councillor' abandoned the sensational tone that Suvorin's readers liked. It is a work that looks back to Anton's childhood in the country around Taganrog and that injects for the first time an element of nostalgia for a lost idyll, which is to colour much of Chekhov's mature prose.

Kiseliov and all Babkino were calling for Anton. Mosquitoes whined; goldfinches sang. Kolia took his paints and brushes, but left his toothbrush and his sackcloth trousers with Anna Golden. Anton hoped that the artist would win over the lover, and ignored letters from Franz Schechtel, raging at Kolia's drunken binges. By 29 April Kolia hurt Schechtel more: he forced Lentovsky, for whose theatre the architect and painter were commissioned, to disgorge another 100 roubles and promptly vanished to Babkino, making sorties to Moscow only for debauchery. Schechtel raged and despaired; he even tried to lure Kolia by putting a letter in an envelope marked 'contains 3000 roubles': 'Friend! I have two overcoats, but fuck-all money – but there'll be some soon . . . if you'd come and see me for a minute . . .'[3] Schechtel complained to Anton of Levitan's dissipation, too; fornication did not stop Levitan painting, but Schechtel complained to Anton:

> Levitan is ploughing and sighing for his bare-bottomed beauty, but the wretch is only human: what will it cost him on quicklime, disinfectant, eau de Cologne and other chemicals and how much trouble to treat his amorous slut and make her fit to receive his thoroughbred organ? . . .

Levitan arrived late in Babkino: he was detained in the Crimea, whence he wrote to Chekhov: 'What made you assume I'd gone off with a woman? There is screwing here, but it was there before I arrived. And I'm not hunting for fine picturesque pussy, it just happened to be there (and, alas, has gone).'[4] Once Kolia and Levitan were at Babkino, the fun began. On 10 May Anton reached Moscow from Petersburg; the next day he took his mother, sister and Misha to Babkino. They painted, fished, bathed, and played: Levitan would dress as a savage Chechen, or the Chekhov brothers would hold mock trials of

Kolia and Levitan for drunkenness and debauchery. Anton composed 'Soft-Boiled Boots', illustrated nonsense worthy of Edward Lear, to amuse the Kiseliov children. Somehow he found time to dispense medicine, and write for *Fragments*, *The Petersburg Newspaper* and *New Times* – comic classics, such as 'Novel with Double Bass'. Anton wrote his first philosophical stories, such as 'The Dreariness of Life', where activists and quietists debate what a civic-minded Russian ought to do. In Chekhov's world, unlike the world of Dostoevsky or Tolstoy, neither party wins the debate: there is an ideological stalemate. This summer Anton was groping for a new type of story, that would evoke the futility of words and thoughts. In 1886 he wrote far less than in 1885, but he was preparing himself for the real mastery of his prose of the following year.

No sooner was Kolia rescued from Anna Golden's bed and Moscow's drinking dens, than Aleksandr burst back into Anton's life. On 21 May 1886, in Novorossiisk, Aleksandr dictated a letter for Anton: Anna added a desperate postscript of her own:

> For God's sake, suggest what we can do. Aleksandr suddenly went blind at 5 p.m.; after dinner he went to bed as usual, after drinking a great deal, then he woke at 5, came out of the room to play with the children and asked for water, sat down on the bed and tells me he can't see.

Kolia insisted that Aleksandr was acting, but the act was convincing: Aleksandr was given leave to go to Moscow and Petersburg for treatment. On 3 June he arrived at Vania's schoolhouse in Moscow. From there Pavel wrote to Anton:

> I ask my children to look after their eyes above all things, do your reading by day, not by night, act sensibly, to be eyeless is bad, to beg alms and assistance is a great misfortune. Kolia and Misha, look after your eyes. You still have to live long and be useful to society and yourself. If you lose your good sight it is disagreeable to me to see. Aleksandr can see nothing, he is handed bread and a spoon and that is it. These are the consequences of wilfulness and of letting his reason incline to the bad.

Aleksandr, Anna, their illegitimate sons, and Anna's elder children, who drifted in and out of her care, lasted two months with Pavel and

Vania in the school house. Pavel kept calm. Aleksandr was drying out, and his sight was returning. On 10 July 1886 he told Anton:

> Imagine, after supper, I was banging away with my equine penis at the 'mother of my children'. Father was reading his *Monastic Rules* and suddenly decided to come in with a candle to see if the windows were locked ... He solemnly went up to the window, locked it as if he hadn't noticed anything, had the sense to put out the candle and left in the dark. I even fancied he said a prayer to the icon.[5]

In mid July Kolia vanished again – to cousin Georgi and Uncle Mitrofan in Taganrog. Aleksandr and his family came to Babkino. Anton was aghast: he wanted other company. He failed to lure Franz Schechtel from Moscow, even though he exhorted him, 'living in town in summer is worse than pederasty, more immoral than buggery'. Anton moved twenty miles south to Zvenigorod, ostensibly to depute for Dr Uspensky at the hospital. After Petersburg, Chekhov felt imposed upon by his brothers. Fame brought bitter poison: the prestigious *The Northern Herald* reviewed *Motley Tales*: '[Mr Chekhov] will like a squeezed-out lemon inevitably die, completely forgotten, in a ditch ... In general Mr Chekhov's book is a very sad and tragic spectacle of a young talent's suicide ...' Chekhov never forgave N. K. Mikhailovsky, to whom he attributed this review.[6]

The more he felt put upon, the greater his need for Masha. Now she had her diploma, she had grown confident. She had a profession for the coming twenty years: she taught part-time in Moscow in the prestigious Rzhevskaia girls' grammar school, run by a family of farmers and thus known as the 'Dairy School'. Masha was now more than an agency by which Anton could meet strong-minded, intelligent young women. Evgenia was surrendering the household to her. In early August 1886 it was Masha who left Babkino to seek a quieter flat for the family. Like many a sister in the nineteenth century, she was a handmaiden so prized by her siblings that cousin Georgi proclaimed to Anton: 'I have concluded from all the attractive stories from Misha that she is your goddess of something kind, good and precious.'[7]

More servant than goddess to her brothers, Masha's first conflict of interests arose in Babkino in summer 1886. Taught by Levitan, Masha was painting very fine water-colour landscapes and portraits.

Levitan made hundreds of propositions to hundreds of women, but only one proposal. Seventy years later, at the age of ninety-two, Masha recalled it:

> Levitan dropped to his knees in front of me and – a declaration of love ... All I could do was turn and run. The whole day, I sat distraught in my room crying, my head deep in the pillow. Levitan, as always, came to dinner. I stayed in my room. Anton asked everyone why I wasn't there ... He got up and came to my room. 'Why are you howling?' I told him what had happened and admitted I didn't know what to tell Levitan, and how. My brother replied: 'Of course, you can marry him if you like, but remember that he wants women of the Balzac age, not girls like you.'

Whenever Masha referred proposals to Anton, she received a strong negative signal. Anton never expressly forbade her to marry, but his silence and his actions, if necessary, behind the wings left her in no doubt how much he disapproved and how deeply he was dismayed.

Anton could stop his sister marrying, but he could not keep his girlfriends on stand-by. Despite chocolates from Petersburg, Dunia Efros kept her distance; Olga Kundasova fell instead for Professor Bredikhin, at the Moscow observatory. Lily Markova vanished to Ufa, among the Bashkirs in the Urals foothills. Finally, in Petersburg, she accepted the artist Sakharov. Aleksei Kiseliov thought Anton's love life hilarious and celebrated it in verse that was recited all around Babkino.

> *To A. P. Chekhov*
> Sákharov got married
> And he was not thrilled
> When he found that Lily
> Was already drilled.
> Who? he'd like to know.
> The truth is what he's after.
> But Lily and Anton
> Can't hold back their laughter.
> The groom is coming, scowling,
> And if he gets his hands on
> That wretched whoring Chekhov,
> He'll loudly thump Anton
> And give him such a thrashing

So that he'll remember
To keep off others' brides
With his dripping member.[8]

Others saw Anton as a threat to the married. When Bilibin's wife, Vera, read a story Anton wrote that August for *New Times*, 'A Misfortune', she told her husband that the ruthless seducer of the married heroine was Chekhov himself. Vera Bilibina refused to greet Anton when he visited the house. Four years later Bilibin deserted her for Anna Arkadievna Soloviova, a secretary at *Fragments*. Vera always felt that Anton had exerted a pernicious influence on her husband.

TWENTY

Life in a Chest of Drawers
September 1886–March 1887

MASHA AND MISHA rented from a surgeon, Dr Korneev, new premises for the family: a two-storey brick house, eight rooms for 650
roubles a year, on the west side of the Moscow Garden Ring, then a
country road where a horse tram passed once an hour. Anton moved
in on 1 September 1886. Here the Chekhovs spent nearly four years.
The only Chekhov residence in Moscow to be made into a museum,
its fussy red-brick façade reminded Anton of a chest of drawers. Anton
lived like a gentleman in his study and bedroom. On the ground floor
was an enormous kitchen and pantry leading to the chamber maid's
and cook's rooms. Upstairs Masha's room adjoined the drawing
room; her guests' siren voices lured Anton up from his study. The
dining room was also upstairs: the tramp of feet on the stairs never
ceased. Under the stairs the ageing whippet Korbo dozed. Pavel visited
daily, but slept at the warehouse or at Vania's, a few minutes' walk
away.

Anton was spending more than he earned. He pawned his watch
and the gold Turkish lira the Ianovs gave him after their typhus. His
short pieces at this period show him preoccupied with status. A story,
'The First Class Passenger' is told by an engineer whose mistress, a
mediocre actress, gets all the attention when the bridge he built is
opened. Anton, too, felt he deserved better. His skit, 'A Literary Table
of Ranks', ranks writers on the 13-point scale of the Russian civil
service: the highest rank of 'Actual State Councillor' is vacant. Next
highest are Tolstoy and Goncharov, followed by the gruesome satirist
Saltykov-Shchedrin and the defender of the peasants Grigorovich.
Below them come the playwright Ostrovsky and novelist Leskov,
together with the melodramatic poet Polonsky. The *New Times* journalists – Burenin and Suvorin – are ranked with a real genius, the
young story writer Vsevolod Garshin. At the bottom, the anti-Semitic

Okreits, known to Chekhov as Judophob Judophobovich, is left with no rank at all.

Women guests exerted *demi-monde* charm, but Anton's correspondence for the year to come shows that, for once, he was unresponsive. Only Maria Kiseliova evoked any reaction: she rebuked him for his dissipation and lubricious stories. On 21 September he undid any illusions she might have about his hedonism:

> I am living in the cold with fumes from the stove ... the lamp smokes and covers everything with soot, the cigarette crackles and goes out, I burn my fingers. I could shoot myself ... I write a lot and take a lot of time over it ... I've ordered the doctor's sign taken down for the time being! Brrr ... I'm afraid of typhus.

On 29 September he wrote to her again:

> Life is grey, no happy people to be seen ... Kolia is living with me. He's seriously ill (stomach hæmorrhages that exhaust him to hell) ... I think that people who feel revulsion for death are illogical. As I understand the logic of things, life consists just of horrors, quarrels and vulgarities ...

The Kiseliovs, too, were desperate: they could not pay off their children's governess. Aleksei Kiseliov wrote on 24 September 1886:

> I sat my writer-wife down and made her write a tearful letter to the Aunt in Penza, saying save me, my husband and children, save us from this hissing hag [*the governess*]. Perhaps she'll take pity and send not just 500 to pay her off but enough to buy us all sweets.

This letter sowed seeds for *The Cherry Orchard*, where Gaev appeals for money to an aunt in Iaroslavl and spends his fortune on boiled sweets.

The Chekhov family is reflected in Anton's fiction of autumn 1886. He acknowledged Pavel's touchy obstinacy, for he sensed it in himself. His story for *New Times* in October 1886, 'Difficult People', relives appalling rows between father and son: they admit that they share a tyrannical temperament. In Anton's second story for *New Times* that month, 'Dreams', a sick convict trudges to Siberia, while his guards know that he will soon die. Anton was thinking of Kolia, if not himself. Kolia had crawled home after writing a desperate note: 'Dear Anton I've been in bed for five days ... vomiting mercilessly and turning my guts inside out.' Doctors in the 1880s deceived TB patients that the blood they coughed was from the stomach or throat, not from the lungs: 'I even thought I had consumption,' Kolia told Anton. Kolia was hiding from death in the arms of Anna Golden or of his mother, or fled them all to his student haunts. Within days Kolia ran away again.

Aleksandr threw himself on Suvorin's mercy. Suvorin gave him work as a copy editor and a freelance reporter, and found him a second job editing *Russian Shipping*. From the latter Aleksandr was soon dismissed, but he was paid enough by Suvorin to bring his family from Tula, where Anna's relatives lived, for the Christmas goose. Aleksandr, as Anton's agent in Petersburg, collected royalties and gossip. He hoped to edit *New Times*, if Fiodorov went to prison, but Suvorin was too canny: Aleksandr remained a hack.

Petersburg, however bad its air for the lungs and its water for the gut, had in spring lifted Anton's spirits: the company of Suvorin, successful writers and lively actresses excited him. At the end of November he went for a third visit, this time taking Masha with him: her gratitude and joy were vehement. In Petersburg Chekhov's new stories were sensations: stories of lost children, such as 'Vanka', or of a lone man and a child ('On the Road'), quenched the public's thirst for Dickensian Christmas sentiments, yet dumbfounded critics with their desolation. Acclaim restored Anton's self-esteem: 'I am becoming as fashionable as [*Zola's*] Nana!' Literature was like fornication. Soon Anton saw himself as an unholy trinity, 'Antonius and Medicine Chekhov, Medicine the wife and Literature the mistress'.

After Petersburg Anton met the festivities in Moscow, from Christmas to his name day, in gayer spirits. Grigorovich visited the Chekhovs then. Vamped by laughing women, he walked the actress Daria Musina-Pushkina to her home and recalled his youth, when he was notorious for seducing the wife of the poet A. K. Tolstoy on a garden swing. In Petersburg Grigorovich told Anna Suvorina, 'My dear, if you only knew what it's like at the Chekhovs: Bacchanalia, my darling.'⁹

Men as well as women were attached to Anton. Bilibin wrote 'I must secretly tell you, I love you,' but as 'the husband of a learned wife' he was tugged out of Chekhov's circle. Unhappy with Vera and with Leikin (for whom he worked until the latter's death in 1906),

Bilibin presented tedious psychosomatic symptoms, and was passed over for new acolytes. Chekhov's new disciple was Aleksandr Lazarev, who signed himself Gruzinsky. A provincial seminary teacher, who aspired to be a writer, Gruzinsky visited the Chekhovs on New Year's Day 1887. He brought with him another schoolteacher-writer, his close friend, Nikolai Ezhov, who worshipped Chekhov just as fervently. The affection of Ezhov, as prickly as his name 'Hedgehog', was to sour in a few years, as he resented Chekhov's ascent and his own obscurity.

An old admirer came to stay: Sasha Selivanova, Anton's pupil in Taganrog, who now taught in Kharkov. Back home, she wrote to Anton, Vania and Misha: 'My heart is torn to pieces, I miss you so much. But I can't say it's torn into three <u>even</u> pieces. One is bigger. Guess which one of you three is the reason? So you all played the part of the holiday husband excellently.'[10] Anton wired back: 'Angel, darling, miss you terribly, come soon . . . Your lover.'

The climax of January was Anton's twenty-seventh name-day party 'with Jewgirls, Turkeys and Ianova girls'. His cousin Aleksei Dolzhenko brought violin and zither. Over the holidays Anton produced only one story with any literary impact or personal input, 'Enemies': a bereaved doctor is tricked into an unnecessary visit and conceives a violent hatred of mankind. Chekhov placed a story in the Moscow weekly *The Alarm Clock*. Once again Leikin was furious with Chekhov for giving *Fragments* nothing in December, when new subscribers had to be lured. Before turning up at Anton's name-day party, he wrote: 'You really have stabbed *Fragments* in the back. Of course, you're not a journalist, you can't fully understand what you have done to me.'[11]

Chekhov no longer felt dependent on Leikin: he told Uncle Mitrofan, 'I am now the most fashionable writer.' Leikin tried to rein Chekhov in: 'Your last piece in *New Times* is weak, in general your little pieces [*for Leikin*] are more successful'. He tried to bind Anton closer, suggesting a tour of the northern lakes or the southern provinces together – a proposal that Chekhov evaded for a decade – promising him a puppy, pestering him with his hypochondria. Leikin was worried about his obesity. Frivolously, Chekhov prescribed two weeks' fasting. Eventually, in May 1888, fed up with Leikin's and Bilibin's hypochondriac missives, he would order: 'Take a French maid, 25–26, and, when you're bored, screw her as hard as you can. That's good for the health. And when Bilibin comes, let him screw the maid too.' Leikin, Russia's most prolific humorist, did not understand such quips, but he forgave Anton and raised his fee to 11 kopecks a line.

At the same time Anton's illusions about Suvorin were dented. In *New Times* Burenin attacked a dying man, the poet Nadson, the darling of radical students, for 'pretending to be bedridden, so as to live at his friends' expense'. Nadson had a fatal hæmorrhage: Burenin was called a murderer. At the same time Suvorin staged a coup by selling out 40,000 copies of a ten-volume set of Pushkin's work a few days after the copyright expired. Kicking a dying man and exploiting an expired copyright earned Suvorin both obloquy for opportunism and admiration for acumen. Anton was dismayed. He thought Nadson 'greater than all other living poets together'; he found that Suvorin had not reserved for him a single set of the Pushkin edition Anton had promised to friends and relatives.

Chekhov began to wonder, too, what his new admirers in Petersburg might want from him. On 29 January 1887 Aleksandr told Anton: 'You are expected – they don't know what – but they expect. Some demand *big and thick*, others *serious*, yet others *real polish*, while Grigorovich is afraid your talent might be changed into petty cash.' Maria Kiseliova was wrestling with *New Times* for Anton's soul. In early January, revolted by Anton's sensational story 'The Slough' and its heroine, a nymphomaniac Jewish swindler, she wrote: 'I'm personally upset that a writer *of your sort*, i.e. gifted by God, shows me just "a dunghill" ... I had an unendurable urge to swear at you and your foul editors who don't care that they are ruining your talent.'[12] Anton defended at length his right to poke about in dunghills: 'A writer must be as objective as a chemist; he must renounce subjectivity in life and know that dunghills play an important part in the landscape and evil passions are as much part of life as good ones.' But Maria Kiseliova had hit her mark. The lubricious, Zolaesque sequence of *New Times* stories came to an end. In February 1887 Chekhov published little, then began a new direction. One story, 'Verochka', in *New Times*, met both Kiseliova's and Suvorin's tastes: the hero has come to a country district and is about to leave; Verochka, the girl whose family has looked after him, is quietly but desperately in love with him, but he lacks the emotional energy to respond to her. Their parting and the hero's failure to propose at the traditional encounter in the garden are scenes that will recur through Chekhov's work, up to *The Cherry Orchard*. The sense of futile waste makes 'Verochka' a story we can call archetypically Chekhovian.

Despite all the poetry in 'Verochka', Anton felt his well running dry. He longed to revisit the south, the scenes of his childhood: he had not seen Taganrog since the Loboda wedding in June 1881. Overlooking Anton's misbehaviour then, Uncle Mitrofan and cousin George in Taganrog, and the Kravtsovs, Gavriil and Petia, in their steppes, pressed him to come. A break from his immediate family and his editors would be a search for new material.

To travel Anton needed an advance from Suvorin, and for that he needed to visit Petersburg. His elder brother's cry for help provided a less transparent pretext for the journey. Aleksandr felt a pariah: Suvorin had forbidden him to sign his work for fear of readers confusing two A. Chekhovs. Although he was offering Kolia a refuge from creditors, vice and police in Petersburg, Aleksandr was himself so penniless that he purloined Vania's coat. He then telegraphed to Moscow that he was fatally ill. On 8 March Anton took the night train. From a hotel room on the Nevsky Avenue Anton wrote to the family:

> Naturally I travelled as tense as could be. I dreamt of coffins, torchbearers, I fancied typhus, typhoid, doctors etc . . . Generally, a vile night . . . My only consolation was my darling precious Anna (I mean *Karenina*) who kept me busy all the way . . . Aleksandr is perfectly well. He was depressed, frightened and, imagining he was ill, sent that telegram.

Anton's journey achieved its real aim. He and Suvorin talked from nine in the evening to one in the morning: Anton left with an advance of 300 roubles, and then wrote to Franz Schechtel, who would get him a free railway ticket to Taganrog and back. 'Whatever happens, even earthquakes, I'm going, because my nerves can't stand it any more.' He collected fees, but told Masha: 'I'd ask you to spend as little as *possible*. I don't know when I'm coming. Aleksandr with his depression and tendency to hit the bottle can't be left until his lady recovers . . .' After cementing his friendship with Suvorin, Anton went to see Grigorovich, diagnosed arterial sclerosis, kissed him and divulged a prognosis of imminent death only to Suvorin. Apart from Aleksandr's household, other things in Petersburg upset Anton. Someone stole his overcoat, so that he froze on the streets. Typhoid was raging: it killed Leikin's porter. By 17 March Anton was back from 'the city of death' in Moscow, determined to leave for the south within the fortnight.

Anton's brothers begged for his attention. Schechtel wrote on 26 March: 'Kolia writes that he's very ill, spitting blood ... Shouldn't we get together at his place tonight?' On 29 March Aleksandr appealed again from Petersburg:

> Anna is in hospital, ward three, Annushka [*the servant*] in ward 8, typhoid, Kolia [*the elder son*] is in Oldenburg's clinic, Antosha [*the younger son*] is being visited daily by a woman doctor. I and my Tanka [*the other servant*] are the only ones on their feet.

Anton had had enough and would not be dragged back to Anna's or Kolia's bedside. On 2 April 1887, swearing his Taganrog cousin Georgi to secrecy, he took the train south.

TWENTY-ONE

Taganrog Revisited
April–September 1887

As Franz Schechtel became a successful architect, he became more careful with his reputation and his money. He got Anton a third-class single to Taganrog – mean payment for the medical attention he had enjoyed. Anton slept, like his cat, 'boots under nose'. At 5.00 a.m. on the first morning he woke in Oriol, and posted a letter telling the family to obey Vania, as the 'positive man of character'. On the third morning, Easter Saturday, the train reached the sea. Anton, Mitrofan and his clan went to all-night Easter service.

Taganrog disillusioned Chekhov; he wrote to Leikin:

> 60,000 inhabitants do nothing but eat, drink, reproduce and have no other interests. Wherever you go, Easter cakes, eggs, Santurini wine, suckling babies, but no newspapers or books anywhere ... The town's location is beautiful in all respects, a splendid climate, masses of fruits of the earth, but the inhabitants are hellishly inert. Everyone is musical, gifted with imagination, highly strung, sensitive, but it's all wasted. There are no patriots, no businessmen, no poets, not even any decent bakers.

After six years' increasing gentility in Moscow, Anton found Mitrofan's house foul. 'The lavatory is in the back and beyond, under the fence,' he told the family. '... There are no spittoons, no decent washstand ... the napkins are grey, Irinushka [*the servant*] is grubby and gross ... so you could shoot yourself it's so bad!' He went to see the house where he had spent the last five Taganrog years and reported: 'Selivanov's house is empty and neglected. It's a dreary sight and I wouldn't have it at any price. I'm amazed: how could we live in it?!'

For eight years Anton had not been parted for so long from his mother and sister. He wrote a diary of this sentimental journey and posted it in instalments. He saw old teachers – Diakonov, the deputy-head, still 'as thin as a viper', Father Pokrovsky now 'the thunder and lightning' of the church. He asked after girlfriends – a jealous husband kept one away; other girls had eloped with actors. He visited the wives of his Moscow colleagues, Saveliev and Zembulatov; he drank wine with local doctors, now trying to turn the town into a seaside spa. He hid from the police informer Anisim Petrov, who was now a member of Mitrofan's Brotherhood.

Dirt and stress brought on diarrhœa and hæmorrhoids; the weather, bronchitis. Running from Anisim, Anton was almost crippled by a varicose vein on his left leg; drinking with an old school friend, Dr Eremeev, made him too ill to appreciate Taganrog's girls. Only cousin Georgi pleased Anton: he rarely went to church, he smoked, talked of women and worked hard at a shipping company.

Two weeks' celebrity in Taganrog was enough for Anton, and he left for the steppe town of Novocherkassk, to be best man at the wedding of Dr Eremeev's sixteen-year-old Cossack sister. First he stayed with the Kravtsovs at Ragozina Gully. Riding and shooting, drinking sour milk and eating eight times a day, he could 'cure 15 consumptions and 22 rheumatisms'. At the wedding, in borrowed clothes, he teased the girls, drank the local pink champagne and stuffed himself on caviar. The journey from Ragozina Gully to Novocherkassk and back was slow; he waited eight hours for a connection. On the way there he slept in a siding, on the way back, 'I went out for a pee and pure miracles outside: the moon, the boundless steppe with its barrows and wilderness; the quiet of the grave, the carriages and rails stand out in the twilight – you'd think the world had died.' At Ragozina Gully he rode fifteen miles to fetch the post. It did not make him homesick. Leikin reported on Palmin's misfortunes and was annoyed that Chekhov should complain of his own diseases: 'For a doctor that is not good at all. Your illness, though a nuisance, is not at all danger-ous. As for my health, turpentine helps to expel the gases.'

On 1 May Suvorin's fourth son, the twenty-one-year-old Vladimir, shot himself dead. Aleksandr sent a postcard, discreetly in Latin: 'Plen-issima perturbatio in redactione. Senex aegrotissimus est. Dolor communis . . .' Suvorin felt guilty for ignoring his son's play, *An Old Eye Is No Bar to the Heart*. He recalled his first wife's suicide and blamed himself for both deaths:

Yesterday Volodia shot himself ... Eternally alone, eternally by himself. Yesterday I listened to his strange comedy – everywhere clever, original. He would've been a talented man. And again I failed to do a thing.[13]

Leikin wrote to Anton a week later: '[*Vladimir*] just left a note to say that he was fed up with life and supposed that the next world is better than this. Poor Suvorin, completely shattered with grief, was taken yesterday to his estate in Tula Province.' A theme of *The Seagull* was born. Chekhov felt for Suvorin. Suvorin's sons were as doomed as Chekhov's elder brothers – despair linked the two men.

The Chekhovs celebrated Easter loudly, but without Anton. Pavel reported:

> Officer Tyshko came, and Dolgov, who drank three bottles of beer and nearly smashed the piano with his heavy blows. He played well, with verve. Then Mr Korneev and Mlles Ianova, Efros and Korneev's niece and in the evening Korneev's children, who amazed me with their gutter language ... I remain your loving P. Chekhov.

The family was reassured by Kolia: he agreed to spend the summer with them in Babkino. Aleksandr, however, sent them appeal after appeal from Petersburg. His sons had typhoid, but no hospital would take in children who had no birth certificates. Meanwhile, Aleksandr could not cope with his idle, thieving servant girls. He begged Vania and Masha to send out their mother: 'The poor children shriek, ask for the "potty" and dirty the bed. I'm out all night. Really it wouldn't be wrong for mother to come.'[14] Speaking for the whole family, Kolia protested to Masha:

> When a few years ago little Mosia fell ill in Taganrog, mother went to visit the sick little girl and look after her and what happened? Mother was exhausted, gave it up as a bad job and Aleksandr tore his hair and went to church to weep ... If we send mother to Petersburg, the same will happen again, mother will be <u>unhappy</u> and Aleksandr's life <u>poisoned</u>.[15]

Whenever Aleksandr's illegitimate family called for help, the Chekhovs hardened their hearts. They detested Anna and her children by Aleksandr, and would do so until the last of them perished. Aleksandr had to fend for himself; in May his mother and sister left for the country.

*   *   *

On 5 May Anton went north to the monastery at Sviatye Gory (Sacred Hills) southeast of Kharkov, where 15,000 pilgrims congregated after Easter. The monks gave him a room with a stranger, perhaps a police spy, who told Anton his life story. The impression made on Chekhov by just two days and nights at Sviatye Gory was overwhelming – the hillside forested setting, the church services, the fervent pilgrims. The stories stemming from his travels in the south are infused with a psalmodic reverence for nature, for the pathos, liturgy and clergy, if not the dogma, of Orthodox Christianity. On his way back from Sviatye Gory to Taganrog he met childhood friends: Sasha Selivanova, and Piotr Sergeenko, who would fifteen years later change his life. By 17 May Chekhov was back, penniless, in an unseasonably chilly Moscow: he summoned Schechtel for a frank conversation about the Ianova sisters and sexual frustration, and borrowed 30 roubles. Then Anton joined his mother, sister and Misha in Babkino.

Suvorin, disabled by bereavement, had neglected the publication of Chekhov's new book of stories, *In the Twilight*. Anton had to write more for *New Times* in order to pay off Suvorin's advance, and Leikin only received four small stories from him that summer. *The Petersburg Newspaper*, which paid better and allowed more scope, got nine stories, notably 'His First Love', which Chekhov later worked up into a study of adolescent suicide, 'Volodia'.

The need to recoup Suvorin's advance gave the motivation and the journey south the material for the finest prose of the time in Russia. The first prose-poem (a *'quasi symphony'*) of steppe nature, 'Fortune', introduces the motif of the breaking string that punctuates *The Cherry Orchard*, an ominous mine shaft catastrophe deep beneath a doomed landscape. Chekhov could stake a claim to be Russia's first 'green' writer. Even the acerbic Burenin wrote a panegyric; copies of *New Times* were stolen from Petersburg's cafés. In 'Tumbleweed', the July story for *New Times*, the police agent that Anton met at the monastery became the baptized Jew – 'a baptized Jew, a doctored horse, a pardoned thief – all worth the same.' Here too is a 'breaking string' – a falling mine-bucket which cripples the hero.

Chekhov's rootless Jew is the culmination of a series of intelligent well-meaning unfortunates who had dominated Russian fiction, the so-called 'superfluous men' whom Pushkin and Turgenev had created. Chekhov won recognition for renovating a tired tradition, but tributes to his genius were loudest among musicians, who felt most acutely the musical nature of his prose in its rhythms and the sonata-like structure, where the end recapitulates the beginning after a central development. In May Tchaikovsky was struck by the ecclesiastical story, 'The Laymen' (later known as 'The Letter'): he wrote a letter, that went astray, to Chekhov and also to his brother Modest about it. Through Modest, Piotr Tchaikovsky was to meet the Moscow Chekhovs.[16]

Anton would not see Anna in Petersburg: he diagnosed by post from Babkino, guessing from Anna's medicines and temperature that TB underlay her typhoid. Anton made only one short trip that summer to Moscow to spend a few days with admirers such as Ezhov and Gruzinsky. Gruzinsky was the only person to recall Anton Chekhov in a rage. *The Alarm Clock* was printing Anton's sketch, 'The Diary of a Volatile Person', in three parts; when Anton found that they had cut his copy, he exploded like his character and left the deputy editor stunned by authorial fury. Ezhov, however, recalled a milder man:

> He had a weak voice. His laughter showed that Chekhov was not inclined to get angry. When writing he suddenly smiled. This smile was special, without the usual proportion of irony, not humorous, but tender and soft, a smile of authorial happiness.[17]

After a few days Anton had to return to Babkino. He was keeping Kolia under guard, while helping Dr Arkhangelsky with a study of Russia's psychiatric institutions – work that would bear fictional fruit five years later. At the end of July Kolia broke free. Schechtel reported from Moscow:

> We had a heart-to-heart and finally he admitted that he has to abandon his 'big slag' and that this is the only way of burning his boats and, . . . after giving his appearance, very bedraggled recently, a gentlemanly veneer, to re-enter society . . . That same evening blood gushed, real blood, there's no doubt about it, I saw him spit it. The next day was worse – today he's sent a note; he asks me to send a doctor, he's bleeding to death.

Anton did not rush to Moscow, but Kolia was moved to the Korneev house after promising not to infest it with fleas. Anton stayed at Babkino until September, picking gooseberries, raspberries and mushrooms. Inspired by the south, needing money from *New Times*, he wrote his stories of the steppes. Other pursuits were out of the question, he told Schechtel: 'I could devour a whorelet like Nadia [Ianova] ... In Babkino there's still nobody to screw. So much work that there's no time even for a quiet fart.'[18]

In September Moscow's writers returned to their desks. Palmin boasted of implausible amorous adventures on the Volga. Anton had no love affairs to ponder. His third and last story inspired by the steppes, 'Panpipes', evoked the doomed rivers and forests of the Don basin, and irritated critics who wanted more humanity, morality and plots in fiction. Mikhailovsky, the *Northern Herald*'s purveyor of opinions to the intelligentsia, went for Anton's collection, *In the Twilight*, which Suvorin had just published in book form:

> Questions without answers, answers without questions, stories with no beginning or end, plots with no dénouement ... Mr Chekhov should turn on his work lamp in his study to light up these half-lit characters and dispel the gloom that conceals their silhouettes and contours.

A man whom there were few to praise, worried by debt and by his brothers, Anton fell into gloom.

TWENTY-TWO

Ivanov *in Moscow*

September 1887–January 1888

IN SEPTEMBER 1887 Anton wrote a letter apparently so suicidal that Aleksandr destroyed it, responding:

> You write that you're alone, have nobody to talk or to write to . . . I deeply sympathize with all my heart and soul, for I am no happier than you . . . One thing in your letter I can't understand: lamenting that you hear and read only lies and more lies, petty, but endless. What I can't understand is why you're hurt by it and driven to moral vomiting by an overdose of vileness. Undoubtedly you're a clever decent person, don't you realize that in our age everything lies? . . . I don't deserve the order of St Anna [*his sick and unloved wife, Anna, and a civil service award*], but it's hung round my neck and I wear it workdays and holidays.

The answer, Aleksandr told his brother, was to move to Petersburg, but Anton now found Petersburg repellent. Suvorin was still in the country, mourning, while the 'Zulus' as Anton dubbed the journalists of *New Times*, were lambasting Darwin or Nadson. He salved his conscience by fancying that he and his brother counterbalanced the reactionaries. Suvorin saw no conflict, saying: 'Chekhov did not condemn *New Times*' political programme, but angrily argued with me about Jews . . . If *New Times* helped Chekhov to get on his feet, then it is good that *New Times* existed . . .'[19] Suvorin never doubted that his affection for Anton was reciprocated: 'If Chekhov loved me, he did so for something serious, far more serious than money,' he was to say to Doroshevich. Nevertheless, Suvorin did not always shield Anton from his underlings' attacks, even if he sometimes defended Anton against them: 'Chekhov is a very independent writer and a very independent man . . . I have facts from his literary life to prove what a straight, good and independent man he is.'[20]

Other Petersburgers irritated Anton. He wrote less for *Fragments*:

Leikin and Bilibin bored him, whining about each other – hen-pecked Bilibin's anaemia and anorexia; Leikin's deviousness, obesity and hysterical fits. Babkino, not least Aleksei Kiseliov's sexual frustration, was also becoming tedious.

Anton was short of money too. For 150 roubles he sold the Verner brothers, typographically Moscow's most innovative printers, the rights to fourteen of his comic stories; he was waiting for Suvorin to market a more substantial book. In Russia in the 1880s it was more profitable to write full-length plays: a playwright received two per cent of the gross takings for each act of a play. To be performed in the State theatres, a play had to pass many hurdles. In Moscow there was one reputable private theatre: Korsh's. Lily Markova had acted there, as had Daria Musina-Pushkina, Masha's friend. Chekhov made fun of a 'preposterous' drama at Korsh's theatre. Korsh challenged him: 'Why don't you write a play yourself?' Korsh's actors told Chekhov he would write well: 'You know how to get on people's nerves.'[21] Chekhov agreed to write a play, and then join the Russian Society of Dramatists and Operatic Composers.

Chekhov's title, *Ivanov*, was a clever ploy. Ivanov is a surname as common in Russia as Smith in England, and the play could bring one per cent of the population to see their namesake. Ivanov, a bright intellectual (we are told), spends all four acts of the play in manic depression. The Jewish girl he has married and cut off from family and religion is dying of TB; he falls for the daughter of his creditors. Self-hate overcomes him. For the Korsh theatre *Ivanov* at least had melodramatic curtain falls: Act 2 ends with the sick wife catching her husband embracing his new love; Act 3 ends with his telling her the doctor's prognosis, and the play ends with the hero's death – by heart attack and later, Chekhov decided, by bullet. Modern audiences are more enthralled by Ivanov's conflicts with the priggish doctor who denounces him and the evil steward who eggs him on – three central male figures suggesting one multiple personality. Chekhov himself saw the play as charting a mental disease, but he was to baffle actors who wanted to know only whether Ivanov is villain or victim? Chekhov bemused them by subtitling the play 'Comedy'.

Ivanov, his 'dramatic miscarriage', was written in ten days. Chekhov shut his study door and upset Nikolai Ezhov by his 'pensive, taciturn, somehow disgruntled' mien. Ezhov was the first outsider to read the play out: Chekhov listened with detachment. Ezhov praised it to Chekhov's face, but privately reacted 'with amazement, since instead of the expected cheerful comedy in the Chekhov genre I found a gloomy drama crammed with depressing episodes . . . Ivanov seemed unconvincing.'[22] Chekhov was happy: the play was: 'light as a feather, without a single longueur. An unprecedented plot'. Korsh liked it too, and Davydov, who was to play the lead part, kept Chekhov up until three in the morning, enthusing. Twenty years on, he wrote: 'I don't recall any other work captivating me like this. It was as clear as anything that I was seeing a major playwright laying new paths.'[23]

The first performance on 19 November 1887 launched Chekhov as a dramatist. He had produced something 'big', 'serious', though – as he saw himself – unpolished. Leikin was a mean-spirited and uncalled-for mentor: he slandered Davydov, and told Chekhov to stay away from rehearsals. The first night went awry: Chekhov was aghast. Only Davydov and Glama, who played Sarra, knew their parts, and the minor actors were drunk. Nevertheless the audience applauded and the author took three curtain calls, though the finale with Ivanov's coincidental heart attack at his second wedding bewildered them. For the second performance four days later, Chekhov tinkered with this act. Piotr Kicheev, the literally murderous editor who had never forgiven Anton for deserting *The Dragonfly*, went for the jugular: 'deeply immoral, cynical rubbish . . . the author is a pathetic slanderer of the ideals of his time. [*Ivanov is*] not a hero of the times we live in, but just an outright blackguard, trampling on all laws, God's and man's.' Surrounded by beer bottles and duck dung, Palmin wrote to Leikin: 'In all the scenes there is nothing comic and nothing dramatic, just horrible, disgusting cynical filth, which creates a revolting impression.'

Ivanov had one more performance in Korsh's theatre. Critics praised it only enough to ensure that the play toured the provinces. For 400 roubles Chekhov endured embarrassment which coloured his attitude to the theatre. Disapproval incited in him a love-hate relationship with drama; he would respond with plays that were time bombs for stage conventions and poison for actors. The more he was lectured on conventions, the more he would flout them. In the failure of *Ivanov* lie the seeds of the success of *Uncle Vania*.

Chekhov was to flee the city after almost every new production of his plays. Four days after the third performance of *Ivanov*, he went to Petersburg. He brought *Ivanov* for Suvorin to read. This time, however, he slummed with Aleksandr and his family, all recuperating from typhoid. Aleksandr's life outdid Ivanov's: Anna, facing death, missing her eldest son and her daughter, was jealous of Aleksandr, who thought only of sexual frustration. Aleksandr's household, despite two servants and the salary that Suvorin paid him, was sunk in filth and poverty; the two infant boys were retarded, locked in a world of their own. Anton wrote home, as his own high-minded character in *Ivanov*, Dr Lvov, might have written: 'Anna is ill (tuberculosis). Filth, stench, weeping, lying; stay a week with Aleksandr and you'll go crazy and get as filthy as a floor-rag.'

After three days he left for the Leikins, to wash, sleep and relax. From Leikin he moved to the Hotel Moskva. Living in luxury among strangers, he could make women friends, but he was also freer to make new men friends. In St Petersburg he acquired two more lifelong acolytes, as he had previously acquired Ezhov and Gruzinsky. One was Ivan Leontiev-Shcheglov, the grandson of an army general, who wrote as Shcheglov ('Goldfinch'), following the fable by Krylov: 'Better to sing well as a little goldfinch, Than badly as a nightingale.' The other was Kazimir Barantsevich, a ticket inspector on Petersburg's trams, who had six children and spent his nights writing. Pathologically modest, Barantsevich had no mirrors in his house. He wrote about heroes with lives even grimmer than his own: but for Chekhov, he would never have left Petersburg.

Bilibin, Shcheglov and Barantsevich in Petersburg, Gruzinsky and Ezhov in Moscow, were not just friends and admirers; they were horrible warnings of the price of failure for a Russian intellectual. Trapped by bad luck, poverty or mediocrity into being part-time writers, they seemed to Anton like animals in a menagerie. As Vagner, a zoologist, would tell Anton, they saw Chekhov as the elephant in the zoo. Their admiration became envy only when the elephant broke out of the zoo. The other animals stayed caged, dispirited, cannibalistic. It was Suvorin, the kindly keeper who fed and doctored the menagerie, who singled out Anton for release, raising his payments from 12 to 20 kopecks a line, allowing Chekhov more space, preparing to launch him in the 'thick' literary journals. By 1888 Chekhov would enjoy the freedom to write as he wanted, and was distinct from the caged literary animal. As Chekhov reported to his family on 3

December 1887, Suvorin was enthusiastic about *Ivanov*: 'Everyone is waiting for me to put the play on in Petersburg and is confident of success, but after Moscow I am so repelled by my play that I can't possibly make myself think about it: I can't be bothered . . .'

Chekhov's success in Petersburg was crowned by the wide popularity of his latest stories in *New Times*. The story of starving cattle, 'Cold Blood', based on a miserable business failure of a Taganrog cousin, won Anton an accolade from the Petersburg Society for the Protection of Animals. 'The Kiss', set in an artillery regiment (officers like those Chekhov invented for *Three Sisters*), won admiration from the military. The hero is a shy officer, kissed in the dark by a woman who mistakes him for someone else and whose identity he never discovers. Chekhov had studied the battalion in Voskresensk so well that his readers believed he must be a serving officer. The greatest sensation, however, was aroused by 'Kashtanka', the story of a dog, conscripted into a circus, that recognizes his owner in the audience. It was the first Chekhov story to be published as a book.

Anton's public was now far wider than the *New Times* readership. Suvorin now needed him more than vice versa. Other grand old men took a liking to Chekhov. One was the aristocratic radical, Aleksei Pleshcheev, who had mounted the scaffold with Dostoevsky, and still wrote an occasional inspirational civic poem. Pleshcheev was for his remaining years Chekhov's most perspicacious critic. Like Suvorin, Pleshcheev hinted that he would like Anton as a son-in-law, but Anton returned, unbetrothed, to Moscow on 17 December. Bilibin wrote his greetings for New Year 1888: 'Gruzinsky tells me that you are radiating all the colours of the rainbow after your Petersburg impressions.'

On Suvorin's advice, and to appease the censorship, Chekhov revised *Ivanov*. He now called the play a 'drama', but Act IV was intractable: How could Ivanov die a convincing death?

TWENTY-THREE

The Death of Anna
January–May 1888

CHEKHOV ALLOCATED all January 1888 to a masterpiece, 'Steppe'. *The Northern Herald*'s editor Evreinova (who reminded Anton of a 'roast starling') had given him carte blanche on length, subject, and fee. Chekhov had 500 roubles as an advance and another 500 on publication for a story of 120 pages. His income was trebled: never again did the Chekhov family know penury, though they sometimes spent more than they earned. *The Northern Herald* was not censored: Anton was free. The pressure of weekly or fortnightly stories for three Petersburg journals receded: he fed *New Times*, but starved *Fragments* and *The Petersburg Newspaper*.

'Steppe' flaunts all conventions for extended prose: instead of a plot, we have a boy's journey across the Ukraine, from Taganrog to Kiev, accompanied first by a friendly priest, Khristofor, then by carters, and encountering a cross-section of humanity – an embittered Jew, a Polish countess, peasants rebellious and submissive. Nature – ponds, insects, a storm – overwhelms the boy's mind: he succumbs to a fever. The work has a musical structure: it is a symphony, with a storm and a pastorale as haunting as those in Beethoven's Sixth Symphony. Spellbound by memories of his own childhood in the steppes, Chekhov also had Gogol's 'Sorochintsy Fair' and Turgenev's prose poetry in mind as bench marks. 'Steppe', unmatched until Katherine Mansfield's 'Prelude', is the first work by Chekhov that we can call a classic.

Pleshcheev read the manuscript in ecstasy. In February 1889 it was published. It left musicians, painters and writers awe-struck: Vsevolod Garshin, the most original of younger prose-writers, had met his peer. Critics, notably Ostrovsky (the playwright's brother) risked their necks in praise. Suvorin, Aleksandr reported, 'left his tea undrunk. Anna Suvorina brought him three fresh cups when I was there'. Suvorin's cronies, however, distanced themselves. Aleksandr passed on the comments of Burenin, the *New Times* journalist who was most trusted by Suvorin:

> Such descriptions of the steppe as yours he has read only in Gogol and Tolstoy. The storm that gathers and does not burst is the height of perfection. The characters, except for the yids, are alive. But you don't know how to write long stories . . . 'Steppe' is the beginning, or rather the prologue, of a big piece you will write.

Leikin tried to dispirit Chekhov: 'Hanging is too good for those who advised you to write long pieces. A long piece is good when it's a novel or tale with a plot, a beginning and an end . . . Anyway, I stopped reading about 25 pages before the end.'

Unlike his experience with *Ivanov*, Anton was sociable and cheerful all the time he was writing 'Steppe', although he wondered at his story, almost unique in his work for its lack of love interest. 'I can't do without women!' he exclaimed in a letter to Shcheglov.

He found two days to write a melodramatic short story, 'Sleepy', about a skivvy who murders her mistress's baby so that she can sleep (a story that Katherine Mansfield would later plagiarize). He threw off two short plays, the Beckett-like monologue for a superannuated actor alone in the theatre, *Kalkhas*, later called *Swansong*, and the first of his fine farces, *The Bear*, which he later dubbed *The Milch-Cow* for its profitability. Friends noted Chekhov's soaring self-esteem, and other changes: his flowing hair, and quizzical smile. Gruzinsky wrote to Ezhov in February 1888: 'Chekhov really looks like Anton Rubinstein . . . a coolness has sprung up between Bilibin and Chekhov.' Bilibin stopped signing himself 'Your Victorina', but Anton's new friend, Ivan Shcheglov, became more affectionate: 'No Frenchwoman can caress so seductively as you can.'

Friends still called on Anton's medical skills. Grigorovich, after Chekhov had examined him, decided to stave off death in Nice: from there he sent Chekhov ideas for stories. From Petersburg Aleksandr issued desolate bulletins about Anna. Surgeons and doctors disagreed. Aleksandr was tormented by temptation as well as remorse – the secretary at *New Times* had soft black eyes. He asked Anton for moral guidance. Anna's terror of death overcame her inhibitions: she pleaded with her mother-in-law:

> I beg you, take pity on your grandchildren, come to Petersburg and

stay with us. I've been ill for a long time and now the doctors think I must have an operation, that I have an abscess or echinococci [*bacteria*] (ask Anton he will explain) on the liver and I have to have them cut out. God knows how the operation will end, but I'm terribly afraid and at best I shall have to be in hospital for a long time. Who will be with my children then? ... If I had fallen ill in Moscow I wouldn't be so afraid, but here I'm utterly alone and I am so miserable. Do me one more favour, light a candle to the martyr St Panteleimon for me in the chapel and pray to the Healer for me. My regards to Pavel Chekhov and ask him to say a prayer ... I thank Anton for his sympathy ...[24]

Botkin, the most distinguished surgeon in Petersburg, examined Anna. There was a brief remission, but by 4 March it was clear that she was dying of tuberculosis of the liver.

Kolia's existence was also threatened not just by disease but by the authorities, for he had evaded conscription. All communications, even from his brothers, went via Anna Ipatieva-Golden. Putiata, Anastasia Golden's first husband, and virtually a brother-in-law, was destitute and dying: Anton felt obliged to offer him treatment and money. The indigent and importunate spoilt Anton's mood. He wanted to go back to Petersburg so badly that, after Lucullian nights together, he shared a train compartment with Leikin. He told his brother Misha that March:

I had a bad journey, thanks to Leikin the chatterbox. He wouldn't let me read, eat or sleep. All the time the bastard boasted and pestered me with questions. As soon as I drop off he touches my foot and asks, 'Did you know that my "Bride of Christ" has been translated into Italian?'

At the Hotel Moskva Pleshcheev, Shcheglov and Anton's new editor, Evreinova, were waiting. The next day he moved in with the Suvorins, with mixed feelings, as he suggested to Misha:

A grand piano, a harmonium, a divan with a bustle, Vasili the footman, a bed, fireplace, a chic desk – these are my conveniences. As for the inconveniences, they are beyond counting. For a start, I am deprived of the chance of coming home under the influence and in female company ... before dinner a long talk with Mme Suvorina about how she hates humanity and her buying today a jacket for 120 roubles.

After dinner a talk about migraine, then the kids can't take their eyes off me and wait for me to say something unusually clever. They think I'm a genius because I wrote the story of Kashtanka. The Suvorins have named [*after the animals in the story*] one dog Fiodor Timofeich, another Auntie and a third Ivan Ivanych.

From dinner to tea we have pacing of Suvorin's study from corner to corner and philosophy; the spouse interrupts the conversation out of turn and puts on a bass voice or imitates a barking hound.

Tea. At tea we talk about medicine. Finally I'm free, sit in my study and can't hear voices. Tomorrow I'm running away for the whole day: I shall be with Pleshcheev . . . By the way I have my own loo and back door – if I didn't I might as well lie down and die. My Vasili is dressed better than me, has a genteel physiognomy and I find it strange that he walks reverently on tiptoe around me and tries to anticipate my wishes.

On the whole it's awkward being a man of literature.

I want to sleep but my hosts go to bed at 3 a.m.

Anton called on Aleksandr: he was amazed to find the children fed and clean, and his brother sober. Anton climbed endless stairs to see Vsevolod Garshin. Garshin was out.[25]

After one week, Anton took the train to Moscow, unaware that on 19 March 1888, in a fit of depression, Vsevolod Garshin had killed himself by hurling himself down the stairs Anton had climbed. Ever since his traumatic experiences as a soldier in the Turkish wars twelve years before, Garshin had distilled his madness into stories of obsession, such as 'The Red Flower'. Marriage to Russia's only woman psychiatrist did not save him. Garshin's funeral was as grotesque as his death: Leman, an author of a manual on billiards, usurped the ceremony with an inept oration; *New Times*, which scorned radical writers, was represented only by Aleksandr Chekhov. A quarrel over two commemorative books sucked Chekhov into literary politics. All that came of the controversy was that Chekhov got to know one significant contemporary, Korolenko, the literary lion of Nizhni Novgorod. Garshin's prose of alienation was, however, to influence Anton's later work.

Spring made Anton yearn for the country, but Orthodox Easter was late that year – 24 April – and, Anton explained to Korolenko: 'Anyone absent during the Easter holiday is considered by my household to be in mortal sin.' He had many invitations: to explore the

Volga with Korolenko, the far north with Leikin, or Constantinople with Suvorin. Babkino now palled. Was it proximity to importunate visitors, or boredom with prurient Aleksei Kiseliov and prudish Maria? In April, to soothe the Kiseliovs, Anton agreed to house their son Seriozha when he went to school in Moscow in the autumn, leaving him free to spend July in the Crimea at Suvorin's new seaside house outside Feodosia, before setting out with Suvorin's eldest son, 'the Dauphin', across the Black Sea to Georgia, and perhaps the Caspian to Central Asia. He would leave his family behind. The dacha he had in mind for them in May and June was in the Ukraine.

Kolia's friends at The Eastern Furnished Rooms, by the conservatoire, included two hapless musicians who were to become Anton's companions. One, Ivanenko, had come to Moscow to study piano and found all the conservatoire pianos allocated; he took up the flute, and made forays into literature, signing himself 'Little Ius', a redundant letter in the Cyrillic alphabet. The other was the cellist Semashko, whose lugubrious playing was the butt of the Chekhovs' jokes. Ivanenko and Semashko came from northeast Ukraine, near the town of Sumy. They put Anton in touch with the Lintvariov family, who, like the Kiseliovs, supplemented their income by renting summer cottages. Their estate, Luka, lay outside Sumy, on the river Psiol in hilly wooded countryside, warmer than Babkino, and even better for fishing.

At Easter, Misha, on his way to Taganrog, was deputed to make a detour to Sumy and report on the Lintvariov estate. He recalled:

> After the stylishness of Babkino, Luka made a terribly mournful impression on me. The manor house was neglected, the courtyard had a puddle which seemed never to dry up, with the most enormous pigs wallowing in it and ducks swimming about, the park was more a wild, untended forest, and there were graves in it; the liberal Lintvariovs saw my student uniform and from the start treated me like a pariah.

Anton had already invited half literary Petersburg to stay with him: he was not deterred. Pleshcheev intended to come, so did Suvorin, before taking Anton to the Crimea. Anton bought tackle: he and Suvorin would fish the Psiol together.

Despite Aleksandr's pleas, Anton refused to go to Anna's bedside, and called him a 'loathsome blackmailer':

Urgent medical help is required. If you won't take Anna to Botkin then at least visit him yourself and explain what's the matter ... I doubt if mother will come, for her health is not all that good. And she has no passport. She has the same passport as papa, that would mean long discussions with father and going to the police chief etc.

The family's postscripts were no comfort: 'Greetings!!!!! N. Chekhov. Mother grieves she can't come.' and: 'My regards, I kiss you, Anna and the children, Masha.' Aleksandr painted for Anton a picture of domestic hell:

> The children are running wild: howling, cowering, trying to get to their mother who either cries over them or chases them away. When I get home from the office, more trouble: she demands to see the vile woman I am going to marry, who intends to poison Kolia and Antosha for the sake of her own future children. She demands this woman be searched for behind the door, in the wardrobe, under the table ... Just imagine the night, the ravings, the loneliness, the impossibility of consoling her, the crazy words, the sudden transitions from laughter to crying, the children crying in their sleep after being frightened all day. Judge, you Herod's Æsculapius, what a time I'm having and what grief that mother won't come.

Aleksandr's siblings showed more concern for strangers. Masha brought home a twelve-year-old boy she found begging. She and Anton gave him money, got him boots from the school where Vania worked, and gave the boy a train ticket to Iaroslavl and a letter to the local celebrity, the poet Trefolev (who looked 'like a plucked crow'). Only Pavel softened to his son:

> Dear Aleksandr ... I sympathize with your grief, but unfortunately can send you nothing, I can only pray, and I advise you to rely on God. He will arrange everything for the best. I wish Anna a Happy Easter and with all my heart a quick recovery, I ask her to forgive me and to forget the past ... Your loving father, P. Chekhov.

Anton was dreaming of catching perch-pike in the Psiol, 'nobler and sweeter than making love' he told Pleshcheev. Misha was with Uncle Mitrofan: 'Mummy! I'm in Taganrog! happy, cheerful, calm, pleased.'

Aleksandr despaired: 'Anna's days are numbered and the catastrophe is inevitable ... Please ask our mother and her sister if they'll take the children ...' But Anton was adamant in his refusal:

If I add two rooms for the children, nurse and children's junk, then the flat will cost 900 ... Anyway, in any spacious flat we would be crowded. You know I have an agglomeration of adults living under one roof simply because, thanks to incomprehensible circumstances, we can't go our own ways ... There's my mother, sister, the student Misha (who won't leave even when he graduates), Kolia, who is doing nothing and has been jilted by his paramour, drinks and lies about undressed, our aunt and [her son] Aliosha (the latter two just use the accommodation). Add to this Vania hanging about from 3 p.m. to the early hours and all day on holidays, while papa comes for the evenings ... These are all nice, cheerful people, but they are selfish, they make claims, they are usually talkative, they stamp about, they have no money ... I refuse to take on anyone else, let alone somebody who has to be brought up ... Tear this letter up. You should make it a habit to tear up letters, they are scattered all over your apartment. Join us in the south in summer. It's cheap.

The children, Anton suggested, could be left with Aunt Fenichka, who would live in the Korneev house, while the Chekhovs were in the country. Aleksandr had to accept these brutal terms. Anton wrote far more mildly about his dependants to his 'dear Captain' Shcheglov on 18 April:

I too have a 'family circle'. For convenience I always take it with me like luggage and am as used to it as a growth on my forehead ... it's a benign, not a malignant growth ... Anyway, I am more often cheerful than sad though, if I think about it, I am tied hand and foot.

Evgenia worried only about her summer in the country, and wrote to Misha: 'It's a pity our dacha is not a success, it's too late now, the luggage was sent at Easter ... you wrote little about servants, what the prices are in Sumy, how much they're paid a month.'

On 7 May 1888 Anna took the last rites in Petersburg, while the Chekhovs reached Sumy by train and took a carriage two miles to Luka. Their hosts were friendly, the house comfortable, the weather hot and the setting unspoilt. 'Misha was talking rubbish,' Anton wrote, inviting Vania and Pavel to join them in 6 weeks' time and bring vodka. He invited Shcheglov and wrote again to Vania specifying fish hooks. To Leikin he praised the civilized Ukrainian peasantry. Here, after the diseased and degraded peasants around Babkino, he could forget he was a doctor. Soon the Chekhovs were joined by guests. The arrival of the legendary Pleshcheev thrilled the Lintvariovs: for three weeks they treated him as a god. Belatedly Anton remembered his brothers. On 27 May he told Aleksandr to make Aunt Fenichka his children's guardian, and not to pay Anna's doctors: 'If they are waiting for the autopsy to make a diagnosis, then their visits were absurd and the money they dare to take off you cries unto heaven . . . My regards to Anna and the kids.' The next day, before this callous letter had arrived, Aleksandr sent Anton a note:

> Today at 4.15 a.m. Anna died. Knoch will do the autopsy tonight. After the funeral I shall immediately take the children to Auntie in Moscow and will join you in Sumy. Then we'll talk it all over. Be well for now. Regards. Yours, A. Chekhov.

TWENTY-FOUR

Travel and Travails
May–September 1888

THE LINTVARIOVS were very unlike the Kiseliovs. The Kiseliovs had the rakishness and the loftiness of the nobility; the Lintvariovs were principled gentry, hardworking landowners and good employers, radicals ready for self-sacrifice. All they had in common with the Kiseliovs was impecuniousness.

The head of the Lintvariov family was the mother, Aleksandra. She had five adult children, three daughters and two sons. The eldest daughter, Zinaida, impressed Chekhov. He told Suvorin:

> A doctor, she is the pride of the family, and the peasants say, a saint . . . She has a brain tumour; this has left her completely blind, she has epilepsy and constant headaches. She knows what to expect, and talks about her imminent death stoically with striking calm . . . here, seeing a blind woman on the terrace laughing, joking or listening to my *In the Twilight* being read, I start to think it odd not that the doctor will die but that we don't sense our own death.

The second daughter, Elena, plain and assumed unmarriageable, was also a doctor. Natalia, the youngest, was full of song and laughter: she identified with the peasantry, and not only spoke but also taught Ukrainian (then forbidden). The elder son, Pavel, under house arrest for radical activities, was married and expecting his first child. The youngest son, George, was a pianist, enthralled by Tchaikovsky's music and Tolstoy's morality: his career was also curtailed by political activism. Letters sent to Luka, even to Chekhov, were intercepted by the secret police. The Lintvariovs expected intellectuals to devote themselves to the people. Discussions at Luka, despite Natalia's vivacity, had little of Babkino's frivolity. There were no drinking bouts, no romps with peasant girls. The innocent ambience and idyllic setting were to infiltrate a few of Chekhov's works, notably *The Wood Demon*, and give them a Utopian colouring.

The house the Chekhovs rented was more habitable than Misha had suggested, despite four dogs that chased the Lintvariov pigs around the yard and burst into the guests' dining room. A Polish girl cooked for the Chekhovs; Evgenia refused to cook, because the kitchen was occupied by another holiday-maker. Anton went fishing and struck up a partnership with a local factory-worker, a keen fisherman. They fished the millponds on the Psiol. The miller's daughter was plump 'like a sultana pudding … such concupiscence, Heaven help me,' Anton wrote to Kiseliov, but gentlemen at Luka did not seduce peasant girls, and Anton was dismayed to discover that Sumy had no brothel. Luka also lacked lavatories: Chekhov's bottom was covered with mosquito bites.

None of the visitors who trekked 400 miles, a thirty-hour train journey, complained. The Ukraine appealed to Russian intellectuals, who felt a yearning for a Shangri-La they could idealize, like the Victorian English love affair with Scotland. Anton's newest acolytes – the writers Ivan Shcheglov, Kazimir Barantsevich, and the flautist Aleksandr Ivanenko – and those whom he revered happily joined him for two weeks at Luka. On 20 May the poet Pleshcheev arrived. Ivanenko played duets with Georges Lintvariov; the local girls rowed Pleshcheev on the Psiol and sang romances to him, Anton monitoring the old poet's pulse and breathing.

Early in June two of Anton's brothers, Vania and Kolia, came. Kolia was subdued, for in Moscow he had vanished with Franz Schechtel's money and materials; Schechtel, as architect for a church that Kolia was helping to restore, was facing a fine of 150 roubles for each day's delay. 'I pity myself in the extreme,' he wrote. 'Kolia is not worth pitying.' Aleksandr came to Moscow and left his infant sons with Aunt Fenichka. There, Gruzinsky reported on 21 June, order had disintegrated: 'On the steps of your apartment I saw a charming young maid with a charming young man on her knees (usually it's the other way round).'[26] Aleksandr hurried to Sumy, but was quarrelsome and drunk. He mounted the stage of the little Sumy summer theatre and helped the hypnotist and the conjurors: the audience laughed, but Anton removed him. Then Aleksandr wrote a proposal of marriage to Elena Lintvariova, presuming her desperate enough to accept a widowed alcoholic with two retarded sons. Anton tore the letter up. Aleksandr stalked off to the station at two in the morning. In Moscow he accused Aunt Fenichka of poisoning his children. He took them to the Petersburg flat, which had been stripped bare by two dismissed servant girls, and there lapsed into alcoholic stupor. (Some time elapsed before the two little boys were rescued and sent for a few weeks to Aunt Fenichka in Moscow.)

Kolia and Pleshcheev left two days after Aleksandr walked out. Kolia, after a third-class journey cramped among the household goods of other returning holiday-makers, went to his sick-bed in Anna Ipatieva-Golden's house: from here he tried to extort money from Suvorin to illustrate 'Steppe'. Pleshcheev returned (forgetting his nightshirt) first-class to his genteel apartment in Petersburg. The gap was filled by Misha, back from Taganrog, who now felt closer to Mitrofan's family than his own, particularly to his cousin Georgi.

Anton thought of buying a ranch in the Ukraine for a few thousand roubles. There, he fantasized, he could write, found a spa for other city writers, and practise medicine. Earning 500 to 1000 roubles from each new story or play, Anton could be a man of property. A farmer friend of the Lintvariovs, Aleksandr Smagin, had taken a fancy to Masha, and offered to help find Anton a property near his own estate in Poltava. The Lintvariovs harnessed four horses to their antiquated carriage: Anton with Natalia Lintvariova, her brother George and a girl from Poltava set off to the Smagin estate. Anton started a ten-day tour of the market towns of the northern Ukraine that Gogol had made famous fifty years before. For three years Anton considered properties, but every deal fell through. The 250-mile tour left Chekhov a lover of all things Ukrainian. When he returned to Sumy he was buoyant.

Nightingales hatched their young in the window frame. More visitors came. Anton had asked Gavrilov to give Pavel two weeks' leave from the warehouse. Gavrilov was happy to employ the father of a famous man: his demands on Pavel were nominal, though Pavel liked helping Gavrilov reckon his million-rouble annual profit. On 26 June Pavel arrived, to celebrate his name day jointly with Pavel Lintvariov, an event that contributed touches to Chekhov's story 'The Name-Day Party'. Of the acolytes, only Kazimir Barantsevich came for long. He and Anton caught crayfish together. Barantsevich left, forgetting his waders and a pair of trousers. He wrote a thank-you letter: 'Not a day passes without my thinking about suicide (except for my short stay with you).'

Anton missed Suvorin. Sending Anton his comedy *The Theatrical Sparrow* for comment, Shcheglov said the same: 'I occasionally have Suvorin-schmerzen; it's so wonderful to talk to him now and then – he is sensitivity itself.' After three days by train and boat, on 13 July 1888, Anton was greeted by the Suvorins at their villa in Feodosia. For nine days they bathed, lay in the sun, strolled and talked. Anton wrote neither letters nor fiction: the relationship absorbed him totally. Here they sketched out the play that would later become *The Wood Demon*. Anna Suvorina watched:

> We lay on the baking-hot sand or on moonlit nights watched the boundless sea . . . My husband and Anton when they were together chatted or exchanged stories all the time . . . We introduced Anton to Aivazovsky [*the painter*] . . . Aivazovsky's beautiful second wife, an Armenian, wore a white housecoat and her long black hair, still wet after bathing, flowed loose; lit by the moon she was sorting out roses, freshly picked and strewn over the table, into baskets. Anton said, 'It's a magic fairy tale.'

Chekhov wrote nothing that summer, although he was planning a novel. Suvorin's munificence overwhelmed him: rowing boats for fishing on the Psiol, money to buy an estate, a daughter, a partnership in the publishing business, co-authorship for a new play, worldly wisdom, state secrets. Anton made light of Suvorin's offer of his eleven-year-old daughter Nastia, and borrowed a sum too small to embarrass himself, but large enough not to offend Suvorin.

Anton ignored everything else. In Moscow Vania was searching for quarters for himself and Pavel. The Korneev house was a shambles. Vania told his mother:

> There is a lot of dust and rubbish from well-known persons in your apartment, but what there really are a lot of are *cats*. For want of anything to do, Auntie talks to them, feeding the poor animals on buns and milk, all the pussy cats have names, the littlest is called Paper Bag.

At 4.00 a.m. on 23 July 1888, Anton set sail with Aleksei Suvorin junior, the Dauphin, for the Caucasus. In heavy seas Anton lost his footing and grabbed the telegraph machine to stop his fall. In the confusion on the bridge the ship, the *Dir*, narrowly missed another boat.[27] Anton and the Dauphin set off across Georgia for the Caspian sea, aiming to reach Persia via Bukhara. A new disaster struck Suvorin. The Dauphin had telegrams: his third brother, Valerian, was ill. Valerian had turned up, complaining of headaches, at Zvenigorod, where Anton would have been working, had he accepted Kiseliov's invitation to Babkino. Here Anton's colleague, Dr Arkhangelsky, diagnosed diphtheria and ordered a trachæotomy. A call to a Moscow surgeon went astray: Valerian died in Zvenigorod on 2 August 1888.

The Dauphin and Anton raced back to the Crimea. Suvorin junior hastened to his father. Anton avoided the bereaved Suvorins and returned to the Lintvariovs and the river Psiol. The Dauphin wrote to Anton on 12 August 1888:

> I found our father completely shattered and tired, as if after an attack of mental illness ... Now everything seems impossible, futile ... My father is trying to follow common-sense prescriptions, trying to live 'a normal life', is doing the bookshop accounts, going to the building site ... We expected you here, I did my best to make excuses for you.

Appeals for compassion came from Moscow as well as the Crimea. Aunt Fenichka wrote to her sister on 11 August:

> I grieve for the children now that Anna is no more and I wake up at night and think about them ... I can't bear it, when the child [*little Kolia*] misses his mother.' He can't talk and told me – he shows me with his hands – how mama was dressed and put in the coffin and then buried in a hole in the ground, shows me with his hands and simply I have never known such grief; I just cannot calm myself. Anna was a dear and I was quite certain that her relatives would take them in and not let them live like this. I pray that Our Father in Heaven will soften Anton's heart ... poor Shura [*Anna's 16-year-old son*] cried a lot for his mother and fell unconscious, and the daughter [*the eleven-year-old Nadia*] cried a lot.

Anton could not cope with any more demands on his sympathy, his living space, or his purse. His nephews, for whom he felt scarcely more affection than did Pavel, were abandoned to their drunken father, and Suvorin to his wife and surviving sons.

Since 'Steppe' in March Chekhov had not maintained his

reputation. He was ashamed of 'Lights', his second story, which was to appear in *The Northern Herald.* (He excluded it from his collected works.) Inspired by revisiting Taganrog, it tells the story of a successful provincial who returns to the seaside town where he grew up. The local girls pine for the boys who abandoned them for the metropolis: they endure loveless marriages. The narrator seduces a girl, Kisochka, whom he once revered. The work to which Anton devoted most thought but which never saw the light of day was an unwritten novel. The hints that survive in others' recollections and Anton's letters suggest that it was based on the life of the Lintvariovs. Perhaps it was recycled into *The Wood Demon* and the stories which Chekhov wrote, when inspiration returned, in the autumn. The company of writers all summer had left Anton so irritated, and the suffering of others weighed so heavily, that his novel was abandoned.

Physically and spiritually exhausted, but desperate to write, Anton returned to Luka. On 2 September 1888 he and his family returned to the Korneev house in Moscow, evicting Aunt Fenichka (who returned to her cramped quarters) and her stray cats and dogs.

TWENTY-FIVE

The Prize

October–December 1888

BACK IN HIS STUDY, Chekhov began a busy autumn. The house was noisier: Seriozha Kiseliov stamped upstairs when he came back from school. There was now a family retainer, the cook Mariushka Dormidontovna Belenovskaia, already over sixty, who would serve Anton for the rest of his life.

The protests about Kolia's dereliction were loud. Early in October 1888 Schechtel (who had suffered financially) voiced to Anton everyone's thoughts:

> That Kolia is feeling bad, and very bad, is obvious – I wouldn't give tuppence for his life expectancy. I can positively affirm that he is incorrigible. With tears in his eyes he assured me that he could see and sense the evil which his Big Slag [*Anna Golden*] causes him, that from this instant he is breaking with her forever, he will see people, dine, lunch, work. Excellent: I almost believed him; for a few days he behaved just like the Kolia of old, he came to see us every day. Apart from a little glass of Sauternes he drank nothing. Whom he was trying to deceive, I now can't understand. The other side of the coin: constant vodka, salami (Luxus) and Slag [*Anna*] every day. No inclination to work. He fancied the idea of painting my wife's portrait. All right – a mass of money has been spent – I don't know what will happen; so far the canvas is standing in a virginal state.

Three weeks later, Schechtel said, Kolia had taken 100 roubles and an iconostasis: 'He definitely suffers from a mania which lets him see all his actions, some criminal, through rose-coloured glasses . . . I'm sorry to bother you, but what can I do? . . . *Return the inconostasis to my messenger.*'

The next warning came in a note from the landlord, Dr Korneev, to Misha:

> Tell me where your brother the artist Kolia is sleeping. Today there

was an <u>incident</u>. I caught a fellow looking into your windows. As a vigilant landlord I gave the lad a fright ... He admitted he was Kolia, that he'd taken a room in Medvedev's lodgings and, he said, <u>he didn't know</u> where he'd spent the nights for three weeks and he had no papers! I tell you in such detail in case there's trouble and you have to pay a fine.[28]

Chekhov appealed to Suvorin's son-in-law and legal expert, Kolomnin, to see if Kolia could get a certificate of exemption from military service. The crime of having hidden was inexpiable; none of Kolomnin's suggestions would save Kolia. Schechtel persisted in salvaging. At the end of November he wrote:

I sent two telegrams to the Big Slag – no answer. Clearly, he's not there. Has he been to see you? Just let him give me back the boards – I don't want anything else. Why does he punish me twice over! Perhaps he'll sort himself out and work; I am ready to forget everything if only he'd work.

Through Aleksandr in Petersburg, Anton traced Kolia to a new woman. Not until the approach of Easter 1889, did the family hear from their black sheep again.

After he had left Sumy in a huff, Aleksandr twice wrote to Masha asking secretly whether he might marry Elena Lintvariova. Masha told Anton, who defended a vulnerable colleague and comrade, as he always felt Elena to be, from his brother. He told Aleksandr:

Above all, you are an 84° proof hypocrite. You write 'I want a family, music, affection, kind words when I'm tired after ... running round fires etc.' ... you well know that family, music, affection and kind words come not from marriage to the first woman you meet, even if she is very decent, but from <u>love</u> ... you know Elena less than the man on the moon ... As for Elena, she is a doctor, a landowner, free, independent, educated and has her own views. She may decide to get married of course, for she is just a woman, but she won't get married for a million roubles if there is no <u>love</u> on her part.

Aleksandr capitulated. Suvorin set aside his own misery and remonstrated with Aleksandr. Aleksandr remained for some months, under Suvorin's influence, sober.

Soon, Aleksandr found 'affection' for himself and a mother for his sons. Natalia Golden, Anton's old love Natashevu, re-entered the

Chekhov circle. Aleksandr's letter to Anton of 24 October 1888 had a sting in the tail: 'Natalia is living in my apartment, running the household, fussing over the children and keeping me up to scratch. And if she crosses sometimes into concubinage, that's not your business.'

New Times had printed an article on the dying Putiata. Into the office came Natalia to ask where Putiata was living. (Her sister Anastasia was Putiata's estranged wife.)

> We got chatting. I invited her to visit and have a look at my boys. She agreed, visited and after a few evenings spent between 'the widower and the maid' the end result is that we are living together. She has one room, I have the other. We live, we curse each other from morning to night, but our relationship is entirely conjugal. She fits me like a glove. If our parents, whose old age I intend to console by exemplary behaviour, don't view this 'intimacy' as incest, fornication and onanism, then I have nothing against marriage in church.

Anton received a wry note from Natalia:

> Dear Anton, I know that this letter will astound you greatly, but I'm just as astounded. The things that happen! I would love to know your opinion about all that has happened. Sincerely devoted to you, N. Golden.[29]

Anton answered nothing, until he had another death to announce in Latin, that of Korbo the whippet. The decrepit dog's death in early November took the brothers back to their early days in Moscow in 1877 and brought them together more than the transfer of Natashevu's affections. Aleksandr confessed to purloining money from Anton's earnings from *New Times*. He appended condolences in Latin from his dog, Gershka-Penchuk, who had outlived Korbo.

Within a week Natalia, who, like the other Golden sisters, had a gargantuan appetite for food and sex, was more than Aleksandr could cope with:

> I could put under her portrait the inscription I saw in childhood in an inn on a picture which showed gorillas grabbing and gnawing at negro women while Englishmen in bowler hats fired guns at them. The inscription is simple but expressive: 'This passionate and sensual beast . . .'

All autumn 1888 Anton received letters from 'the Dauphin'. The Dauphin, an apologist of pogroms, sent anti-Semitic ravings.[30] The only effect was to confirm Anton's own respect for Jews and to sow doubts about the whole Suvorin empire's noxiousness. On his other favourite topic the Dauphin found a more sympathetic ear: 'Never marry, Anton, for longer than three months, and if you do, leave your wife before she is thirty, for after thirty a woman, even the most selfless, sees her husband primarily as a convenience.'

Suvorin senior, who had over the past year done little more than tinker with his villa and organize the publication of two books of Chekhov's stories, shook off his torpor at the end of September. He spent a day with Anton in Moscow before going to Petersburg to take control. Suvorin confirmed what Anton already knew: the Russian Academy's 1888 prize for literature was half his. Even before 'Steppe' was published, the committee – run by Grigorovich – had ensured the outcome in Anton's favour. The 500 roubles, added to the income from increased sales of Anton's books, *In the Twilight* of 1887, and, now, *Stories*, pulled the Chekhovs out of debt. Suvorin came to congratulate him, followed by Anna Suvorina. Visits from the Suvorins were prestigious, but made Anton a target for Moscow's radicals who fell upon any intimate of *New Times*.

Suvorin found a distraction after his two sons' deaths: he started a theatre. For the next two decades he surrounded himself with pretty actresses and more or less talented playwrights, while *New Times* slid into the hands of the Dauphin. Now Suvorin had a play of his own to produce in Moscow, *Tatiana Repina*. Suvorin and Chekhov agreed to produce each other's plays in their respective cities. Chekhov was to see *Tatiana Repina* through rehearsal at Korsh's theatre, while Suvorin would have *Ivanov* performed in Petersburg, a crucial début for Chekhov. Anton overhauled his play again.

Anton's letters to Suvorin became longer, and more frequent; the relationship was closer than ever. On 14 October 1888 he revealed his secret, but pretended that he was not seriously ill:

> Every winter, autumn, spring and every wet summer's day I cough. But all this frightens me only when I see blood: in blood that flows from your mouth there is something ominous like a red sunset ... consumption or any serious lung illness is recognized only by a syndrome and I happen not to have that syndrome; blood sometimes

pours from a lung all day, it gushes, the household and patient are horrified and it ends with the patient not dying – more often than not.

Only four days before Anton had had another hæmorrhage.

Rather than TB Chekhov preferred to discuss sex with Suvorin. He had written a story, 'An Attack', after some pressure, to commemorate Garshin. Chekhov chose a controversial topic: the brothels of Sobolev Lane. The story has a simple 'three friends' plot: three students trawl the brothels; one is so convinced that prostitution is evil that he preaches on the streets. His friends take him to a psychiatrist who tells him it is he, not society, which is sick. The two 'healthy' students resemble Schechtel and Levitan; the rebel resembles Kolia. The narrator sides with the rebel, who is very much in 'the Garshin spirit', pure, ardent and on the verge of insanity. It is the first Chekhov story where we ask if the sane are the real madmen. Anton found his own experience of prostitution as a medical student a cause for ambiguous feelings. To Suvorin he wrote, on 11 November 1888: 'I talk a lot about prostitution, but decide nothing. Why isn't anything written about prostitution in your paper? It's the most terrible evil.' To Pleshcheev (whose views were as broad-minded as Kiseliov's) Chekhov wrote the next day in a different tone: 'As a medic I think that I described the mental pain correctly, following all the rules of psychiatry. As for the girls, I used to be a great specialist in that department in days of yore.' To Shcheglov in late December Chekhov showed complete tolerance: 'Why do you so dislike talking about Sobolev Lane? I love people who go there, although I go as rarely as you do. One mustn't disdain life.'

That autumn the disparity between sex in real life and sex in literature irritated Anton. When Suvorin praised Zola's expertise, Chekhov responded angrily:

> I have seen quite a few wayward women and have sinned many times personally, but I don't believe Zola or that lady who told you, 'Wham-bam, and it's done.' Dissipated people and writers like to make out they are gourmets and fine connoisseurs of fornication; they are daring, decisive, inventive, they have sex 33 different ways, on virtually everything but a knife edge, but all that is just talk, in fact they have sex with their cooks and go to one-rouble brothels ... I have never seen a single decent apartment where circumstances

would allow you to topple a woman dressed in a corset, skirts and a proper dress onto a chest or a divan or the floor and have sex with her without the servants noticing. All these terms for doing it 'standing up', 'sitting down' and so on are nonsense. The easiest way is on a bed, and the other 33 are difficult and feasible only in a hotel room or a shed ... If Zola himself had sex on tables, under tables, on fences, in dog kennels, in mail coaches or saw with his own eyes others doing so, then trust his novels, but if he wrote on the basis of rumours and friends' stories, then he was hasty and careless.[31]

Rather than discuss such matters on paper, the Suvorins invited Anton and Masha to Petersburg. The Dauphin expected Chekhov to come home drunk: 'Let your sister have your rooms, you take the library ... the one near the hall. I recommend the divan there. A separate entrance. When you come in at night, try to fall to the left and you'll hit the door.' By early December Anton and Masha were installed at the Suvorins'. Anton talked all night with Pleshcheev, Modest Tchaikovsky, Davydov and George Lintvariov. On 11 December Anton went with Suvorin to the first night of *Tatiana Repina*. The next day he read his story 'An Attack' to the Literary Society. He avoided public readings, not just out of shyness but because he would lose his voice after only a few minutes: an ominous symptom of TB. Fortunately Davydov took over. Anton tried to explain *Ivanov* to uncomprehending professionals. In that fortnight in Petersburg the crucial meeting was with the composer Piotr Tchaikovsky: like Levitan and, in the future Rachmaninov and the painter Repin, Tchaikovsky proved that musicians and painters best understood Anton's art.

Anton spent time interceding for others: introducing George Lintvariov to Tchaikovsky ('nice, not at all like a demigod', Anton asserted), persuading editors to pay Maria Kiseliova more for her children's stories. He found no time for Grigorovich, and hurt his feelings. His most traumatic experience was a visit, without Masha, to see Aleksandr. He was not jealous: over the years Natalia Golden's serpentine figure had filled out and now her black tresses were hidden under a headscarf. Nevertheless, although Anton had never protested at his brother's abuse of Anna Sokolnikova, Aleksandr's drunken, obscene bullying of his old love Natashevu outraged him. He left the house after a row and got drunk. Suvorin had to guide him to bed.

Back in Moscow, Anton, on Aleksei Suvorin's behalf, cast *Tatiana Repina* at the Maly theatre. He decided that 'actresses are cows who fancy they are goddesses . . . Machiavellis in skirts'. Suvorin was producing *Ivanov* at the Aleksandrinsky theatre in Petersburg. Anton became as ruthless as any producer. 'The women are devious. Don't reply to their telegrams and letters, if you get any, without my say-so,' he ordered Suvorin. The stress of fighting theatrical egos made his hæmorrhoids painful. He was fighting for Suvorin, and, through Suvorin, fighting Petersburg actors' incomprehension of even the revised version of *Ivanov*. Anton sent Suvorin medical graphs of Ivanov's depression. He felt he would never win unstinted praise: Petersburg loathed psychological drama.

The prize and the play overshadowed new trends in Chekhov's prose. 'The Attack' was not his only puritanical Tolstoyan indictment of society. In another story, 'The Princess', an ascetic doctor accuses a princess of masking her hypocrisy as charity. A very substantial story 'The Name-Day Party', like Katherine Mansfield's 'The Garden Party', gets at the private falsity which underlies a public celebration; 'The Name-Day Party' ends dramatically, with a thunderstorm to wash away the party and a miscarriage to shock the heroine out of her pretences. All three stories are studies of lies and the way in which physiology reveals the lie. The techniques are Tolstoy's: the author monitors the character's body language and makes the simpleton soothsayer to the sophisticate. Nobody foresaw that Chekhov, after weighing Tolstoyanism, would reject it. The liberal and hedonistic elements in Chekhov's make-up rebelled against Tolstoy's puritanism, just as Chekhov's expressive understatement was ill suited to Tolstoy's lapidary edifying style.

One short article said more than anything else about Chekhov's intentions and aspirations. In October 1888 the explorer of China and Tibet, Nikolai Przhevalsky, now known as the discoverer of Przewalski's horse, died by a remote lake on the border of Kirgizia and China. He died as Tchaikovsky would, sick with homosexual love, after drinking infected water. Chekhov wrote an unsigned obituary for Przhevalsky in *New Times*, praising his heroism, saying that one Przhevalsky was worth a dozen educational institutions and a hundred good books. Chekhov had not read Przhevalsky's last book in which the explorer recommends exterminating the inhabitants of Mongolia and Tibet, replacing them with Cossacks, and starting a war with China. What aroused Chekhov's enthusiasm was the image of the lone traveller deserting family and friends, trekking to the ends of the earth to die.

TWENTY-SIX

The Petersburg Ivanov
January–February 1889

IN THE NEW YEAR OF 1889 Suvorin and Chekhov were like twins: they produced each other's plays; they planned to write together *The Wood Demon*, a country comedy, dividing between themselves the characters and the acts. Suvorin would come to Moscow for *Tatiana Repina*; then Anton would see *Ivanov* performed in Petersburg. All Petersburg was gossiping about their relationship. 'Suvorin the Father, Suvorin the Son and Chekhov the Holy Ghost,' they quipped when the two friends appeared with the Dauphin.[32] Rumour had it that Suvorin paid Anton 6000 roubles a year; that either the eleven-year-old Nastia Suvorina or Pleshcheev's daughter Elena was to be Anton's bride. No Chekhov brother was yet married, unlike all Anton's doctor friends, and nearly all his acolytes, Bilibin, Shcheglov, Gruzinsky, Ezhov. Anton pleaded poverty. Evreinova's joke at *The Northern Herald* became a rumour: Chekhov was betrothed to Sibiriakova, a millionaire widow.

Anton prepared for Suvorin's arrival, searching the Moscow hotels for a suite with central heating. He could not shake off his horror at Aleksandr's treatment of Natalia. On 2 January 1889, as he had done with Kolia two years before, he spared his eldest brother nothing:

> I was driven from you by your *horrible*, completely unjustified treatment of Natalia and the cook . . . Constant foul language of the lowest sort, raising your voice, reproaches, rows at lunch and dinner, constant complaints at your hard labour and cursed life – isn't that an expression of coarse tyranny? However pathetic and guilty the woman, however intimate she is with you, you have no right to sit in her presence with no trousers on, to be drunk in her presence, to use language that not even factory workers use when they see women around . . . No decent husband or lover would let himself talk coarsely to a woman about pissing, about lavatory paper, to

make an ironic joke of their relations in bed, to poke about verbally in her sexual organs. This debauches a woman and distances her from God in whom she believes. A man who respects a woman, who is well-bred and loving, will not appear in front of the chambermaid without his trousers, shouting at the top of his voice, 'Katka, bring the piss-pot!' . . . Between the woman who sleeps on clean sheets and the woman who dosses down on dirty sheets and roars with laughter when her lover farts is the same distance as between a drawing room and a pub . . . You can't get away with obscenities in front of the children, insulting the servants or spitefully telling Natalia 'Clear off and go to hell! I'm not keeping you.'[33]

After this salvo, Natalia got the upper hand in her marriage: Aleksandr drank, the flat was sordid and the children unhappy, but he never abused her again. Anton was, in Natalia's eyes, her rescuer.

In a letter that January, Anton told Suvorin he was glad he had not written a novel – perhaps the novel which has been lost – when he still lacked 'a feeling of personal freedom', although, looking back at his life so far, he saw it as a victory:

What writers of the gentry had free from birth, we the underclass have to pay for with our youth. Why don't you write the story of a young man, the son of a serf, a former shop boy, chorister, schoolboy and student, brought up on deferring to rank, on kissing priests' hands, submitting to others' ideas, thankful for every crust, thrashed many times, who tormented animals, who loved having dinner with rich relatives, who was quite needlessly hypocritical before God and people, just because he knew he was a nonentity – write about this young man squeezing drop by drop the slave out of himself and waking one fine morning feeling that real human blood, not a slave's, is flowing in his veins.

Slave's blood still ran in his brothers' veins. Aleksandr was bonded to Suvorin's *New Times*, Vania to the inspector of primary schools, Misha, shortly to graduate, to the Tax Inspectorate, Kolia to drink and drugs. Anton alone seemed free.

Anton extended his charity to other derelicts. Despite Palmin's drunken slanders – he had spread rumours to Leikin that Anton was mad and suicidal – Anton rode out to treat him for a cut, and was touched by Palmin's gift of a bottle of Ylang-Ylang perfume. Anton visited the dying Putiata, and discreetly placed an envelope of banknotes under Putiata's pillow. Putiata was more embarrassed than relieved: 'as a poor man with a family you ought not to have done this.'

On 10 January 1889 Suvorin came to Moscow to watch rehearsals of *Tatiana Repina*. It had mixed success, but one critic, Vladimir Nemirovich-Danchenko, who was in the next decade to be cofounder of the Moscow Arts Theatre and a close associate of Chekhov, did protest at Suvorin's provocative prejudices: 'Why did the author have to put two Jews as the most antipathetic figures on stage? . . . Why did the author have to deal so inappropriately with the women's question?' For the time being Suvorin's anti-Semitism and sexual chauvinism did not impair his friendship with Anton. They celebrated Tatiana's day so thoroughly that Anton's hand still shook when, the next day, he wrote to Lily Markova, now Sakharova.[34] The following week Suvorin and Chekhov set off together for Petersburg. Chekhov had a contract with the Aleksandrinsky theatre for 10 per cent of the gross from *Ivanov*, and sold them the rights to *The Bear*. *Ivanov* had been passed, after further revision, by the censor for the Imperial Theatres, but the play's defenders were faint-hearted. One Petersburg theatre-goer, the playwright Sazonova, records: 'Davydov and Sazonov are both unwilling to act in the play, all its absurdities and inconsistencies are even more striking.'[35] Anton spent evenings arguing with Davydov that the new version, where the doctor taunts Ivanov into suicide, was plausible. Despite the difficulties with *Ivanov*, made worse by the author attending the rehearsals, Anton thought about future plays. He contemplated joint authorship of a farce with Shcheglov: they improvised a plot.[36] Suvorin and Anton did the literary rounds: a surreptitious sketch by Repin shows Chekhov bored to tears and Suvorin smouldering with anger at a meeting of the Society of Russian Writers.

Anton went to see Khudekov, the editor of *The Petersburg Gazette*: Khudekov's wife attracted Anton, but it was Khudekov's sister-in-law who responded. Lidia Avilova, mother of two and writer of children's stories, was infatuated. She had little encouragement – Anton avoided affairs with married women with children – but saw herself as the love of Chekhov's life, encrypted into Chekhov's fiction. Other female company was uncomplicated. Pleshcheev and Shcheglov left Anton free tickets to go out with George Lintvariov to the Prikazchik club:

'If you're going there for "erotic" purposes, we are superfluous.' With Nastia Suvorina Anton established a joking avuncular relationship.[37] Only Grigorovich still hoped to see them married. Anna Suvorina recalled: 'My daughter was interested in anything but famous writers. Anton often told her that he wouldn't mind doing what Grigorovich wanted but on condition "Nastia, your daddy has to give us a dowry: his publishing firm as my property and his monthly magazine ..."'

On 31 January 1889 the Petersburg première of *Ivanov* took place. It had, even its enemies admitted, great success. Davydov's obesity expressed Ivanov's moral paralysis. Russia's unhappiest actress, Strepetova, put her suffering into Sarra. They brought the house down at the end of Act 3. Strepetova could not stop crying. Anton momentarily felt the cast were 'kith and kin'. Modest Tchaikovsky, Bilibin, and Barantsevich were moved. Many proclaimed the play the equal of Griboedov's or Gogol's dramas. Some had doubts: Shcheglov's diary noted 'drafts blowing across the stage, the author's inexperience and the absence of finish.' Suvorin felt that Ivanov's character never develops, that the women characters were sketchy – allegations which Anton repudiated. Lidia Avilova, however, was watching him intently at the party backstage:

> Anton kept his word and sent me a ticket to *Ivanov* ... How he stood, strained and awkward, as if he was tied down. And in that glimmer of a smile I sensed a morbid tension, such tiredness and anguish that my arms drooped with helplessness. I had no doubt, despite the noisy success, that Anton was dissatisfied and unhappy.

Anton fled to Moscow before the second performance on 3 February. The play had only five performances that season, although every house enthused. More sober evaluations came by post. Vladimir Nemirovich-Danchenko, then a playwright, but not yet a director, spoke for posterity on *Ivanov*:

> You are the most talented ... and I subscribe to this without the slightest feeling of envy, but I shan't consider *Ivanov* to be among your best work ... but to be among the original drafts of beautiful pieces.[38]

Ivanov brought Anton two new friends. Nemirovich-Danchenko was in ten years to be the interpreter of Chekhov's drama and then a close friend of Anton's wife. The other was Pavel Svobodin, who played

Ivanov's uncle Shabelsky. Svobodin was bewitched by Anton for the rest of his short life. Svobodin and Anton were two over-worked consumptives, with contradictory streaks of idealism and cynicism. Svobodin believed in Chekhov's genius and, with Suvorin, pushed Anton into finishing his next play, *The Wood Demon*.

In Moscow Anton tried to help his less fortunate friends Gruzinsky, Ezhov and Barantsevich: he offered to revise their work, he persuaded Suvorin to take them on, but the acolytes felt insecure when they visited the Chekhovs in the winter of 1888–9. Gruzinsky, normally a good-natured man, resented the claims that Kolia, Vania, Masha and Pavel had on Anton. He and Ezhov loathed losing at whist to Vania (a game that Anton refused to learn). They disliked Masha and found Pavel sinister. Gruzinsky's letters to Ezhov snarl:

> Ivan Chekhov is a weird character and, as Bilibin says of his older brother Aleksandr, 'a crooked personality' . . . I don't like Chekhov's father. Yes, certainly he was a tyrant and a wild beast. That sort almost always develop into 'unctuous' types . . . Maria Chekhova in passing argued that there is nothing more selfish than talent and genius. That was an allusion to her brother who is bursting his guts for them.[39]

Ezhov saw Anton's parents in a poor light. He recalled Easter 1889:

> Once Chekhov told his friends at tea: 'Do you know, gentlemen, our cook is getting married. I'd like to take you to the wedding, but I'm afraid the cook's guests will start beating us up.' – 'Antosha,' remarked his mother, 'You should read them your poetry and they won't.' Chekhov . . . suddenly frowned and said, 'Mother still thinks I write poetry.'[40]

It was true that Anton's parents may never have read, or listened to, a word of his stories or plays. Ezhov was as envious as he was protective, and he soured his crony Gruzinsky, who complained to Ezhov:

> Anton Chekhov is strange: he says it's terribly easy to go to Petersburg. His talent gives him perverted ideas about money . . . He asked me how much Leikin was paying me. [*Anton said:*] 'Too little, awfully little . . . I get 70–80, once I got 90 roubles.' And I'm grateful for 40!

Anton found celebrities better company. Pleshcheev came to Moscow to celebrate his birthday and Shrovetide: he gorged on pancakes.

Anton summoned his colleague Dr Obolonsky to treat the elderly poet. Suvorin promised to come and watch his *Tatiana Repina*, which, unlike *Ivanov*, was still running. He sent a balalaika (with no strings) and some photo-portraits of Chekhov; then came a telegram from Anna Suvorina: 'HUSBAND NOW LEFT FOR MOSCOW DON'T FORGET MEET HIM CHEER HIM AND AMUSE PROPERLY BUT SAME TIME REMEMBER ME.'[41] Suvorin did not stay long. Renewed links encouraged the Dauphin to resume writing to Anton: he kept off Jews but, in the spirit of *New Times*, praised the Cossack Ashinov for invading the Horn of Africa. Anton, with embarrassment, confessed that he knew two of the invaders.[42] The Dauphin also reported that their Tatar neighbour in Feodosia had seen *Ivanov*: the play had induced a fit of hysterics in a lady in the audience.

Ivanov brought in nearly a thousand roubles: 'A play is a pension,' declared Anton. The Chekhovs made merry. Leikin pricked the bubble and told Chekhov that he had lost money by putting the play on late in the season (State Theatres closed on the first day of Lent), that his play gave actors no breaks for applause. Leikin added every drop of gall he could: he reported Palmin's wild slanders. Anton responded:

> I haven't seen Palmin *once* this month. How does he know I am losing blood, ill and afraid of madness? I haven't had any hæmorrhage, thank God, since I left Petersburg (only just a little) ... I have no reasons to fear sudden insanity for I don't drink vodka for days on end, I don't go in for spiritualism or masturbation, I don't read the poet Palmin.

Palmin, when challenged, told Leikin that his information came from Kolia. Leikin's dogs, not his opinions, interested Anton. Leikin had acquired a pair of dachshunds and was so much in love with them that he finally had to promise puppies to Anton.

Friendly with so many of the Lintvariov circle, the Chekhovs were bound to return to Luka that summer. Anton began composing *The Wood Demon* in his head, to write in its natural setting, the Lintvariov estate and the mills on the Psiol. He spent money: he bought a set of Dostoevsky and read it, apparently for the first time: 'good, but very long and immodest. A lot of pretensions.' For fun Anton then composed his most extraordinary play: a sequel to Suvorin's *Tatiana*

Repina. Chekhov shows Suvorin's hero, who drove Repina to suicide, marrying in church: the marriage service is ruined by a mysterious lady in black who takes poison, and 'the rest I leave to the imagination of A. S. Suvorin'. The genius of Chekhov's parody sequel lies in the mingling of casual gossip by minor characters with the text of the liturgy which Chekhov knew so well. Anton sent the play to Suvorin: Suvorin went to his print room and had two copies printed, one for himself and one for Anton.

This playful gift for absurdly mixing trivial and serious speech was to lead to two elements that mark out Chekhov's mature drama: inconsequential conversation acting as a counterpoint to tragic utterances, and a plot which hangs on a character who has died before the action starts and about whom we shall never be told the truth. The corpse of Tatiana Repina haunts Chekhov's gift to Suvorin, just as the professor's first wife haunts *Uncle Vania*, Colonel Prozorov the *Three Sisters*, or Ranevskaia's drowned son *The Cherry Orchard*.

TWENTY-SEVEN

A Death at Luka
March–June 1889

CHEKHOV TOOK UP his novel. He also made a mysterious trip to Kharkov, ostensibly to look at a ranch for Suvorin, but perhaps in response to Lily Markova's (now Sakharova) invitation. The trip was, to judge by the hellish aura around Kharkov in his fiction, disagreeable. When Anton returned to Moscow on 15 March 1889, the horse-trams had stopped and blizzards had piled snowdrifts five feet high in front of the house. His mother showed him a postcard from Kolia:

> 11 March 1889 . . . Dear Mama, Illness has prevented me from visiting you. Two weeks ago I caught a bad chill: I was shaking with fever and my side was hurting desperately. But now, thanks to quinine and various ointments I am better and hasten to work to make up for lost time . . .[43]

TB had struck Kolia's intestines. Anton diagnosed typhoid as well. On 29 March Anton, unsure of himself, summoned Nikolai Obolonsky again to Kolia's bedside, back at Anna Ipatieva-Golden's house: Anna told them that Kolia had not touched alcohol for two months. For ten days, longing to escape, Anton visited the feverish emaciated Kolia. It took four hours to cross Moscow's thawing snow to see him.

Anton brought Kolia home. Kolia described his rescue to a Taganrog friend:

> My brother sent me broth. Then on Easter Saturday a carriage was sent for me, they dressed me, and sent me to my mother and family. Almost nobody recognized me. They immediately put me to bed. At 2 a.m. on Easter Sunday everybody celebrates, shouting, noise, drinking wine, and I am lying out of the way, an outcast. The week after Easter there was a concilium with Karneevsky [*Korneev?*] and it was decided that I should eat as much as possible, drink vodka, beer, wine, and eat ham, herring, caviar.[44]

Anton could only muse about his unwritten novel, a work 'with all thoughts and hopes of good people, their norms and deviations, the framework being freedom'. Little freedom was in prospect. There was no money to take Kolia to a warm climate where he might rally, and he could not get a passport. Anton sought consolation in the stoic maxims of Marcus Aurelius, a book he marked heavily with his pencil.

Meanwhile the servants made merry. Pavel and Evgenia were giving their cook, Olga, away in marriage. In late February, at the betrothal, the kitchen had rung with the sound of the harmonica and stamping boots. On 14 April, while Kolia lay moribund upstairs, the wedding feast began. Anton did not feel festive. He invited Schechtel to take leave of Kolia, who was now able to stand, and sent Misha and their mother to prepare the arrival of patient and doctor in the Ukraine. After he had seen them off, Anton went to a meeting of the Dramatic Society and afterwards, he confided in a letter to Dr Obolonsky,

> looked at the dawn then went for a walk, then I was in a foul pub where I watched two crooks play an excellent game of billiards, then I went to the sordid places where I chatted with a mathematics student and musicians, then I returned home, drank some vodka, had breakfast and then (at 6 a.m.) went to bed, was woken up early and am now suffering.

Posting that letter, Chekhov took Kolia to the station and, in a first-class sleeping car, made the journey to Sumy. For the first time in months Kolia slept and ate well. Masha followed a few days later with shoes, a string for the mandolin, and paper and frames for Kolia. Despite, or because of, Kolia's illness, many friends were invited down: Davydov, Barantsevich, the cellist Semashko, not to mention Vania. Suvorin proposed to call on his way to Austria and France. Anton told him: 'How I'd love to go now somewhere like Biarritz where music is playing and there are lots of women. Were it not for the artist, I'd chase after you.'

Aleksandr was not invited. Anton sternly told him that money was the only practical help. Aleksandr offered to marry Natalia – she would not risk pregnancy until she was married. Aleksandr became the first Russian male recorded buying a contraceptive. On a chit for Anton's eyes alone he wrote, on 5 May:

Engulfed by carnal lusts (after long abstinence) I bought in a chemists' a condon (or condom – the devil knows) for 35 kopecks. But as soon as I tried to put it on, it burst, probably from fear at the sight of my shaft. So I had no luck. I had to tame the flesh again.[45]

Kolia was too weak to flee. By day he sat, or lay in a hammock, sunbathing in the orchard. He ate for four, but could not digest food and could hardly walk. He coughed incessantly and he quarrelled with his mother. Other people's deference to the dying made him more capricious. He was given creosote, ipecacuanha and menthol. Death cast a pall over the Psiol: the fishing and the songbirds lost their appeal. Anton tried to distract himself. He dreamed of Mlle Emilie, the Suvorins' governess; he went to the Sumy theatre that Aleksandr had disrupted the previous year; he buried himself in work. He wrote the first act of *The Wood Demon* to an outline agreed with Suvorin: the core of this play, which eventually became *Uncle Vania*, is in the doctor-landowner who finds ecstasy in planting a birch tree, but there was little drama yet. The original plan was based on the Suvorins. The elderly professor, his young second wife, his daredevil son, two children called Boris and Nastia and a French governess called Mlle Emilie are the Suvorin family transferred to Luka; the idealists and cranks who cross their path have aspects of the Lintvariovs and the Chekhovs. From the start, the material is unstageable, for it is as rich and broad as *Middlemarch*. Suvorin would soon back out, but Chekhov persisted.

On 8 May Suvorin arrived for six days, on his way to more comfortable summer quarters. His arrival caused as much tension as that of the professor in *Uncle Vania*. The Lintvariovs, principled radicals, ostracized Suvorin (not that this stopped them from later asking Suvorin to send their village school free books). Anton was torn between two sets of friends. Worse, Kolia begged Suvorin for an advance for book cover designs. (Anton forbad Suvorin to pay him.) Meanwhile Kolia's mistress, Anna Ipatieva-Golden, at her wit's end near Moscow, was begging both Suvorin and Anton for financial help and a job.

Suvorin promised Anton 30 kopecks a line for the novel. He tactfully talked of buying a dacha nearby, but soon left for his villa in the Crimea. From there he discussed with Anton Paul Bourget's novel, *The Disciple*. Suvorin sympathized with Bourget's attacks on free-thinkers as the godfathers of anarchy and murder. Russian readers, said Anton, liked Bourget only because French culture was better: 'a Russian writer lives in drainpipes, eating slugs, making love to sluts and laundresses, he knows no history, geography, natural sciences.' Anton wrote grimly to Leikin: he yearned for a time 'when I shall have my own corner, my own wife, not somebody else's ... free of vanity and quarrels.'

Kolia also longed to be elsewhere. He wrote letters, mostly unposted, in all directions, begging for help. Kolia wanted to be back in his birthplace:

> I definitely need to visit Taganrog <u>on business</u> and, while I'm there, <u>bathe in the sea</u> ... Get me a <u>ticket</u> from Kharkov to Taganrog and back ... The class of ticket should correspond to my social position and take account of my weak state. In exchange I'll send you a woman's head painted in oils (very nicely done, I don't want to part with it) ... I impatiently wait for a letter with 'Yes' and 'No' but with no 'ifs' etc.[46]

Kolia still had a sharp eye and steady hand. He wrote a calligraphic masterpiece to Dr Obolonsky, and illustrated it with a stout passenger in a first-class compartment and a train steaming across the steppes.

Misha's letters to his cousin Georgi draw a veil over Kolia. He had to give up revisiting Taganrog: 'The poor man is so bad that really it would be awkward to leave him.' As Kolia declined, Misha ignored him. On 29 May 1889 he told Georgi:

> If you knew how good our evenings are, you'd drop everything, dacha, family, and come straight away to us ... The smell of flowering lime trees, elder and jasmine and the scent of newly mown hay, scattered over our terrace for Trinity Day and the moon, like a pancake hanging over us ... Next to me Masha is sitting, just back from Poltava, and a little further is nice Ivanenko. Both are reading. Through the open window come the conversations of Suvorin, who's come to stay with us, and ... Anton ... Semashko has taken a room with us for the whole summer, so all summer we shall be enjoying music.

At the end of May the irrepressible actor Pavel Svobodin came, but could not bear the spectre – he too was dying of tuberculosis. He took a train back for Moscow, but Vania persuaded Svobodin to turn back and give the Chekhovs moral support in a seemingly interminable vigil. Kolia, Anton reported to Dr Obolonsky on 4 June, was bed-ridden, losing weight every day. He was taking atropine and quinine, dozing, sometimes deliriously. A priest gave last rites: Kolia confessed to maltreating his mother. Then he wrote with frenzy: graphic child-hood memories, letters to Uncle Mitrofan and Suvorin, begging for loans, promising paintings.

Aleksandr insisted on coming: he gave Suvorin a reason so odd that Suvorin passed it to Anton: 'ambulatory typhoid' became the Chekhov term for alcoholism:

> I am fettered to my bed. I had ambulatory typhoid. I was able to walk, attend events and fires and give the paper reports. Now the doctor says I have a relapse. The doctor is urging me south; give me leave and the right to take 2 months' salary (140 roubles) in advance.[47]

At 2 p.m. on 15 June Aleksandr arrived with the children and Natalia, and for one hour all five Chekhov brothers were together. After two harrowing months on duty, sleeping in the room next to Kolia, Anton suddenly snapped. Taking Vania, Svobodin, and George Lintvariov with him, at 3 p.m. he took the carriage to see the Smagins, a hundred miles away in Poltava. Evgenia, exhausted, could not cope; Misha refused to recognize Kolia's agony and went to an annexe to sleep. Aleksandr alone nursed Kolia for two nights. Anton had left no mor-phine, and few medicines. The three local doctors – including two Lintvariov daughters – stayed away.

In a long letter to Pavel (who was not summoned to Sumy that summer), Aleksandr showed himself at his best.

> As I drove up to the manor house I met Anton in the courtyard, then Masha, Vania and Misha came onto the porch. Mama met us in the hall and began kissing her grandchildren. 'Have you seen Kolia?' Vania asked me ... I went into the room and saw that instead of the old Kolia a skeleton was lying there. He was horribly emaciated. His cheeks had sunk, his eyes fallen in and shining ... To the last he didn't know he had TB. Anton hid it from him and he thought he just had typhoid.
>
> 'Brother, stay with me, I'm an orphan without you. I'm alone all the time. Mother, brothers and sister come to see me, but I'm alone.' ... When I lifted him from the bed onto the pot I was always afraid

that I might break his legs . . . The next morning I went crayfishing in the river, not for the crayfish but to get strength for the next night.[48]

Kolia talked of living in Petersburg with Aleksandr and said that he loved his father.

At supper I said 'God grant Kolia lives till morning' . . . Our sister said I was talking rubbish, that Kolia was alive, would go on living, that he often had these attacks. I calmed down . . . Everyone went to bed . . . Kolia was completely rational. He kept going to sleep and waking. At 2 in the morning he wanted to go outside; I tried to lift him onto a wheelchair but he decided to wait and asked me to fluff up his pillows. While I was doing that he burst like a fountain. 'Look, brother, I've shat myself like a baby in bed.' At 3 a.m. he became very bad; he began choking on mucus . . . Around 6 a.m. Kolia started choking. I ran to the annexe to ask Misha what dose to give Kolia. Misha turned over in bed and replied, 'Aleksandr, you keep exaggerating.' . . . I raced back to Kolia. He seemed to be dozing. At 7 a.m. he spoke. 'Aleksandr lift me. Are you asleep?' I lifted him. 'No, I'm better lying.' I laid him down. 'Lift me up a bit.' He offered me both arms. I raised him, he sat up, tried to cough but couldn't. He wanted to vomit. I supported him with one arm and tried to get the pot from the floor with the other. 'Water, water.' But it was too late. I called, shouted 'Mama, Masha, Nata [*Natalia Lintvariova*].' Nobody came to help. They ran in when it was all over. Kolia died in my arms. Mama came very late and I had to wake Misha to tell him that Kolia had died.

TWENTY-EIGHT

Shaking the Dust
June–September 1889

THE DEATH OF KOLIA on 17 June 1889 shook Anton to the core: for years to come he hinted how much he was haunted by it. He knew: last year Anna, this year Kolia, in a year or two Fenichka, Svobodin, and then himself, not to mention a dozen other friends, would die of the 'white plague'. He became restless and could not stay in one place more than a month.

As soon as Kolia died, the family summoned him back to Luka from the Smagins. He wrote to Pleshcheev:

> For the rest of my life I shall never forget that filthy road, the grey sky, the tears on the trees; I say never forget because a ragged peasant came from Mirgorod that morning with a soaking wet telegram: 'Kolia dead.' You can imagine my feelings. I had to gallop back to the station, take the train and wait at stations for eight hours at a time ... I remember sitting in a park; it was dark, terribly cold, hellishly dreary; behind the brown wall where I was sitting actors were rehearsing a melodrama.

The Lintvariovs took charge. Elena led Masha and Evgenia away, while peasant women laid out the body – 'dry as tinder and yellow as wax', Misha noted – on the floor. The church bells rang; the priest and cantor held a requiem. Elena offered money for the burial; Aleksandr found a carpenter to make a cross. Aleksandr's two boys spent the night with their grandmother. Masha was taken in by the Lintvariovs. Three old women from the estate kept vigil over the corpse, while the cantor chanted psalms. At noon the next day a white coffin lined with brocade came from Sumy: Kolia was lifted in. Evgenia, in black, prostrated herself by the coffin. Letters and telegrams were sent off. Misha went to Sumy to find a photographer. That evening Anton returned. Misha flared up at Aleksandr and Natalia, and demanded that they move to separate quarters. After Kolia's death the two brothers loathed each other. Aleksandr wrote a note asking Anton to intervene.

After another vigil with whispering old women and a chanting cantor, a truce reigned. The Lintariovs had Kolia buried in their graveyard, on the hill behind the dacha where he had died. Misha described the funeral to Pavel in Moscow:

> Mother and Masha were sobbing so much that we couldn't bear to look at them. When we took the coffin out Masha and the Lintvariov girls carried the lid, while six of us – Antosha, Vania, Sasha, I, Ivanenko and George Lintvariov carried the coffin. We said a prayer for the dead at each corner of the church. There was a solemn matins, the church was fully lit and everyone held a candle. While matins was said a cross was taken to the cemetery and all the furniture was removed from the house and the floors were scrubbed ... A mass of people followed the coffin, with icons, as in Taganrog: like a procession with the cross. At the cemetery, when we took our leave, everyone was sobbing, mother was in anguish and couldn't be parted from the body ... all the ordinary people in the funeral were issued a pie, a headscarf and a glass of vodka, while the clergy and the Lintariovs had lunch and tea. After dinner mama and I went back to the cemetery, mama grieved, wept, and we went back.[49]

Aleksandr's account to his father adds one detail: 'Everyone is howling. The only one not crying is Anton and that is awful.'[50] Anton refused to weep, perhaps for fear his grief might turn to self-pity. The new cross, with Kolia's name painted by Misha, could be seen for miles around from the north, the west and the south.

Obituaries were printed; Kolia's friends forgot their grudges. Diukovsky, the school inspector, who had loved the Chekhovs from their first Moscow years, declared that Kolia was 'my only friend, the most disinterested and sincere of men'. Franz Schechtel wept for a 'lost brother':

> It's good that he spent his last, perhaps his happiest, days in his family; and, had he not broken with his family for that nomadic life, which drew him so much, he would most probably have been healthy and happy.[51]

Gruzinsky wrote to Ezhov:

199

I'm sad, Hedgehog, sad, as if he were one of my close relatives ...
Peace to the disorderly but talented and dearest of artists ... Poor
Anton![52]

There were requiems and tears in Taganrog. In Moscow Pavel showed
fortitude:

Dear Antosha, At your aunt Fenichka's request I send 10 roubles
belonging to Aleksandr. I read your letter to your aunt, it is very
joyful for my parental heart that Kolia took Last Communion and
that the burial followed Christian rites. I sincerely thank you for the
love which you showed your brother Kolia with respect to the burial
and memorial. For this God will show you much mercy and health.
Fenichka is grieving, groaning and coughing, she hadn't known
about Kolia's death, I hadn't told her. Kolia's obituary is in *News of
the Day* ... I should like to visit Kolia's grave, to look and say a
prayer. May he rest in peace.[53]

Three days later Anton took the family thirty miles to spend a few
days at the monastery of Akhtyrka, where they had, only weeks before,
clowned and laughed with Natalia Lintvariova and Pavel Svobodin,
and Anton had announced himself to the monks as Count Wild-Boar.

When Anton returned to Luka, there were tempting invitations.
He was expected by Grigorovich and the Suvorins in Vienna, for a
tour of Europe. The actor-manager Lensky and his wife Lika Lenskaia
had taken the Moscow Maly theatre on tour to Odessa and invited
Anton to recuperate there. Telling Suvorin he was 'yours to the end
of my days', on 2 July Anton (with Vania) set off not to Europe but in
the opposite direction. Two days later they were dining with Lensky's
actors. A journalist greeted Anton: it was Piotr Sergeenko, a Taganrog
schoolmate, who took Anton to see Odessa's rising star, Ignati Potapenko. Potapenko sang, played the violin, told funny stories and wrote
plays. Four years later Potapenko was to become an *alter ego*, both
genial and sinister, in Anton's life, but now he was 'the god of
boredom'.

The actresses were kindly goddesses. Anton drifted to room 48 in
The Northern Hotel: there Kleopatra Karatygina and Glafira Panova
dispensed tea, chatter, flattery, flirtation and consolation. The only
'older woman' in Chekhov's life, Kleopatra, at forty-one, was neither
sociable nor pretty. Known as 'Beetle', she was the thinnest and most

ill-used actress in the Maly. She knew she would never play Ophelia: she played Death in *Don Juan*. Homeless, widowed young, she understood Anton's unhappiness. Her description of Chekhov that summer has gentle irony as well as motherly concern. She first saw him on the sea-shore:

> A young man, handsome, elegant, a pleasant face, with a small bushy beard; wearing a grey suit, a soft pork-pie hat, a beautiful tie and a shirt with a frilly neckline and cuffs. Overall, an impression of elegance but ... O horror!! he was holding a big one-pound paper bag and nibbling sunflower seeds (a southerner's habit).[54]

'Antony and Cleopatra' were the talk of the town, but Glafira Panova, a pretty debutante of nineteen, also fascinated Anton. To Vania, who had gone back to Luka, he described his ten days in Odessa:

> At 12 I take Panova to Zembrini's for ice cream (60 kopecks) and trail after her to the milliner's, the shops for lace etc. The heat, of course, is unbelievable. At 2 I have been going to Sergeenko's and then to Olga's for borshch and sauce. At 5 tea with Karatygina, which is always very noisy and fun; at 8, after tea, we go to the theatre. Offstage. Treating coughing actresses and planning the next day. Lika Lenskaia alarmed, afraid of spending money; Panova, her black eyes searching for whomever she needs ... After the show, a glass of vodka in the buffet downstairs and then wine in a cellar, waiting for the actresses to gather for tea in Karatygina's room. More tea, we take our time, until 2 in the morning and gossip about the most devilish things ... I'm completely feminized. I've practically been wearing skirts and not a day has passed without virtuous Lika Lenskaia telling me with a meaningful look that Medvedev [*the director*] is afraid of letting Panova go on tour and that Mme Pravdina (also virtuous but a very nasty person) is gossiping to everyone and about her, Lika, for supposedly conniving at sin.

To Anton's horror, the Lenskys, supposing Anton had seduced and compromised Glafira Panova, tried to engineer a marriage between him and the girl, but, Anton insisted years later to Olga Knipper, he 'had not seduced a single soul'. He asked Kleopatra Karatygina in Petersburg in January 1890: 'Why is that Lenskaia poking her nose in where it's not wanted? Actors and artists should never get married. Any artist, writer, actor *loves only their art, is entirely, only absorbed by it.*'

Kleopatra's relations with Chekhov began lightly. Chekhov brought laughter into her life. When she complained about playing skeletons and death, Chekhov gave her a prescription; she was taking it to the chemist's when she saw that it was for 'poison for Pravdin and Grekov', the Maly's lead actors. She fell in love; Anton's friendship was not disinterested. Karatygina had spent half of her life in Siberia, partly as a governess in Kiakhta on the Mongolian border, and she sowed in Anton the seed of an idea. He questioned her about Siberia.

Anton ignored Suvorin's telegrams, although Grigorovich met the train from Russia at Vienna Hauptbahnhof day after day. Grigorovich wrote to Suvorin: 'Chekhov has absolutely no languages and is unused to foreign travel ... he hasn't been treating us like a European ... He's a Slav, disorderly with no firm support to help him control himself ... I'm now angry with him.'[55]

Anton was in fact on a boat to the Crimea. At Luka, meanwhile, he had missed an event. Less than four weeks after Kolia's death, Aleksandr wrote to Pavel:

> Dear Papa, I have kept the promise I made you. Today at 12 I married Natalia Golden. Mama and Misha gave their blessing. Father Mitrofan conducted the wedding. After the wedding we went to Kolia's grave.

Aleksandr's timing is matched by an implausibility in the play which Chekhov was writing: Act 3 of *The Wood Demon* ends with the suicide of Uncle Georges; in Act 4, two weeks later, the cast celebrates marriage. The Chekhovs, teeth gritted, accepted Aleksandr's marriage. Natalia, too, had demanded marriage: since she had arrived as 'children's maid' at Luka, she had found her humiliating status excruciating, even more so perhaps than hearing Anton use her pet-name Natashevu for another Natalia, Natalia Lintvariova. Aleksandr, Natalia and the children left for Petersburg. In Moscow Fenichka had to beg Pavel: 'Natalia asks for 2 roubles, she hasn't got the fare, as soon as they get home she'll send it, she has 50 roubles hidden from Aleksandr.'[56] Not for fifteen years did Aleksandr and Natalia visit their relatives *en famille*. Natalia Golden, no longer a concubine but the wife of a Chekhov, was still a pariah.

On 16 July 1889, reeling from the heavy seas, Anton landed at Yalta. There another three sisters entered his life. With a troupe of actors in Yalta was the widowed Mrs Shavrova and her three daughters, Elena, Olga and Anna. Elena was a precocious fifteen. She accosted Anton in a café; she had written a story 'Sophie', about a Georgian prince's love for her mother. Anton rewrote it for her, making the prince in love with the daughter. Chekhov had opened a school of creative writing – a task he liked, even if the pupil was not a pretty girl. A flirtation started with Elena: a Biblical seven years would pass before she offered Anton her body.

Anton stayed three weeks in the Crimea. When he was not charming the Shavrova girls, he mused aloud to aspiring writers: one, the twenty-four-year-old Ilia Gurliand, noted Chekhov's rules for drama:

> Things on stage should be as complicated and yet as simple as in life. People dine, just dine, while their happiness is made and their lives are smashed. If in Act 1 you have a pistol hanging on the wall, then it must fire in the last act. There's nothing harder than to write a good farce.

Friends at home and abroad were, like Grigorovich, aggrieved; the actor Pavel Svobodin wrote, 'Villain, to drop Rome for Deribasova street in Odessa.'[57] Leikin asked: 'I was flabbergasted, how could you head abroad, not reach the frontier and turn away. What weak will! How could you fail to take a ticket to Vienna . . . I have spent two weeks in Yalta. It is a bandit town.'[58]

By August Anton was sated with women. He told Pleshcheev that they now all seemed ugly, Masha that they all smelt of ice cream. Pavel was writing to Anton c/o the Suvorins in Paris, but Anton did not go abroad. He did not know where Suvorin was, he had no money and he had to write. He had promised Svobodin *The Wood Demon* and *The Northern Herald* a long story. Besides, his unruly father had to be quelled – Pavel was harassing Anna Golden for Kolia's paintings. By 11 August 1889 Anton was back at Sumy, with Misha, Masha and Evgenia. Vania was back in Moscow, where, Pavel reported, Aunt Fenichka had taken a turn for the worse. Kolia's death had broken her heart, and Gavrilov demanded, on pain of dismissal, that her son Aliosha stay in the warehouse. Nobody nursed her.

For a fortnight Anton worked at 'My Name and I', his bleakest and most powerful piece so far, later titled 'A Dreary Story'. Told by a professor of medicine, incurably ill, it surveys life with the despondent wisdom of Solomon. The professor is alienated from the wife he loved, the students who adore him, even the actress to whom an ambiguous affection binds him. He loathes his daughter's music and her fiancé. His disillusion with all things Russian is so wittily expressed, his fear of death so moving that the reader forgives him the torture he inflicts on others. Readers saw parallels with real medical luminaries, or read the story as a retort to Tolstoy's recent *Death of Ivan Ilyich*. The despair implicit in Chekhov's story, however, was the aftermath of Kolia's death. Not yet thirty, Anton felt like his moribund professor.

The play that Anton, at Pavel Svobodin's insistence, struggled to write also centres on an elderly professor. This professor is, however, a nuisance and a pedant, and *The Wood Demon* is hopeful, not despairing, even though a central character, Uncle Georges, kills himself. Only the 'Wood Demon', a highly strung doctor, saving forests from the professor's predation, has any autobiographical input. *The Wood Demon* however is strikingly clumsy and tedious. Anton, inspired by his own thoughts of death, was unable to make a drama out of another person's idyll. His finest prose and most awkward drama arose at the same desk. Death infiltrated other work: revising for Suvorin the story of an unhappy adolescent, 'His First Love', for a new book, Chekhov retitled it *Volodia*. Like Suvorin's Volodia two years before, the fictional Volodia, too, shoots himself dead.[59]

On 3 September 1889 Valentina Ivanova, a schoolteacher who admired Anton and for whom Vania pined, packed the Chekhov bags. At four on a freezing morning, the surviving Chekhovs and Marian Semashko said goodbye to the Lintvariovs. The death of Kolia had brought them close: Aleksandra Lintvariova refused rent for that summer. Anton felt an enduring affection for them: 'If it were acceptable to pray to sacred women and maidens before the heavenly angels take their souls to heaven, I'd long ago have written a psalm to you and your sisters,' he told Elena. The Chekhovs took a slow train for Moscow. In their carriage sat Professor Storozhenko, Masha's examiner. Chekhov made Masha's embarrassment worse: 'I talked loudly about working as a cook for Countess Keller and what nice masters I had; before I took a drink I bowed to mother and said I hoped she'd find a good position in Moscow. Semashko pretended to be a valet.' In November 1889 Chekhov would tell Suvorin, and his play would prove it, 'I have it in for professors.'[60]

IV

Années de Pèlerinage

I sometimes feel now it is just possible that, setting off on his journeys, he was not looking for something so much as running away from something . . .

V. Nabokov, *The Gift*

TWENTY-NINE

Exorcizing the Demon
October–December 1889

IN MOSCOW Kleopatra Karatygina awaited Anton: she had left the Maly theatre and was looking for a new company. Her letter of 13 September sets the tone: 'Hellishly elegant writer! . . . Dear man, for old time's sake come and see me and don't forget to bring the photo you promised.'[1] In November a grateful Elena Shavrova arrived in Moscow: Suvorin had printed her story, 'Sophie'. Her mother wrote to Anton 'If you remember your Yalta friends, come and see us: the Slav Bazaar No. 94.'[2] By December the Shavrovas were living on the Volkhonka, only twenty minutes from the Chekhovs. Anton deputed Misha to see Elena. Olga Kundasova frequented the Chekhov household: she was teaching Masha English; she later tried to teach Anton French. The house resounded with loud female voices: Olga Kundasova laid down the law, Natalia Lintvariova stayed three weeks in November, infecting Anton with her laughter. A piano teacher, Aleksandra Pokhlebina, nicknamed 'Vermicelli', was an inconspicuous visitor, nursing a passion for Anton that later exploded into paranoia.

A new woman entered Anton's life. She was, like Masha, a Guerrier student teaching at the Rzhevskaia girls' school. She was Lidia Mizinova: the Chekhovs called her Lika, after the actress Lidia (Lika) Lenskaia. Only nineteen when Masha introduced her, Lika is best described by the writer and familiar of the Chekhovs, Tatiana Shchepkina-Kupernik, a connoisseur of female beauty:

> A real Swan Princess from the Russian fairy tale. Her ash-blonde flowing locks, her wonderful grey eyes and 'sable' eyebrows, her extraordinary softness and elusive charm, combined with total absence of affectation and an almost severe simplicity, made her spellbinding.

Masha recalled:

People could not take their eyes off her. My girl friends often stopped me and asked, 'Chekhova, tell me, who is that beauty with you?' . . . Lika was always very shy. She huddled against the hat stand and half-covered her face in the collar of her fur coat. But Misha managed to get a look. He entered Anton's study and said, 'Listen, Anton, there's a really pretty girl come to see Masha! She's in the hall.'

Lika was of genteel family: her mother was a concert pianist, Lidia Iurgeneva, but her father had deserted the family when she was only three. Lika was brought up by a great-aunt, Sofia Ioganson, 'Granny'. She was not content to be a teacher. She wanted to be an actress, but inveterate stage fright frustrated her. Her charm and wit were undermined by an inability to protect her interests, which made her vulnerable to ruthless men. Eighteen months earlier, she had written Anton a heart-felt anonymous fan letter.

No woman yet affected Anton as much as another visitor, Piotr Tchaikovsky. Tchaikovsky had loved Chekhov's prose (and Chekhov his music) for two years. He called on 14 October 1889: they agreed to collaborate on an opera, *Bela*, about the abduction of a Circassian princess by a Russian officer, based on part of Lermontov's *A Hero of our Time*. Anton gave Tchaikovsky his books, inscribing his latest collection, entitled simply *Stories*, 'from your future librettist'. Tchaikovsky responded with a photograph 'from your ardent admirer.' When the composer left, he forgot his cigarette case: Semashko the cellist, Ivanenko the flautist and Vania the schoolteacher each took a cigarette and solemnly smoked it before letting Anton post the case back. Tchaikovsky responded by sending a season ticket to the Russian Musical Society's symphonic concerts in Moscow, a ticket which Masha used. Anton dedicated his new collection of stories *Sullen People* to Tchaikovsky. Literary friends were bemused. Gruzinsky grumbled to Ezhov: 'Why should Chekhov dedicate a book to Tchaikovsky? He ought to dedicate it to Suvorin, oughtn't he?'[3]

Suvorin had forgiven Anton his failure to meet in Vienna. Others had not. Grigorovich was telling the Suvorins that there were now better writers, and that Anton had libelled the Suvorins in *The Wood Demon*. Anton blustered:

You're not in the play and can't be, although Grigorovich with his usual insight sees the opposite. The play is about a bore, egotistical, wooden, lecturing on art for 25 years . . . For God's sake don't believe these gentlemen who ... ascribe to others their personal foxy and badgery features. Oh how glad that Grigorovich is! And how pleased they'd be if I'd put arsenic in your tea or turned out to be a secret police spy.

Grigorovich never quite forgave Anton for all the trains he had met in vain. Anna Suvorina, however, on 12 November 1889 accepted Anton's apology: 'I know, and they say, you're in love again. Is it true or not? That was the only explanation I had for your botched journey abroad and the only reason I forgave your *bad manners*. O how furious I was with you!'⁴ Anna, unlike Suvorin, was amused to see her family in the play.

In November 1889 *The Northern Herald* saved itself from extinction by printing Chekhov's 'A Dreary Story'. The work made a tremendous impact. Chekhov had found a voice and a viewpoint in his disillusioned professor of medicine: the existentialism of a man dying in a world from which he is totally alienated seemed a generation ahead of Tolstoy. The Petersburg Professor of Medicine, Botkin, died of liver cancer that winter, and Chekhov's work seemed prophetic. Even Leikin conceded: 'Charming. It is your best piece.' Anton proudly inscribed a copy to the playwright Prince Sumbatov:

> From a successful author who's
> Managed to combine and fuse
> A soul at peace, a mind on fire,
> The enema tube and poet's lyre.

The Wood Demon was, however, to be widely deplored. All autumn Pavel Svobodin pestered Anton to complete it by the end of October for his benefit performance in Petersburg. His letters to Anton that autumn are frantic:

> I'm superstitious and afraid of November every year, that's the month for disasters in my life (I was married on 12 November 1873) and therefore ... in November – it's better to have no play at all ...
> I hope you were lying when you said you'd thrown two acts of *The Wood Demon* into the Psiol ... God forbid!!!
> We really have to spend two weeks living together, or at least see each other every day – and the Wood Demon would sprout. You would go fully armed after him into the forest and I would part the thorny branches in your path, clear the trail and the two of us would

find him and drag him out . . . for the sake of God who created the Psiol, write, Antoine!

Svobodin set his benefit night for 31 October. In mid October Svobodin took a train to Moscow, grabbed the script and went back; his family copied out the play to submit to the Theatrical-Literary Committee of the Aleksandrinsky Theatre.

On 9 October Svobodin read the play to the committee, which included one man disillusioned with Anton, Grigorovich. The committee rejected *The Wood Demon*, not simply because Grigorovich was hostile. They were unhappy on many counts: a university professor was vilified, in a country where professors had the rank of general (within living memory a student had been flogged to death for assaulting a Moscow professor). They also wanted a 'safe' play, for the heir to the throne was to attend Svobodin's benefit performance, and *The Wood Demon* was unorthodox, undramatic, and obscure.

Svobodin cancelled his benefit night, telling the editor Vukol Lavrov that *The Wood Demon* might be 'boring, drawn-out, strange', but was worth double the hackneyed vulgarities the Aleksandrinsky audiences preferred.[5] He begged Anton:

> Dear friend, go to your 22-rouble wash-stand, have a wash and a think, couldn't something be done with *The Wood Demon* so that it appeals not just to me and Suvorin . . . but to those who advised you to burn it?

Svobodin dared to be frank. Suvorin's comments are not on record. The actor Lensky was brutal:

> I'll say one thing: write stories. Your attitude to the stage and to dramatic form is too contemptuous, you respect them too little to write drama . . .

Pleshcheev, the following spring, delivered judgement:

> This is the first piece by you that has left no impression on me . . . As for Voinitsky, strike me dead, I can't understand why he shot himself.

Anton felt he might as well take 500 roubles advance from the Abramova troupe in Moscow. They hurriedly rehearsed. The male actors did not know their parts, the women couldn't act. At the première on 27 November 1889 the audience booed. A claque from Korsh's theatre wolf-whistled to punish the breakaway author and actors. The reviewers were scathing: 'boring', 'pointless', 'clumsily constructed'. Chekhov withdrew his play and refused to print it, though 110 lithographed copies were circulating in the provinces. Seven years would pass before, by a mixture of alchemy and surgery, he transmuted *The Wood Demon* into *Uncle Vania*.

Anton had expected to live for three to four months off *The Wood Demon*, and was now in financial straits. He had only one other publication of any significance that autumn: 'Ordinary People', later the first half of 'The Literature Teacher'. A schoolteacher in a dead provincial town, seduced by the prospects of wealth, decides to marry one of his ex-pupils. Allusions to real figures link the story to Chekhov's stay with the Suvorins and their children in the Crimea in summer 1888, and to the offer of little Nastia as a bride: the story is a coded 'no, thanks' to Suvorin[6] (who without comment printed it in *New Times*). *The Northern Herald* took time to pay for 'A Dreary Story'. The sales of three books of stories, constantly reissued by Suvorin, and the 'pension' from *Ivanov* and the farces Anton had written, kept the Chekhovs solvent.

Family life seemed to settle: Aleksandr in Petersburg was married and sober; Vania lived in his schoolhouse with Pavel; Misha was with the Suvorins in Petersburg and soon to leave home. Aunt Fenichka was meekly dying. Of Kolia only debts remained: his paintings vanished into his creditors' hands. Anton and his brothers agreed to pay off the monetary debts. There were other liabilities: Anna Ipatieva-Golden, as Kolia's common-law widow, wrote on 30 November 1889:

> There's not a soul in Moscow I could turn to, I can't ask my family, they're all (except for Natasha) virtually dying of hunger. The fact is I am stuck even now *in the country* at Razumovskoe with no firewood, no fur coat and so I appeal to you, for Christ's sake, send me 15 roubles.[7]

Anton gave her money, and asked Suvorin to give her work. The Suvorins, however, demanded a hefty deposit from those employed in their bookshops: Anna was unemployable. After another hand-out she resumed her old job as companion to unmarried mothers and landlady to students. Anna's gratitude was effusive: 'I wept with gratitude, that is from feeling your kindness to the point of tears. And I'd never thought you were like that.'

Anton began an affair with Kleopatra Karatygina. He took her, at her request, to see *Les Huguenots*, and prescribed her laxatives. Never did he bring her home or mention her. He also saw Glafira Panova, sometimes at the same address and time as Karatygina. She was clearly in his mind when he wrote to his editor, Evreinova, at *The Northern Herald* and mused about settling down 'with a nice little actress', or to Suvorin, for whom he drew Glafira's foot: 'I have known actresses who used to be ballerinas. Yesterday, before a stag night, I visited one such actress. She now despises ballet and looks down on it, but she can't get rid of her ballet body movements.'

Writing to Elena Lintvariova, Anton laughed at commitment: he signed himself 'A. Panov', to make fun of the rumours that he was to marry Glafira Panova. Kleopatra had agreed to humiliating conditions from her 'hellishly elegant writer': she was not to talk about the relationship in case Anton's mother and sister found out. Glafira had more pride, Kleopatra wrote:

> Glafira is with me . . . She asks me to tell you that if you grudge 20 kopecks, she takes on the travel costs . . . everything she would like to throw at our bosses will be thrown at you. Although, as she says, you will get what you deserve. In a word, you are going to be bawled out, she doesn't care that you're a fashionable writer and hellishly elegant. So if you wish to make up for your *negligence* towards her come and fetch me (if you're not embarrassed to drive down the street with an actress nobody wants) . . . You are ordered to come on Monday from 12 to 2. You are to have your hair curled and to put on a pink tie.

Glafira left for Petersburg. Karatygina followed, clutching letters of recommendation and a copy of 'A Dreary Story' (a work she loathed for its portrayal of acting as moral perdition) inscribed 'For the famous actress K. K.'s bloody nerves, from her doctor'. About this time Anton confided in Vladimir Nemirovich-Danchenko that he had seduced a married woman and found her to be a virgin. (He also told the playwright that none of his affairs had lasted more than a year.)[8]

Anton hated being a 'fashionable writer': when an admirer in a restaurant started to recite a page by heart, he hissed at his companion, 'Take her away, I have a knuckle-duster in my pocket.' He felt ill all autumn: he told Dr Obolonsky that he had 'flu, Mesopotamian plague, sap, hydrophobia, impotence and all sorts of typhoids'. At his desk Anton was as paralysed as his professor of medicine. Instead of picking up the discarded novel, he encouraged Suvorin to send him unsolicited manuscripts to sift. Some of the beneficiaries were the young men and women who had accosted him in the Crimea. Ilia Gurliand had his story of a civil servant 'Gorshkov' polished and published. Anton took Elena Shavrova's next story, 'The Chorus Girl', about a girl seduced and abandoned by an actor who has another mistress. Anton recognized the protagonists. He told Suvorin:

> I've made the middle of 'The Chorus Girl' the beginning, the beginning the middle, and I've put on a totally new ending. When the girl reads it she'll be horrified. And mummy will give her a thrashing for an immoral ending ... The girl is trying to portray an operetta troupe that was singing this summer in Yalta ... I used to know chorus girls. I remember a 19-year-old whom I treated and who flirted splendidly with her legs. For the first time I noted their skill at demonstrating the beauty of thighs without undressing or kicking up their legs ... Chorus girls felt awful; they went hungry, whored out of poverty, it was hot, stifling, people smelt of sweat, like horses. If even an innocent girl had noticed and described that, then you can judge their position ...

On literature Chekhov sounded as embittered as his dying professor in 'A Dreary Story' or his neurotic *The Wood Demon*. On 27 December 1889 he berated the intelligentsia to Suvorin:

> The best modern writers, whom I love, serve evil, since they destroy. Some of them, like Tolstoy, say 'Don't have sex with women, because they have mucous discharges; woman is revolting because her breath smells.' ... these writers ... help the devil multiply the slugs and woodlice we call intellectuals. Jaded, apathetic, idly philosophizing, a cold intelligentsia, which ... is unpatriotic, miserable, colourless, which gets drunk on one glass and visits 50-kopeck brothels.

Anton defended only medical science:

> A society that doesn't believe in God but is afraid of omens and the devil, which denies *all* doctors and then hypocritically mourns Botkin

and bows down to [*Professor of Medicine*] Zakharin, should not dare hint that it knows what justice is.

Suvorin realized what was coming: Anton was abandoning Literature his mistress for Medicine his wife.

THIRTY

Arming for the Crusade
December 1889–April 1890

BY THE END OF 1889 Anton had resolved to make a long journey – from which he thought he might not return – over Siberia to the edge of the Russian empire, the island of Sakhalin, Russia's grimmest penal colony. His family and friends had hints – his ardent obituary of the explorer of Central Asia, Nikolai Przhevalsky; his reading of Misha's old law-lecture notes, geography textbooks, maps, political journalism; contact with administrators of Siberia's prison empire. Ever since childhood Anton had been an avid reader of explorers' biographies and geographers' descriptions. Now, shaken by Kolia's death, he was seeking to emulate Przhevalsky's heroic exploits. After *The Wood Demon*, the writer felt humiliated, and the doctor-scientist in his personality took the lead. Not for the last time, Anton's entangled love life made the life of a solitary wanderer seem particularly alluring to him.

After the first performance of *The Wood Demon* friends expected Chekhov to flee, as he had after both premières of *Ivanov*, to the other capital city, but Anton put off his New Year visit to Petersburg. The Suvorins drank Anton's health in his absence. He had fled to the Kiseliovs at Babkino. He composed for Maria Kiseliova an opening line of a story 'On such and such a date hunters wounded a young female elk in the Daragan forest' and left the rest for her to write. Anton, however, had an ulterior motive for going back to Babkino: he needed to talk to Maria's brother-in-law, a Senator Golubev, who could get him a berth on a ship that returned via China and India from Sakhalin to Odessa. In exchange for the Kiseliovs' help he agreed to examine Maria's father who was dying in Petersburg.

Around 4 January 1890, Chekhov took horses from Babkino and rejoined the railway north: he went to Petersburg with Maria Kiseliova and her younger daughter. In Petersburg, too he had business: he wanted to ask the Department of Taxes to give his brother Misha a job, and Kleopatra Karatygina asked him to persuade Suvorin to give her work. Above all, he needed official support for his journey to Sakhalin.

Anton spent a month lobbying in the city. Suvorin's name opened the doors of ministries and the prison administration, but Suvorin disapproved of Chekhov's journey: it was hazardous, and would take his closest friend away for a year. Chekhov saw the director of prisons, Galkin-Vraskoi, who, when Anton undertook to review his report, promised that Siberia's prison gates would be opened to Chekhov (and then sent a secret telegram to ensure the opposite). Suvorin gave Anton a newspaper correspondent's card.

Chekhov's plans were praised in the newspapers. Many Russian writers had made involuntary, often one-way, journeys to Siberia; none had undertaken voluntary exploration. This journey to the heart of evil was a Dantean exploit that rehabilitated Chekhov in radical eyes. They hoped Chekhov would discover on Sakhalin a set of coherent 'ideals'. Perhaps Anton's main reason for making this suicidal journey was to silence accusations that he was indifferent to the suffering he portrayed. The Russian Zolas – Korolenko and Ertel – withdrew their strictures. The animals in the literary zoo were envious of Chekhov's limelight; some of them were even glad that he would be out of the way for the rest of the year. From Petersburg Gruzinsky wrote to Ezhov (in Moscow playing whist with Vania and Misha): 'It's excellent that Chekhov is going; Sakhalin is not the point, the point is travelling the great oceans and meeting prisoners.' The right wing, however, sneered: before Anton set off, Burenin wrote:

> The talented writer Chekhov
> To distant Sakhalin trekked off.
> He searched its grim quarries
> For ideas for stories,
> But finding there a total lack,
> Took the earliest steamboat back.
> Inspiration, says this fable,
> Lies beneath the kitchen table.

Obsessed with his expedition, Anton lost interest in his elder brother. When Suvorin asked, Anton demurred:

I don't know what to do with Aleksandr. It's not just that he drinks. That would be all right, but he is inextricably stuck in surroundings where it is literally impossible not to drink. Between us: his spouse also drinks. Grey, nasty, gloomy . . . And that man since he was 14, practically, has wanted to marry. All his life he's been marrying and swearing that he'll never marry again.

Anton alternated hard work with frivolity. He read everything about Siberia. Suvorin had a collection of forbidden books, which included pamphlets on political prisoners, as well as Tolstoy's diatribe against sex and marriage, *The Kreutzer Sonata* – a book it was hard to ban, since Tsar Alexander III had liked it. Anton went to Shcheglov's name-day party; he went with the Suvorins and their Trésor to the Petersburg Dog Show. Shcheglov was exhausted by the parties until three or four in the morning. Anton had surreptitious encounters with Kleopatra Karatygina. He channelled her energy into making notes on Siberia and Sakhalin, some from the Public Library, some from her own experience. She gave him lists of friends to tap for hospitality; she taught him Siberian etiquette – never ask why anyone is in Siberia; she gave him the dates for navigation on Siberia's rivers; for his birthday she made him a travelling pillow – 'for when you're sick on the boat'. In return she wanted affection. Her weapon was Anton's anxiety not to be found out: 'Where did I put the letter to you? Which envelope did I put it in? . . . The letter to my sister!'[9] When Anton's family did find out, Kleopatra denied responsibility: 'If your mama and sister find out your *secret d'un polichinelle* of course it isn't my fault. You did ask me not to blurt things out in Moscow.' Like Olga Kundasova, Kleopatra resigned herself to being unloved. She wrote dozens of notes, some in doggerel, some reproachful. She touched Chekhov for loans that she never repaid. She hoped that his dream of 'a room to share with Lika Mizinova' would prove a curse.

Anton and Suvorin clung to one another: they travelled back to Moscow together, and Suvorin took a room in the Slav Bazaar. They discussed illness, real and imaginary. One night they watched Racine's *Phèdre*; the next they went to the Literary Society's fancy dress ball; the following night they dined with Grigorovich, and healed the breach between him and Chekhov. As Anton recuperated from his 'Sakhalin fever', his women, and libraries, he summed up his Petersburg month to Pleshcheev: 'I think of the sins I have committed, of the thousand barrels of wine I have drunk . . . In one month in Petersburg I committed so many great and petty deeds that I should be both promoted to general and hanged.'

The Suvorins left. Anton lacked congenial company. Levitan was in Paris, from where he complained of 'psychopathic' impressionists and women 'overworked by centuries of screwing'.[10] Anton studied atlases, ancient and modern, and dreamed of river boats. 'I feel like crossing 12 or 18 months out of my life,' he told one journalist. He wrote just one story for *New Times*: 'Devils', later 'Thieves', portrays a nest of horse thieves in the steppes. Suvorin was upset that Chekhov romanticized criminals. Anton just edited Suvorin's unsolicited manuscripts, and compiled a geographical introduction to a future book on Sakhalin. In Moscow he sent Masha, Olga Kundasova and Lika Mizinova to the Rumiantsev Museum (now the Russian State Library) to copy what he had marked about Sakhalin and Siberia in hundreds of journals and books. From Petersburg, from Aleksandr and from Kleopatra, came facts, opinions and pleas. Karatygina reverted to a motherly style:

> Forgive me for poking my Roman Catholic profile where I shouldn't, but I am awfully reluctant to have you in my Siberian kingdom playing the part of a hopeless floating point (out of boredom and ignorance) and therefore I have taken it on myself, my bold child, without your knowledge, to get for you letters of recommendation.

Anton was deeply upset that February by a reminder of Kolia's death:

> Ezhov was sitting at the table crying: his young wife is ill with consumption. He has to take her south quickly. I asked him if he had money, he said yes. He spoilt my mood with his tears. He reminded me of certain things, and anyway I'm sorry for him.

Of the many forces that pursued Chekhov to the Hades of Sakhalin, 'certain things' – i.e. Kolia's ghost – were the most persistent, if not the avowed motives.

From intimations of mortality Anton was rescued by Lika Mizinova. She and Anton began to exert a pull on each other. Granny Sofia's diary traces day by day Lika falling in thrall:

> 5 March. Monday. Lika at 8 p.m. went to the Chekhovs, she came back at 3 a.m., very pleased that she had been there . . .

218

10 March. Saturday. Lidia [*Lika's mother*] is writing ... advice for Lika, to bring her to her senses, to pull her back from an idle, disorientated life, she is never home and every night comes back late; she doesn't like the house or home life. This upsets us terribly, especially her mother, and it's impossible to talk to her, she starts yelling immediately and it ends with her walking out angry with family life, saying that it's hell, not life.

13 March. Tuesday. Lika has been out and about until 2 a.m., she went to the Rumiantsev museum to make notes about Sakhalin island ...

28 March. Wednesday. I happened to make the acquaintance of the mother of Maria Chekhova, Lika and I met her in the arcade, very nice, simple manners, we were introduced and had a chat there and then.

29 March. Thursday. Lika was to go to All Night Vigil at some nunnery with her girl friends. She deceived us! She went with the Chekhovs and came back at 1.30 a.m.

31 March. Saturday. The brazen Kundasova appeared to ask us to let Lika come to the Chekhovs, to which Lidia [*her mother*] said that we had a long-standing custom of a family Easter at home ...

5 April. Thursday ... We liked Anton very much – he's a doctor and a writer, such a nice personality, simple manners, considerate ...

21 April. Saturday. Today, finally, Anton Chekhov is setting off. So Lika will have some rest. At 1 Anton came to say goodbye. His family and many friends, among them Olga Kundasova, she really is infatuated, are off to the station at 7 to see him off. He spent half an hour with us and set off with Lika ... I'm afraid, is our Lika involved with him? It looks very like it ... But he's a fine man, an alluring personality.[11]

Anton was swamped with affection on the eve of his departure. He told Suvorin 'such girls that if I rounded them all up to my country cottage I'd have a really wild ball, pregnant with consequences.'

It was easier to part with his brothers and men friends: he promised to bring back Manila cigars and ivory carvings of naked Japanese girls. Shcheglov, Ezhov and Gruzinsky lauded Anton's courage. Pavel Svobodin declared that he would be called Chekhov of Sakhalin. Anton fobbed off Misha, who fancied meeting in Japan and returning to Russia together. Lily Markova's husband, Sakharov, asked to be the expedition's artist (for a fee of 1000 roubles): the husband of an ex-mistress was no travelling companion for Anton in Siberia: he begged Suvorin to put Sakharov off the idea.

Suvorin could not see the point of the crusade, of expense, suffering and wasted time. To him Anton addressed a fiery missive:

> You write that Sakhalin is of no use, no interest to anyone. Can that be true? Sakhalin can be useless and uninteresting only to a society that does not exile thousands of people there and spend millions on it. After Australia in the past and Cayenne, Sakhalin is the only place where criminal colonization can be studied ... Sakhalin is a place of the most unendurable sufferings free or enslaved man can endure ... I'd say that places like Sakhalin should be visited for homage, as Turks go to Mecca ... We have rotted alive millions of people, rotted them for nothing, without thinking, barbarically; we have herded people through the cold in fetters tens of thousands of miles, infected them with syphilis, debauched them, bred criminals and blamed all this on red-nosed prison warders. All educated Europe now knows that it's not the warders but all of us that are guilty, but we don't care, we're not interested.

Rarely had Anton been so emotionally stoked up. He felt mortally insulted by a reviewer's phrase 'priests of unprincipled writing like Mr Chekhov' in the March issue of the radical monthly *Russian Thought*, and raged to Vukol Lavrov, its editor:

> I would not reply even to slander were it not that I am soon leaving Russia for a long time, perhaps never to return, and I have not the strength to refrain from replying ... After your accusation not only are business relations but the most ordinary nodding acquaintance between us is impossible.

Had Chekhov perished on Sakhalin, *Russian Thought* would have been blamed, as Burenin was blamed for killing Nadson. It was to take two years' diplomacy by Pavel Svobodin to undo the damage done to Chekhov and to *Russian Thought* by a careless remark and Anton's pride. Anton left in high dudgeon and high spirits.

On 21 April, fortified by three glasses of Santurini wine from Dr Korneev, he took the train to Iaroslavl. Here he took a river boat down the Volga and up the Kama into the Urals. He left his mother Masha and Lika weeping at the station. (He had told them he would be back in September, knowing well that he would be away until December.) Lika was left a photograph inscribed: 'To the kindly creature I am running from to Sakhalin and who scratched my nose ... P.S. This inscription, like an exchange of cards, obliges me to nothing.'

Chekhov dropped hints in Siberia that he and Lika were betrothed.

Friends travelled with Anton the first thirty miles to the St Sergei monastery: his brother Vania, the Levitan *ménage à trois* – the mistress Sofia Kuvshinnikova and her husband Dr Kuvshinnikov (who gave Anton a bottle of cognac to open on the Pacific Ocean). Olga Kundasova stayed on the train as far as Iaroslavl and accompanied Anton down the Volga. Next day, when they had passed Kineshma, she disembarked.

Anton was at last truly alone, travelling into unknown territory.

THIRTY-ONE

Crossing Siberia
22 April–June 1890

STEAMING DOWN THE VOLGA to Nizhni and up the Kama to Perm, his stomach churning from the farewell, Chekhov wrote greetings to friends and instructions to family. At Perm the river journey ended; here, on the slopes of the Urals, heavy rain turned the snow to mud. Chekhov arrived at Perm at 2.00 a.m.; the train across the Urals left at six in the evening. A 200-mile train journey took all night to Ekaterinburg. Here Anton had the addresses of his mother's relatives. One visited Anton in the American Hotel, but did not invite him to dine.

Anton stayed three days in Ekaterinburg reconnoitring. The railhead ended another 200 miles east at Tiumen. America had been joined coast-to-coast for twenty years; Russia had no Trans-Siberian railway. From Tiumen Chekhov hoped to spare himself 1000 miles overland through blizzards and floods to Tomsk: ships went down the Tobol and the Irtysh and then upstream, southeast up the Ob and the Tom, to Tomsk, from where travellers had to go overland. Siberia's major rivers flow from south to north, and travellers head from west to east. The great Siberian road was a rutted belt of mud, snow or dust (depending on the season), interrupted by ferry crossings over wide, dangerous rivers. Prisoners and exiles and the crude birch-pole carts (*tarantasy*) of officials and carters were the traffic.

To reach the Russian Far East – Vladivostok, Kamchatka or Sakhalin – by sea a Voluntary Fleet had been launched by public subscription. Anton, in Nikolai Przhevalsky's footsteps, was crossing the hard way. Arriving in Ekaterinburg on 28 April, he was told that until 18 May no passenger ships could leave Tiumen: ice obstructed the Tobol, but the Irtysh had already melted and flooded for miles. He had left two weeks too early or four weeks too late. Nevertheless, on 1 May Chekhov took the train, pursued by furious blizzards, to Tiumen. Here he bought a cart, and hired horses to Tomsk.

Anton kept a pencilled diary. He wrote few letters: he was too bruised and exhausted, wet and cold, and the post to Russia took weeks. He was also ill-equipped. Misha had bought him a wooden trunk which crashed about the cart as it bumped over the ruts and lumps of ice and nearly brained him. Others had soft leather bags as mattresses to sleep on or cushions to brace against. Only the thick leather coat that Aleksei Kiseliov had provided protected Anton's body from hypothermia and broken bones when he was flung from the cart. The revolver he had brought he never even drew. Though Siberia was full of prisoners, escaped and settled, its lonely roadhouses were cleaner and friendlier than European Russia's inns. He starved. On Russia's rivers he gorged himself on sterlets. In Siberia, in spring, there was only bread, wild garlic and coarse powdered tea. Evgenia had given Anton a portable coffee stove and coffee: it took him three weeks to learn how to brew up.

On 7 May, paying his drivers double or treble the standard tariff, he reached the shores of the Irtysh, 450 miles in four days by cart from Tiumen. He was now stranded: the roads were so flooded that he could not turn back, and the winds so furious that the ferryman would not row across. He wrote not to his mother, who feared for his life, but to Maria Kiseliova, who had in her letters been hinting for years that suffering would do him good:

> A second troika, also at top speed; we veer right, it veers left. 'We're colliding' flashes in my head. One instant and a crashing sound, the horses entangle in a black mass, my cart is on its rear, I tumble to the ground all my suitcases and bundles on top of me. I leap up and see a third troika. My mother must have been praying for me last night. If I had been asleep or the third troika had come straight after the second I'd have been crushed to death or crippled ... I feel a complete loneliness that I have never known before.

It took a week to reach Tomsk: this time the flooded Tom held him up. It was the coldest May in Siberia for almost forty years. Not a leaf on the birches, not a blade of grass on the ground, and three inches of snow. Only flocks of geese and ducks heralded spring. At Tomsk Anton recuperated for a week. He wrote at length to his family: there were no murders in Siberia; men did not beat their wives;

'even' the Jews and Poles were decent farmers; the beds were soft, the rooms were clean. The bread and the salty soup of half-cooked duck innards, however, unsettled Anton's stomach.

Anton mentioned the crash that nearly killed him. He told 'sweet Misha' it was as well he had declined his offer of company. In Tomsk, before the even worse overland stage – 1100 miles to Irkutsk – he ordered a wickerwork superstructure for his cart. The streets were swamped with mud; there was only one bathhouse. Chekhov was the first traveller of the season, and in central Siberia travellers on pleasure were objects of curiosity and hospitality. Sitting in his hotel room, writing to Suvorin, Anton was interrupted by a man in uniform with long moustaches, Arshaulov, police chief of Tomsk. They got talking: the police chief ordered vodka. Anton read Arshaulov's literary efforts and wrote him a letter of recommendation to Suvorin.

Arshaulov took Anton around the brothels of Tomsk. They got back to the hotel at two in the morning. The experience had not been gratifying: 'Tomsk is a boring, drunken town; no beautiful women at all, Asiatic lawlessness. The only notable thing about this town is that governors die.' For the return journey travellers in Tomsk advised an American boat via San Francisco and New York, rather than the austerity of the Russian Voluntary Fleet.

On 21 May Anton left Tomsk, in company. Three army officers – two lieutenants and a military doctor – travelling east by sledge on official business offered to share expenses with Anton. They were rough, sometimes obnoxious company, but they gave the novice traveller confidence. One of them, Lieutenant von Schmidt, had been sent to Siberia (where he was to have a successful career) for beating up his batman. Garrulous and abusive, he may have inspired some of the features of Lieutenant Soliony in *Three Sisters* – the most Siberian of Chekhov's plays. Von Schmidt took to Anton (and later wrote him an apologetic letter): he suggested Anton find himself female company:

> 'I can't,' he [*Chekhov*] said, 'I have a bride in Moscow.' Then after a short silence he added in an odd voice, as if thinking aloud: 'Only I doubt if I'll be happy with her – she's too beautiful.'[12]

Lika was on Anton's mind. He was to tell his host on Sakhalin, Bulgarevich, that he planned to marry. His letters to Lika constantly invent little tasks for her, he enquires after her admirers, he teases her by proxy. But Lika, or as Anton now called her *Jamais*, did not write. She was being escorted by the flautist Ivanenko and by Anton's younger brothers – none of whom Anton took seriously enough to feel jealousy. Through the Chekhovs, however, Lika knew Sofia Kuvshinnikova and her lover, Levitan. Of all Chekhov's circle Levitan was the most irresistible womanizer, and gave Anton cause to fear for Lika's fidelity.

The Chekhov family scattered all over Russia as soon as Anton was away. It was as if in Anton they had lost their centre of gravity. School ended in May: Masha and her mother stayed with the Lintvariovs, taking a wreath for Kolia's grave. Misha went with them but the very next day left for Taganrog. After his return to Luka, Masha would venture with Natalia Lintvariova for a month in the Crimea. Pavel too was on the move, to stay with Aleksandr's family in Petersburg and even to travel with Aleksandr to Finland.

The Chekhov family had shrunk to just Masha, Anton and their parents. Neither parent was sure that Anton would return. The 'chest of drawers' house seemed absurdly large, and the family surrendered the tenancy: they would look for new quarters in September. Vania had, again by bad luck, lost his job, and could find a post only in the peat bogs of Vladimir province, 150 miles from Moscow. Misha from September would be a tax inspector 200 miles south of Moscow. Aunt Fenichka was only just alive.

Ivanenko wrote to Anton at the end of May: his letter reached Sakhalin months later, so that Anton did not realize how badly his family coped without him. Masha and Evgenia fell ill with distress.[13]

The move to the country was joyless. Masha found herself in love with George Lintvariov and her feelings unreciprocated. Worse, Misha had quarrelled with the Lintvariovs. Masha, nevertheless, had to stay there all May.[14]

By the end of May, when Misha had returned from Taganrog, Masha set off with her friend 'Natashevu' Lintvariova for a happy month, free of parents and brothers, in the Crimea. On 20 June she wrote to Pavel: 'Thanks to Antosha, I'm very happy to be in such a wonderful fairy tale place. I had a telegram from Irkutsk asking me not to grudge the money, that he's well and rich. Thanks to him I have many friends in Yalta.'

Others were unhappy. Vania was angry that Misha had abandoned Evgenia for Taganrog, and he reported to Masha on Lika:

> She is obeying her mama and stays home, not leaving the house after six. Amazing ... Things are bad with her, she has no job ... I want to drag Lika off to the Sparrow Hills, but doubt she will submit: she is awfully obstinate. Kuvshinnikova left with Levitan 4 days ago for the Volga.

Lika had given up her dreams of being an actress and singer. She was shortly to take up work as a clerk in Moscow's town council offices.

Far worse, however, was the plight of Ezhov. He wrote on 10 June:

> My wife Liudia died on 3 June at 4.30 a.m. I don't know where you are, Anton, but I'm in the cold tundra and there's not a spark of hope of my life being happy or making sense. Liudia loved me like nobody else. My tiny successes were happiness for her. On the evening before she died her face was worn out with disease, and she never took her loving eyes off me as if asking, 'Save me, save me!'

Letters reached Anton too slowly to be worth answering and he stoically accepted his inability to help or console his correspondents. The telegraph linked Europe and Siberia, but the Chekhovs were too thrifty to send telegrams, however much Anton begged them to do so. (He was sparing himself, however, the expense of telegrams.) Anna Suvorina telegraphed to the river boat Anton was catching in eastern Siberia, discreetly but flirtatiously encoding Anton as Mikita and herself as Marina:

> HUSBAND ODESSA WHAT CAN I SAY GLAD YOUR SUCCESS GRIEVE YOU NOT HERE WHO PROMISED WRITE GOD HELP YOU MIKITA NO HAPPINESS FOR YOU MARINA.

After 400 miles Anton reached the banks of the Yenisei. At Krasnoyarsk, mountainous forests replaced the desolation of the Siberian plains. The road was atrocious: hemmed in by hills, the driver could not avoid the ruts and holes. It took two weeks to reach Irkutsk, the capital of Siberia. All roads ended. Anton put his cart up for sale. He stayed at Irkutsk a week, drawing money, writing letters. He liked the city – 'just like Europe' – but his companions were spending his money as well as their own on drink. They sickened him. Anton pined. He thought again of buying a ranch; he longed for female company, and wrote to Masha:

> I must be in love with *Jamais* [*Lika*], since I dreamt of her last night. Compared with these Siberian Parashas [*the name also means chamber pot*], all these whorefaces that don't know how to dress, sing or laugh, our *Jamais*, Drishka and Gundasikha [*Lika, Daria Musina-Pushkina, Olga Kundasova*] are queens. Siberian ladies, married or not, are frozen fish. You'd have to be a walrus or a seal to have fun with them.

Irkutsk was hard to leave. When they finally reached Lake Baikal, the ferry had gone. Anton complained:

> We searched the village all evening to buy a chicken, but didn't find one. But there is vodka! Russians are terrible pigs. If you ask why they don't eat meat or fish, they explain that there is no transport, roads are bad etc., but there's as much vodka as you like even in the remotest villages.

The next day Anton spotted smoke from the funnel of a small boat; after appalling discomfort it disembarked them on the eastern shore of Lake Baikal. A week later, on 20 June, Chekhov, *Homo sachaliensis* as he now called himself, made Sretensk and boarded the *Ermak* an hour before it departed. Relief – no more rutted mud tracks – made Anton euphoric.

On the *Ermak* Anton read his telegrams from the Suvorins; he was free of Lieutenant von Schmidt, there was a washroom (where the crew's pet fox watched the passengers' ablutions). He gazed at the wild shores of the Amur, and spied on the Chinese villagers on the right bank. The steamboat shook, it ran aground in two and a half feet of water and the crew took a day and a night to repair the holes. The Far East of the Russian empire, recently acquired from China, was another land. The monsoon climate made it lush in summer. The Manchurian border brought it prosperity. Above all, there was freedom. Anton told his family: 'Here people are not afraid to talk loudly. There's nobody to arrest them here and nowhere to exile them to, you can be as liberal as you like . . . A fugitive political prisoner can freely take a boat to the ocean.'

On 27 June, intoxicated with the Amur air – 'free and warm' – Anton reached Blagoveshchensk. He was bewitched by the Chinese traders and Japanese girls. In a Blagoveshchensk brothel, as a letter to Suvorin shows, Anton was happy:

> a nice clean room, sentimental in an Asiatic way, furnished with bric-à-brac. No ewers, no rubber devices, no portraits of generals ... The Japanese girl has her own concept of modesty. She doesn't put out the light and when you ask what the Japanese is for one thing or another, she gives a straight answer and as she does so, because she doesn't understand much Russian, points her fingers and even puts her hand on it. What's more, she doesn't put on airs or go coy, like Russian women. And all the time she is laughing and making lots of *tsu* noises. She is amazingly skilled at her job, so that you feel you are not having intercourse but taking part in a top level equitation class. When you come, the Japanese girl pulls with her teeth a sheet of cotton wool from her sleeve, catches you by the 'boy' ... gives you a massage, and the cotton wool tickles your belly. And all this is done with coquetry, laughing, singing and saying *tsu*.[15]

Anton touched foreign soil when he crossed the Amur to the Chinese port of Aigun. Then he took the *Muraviov* down to the Amur, to the ocean at Nikolaevsk on the final stage of his journey to Sakhalin.

THIRTY-TWO

Sakhalin

June–December 1890

CHEKHOV SHARED HIS CABIN to Nikolaevsk with a Chinese citizen, Sung Liu Li, who chattered about decapitation and appended his greetings in Chinese when Chekhov wrote to the family. Turning northeast along the Amur, the boat brought Anton into a bleak land-scape, the gateway to the penal settlement. Nikolaevsk had no accommodation and Anton had to board another ship to sleep. After a week he set sail in the steamer *Baikal,* with soldiers and a few prisoners, across the shallow straits to Sakhalin. The *Baikal* soon stopped: the sandbanks were too treacherous to navigate and Anton was rowed ashore at Cape Jaore. There, tormented by the mosquitoes, he stayed for two days at the lonely house of a naval officer and his wife. Then, at 5 a.m. on 11 July 1890, after eighty-one days' travelling, Chekhov finally disembarked at Aleksandrovsk, a cluster of wooden buildings that housed the administration for the prison colonies of central Sakhalin. At dinner in the prison he was introduced to a man who was, Anton said, the spitting image of Ibsen – the prison doctor Dr Perlin, who later took Anton as a lodger.

Anton's reading had ill prepared him for the island. Six hundred miles long, but with a land area of Scotland, Sakhalin is a hilly sliver of Arctic tundra, thinly covered with coniferous scrub. For half the year the temperature is below 0°C; for the other half chilly fog and rain alternate. The island barely supported a few thousand aborigines, Gilyaks and Ainu, who lived off berries, seeds and fish. A little coal was mined to supply passing ships, but Sakhalin's only use to Russia was as a penal colony that hardened criminals would fear. Nothing could convey the awfulness of Sakhalin: its bogs rendered impassable by tree-roots, its cold, rain, fog and murderous insects. The officials disingenuously claimed to know nothing of his arrival (despite the newspaper reports and government telegrams they had received).

They lived in a dream world. General Vladimir Kononovich, the island's governor, promised full cooperation[16] as soon as the visit of Baron Korf, governor of the whole Amur and Sakhalin province, was over. A week later, Korf dined with Anton and Kononovich. Both governors seemed liberal: they deplored corporal and capital punishment, perpetual servitude and exile. Baron Korf had not visited Sakhalin for five years and proclaimed himself delighted by its progress; Kononovich apparently knew nothing of the daily floggings, the embezzlement of food and medicine, the enforced prostitution of women, the murder of native Gilyaks – barbarities which Anton heard of in his first days on the island.

Kononovich was forced to retire: he was too humane a man for the government, although he closed his eyes to his subordinates' misdeeds. Dr Perlin, disloyal by nature, was an excellent informant, though an uncongenial host. After a month Anton moved in with a young civil servant, Daniil Bulgarevich. Bulgarevich's brother had been exiled to Siberia for political offences: Daniil was a decent, melancholy individual. His household was the hearth from which Anton worked. Like many officials and prisoners, Bulgarevich showed the best of his character to Anton. Anton's medical training ensured that he hid his revulsion and relaxed prisoners and guards. They talked. Anton was the only Russian on the island who was neither prisoner nor jailer. Exiles wept and gave him presents. From his dwindling funds he dispensed charity – he bought one exile a heifer. Psychopathic killers and sadistic guards were equally responsive. They showed a humanity that their colleagues, after Chekhov published his book, found incredible.

The 10,000 prisoners, the 10,000 men and their families who guarded them, the few thousand released prisoners and exiles who tried to farm the intractable Sakhalin bogs, the few hundred aborigines, Gilyaks and Ainu, who had survived the diseases brought by the Japanese (who had territorial claims to Sakhalin) and Russians and the savage plunder by escaped convicts and renegade guards, lived in hell. Until 1888 exile to Sakhalin was for life; even in 1890 exiles were allowed to resettle only in eastern Siberia. The guards, too, were likely to succumb to disease or violence on the island. In late July Kononovich let Chekhov print 10,000 questionnaires in the island's print shop and interview prisoners and exiles. All August Anton sur-

veyed the west coast around Aleksandrovsk and the Tym river valley
that runs north from the centre of the island to the Sea of Okhotsk.
In mid September he took a boat to Korsakovsk in Aniva Bay on the
south side. At Korsakovsk Anton found hospitality with the Feldmans,
a family of policemen and prison officials. Despite their notorious
brutality, they showed their best side to Chekhov. Aniva Bay was
cosmopolitan: Anton picnicked with the Japanese consul, and met
shipwrecked American whalers.

The cards that Chekhov distributed to prisoners and exiles recorded
name, address, married state, age, religion, place of birth, year of
arrival, trade, literacy, source of income, diseases. They provided statistics that the Russian authorities lacked. In poor health, in two
regions, each of 10,000 square miles, travelling on foot over treacherous paths, Anton collected data for 10,000 individuals in one short
Arctic summer. In August and September 1890 the sun shone exceptionally often on Sakhalin, but Anton's achievement, nevertheless, was
Herculean. He recorded hundreds of conversations with men, women
and children of every status and nationality (though he met few aborigines); he inspected farms, mines, hospitals; he watched floggings. If
he had the wherewithal, he treated the sick. He arrived too late to
witness a mass hanging; the death penalty for murder had been abolished in Russia, but on Sakhalin murderers were hanged.

Chekhov's indignation focused on the plight not of the prisoners
or guards, but of the children. The schools were closed for the summer, but, even when they were open, they were clearly as fictitious
as the hospitals, where there were no scalpels or medicines and the
doctors spent the money on brandy for themselves. Chekhov remonstrated with Kononovich: he made his officials order textbooks from
Suvorin and telegraphed Vania to send school programmes and books.

Anton sent a few telegrams home: he accustomed his mother to
the idea that he would be back later than he had originally said. At
the end of his stay he received a letter from her:

> Dear Antosha, look after your health, don't risk travelling by horse
> at night, boats are also dangerous . . . Excuse me Antosha for asking,
> please bring if you can a collar for Masha, I think it's called Arctic
> fox, I don't know what fashions you have there, and 4 sables for
> me.[17]

Anton learnt that he now had no home in Moscow, that Vania had lost his job, that Ezhov was widowed, that Ivanenko was writing to Lika, and that Olga Kundasova had vanished. In two and a half months on the island he sent only one substantial letter to Russia, to Suvorin, as he sailed to the south of the island. It is a wary letter:

> I don't know what will come of it, but I have done quite a lot. There'd be enough for three dissertations. I got up every day at 5 a.m., went to bed late and every day was tense with the thought that I had still a lot to do, and now that I have finished forced labour, I have the feeling I have seen every small detail but missed the elephant ... I have visited all the famous. I witnessed a flogging, after which I dreamt of the executioner and the revolting flogging-horse for three or four nights. I chatted with men fettered to wheelbarrows. Once I was having tea in a mine and the former Petersburg merchant Borodavkin, sent here for arson, took from his pocket a teaspoon and gave it to me, and as a result my nerves were upset and I promised never to go to Sakhalin again.

The Chekhovs received a telegram dated 12 October 1890 from a ship of the Voluntary Fleet, *Petersburg*: 'Unloaded convicts, left Korsakovsk 10th, will pick up Anton Pavlovich Chekhov, leaving [*for*] Odessa 13th.'[18] In Vladivostok Anton got a foreign passport from the chief of police, and telegraphed to Aleksandr in Petersburg, the only sibling whose address he had: 'Sailing Singapore Chekhov'.

The family had endured its own Sakhalin. They knew little of Anton's adventures. In his absence they sought protection from Suvorin. On his way to his Crimean villa, Suvorin called on Masha. He offered both her and Vania work; he invited Misha to Feodosia. Misha was, thanks to Suvorin, a tax inspector, but he was unhappy in his provincial hotel room. All Anton's siblings were under Suvorin's wing. Only Evgenia felt abandoned. All July at Luka she nagged Pavel:

> for God's sake, ask Vania to find us a flat, we are leaving here on the 2nd [*of September*] and I'm worn out with worry ... we need money badly ... Masha sent a letter to Aleksandr the day after we had his letter and he still isn't sending us any money.[19]

In September Evgenia and Pavel found new quarters. Olga Kundasova came to live there for a few weeks; Suvorin called twice. Pavel, quelled for once, described to Vania the shouting matches between the reactionary tycoon and the radical feminist, whom Suvorin called 'Psycho-path!' The Chekhovs moved again, but this house was expensive and small. Evgenia wrote to Vania on 8 October:

> On 4 October we moved to new quarters, Malaia Dmitrovka. Fir-gang's house, a detached house, 2 floors, 800 roubles. Antosha and Masha upstairs, two rooms, downstairs papa and I and the dining room, you're welcome to come, you'll be fed, it's hard for you and I miss you and I'm very sorry, Misha went to Efremov on 1 October, he'll stay there 2 weeks and then be transferred to Aleksin, some-where the other side of Serpukhov, no news from Anton, we don't know where he is, we meant to telegraph Suvorin to ask, we don't know where Suvorin is either, we are all exhausted . . . I'm sorry for Masha, she has been most unhappy of all. If I miss anyone it's you. I keep mourning, my lovely hawks have all flown the nest. Lika Mizinova has been in the country for two weeks . . . Fenichka is barely alive, she can't hold anything.[20]

The new Moscow flat with its two servants, the elderly retainer and cook Mariushka and a new chambermaid, never felt like home. The carters had broken Evgenia's sewing machine and Masha's wardrobe. From Petersburg (where he was entertaining Pavel) Aleksandr urged Masha:

> Dearest Sister, Why are you moving like matchmakers almost every day from one flat to another? . . . Nobody knows where Anton is now. Probably he's not even writing to Suvorin . . . What ties you and mother to Moscow? Essentially, apart from many years' habit, nothing. Come and live with me in Petersburg. I have been saying this to Vater in Petersburg, but he has some weighty considerations on this account.[21]

Natalia added: 'Dear Masha, I am sincerely sorry for you, now you are completely alone, but God grant Anton will soon arrive and you will have your happy days.' The telegram from Vladivostok with news of Anton's return relieved Masha. She told Misha:

> We are very pleased with the flat, we have settled very well indeed, come and look. The day before yesterday Suvorin came. He came specially to offer me a post in his bookshop, at first just as a shop assistant . . . I was very pleased of course, but remembered that Anton might not be especially pleased . . . I asked Suvorin to wait for Anton to arrive.[22]

The literary world could relax in Chekhov's absence. Only a few travel sketches from Siberia had appeared in print under his name. The dramatist and editor V. A. Tikhonov recorded in his diary:

> What a powerful, sheer elemental force Anton Chekhov is! But how many enviers he has attracted from among our authors . . . The most repellent in this respect is Shcheglov; he slobbered over Chekhov as a most devoted friend; now he has started hissing at him behind his back.[23]

Chekhov enjoyed the *Petersburg*, a sturdy 300-foot steamer built in Scotland twenty years before. It was lightly loaded – no prisoners ever came back from Sakhalin. Leaving Vladivostok on 19 October 1890, the ship held a mere 364 sailors, soldiers and guards, relieved from service in the Far East. The American whalers were to be dropped at Hong Kong. A few passengers occupied the cabins. One was Father Irakli, a Buriat Mongol who had been given a free passage to Russia to report in Moscow on his missionary work with the Gilyaks and Ainu. The Captain appeared only during a storm in the China Sea and told passengers who had revolvers to keep them loaded, since death by shooting was preferable to death by drowning. A midshipman Glinka struck up an acquaintance with Anton: he was the son of a Baroness Ikskul who in Petersburg had given (and broken) a promise to use her power to smooth Anton's passage.

Sakhalin was the evil face of colonialism; Hong Kong impressed Chekhov as the opposite. The ship stayed there eighty hours. Anton told Suvorin, on his return:

> A wonderful bay, such movement on the sea as I have never seen even in pictures; nine roads, horse-trams, a railway up the mountain, museums, botanical gardens; wherever you look you see the English-men's most tender concern for their employees, there is even a sailors' club. I . . . was annoyed to hear my Russian companions cursing the English for exploiting the natives. I thought: yes, the English exploit the Chinese, the Sepoys, the Indians, but they do give them roads, piped water, museums, Christianity, you [*Russians*] exploit them and what do you give them?

As they crossed the China Sea, the storms died away. On 20 October, just one day into the voyage home, one soldier died of 'acute pneumonia' in the ship's hospital: his body was thrown overboard in a sailcloth shroud. As they left Hong Kong, on 29 October, another soldier died and was buried at sea. Anton's mood plunged. He barely remembered Singapore for the tears that he was holding back (although in his few hours on shore he ordered a Javanese pony as a present for Suvorin).

Burial at sea inspired Chekhov to write the first fiction he had composed for a year, 'Gusev', an awesome portrayal of nature's indifference to death. The grim philosophy of 'A Dreary Story' was now matched with the vision of nature in 'Steppe': Chekhov's post-Sakhalin phase had begun. The story had the by-line Colombo. Fifty-eight hours spent in Ceylon, the legendary Eden, revived Anton's spirits. He took a train to Kandy in the mountains, and watched the Salvation Army: 'girls in Indian dresses and glasses, drum, harmonicas, guitars, a flag, a crowd of bare-arsed little boys ... Virgins sing something wild, and the drum goes boom boom! And all that in the dark, on the shores of a lake.' After the Salvation Army Kandy offered something more to his taste:

> I was sated to the throat with palm groves and bronze-skinned women. When I have children then I shall tell them not without pride, 'You sons of bitches, in my day I had intercourse with a black-eyed Indian girl ... and where? In a coconut plantation on a moonlit night.'

This was the exploit of which he was to boast to his Petersburg friends – 'the real charmers are coloured women,' he told Ezhov.[24]

There was another transaction in Colombo. Midshipman Glinka and Chekhov went to an Indian animal-dealer and each bought a tame male mongoose; Chekhov went back to the dealer and bought another animal, too wild to handle and sold as a female mongoose. With these animals they returned to the *Petersburg*. On 12 November 1890 the ship left Colombo. Thirteen days passed without a port. Midshipman Glinka and Anton Chekhov sat on deck with their mongooses. In late November Chekhov passed through the Suez Canal. Pavel wrote: 'Greetings to Holy Palestine, in which the world's Redeemer lived. You will be passing Jerusalem'. Uncle Mitrofan was so moved, Georgi reported, that 'my father put Anton's letter on the chest of drawers, covered it with his hat and went to church.' Pavel was tracing Anton's journey on a wall map of Siberia; he wrote to Vania just before Anton docked in Odessa: 'I think only about Antosha, may he return safe and sound. Such separation is unbearable. Come and meet him. Misha will come too.'[25] Anton saw Mt Sinai, and then sailed past the island of Santurini which supplied Taganrog with wine. On 2 December the ship reached Odessa. After three days' quarantine the passengers disembarked. Anton, Glinka, Father Irakli and the mongooses took the express to Moscow. On 7 December Evgenia and Misha intercepted the train at Tula. Misha recalled:

> We found Anton dining in the station restaurant with Midshipman Glinka . . . and a strange looking man, an aborigine with a broad, flat face and narrow slanting eyes. This was the chief priest of Sakhalin, monk-priest Irakli . . . wearing an ordinary suit of an absurd Sakhalin cut. As they ate, the mongooses stood on their hind legs and kept peeking at their plates. The Sakhalin priest, his face as flat as a board and without a hint of facial hair, and the mongooses seemed so exotic that a whole crowd gathered around the diners, gawping at them. 'Is he a Red Indian?' 'Are they apes?' came the questions. After a touching reunion with the writer, mother and I got in the same carriage and the five of us set off for Moscow. Apart from the mongoose Anton had brought in a cage a very wild female mongoose which soon turned out to be a palm cat.[26]

Misha and Anton drank and played with the mongooses for the four hour journey. Father Irakli and Midshipman Glinka's mongoose stayed with the Chekhovs for some time. The Firgang house was crowded. Pavel now came home every evening. (He was soon to retire from Gavrilov's warehouse.) While he put up with the mongooses, which dug up potted plants and scrabbled in his beard, the palm cat was unbearable. It would emerge at night and bite the twitching feet of any guest sleeping in the dining room. (For Pavel, Anton's 'mongooses' were a bench mark of animal delinquency.) The male mongoose was christened Svoloch, best translated as 'Sod'. Sod and Suvorin were uppermost in Anton's mind. Sick with the change of climate (he had a cold, constipation, hæmorrhoids and, he claimed, impotence), he stayed at home and wrote letters. He told Leikin that mongooses were better than dachshunds, 'a mixture of rat and crocodile, tiger and monkey'. To Shcheglov he wrote:

> If only you knew what lovely animals I brought from India! They are mongooses, the size of half-grown kittens, very cheerful lively

beasts. Their qualities are: daring, curiosity and affection for man. They fight rattle snakes and always win, they are afraid of nothing and nobody and, as for curiosity, there isn't a parcel or package in the room they don't open; when they meet anyone they first of all poke around in pockets to see what's there? When they're left alone in the room they start to cry.

He did not mention mongooses to Suvorin: instead he confessed his disillusionment with humanity – after Sakhalin his contempt for the Russian intelligentsia extended to Suvorin's closest collaborators:

> I passionately want to talk to you. My soul is seething. I want nobody but you, for you are the only one I can talk to . . . When shall I see you and Anna? How is Anna? Greetings to Boria and Nastia; to prove I have been a convict I shall, when I come to see you, attack them with a knife and yell wildly. I shall set fire to Anna's room . . . I embrace you and all your house warmly, except for . . . Burenin who . . . should long ago have been exiled to Sakhalin.

For a month Anton was too ill to leave the house, let alone visit Petersburg. He spent Christmas and New Year with his family.

THIRTY-THREE

The Flight to Europe
January–May 1891

ANTON SPENT DECEMBER 1890 sorting out boxes of cards and papers from Sakhalin and revising his story 'Gusev'. Winter in Russia that year was harsh: Moscow plunged to minus 30°, in Taganrog snow reached the eaves. Irregular heart beats and a cough kept Chekhov awake; by day hæmorrhoids made sitting painful. The house was crowded – Vania had caught typhoid in the marshes of Sudogda and came to recuperate. Mentally, Anton had changed. His fiction was to show how Sakhalin had destroyed his respect for authority and strong men. His affection for Suvorin survived, but he now felt contempt for *New Times*. He rarely referred to Sakhalin in his fiction, but his confirmed distrust of ideology, and his preference for unspoilt nature over spoiled humanity are Sakhalin's legacy. Chekhov's remarks to Suvorin that December echo those he would give to his fictional heroes: 'God's world is good. One thing is not good: us.'

Lika Mizinova, Olga Kundasova – who brought her seventeen-year-old sister Zoe along – and the piano teacher Aleksandra Pokhlebina all danced attendance on Anton. In the Crimea Masha had met Countess Klara Mamuna: she became Misha's fiancée, but for a year she too focused on Anton. In Petersburg others were waiting. New rumours of impending marriage were spreading. While Anton was away, the old poet Pleshcheev had unexpectedly inherited two million roubles from a cousin who died intestate. His daughter Elena became an heiress. All Petersburg, from Anna Suvorina to Aleksandr Chekhov, urged Anton, half in jest, to propose.

To Burenin the journey to Sakhalin had been radical posturing by a failed talent. The radicals, however, acclaimed a politicized Chekhov. 'Gusev' won praise all round: the story's hero, a doomed tubercular soldier buried at sea, was seen by the left as a victim of a ruthless system and by the right as a model of Christian resignation. Tchaikovsky was moved. Natalia's dentist refused to accept payment from her, as Chekhov's sister-in-law. Two years late, the Dauphin sent a promised gift of Santurini wine, with a letter in fine Latin, ending: 'Dii te servent, nymphae ament, doctores que ne curent. Tuus A.[27] The Gods were not obliging, and Anton would not let any doctor treat him, but the nymphs were loving. The Dauphin's wine helped Anton cope with his friends' misery.

Ezhov was still suicidal after his wife's death; he survived because he now wrote for Suvorin, and, vouched for by Masha, was teaching drawing to girls in a school run by a Madame Mangus [*Mongoose*].[28] Ivanenko, his sister-in-law dead, his brother dying of TB, had lost hope and abandoned his flute, while Zinaida Lintvariova, ill with a brain tumour, Ivanenko reported, 'is sincerely and patiently waiting for her end. She keeps asking with great interest after you and your family, the poor woman cannot bear it.'[29] The 'white plague' struck old friends in Taganrog. Death was gathering in Aunt Fenichka in Moscow and Anton's friend the actor Svobodin in Petersburg. After watching a soldier die on board the *Petersburg*, how could Anton not think of his own inevitable end? Nor had he forgotten Anna and Kolia: in March 1891 he put in his new notebook: 'The trouble is that both these deaths (A. and N.) are not an accident and not an event in human life, but an ordinary thing.'

On 7 January Anton went to Petersburg for three weeks, Shcheglov could see that he 'was ailing', but Anton wanted a 'feast in the time of plague'. On arrival he went with Svobodin to Shcheglov's name-day party, and panicked the gathering: he was announced as an emissary of the Chief of Police. Anton became drunk and arrogant. Shcheglov records words[30] that foreshadow Chekhov's Dr Astrov (in *Uncle Vania*) who, drunk, 'does the most difficult operations and has his own philosophy'. He boasted that he would seduce his Petersburg admirer, the virtuous Lidia Avilova. He laid down the law to Shcheglov: 'The theatre should be like the church – the same for the peasant and the general . . . You ought to have an affair with a dark-skinned woman.' The next day Anton saw Tolstoy's comedy *Fruits of Enlightenment*. Stanislavsky directed it, and Vera Komissarzhevskaia made her début. Anton had no idea who they were. Carousing with friends, Anton exhausted himself and his hosts.

The Suvorins' telephone broke down under the strain of Anton's social whirl. Anton evaded Kleopatra, but took up with another actress, Daria Musina-Pushkina, once of Masha's circle. Daria had come to Petersburg to escape her fiancé and meet another suitor. She lived in the same building as the Suvorins, and was eager to have Anton as an escort. Daria besieged Anton with notes:

> Listen, cockroach, I couldn't resist the temptation and am coming to Svobodin's ... I won't deny that I'd very much like you to come and fetch me, not me fetch you, but I know how stubborn you are ...

> Darling Anton, if you came and saw me right now, how I should thank you, because I'm alone, terribly unhappy.

> Little cockroach, aren't you ashamed to ask if it's too late? Remember the saying: 'better late than never.' ... But all the same you're better than I thought. Cicada. I expect you – you'd better come![31]

In Petersburg there were women who disliked Anton: Zinaida Gippius, already a literary lioness, baited Chekhov: listening wide-eyed, she disingenuously asked: 'Does your mongoose eat people?'

For his Moscow womenfolk Anton found answers. He told Masha: 'I've been talking to Suvorin about you: you will not be working for him – I've decided. He is terribly fond of you, but in love with Kundasova.' Elena Shavrova rejected Anton's advice to change her pseudonym, and abandon her drama course. 'I'll make my breakthrough anywhere,' she asserted. The more she was opposed, the tougher the sixteen-year-old Elena got.[32] She persuaded Anton to make Suvorin pay her 8 instead of 7 kopecks a line for the stories she was feeding *New Times* after Chekhov had revised them.

Lika Mizinova, however, wanted Anton, body and soul. She resumed the romance and set the tone for the coming nine years in her first letter to Anton in Petersburg:

> Today in the Council I wrote you a long letter and I'm glad I couldn't send it, I've just read it and am horrified – sheer weeping ... I've been coughing blood (the very day after you left). Granny is angry with me for going out and not looking after myself, she prophesies consumption – I can just imagine you laughing about that ... When you get back don't forget to go to Vagankovo cemetery to say hello to my remains ... In the morning I could write such a

gloomy letter, now I think it's all rubbish I shall enjoy upsetting you
... write a letter without the usual little sarcasms ... surely I deserve
something other than irony?[33]

Anton's response was remorselessly teasing:

> As for your coughing ... stop smoking and don't chatter in the
> street. If you die, Trofim will shoot himself and Spotty-face will get
> puerperal convulsions. I'll be the only one glad of your death. I hate
> you so much that just the memory of you is enough to make me
> utter sounds like your granny 'Eh ... Eh ... Eh'. I'd gladly scald
> you with boiling water ... My lady writer, Misha's friend [*Elena
> Shavrova*], writes to tell me 'Things are bad – I am seriously thinking
> of leaving for Australia.' You to the Aleutian islands, she to Australia!
> Where am I to go? You've grabbed the better half of the earth.
> Farewell, villainess of my heart. Your <u>Well-known Writer</u>.

A few days later, sending him birthday greetings, Lika tried a different
tack: 'I've just got back from your family ... I'm writing in the dark
and what's more after Levitan saw me home! And whom are you
seeing home?' Anton relented a little. His reply ended: 'Bibikov [*a
consumptive poet whom Anton knew*] ... saw you and my sister and
wrote to Petersburg "at Chekhov's I saw a girl of amazing beauty."
There's a pretext for you and Masha to have a quarrel, even a fight.'
    Lika's next letter, on 21 January 1891, was the first (and almost the
last) that she wrote to Anton in the intimate *ty* form:

> Knowing your meanness, my dear Antosha, and wishing to hang on
> to a chance to write to you, I am sending you a stamp which I had
> much need of. Will you come back soon? I'm bored and I dream
> of meeting you as the sterlets in the Strelna [*park*] pool dream of a
> pure transparent river. I don't know how to be tactful and when I
> try to be it doesn't work out. But all the same come on the 26th
> and you will see that I can be tactful not just verbally ... So I expect
> you, I hope, that you will give me at least ½ an hour! She can't have
> it all! For my love I deserve ½ an hour. Goodbye, I kiss you and
> wait. Yours for ever, Lika Mizinova.

Olga Kundasova, scolding the great men of Moscow and Petersburg
in their dens, or Elena Shavrova, cajoling and wheedling, left Anton
in total command of himself. Lika got under his skin, as no other

woman had done. His responses to her are always ironic, never passionate or jealous, but their frequency, length and extravagance betray the disturbing effect Lika had on him.

Anton called on his brother Aleksandr. He told Masha: 'His kids made a very good impression on me . . . Aleksandr's spouse is a kind woman, but the same stories happen every day as at Luka.' Anton's sober days in Petersburg were spent lobbying for Sakhalin's children. Through Koni, the radical lawyer, he contacted Princess Naryshkina who ran the Imperial children's charities: orphanages were set up for 120 of Sakhalin's child beggars and prostitutes. Through Vania and Suvorin, Anton had thousands of books sent to Sakhalin: the authorities paid. Chekhov, loth to meet aristocrats, made Suvorin and Koni talk to influential courtiers.

In Petersburg Anton began his monograph *The Island of Sakhalin*: he wanted it to be dry and impersonal. He would publish it only in its entirety to heighten the impact. The Siberian penal system and Sakhalin were in the news: an illegal Russian edition of the American George Kennan's survey of Siberia's prisons had been circulating. A work so anti-establishment as a survey of Sakhalin could not expect to be published by Suvorin. Anton's unbroken association with *New Times* puzzled the radicals even more. One political exile (Ertel) told another (Vladimir Korolenko): 'Pity that Chekhov is tied to that nest of robbers.'

At the end of January Anton returned to Moscow. He began a new story, 'The Duel': it grew as long as a novel. He nursed the mongoose which a Russian winter had made too ill to break crockery or leap on the table. He consoled Olga Kundasova, tantalized Lika Mizinova and flirted with Daria Musina-Pushkina (who had followed him back to Moscow). When the mongoose recovered its *joie de vivre* the flat seemed too small.

Anton endured two cramped weeks. Suvorin came to Moscow and took him to dinner and the theatre. Then Anton decided they should take the European tour that he had missed two years previously. On 5 March he wrote to Suvorin: 'Let's go!!! I agree, wherever and whenever you like.' Accounts at *New Times* were chaotic: Anton believed he was still 2000 roubles in Suvorin's debt, but he would not stay in Moscow working the debt off. He prevaricated: he assured his family that he would be back for Orthodox Easter. Elena Shavrova begged him to stay. Lika, snubbed, was proudly silent. Vania pleaded with him to come to Sudogda, where Vania's only friends were his pet starlings and canaries.

On 11 March Anton left family, mongoose and friends for Petersburg. (Kundasova and Musina-Pushkina also made their way there.) At 1.30 p.m. on 17 March, Suvorin, the Dauphin, and Anton – Father, Son and Holy Ghost – took the Petersburg–Vienna express. Daria Musina-Pushkina spotted them on their way to the station: 'I was riding down the Liteinaia and met you travelling in a cab, and you looked straight at me but for some reason didn't greet me.' Anton's pince-nez was broken, so he had left it behind in Moscow. As a result, he had trouble recognizing friends, and no doubt a blurred view of Europe.

Neither did he understand all he heard. Anton had only schoolboy German. He was to tell Ezhov, 'I speak all languages except foreign ones. Getting from one station to another in Paris is for me a game of blind man's buff.' The Suvorins bore the brunt of the expense, decided the itinerary and did the talking. On the one hand Anton liked being treated 'like a kept woman' – he called himself the 'Nana of the Railways' and enjoyed the physical comforts: the Pullman sleeping cars with mirrors, carpets and soft beds; the flushing lavatories. He was amazed, as he had been on the Amur, by free speech – frank conversations with strangers in Moscow could lead to trouble with the secret police. In Vienna, he told his family, 'It is strange that you can read and talk about whatever you want.' On the other hand, he was quickly soured: when he crossed the border into Austro-Hungary his only note was 'A lot of Yids. The customs charged more than my tobacco cost.' As he came over the Alps to Venice, he declared them inferior to the Caucasus or the mountains of Ceylon.

Venice, however, aroused his enthusiasm: Desdemona's house and Canova's tomb sent Anton into ecstasy. He told Vania: 'For a Russian, poor and degraded, here in the world of beauty, wealth and freedom, it is not hard to go mad ... when you stand in church listening to the organ you want to convert to catholicism.' In Venice Zinaida Gippius turned up and pricked the bubble. Like many Petersburg snobs, she felt impelled to put provincial upstarts down, and wilfully misinformed Anton that the hotel charges were by the week, not the day. She noted in her diary that he was 'A normal provincial doctor.

he had fine powers of observation within his limits, and rather coarse manners, which was also normal.'

By 30 March the party was in Rome. Anton was wan. He asked the hotel porter, Suvorin claimed, for the address of Rome's most luxurious brothel. He reported to Uncle Mitrofan that the Vatican had 11,000 rooms; later he said that Rome was just like Kharkov. Letters home ask only after the mongoose. About Lika and her cough, or the convalescent Vania and his dormitories full of workers' children, he did not enquire. On 3 April the Suvorins and Anton went to Naples; on the 6th they toured Pompeii. Years later Suvorin recalled:

> He was little interested in art, statues, pictures, churches, but as soon as we got to Rome he wanted to get out of town, to lie on the green grass. In Venice it was the originality, most of all the life, serenades, not its Doges' palace and so on, that held him. In Pompeii he wandered bored over the open city – it is boring in fact – but immediately he took pleasure in riding a horse to Vesuvius over a very difficult route and kept edging towards the crater. Abroad, cemeteries interested him everywhere – cemeteries and circuses with clowns, which he saw as real comedians.[34]

The party then took the coastal railway to Nice, a city Anton little suspected was to become a second home (it was a resort for Russians, rich and sick, and the Russian navy). Lika did not write. Pavel reported: 'The mongoose is well, its behaviour is incorrigible but deserves leniency.' To Vania Pavel was franker: 'The mongoose gives us no peace, it bit off a piece of mama's nose in the night, she was frightened when she saw the blood. Now it has healed.'[35] Anton wrote back. He confessed that he would miss Easter. He and the Dauphin discovered Monte Carlo. For several days they took the train there to play roulette. In two days Anton lost 800 francs.

Three days later the party took the express to Paris. Anton celebrated Easter in the Russian Orthodox church, amazed that French and Greek Christians should be singing the Bortniansky anthems he had sung as a boy in Taganrog. May Day in Paris gave Anton food for thought. He mingled with a crowd of rioting Paris workers and was himself manhandled by the police. Three days later he sat in the public gallery of the French parliament and listened to something unimaginable in Russia – deputies calling on the Minister for the Interior to account for the deaths of seven workers. Paris, as much as Sakhalin, developed Anton's political consciousness. Meanwhile Suvorin decided to commission a bronze bust of himself (which he was later to present to Chekhov), and while the sculptor carved, Anton and the Dauphin toured the nightclubs and watched naked women. On 2/14 May Anton was back in Moscow.

THIRTY-FOUR

Summer at Bogimovo
May–July 1891

ANTON STAYED ONE DAY on the Malaia Dmitrovka. (Of the twenty months that the family rented Firgang's house, Anton lived there fewer than five.) The day after his arrival Evgenia, Masha, Anton and Sod the mongoose left for a dacha that Misha had found them near Aleksin on the river Oka, a beautiful region of wooded hills that was somewhat fancifully called the 'Russian Switzerland'. Probably the palm cat came to a sticky end that spring. Floor-polishers came to the Firgang house while Pavel was in charge and flushed it from its lair beneath the wash-stand: one workman, his little finger badly bitten, reacted violently.[36]

Pavel retired on 30 April 1891. With his sons in Petersburg, Sudogda, Aleksin and Nice, he portrayed his future as bleak. His employer of the last fourteen years, Gavrilov's parting remark was, 'Your children are bastards'.[37]

Cousin Aliosha Dolzhenko also left Gavrilov – for a more generous employer. As his family left for the country Pavel told Vania:

> I remain in Moscow to put the flat in order. Antosha had brought you remarkable gifts: a purse with two French gold coins, paper and envelopes from the Louvre shop ... I can choose my life and my locality. I think it best for me to spend my days among my own family, rather than in coarse and rude society. All this time I have been living for the family and have laboured for it, I have left the Slough of Gavrilov without a penny, I hope that my family will not leave me penniless ... I shall be well fed, clothed and not want for anything.[38]

The dacha, surrounded by woods, was just across the river Oka from Aleksin. There were no latrines – Anton was constantly running to a gully – the house was cramped and trains noisily crossed the Oka on a rickety bridge. When Pavel arrived three days later, conditions were intolerable. The mongoose was breaking crockery and uncorking bottles. Chekhov could not work: 'Writing, I'm like a crayfish sitting in a trap with other crayfish.'

After a breach of three months in their relationship, Lika brought Anton salvation. She arrived with Levitan by river-boat; she flaunted the painter all summer to flush Anton out. Anton reacted only with more irony: he openly referred to Levitan as Phaon, to Levitan's mistress Sofia Kuvshinnikova as Sappho, and to Lika as Sappho's young rival Melitta.[39] On the boat Lika and Levitan were accosted by a local landowner Evgenii Bylim-Kolosovsky, a tiresome idealist with a large estate at Bogimovo, ten miles from Aleksin. Bylim-Kolosovsky needed sympathetic ears and a supplementary income: when he heard that the Chekhovs were dissatisfied with their quarters he sent two troikas to fetch them to Bogimovo, where he offered them the upper storey of the manor house for the summer. Masha recalls: 'We saw a large neglected estate with an enormous two-storey house, two or three cottages and a splendid old park with avenues and ponds.'

Amenaisa Chaleeva, a toothless red-head ('dim and vicious', decided Anton) was Bylim-Kolosovsky's mistress and ran his model dairy. She recalled Chekhov:

> A man who looked about thirty, pale, thin, seemingly very pleasant. A home-made sailcloth jacket, a broad grey hat. I thought, he can't afford our dacha – 160 roubles for the summer ... We enter the drawing room, a long room with windows looking out on a lime avenue, columns in the middle, a parquet floor, long leather divans along the walls, a big round table, a few ancient armchairs. The man saw all this and even cried out with pleasure: 'Oh I've been looking for something like this! And the parquet squeaks with age, the divans are antediluvian ... What happiness. This will be my room and I'll work here.'[40]

In the move from Aleksin to Bogimovo the mongoose vanished into the woods. Anton stirred up neighbouring landowners. The one reply was distraught:

> Dear Mr Chekhov, I inform you of the terrible grief that has struck me today: at 6 this morning my father died of acute pneumonia. I have asked many people in Seianovo about the mongoose, but it hasn't turned up.[41]

Lika and Levitan had left. Anton, his affections revived, invited Lika back to Bogimovo; he also invited Suvorin, Vania and Aliosha Dolzhenko. Bogimovo, which still stands, was magnificently placed near the top of a steep hill. Great windows to the west overlooked a stream; the morning light came through equally large windows and the park on the east. Anton established an arduous regime. He rose at 4.00 a.m., made coffee and worked while the household slept until eleven. Then they walked, played, lunched, gathered mushrooms, caught fish and rested. Anton sat down to work again at three and worked until dark, at 9.00 p.m., after which came supper, cards, bonfires, charades, arguments, personal and philosophical, and visits to neighbours. On Mondays, Tuesdays and Wednesdays he wrote *The Island of Sakhalin*; on Thursdays, Fridays and Saturdays 'The Duel'; on Sundays he composed bread-and-butter fiction, such as 'Peasant Women', a story of indignant women listening to a traveller telling them how he drove a neighbour's wife to her death. He kept up a furious rhythm, with only two or three hours' sleep a night, for three months, despite toothache, stomach upsets and coughing.

As well as Sod, Anton had mislaid Lika. His invocations lost their power. Signing himself as a laxative mineral water, Hunyadi Janos, he appealed:

> Golden, mother-of-pearl, fil d'Écosse Lika! The mongoose ran away the day before yesterday and will never ever return. He's kicked it. . . . Come and sniff flowers, catch fish, go for walks and howl. O, fair Lika! When you watered my right shoulder with your howling tears (I've removed the stains with benzene) and ate our bread in big slices and our beef, we were greedily devouring your face and the back of your neck.

It was Levitan who answered, not altogether in jest:

> Everything, beginning with the air and ending, God forbid me, with the most insignificant bug on earth, is imbued with the divine Lika! She isn't here yet but she will be, for she doesn't love you, the tow-haired, but me, the volcanic dark-haired man, and she will only go where I am. It hurts you to read this but love of truth prevents me from hiding the fact. We have settled in Tver province near the estate of Panafidin, [*Lika's uncle*] . . . I'm a sheer psychopath! You'll find it interesting if you come – wonderful fishing and our rather

248

nice company, consisting of Sofia [*Kuvshinnikova*], me, the Friend and the Vestal Virgin.

Suvorin came for a few days and contemplated buying a neighbouring estate, a house with a mezzanine, where he might spend summers next to Chekhov. Masha fell ill with symptoms of typhoid. This concerned Levitan, who wrote again:

> Lika says that if there were anything serious about Masha's illness you wouldn't have written in such a playful tone. How did you lose the mongoose? What the devil is all this? It's simply obscene to bring an animal from Ceylon only to lose it in Kaluga province!!! You are all phlegm – to write about Masha's illness and the loss of the mongoose in cold blood as if they were only to be expected!

Sofia Kuvshinnikova (like Zinaida Gippius, she loathed Chekhov as he loathed her) added reproaches:

> I don't understand how you could let this little foreign mongoose go to his doom. I am beginning simply to think that you, Chekhov, were terribly envious of its popularity and so neglected your rival on purpose!

Anton felt deserted: first by Lika, then by Sod, and now by his sister, for Masha soon recovered and left for Sumy to be with Natalia Lintvariova.

Anton was discussing sex by letter with Suvorin. In mid May 1891 Petersburg buzzed with the delinquencies of a schoolgirl, daughter of a senior civil servant: her lover's trial went into closed session. Suvorin knew the details. Anton reacted by saying that nymphomaniacs should be incarcerated, and that the schoolgirl, 'if she doesn't die of consumption, will be writing edifying tracts, plays and letters from Berlin or Vienna – she has an expressive and very literary style.'[42] Suvorin responded with another letter on the depravity of modern schoolgirls. On 27 May Anton pointed out that they were no worse than Shakespeare's fourteen-year-old Juliet. He added: 'By the way, about little girls' but the next fourteen lines are so heavily inked out, by Suvorin or Masha, that Anton's views remain unfathomable. In him, as in Suvorin, prurience and prudishness alternated unpredictably. Anton, like Suvorin, appreciated female sexuality, but unlike

Suvorin, feared sex as an addiction which, were he to surrender to it, would annul his freedom and stifle his creativity.

On 2 June hunters on the other side of the Oka found an animal hiding in a crack in a quarry. It came out to greet them and they recognized it as Chekhov's mongoose. Sod was captured and taken to Bogimovo, where he enjoyed prancing with the children of the neighbouring families. When Anton spotted a snake in the grass, Sod was brought out to show his prowess.

June 1891 was an exotic pastorale. Lika and Anton resumed their correspondence in mid-June, Anton teasing, Lika pretending to be evasive. She spent a few days in Moscow vainly looking for a better flat for the Chekhovs; back with Levitan, she stressed that Sofia Kuvshinnikova watched, that she was too unwell to go outdoors in the evening. Anton told his 'enchanting, amazing Lika' to come, despite 'being carried away by the Circassian Levitan' or 'things will go badly'. He sent her a photograph of an officer on the *Petersburg* and signed it 'Your Petia'. Lika did not come. Her assurances of her innocence were unconvincing:

> We have a splendid garden and what's more Levitan, whom, anyway, I can only lick my lips at, since he doesn't dare come near me, and we're never left alone. Sofia is very nice; she is now very kind and utterly sincere with me. Clearly, she is now quite sure that I cannot be a danger to her.[43]

Sofia Kuvshinnikova, everyone knew, had lasted so long because she put up with Levitan's polygamy. At the height of summer, however, Sofia Kuvshinnikova left Zatishie. Levitan was untrammelled: Lika gave him her photograph. At the end of July 1891 Anton sent Lika one last letter, but signed it Masha (the handwriting is Anton's), as if his sister had written it: 'If you have decided to break off your touching triple alliance for a few days, then I'll persuade my brother put off his departure [*for Moscow*] . . .' Lika was silent. Suvorin returned briefly, advising Anton not to marry Lika.[44]

Anton's reaction to what he regarded as Levitan's seduction of Lika was vicious but hidden. His letters stopped. Instead, on 18 August, although work on *The Island of Sakhalin* was far from complete and his long story, 'The Duel', had only been despatched to Suvorin that day, he wrote to a Petersburg lawyer called Chervinsky. He asked him to find out from the editor of *The Cornfield* how much they would pay for 'a suitable little story'. Chervinsky took the idea to Tikhonov, editor of *The North*. Chekhov's revenge on Levitan, Kuvshinnikova and Lika now had an outlet in a story that would be known as 'The Grasshopper'. (Anton's host, Bylim-Kolosovsky, was to wait three years to be even more cruelly caricatured.)

As 'The Duel' neared completion, Anton was inspired by a tenant of Bylim-Kolosovsky. An entomologist, Dr Vagner, whom the locals called 'Spider', was embroiled in a polemic between biologist Professor Timiriazev and Moscow Zoo, where amateurish 'experiments' were carried out on the animals by a Professor Bogdanov. From Vagner, a vehement Darwinist, Anton borrowed many features and arguments for the protagonist, von Koren, of 'The Duel'. Chekhov also edited and extended Vagner's own diatribe against Moscow Zoo into a sketch called 'The Tricksters'.

Bogimovo turned cold as August ended. Chekhov had to face the autumn. Aunt Fenichka, camping in the Firgang house, wrote to her sister for the last time:

> Dearest sister don't send any more, I cannot cook at all, we simply weep . . . on the Feast of the Holy Apostles I made soup and on Sunday I was very ill, now I want Ukrainian cherry pie I have no strength . . . don't invite me, take me to a small flat, here I can't cope . . . everything is bitter in my throat and I've been miserable so long.[45]

Anton wrote back to her son, briskly telling him to feed her olives, baked fish and cough powders, asking why he had not called a doctor. A month passed before Anton visited his dying aunt. In August he travelled to Moscow for a day, not to treat Aunt Fenichka, but to inspect the zoo for his article.

On 28 August Pavel arrived in Moscow: he moved Aunt Fenichka and Aliosha out of the house and swept it clean, grateful at least that Fenichka's dog Kartuzik had exterminated the rats which Sod had spared. Pavel too was moving out, for, thanks to Suvorin, Vania had a job in a Moscow school with magnificent accommodation. Anton's heart was with the Suvorins. He consoled Suvorin over the sudden death of his manservant from a 'twisted gut' (in today's terminology, intestinal gangrene); he reassured him over the Dauphin who, fearful that he had TB, had gone to the Volga to drink fermented mares' milk; he congratulated both Suvorins on their womenfolk, who left them to holiday as they wished, and concluded, in accord with the Suvorin philosophy:

> In women I love above all beauty, in the history of mankind culture … in the form of carpets, sprung carriages and witty thinking.

THIRTY-FIVE

'The Duel' *and the Famine*

August 1891–February 1892

ON 16 AUGUST 1891, her thirty-sixth birthday, Aleksandr's wife Natalia had given birth to a boy, Mikhail. Pavel exalted in his first legitimate grandchild:

> The Chekhov surname has expanded in the North and the South 'Magnify, o Lord, and visit this vineyard which Thy right hand hath planted.' I arrived here early as the Baptist to make ready the way and clear the Mansions, in which we shall live like herrings in a barrel.[46]

Aleksandr cherished his baby son: he paid for a designated cow to provide milk of proven origin, but the Chekhov-Golden family was not happy for long. Anastasia Golden, the eldest and once most prosperous sister, was destitute. Pushkariov, her consort, had lost all his money. Anastasia and her children moved in with Anna Ipatieva-Golden, who begged Anton:

> If 30 roubles doesn't come, we'll all be out on the street. Anton, for the sake of everything holy, help us, I expect we will pay it back, though not soon, and it's hard to ask others, you're different, nobody will know and neither Pushkariov's nor our pride will suffer.[47]

Anton appears to have sent money, but the Goldens' mother went to live with Aleksandr and Natalia. Called 'Gagara' she spent eight years, as Aleksandr put it, 'applying for admission to the Elysian fields'.

Anton was preoccupied by death. Leonid Tretiakov, the Chekhov brothers' student friend, had died of TB. That autumn Kurepin, the editor of *The Alarm Clock*, who had nurtured Anton's early work, was dying of cancer of the neck; Aunt Fenichka's days, Anton told Suvorin, 'are numbered. She was a glorious woman. A saint.' On 25 October Fenichka died.[48]

Suvorin and the Dauphin had come to stay in the Slav Bazaar in

Moscow, only to catch flu and infect Anton. Anton felt so ill that he gave up vodka for good. Suvorin and Anton were both depressed by bereavement. Suvorin had lost his man-servant; Anton had been to three funerals that autumn; Zinaida Lintvariova had died at last and Anton had written her obituary. Anton expressed his despair so vehemently to Aleksandr that his brother destroyed the letter. Aleksandr, who had won respect for two articles on dosshouses and lunatic asylums, responded sympathetically:

> I deeply and sincerely want to warm you with affection. Poor man, you really have a lot on your shoulders. Your last letter (sealed) created such an impression that my wife burst out howling, and my spectacles clouded over. My dear Antosha, there's nobody to take pity on you. You lack the affection that is given to anyone who loves a woman.

Anton, however, shut out women's affection. Elena Pleshcheeva was lost, betrothed to a Baron von Staël. Kundasova had gone to Batum on the Black Sea (hoping he might join her). Lika was ostracized for fickleness. Anton would not see Elena Shavrova. On 16 September 1891 he told her off for her story 'Dead People', where 'gynæcologists were cynics' and 'old bachelors smelt like dogs':

> Gynæcologists have to deal with a frenzy of tedium that you couldn't even dream of and which . . . you would find smelt worse than dog . . . All gynæcologists are idealists . . . I dare to remind you of justice, which an objective writer needs more than air.

When Elena called, Anton announced that he was 'not at home'.[49] Lika, feeling drawn to Anton again, was made to feel unwanted, and complained to Granny: 'I see the Chekhovs, and Sofia Kuvshinnikova too, rather seldom . . . I repent not staying for the winter in Pokrovskoe [the family country estate]. Sometimes I want so much to see you and get out of here.'[50] Lika left the city council; she had seven pupils in the Rzhevskaia school and a few private lessons. Her father had surfaced and was promising her money. She had hopes of studying to be a singer, but, ignored by Anton, she lapsed into hypochondria. All winter she complained to Granny of consumptive symptoms.

Anton's male friends needed him too. Ivanenko the flautist sought work: 'If you reject my request, please send the revolver which we bought together and if you don't, then I'll still borrow one.'[51] Anton asked Tchaikovsky to find Semashko the cellist a place in the Bolshoi opera orchestra. Others appealed in vain. In early November 1891 Gruzinsky wrote: 'I sit and grieve, Anton! My wife has caught a chill looking after her sick sister. The sister is better, my wife has collapsed and something serious has begun . . . Not visiting the healthy, perhaps you call on the sick?'[52]

Anton gave all his attention to the novel-length story he had sent Suvorin. Suvorin wanted to call it not 'The Duel' but 'The Lies'. Anton stuck by his title. Here was a story far more traditionally Russian than his preceding fiction: two heroes – one with a faintly Polish name, Laevsky, the other distinctly Germanic, von Koren – each preach a set of ideas, one lazily Slavonic, the other manically Germanic, and fight a duel. The novelty of the story is that the author's sympathies lie with neither set of ideas, even though he loves both his characters. Nobody would know from 'The Duel' that Chekhov had been in Sakhalin: the setting resembles Sukhum or Batum on the Caucasian Black Sea coast, and recalls Chekhov's tour with the Dauphin in 1888. The story opens and closes with the sea drowning out the hero's words. The positive figures are the natives who gather in harmony while the Russian colonists quarrel, the naïve deacon who interrupts the duel, and the forbearing doctor who mediates between Laevsky and von Koren. Sakhalin's indigenous Ainu and the Buriat Father Irakli contribute only a few touches to 'The Duel'.

'The Duel' has a satisfying plot. Laevsky has come to the Black Sea with another man's wife, Nadezhda. When he finds her husband has died and he will have to marry her, he tries to borrow money to flee. The marine biologist Von Koren has come to prepare for an expedition. Laevsky parodies Tolstoy's ideas on the wickedness of women to justify his cowardice. Von Koren argues that love of humanity requires helping natural selection by killing off the weak. To justify his scientific outlook he proposes to kill Laevsky in a duel. The climax is as conventional as the conflict. Nadezhda is physically and morally sickened, and when Laevsky finds that she has been prostituting herself to pay the shopkeeper's bill, he too is profoundly shaken. The shock of the duel alters everyone: Laevsky and Nadezhda are reformed, Von Koren is chastened into admitting that 'nobody knows the real truth.' The instinctive faith of Dr Samoilenko, the deacon and the natives survives the wreck of intellectual structures. The upbeat ending is not very cogent; the story is shackled to fashionable ideas of the time – Tolstoy's asceticism and Darwin's 'struggle for existence'. Laevsky's hysterical, good-natured delinquency recalls Aleksandr Chekhov; von Koren has the megalomania of Przhevalsky, the logic of Dr Vagner and even Anton's own toughness. Yet we can sense the protagonists, von Koren and Laevsky, activist and quietist, as two sides of Chekhov, against a background of indifferent nature. From now on he would write works which argue ideas, not until the authorial mouthpiece is victorious, but until the reader senses that all ideas are futile.

Suvorin liked 'The Duel' so much that he allowed it to fill the literary supplement of *New Times* for most of October and November, and although Chekhov made enemies in Petersburg – there was after all no room for other contributors – his reputation as Russia's greatest living storyteller was now established. His second publication that autumn, the anonymous polemic 'The Tricksters', appeared in *New Times* on 9 October 1891. It created a scandal which persuaded the Imperial Society for Acclimatizing Plants and Animals to rebuild Moscow zoo along the lines of Hagenbeck's Hamburg zoo, and buy new, healthy animals.

When Anton had described Fenichka dying, he had mentioned, with mounting irritation, the mongoose leaping. 'I'm auctioning the mongoose,' he wrote to Natasha Lintvariova. Anton now showed two faces. In 'The Tricksters' he raged:

> The Moscow public calls the Zoo 'the animals' graveyard'. It stinks, the animals die of hunger, the management hands its wolves over for wolf-baiting, it's cold in winter . . . there are drunken rowdies and animals which are not yet dead of hunger can't sleep.

Anton's letter to the Zoo director on 14 January 1892, however, ingratiates:

> Last year I brought from Ceylon a male mongoose (*mungo* in Brehm). The animal is utterly healthy and in good spirits. As I am leaving Moscow for some time and cannot take it with me, I humbly ask the Management to accept this animal from me and to fetch it today or tomorrow. The best way of carrying it is a small basket with a lid and a blanket. The animal is tame. I have been feeding it on meat, fish and eggs.

Thanks to Suvorin's indiscretion, it was widely known that Chekhov was the author of 'The Tricksters', but Dr Volter of the zoo did not question why the zoo's most articulate enemy should offer them a free mongoose. He sent for it, and reported: 'The mongoose has arrived safely and does not seem to have frozen. I hasten to carry out my promise about a free ticket to the zoo.'[53] Poor Sod was visited by Masha, using the free ticket. Sod put his paws through the bars and removed her hair-combs. He survived two years in this 'animals' grave-yard'. No mongoose is listed among the fallen and sick for 1892, but there is no mongoose in the zoo's inventory for 1895. Sod, like Lika, could reflect on the fate of those who loved Anton, but whose demands for a response were too insistent.

Living in a crowded flat with a mongoose meant to Chekhov remoteness from reality and 'the people'. The revealing remark, to Suvorin in October, is: 'There is nothing I love so much as personal freedom.' Freedom from being crowded by others made the dream of a country estate an obsession. Anton had a substantial income, not just from 'The Duel' but from editions of collected stories and from farces, and Suvorin was eager to advance or underwrite money. Anton could spend 5000 roubles and mortgage a property for much more. Aleksandra Lintvariova and the Smagin brothers were put on alert, Anton relying on Aleksandr Smagin's love for Masha as an incentive to drive him around the farms of Mirgorod. All through December 1891 Smagin bargained with Ukrainian landowners. Just before Christmas, Anton sent Masha down to inspect a short list, make decisions and exchange contracts. Masha was flustered by the responsibility, yet seized the reins of power. Ukrainian farmers, however, did not like dealing with a woman. By New Year's Eve Masha was exhausted and begged Anton to come in person. She went back to Moscow empty-handed.

When she returned Anton was gone. He was seeing in the New Year with Suvorin in Petersburg. While Masha faced blizzards in the Ukraine, Anton relaxed for a fortnight. He and Suvorin were up until 4.00 a.m. drinking champagne with the actress Zankovetskaia; in the afternoons they tobogganed down ice mountains. They wanted diversion: they had both spent much of October and November too ill with flu to leave their bedrooms.

Now Anton's closest actor-friend, Pavel Svobodin, announced his imminent death:

Are you sleeping peacefully opposite my windows, across the road, in Suvorin's house? ... What sort of actor am I, when I have, on stage, such attacks of convulsions and spasms in the chest, throat and left elbow that I can't even call for help? Well sir, and what do I do with three children?[54]

Svobodin was not deceived when Anton told him that 'his disease was trivial.' Two and a half years had passed since Kolia's death, and Anton still sought oblivion in selfless work on behalf of the suffering prisoners of Sakhalin. Sakhalin remained a life's cause: he was despatching books and school programmes there, and contributing a chapter, 'On Escapees and Tramps', for charitable publication. Now Anton found a new cause. In central Russia the harvest of 1891 had failed; the government discouraged any intervention. The conservative *New Times* was one of the first newspapers to call for famine relief. By November peasants were eating grass; terrible hunger was imminent. Anton raised the alarm. Masha's pupils raised funds. Lika contributed 34 kopecks. Dunia Efros gave a rouble and demanded a receipt. Suvorin, moved by the hunger in Voronezh, his native province, did not blame the peasants for improvidence and even cooperated with rival newspapers. His children contributed their pocket money. Anton, helped by Pavel Svobodin in Petersburg, exacted contributions from friends. (His notebooks show that doctor-friends offered roubles, writers kopecks, while the Writers' Charitable Fund, with 200,000 roubles' capital, refused to give the 500 he asked them for.) Petersburg knew of Chekhov's campaign and marvelled at Suvorin's involvement in a cause so radical.

Anton discovered that Lieutenant Evgraf Egorov, Masha's old admirer, with whom the Chekhov family had quarrelled eight years ago, was now (like Aleksei Kiseliov in Voskresensk and Aleksandr Smagin in Mirgorod) a 'rural captain' (a post that gave men enormous power over the peasantry) fighting the famine in Nizhni Novgorod province. Egorov opened soup kitchens for children and devised a practical charity. He used funds to buy horses from the peasants, so that they could buy food and seed-corn. The horses were then kept until spring and sold back on credit, thus saving the animals on which the peasants depended. Egorov welcomed Anton: 'You shouldn't even have mentioned our old misunderstanding; such a petty incident cannot break a relationship.'[55]

In November, while Anton was too ill to move, he had begun a story 'The Wife' (originally entitled 'In the Country'), in which a doctor, despite the enmity of his estranged wife, devotes his energies to famine relief. He now offered it to *The Northern Herald*, instead of 'My Patient's Story', which had no hope of passing the censor.[56] To the amazement of editor and author, the censor did not alter a word of 'The Wife', despite the politically tabu subject of famine. The only shocks were registered by telegraphists as Chekhov and his Petersburg editor decided on the title: 'Let me leave the wife.' – 'All right, leave the wife. Agreed.' 'The Wife' is weak – like other Chekhov stories where a saintly doctor wars with an unprincipled woman, for personal martyrdom sours the altruism, but it achieved more publicity for famine relief than any manifesto.[57]

There were uproarious parties in Petersburg. Nobody slept much. After a party on 5/6 January which broke up at six in the morning, Anton was led on foot by his fellow guests all over the freezing city from one cathedral to another to celebrate Epiphany. On 10 January, exhausted, he arrived in Moscow. Four days later, just before the man from the zoo came for Sod, Anton was off in one of the worst winters ever to the wilds of Nizhni Novgorod. He drove through starving villages and was received by the provincial governor. The governor retracted his blame of the peasants for their own misfortune and drove Chekhov to the station on his own horses. A week later Anton was in Moscow, ill with pleurisy, and sick at heart at his discovery that so much of the famine relief was being embezzled.

Masha had failed to find a country estate. What she dared not at first tell her brother of was a marriage proposal from Aleksandr Smagin on 10 January 1892:

> My desire to be your husband is so strong that neither your love for George Lintvariov nor your negligible affection for me would stop me from fulfilling this desire, assuming you agree to it. The insurmountable obstacle to this desire is my disease [*unknown* D.R.] ... If you don't believe me I shall write to Anton about my health ... And I shall send you his answer. Anyway, sooner or later, I shall tell him about <u>my</u> feelings for you ... I am not afraid either of Anton's judgement – I want it.[58]

Anton's only overt objection to Smagin had been his 'tragic' handwriting, no trivial matter to a man who often joked 'the main thing in life is good handwriting.' Covertly, however, using arguments that none of the victims ever divulged, Anton took aside every one of Masha's suitors and dissuaded them. To Masha Anton had only to give a silent look signifying dismay or disapproval for her to reject any man's proposal.

Anton was desperate to quit Moscow; he instructed Masha with the help of Misha, now in Moscow, to buy an estate advertised in the Moscow newspapers for sale. It was not in the warm Ukraine but just forty-five miles south of Moscow, six miles over rough roads from a railway station. Too ill to inspect it, Chekhov nevertheless left on 1 February for another famine area. He met Suvorin at the Slav Bazaar. To kill two birds with one stone, he invited Elena Shavrova to join them: she thought Anton 'in the nicest, most amiable mood, so young and full of the joys of life.'[59]

Suvorin was grim and out of his depth in any enterprise so radical as famine relief. Anton was dragging him off to Voronezh, to make the governor adopt Egorov's horse-buying scheme. They found matters no better than in Nizhni: bread ovens, wheat and fuel were being distributed, but there was no fodder for the horses that were being bought up in order to give the peasants money for seed corn. Suvorin's sister Zinaida still lived there, and was helping with famine relief, but Suvorin saw no point in his visit. For the first time, he annoyed Anton. Suvorin, Anton told Masha, talked rubbish. (In Petersburg Anton had complained to Shcheglov of 'the senselessness of Suvorin's charitable work'.) After a week visiting Suvorin's (but not Chekhov's) ancestral villages, they returned north. Suvorin went back to Petersburg.

By mid February starvation and cold had killed perhaps a million Russian peasants: it was too late for charity. Previously, Anton had played the role of public-spirited landowner, as well as journalist. Now the role was real. Misha had bought on his behalf the estate of Melikhovo. Nearly 600 acres of birch woods and pasture, with a small wooden house and outbuildings in some dilapidation, Melikhovo was priced at 13,000 roubles, of which 5000 had to be paid outright, the rest over ten years. Misha mortgaged the property with the Land Bank, and after his machinations the Chekhovs owed only annual repayments of 300 roubles and 5000 roubles to Suvorin, which new editions of Anton's books were to pay off. *Sullen People* was into its third edition, *In the Twilight* its fifth: Anton's income reached 1000 roubles a month. Naïvely, the Chekhovs believed that farming 600 acres would be cheaper than renting a flat in Moscow. Pavel expressed his approval to Anton: 'Your mother wishes her children to buy a country house ... God will help in this matter ... His holy Will be done.'[60] Aleksandr was fired with envy. He proposed settling nearby, for he had new-found prosperity. Prince Sheremetiev had appointed him editor of the fire brigade's journal *The Fireman* and installed a telephone in his flat. Anton joked that Aleksandr, as an inveterate bed-wetter, would be good at putting out fires, but Aleksandr was sacked after only three issues of the magazine and his telephone was removed.

Anton visited his estate – on which rested all his hopes for privacy, inspiration, health, and contact with 'the people' – only after contracts had been exchanged, on 26 February. A blanket of snow concealed the boundaries, the untilled soil and neglected woodlands. The vendor was unprepossessing: the artist Sorokhtin lived there with his wife, mistress and their ragged children, in what was more like an Australian squatter's shack than a Russian gentleman's manor. It crawled with bedbugs and cockroaches. Sorokhtin had put up outbuildings and fences, but farming bored him. He wanted his 5000 roubles in cash, to leave for the warmth of the Crimea and paint. The Chekhovs had signed the papers. On 1 March Pavel, Misha and the baggage moved to Melikhovo. Anton came a few days later.

V

Cincinnatus

They would wake to the song of the lark, to follow the plough, they would take a basket to gather apples, watch butter being made, grain threshed, sheep shorn; they would look after the beehives, would take delight in the lowing of the cows and the smell of new-mown hay. No more writing! No more bosses! No more rent to pay!

Flaubert, *Bouvard and Pécuchet*

THIRTY-SIX

Sowing and Ploughing
March–June 1892

EIGHTEEN MILES from a post office, six miles from the station over rutted ice, Anton felt, on 4 March 1892, like the Roman dictator Cincinnatus who left Rome to till the soil. Until the snow melted, while the family scrubbed floors, papered walls, bought horses, tack, seed and saplings and hired workmen and servants, he was aghast at his decision.[1]

The Chekhovs' 'manor house' was a single-storeyed L-shaped wooden building with no bathroom or privy. An outbuilding served as a kitchen. The best room, open to the south and the west, was designated as Anton's study: Pavel and Masha decorated it in time for Anton's arrival. Across the drawing room was Masha's room. A narrow corridor ran one side of the L, leading to Anton's and Pavel's bedrooms, the dining room, and Evgenia's room. When guests tarried, the layout would prove awkward. The largest rooms, Anton's study and the drawing room, with its balcony, were crowded when more than five – including family, guests and servants – were there. In a few weeks the house was habitable, if sparsely furnished. Pavel's room was crammed with icons and ledgers and smelt of incense and of medicinal herbs; Masha's room was like a nun's, dominated by her brother's portrait; Evgenia's bedroom was filled with a trunk, a wardrobe and a sewing machine. The drawing room was furnished with Sorokhtin's unplayable piano.

Sorokhtin had left no hay, and the three horses starved on straw. One was unruly, one moribund; an elderly mare was the sole transport. The cow gave no milk. The farm dogs, Sharik and Arapka (Ball and Nigger), had two puppies, which Anton named Muir and Mirrielees, after the Moscow department store. When the ice melted, the pond turned out to be a cesspit and Anton's carp fingerlings all died. The river Liutorka was two miles away, so that water came from a dilapidated stirruppump. When the Chekhovs woke up on Sunday 29 March, they had a new view: the house next door had burned down, and only a smoking pile of beams remained. Anton quickly installed a new well-bucket, a hand-pumped fire engine and a bell, and planned a pond as big as a lake by the house. The Chekhovs had brought the sixty-seven-year-old Mariushka: they recruited cooks, maids and a driver from among the Melikhovo peasants.

By mid April the roads would be impassable with floodwater. The Chekhovs had to hurry if they were to start farming. Hay, straw, seed, ploughs, horses, poultry had to be bought, begged and borrowed. Debts spiralled. Anton had brought manuals of agriculture, horticulture and veterinary science. Despite their grandparents' peasant blood, the Chekhovs blundered, to the amusement of the peasantry and the neighbours, like Flaubert's Bouvard and Pécuchet. Their best ploy was to make Misha farm manager. Misha deserted his tax office, bought six horses with his own money and oversaw peasants and contractors. Pavel happily took to the role of gentleman, leading peasants to the barn and stables 'as if he were taking them to be thrashed', forcing visitors to wait because 'the masters are dining', patronizing the clergy.

When Chekhov's fictional city-dwellers plough and sow, they are driven out by the peasants' hostility. Anton's initiation was easier. He let the peasants drive cattle down the track that cut his estate in two, and even moved his fence. The peasantry did not at first come round: one of the Chekhov mares, left out at night, was switched for a moribund gelding. Only when Anton set up a free clinic, visited the bedridden, and gave the peasants the right to cut hay in his forest, did he win trust. Of the neighbouring gentry the nearest to Melikhovo were outcasts: the Varenikovs – she ten years older than her lover – were keen farmers who wanted to buy Chekhov's arable land, urging him to build a more habitable home in the 300 acres of woodland that would be left. A mile away was Vaskino, the mansion of Prince Sergei Shakhovskoi, a magistrate and the stentorian and Herculean grandchild of a Decembrist rebel.

The Lintvariovs, Smagins and Ivanenko sent cattle from the Ukraine, and lent ploughshares. Smagin sent hundreds of roubles' worth of seed-corn so that rye and oats could be planted once Misha's horses had ploughed. Smagin's help had a price. Masha's version runs:

Although it is hard to say now whether I loved him then, I thought hard about getting married ... I went to the study and said, 'You know, Anton, I've decided to get married ...' My brother naturally realized to whom, but he made no reply. Then I sensed that he found this announcement unpleasant, although he remained silent.

Smagin's proposal was Masha's third; she was nearly twenty-nine and it could be her last. Anton told Suvorin, who told Olga Kundasova: Petersburg and Moscow were abuzz. Smagin was coming to Melikhovo on 23 March: Masha left to teach in Moscow, and only returned a day or two before Smagin left. Smagin grasped that this flight meant a refusal, and spent two days chatting about farming: he kept his promises and sent the Chekhovs bags of seed, but he seethed. On 31 March 1892 he wrote to Masha:

It cost me great efforts to refrain from having a scandalous row at Melikhovo. Do you realize that I could have crushed you there – I hated you ... only Anton's constant hospitable welcome saved me.[2]

On 28 July 1929 Smagin was to write:

although a whole lifetime has passed since 25 March 1892 ... for me you remain the most enchanting and incomparable woman. I wish you health and a long life, but I should like to meet you again before I die.[3]

Anton later told Suvorin that his sister was 'one of those rare, incomprehensible women' who did not want to marry, but some years were to pass before Masha became sure that marriage would give her less happiness than her position as her brother's amanuensis. In later life she told her nephew Sergei that she had never really been in love with anybody.[4]

That spring Anton was as ruthless with his own suitors as with Masha's. Before Easter none of his women friends ventured out to Melikhovo. Few even wrote, so bruised were they by his departure. Anton, busy planting an orchard, had little time for correspondence, but on 7 March he sent a long misogynistic letter to Suvorin:

Women are most unlikeable in their lack of justice and because justice is organically alien to them ... In a peasant family the man is clever, reasonable and fair and God-fearing, while the woman is – God help us!

Anton lost Elena Shavrova's manuscript, and sent her fee to famine relief. He recommended her to a dilettante editor, Prince Urusov, but not as a writer: 'She gives a sort of lisping first impression – don't let that bother you. She has a spark and mischief in her. She sings gypsy songs well and can handle her drink. She dresses well, but has a silly hair style.'

Masha, 'with remarkable self-sacrifice', Anton commented, spent the weekend planting out the kitchen garden and her weekdays teaching at the 'Dairy' school. The school was in financial straits, so that Masha worked unpaid. None of her friends came to Melikhovo. Anton's note to Lika was as frosty as the weather:

> Masha asks you to come the week before Easter and bring perfume. I'd buy it myself but I shan't be in Moscow until the week after Easter. We wish you all the best. The starlings have flown away. The cockroaches haven't left,[5] but we've checked the fire engine. Masha's brother.

Two days later, he teased Lika that she would again take a summer dacha with Levitan and Kuvshinnikova. His letter ended half flippant, half appealing, paraphrasing Lermontov: 'Lika, it's not you I ardently love! I love in you my former suffering and my lost youth.' On 2 April Anton sent Masha an Easter shopping list, ending: 'Bring Lika.' Lika came, deserting her family's Easter reunion.[6] Hard on Lika's heels came Levitan. The Chekhovs brought a priest from the monastery to take the Easter service in Melikhovo church (which had no clergy): the family and guests acted as choir and Pavel relived his Taganrog days as cantor. Anton kept Lika and Levitan apart: the two men went shooting for two days after Easter Sunday, until an incident that foreshadows *The Seagull*. Anton confessed to Suvorin:

> Levitan fired at a snipe; the bird was winged and fell in a puddle . . . Levitan wrinkles his brow, shuts his eyes and asks in a trembling voice: 'Dear boy, bang it on the head with the gunstock.' I said I couldn't. He keeps nervously twitching his shoulders, his head trembling, begging. And the snipe is still looking bewildered. I had to do as Levitan said and kill it. One fine lovelorn creature less, and two fools go home to supper.

When Levitan went home next day, he discovered that Anton had treated him less mercifully than the snipe. 'The Grasshopper', in *The*

Performing Artist, set all Moscow tittering or seething. The 'heroine' of the 'little' story, 'The Grasshopper', is a married woman (with the features of Lika and the circumstances of Kuvshinnikova) who has an affair with a lecherous artist, very like Levitan; the 'grasshopper' heroine's husband, a saintly doctor (who faintly recalls both Dr Kuvshinnikov and Dr Chekhov), is driven literally to self-destruction by the situation. Dr Kuvshinnikov was alive and well, but his loving tolerance (recognized by his wife in her diaries) imbues the fictional doctor. Sofia Kuvshinnikova, forty-two, swarthy, and a serious painter, saw herself in the heroine, despite Anton's heroine being, like Lika, twenty, blonde and without artistic talent. Others also felt libelled. The actor Lensky, who frequented the Kuvshinnikova salon, and had told Chekhov not to write drama, recognized himself in a minor character.

Sofia Kuvshinnikova never spoke to Anton again; Lensky did not speak to a Chekhov for eight years. Levitan wanted to fight a duel and did not meet Anton for three years. (Levitan had other worries. The police were expelling Jews from Moscow, and he fled 150 miles east, until Dr Kuvshinnikov, a police surgeon, secured his return.) Levitan's relationship with the Kuvshinnikovs broke down. Sofia marked the summer of 1892 as their last. Dr Kuvshinnikov kept a discreet silence, but he never spoke to Anton again.

Lika was as badly hurt as the Kuvshinnikovs and Levitan, but she was in love and, in this matter, was wiser than Anton:

> What a savage you are, Anton ... I know full well that if you say or do something hurtful it's not out of any wish to do it on purpose, but because you really don't care how people will take what you do ...[7]

Neither Lika's reproaches, nor the loss of Levitan, a friend of ten years, seemed to mean much to Anton. Nor did the visit of his ex-fiancée Dunia Efros (now married to Konovitser, a lawyer from Taganrog *gimnazia*). Anton wanted to see only Suvorin and Pavel Svobodin. Suvorin came on 22 April (a day after Dunia Efros left). Suvorin, who owned a palatial mansion in Petersburg and a fine villa in the Crimea, could not stand the ill-heated smoky rooms, with no W.C. and no sprung carriage to take him to the station. On the 24th he took Anton to Moscow to spend three days in luxury at the Slav

Bazaar. While Suvorin slept, Anton wrote. Melikhovo was modernized over the next five years, but it was hard to persuade Suvorin to go there again: if he passed on his way south, he met Anton at Lopasnia station.

Anton returned to Melikhovo with Svobodin, just as Pavel was consecrating the sowing of thirty acres of oats. Apart from the Dauphin, Svobodin was the only guest at the end of April 1892. He returned in late June. The family planned to build him a cottage. Until the theatre season opened, Svobodin devoted himself to Anton, for whom he felt, both as actor and patient, admiration and affection.

Anton wrote his new work, 'Ward No. 6', for a Moscow journal, *The Russian Review*. The editors had paid a 500-rouble advance and would print whatever Chekhov sent, but they disliked the gloom and radicalism of the story. The obvious journal for such a work was the left-wing *Russian Thought*, but Anton had quarrelled with its editors, Vukol Lavrov and Viktor Goltsev, two years before. Svobodin's tact now reconciled Anton to men who had called him 'unprincipled', but it took until 23 June to get Chekhov to transfer his story from *The Russian Review*, and to conjure an apology from Lavrov. Svobodin pitched Chekhov into the camp of *Russian Thought*, the *bête noire* of Suvorin's *New Times*. Anton could do little in return. Svobodin's heart had tired of pumping blood round tubercular lungs. On 25 June 1892, after Svobodin had left, Anton told Suvorin:

> He has lost weight, gone grey, his bones are showing and when he's asleep he looks like a dead man. Extraordinary meekness, a calm tone and a morbid revulsion for the theatre. Looking at him I conclude that a man preparing for death cannot love the theatre.

Dramaturgy too was stale. On 4 June 1892 Anton complained to Suvorin: 'Whoever invents new endings for plays will open a new era. The damned endings won't come! The hero either gets married or shoots himself.' All Chekhov could write was a story of illicit love and family conflict, called 'Neighbours', with a sidelong glance at the Varenikovs next door to Melikhovo.

'Ward No. 6' depleted Anton's creative resources. Set in the psychiatric ward of a remote hospital, the story is a bleak allegory of the human condition. There is no love interest. The plot is a Greek tragedy in its violent reversal of fortunes. Like 'The Duel', it confronts activist with quietist. Now the activist is not a scientist, but a madman, Gromov, who has been incarcerated for proclaiming that truth and justice must triumph one day. The quietist, Dr Ragin, is drawn into dialogue and borrows every excuse devised by Marcus Aurelius or Schopenhauer for condoning evil. By consorting with a madman, Ragin alarms his superiors: he is trapped into his own ward, where, after a beating from the charge nurse, he dies of a stroke. Gromov has to go on living. Chekhov set his story among nettles and grey fences. Suvorin disliked it, but the elderly novelist Leskov recognized its genius, exclaiming 'Ward No. 6 is Russia.'[8]

Work so harrowing left a void. The *Island of Sakhalin* lay untouched. A worried editor, Tikhonov, wrote in March 1892, 'I hope that you won't stop writing, like some Cincinnatus'. Fears were well-founded. Chekhov saw medicine and physical labour as salvation. Yet another young writer whom Anton knew, Bibikov, died destitute in Kiev. In Petersburg Barantsevich, Bilibin and Shcheglov moaned to Anton. Tilling the soil gave Anton only the illusion of health. When not planting trees, catching mice to release in the wood, or digging a pond, he slept exhausted. For Leikin he wrote a few trivia, to pay for the dachshunds that Leikin had promised. Anton toiled from five in the morning until after dark. He was as happy in Melikhovo as he ever would be. He ordered almost every freshwater fish of Russia: his pond was an ichthyological museum. He planted fifty cherry trees from Vladimir – the real cherry orchard preceded the fictional one. He summoned stove-makers from Moscow, bought a sprung carriage for the journey to the station and dreamed of building a house in the woods, where he would tend trees and keep chickens and bees. Small disasters brought him down to earth: bad weather and the deaths of a horse, of his only drake, and of the hedgehog that hunted the mice in the barn.

Leikin, himself a recent landowner, sent cucumber seeds and endless advice. Franz Schechtel, a man of many hobbies, sent eggs which hatched into fancy poultry. He also sent mare's tail, a medicinal weed.[9] Chekhov told him on 7 June: 'The ground is covered with little penises *in erecktirten Zustande*. Some places now look as if they'd like to screw . . .'

Cousins from Taganrog and Kaluga expressed their amazement that a Chekhov had joined the landowning gentry. Women friends wondered at Anton's empire. They crowned him 'King of the Medes', a title as apt as Cincinnatus. Aleksandr's envy of 'Cincinnatus' bothered Anton. All spring his elder brother begged for land on which to build. Anton hedged, horrified lest Natalia come near. In early April Natalia's year-old Misha nearly died of the convulsions that had killed Aleksandr's first-born Mosia: 'My wife is destroyed, and I walk about like a cat scalded with sulphuric acid,' Aleksandr wrote. The doctor, Aleksandr hinted, advised a climate warmer than Finland and cooler than Taganrog – near Anton:

1) By the way I have absolutely given up drinking . . .

2) I can't let a rootless, if good, person like my wife go where she wants, as I know from experience. Even less can I let her go to her sisters' . . .

3) Therefore wouldn't there be a hut, a house, or something similar, near your estate for the summer? . . . It would only be on the absolute condition that nobody of my family dares to get into your house. My wife herself insists on that. If granny wants to take the infants in, that is her business. The infants and my wife will not be coming to see you uninvited . . . Natalia says that . . . our mother is not fond of her.

In the last week in June Aleksandr brought his two elder boys, now aged eight and six, to Melikhovo. He took photographs, and neither argued nor drank. Natalia was not invited, though she had fed Pavel and Anton in Petersburg, and shopped with Masha in Moscow.

In summer the 'Dairy' school closed for the holidays and Misha's tax office in Aleksin condoned his absences. Women friends of Vania and Misha visited. Countess Klara Mamuna, who had befriended Masha in the Crimea two years ago, came to play the piano. She flirted with both Misha and Anton, but seemed, before the summer ended, to be Misha's fiancée. Aleksandra Liosova, a lively and beautiful local schoolteacher, 'the fair daughter of Israel', was to be engaged to Vania, but photographs and letters show that it was Anton who drew her. Natalia Lintvariova alone caused no tension: she avoided flirtation.

Olga Kundasova, as she watched Anton become more and more involved with Lika Mizinova, had begun to show symptoms of manic depression. After astronomy and mathematics, she now took up psychiatry – as therapy for herself, and as a career. In August 1892 Olga made her promised visit. She made friends with a local woman doctor, Pavlovskaia, and became both outpatient and assistant to Dr Iakovenko at Meshcherskoe psychiatric hospital ten miles away. Anton's affection was rekindled. 'Kundasova seemed cleverer in the country,' he told Suvorin and in May declared: 'I should be very, very glad to see Kundasova, as glad as seeing a heavenly angel, and would build a separate cottage for her here.' Their intimacy, to judge by the fragments of evidence, remained troubled. Olga responded to a gift:

> I implore you to treat me, if not gently (that's not in you), then not exactingly and not roughly. I have become impossibly sensitive. In conclusion let me tell you that you have no grounds for fearing a long stay by such a psychopath as O. Kundasova.[10]

The piano teacher Aleksandra Pokhlebina, nicknamed 'Vermicelli' for her skinny figure, also visited. Her love for Anton rapidly became demented. Lika Mizinova was unperturbed by these rivals. She knew that Anton preferred her shy beauty, her contralto and her cantaloupe-yellow jacket to Kundasova's intellect and severe black dresses. She was amused as Anton desperately evaded 'Vermicelli'. Lika may have been helpless in love, unable to break free or to secure a response, but she had studied Anton: she guessed that by autumn he would be restless. By June, in fact, he was sounding out Suvorin about a journey to Constantinople; the Lintvariovs were calling him to Sumy. Disillusion creeps into Anton's jokes to Natalia Lintvariova on 20 June 1892:

> We're finished, there will be no oats ... Daria the cook, though quite sober, threw out all the goose eggs: only three of the enemy [the geese] hatched out. The piglet bites and eats the maize in the garden. The dear ponies ate the cauliflowers at night. We bought a calf for 6 roubles, it bellows in a deep baritone from morning til night ... In a word, the King of the Medes can only utter a wild warrior cry and flee to the wilderness ...

Lika acted. She dismissed her suitors, and asked her father for railway tickets to abduct Anton. She told him on 18 June 1892:

> Throwing aside all pride, I'll tell you I am very sad and want to see you very much. There will be tickets to the Caucasus, that is separate ones for you and me ... From Moscow to Sevastopol, then from Batumi to Tiflis and finally from Vladikavkaz to Mineral Waters

and back to Moscow. Be ready for the beginning of August, only for the time being please don't tell any one at home about the tickets.

Anton beat a quick retreat:

Write and see that nothing is done about tickets until the cholera in the Caucasus is over. I don't want to hang about in quarantine ... Are the dragoons at Rzhev courting you? I permit you these attentions, but on condition that you, darling, come no later than the end of July. Do you hear? ... Do you remember us walking across the fields? Until we meet, Likusia, darling little Cantaloupe. All yours, The King of the Medes.

To the non-committal King of the Medes, the cholera epidemic now creeping to Russia from the Caspian Sea was a convenient excuse not to depart. In his letter to Suvorin, however, Dr Chekhov played the cholera down as more sensation than danger.

THIRTY-SEVEN

Cholera

July–September 1892

AFTER FAMINE, cholera struck Russia's heartland. With unusual alacrity the authorities marshalled doctors. Anton did not wait to be asked. On 8 July 1892 he offered to man a village clinic. He forwent a salary: the Serpukhov health commission thanked him, but denied him even a nurse. Council funds had to be topped up by the rich: Anton begged the owners of the tannery and cloth mill, the archimandrite of the monastery and the aristocracy for funds to build quarantine barracks. The archimandrite refused, while Princess Orlova-Davydova – Anton never hit it off with the nobility – treated him like a hired hand.

Anton was soon on good terms, however, with Doctor Vitte in Serpukhov. One local doctor, Dr Kurkin, was an old acquaintance. Few supplies were available, but the Serpukhov authorities ordered the latest anticholera equipment: thermometers, large Cantani syringes for injecting fluids under the skin, tannin enemas to disinfect the gut, carbolic acid, castor oil, calomel, coffee and brandy. All summer Anton rode round twenty-five villages, over dusty or muddy tracks, checking sanitation, treating the dysentery, worms, syphilis and tuberculosis endemic among the peasantry, falling into bed exhausted every night, rising with the sun. Grateful patients gave him a pedigree pig, and three pairs of suede gloves for Masha. Anton's Sakhalin experience served him well. With Dr Kurkin he inspected factories in nearby villages. Three times they inspected a tannery that was polluting the rivers and shamed the owners into action, if only cosmetic. In this fallow creative period, Chekhov saw environmental degradation, human misery, complacency and failed ideals – material for new fiction. The cholera never came to Melikhovo. A neighbouring district had sixteen cases, four fatal.[11] Anton's energy won commendation and he was sucked into the committees for improving the lot of the peasantry. From cholera officer he would become medical officer of health, and builder of schools, libraries, post offices, roads and bridges over 100 square miles.

Anton's medical duties left him little energy for the harvest, but with the loan of machinery from Prince Shakhovskoi, and Masha toiling in the kitchen garden, a little of what they sowed was reaped, even though the geese and cows helped themselves to the cabbages. Anton found it odd to pick cherries and not be beaten for it. Visitors were few. Muscovites feared the cholera, and Anton's friends knew that he came home only to sleep. He visited Moscow just once between 16 May and 15 October, although trains ran every three hours and reached the city centre in two to three hours. The devoted Gruzinsky and Ezhov, despite invitations, stayed away. Ivanenko the unemployed flautist came to live in Melikhovo until autumn 1893; he was enthusiastic but incompetent – Chekhov called him *nedotiopa* ('ninny'), the sobriquet of Epikhodov, the manager in *The Cherry Orchard*. Prince Shakhovskoi gave Ivanenko a sinecure as secretary, and he would accompany, on piano or flute, any visitor who sang. One relative came for a week with his son: Piotr Petrov, the husband of Anton's cousin Ekaterina Chokhova.[12]

Lika could not accept Anton's excuses for not travelling. Anton deflected her again: he entrusted her with Sudermann's play *Sodom's End* to translate: he would edit it for the stage. Lika just passed the play to a German woman friend, which angered Anton. All summer they struggled by letter; he played her like a fish he was reluctant to land; she took the bait and could not tear out the hook. They swore devotion and indifference to each other. Anton blew hot and cold on 28 June:

> Noble, decent Lika! As soon as you wrote to me that my letters did not tie me in any way, I breathed a sigh of relief and now I am writing you a long letter without fear of some aunt seeing these lines and marrying me to a monster like you . . . Do you dream of Levitan and his black eyes full of African passion? Are you still getting letters from my 70-year-old rival and hypocritically answering them? A big crocodile is inside you, Lika, and really I do well to follow common sense and not my heart, which you have bitten. Get away from me! Or no, Lika, whatever the consequences, let your perfume make my head spin and help me tighten the lasso you have thrown round my neck . . . don't forget your victim, The King of the Medes

On 2 July 1892 Lika wrote: 'Why do you want so intensely to remind me of Levitan and my "dreams"? I think *about nobody*. I want nobody and I need nobody.' And the next day: 'O how I'd like (if I could) to tighten the lasso as hard as I can! But I've bitten off more than I can chew! For the first time in life I have no luck!'

On 16 July Anton teased her mercilessly about growing old in a *ménage-à-trois* with a balding Levitan and a hard-drinking Kuvshinnikova. He invited Lika to Melikhovo: the cholera had attracted interesting young men. He promised to knock bad habits out of her. 'Above all I shall shield you from Sappho.' After refusing to travel with her, Anton now mused about going to the Crimea on his own. She spent August, furious, with Granny at the family estate, Pokrovskoe. Lika summed up Anton, the summer and cholera on 3 August: 'The cholera hasn't come yet . . . Anyway, I doubt if you'll move yourself for anyone, especially not for me – well, I'm not offended! Farewell.' One of Anton's replies was too abusive to send. Lika distracted herself with suitors. She wrote to Masha on 18 July: 'In Moscow I've been seeing all my lovers (excuse the expression, but it's your brother's).'[13] Nevertheless, Pavel's diary records,[14] she travelled 150 miles from Pokrovskoe to Melikhovo to see Anton on 14 September. Whatever transpired, they stopped writing to each other for three weeks.

As soon as Lika retreated, another woman desperately in love with Anton asserted herself. Aleksandra Pokhlebina, 'Vermicelli', was very determined. A piano teacher who tied brass weights to her pupils' wrists and elbows, she turned the screw on Anton:

Half the summer has passed and nothing has been talked over . . . You might have forgotten about my existence, there is nothing amazing about that, but once it is an affair of the heart, I felt it can't be forgotten . . . I think you will not wish to embarrass me in front of my family.[15]

On 3 August, after an evasive response, she wrote again:

So you're fed up with me! I can just imagine you looking at the signature and saying Oh My God, she's writing again. Unfortunately for you I care too much about you.

She had no reply, and wrote on 28 August:

I rather need to see you – yesterday I had a letter from my family and I have something to tell you about business . . . Yesterday I saw Masha and I heard from her a great many unpleasant things about you.

Anton said nothing, and Pokhlebina smouldered. Olga Kundasova lost control. Established with Dr Pavlovskaia nearby, she made two brief visits to Anton that summer. On 25 August her letter about medical matters veered towards the personal:

Come on Friday and Saturday with Masha, I can assure you by all that is dear to me in this world that you will feel better at my place than I did at yours. Really, was it worth my coming for the sessions you awarded me?

Anton was not the only member of the household to fear the post. On the same day Smagin wrote to Masha with similar passionate resentment. He resigned his post as country magistrate, he complained of consumption. Smagin was equally scared of a visit and of a final breach. He wrote to Masha on 19 August 1892:

I still haven't forgotten the reception I had in March in Moscow province. Your request about burning your letters I shall not carry out, and in the event of my death I shall make arrangements . . . You can rest at ease: nobody will dare to read a single line of yours. You are very unkind.

Three women judged the right tone to take with Anton: Natalia Lintvariova, Vania's fiancée Aleksandra Liosova and Misha's love, Countess Mamuna. Liosova concealed her interest in Anton. Mamuna made a joke of hers. On 15 September she wrote: 'Why not see me in Moscow and share my isolation? . . . It's not bad to be carried away by both Chekhov brothers!!!'[16] Misha, Masha and the Chekhov parents brought harmony into Melikhovo. Morning and evening Pavel recorded in the family diary the outside temperature. An odourless earth closet was installed; the Chekhovs acquired pigs, calves and a pair of prolific Romanov sheep. Gherkins were pickled; potatoes were buried for the winter; double glazing was fitted; the Assumption and Dormition were celebrated with a liturgy. Misha lauded Cincinnatus's realm in a letter to cousin Georgi in Taganrog:

I have six horses here, we shall go riding, I shall take you over our virgin forests where you can go for three miles and all the land is <u>ours</u>. My rye is magnificent, but the oats and grass have been burnt by the heat and drought, while my sister's kitchen garden is a wonder to behold; she has 800 head just of cabbage. We have made hay . . . and if you could see the cartloads come into the yard and it being piled into stacks![17]

Misha wrote to Uncle Mitrofan on 7 October 1892:

Antosha is sitting in his room and has locked himself in, he is stoking the stove, the stove is warming up and he is freezing. He'll freeze and freeze then come out and say, 'What weather! Mama, isn't it time for supper?'

Misha tended to paint a rosy picture. He did not mention the servants. Two were dismissed – Pelageia had been robbing family and guests, and Daria had murdered the goslings – and others were hired – Olga and two pert Aniutas, Chufarova and Naryshkina. Vania and Aleksandr could not share Anton's life among the country gentry. Vania was now head teacher at a Moscow school, on the Basmannaia, a post he held for years to come. Pavel set off to Petersburg to stay with Aleksandr; on the way he reported Vania's privations to Anton:

he has a room for visitors, but you have to sleep on the floor, his bedstead was left at Melikhovo . . . and he can't buy one, he has no money. Vania acts energetically at his school, putting everything in order, trying hard. The school is terribly neglected, there is dirt everywhere, the walls, the floors, the window frames are old and frail and the double glazing hasn't been put in yet. He runs round all the classrooms alone and gives the women teachers instructions, they at first looked askance.[18]

Using a free railway ticket from Gavrilov and posing as a Customs official, Pavel arrived in Petersburg. He saw little of Aleksandr and his children but he attended every important church service in the city. He stayed for more than two weeks. Although he tolerated his daughter-in-law, conflicts arose, Aleksandr reported, over the soup, in which Natalia boiled one onion, for which both Pavel and Natalia's mother, Gagara, fought. Aleksandr was drinking less, but poverty bothered him. He asked Suvorin to increase his 5 kopecks per line.

Suvorin merely scribbled on the request: 'Who among my reporters [*apart from you*] is paid a salary?'[19]

Anton neglected literature, but in Moscow Pavel Svobodin ensured that his name still appeared in print. After 'Ward No. 6', *Russian Thought* was to print 'An Anonymous Story'. (Both stories had been written a year before.) Anton found another editor – Chertkov, grandson of the man who had sold the Chekhov family their freedom. This Chertkov, Tolstoy's closest acolyte, published reprints for the masses and, despite poor recompense and poor proof-reading, Chekhov sold him the more radical stories. Monthly journals gave Anton large advances, to shame him into writing. Despite the cost of rebuilding Melikhovo, the income from advances and Chertkov's reprints kept Chekhov solvent. Anton was grateful for Svobodin's selfless work in placing Anton's stories with *Russian Thought*: 'serious illness has forced him to undergo a spiritual metamorphosis,' he told Suvorin. Svobodin handled the tricky withdrawal and re-offering of 'Ward No. 6', and he offered Anton sympathy. He complained only of the theatre, saying he acted only to pay 'tailors, butchers, decorators, lamp-makers, cabs, innkeepers and loan-sharks'. On 9 October 1892, Suvorin wired Anton: 'Svobodin just died during performance play *Jokers* come dear boy.'

THIRTY-EIGHT

Summoned by Suvorin
October 1892–January 1893

THE ILLEGITIMATE SON of a groom, Svobodin had dominated the Petersburg stage. He died from TB at the age of forty-two. Vladimir Nemirovich-Danchenko was there:

> Svobodin fell down in the doorway. Perhaps the audience took this to be an extra effect, not in the stage directions. It was the first deadly attack. Svobodin still had enough strength to come out for two curtain calls. Then he went to his dressing room, began changing for the last act and suddenly, clutching his throat, shouting 'Tear it, tear it' fell on his back.

Anton was handed Suvorin's telegram as he left for his clinic. He told Suvorin of Svobodin's love for him, rather than his for the actor, and he did not go to the funeral. He had attended too many. In Petersburg he wanted to talk only to Suvorin. In any case, cholera required him to stay: new cases had occurred only eighteen miles away.

In Petersburg Pavel, an eager mourner, told Anton on 12 October 1892:

> I attended Requiems twice with the numerous presence of his admirers at the Volkovo cemetery, the sung requiem was solemn ... for his two visits to us at Melikhovo I said a heartfelt prayer for his soul's peace ... The last time he had not wanted to leave us, he kept taking his leave ...
>
> Aleksandr and his family send their regards and he asks you to sell him 12 to 15 acres of land to build a House just in case for his family, for his family is multiplying and he proposes to make himself a settlement. I am very pleased that sobriety, love, harmony, peace and calm have settled in their family. God grant that we be the same.

Aleksandr had forsworn not only alcohol, but also meat. Anton's publication in the 'enemy' *Russian Thought* made Aleksandr fear for his job, all the more since Suvorin, sliding into depression, was letting his paper slip into the hands of the Dauphin, who loathed Aleksandr. Anton had to mend fences with Suvorin: over eighteen months he had written nothing for him.

Anton was content among the peasantry, his Serpukhov colleagues, and even his neighbours. Only police officials repelled him. Siren voices called Anton to Moscow. Lika was desperate for comfort. On 8 October she broke her silence and appealed:

> I am burning my life, come and help as soon as possible burn it out, because the sooner the better ... You used to say that you loved immoral women – so you won't be bored with me, either. Even though you won't answer my letters, now perhaps you will write something, because writing to a woman such as I'm becoming really doesn't put you under any obligations, and anyway I am dying, perishing day by day and all *par dépit*. Oh, save me and come! Till we meet. L. Mizinova.

Vania had cleaned up his school house, and the Chekhovs had accommodation. On 15 October 1892, when cholera was declared vanquished, Anton came to Moscow for two days. He dined with his editors and erstwhile enemies, Vukol Lavrov and Viktor Goltsev, but spurned Gruzinsky and Ezhov. He must have contacted Lika, for at the weekend, classes over, Lika and Masha left for Melikhovo, followed by Anton with Pavel.

Lika had, however, received little comfort. Anton told Suvorin that he was bored without 'strong love', and Smagin 'there are no new attachments and the old are gone rusty'. Anton wanted to travel even further than in 1890: he would write all winter to earn the fare to Chicago to visit, with the Dauphin, the 1893 International Exhibition. First he had to go to Petersburg. Anna Suvorina summoned him twice:

> Anton, has my image utterly vanished from your heart? Do you really not want to see me? I suddenly felt a terrible desire to meet you and talk ... Can you really not get over Lenochka Pleshcheeva choosing somebody else? Well it was all your own fault and who could have supposed afterwards!!! Come, my dear Anton, I'll find you a bride here.[20]

The next day (26 October) Anna wrote:

> ... now I'm writing seriously with an outright demand that you come. Aleksei [*Suvorin*] is unwell, he has fainting fits, Liolia [*the Dauphin*] and I are at our wits' end and awfully worried. We ask you to help us.

Anton did not come. He told Suvorin, in the callous tone of the doctors in his plays, to take valerian, and to carry a folding chair wherever he went. Suvorin's desperate reply, however, panicked Anton. He told Shcheglov that he was rushing to Suvorin's bedside, for fear of a death 'that would age me about ten years'. On 30 October 1892 Anton went to Petersburg. News of Suvorin's illness spread through Moscow.[21]

Anton found Suvorin physically well: the only visible cause for depression was that the ceiling of his mansion had collapsed. He and Anton talked, drank and ate oysters.[22] When Suvorin fell silent, Anton reviewed manuscripts for the Dauphin. One was a ghastly survey by Dr Sviatlovsky called *How Doctors Live and Die* – suicide, tuberculosis and typhus.

Back in Moscow on 7 November, Anton felt ill: to save money he had travelled third class, and was choked by cigar smoke. The road to Melikhovo, now under snow, was passable, and the next weekend the Chekhov brothers' women friends, Lika, Countess Mamuna and Aleksandra Liosova, descended. Lika did not enjoy her stay: she was sought out only by Countess Mamuna, who did not want to be alone with Misha. Lika returned to Moscow with Masha the following Tuesday. In Moscow she met a new friend of Anton's, the young poetess Tania Shchepkina-Kupernik. This was a new blow to Lika, and her letters, by late November, become plaintive: 'I am annoyed that I ... went to Melikhovo ... and again I have no idea where to get away from anguish and the realization that no one needs me.' Anton refused to respond seriously: Masha had seen Lika at a symphony concert in a new blue dress. He answered with a spoof from one of 'Lika's Lovers' to another:

> Trofim! If you, you son of a bitch, don't stop chasing after Lika, then, you sod, I shall stick a corkscrew up the bit of you that rhymes with farce. You turd! Don't you know L. is mine and that we have two children?

As November ended blizzards cut Melikhovo off. Anton wrote *The Island of Sakhalin* and reports on the Tolokonnikovs' tannery at the nearby village of Kriukovo. Lika's phrase, *par dépit*, also inspired him. He began 'Big Volodia and Little Volodia': a young woman, married *par dépit* to an older man, is seduced by a younger man. Neither loves her. That freezing week Anton wrote a passionate *apologia* for his own 'mediocrity' to Suvorin. (Suvorin had read 'Ward No. 6' with all the more distaste because it was in *Russian Thought*.)

> You are a hardened drunkard and I have treated you to sweet lemon-ade and while you grant lemonade its due, you rightly note that lemonade has no spirit. There is none of the alcohol which would make you drunk and enthralled ... The reasons are not stupidity or mediocrity or arrogance, as Burenin thinks, but a disease worse for an artist than syphilis and sexual exhaustion. We haven't got 'it', true, and so, if you lift up our muse's skirt, you will find a flat place. Remember, that writers whom we call great or just good and who make us drunk have one common, very important feature: they are going somewhere and calling you with them, and you feel not with your mind but your whole being that they have a goal, like the ghost of Hamlet's father.

Suvorin was so bewildered by the letter that he asked his Petersburg crony, Sazonova, if Chekhov had gone mad. Sazonova, yet another Petersburg woman who did not take to Anton, wrote in her diary that, on the contrary, Chekhov was 'all there'; to Suvorin she berated Chekhov for not taking life as it came. Suvorin sent her letter to Anton, who sneered that Sazonova was 'a person who is far from life-enhancing'.

December's stiller weather brought fresh company every day – old friends like Kundasova, as well as casual visitors who shamelessly ate the Chekhovs' food, bedded down in their drawing room and bearded the writer in his den. Suvorin, addicted to painkillers, now appealed for help. Anton went back to Petersburg. On 20 December, as blizzards hit Melikhovo, he came into the warm. He stayed away from family and Moscow for over five weeks – well past his name day. Anton brought Suvorin his last gasp for *New Times*, a Christmas story called 'Fears'. He dined with Leikin. Moscow friends were hurt that Anton did not even mention his passing through. In Moscow he called on Lika and Masha for a few minutes only, but took the actress

Zankovetskaia to the music hall.[23] He did not warn Aleksandr and Natalia that he was coming to Petersburg.

Anton wrote to Lika, inviting her to Petersburg, knowing full well that she was too shy to come to the Suvorins, with whom Chekhov so frankly discussed his private affairs. Anton taunted her: he was dreaming of Countess Mamuna, he liked the idea of telling his friends that a blonde was being unfaithful to him. On 28 December he enclosed a newspaper cutting, should Lika wish to marry '*par dépit*':

> Wishing to marry, there being no suitable brides in our area, I invite girls desiring marriage to send their terms. The bride must be no older than 23, blonde, good-looking, of medium height and of lively, cheerful character; no dowry required. Apply to Evgeni Insarov, Almetevo, Bugulma district.

Lika replied by return of post:

> *Par dépit* I am burning up my life now! . . . and if you tell your friends at supper that a blonde is being unfaithful to you, that will probably amaze nobody, since I shouldn't think anyone would suppose that someone could be faithful to you.

Anton was supping with literary friends that night and the next four. Sergeenko tried to recruit Chekhov into a club of twelve – writers, painters, composers – for suppers, teas and story-telling. In Petersburg the temperature was $-35°C$. (At Melikhovo, too, it was colder than anyone could recall.) Party-going and terrible cold took their toll. Suvorin's house turned into a sickbay. Anton coughed uncontrollably, but treated everybody else. Suvorin had flu and otitis. Anton bandaged Emilie Bijon's leg: the governess had fallen off a wardrobe. He introduced to Petersburg a Moscow tradition: Tatiana-day celebrations with Suvorin, Grigorovich and Leikin, Barantsevich, Ezhov and Tikhonov. 'We drank little, but it was an extremely lively dinner,' recorded Leikin. Anton announced: 'We must all unite, or they'll pick us off one by one.'[24]

Accounts at *New Times*, controlled by Suvorin's eldest son, Mikhail, were a muddle. Anton needed to offset the 5000 roubles in advances and loans he had taken from Suvorin. He wanted to pay off Natalia Lintvariova, who had lent him 500 roubles to buy seed and equipment for Melikhovo. He was puzzled: no matter how many of his books Suvorin sold, he seemed to be in debt. At Suvorin's, he wrote only a short discourse, 'What Disease Did Herod Die Of?', and an enquiry on behalf of the painter Repin into whether the moon shone on Gethsemane.

Even in Petersburg Anton could not escape the demands on his time, pocket and affections. Pavel, who received a pension through Suvorin's office, ostensibly from his sons, angry that payment was late, protested to Aleksandr:

> I am the father of famous children. I must in no way find myself embarrassed or humble myself before anyone. I shall not go begging from anybody. It is a disgrace! I need freedom, I shall live where I wish, I shall go whither I wish, and I need money for that.[25]

Lika lamented still more loudly on 15 January 1893:

> I haven't seen Masha since December ... You say that you will come on a Monday? That's stupid – there are Mondays in March and July and that explains nothing ... I am counting the days and hours which must pass before the happy moment comes when I see you. Your Likula.[26]

Anton felt he had to surrender to Lika, and to return home. On Sunday 24 January 1893, just before he left, he reluctantly dined tête-à-tête with the sister of Maria Kiseliova – Nadezhda Golubeva, a senator's wife and amateur writer. Anton had last met her at Babkino in the summer of 1887. Anton was forthright with Nadezhda: neither her nor Maria's writing was any good, because it was done without sweat; his own success came not from genius, but luck and toil. Nadezhda observed Anton closely:

> He cast a quick eye around the room; I understood that look and hastened to tell him that my husband would not be dining with him as he was away. Chekhov brightened up suddenly and barked out as of old: 'Oh, how glad I am! You know, Nadezhda, I don't have your husband's good manners. My papa and mama sold herrings.' ... Chekhov was turning the napkin in an astoundingly odd way, as if it irritated him terribly, he crumpled it, twisted it, finally put it behind him. He was on tenterhooks. I couldn't understand what this all meant. Suddenly he fired: 'I'm sorry, Nadezhda, I'm not used to sitting down to dinner, I always eat as I walk ... In the last six years I've aged by twenty years.' ... There was such tiredness in his face!

I thought: the springtime of his life has passed, there has been no summer, autumn has come straight away.[27]

That tired disillusionment is equally strong in Shcheglov's diary entry for the next day: 'Chekhov and Co. is not literature, but [*quoting Nadson*] "Our useless ant hill, our world of pygmies not of men."'[28] On 26 January 1893, Anton was back in his Moscow ant hill, climbing the stairs to see Lika. After nearly three years' evasion, she must have felt, Anton had surrendered.

THIRTY-NINE

Sickbay
February–March 1893

ANTON HAD ENJOYED PETERSBURG so much that he thought of renting an apartment there. In the frozen countryside, he forgot such frivolity. Pavel, after watching the cow give birth, collapsed and prepared to die. Anton fetched Masha, delirious with a temperature of 40°C, from Moscow. She grew worse, and Countess Mamuna came down to nurse her. Lika, always ill at ease in times of crisis, stayed away. Then Anton himself fell ill. He wrote to Aleksandr on 6 February 1893:

1) Father is ill. He has bad spinal pains and numb fingers. Not continuously, it comes in attacks like angina. The symptoms seem to be senile. He needs treatment, but 'his lordship is dining' furiously, rejecting moderation: pancakes all day, hot flour dishes for supper and all sorts of rubbishy snacks. He says 'I'm stricken with paralysis', but won't obey.
2) Masha is ill. She was in bed for a week with a high temperature. We thought it was typhoid. Now she's better.
3) I have flu. I am doing nothing and am irritable.
4) The pedigree calf has frostbitten ears.
5) The geese pecked off the cockerel's comb.
6) Visitors keep coming and staying the night.
7) The rural authorities are demanding a medical report from me.
8) The house has subsidence and some doors won't shut.
9) The sub-zero temperatures continue.
10) The sparrows are copulating.

Now Anton needed Aleksandr's help. While in Petersburg Anton had found he had no right to live there. A humble townsman, no longer a Moscow resident, he needed a permit to reside in either capital city. He had to obtain *dvorianin* (noble) status to enjoy full civic freedom.

Suvorin found the solution and Aleksandr did the work. Aleksandr lobbied with the Medical Department of the Interior Ministry to appoint Anton a supernumerary civil servant. Now, like Aleksandr and Vania, he had rank and civic rights. Employed by a Petersburg ministry (he forwent a salary), Anton could reside only in Petersburg; to reside in Moscow as well, he had to take leave or, better, retire. The first half of 1893 was spent securing appointment, the second retirement. Then Anton Chekhov could live and travel anywhere. (His parents still needed, to reside in Melikhovo, an annual passport issued by the police in Taganrog.) Aleksandr's reward was to be invited, with his elder boys, but without Natalia, to Melikhovo. Now that Misha was two, Natalia's passion fixed on her son; her stepsons were left to Aleksandr's care. Aleksandr won little sympathy or thanks from Anton. He sent photographs, taken at Melikhovo or printed from Sakhalin plates. Anton grumbled that he had no room to display them and that he despised Aleksandr's hobbies, fretwork and photography.

Lika reappeared. In February, as the patients in Melikhovo recovered, she came with Masha for weekends there. In March she spent a whole week, from the 23rd (her name day) to Easter Sunday, but Anton was still hard to lure to Moscow. She wrote on 1 April 1893: 'I've made you some perfume, if you don't come soon, I'll give it to somebody else . . . All men are bastards. Come!' Pavel set off to see Vania and do the rounds of Moscow's churches. Masha and Anton took over Pavel's diary and parodied his lugubrious style:

> 18 March: −1°. Glory to God, all have left and only two, myself and Mme. Chekhova remain. 19: Masha and Mizinova came . . . 20: Mama dreamt of a nanny goat on a chamberpot, this is a good sign. 21 Sunday: Semashko came. We ate roast udder. 22 We heard a lark. A crane flew by in the evening. Semashko left. 23 Mama dreamt of a goose in a priest's hat. This is a good omen. Masha's belly aches. We slaughtered a pig. 24. We made sausages.

Anton was again hiding from admirers. In February Aleksandra Pokhlebina had lost her pupils and her sanity. She raved that a morphine-addicted rival for Anton's affections had hired men to attack her. Anton heard from her again in March 1893: 'Just the thought that you don't care about my suffering drives me mad, I feel I won't survive.

If you really don't care what happens to me, then at least pretend, make believe that you like me . . .' Pokhlebina's life and Anton's peace of mind were saved when her family set up a metallurgical plant, and she went to work there. Anton also persuaded *The Performing Artist* to publish her eccentric *New Ways of Getting Piano Technique.*

War broke out between the two camps, Suvorin's and Lavrov's, in which Chekhov had pitched his tents. *Russian Thought* accused the Suvorins of profiting from the Panama Canal scandal.[29] On 1 March Anton went to Moscow, with Lika, and calmly drank five glasses of vodka with Lavrov at *Russian Thought.* On the 5th, two days later, the Dauphin came to *Russian Thought*, struck Lavrov, and took the night train back to Petersburg. Suvorin was as upset by the distress that 'Liolia', his darling Dauphin, had undergone as by public hostility to all Suvorins. Two weeks later Suvorin, Grigorovich and their wives set off for Vienna. Suvorin spent most of 1893 abroad.

Anton was not only deprived of a friend, but his most important relationship was damaged. Few of his letters reached Suvorin that spring and summer: the Dauphin and his brother were intercepting their father's mail. *New Times* turned vicious as the Dauphin took over. Aleksandr trembled for his job: the Dauphin would not speak to him or print him. The office of *New Times* felt that Anton's involvement in *Russian Thought* was black ingratitude to Suvorin, his maker. The Dauphin claimed that Anton had written abuse to his father. Hearing of the assault on Lavrov, Chekhov told Masha on 11 March:

> So between me and Suvorin [*junior*] everything is now finished, even though he is writing me snivelling letters. A son of a bitch who swears at people every day and is famous for it, struck a man for swearing at him.

Anton told Aleksandr that the breach was only partially mended:

> The old building has cracked and must collapse. I'm sorry for the old man, he wrote me a penitent letter; probably, I shan't have to break with him permanently; but as for the office and the Dauphin's clique, there seems little chance of any sort of relations with them.

New Times had lost Chekhov as a writer. It was to lose all its respectable contributors, and its verve degenerated into chauvinism. Even its editors resigned, went mad, or wrote anonymous denunciations. As Suvo-

23. LEFT The actors
Pavel Svobodin and
Vladimir Davydov
with Anton and
Suvorin, January 1889

24. BELOW Repin's
drawing 'Literary
Society' in St
Petersburg, 1889
shows Anton second
from right and
Suvorin far right

25. Anton Chekhov, January 1890
inscribed to Kleopatra Karatygina
'from the artist on tour in Odessa'

26. ABOVE Lika
Mizinova in the early
1890s

27. LEFT At the
Korneev house before
setting off for Sakhalin,
April 1890;
back row Aleksandr
Ivanenko, Vania, Pavel;
middle row Masha
Korneeva (the land-
lord's daughter). Lika
Mizinova, Masha,
Evgenia, Seriozha
Korneev; *front* Misha
and Anton

28. ABOVE Convicts being fettered on Sakhalin

29. BELOW Anton on a picnic with Japanese consular officials on Sakhalin, October 1890

30. RIGHT Levitan with gun-dog, early 1890s

31. TOP The house at Melikhovo
(painting by Simov)

32. ABOVE Masha, Anton, Vania behind,
Aleksandra Liosova (Vania's fiancée),
Misha, Aleksandr Smagin (Masha's
suitor), 25 March 1892

33. RIGHT Cousin Aleksei Dolzhenko,
Anton in wheelbarrow, Misha behind,
Giliarovsky pushing, Vania at right at
Melikhovo, Easter 1892

34. ABOVE LEFT With Pavel Svobodin at Melikhovo, June 1892

35. ABOVE RIGHT Aleksandr *left* and Vania at Melikhovo, July 1892

36. BELOW Aleksandr's sons Kolia and Tosia by the stables at Melikhovo, July 1892

37. LEFT Pavel and Evgenia at Melikhovo, July 1892

39. BELOW Natalia Golden-Chekhova with son Misha, 1893

38. Anton with neighbours and colleagues: *standing* Dr Kurkin, Dr Vitte, Prince Shakhovskoi; *sitting* Anton, Dr Kashintsev, Misha, Khmeliov (Serpukhov council), summer 1893

41. Elena Shavrova, *c.* 1894

40. 'The Temptations of St Antony': Tatiana
Shchepkina-Kupernik, Lidia Iavorskaia and Anton, late 1893

42. Masha and Natalia Lintvariova painting watched by artist Sakharov at Luka, *c.* 1894

43. LEFT Masha in the garden at Melikhovo, *c.* 1894

44. BELOW Anton, Mamin-Sibiriak and Ignati Potapenko, 9 January 1896

45. Sonia and Vania Chekhov with their son Volodia, 1896

rin senior failed to hold back the anti-Semitic barbarities of *New Times*, the breach affected the two men personally. Anton dropped the idea of going to the Chicago Exhibition because the Dauphin intended to come.[30]

Olga Kundasova, crossing Russia from Novocherkassk, where she researched into mathematics, to Moscow and Petersburg, where she disseminated her findings, felt more for Suvorin. On 10 March she appealed to Anton:

> Anton, Suvorin was about to go to Feodosia today, but has put it off. I have, by the way, given him a[*nother*] letter addressed to you and written that he must not be left alone in his present nervous state. I even suggested that you should accompany Aleksei to Feodosia. Be a good friend, do that and distract him if only a little bit ... He wants to call you out to Lopasnia station. So be ready. I ask just one thing: not a word to him about the letter which you will have from his hands. Tear it up.

Anton replied to Kundasova so strongly about his own shattered nerves that she did not dare show the letter to Suvorin. Soon, however, Suvorin was in Vienna listening to Grigorovich's tales of sexual exploits. In late March he was ill in Venice, nursed by the Grigoroviches. In mid April the Grigoroviches and Anna Suvorina turned back. Suvorin bought himself 1650 francs worth of furniture and began a lonely peregrination to Biarritz and Paris.

Unlike Anton, his younger brothers had decided to marry. After November 1892 Vania's fiancée, Aleksandra Liosova, had stopped coming to Melikhovo, but by Easter 1893 Vania was betrothed to Sofia Andreeva, a teacher at the Basmannaia school – 'a long-nosed gentlewoman from Kostroma', Anton sneered. (Liosova later told Anton 'Ivan asked me not to meet him again, for his hatred for me is too great.') Countess Mamuna continued to visit Melikhovo, where Misha, to Anton's irritation, lived throughout 1893, employed at a tax office in nearby Serpukhov. Less was said of Misha's engagement to Mamuna, although he visited Moscow to see what the family jokingly called 'the government offices – brunette in a red jacket'. On 26 April Anton, however, told Suvorin:

> At Easter the countess writes she is off to see her aunt in Kostroma. There have been no more letters until recently. Misha yearns, hears

she is in Moscow, goes to see her and, O wonders, sees people hanging about the windows and the gates. What is it? It turns out there is a marriage in the house, the countess is marrying some goldminer. How's that? Misha comes back in despair and thrusts under my nose the countess's tender letters, full of love, asking me to solve this psychological problem.

Anton had discovered Kipling's substitute for women, and told his architect friend Franz Schechtel in March 1893:

> Dear Franz, can you imagine, I smoke cigars ... I find they taste far better, they're healthier and cleaner, although, more expensive. You're an expert in cigars, I'm still an ignoramus and dilettante. Please instruct me: what cigars should I smoke and *where in Moscow* can I buy them? I now smoke Petersburg Ten-Kate, called El Armado, Londres, made there from imported Havana tobacco, strong; you can judge their length by ... [*Schechtel blacked out a phallus*]

Schechtel, who was now a rich and fashionable man, sent back a hundred Havana cigars from Riga. In gratitude Anton called on Schechtel on 1 May 1893 and left him a banded cigar with instructions: 'It must be smoked not just standing and with hat doffed, but also "God Save the Tsar" must be played and gendarmes must prance around you.' The best cigar in the world, however, provides only an hour of bliss. Leikin had promised Anton his heart's desire. The arrangements kept on falling through, but finally, on 5 April, as Leikin's diary shows, Anton's desires were met:

> Khudekov's servants are taking the Khudekov birds from the Bird Show to the country, to Riazan province, and will at the same time deliver, it's not out of their way, two dachshunds to Chekhov in Moscow.

FORTY

Dachshund Summer
April–August 1893

ON THURSDAY 15 APRIL Masha brought to Melikhovo 5 lb of lard, 10 lb of pork breast, 10 lb of candles, and two dachshunds. She named the blackish dog Brom (*bromine*) and the tan bitch Quinine (Anton christened them Brom Isaevich and Khina Markovna.) They were frozen on the cart journey, after a week in Vania's house, where they had been banished to the privy. Anton thanked Leikin:

> The dachshunds have been running through all the rooms, being affectionate, barking at the servants. They were fed and then they began to feel utterly at home. At night they dug the earth and newly-sown seed from the window boxes and distributed the galoshes from the lobby round all the rooms and in the morning, when I took them for a walk round the garden they horrified the farm dogs who have never seen such monstrosities. The bitch is nicer than the dog ... But both have kind, grateful eyes.

The dachshunds spent the day chasing hens and geese out of the garden. Anton told Leikin 4 August 1893:

> Brom is nimble and supple, polite and sensitive, Quinine is awkward, fat, idle and cunning. Brom likes birds, Quinine digs her nose into the ground. They both love to cry from excess of emotion. They know why they are punished. Brom often vomits. He is in love with a farm bitch. Quinine, however, is still an innocent maiden. They love going for walks across the fields and in the woods, but only with us. I have to smack them almost every day: they grab patients by the trousers, they quarrel when they eat, and so on. They sleep in my room.

Misha was amazed by Anton's affection:

> Every evening Quinine would come up to Anton, put her front paws on his knees and look into his eyes pathetically and devotedly. He

would change his expression and say in a broken old man's voice: 'Quinine! You poor old thing! You ought to go to hospital, you'd feel better there.' He spent a whole thirty minutes talking to the dog and made everyone in the house helpless with laughter. Then came Brom's turn. He too would put his front paws on Anton's knee and the fun would start again.

In late April the starving cows and sheep left the sheds to graze with the communal flocks. Ploughing and sowing started. The Chekhov family was up from dawn to dusk. Warm weather brought patients with sores, wounds and mental illness. Epidemics of scarlet fever and measles raged; it was also a critical time for tuberculosis victims. Anton barely mentioned his own cough, but wrote about his patients. The Tolokonnikovs, peasants turned mill-owners, disgusted him: after a vigorously celebrated marriage Chekhov was summoned urgently for the couple's inflamed genitals; another old man demanded treatment for his aching balls after marrying a young bride.

Once again the authorities feared cholera, and Anton was asked not to leave the district for more than a few days. This time the council paid for an assistant, a *feldsheritsa* (paramedic) called Maria Arkadak-skaia. Her notes alarmed Anton. On 11 July she wrote 'send me cocaine, my teeth are killing me'. By August, when cholera was only twelve miles away, Maria was so addicted to morphine that Chekhov could not leave her in charge for a day. In early August he put her in Iakovenko's asylum at Meshcherskoe – Iakovenko took only Anton's more interesting cases – and coped alone. Anton needed morphine too, he told Franz Schechtel on 19 April 1893: 'I have hæmorrhoids, awful, like grapes, growing in bunches from my behind . . . from the part of me which my father used to thrash.' He steeled himself for an operation in Moscow but became too ill to travel:

> I have two dozen or so diseases, with hæmorrhoids the main one. Hæmorrhoids make the whole body very irritated. These ailments affect one's psyche in the most undesirable way: I am irritated, I turn nasty etc. I am treating it by celibacy and solitude . . .[31]

Hæmorrhoids were his excuse for not seeing Lika: 'a general's disease – can't travel,' he told her. The dachshunds, not Lika, were caressed that spring.

Anton complained to Aleksandr that Suvorin was not getting his letters. The Dauphin demanded that Anton edit Aleksandr's copy for *New Times*, but the brothers would not let the Dauphin sow discord between them. That summer they were closer. Aleksandr was unhappy with Natalia, and saw her and the children only at weekends forty miles outside Petersburg. After five months without alcohol, he was suffering again from 'ambulatory typhoid', and from toothache, which he treated with a mixture of resin, ether, ammonia and menthol that Anton prescribed. For Anton's ills Aleksandr, on 15 May, prescribed marriage:

> When you decide to get 'hitched', then things will be fine up top. A wife must not argue. 'Shut up!' deals with that ... All you have to do is follow the general law, submit to Aunt Liudmila's desires and take some lessons in God-fearing coitus from Uncle Mitrofan.

Aleksandr came to Melikhovo for a week in June: he found the suppressed unhappiness of its inhabitants unbearable. On 9 June 1893, as he waited at Lopasnia for the train to Moscow and Petersburg, he scribbled a rambling letter (which Lika, who was arriving, took with her to Melikhovo):

> I left Melikhovo without saying goodbye to the Tramontano [*their nickname for Pavel*]. He was asleep, so let him be. May he dream of smoked sturgeons and olives ... I suffered all the time I watched you, the foul way you live ... In [*mother's*] opinion you are a sick man ... and the dogs, damn them, she isn't going to feed them any more ... The only way to stop all these misunderstandings and mutual insults, tears, inevitable suffering, muffled sighs and bitter tears is your final decision, only your departure. Mother absolutely can't understand you and never will ... Throw everything up: your dreams of the country, your love of Melikhovo and the labour and feelings ... What sense is there in the Tramontani eating up your soul as rats eat tallow candles? ... You and our sister have a false relationship. One kind word from you with a sincere note and she is all yours ... Lika is approaching. I have to finish.

After Aleksandr had gone (leaving in the new pond a bottle with a polyglot message from a shipwreck), Evgenia went to a convent for three days' retreat. Only those who were closest to Anton, as was Aleksandr, understood how irritable physical pain, mental stress and loneliness made him and how much he could, without intending to, torment his mother and sister.

In summer 1893 Anton wrote almost nothing new. He denied that he was writing a comedy about Siberian exiles and their jailors. He kept up his reputation with old work. When *Russian Thought* published 'An Anonymous Story', in March 1893, few readers knew that Chekhov had abandoned it five years before, before taking it up again, because of its political theme. A revolutionary (the anonymous narrator) is planted as a servant to spy on a minister's son, but reneges on his mission and elopes with his target's mistress, who dies abroad of TB (only three heroines in all Chekhov's mature work die, and two of TB). When the narrator returns to Russia, he surrenders the heroine's baby girl to the enemy. 'An Anonymous Story' is Chekhov's only story with revolutionaries, aristocratic protagonists, or a Petersburg setting: the work is more like Turgenev's than Chekhov's. Anton's own world is better reflected in 'Big Volodia and Little Volodia', whose forlorn heroine might have suggested to Lika Mizinova that she was Anton's raw material, not muse. Many more times she would see her vulnerable character and unlucky fate mirrored, even anticipated, in Anton's fiction.

In 1893 Anton's reading was as important as his writing. Zola's novel *Dr Pascal* was serialized in Russia. Dr Pascal devotes himself to the welfare of mankind, defending humanism against the Christian piety of his niece Clotilde. She nevertheless comforts him and becomes his mistress. Anton's life at Melikhovo with Masha seemed to outsiders an idealization of *Dr Pascal*. No wonder that he discussed the novel heatedly with Suvorin, once communication between them was re-established. There was one 'happy' event at Melikhovo: on 9 July Vania married Sofia in the local church. Six weeks later, Anton was telling Suvorin that he felt crowded by the presence of Vania, his wife and the homeless flautist Ivanenko. Real inspiration visited Anton once, after a heavy dinner. He awoke from a nightmare, telling Misha he had dreamt of a black monk. Into 'The Black Monk' he wrote at the end of 1893 comes imagery from his orchard, where workmen desperately tried to shield the blossom from frost. A story of overwork leading to madness and TB, it shows Vsevolod Garshin's ghost working on Chekhov. It needed a musical theme for the plot to crystallize.

The bringer of music to Melikhovo in August 1893 was Ignati Potapenko, and the bringer of Potapenko was Suvorin. By May Suvorin was in Paris, seeking distraction in Le Moulin Rouge, with the doctors of La Salpêtrière, or in jewellers' shops. Only on 7/19 June does his diary show animation:

> Back at my hotel I found a letter from Potapenko asking me for 300–400 roubles. Today I gave him 300 roubles ... Maria [*Potapenko's second wife*] ... said that she needed treatment, some operation had to be done, but they had no money. Potapenko works a lot, far too hard, and doesn't conceal from himself that this is wearing him out; but he works fast.

Potapenko invited himself and Sergeenko to Melikhovo. Anton groaned: he recalled Sergeenko taking him to see Potapenko,' 'the god of boredom', in 1889. Sergeenko had proved unmitigated tedium – all 1893 he had urged Anton to make a pilgrimage with him to see Tolstoy. Anton resisted, fleeing a Moscow bathhouse when he found that Tolstoy was there. He wanted to see Tolstoy alone, and hid from Sergeenko and even Tolstoy's son, Liovushka.

Patients died. A rainy summer washed away the harvest. With Sergeenko, Potapenko arrived on 1 August and, as the god of amusement, lightened Anton's gloom. He plunged into everything, even the muddy pond Anton had dug. Anton recanted to Suvorin (who warned that Potapenko might be a crook): 'My Odessa impression misled me ... Potapenko sings very nicely and plays the violin, he and I had a very interesting time, quite apart from the violin and drawing room songs.' In Anton's phrase, the 'crow' of Odessa had become the 'eagle' of Moscow. Anton talked as intimately to him as to Suvorin. Potapenko became an *alter ego* in a few days. He fell under Anton's spell and respected his secrets. Potapenko recalled:

> The head of the house was Anton. His tastes dominated everything, everything was done to please him. He treated his mother with tenderness, but showed his father only filial respect ... And he said that his father had been a cruel man ... He had cast a pall on his childhood and aroused in his soul a protest against the despotic imposition of belief.[32]

Anton, for all his memories of enforced church services, sang with Potapenko: 'not love songs but church music ... He had a fairly resonant bass. He knew the liturgy extremely well and loved improvising a family choir.' Again, as she had used Levitan, Lika used Potapenko to arouse Anton. Lika joined the men, singing to the accompaniment of Potapenko's violin. The music was Braga's 'Wallachian Legend'. The main motif of 'The Black Monk' was born, and the form too, for as Shostakovich noted, 'The Black Monk' has a perfect sonata form. Potapenko and Lika were thrown together; other harmonies, as ominous as those of Braga's 'Legend', were born.

That summer Potapenko was a *deus ex machina* in many of Anton's plots. In Petersburg he made Suvorin's accountants recalculate Anton's debt: instead of owing Suvorin 3482 roubles, Anton found he was owed 2000 and could abandon a plan to sell Suvorin ten years' rights to his books.[33] Potapenko prided himself on extracting money from publishers. He was paying for a sick second wife in Paris and an embittered first wife in the Crimea. Potapenko's unsinkable temperament made all problems, even Anton's, a pretext for merriment. He made things work. Anton's hæmorrhoids, coughing, and the depression, which Aleksandr's letter had tried to pinpoint, vanished.

On 30 July/11 August, in Stuttgart, coming home, Suvorin wrote a poem that showed in what deep gulfs he was drowning. It ends:

> I feel the flies are crawling
> Over the membrane of my brain . . .
> 'It's not flies sitting in your head,'
> The surgeon answers with a laugh.
> 'Old age has come, and your brain
> Is being eaten all the time
> While water is filling up the holes.'

Suvorin reached Petersburg in August; he described his symptoms to Anton. Anton told him not to worry and Suvorin took the train, alone, back to western Europe.

FORTY-ONE

Happy Avelan
October–December 1893

NOT UNTIL LATE OCTOBER could Chekhov visit Moscow. He made only day trips to Serpukhov, to council meetings, or to meet Olga Kundasova. After Potapenko's arrival, his mood remained buoyant, despite the washed-out harvest. A new well was dug; fish swam in the new pond; there were watermelons from the kitchen garden. *Russian Thought* began serial publication of *The Island of Sakhalin*. (Its publication as a book was to come afterwards.) Despite its understated quality, it earned Chekhov esteem: he was now a conscience for the nation, like Tolstoy.

The desire to revisit Petersburg receded – Anton was not to go there for nearly two years. Suvorin was abroad, talking to novelists he published in Russia: Zola and Daudet. Aleksandr, after being so outspoken, was ignored. After Potapenko, Anton was seeking new confidants and setting aside old friends. He was apparently unmoved when the poet Pleshcheev died of a stroke in Paris. Some of the women who loved Anton recognized a change, and stood back: in autumn 1893 Olga Kundasova wrote:

(25 September) I don't think it's bad for you to be in solitude.
(17 November) I want, and I don't want, to visit you. One lives mostly on illusions and feels even worse when they scatter. Devoted to you with all my soul, Kund.

Both Olga Kundasova and Suvorin recognized that they had in common not only a love for Anton, but symptoms of mental illness, manic depression. Kundasova sought treatment, while Suvorin sought distraction. Despite their diametrically opposed political views, Kundasova and Suvorin had respect, even affection, for each other and, for the next decade, gave each other support. Suvorin's support was monetary, which Olga nearly choked on. 'Don't think that I am charmed by *the prospects of free provision at others' expense.*'[34]

Another woman also withdrew from Anton on 16 October 1893: 'I feel I shall write a lot of various stupid things today, so – farewell! With far more than respect, Aleksandra Pokhlebina.'

Once autumn came, Lika visited less often. A more varied social life, as well as teaching in the Rzhevskaia School, kept her in Moscow. Acolytes also retreated. Bilibin, Shcheglov and Gruzinsky all felt neglected. Ezhov was becoming demented: 'Critics have started leaping from behind gates, biting my trousers ... I've become a complete swine and write to you like a drunken peasant.'[35] All editors slammed their doors in Ezhov's face after he offered *Amusement* a sketch called 'The Sad Boy'. Two women ask a street urchin where he lives: '"In a cunt," replied the rude boy and went his way.'

Grim news came from Petersburg. On 25 October Tchaikovsky died, apparently of cholera. Suvorin, who recorded every scrap of gossip, had noted Tchaikovsky living as man and 'wife' with the poet Apukhtin, but heard not a whisper about suicide or homosexual scandal. All Russia felt bereaved and blamed, if anyone, Dr Bertenson who failed to save the composer. Anton took Tchaikovsky's death as calmly as Pleshcheev's. On the same day he heard from Aleksandr of his own demise:

> You, my friend, are dangerously ill with consumption and will soon die. Rest in peace! Today Leikin came to our office with this sad news ... he shed bitter tears while he spoke, claiming that you had confided to him alone in the world the tale of your so early extinction from an incurable ailment.

Aleksandr warned Anton that if he didn't die soon, he would be accused of publicity-seeking.

Anton leapt into action as if to scotch the rumours and to live to the full. On 27 October 1893 he broke free to Moscow and stayed until 7 November. On 25 November he was back in Moscow for four weeks, ostensibly to read the proofs of *Sakhalin*. In Moscow Anton had a new nickname, 'Happy Avelan'. In France the Russian Admiral Avelan was received with Bacchic hospitality, to celebrate the new Franco-Russian alliance. Anton, like Admiral Avelan, began to relish wine, acclaim and beautiful women. Lika's happiness was soon undermined by the knowledge that she was now one of several women in Anton's life.

Anton-Avelan's 'squadron' included Potapenko, Sergeenko, the superman-reporter Uncle Giliai (Giliarovsky) and the wheezing editor of *The Performing Artist*, Kumanin (whose life the squadron's expeditions shortened). They haunted the Loskutnaia, Louvre and Madrid hotels. They were entertained by Lika and her friend, the budding opera singer, Varia Eberle. Two women from Kiev also joined them.

One was Tania Shchepkina-Kupernik. Nineteen years old, less than five foot tall, the daughter of a rake, the lawyer Kupernik, she had the blood of Russia's great actor Shchepkin in her veins. She was already famed as a verse translator from French and English: she singled out plays with a strong female role – *Sappho*, *The Taming of the Shrew*, *The Distant Princess*. She was a Sapphic love poet. Misha Chekhov already knew her; now she moved into Anton's life. Tania charmed men, too, and Anton would value her above any other woman writer. She was called 'topsy-turvy' (*kuvyrkom* sounded like Kupernik) for her impetuosity.

Tania lived in the Hotel Madrid, which was linked to the Hotel Louvre through corridors (known as the 'catacombs' or 'Pyrenees'). In the Hotel Louvre lived the love of Tania's life, also from Kiev, the twenty-three-year-old actress Lidia Iavorskaia. Their love affair began as loudly as it ended: Tania had come to deny that she had slandered Lidia in Kiev. For 1893 and 1894, Lidia's heart was Tania's, although she devoted the rest of her person to her manager, Korsh (of the Korsh theatre), to a lover in the Customs Department, to Anton Chekhov and, perhaps, to Ignati Potapenko. Like Tania, Iavorskaia was a vivacious polyglot. Her background was darker. Her father, Hübbenett, of Huguenot origin, was Chief of Police in Kiev and, like her, promiscuous, self-important, vindictive, yet generous. Hübbenett helped Iavorskaia literally to force herself on stage. Sensuality made up for shallowness. In Moscow she hypnotized Korsh into hiring her as *La Dame aux camélias*. Lidia Iavorskaia stormed through Anton's life: she aroused both lust and disgust in him. The 'sirens of the Louvre', however, romped with Isaak Levitan, who called them his 'little girls', and Anton found this off-putting.

Avelan's expeditions to theatres, restaurants and long sessions in hotel rooms were fuelled by the passion between Tania and Lidia Iavorskaia. Iavorskaia destroyed Tania's letters; Tania kept everything. Bits of paper and card, in Russian and French, in prose and verse, show Lidia responding to the poetess's affection:

> let's go ... I await you. I kiss you as strongly as I love you. Lidia ...
> Cette nuit d'Athènes était belle. Le beau est inoubliable. Cher poète, si vous saviez quel mal de tête ...
> J'attends le vice suprême et je vous envoie votre dot.
> Ma petite Sappho. Venez immédiatement, urgent ...[36]

Anton saw Lidia act Napoleon's mistress Katrina Hubsche in Sardou's *Madame Sans-Gêne*. He raved to Suvorin on 11 November 1893:

> I spent two weeks in intoxication. Because my life in Moscow has been nothing but feasts and new friendships, they call me Avelan to tease me. Never before have I felt so free. Firstly, I have no flat – I can live where I want, secondly, I still haven't got my passport and ... girls, girls, girls ... Recently frivolity has taken me over and I feel drawn to people as never before, and literature has become my Abishag [*King David's comforter*]

In the same letter Anton asserted that all thinkers are impotent by forty: sexual potency, he implied, was for savages, even though he hoped, in Apuleius' phrase, to go on 'drawing his bow'.

Both Tania and Lidia did their best. After he left on 7 November Tania sent him a poem (drafted on the back of one of Lidia's love-letters to her):

> All, all our dreams see Avelan
> All that we see recalls this man,
> Through the rosy mist he looms
> And quietly sails into our rooms.[37]

Tania wrote her Avelan notes on Lidia's behalf as her own. One sent to room No. 54 at the end of November runs: 'Perhaps you will honour with your presence the modest room No. 8. And I shan't say how happy the hostess will be. Tatiana K.' Iavorskaia set her sights on Anton and frightened Lika. Lika enjoyed the party, and even added her phrases to joint messages to Anton, but, embarrassed, humiliated, even shocked, she now wanted out. Anton had that summer claimed he was too old to be a lover; now she saw him in thrall to the 'sirens of the Louvre'. On 2 November she fired across his bows:

> I also know your attitude – either condescending pity or complete neglect ... don't invite me to your place – don't meet me! – that's not so important for you, but it may help me to forget you. I cannot leave earlier than December or January – otherwise I would go now ...

Two days later, when Anton was back in Melikhovo, Lika wrote:

> I got to bed at 8 a.m. Mme Iavorskaia was with us, she said that Chekhov is a charmer and that she definitely intended to marry him, she asked me to help and I promised to do everything for your mutual happiness. You are so nice and accessible that I thought I wouldn't find it hard.

Lidia met Anton at Masha's empty flat (Masha was in Melikhovo). In spring 1894 she recalled the talk they had one November night:

> I was fleeing a man who was harassing me and I threw myself on your hospitality ... You kept asking me 'what was I after?' When revulsion and pity for the man battled inside me, you, an artist, as a psychologist, as a human being, told me about a person's right to dispose of their affections, to love or not to love, freely submitting to inner feeling.[38]

Lidia Iavorskaia extracted a promise of a play for her, to be called *Daydreams*.

The sirens had made Anton forget Suvorin. He wrote on 28 November: 'For mysterious reasons I shall not stay with you but in the Hotel Russia on the Moika.' Suvorin was badly upset. A draft of his reply runs:

> 30 November 1893. 7 a.m. Yes, 7 a.m. Things are bad, dear boy, I don't sleep at all and I don't know how and when it will end ... When can I summon you to Petersburg? Well, if you stay in the Hotel Russia in the back and beyond, might you not as well be in Moscow, from my point of view, at least? It may be more advantageous for you, though I don't think we were much bother to you, but this really is hateful to me ...[39]

Anton's next letter to Suvorin was a kick in the teeth. He had met the Moscow publisher Sytin and liked 'the only publishing firm in

Russia that has a Russian smell about it and doesn't push the peasant-customer about'. He drew up a contract with Sytin, receiving 2300 roubles for the book rights to old stories. Anton's publications were now in Moscow, not Petersburg, journals. The new editor of *The Northern Herald*, Liubov Gurevich, gave up all hope of persuading Chekhov to give the journal a major work: in November 1893, to Chekhov's fury – he cursed her Jewishness – she insisted on immediate repayment of 400 roubles she had advanced: Anton telegraphed Suvorin, who paid without demurring. Anton rarely paid back an advance. Shcheglov's diary boasts: 'There are four kings of advances: me, Chekhov, Potapenko and Sergeenko.'[40]

On 19 December, Anton felt ill. He stood Lika up – she had expected to see him – and left for Melikhovo. The clan gathered: Vania brought Sofia down. Lika was invited for the holidays. Her acceptance of 23 December 1893 had a new name in it, Ignati Potapenko's:

> Dear [*crossed out*: Igna...] Anton, I keep travelling and travelling but I can't get to Melikhovo – the cold is so terrible that I dare to beg you (of course, if this letter reaches you) to send something warm for me and Potapenko, who at your request and out of friendship for me will accompany me. Poor man! ... At the Ermitage they keep asking why you haven't been seen there so long. I answer that you are busy writing a play for Iavorskaia's benefit night.

Potapenko added a postscript, asserting his right to bring Lika to Melikhovo.[41] Ivanenko warned Chekhov that Christmas:

> Hurry to Moscow and save *her* from perdition, not me but *her*. You are awaited like a god. Lika is very fond of white and black beer and a few other things that are her secret and which she will reveal to you.[42]

Anton did nothing to save Lika, who now understood that she was being handed over. On 27 December cousin Georgi arrived from Taganrog. Pavel had gone to Moscow to attend as many church services as he could. Anton wrote to his editor at *Russian Thought*, Viktor Goltsev: 'Potapenko and Lika have just arrived. Potapenko is already singing. But so sadly, you can't imagine!' Anton ended: 'Lika has started singing too.'

FORTY-TWO

The Women Scatter
January–February 1894

ON NEW YEAR'S DAY 1894, Potapenko and Lika left Melikhovo together: Anton told Suvorin the next day:

> I can't take any more guests. Though there was one pleasant guest – Potapenko, who sang all the time ... In the dining room the astronomer [*Kundasova*] is drinking coffee and laughing hysterically. Ivanenko is with her and in the next room my brother's wife, and so on.

As guests and relatives left, they were met in Moscow by Pavel, happier that winter in the company of Vania, his 'positive' son. Pavel stayed in Moscow until 10 January: in Moscow, not Melikhovo, Aleksandr met his father. The last irksome guest left Melikhovo for Taganrog on Tatiana's day, 12 January, when Anton reappeared in the city, in the Hotel Louvre, room No. 54, near his sirens. Anton's brother, Misha, whom Anton made feel unwanted at Melikhovo, decided to leave for good. Despite his work on the estate, Anton was disparaging him for selfishness. (Potapenko also took a dislike to him, calling him 'enigmatic, like all tax inspectors'.) Misha applied for a transfer from Serpukhov tax office. On 15 February 1894 he went for an interview in Uglich, a northern city where mediæval Tsars had exiled undesirables. Misha was appointed tax inspector in Uglich and left Melikhovo for good on 28 February. His labour at Melikhovo was distilled into a manual for smallholders, *The Granary, A Dictionary of Agriculture*. A year passed before *The Granary* was published by *Russian Thought*. It sold 77 copies in four years.

Anton's fallow period was over: from 28 December 1893 to the first week of January 1894, Moscow readers had a new instalment of *The Island of Sakhalin*, and three stories, 'Big Volodia and Little Volodia' in the newspaper *The Russian Gazette*; 'The Black Monk' in *The*

Performing Artist, and 'A Woman's Kingdom' in *Russian Thought.*
None of the stories was acclaimed: the editors of 'Big Volodia and
Little Volodia' took fright at the story's sexuality and cut it. (Anton
gave his French translator, Jules Legras from Bordeaux, the manuscript for a full version in French.) 'The Black Monk' only later
became famous – the first Chekhov story to be published in English.
Its medical expertise in the study of TB and megalomania is striking,
even though its plot is a tragic love story. A brilliant academic marries
the daughter of the man who brought him up, and then, mad and
sick, deserts her. The story has a Hoffmanesque mix of music (Braga's
elegy) and of the supernatural (the vision of a black monk). But it is
as pregnant with political meaning as 'Ward No. 6' or *The Cherry
Orchard,* for much of the story centres on a great orchard, which goes
to rack and ruin together with the hero. No reader could fail to align
the tyrannical gardener, the hero's father-in-law with autocracy, or
the mad hero with rebellion, and Russia with the orchard – an association that would become explicit in *The Cherry Orchard.* 'The Black
Monk''s publisher, Kumanin, told Shcheglov, however: 'Very watery
and unnatural. But, you know, Chekhov is still a name. It would be
awkward not to print it.'

'A Woman's Kingdom' is a new departure: in three episodes set in
an iron foundry it sketches the disparity and parallel between the
workers' misery and the desolation of the owner, a young woman.
The story shows the influence of Zola and Dostoevsky – Zola in his
portrait of an industrial hell, Dostoevsky in the heroine's disastrous
attempt to mete out charity. If Sazonova's guess in her diary is right,
and the heroine is based on Anna Suvorina, then the iron foundry is
an allegory of the Suvorin empire. The radicals saw none of this:
they felt that Chekhov's depiction of the foundry was 'immoral' and
'obsessed with detail', and for the critics 'The Black Monk' was too
melodramatic a psychiatric case history. Anton was disappointed that
his new works aroused muted reactions. In vain Suvorin lobbied for
The Island of Sakhalin to be awarded a prize, while Moscow University
rejected the work as a thesis that would entitle Chekhov to lecture
on social medicine.

Spurned by critics and academics, Anton connived, to say the very
least, at being superseded in Lika's affections too. Olga Kundasova
noticed an opportunity to regain Anton's love and made herself known

at the end of January 1894: 'If you want to behold me at your place, send horses to meet the post-train and collect your mail on Friday 4 [*February*]. I shall stay the night and then leave for Meshcherskoe. Until we meet beyond the tomb.' Anton told Suvorin she was mad. She did not come. Although she was still attached to Iakovenko's hospital, a year passed before she re-entered Anton's life.

Everyone at Lopasnia and Melikhovo noticed that on 29 January and 22 February Lika Mizinova came and left not with Anton, but with Ignati Potapenko. On Anton's thirty-fourth birthday, 16 January 1894, and for one last time, on 25 February, she saw Anton without Potapenko. When she and Potapenko left Melikhovo on 31 January they took with them on the sleighs to the station what was to be Anton's standard consolation present, two puppies from Quinine, who had mated in the kitchen with one of the farm dogs, Catarrh. The closer Potapenko became to Lika, the more Anton lauded him. 'You are absolutely wrong about Potapenko, there's not an ounce of deviousness about him,' he told Suvorin on 10 January. Potapenko and Lika were not deceiving Anton. Potapenko invited 'Signor Antonio' to celebrate Tatiana's day in Moscow and warned Anton: '(8 January) . . . Lika is away travelling, as a consequence of which I am pining, since I am almost head over heels in love with Lika.' Potapenko was writing frantically to finance his new life. He went on acting as Anton's agent, collecting royalties, handling manuscripts, even in mid February negotiating with the hard-headed publisher Adolf Marx an advance for a novel that Anton would write by 1895 for the popular monthly journal *The Cornfield*. On the back of Marx's letter of agreement, Potapenko wrote to Chekhov:

> I told him I thought Chekhov needed to get away to some blissful country but is prevented by worries about family business . . . Anton, dear boy, go away somewhere to clear skies, to Italy, to Egypt, to Australia, does it matter? It's vital, for I notice a weariness in you . . . Forgive my interfering in your life, but I love you almost as I would a girl.

Lika's letters hinted that Anton could still retrieve her:

> I am completely in love with Potapenko! What can we do, daddy! All the same you will always know how to get rid of me and dump me on somebody else! I am sorry for poor Ignati – he had to go

such a long way (that is, to Melikhovo) and, worse, talk! Awful! Ask him to forgive you for submitting him to such a punishment for two days.

(22 January) Dear Anton. I have something important to ask you. When I was in Melikhovo I forgot my cross and I feel very bad without it . . . For God's sake, tell Aniuta to have a look and then you wear it and bring it to me. You must wear it, or else you will lose it or forget it some other way. Come and see me, uncle, and don't forget about me. Your Lika??

In Anton's notes to Lika, on 20 and 21 February, when he, Lika and Potapenko were together in Moscow, a note of regret, even desire creeps in:

Lika, give me your little hand [*in Russian 'ruchka' also means 'pen'*]; the one I was given smells of herring. I got up a long time ago, I had coffee at Filippov's. A. Chekhov . . .

Darling Lika, today at 6.30 p.m. I shall leave for Melikhovo. Would you like to come with me? We'd return together to Moscow on Saturday. If you don't want to go to Melikhovo, come to the station.

A day after Anton, Lika came to Melikhovo for five days with Potapenko. In the last days of this strange menage Lika conceived a child by Potapenko.

Masha became resentful. She felt angry at what she believed to be Lika's desertion and Potapenko's betrayal of Anton; at the same time she envied Lika her passionate love life. Masha made the new couple feel awkward. On 25 January Potapenko and Lika left Melikhovo; the next day Anton followed them to Moscow. Anton and Potapenko stayed with Suvorin in the same apartment. On 27 January, Potapenko left Moscow for Petersburg and Paris, where his second wife was waiting. He made Masha a present of English watercolour paints and a disquisition on how women artists might eventually rival men. Masha was icy. On Tuesday 1 March 1894 Lika appealed to her:

Dear Masha. Take pity on me and come for God's sake to say goodbye for ever to an unfortunate woman like me. On Saturday evening I am leaving, first for home, and from there straight to Paris. The affair was settled only yesterday . . . Surely your dressmakers would let you say goodbye to a person whom you used to consider a close friend! No, joking apart, I somehow hope you will want to meet me . . .[43]

By 15 March 1894 Lika was in Berlin, on her way to join Potapenko in Paris.

Anton decided to leave the frozen north himself. He made enquiries about a sunny hotel room at Gurzuf, near Yalta in the Crimea, to spend a month recuperating in the warmth, while Masha and Pavel coped with ploughing and sowing. In five days of February spent in Moscow, Anton rejoined a *ménage-à-trois* with Tania and Lidia Iavorskaia in the Hotel Louvre. He posed for a photograph in which the two women look adoringly at him, while his attention has been caught by the photographer: the picture became known as *The Temptations of St Antony*. Iavorskaia's adoration had a price. She wrote on 1 February:

> On 18 February I have my benefit night in Moscow . . . I hope you remember the promise you made to write me at least a one-act play. You told me the plot, it is so entertaining that I am still under its spell and have decided, for some reason, that the play will be called *Daydreams*.

Anton never wrote a word of *Daydreams*. Tania, instead, wrote for her a one-act comedy called *At the Station*. She wanted to present Iavorskaia with a framed blotting-pad – the frame to be engraved with autographs from her admirers. Anton refused to inscribe his name on it. Levitan had offered. 'Believe in yourself, I. Levitan', and Anton would not join his old friend, even on a piece of silver.

In February 1894 the managers of the Hotel Louvre and Madrid decided that the comings and goings through the 'Pyrenees' brought the hotels more notoriety than profit: Tania and Iavorskaia were asked to leave. By April they were living as lovers in the Vesuvius Hotel in Naples.

On 2 March, after seeing Potapenko off to Petersburg, Anton left for the Crimea. He steamed past Melikhovo without stopping at Lopasnia station.

VI

Lika Disparue

Ariane, ma sœur, de quel amour blessée
Vous mourûtes aux bords où vous fûtes laissée!

Racine, *Phèdre*

The spirit in which Albertine had left was doubtless
like that of peoples who use a demonstration of
their armed strength to further the work of their
diplomacy.   Proust, *Albertine disparue*

FORTY-THREE

Abishag cherishes David
March–June 1894

IN MARCH 1894 the Chekhov squadron scattered south and west from Moscow and Melikhovo. On the 4th Anton came ashore at Yalta, storm-tossed but not seasick. Instead of the tiny resort of Gurzuf, he chose Yalta. Settled in a hotel, he had a telegram from Tania and Iavorskaia in Warsaw. Masha wrote on 13 March: 'I was sad to see Lika off and I miss her very badly. Be well and don't cough . . . Mother asks, should she slaughter the bigger pig for Easter?' Lika Mizinova and her 'chaperone' Varia Eberle joined Potapenko in Paris on 16 March: Lika wrote to Anton from Berlin on the 15th:

> I shall die soon and shan't see anything more. Darling, write for old time's sake and don't forget that you gave me your word of honour to come to Paris in June. I shall wait for you and if you write, shall come and meet you. You can count on accommodation, meals and all comforts from me: only the travel will cost you anything. Well, till we meet, hurry, till we meet, definitely in Paris. Don't forget the woman you rejected, [*wavy line*] L. Mizinova.[1]

Anton was in no hurry even to reply. He merely told his French translator (while ordering 100 bottles of best Bordeaux) to look up Potapenko and 'a plump blonde Mlle Mizinova' in Paris. Anton slept till eleven in the morning, and in the evenings chatted to the intellectuals who, hoping for an early spring, were in Yalta for the good of their lungs. They offered no stimulation, although Miroliubov, an opera singer,[2] and an actress adopted Anton and took him over the mountains. Through Miroliubov Chekhov met a medical colleague, Dr Sredin, as consumptive as his patients. Only a few officials fostered culture in Yalta, a seaside town too small to support more than a bookshop, amateur theatricals and a three-form girl's grammar school.

Lika had jumped from one *ménage-à-trois* into another. Potapenko's wife was waiting in Paris. Lika told 'Granny' that she was settled in a pleasant house with a life on Rue Hamelin, seeking a singing teacher. To Masha she was frank: 'Ignati said that he found his spouse very ill and thinks that she has consumption, but I think that she is faking again.'[3]

Lidia Iavorskaia was happier in her new love life, but in Milan she received a letter which her spurned lover, a customs official, had written to her father, Chief of Police Hübbenett. It ran:

> Your daughter has left for Italy with Madame Shchepkina-Kupernik, this departure naturally forces me to burn my boats and I shall not direct a single word of reproach at your daughter. Her liaison with Shchepkina-Kupernik has become a *vile* legend in Moscow, and no wonder ... nobody can pass undefiled by contact with her.[4]

On 23 March Lidia scrawled a letter to Anton, asking him to protect Tania's name. She was proud to be loved by Tania and wanted Anton to use his connections in Petersburg to silence her former lover in the Customs department.

Far from friends, Anton could write again. He was preoccupied with his shortest mature story, 'The Student' – a work which he himself singled out for its concise perfection, as Beethoven did his Eighth Symphony. A student priest crossing a valley before Easter awkwardly retells the betrayal of Christ to two peasant widows, mother and daughter. The women cry, and he intuits a connection between their misery, the tragedy around Christ, the human condition and history. The priest once again represents the creative writer, communicating a force he cannot comprehend to others even more helpless. Poetic economy and subtle symbolic detail distinguish 'The Student'. This is 'late Chekhov', where the protagonist's and the author's eyes become one, and where all is evoked, not stated. Solitude had sprung an inner lock. His friends and mistresses scattered, Anton found an affinity in his fictional characters, and his prose develops an intimate warmth.

Anton had shaken off ideological constraints, too. He told Suvorin:

> Perhaps because I've stopped smoking, Tolstoy's morality has stopped moving me, in the depth of my soul I am hostile to it, and that of course is unjust. Peasant blood flows in me, and you can't astound me with peasant virtues. Since I was a child I have believed

314

in progress and could not do otherwise, since the difference between the time when I was thrashed and the times when thrashing stopped has been enormous. I love clever people, sensitivity, politeness, wit . . . I was affected not by the basic propositions, which were known earlier, but the Tolstoyan way of expressing oneself, the didacticism and probably a sort of hypnotism. Now something in me protests; calculation and justice tell me that electricity and steam show more love for humanity than chastity and vegetarianism.

Sleeping better (and alone), not smoking, drinking little, Anton was bored in Yalta. His heart showed only physical symptoms, arrhythmia. On 27 March 1894 he wrote curtly to Lika: he was not coming to Paris, he told her, and Potapenko should buy her a ticket home. Irony drowns affection:

Dear Lika, when you are a big singer and have a good salary, give me alms: make me your husband and feed me at your expense, so that I can be idle. But if you are dying, then let Varia Eberle, whom as you know I love, do it.

We hear the first hints of *The Seagull*, to which Lika was to contribute so much. As Trigorin tells Nina in the play, Anton tells Lika:

Not for a minute am I free of the thought that I must, am obliged to write. Write, write and write.'

To write and write was not easy in a hotel room: visitors were importunate. One even removed the manuscript of *The Island of Sakhalin* to read at leisure.

Money was running out. Yalta was dearer than Nice. Anton sold his moulting fox-fur coat, and told Masha to send horses to Lopasnia station for the 10, 12 and 15 April. He arrived a week earlier, to a Melikhovo baking in the sunshine that had eluded the Crimea.

In Anton's absence, Pavel had bustled. He supervised confession, communion, christenings and shrivings among the servants, had the priest for dinner and tea, visited the nearby churches and the monastery. Pavel travelled to Moscow to see his sons, Vania and Misha, his nephews Aliosha Dolzhenko and Misha Chokhov, and the clerks at Gavrilov's warehouse. He visited the public baths, bought 'very broad' underpants and attended all the church services he could.

Anton was pleased to find Melikhovo free of guests, but, like Masha, he was upset by Lika's fate. When Anton had encouraged, and Masha condoned, Lika's flight with Potapenko, they had not known that Potapenko's second wife Maria was in Paris. Lika's next letter (3/15 April) said that she was crying, coughing blood, drinking creosote and cod liver oil; her doctor was ordering her to Switzerland. She hated her lodgings, full of foreign girls who wanted to be singers. Potapenko was the cause of her misery:

> I virtually don't see Potapenko, there's no question of coming to Russia with him. Sometimes he comes for half an hour in the morning and, presumably, without his wife knowing. Every day she stages scenes with hysterics and tears every half hour. He attributes it all to her illnesses but I think that it's all pretence and acting! They are off to Italy soon ... To everyone here I am a married lady – Varia has shown your picture to the landlady as that of my husband! The landlady told her to show her, so she had to. So write to me as Mme not Mlle and don't be angry.

Anton wrote and told Potapenko he was a pig. Potapenko replied disarmingly on 10 May:

> What fantasies, dear Antonio, make you think that I am a pig? Suffice it to admit that I am a human being to expect greater piggery than from the very lowest pig ...[5]

Masha hit out harder. She was going to slaughter Ignasha, the lamb that they had named after Potapenko. Potapenko was abject to Masha in June: 'Dear Masha ... I am an all-round scoundrel and what's more a bastard and a cad. People like that are either ostracized or forgiven everything. I advise you to choose the latter. Oh, if only you knew, Masha.'[6]

Anton's disbanded squadron was regrouping in Paris. Iavorskaia and Tania (in a *ménage-à-trois* with the theatre-owner Korsh) introduced themselves to Alexandre Dumas fils and Edmond Rostand. Tania would translate them, Korsh stage them, and Iavorskaia act their heroines. Levitan, too, was in Paris. Nevertheless, Lika, Tania and Iavorskaia all acclaimed Anton as the man they loved. From Naples on 11 April Tania flirted in verse and prose:

> 'You have been with him, stay with us, and when you return to the south of our homeland, tell him about us ... all the wondrous sounds that sing in our hearts, all the kisses that burn on our lips we shall save for the land of snows.' That's what I told the wind ... from

the Girl in Violet [*Tania*]. The Girl in Green [*Iavorskaia*] kisses you (so do I, I swear).[7]

The friendship that Anton wanted to rebuild was Suvorin's, and he invited him after Easter to tour the Volga and the Dnepr together. Anton was seeking health and peace, but on Easter Sunday, 17 April, he collapsed. Four days later he described the attack to Suvorin:

> For a minute I thought I was dying: I was walking with my neighbour Prince Shakhovskoi down the avenue, talking – suddenly something tore in my chest, a feeling of warmth and stifling, a buzz in my ears, I remembered that I'd had irregular heart beats for some time – significant, I think; I quickly moved to the terrace and the guests, with one thought: it's embarrassing to drop dead in front of strangers.

A glass of water miraculously restored him.

At about that time Anton had two ideas to improve his life. He needed a proper mail service: driving six miles to Lopasnia, he could collect only ordinary letters; parcels and registered letters were delivered after a delay from Serpukhov. Guests made unreliable postmen: Anton's letters often lay forgotten in their pockets. Anton made himself an ally of Blagoveshchensky, the mail clerk at Lopasnia station, and lobbied for a full post office. He reactivated his friendship with Bilibin, the secretary of *Fragments*, whose 'real job' was in the Postal Service. Bilibin was not fooled – he wrote to Gruzinsky, 'had a letter from Chekhov, part pleasantries, part business'[8] – but set the machine in motion. Chekhov's second idea, conceived the previous autumn, was to build in the garden a two-storey cottage in Brothers Grimm style for male guests (female guests would stay in the main house). Anton's first architectural venture was entrusted to Masha, now that school was closed for the summer, as subcontractor. She ordered timber and hired carpenters. Pavel quarrelled with the workmen; he was kept off site. His diary for 11 May reads: 'Mid Pentecost. 24° in the shade. A procession with crosses around the village. The Tower of Babel on four legs is being built in the garden.'

Anton that May was comforted by Aleksandra Liosova, the girl who had been Vania's fiancée. Seven months ago, on 30 September 1893 Liosova, for the first time since Vania jilted her, had come with Anton and Lika Mizinova from Moscow. Now she wanted books for the factory school where she taught:

> The daughter of Israel comes to you with a request . . . You haven't responded to my *ardent feelings* with feelings, so oblige me. I should very much like to see you, but fate is cruel. What are you doing, abandoned by the cruel Lika? . . . But Russian women are not like us Israelites. You advised me to call my dog Vomit (it is a lady), but you forgot that I am an old maid and love everything sentimental . . . Be well and try to find *her*, but a woman less beautiful and cruel than Lika.[9]

Ten days later, 23 May 1894, Liosova was ardent:

> Accept ten passionate kisses from me. But to feel their full ardour, first heat your iron as hot as you can and give it 10 French kisses. But I'm afraid the iron won't be hot enough! It's just as well the weather is bad or I'd burn up, a bit of rain puts out a fire . . . 'No, I cannot stop loving you.' But meeting you is impossible . . .

Liosova hoped in a year's time to enter a nunnery 100 miles away; she harped on Lika's fate. Melikhovo frightened her, but her affection was fired by contact. In autumn 1894 Liosova renounced Anton (but not for a nunnery):

> Do you know, I am now completely happy? . . . I want nothing more from life. Tell me something about Lika – she interests me . . . I humbly ask pardon for getting fat and having vulgar red cheeks. By the time we meet I shall try to dry out. Much-respected King David, accept the fiery kiss of your Abishag, as long as you don't have a cold.

Anton was little bothered by women. The pianist Aleksandra Pokhlebina appeared just once in Melikhovo, free of infatuation. Olga Kundasova visited on 5 May, attending with Anton a doctors' conference at Meshcherskoe. She then vanished until the end of the year. Absent women played a more important role in Anton's fiction than in his life. 'Three Years', at first a novel which poured all summer 1894 from his notebooks, incorporates in its two main heroines phrases and traits of both Olga Kundasova and Lika Mizinova: the hero, torn between intelligence that does not arouse and beauty which does not satisfy, embodies Anton's own dilemma.

Chekhov kept at bay the unhappiness of others. His Petersburg editor Tikhonov had been dismissed from *The North* and was destitute. Kumanin of *The Performing Artist* was facing both his own demise and his journal's. Anton was unmoved. His brothers, at least, were living peaceably. Easter brought from Moscow Vania and Sonia, and from Uglich Misha. Pavel had bought the replica of Christ's shroud he wanted. Aleksandr had rented a dacha and no longer perturbed Anton with talk of settling nearby: he brought his two elder sons and left them for a few days at Melikhovo. Only Aleksandr Ivanenko, the Melikhovo court fool, came too often, stayed too long and talked too much.

On 1 June 1894, the day he left, Ivanenko completed his best composition, *An Inventory of Chekhov's Estate in the Village of Melikhovo*:

> *Carts*, 2; Light droshky, 1; Charabancs 1; Passenger sledges, 2; Flat tops, 1; Broken low sledges 1; Bee-hive carts 1; Wickwork cabs for sledges, 2; Wheels for flat-tops, 17; Riding yokes, 4; ordinary yokes, 4; Swingle-trees 3; Sledge shafts, 2; Cart shafts 3 pairs; . . . Axes 3; Chisels, 1; . . . Watering cans, 6; Spouts, 7; . . .
>
> *Horses*: Kirgiz, aged 8, Has overtaken the mail train 100 times and thrown its owner just as often. Has won top prize; Boy, aged 5, A trained horse, dances very elegantly when harnessed up; Anna, aged 98, too old to be fertile, but shows promise every year; bites drivers; Cossack Girl, aged 10, infertile, can't stand bits, has to be harnessed with a bit of rope or gallops off the road; Head-over-Heels, aged 7, calm and patient.[10]

Ivanenko listed five cows, three bullocks, three sheep, a sow and two piglets, three yard dogs. The inventory continues:

> *Dachshunds*: *Quinine*, distinguished by immobility and stoutness (idle and irritable); *Brom*, distinguished by liveliness and hatred of Whitebrow (a yard dog), noble and sincere.
> *Pigeons*: Brown, pedigree, crested, 1 pair; White with black spots (pedigree) 1 pair. *Poultry*: Old ducks, 4; Drakes, 1; Ducklings, 70; Old hens, 30; Chicks, 50
> *Servants*: *Mariushka*, widow of indeterminate age, excellent cook and lover of livestock, cows, bullocks, hens, chicks etc.; *Katerina*, the cow girl; *Efim*, Katerina's son; *Aniuta*, chambermaid, spontaneous nature, aged 16. Loves laughing and dances splendidly (suffers, so Mariushka says, from an 'innard' disease); *Mashutka*, Mariushka's under-cook, covered in freckles, aged 16. Loves bright colours. The

workman *Roman*, has shown punctuality and energy, is polite. Answers briefly: 'yes, sir; no sir'. Has served in the army, no medals. *Parents*: *Pavel Egorovich Chekhov* and his spouse *Evgenia Iakovlevna Chekhova* most happy of mortals! 42 years in lawful wedlock (Hurrah!)

Children:

Anton, lawful owner of Melikhovo kingdom, of the 2nd plot, Sazoni-kha woods, of Struzhkino, King of the Medes etc. etc. Also writer and doctor. Is about to write a tale *The Man with the Big Arse*.

Masha, kind, clever, elegant, beautiful, gracious, short-tempered and forgiving, strict but just. Loves sweets and perfume, a good book, good clever people. Not amorous (has been in love only 1700 times). Avoids handsome young men (soon off to Luka . . .). Recommends to all her friends the theory 'To hell with it.' A remarkable woman about the house: kitchen gardener, flower grower etc . . .

FORTY-FOUR

Potapenko the Bounder
July–August 1894

IVANENKO SAW MELIKHOVO AS EDEN. He left it for what he called a tomb: his tyrannical father was paralysed, his mother crippled, his brother dead, he himself had TB of the throat and now would run a farm that even hard work could not make viable. 'I'll have to live like a humorous badger,' he wrote despondently.[11] Anton's Melikhovo seemed a fairy-tale realm for a man who had come to Moscow fifteen years before to live in two crowded basement rooms.

Shcheglov's diary for 8 July 1894 reads: 'Chekhov on his estate. He is *entitled*, but how enviably happy his life has turned out.'[12] Masha, now that Misha was in distant Uglich, ran the house and estate. Pavel paid tribute to her achievements in the wet summer of 1894: 'On the farm Masha is invaluable for field work, her arrangements are very remarkably clever and calm. Glory to God, she puts any man to shame. Anton reveres her. We're just amazed by her intelligence and order.'[13]

Anton found a week or two sufficient in his kingdom. Incessant rain spoilt the clover that twenty-five peasants had mown. Only uninvited guests came: not Schechtel, Shcheglov, or Suvorin. Misha and Vania, when the tax office and the school released them, gave Anton no pleasure. Vania could not spend the summer with his pregnant wife: he felt despised by her parents, with whom she was staying, but he missed her and found Melikhovo dreary.

Anton tried to lure Shcheglov: 'We are making hay, the perfidious haymaking. The smell of hay makes me drunk and giddy, so that I only have to sit on the stack for an hour or two to imagine I am in the embraces of a naked woman.' The embraces would remain imaginary. Lika was, despite Anton's advice and Potapenko's neglect, not coming home. First she invited her mother, who loathed Potapenko,[14] to Paris, then she told Granny Ioganson that she was moving to Switzerland for the summer.[15]

In mid June 1894 Anton was in Moscow, avoiding his brother Aleksandr and his two nephews in Melikhovo. In Moscow Anton met Suvorin for the first time since February. Suvorin and the Dauphin had come to Moscow to sack the manager of their stationery shop. Anton and Suvorin passed three days and nights together, and agreed to travel. They talked frankly. Suvorin told Sazonova:

> Chekhov is philosophizing as usual, he's very pleasant, as usual, but I don't think he's well. I said to him, 'Why don't you let a doctor take a look at you?' – 'It makes no difference, I have five to ten years left to live, whether I consult a doctor or not.'[16]

Anton longed to travel, and as far from relatives as he could. Deserted in France, Lika hoped he might keep his promise and come. She wrote to Anton on 14 July a letter which he did not receive until autumn:

> Your pictures are placed all round my room and every day I address them with some warm words which I still haven't forgotten. Predominantly they begin with the letter S. [*swine, sod*]. I don't have the custom of hanging my friends' pictures where you put them . . . I'd give 10 years of my life (and I'm thirty [*she was 24*]) to find myself in Melikhovo. Just for a day. But there's no chance of coming before winter. Oh what a swine you are not to come and see us. But above all for not stopping me from going to Paris . . . I should like to have a half-hour chat with you! I think in half an hour you could put some sense into me. Your girl friends Tania and Iavorskaia have finally left Paris. Varia and I are very glad, although in general we kept them away. They were boasting about a letter you wrote them and of course I couldn't resist the pleasure of compromising you and I told them you write to me every day! So there! Everyone has forgotten me. My last admirer Potapenko has also cunningly deceived me and is running off to Russia. But what a b**** his wife is!

Just before Anton received this letter, Ignati Potapenko turned up at Melikhovo: the carpenters had just finished the guest cottage. Anton was, according to Vania's letter to his wife that day, 'ill, horribly depressed'. On Sunday 17 July Potapenko put his side of the story. He left for Moscow the next day. Masha was indignant, but Anton indulgent. Potapenko told neither that Lika was pregnant.

Potapenko was now a source of strife between brother and sister:

when Anton went to Moscow on 22 July, ostensibly to see Suvorin off to Feodosia, he hid from Masha that he had slept in the same flat as Potapenko. Only in September did Misha let their sister know: 'Now it's over, I can confess to an involuntary lie: I did meet Anton and Potapenko in Moscow and my lie was due to the need to hide their secret.' Anton and Potapenko spent five days with 'Grand-dad Mikhail Sablin'[17], an *éminence grise* in the lives of Lika, Potapenko and the Chekhov brothers. Sablin told Tania Shchepkina-Kupernik that Potapenko and Anton were staying with him; the news leaked to Lika. Anton said he was in Moscow to see *The Island of Sakhalin* through the press. In fact, doubting that Suvorin would ever set off for Italy, Anton was planning a journey with Potapenko. He was desperate to travel.

St George, instead of rescuing the maiden (not having received her last letter), was off with the dragon. Anton returned to Melikhovo for six days and on 2 August left with Potapenko for the Volga. Retracing Anton's route to Siberia, they took a boat from Iaroslavl to Nizhni, to sail down the Volga to Tsaritsyn [*Volgograd*], and thence to Taganrog. A fortnight later Anton summed up an idiotic trip to Suvorin:

> In Nizhni we were met by Sergeenko, Lev Tolstoy's friend [*and Potapenko's*]. The heat, the dry wind, the noise of the fair and Sergeenko's chat suddenly stifled, bored and sickened me, I picked up my suitcase and fled in disgrace … to the station. Potapenko followed. We took the train back to Moscow. But it was embarrassing to return empty-handed, so we decided to go anywhere, Lapland if need be. If it weren't for his wife [*the first Mrs Potapenko*], our choice would have been Feodosia, but – alas! in Feodosia we have the wife. We thought, we talked, we counted our money and we went to the Psiol.

On their way to the Lintvariovs, Anton and Potapenko stopped off at Lopasnia for letters. They went on to Sumy without contacting anyone at Melikhovo. On 14 August they brought Natalia Lintvariova home with them. Potapenko then vanished to Petersburg, where he sorted out his own and Anton's finances with Suvorin, found himself a typist, and plunged into the literary cesspit.

Anton's family now demanded his care. On 9 August a son, Volodia, was born to Vania and Sonia: after a harrowing birth the baby was well, but Sonia was ill. Uncle Mitrofan, at fifty-eight, was dying. In

July Anton's pretext for going to Taganrog had been to examine Uncle Mitrofan, debilitated by three years of illness. Fleeing Sergeenko, Anton had also abandoned Mitrofan. At Melikhovo lay a letter that Mitrofan had dictated to his daughters, addressed to Pavel, asking why Anton had not come:

> Our good Taganrog clergy in all the churches are offering ardent prayers for me in my sickness. My pain is in the left side, in the stomach, sometimes in the head, and my legs are painfully swollen, so that without others' help I cannot cross the room, I cannot eat, I have no appetite; my left side stops me sleeping, I sit on the bed almost all night, dozing ... When you receive the news of my departure to eternity, would you, the only relative in all our family who has loved and considers it a duty to think of one's kin, for the rest of your life have offertories said for me.

Christian faith sustained Mitrofan for a month. Anton set off for Taganrog, and stayed not with his uncle but in the best hotel. When Anton appeared at the sickbed, Mitrofan wept with joy and declared he 'was experiencing unearthly feelings'. Anton spent a week, but could not prescribe anything other than the heart stimulants which the Taganrog doctors were giving. Anton declared that he could have helped if he had been consulted earlier. He resolutely refused to discuss his own illness, let alone take measures to treat it.[18] Telling Leikin that the best treatment for eyes was nothing, Anna Suvorina that the boldest treatment for a bad throat was to leave it alone, and advising the singer Miroliubov that to ensure good health one should lie in bed covered from head to toes with a blanket and rub one's body with tincture of blackcurrant buds, Anton was formulating the facetious approach of Dr Dorn in *The Seagull*. All that he did for his uncle's family was to send their elder daughter, the seventeen-year-old Aleksandra, to Moscow to train as couturier. Anton then called on the mayor of Taganrog, and asked him to offer Aleksandra a post of sewing teacher.

On the eve of Anton's departure *The Taganrog Herald* annoyed him:

> Mr Chekhov has been called as a doctor to his seriously ill relative Mitrofan Chekhov, elder of St Michael church. From here the talented writer is setting off to the Crimea, where he has been summoned by Mr Suvorin who has fallen ill and is now living on his estate in Feodosia.

Chekhov went to the *Taganrog Herald* office, where an old school friend, Mikhail Psalti, worked, to protest that he was not Suvorin's doctor. He did not call at Taganrog post office, where Lika's letter of 14 July (addressed to Potapenko, as a man more likely to collect his mail) had lain all August. Then Anton boarded the train for a two-day journey to Feodosia (the direct sea route was too rough).

Anton stayed with Suvorin for four days. It was cold in Feodosia: Suvorin had built a magnificent villa with no stoves. The two men set off, via Yalta and Odessa, to western Europe. At Yalta, where plaster copies of Chekhov's bust were on sale, they dined in the park café. Elena Shavrova, there on her honeymoon, saw them, but was too shaken to speak to Anton.

Deserted among strangers in Switzerland, Lika longed to be rescued. The family in Melikhovo felt deserted, too. Evgenia was worried about her newborn grandson, and Pavel was distressed by Mitrofan. Masha bore the full weight of running a house in disarray. She complained to Misha:

> This is the third week we have been rebuilding the stoves, relaying the floors ... The stove makers get in the carpenters' way, the carpenters in the painters' and Papa gets in everybody's way ... Roman asks for two weeks' leave and he is my only help ... Quinine and Brom are howling, they have nowhere to sleep ... I'm at the end of my tether, Misha, it really is a terrible amount for one woman to cope with! ... I'm also afraid that Anton will be displeased. Never have I felt so much like leaving, throwing up everything, never to come back![19]

Uncle Mitrofan sank into death; his eldest son Georgi gave him water from a teaspoon, while Aunt Liudmila, heavily sedated, wept inconsolably. On 9 August, telegrams reached Melikhovo and Yalta: 'God's will our dear parent died eighth evening. Chekhovs.' Pavel grieved. He wrote to Anton, Vania, Aleksandr and Misha, 'how kind Mitrofan was to everybody ... Now I have no friend.'[20] (Nobody, however, wrote to Mitrofan's and Pavel's sister Aleksandra in Boguchar, nor to any of her children.) Pavel was too busy with building at Melikhovo to attend the funeral in Taganrog. Mitrofan's requiem, one of Taganrog's most memorable services, was conducted by Father Pokrovsky and four junior priests. Pavel was sent a handwritten copy of the

forty-minute speech that one of the Church Brethren made as Mitrofan was buried within the church precinct. It began:

> Before the grave-digger's spade has touched the coffin lid to conceal
> it in the bowels of the earth, so fateful for so many, by the coffin I
> hasten with a final farewell word for the man who lies within. You
> have left us, dear Mitrofan, and left us for ever! . . .[21]

FORTY-FIVE

The Birth of Christina
September–November 1894

ANTON'S SECOND TOUR of Europe with Suvorin was secret. His family was led to believe he was returning after a short recuperation in Feodosia, but Anton was as naïve as Potapenko in hiding his movements. When he and Suvorin reached Odessa on 13 September and left the next day for Vienna, the newspapers proclaimed their arrival and departure. Odessa's actors lamented that they would be staging *Ivanov* without the author. The Odessa authorities refused Anton a foreign passport. Suvorin had to throw his full weight at General Zelenoi, Odessa's mayor: in the night Zelenoi sent two men to break open the passport office and bring Chekhov's documents. From Odessa Anton sent consolations to Georgi and his family; he also warned Masha not to expect him home until October (November, he told Mikhail Psalti at *The Taganrog Herald*) and told her how to save asparagus and tulips from autumn frosts. She was to bring a warm hat to the station when he returned.

The two men reached Vienna on 18/30 September. Lika meanwhile, seven months pregnant, languished in Switzerland. She had moved from a guest house in Lucerne, where English tourists stared at her, into lodgings at Veytaux, on Lake Geneva. With Anton's photographs around her room, lonely and afraid, Lika pretended to be a married woman of frail health in an interesting condition. To Granny she wrote that, despite a chill, she was in paradise. She went to the post office daily. In Vienna Anton bought an inkwell and wrote to Paris:

> You obstinately refuse to answer my letters, dear Lika, but I am still annoying and pestering you with my letters . . . I remember Potapenko telling me you and Varia Eberle would be in Switzerland. If so, write to me where in Switzerland I might find you . . . I beg you, don't tell anyone in Russia that I am abroad. I left secretly, like

a thief, and Masha thinks I am in Feodosia. If they find out I'm abroad, they will be hurt, for they have long been fed up with my frequent journeys.

I'm not very well. I have an almost continuous cough. I seem to have lost my health as I lost you.

Lika did not know where Anton was: two days later she sent a plea to Melikhovo:

Not a trace of the old Lika is left and I think, and I can't refrain from saying so, it is all your fault! Anyway, that's fate, it seems! I'll say one thing, I have lived through moments I thought I would never live through! I am alone! There is not a soul around me to tell all that I am going through! God forbid anyone should experience anything like this! All this is vague, but I think it will all be clear to *you*! You are supposed to be a psychologist! Why I am writing all this to *you*, I don't know! All I know is that I am writing to nobody but you! And therefore don't show this letter even to Masha and say nothing! I am in despair: there is no ground beneath one's feet and one feels somewhere, I don't know, somewhere very nasty! I don't know if *you* will sympathize with me! Since you're a balanced, calm and rational person! Your whole life is for others and you don't seem to want a personal life of your own! Write to me, darling, soon! ... Your promises to come are all rubbish! You will never move.

Now Suvorin and Anton were in Abbazia, then a fashionable Adriatic resort under Austrian rule. It rained constantly and, Anton told Natalia Lintvariova: 'There are crowds of Yids here; they speak Russian.' To Anton, the only friendly Russian face was that of a wet nurse Anton had once treated. Abbazia reminded Anton of Maupassant's *Mont-Oriol*: the journey revived Maupassant's influence in Chekhov's work. On 22 September/4 October he and Suvorin fled to Venice. Lika had replied to Anton, but her letter lay in Abbazia post office, before trailing Anton across Italy:

I warn you, be amazed by nothing! If you don't fear being disillusioned by your old Lika, then come! There's no trace of her left! Yes, just six months have turned my life over, not leaving, as they say, a stone standing! Though I don't think you'll throw the first stone at me! I believe you've always been indifferent to people, their failings and weaknesses! Even if you don't come (very likely, given your laziness), then keep everything I write a secret between us,

328

uncle! You are not to tell anybody anything, even Masha! . . . Are you alone! Or with Suvorin? He is the last person to be told about my existence [*Suvorin was a notorious gossip*] . . . Potapenko wrote that he might come to Montreux between 25–30 September.

The letter reached Chekhov in Nice two weeks late. Anton told Masha, 'Potapenko is a Yid and a swine.' Lika wrote again: 'Darling I'm alone, very unhappy. Come alone and don't talk about me to anybody.'

By now Anton had Lika's last three letters; he could be in no doubt that Lika was pregnant. He needed a new excuse not to come to her rescue. He chose to use Suvorin as a pretext. On 2/14 October 1894, the same day that he denounced Potapenko to Masha, he sent Lika a chilly note:

> I can't go to Switzerland: I'm with Suvorin who has to go to Paris. I'll spend 5–7 days in Nice, then go to Paris for 3–4 days, then Melikhovo. I'll be at the Grand Hôtel in Paris. You had no cause to write about my indifference to people. Don't pine, be cheerful, look after your health. I bow deeply and firmly, firmly shake your hand. Yours A. Chekhov.
> Had I got your letter in Abbazia then I'd have gone via Switzerland to Nice to see you, but now it's awkward to drag Suvorin along.

Potapenko too let Lika down: from Petersburg he came for forty-eight hours to Moscow, not to Montreux: he wanted to talk Masha Chekhova round.

Avoiding Switzerland and Lika, Anton found Europe less thrilling than in 1891. He bought three silk ties, a tiepin and some glass in Venice, and caught nettle rash. In Milan he watched a dramatization of *Crime and Punishment*: he felt that Russian actors were pigs compared with the Italians – an opinion which boded ill for the play he was germinating. He visited first the cathedral, then the crematorium. In Genoa, Anton and Suvorin strolled around the cemetery, then left for what Maupassant called 'the flowering cemetery of Europe', the Côte d'Azur. They spent four days in Nice; here Anton worked on 'Three Years', and 'coughed and coughed and coughed'. He felt misanthropic and told Masha to see that she alone met him at the station when he got back. Suvorin, too, was disgruntled. Sazonova noted: 'A letter from Suvorin in Nice. He and Chekhov are fed up with each other, they are both roaming from place to place and saying nothing.' Suvorin never forgot a spat with Anton on the Promenade des Anglais. He asked Anton why he no longer wrote for *New Times*. Anton curtly told him to change the subject, and his 'eyes flashed'.[22] On 6/18 October Anton and Suvorin set off for Paris. They left Paris three days later, just before Lika came down to Paris from the Swiss Alps to seek new lodgings and a midwife.

After a day in Berlin, Anton arrived in Moscow on 14 October. Autumn rains had made the journey to Melikhovo hazardous, so he stayed there for five days and read proofs. He thanked Masha for her hard work with a ring and a promise of 25 roubles. He sent a note to the Louvre and Madrid hotel, for Tania and Iavorskaia, who, no longer dressed in violet and green, still astounded Moscow's theatre-goers. Anton's note, on a blue card, was in their style: 'At last the waves have cast the madman ashore ... and he stretched his arms to two white seagulls ...' Lidia Iavorskaia responded eagerly:

> Waiting for you is a hot samovar, a glass of vodka, anything you want, and above all, me. Joking apart, please come tomorrow. You will be off to your village and again I shan't see you for ages. And with you I relax from everybody and everything, my friend, my kind, good man.

On 19 October nine degrees of frost hardened the mud roads: Anton returned to Melikhovo, where the family had installed new bedroom floors, a well, a flushing lavatory and new stoves, though they could not raise the temperature in the house that freezing autumn above 15°C. Anton was to stay a whole month in Melikhovo, writing and sleeping in the new guest cottage. Pavel, as he put it, 'moved into His Cell, into the Kingdom of Earth';[23] Franz Schechtel had presented the family with their most valuable possession, an Art-Nouveau mantelpiece. There was one drawback. Anton wrote twice to Masha, who was teaching in Moscow:

> Find out in the shops what the best mouse poison is; the bastards have eaten the wallpaper up to four feet from the floor in the drawing room ... If you can't find mouse poison, bring 1 or 2 mousetraps.

Soon there was little need for Anton or Masha to leave the estate for Moscow. In mourning for Tsar Alexander III, who died on 20

October, Moscow's schools and theatres closed. Until the first snow came, in any case, travelling over icy ruts was torture. One journey to a patient nearby made Anton's 'innards turn inside out'.

Lika, in Paris, believed that Anton was still in Nice. Her last letter from Veytaux eventually reached Melikhovo:

> Lika, in the literal sense, very very much wants to see you, despite my fear that if you ever did have a decent opinion of me it will now change when you see me! But all the same, come! I'm sad, darling, infinitely!

Masha shared Lika's mood. On 10 October Masha had gone to Moscow for an event so distressing that the 10th became a bad omen for her. On 10 January 1895 she wrote to Tania Shchepkina-Kupernik: 'a sad event that happened on this very day three months ago makes my mood quite unsuitable for merriment.'[24] We do not know what this sad event was: had Masha renounced yet another man? Unhappy, sleepless, she stayed away from Melikhovo until 4 November. She did not meet Tania or Iavorskaia. She was taking cod liver oil and putting a cold compress on her heart. When she came, she brought Ivanenko, because she could not face the train journey alone. To judge by his evasive tact, Anton had an inkling of what was behind her anguish – conceivably, she had been seeing Levitan. Anton told Masha to consult his colleague the neurologist Professor Vasili Shervinsky ('and take 5 roubles just in case'): he would help her sleep.

In Moscow Vania, Sonia and the baby Volodia had become a loving trio, closed to outsiders. Misha was unhappy in Uglich, but hoped that his protectors could transfer him to another tax office. Cousin Aliosha Dolzhenko, free of Gavrilov's warehouse, won Anton's respect. He was now a violinist in an amateur orchestra. Aleksandr in Petersburg, however, was distressed, even though little Misha, Natalia believed, was 'something outstanding'. The more affectionate Natalia's postscripts to Anton, the more Aleksandr disparaged his wife: 'Natalia gives birth almost every day to whole ribbons of some tapeworm.' Aleksandr's unhappiness led to new aberrations. On the night of 12 November 1894 he arrived at Melikhovo with Vania and Ivanenko. The next day a note arrived from Natalia:

> Dear Anton, I beg you to write and tell me if my husband is with you. This strange man left when I was out. I am worn out. Where

is he? What's wrong with him? Please, dear Anton, don't show him my letter.[25]

Aleksandr stayed for the celebrations of Tsar Nicolas II's marriage. Anton thanked Natalia wryly 'for letting him come and see me.'

While Aleksandr took refuge at Melikhovo, his wayward behaviour infected the village. A drunken peasant, Epifan Volkov, set fire to the thatched roof of his cottage. Despite Aleksandr's experience with the fire brigade, the hut burnt down, and Volkov was arrested for arson. Otherwise, Anton had an undisturbed November. Only Elena Shavrova accosted Anton, asking him to return six stories which had vanished in Anton's absence. Anton denied having them and told her to rewrite them from memory. This, said Shavrova sulkily, was untrue and impossible.

Prince Shakhovskoi, ruined by debt, had sold his estate of Vaskino to an engineer, Vladimir Semenkovich. The new neighbour seemed at first just a monstrous reactionary,[26] and gave Anton no reason to emerge from solitude. A month in Melikhovo relatively free of visitors, in a cottage apart, gave Anton the conditions he needed to write. When he rose from his desk in the cottage, Anton talked only to his inferiors. Occasionally he helped Masha teach the two maids, Aniuta Chufarova and Mashutka, to read and write. (Anton would soon be a governor and builder of schools.) He was kind to Mikhail Plotov, the schoolteacher in the nearby village of Shchegliatevo, and gave him medical advice, a gun, a gundog and tickets to the theatre. The schoolteacher at the village of Talezh, Aleksei Mikhailov, an even needier figure, was also befriended. Grey at thirty, with four children, Mikhailov spoke only of misery on 24 roubles a month.[27]

In near solitude, Anton completed the book version of *The Island of Sakhalin* and the long story he had pondered since 1891, 'Three Years'. Not since his journey to Sakhalin had he been so absent from literary circles. Viktor Bilibin told Gruzinsky: 'It's said in Petersburg that Chekhov has consumption and that the Moscow doctors have given him only a year to live.'[28] Russia's minor writers, fed by Suvorin's gossip, buzzed with rumours. Gruzinsky told Ezhov, who told Anton: 'Kindest Anton! ... inviting you to my Moscow flat is like sowing semolina and expecting maize to sprout. You are unattainable for us little people. I remain the friend of your youth, now your enemy.'[29]

Anton responded with enough warmth to persuade Gruzinsky and Ezhov to visit Melikhovo before the winter was over. To Lika he gave not a word of encouragement or comfort.

Lika was no longer alone in Paris. Potapenko, pocketing more advances, had rushed there. (He told Masha he was in Kherson province by his father's sickbed.) By early November Potapenko was with the second Mrs Potapenko, on Rue des Mathurins, a couple of miles from Lika. On 9/21 November Lika gave birth to a daughter, whom she named Christina. She coped alone for nine days; she and the baby were both ill. A wet nurse was found. Maria Potapenko offered to bring the baby up as her own. Lika spurned the offer as a ploy to recapture Potapenko. Lika told Masha in February 1895 that Maria Potapenko threatened to kill herself and her own children, and Ignati to shoot just himself.[30] While Lika was still prostrate, Potapenko wrote to Anton from Paris, unusually legibly:

> First: keep my location absolutely secret, for that is essential. Secondly, the following: I have got into a *tout à fait* desperate situation ... here I am shivering with cold and other misfortunes. This is hard to understand for a man who is sitting in a warm house in front of a newly constructed fireplace, but an artist must imagine it. The reason I am here is hard to explain, and better left entirely unexplained. But I can neither leave nor pay certain bills ... throw off your rural laziness and go to Moscow, take these resources, go to the Crédit Lyonnais (or better Junker's) and make a telegraphic transfer in my name to 60 rue des Mathurins, Paris, Potapenko ... save me, or else I shall be thinking about suicide.

The next day Potapenko took his leave of Lika. They never met again. On receiving Potapenko's letter Anton broke his month's retreat. Over frozen ruts he made his way to Lopasnia and Moscow with Aleksandr and Masha. (Aleksandr was being repatriated to Petersburg and Natalia.) Anton sent no money until he returned to Melikhovo four days later and asked Goltsev at *Russian Thought 'in absolute secrecy'* to borrow 200 roubles and either send them 'to the prodigal son', or – which would break the secrecy – ask Suvorin to do so. Potapenko would ask Anton for another 200 roubles in March, but their friendship was suspended. He and Lika were both frozen out of Anton's charmed circle. Lidia Iavorskaia now tried to fire Anton's senses.

FORTY-SIX

O Charudatta!
December 1894–February 1895

'I FIND OBLIVION in the theatre,' Lidia Iavorskaia wrote to Tania in December 1894.[31] The two had brought bold ventures back from Paris and Antwerp and drew Anton into the whirlpool of their notoriety. Iavorskaia created two 'courtesan' roles. She was the laundress whose son becomes Napoleon's marshal in Sardou's 'relentlessly vulgar' *Madame Sans-Gêne*, an apt title for Iavorskaia, and she was the courtesan Vasantasena in the Russian première of *Poor Charudatta*, a Sanskrit drama attributed to King Sudraka. A poor Brahman, Charudatta, helps Vasantasena escape a prince's wiles: Vasantasena is nearly strangled, Charudatta nearly beheaded, but all ends happily. In winter 1894–5, at the sight of Anton, Iavorskaia, posing as the adoring Vasantasena, would sink to her knees, crying, 'O worthy Charudatta'. Anton acquiesced in the game.

The two women had other projects: Chekhov recommended a perfect vehicle for Iavorskaia, Zola's adulterous and lethal *Thérèse Raquin*. For Lidia, Tania had translated Edmond Rostand's parody of *Romeo and Juliet, Les Romanesques*. She showed the text to Anton at Melikhovo; he made fun of Rostand's precious style in Tania's rendering. Anton was at ease in her company, though Tania quarrelled with Anton as often as with Iavorskaia. She accused Anton of prejudice against lesbians, then abjectly apologized. (Anton warned Suvorin that she was underhand.)

On 2 December snow fell; visitors raced from the station on sledges. Tania came for a fortnight and charmed all Melikhovo. Anton drove the dachshunds to a frenzy with Tania's sable. When Pavel left for Moscow, he let Tania write up the diary: she parodied it perfectly. Tania went to pray at the monastery with Evgenia; lost in the snow, she was led back by Prince Shakhovskoi's workman. Laughter rang out all day. On 6 December she was bonded with Anton, as no other woman. They became godfather and godmother of Prince Shakhov-skoi's daughter Natalia: forever Anton was *kum* (fellow godparent, a significant relationship in Russia) to Tania and she was *kumá* to him.

As Anton finished his brooding 'Three Years', Tania's presence cheered him. He wrote notes on the violet or pink paper that Lidia Iavorskaia had brought from Paris. On 18 December, two days after Tania left for Moscow, Anton followed her. Until Christmas Eve, his mother's name day, he settled into room No. 1 (handy for the W.C.) in the Great Moscow hotel, where he was the favourite of the staff, and worked.

'Three Years', the 'novel', for which Potapenko had negotiated terms with Adolf Marx, the proprietor of *The Cornfield*, came out in *Russian Thought* in January and February 1895. The story was, as Anton said to Shavrova and Suvorin, made not of 'silk', but of 'rough cambric'. 'Three Years' – after *Sakhalin*, his longest work since 'The Duel' – was disturbingly naturalist and autobiographical in its evo-cation of the haberdashery firm Laptev and Sons from which the hero breaks free. Laptev, rich and gauche, is not Anton, but his introversion and revulsion against his merchant heritage, his hovering between the 'blue stocking' Rassudina and the idle beauty Iulia, and his reaction to a Rubinstein concert and a Levitan painting make Laptev very Chekhovian. The feckless brother-in-law Panaurov reminds one of Potapenko. Olga Kundasova and Lika also infuse the story. 'Three Years' is a languid work: Laptev breaks his emotional and class ties slowly. The story seems the prelude to a long *Bildungsroman*. Critics ignored its poetry, while friends were shocked at the exploitation of Olga Kundasova's love for Chekhov. Worse autobiographical frank-ness was to come.

In *The Russian Gazette* Chekhov published uplifting Christmas read-ing, 'The Senior Gardener's Story'. Anton had discussed the death penalty in *Sakhalin* and talked about it when he stayed in the Crimea. In this story the gardener tells of a judge who cannot sentence the murderer of the town's doctor, for his faith in humanity makes such a murder unbelievable. The censor cut Chekhov's moral:

> Believing in God is easy. Inquisitors, Biron and Arakcheev [*the Rus-sian empire's cruellest ministers*] believed in Him. No, you believe in man! That faith is possible only for the few who understand and feel Christ.

Christmas was too crowded for comfort at Melikhovo: Dr Kurkin slept in Anton's bedroom, Vania in his study. Anton skulked in Masha's room. After Christmas Anton went to a Yuletide party in the 'violent' ward of the Meshcherskoe hospital and brought Olga Kundasova back with him to Melikhovo. The following night Pavel groaned all night and in the morning announced that he had just seen Beelzebub. New Year's eve was muted. Pavel's diary reads: 'Masha returned from Sumy. There were no visitors. We didn't see in the New Year, we went to bed at 10 after supper. Masha got the lucky penny.'

On the first day of 1895, as the peasants wished the family a happy New Year and received the traditional gallon of vodka, Anton considered his health. He told his cousin Georgi that his cough was so bad he might spend twelve months in Taganrog: could he buy the seaside mansion belonging to Ippolit Tchaikovsky?

The next day Anton received a summons:

> By their majesties' command, issued in Moscow 1 January 1895, Literary General and Knight of the Orders of the Sacred Names of Tatiana and Lidia the First and Private of our Personal Escorts Anton Chekhov son of Pavel is allowed until 3 February to rest in all cities of the Empire and Abroad, as long as he sends two deputies and appears at the set time indicated to carry out double duties.[32]

On 2 January, while the Chekhovs slept, one of their majesties came. Tania recalled:

> On my way to Melikhovo I dropped in on Levitan who had promised to show me some sketches . . . The Levitan that met me in his velvet blouse looked like a Velasquez portrait; I was laden with shopping as always when I travelled to Melikhovo. When Levitan realized where I was going he began, as was his habit, uttering lengthy sighs, saying how unhappy he was about their stupid quarrel and how much he wanted to go there as he had used to. 'What's stopping you?' I said.

After a slight pause, when they arrived, Anton shook Levitan's hand. They talked as if three years' silence had never intervened. The next morning, while Anton slept, Roman drove Levitan to the station. Anton found only a note at breakfast: 'I'm sorry I shan't see you today. Will you drop in to see me? I am ineffably happy to be here at the

Chekhovs' again. I have come back to what was precious and really has never stopped being precious.' Tania and Iavorskaia could now see two ardent courtiers together. On 4 January Anton went to the Great Moscow hotel for over two weeks. Evgenia came too: she was off to Petersburg, to see Natalia for the first time since Kolia's death. The longing to see her first legitimate grandchild had overcome her distaste for her daughter-in-law.

Anton told Suvorin that he was in Moscow: he would not say why he had neither written nor come. He asked on Tania's and Iavorskaia's behalf if Renan's *L'Abbesse de Jouarre* or Ibsen's *Little Eyolf* could pass the censor. In another letter to Suvorin he asserted that Iavorskaia was 'a very nice woman'. He celebrated Tatiana's day and his name day. He watched Lidia act *Madame Sans-Gêne* at Korsh's theatre. Vasantasena gave Charudatta a rug and more:

> Come immediately, Antosha! We thirst to see you and adore you. That is me writing for Iavorskaia, I just love you. Yours Tania.
> I am awfully sad parting with you, as if the best part of my heart is being torn out . . . wrap yourself up in this Tartan rug, it will warm you like my hot kisses . . . Don't forget the woman who loves only you. Your Vasantasena . . . I'm lonely without you . . . I'm in despair. Come, darling. And there's no salad. Order some. I kiss you hard, Lidia.

Anton loved the luxury around Iavorskaia. He wrote to Suvorin that he needed to earn 20,000 roubles a year 'since I now can't sleep with a woman unless she wears a silk petticoat.' In December 1894 Lika offered a more austere affection from Paris:

> I think I'd give half my life to find myself in Melikhovo, to sit on your divan, talk to you for 10 minutes, have supper and just pretend that this whole year had not happened . . . I am singing, learning English, getting old and thin! From January I shall study massage too, so as to have some chance of a future . . . Soon I shall have consumption, so say all who have seen me. Before the end, if you like, I shall bequeath you my diary, from which you can borrow a lot for a humorous story.

After three months' silence Lika and Anton were briefly in touch, but never did either mention Lika's child. It was as if Christina had never been born. On 22 December Lika invited Masha to Paris: 'You vile girl, you lie when you say you want to see me! You are now involved with all sorts of trash, so how can you remember me?' Whom she was calling trash was clear from Lika's letter to Anton on 2 January:

> Well, has Tania settled in Melikhovo and occupied my place on the divan? Is your wedding to Iavorskaia soon? Invite me so that I can stop it by creating a scene in the church ... may all heaven's thunders fall on you if you don't answer. Your Lika.[33]

Olga Kundasova became hyperactive. She no longer held any post. Her friends – Drs Kurkin, Iakovenko and Pavlovskaia, Anton, and Suvorin – financed her; they were worried by her 'conspiratorial' journeys around Serpukhov and Moscow, where she engaged biologists and philosophers in debate. She longed to break free of the psychiatric hospital at Meshcherskoe; she blamed Anton for her headaches, fever and 'unimaginable melancholy', and showered him with notes. He tried to placate her, but her retort on 12 January 1895 had all the virulence of the fictional Rassudina in 'Three Years': 'I'd like to congratulate in person a fully-qualified little Don Juan like you. I attach a stamp for the reply. Yours. O. Kundasova.'[34] Anton endured her reproaches: more were to come. Kundasova recognized that she was ill – '*dementia primaria* to use our terminology. I'm frightened but not desperately so' – but she believed in the prophylactic effects of travel, sleep, food and talk in Melikhovo. Chekhov contacted Dr Kurkin, who wrote to Dr Iakovenko. They agreed not to give Kundasova enough money to go far from Meshcherskoe (where she believed she was a pioneering psychiatrist, not a patient). Dr Kurkin advised Anton 13 January 1895: 'You shouldn't let your "lady friend" out of your sight, for she tends to get entangled in situations from which she cannot disentangle herself.'[35]

Anton's colleagues coped with Kundasova, but, as though the attentions of Kundasova, Tania, Iavorskaia and Lika were not enough, Anton was seeking for another woman. On 30 December he wrote a jocular letter to Aleksandr with one serious request: to find the address of Anton's admirer, the children's writer Lidia Avilova, in Petersburg and to do so 'in passing, without any talk'. Aleksandr gave Anton Avilova's address and Anton slowly prepared for a journey to Petersburg. He had a pretext: Suvorin required Anton's intervention, for, alone among publishers, he had made himself an object of vituperation by refusing to sign a petition to the Tsar for freedom of the press. (The Tsar dismissed the request as 'senseless dreams', the secret police noted the signatories, and Chekhov, as an author printed by radical journals, came under surveillance.) Ostracized by the intelligentsia, Suvorin fell into a depression that even his theatre company, the Literary-Artistic Circle, failed to lift. On 9 January 1895 Sazonova's diary records:

> Suvorin was complaining of his loneliness, that his newspaper and wealth gave him no happiness, that he had known virtually no personal happiness, that life had passed him by. He was so tense, so upset, that I could sense tears in his voice. At times he simply couldn't speak.[36]

Anna Suvorina wrote about the same time:

> Anton, I ask you again to cheer up Aleksei. I'm told you're in Moscow now. Tempt him into coming if only for a few days, while you are there. He is grumbling a lot that you write him only business letters! ... Write him something nice and interesting and cheer him up a little. After all he doesn't love or value anybody but you. He is very melancholy and, worse, doesn't sleep at night. He can't work at all.[37]

Anton responded, twice offering Suvorin the bait of a drive round Moscow's cemeteries. He even offered to introduce him to Tania Shchepkina-Kupernik, but Suvorin was not to be wooed. Anton went back home for just a week. He inspected the false teeth that Aleksandr had bought Evgenia in Petersburg: she would not use them because they had been made on the 13th of the month. Anton left again on 27 January. He spent four days in Moscow, during which time he visited the sick Grigorovich and saw his childhood love Sasha Selivanova, newly widowed, plump, leaving school-teaching for midwifery.

On 31 January 1895 he went to Petersburg. Moscow's Grub Street looked on with envy: Shcheglov's diary records: 'Cruel cold, a thin rag of an overcoat, no money and now I have to write a humorous novel! ... Really you have to become an egotist like Chekhov to manage to get anything done!!'[38] In Petersburg Suvorin gave Anton a copy, printed on fine paper, of the half puritanical, half pornographic novel he had published, *At the End of the Century: Love*, and inscribed it 'from the kind and virtuous author'. Suvorin introduced Anton to Sazonova, the lady writer and diarist to whom he entrusted his secrets:

Suvorin's two confidants backed away from each other. Sazonova recorded: 'We silently shook hands, he advised me not to drink Russian wines and went to his room, gathered a company there and then left to see Leikin.' Sazonova found Anton's hostility adamant. Anton had other agendas. He renegotiated his royalties from Suvorin: now Suvorin paid Chekhov 200 roubles monthly. While Anna's beloved Italian tenors sang, Anton wrote letters, read manuscripts and began a new story in the next room. A prodigious year had begun.

Visiting Leikin, Anton met his neglected acolytes – the melancholy Kazimir Barantsevich and ever-loyal Gruzinsky. He even met Potapenko. Lika weighed on Chekhov's mind, and he consulted Suvorin. Again, Suvorin confided in Sazonova, whose diary later records:

> Chekhov had an affair with the Mizinova girl. He wanted to marry her but it couldn't have been a strong desire because Suvorin talked him out of it [*possibly in 1891* D.R.] Then Potapenko seduced the girl and abandoned her.

Aleksandr and Natalia now lived soberly; Anton willingly went to dine with them. Natalia, domesticated by motherhood and by cooking courses, was overjoyed when Anton divined his nephew Misha's talented, highly strung nature.

In 1895 Lidia Avilova, the sister-in-law of the editor of *The Petersburg Newspaper*, a woman whose address Chekhov had taken such pains to find, became Anton's most deluded admirer. She asked Chekhov for a critique of her story – which he gave with unusual candour. She then ordered a medallion inscribed with the title of one of Chekhov's books, a page and a line number. This she sent anonymously to Chekhov, who duly found the reference to his story 'Neighbours': 'If you ever need my life, come and take it.' Avilova did not know, as Anton left for Moscow on 16 February 1895, that this medallion would be used as a final touch to Chekhov's new play, the cruellest of modern comedies.

FORTY-SEVEN

A Misogynist's Spring
February–May 1895

THE MEDALLION that Lidia Avilova gave Chekhov in February 1895 was an eloquent love token. Anton responded more guardedly than her 'memoirs' imply; he did less for her career than he did for Shavrova's. Anton did not protest at Burenin's verdict that Avilova was better unpublished. When Avilova in turn tracked him down, Anton had erected a defence against Persons from Porlock. Leikin knew Avilova: in Moscow on his way to Melikhovo, he noted in his diary 9 March 1895:

> Went to the Strakhov [*Avilova's maiden name*] library on the Pliushchikha where L. A. Avilova is staying, and had tea with her. She is grieving, ten days ago she wrote a letter to Chekhov from Moscow inviting him there, but he did not appear or reply, she asked in the offices of *Russian Thought* if he was now at his estate, and she was told he had left for Taganrog. I informed her that I was told in *Russian Thought* that he was at his estate, expecting me and I was off to see him tomorrow.[39]

Anton also took care, while in Petersburg, to avoid Shavrova, whose manuscripts he had mislaid. She received not the meeting she craved, but a roasting for maligning doctors in a story about syphilis and the family. The story was in any case unprintable – only medical journals could discuss syphilis. Anton told Shavrova to leave disease to professionals, and write about picnics instead.

In February 1895 Anton sent to a Moscow anthology 'The Spouse', yet another piece about a long-suffering doctor whose life is wrecked by a spendthrift, unfaithful wife.[40] Chekhov's recurrent topic in 1895, an idealist thwarted by an amoral woman, stems from private disillusion and from a more general misogynistic undercurrent in Russian literature at that time. Repeatedly toying with, and then rejecting, the

affections of one woman after another, Anton was not so much searching for his Dulcinea, as reiterating a bitter experience: each liaison
seemed an obstacle to creative and personal freedom. Like Tolstoy,
Anton felt at heart that Schopenhauer was right to assert that 'only
a male intellect befuddled by sexual drive' could worship woman.
Schopenhauer was widely known in Russia and the heroine of 'The
Spouse' is a Schopenhauerian *Weib*, as are Chekhov's next heroines,
in *The Seagull* and in the stories 'Ariadna' and 'Anna Round the Neck'.

When Anton returned to Melikhovo, he avoided the sirens. Tania
had to seek him out at the end of March. Iavorskaia was by March
on tour 300 miles away to the east, in Nizhni. The Moscow critics,
Anton warned Suvorin, 'had hunted her down like a hare' for her
'parody of a countess' in Giacosa's *La dame de Challant*. Anton no
longer wished to share Iavorskaia with Korsh and Tania, while she
could not understand why he was so unresponsive. Feverish with flu
and desire, she pleaded in bad free verse:

> O Charudatta, worthy of envy! . . .
> You don't know how the lively Vasantasena
> Your southern flower, 'little sun',
> Suffers here in the theatre galleries
> Which take 4 roubles a day off her
> And a hotel room so unlike
> Alas that room in the Great Moscow hotel
> In which you and she
> Tasted true bliss.
> My darling . . . I am in no state at all to write to you in prose about
> our feelings, so send Tania to me . . .

At Easter Iavorskaia would make her Petersburg début. She reverted
to the formal *vy* and pleaded the state of the roads as her reason for
not coming to Melikhovo. She still begged Anton to come and join
her in her Petersburg hotel. By 5 April 1895 Anton had not responded;
Iavorskaia cajoled him from Petersburg:

> Put in a word to defend the unhappy one,
> Your beautiful Vasantasena,
> Or Suvorin and the reviewers
> In savage fury will destroy thy lotus
> And tear to pieces thy Vasantasena
> And hurl her wondrous body for the hungry Muscovite

Reviewers to devour. O save me, Charudatta!!
My darling, Happy Easter, I wish you every bliss, bodily and spiritual! I met Burenin, a venomous man in a mask of amiability. We
spoke about you. He asked me if I was in love with Anton Chekhov
(you see, darling, it's obvious to everyone? Yes . . . yes . . . yes . . .)
. . . I want to meet Suvorin only through you. Put in a word for me
with him. Your word works on him just like the word of a much-
loved woman (!)

Anton did not respond or put in a word, but gossiped instead, telling
Suvorin that Korsh was Iavorskaia's chief lover, but did not forbid
her to have affairs. Suvorin saw *Madame Sans-Gêne* and damned Iavorskaia with faint praise. (Both Suvorin's theatre and Chekhov's drama
would take up arms against her histrionics.) Offering Iavorskaia up to
Suvorin, Anton was angling for a protégée of Suvorin's, the Jewish
Liudmila Ozerova, who had had a sensational début in Hauptmann's
mystical and sentimental *Hannele's Ascension*. In early May Chekhov
asked Suvorin where Ozerova would spend the summer: 'Why not
invite me to be her doctor?' Only two years later would Ozerova
respond to Anton's hints.

None of the Chekhovs had put Lika out of their thoughts. Misha
complained to Masha in January that he missed 'educated' girls: 'At
least there used to be Lika, but now she is no more.'[41] Anton wrote
to her for the first time in three months and, apparently, the last for
fifteen. He expected her soon and would come to talk; although he
was aware of her baby, there was 'nothing to write about, since everything is as it was and there is nothing new'. He asked her to bring
gloves and perfume for Masha. Lika now wrote not to Anton, but to
Masha, to Granny and to her mother. For Granny she kept up the
fiction that she was busy studying singing; she assured her mother
'you are my only and my best friend.' To Masha, in letters of 23
January and 2 February, Lika admitted she was thin – her waist was
nineteen inches – she had a French admirer, but could neither sleep
nor drink: her one consolation was that she would die soon. She was
proud only of her baby, who, the wet nurse said, was the spitting
image of Potapenko. She asked if Masha would marry Levitan, now
that Kuvshinnikova had left him. She defended her lover:

I have had one friend and I hope he will remain a friend for both
of us – that is Ignati . . . I had the idiotic illusion that I also had a

343

friend in Anton, but this turned out to be a stupid fantasy . . . I
regret nothing, I am glad that I have a little creature who is beginning
to give me joy . . . I believe Ignati loves me more than anything in
the world, but he is the most wretched man! He has no will power,
no character and what's more he has the bad luck to possess a spouse
who will stop at nothing.

Masha was moved by Lika's sufferings, but she envied her the experience of love and childbirth.

In spring 1895 Lika made a flying visit to Russia, leaving Christina
with the wet nurse in France. Granny Ioganson yearned for Lika: her
diary for 8 and 14 May exults:

> Today is my dear dove Lidiushka's birthday. The Lord send her
> health, happiness and wellbeing for the 26th year of her life . . .
> I'm expecting Lidiusha! She has come, I'm godlessly glad to see her
> – now I shall die easier.[42]

On 12 May Lika went straight from Moscow to Melikhovo. Only
after twenty-four hours, did she go to see Granny in Tver province.
On 25 May Anton went to Moscow and stayed with Vania, who
reported to his wife: 'Anton spends the night with me but vanishes
the whole day on business.' Anton came back to Melikhovo on Sunday
28 May, bringing Lika. She stayed another twenty-four hours, then
vanished until September, to the relief of Vania's wife who was jealous
of the young bohemian women who frequented Melikhovo.[43]

That spring only males flocked to Melikhovo. Dunia Efros, Anton's
fiancée nine years before, married to a lawyer, Efim Konovitser, was
again one of Masha's intimates. They met in Moscow. A year passed
before Dunia and her family were invited to Melikhovo. At Easter
Tania, beloved by Pavel and Evgenia for attending communion, all-
night vigils, and christenings of workmen's children, was the only
female guest at Melikhovo. As family, she was sent lists of produce –
cheese, salami and halva, wine and olive oil – to bring from Moscow.

The only man banned from Melikhovo was Potapenko. He was
hurt that Anton, 'the object of my undying envy', now communicated
with him only on scraps of yellow paper. Potapenko was, however,
busy: he was writing 'an uncountable number of stories and novels'
to pay for his two wives, and Lika, Christina and the wet nurse, quite
apart from paying off his debts to Anton and Suvorin. On 10 March

Leikin, Gruzinsky and Ezhov arrived. Leikin approved Anton's attempts to be, like him, farmer, gardener and dog-breeder. He and Chekhov grew to like each other better. Leikin recorded:

> From Lopasnia station to Melikhovo, where Chekhov's estate is, we drove through a terrible blizzard. You could hardly make out the road markers . . . We drove in two sledges. Me in front, Ezhov and Gruzinsky behind. A pair of horses was harnessed in single file to my sledge. The road was literally swept away . . . when we got to Chekhov's we were buried in snow, icicles in the beard and on our temples . . . Chekhov gave us a full welcome, even came out onto the porch with the servants. Two very young chamber maids, round as dumplings, girls with full-moon faces, grabbed our bags and rugs . . . Chekhov's house is fine, bright rooms, all repainted and re-papered, spacious, with a nook for every member of the family and comfort you won't find even in some Moscow apartments. It is pleasant to see that a fellow writer (I mean a gifted one) has finally escaped penury and become well off. Inside we were greeted by his mother and his brother Misha, the tax inspector, come from Uglich, where he works, to stay a few days. Two dachshunds got under our feet, and I nearly shouted 'Pip! Dinka!', they were so like my own.
>
> After dinner Chekhov took me around the farmyard and outbuild-ings. The latter are decrepit but he has new hewn-wood stables, cow-shed and stores. A bath house is being built. A two-room cottage for visitors has been built and furnished and there were three beds and bedding. A really charming cottage. This is where Ezhov and Gruzinsky spent the night, while I slept on the divan in Chekhov's study.

Ezhov left the next morning, unimpressed. On 31 March he wrote to Leikin:

> I don't like Chekhov's estate: first of all it's in the middle of the peasant village; if there's a fire there the manor won't escape. Sec-ondly, there's no water. The pond Anton showed us is fit only for piglets to bathe in.[44]

Chekhov did not think much of Gruzinsky and Ezhov. He told Suvo-rin that they were 'two young wet blankets who said not a word and spread raging boredom over the whole estate', although Leikin 'has coarsened, become kinder, more jovial – he must be going to die soon.' Leikin was so touched by his reception that he sent Chekhov's dachshunds a picture of their parents and Masha seeds of Siberian buckwheat, which became yet another weed at Melikhovo. The cycle of presents ended with Chekhov commissioning an artist to paint Leikin in oils for only 200 roubles. Overjoyed, Leikin sent seed of his prize beet and cucumbers.

When Gruzinsky and Ezhov were invited back to a green, warm Melikhovo in early June, Ezhov changed his mind: 'I liked it. The bathhouse we saw is finished and, thanks to Anton's kindness, is a resort for all the Melikhovo peasants.' Perhaps Ezhov felt more gracious because he was about to marry again, this time 'a girl of no means'.[45] It took all summer, however, to lure Suvorin, used to greater comforts, to Melikhovo. When he came at the end of August he stayed just one night.

At Easter Ivanenko came. He annoyed Pavel by oversleeping and not kissing the priest. Giliarovsky, the superman-reporter of Anton's student days, visited, Anton received for three days Doctor Korobov, who had boarded with the Chekhovs when he and Anton were first-year students. Nikolai Korobov was now besotted with Nietzsche. Chekhov had once commented: 'I should like to meet a philosopher like Nietzsche in a railway carriage or on a boat and talk the whole night.' Korobov's visit was the next best thing. Nietzschean views and phrases seep into the conversation of Anton's fictional protagonists.[46] His correspondence with Suvorin was also enlivened by sympathy with the latter's pro-German and Nietzschean views, often eccentric: Suvorin advocated compulsory cricket in Russian universities, for example, to defect students from idle radicalism.

Anton and Suvorin longed for each other. Suvorin wanted to sit and walk with Anton, 'silently and idly exchanging the odd phrase'. Anton begged Suvorin to come to Moscow in May: 'we could travel round the cemeteries, the monasteries, the woods at the edge of the city.' But Suvorin's newspaper and, above all, his *théâtre libre*, held him captive, and Anton lacked a pretext to abandon Melikhovo. An estate could only be run if every member 'regardless of rank or sex, worked like a peasant'. Mice were stopped from stripping the bark off the cherry trees; a pig was slaughtered and hams smoked; timber was hauled for a new workman's shed. The summer of 1895 brought a drought as bad as the rains of 1894; the birch leaves were stripped by larvae. Fruit blossom was spoilt by frosts; sudden heat generated mosquitoes 'which bite like dogs'. Anton could not leave Masha with such drudgery again. In vain Suvorin tempted him with the Volga and Dnepr, or Leikin with the lakes and monasteries of the North. He himself longed for the sea, the Baltic or the Azov, but had to stay at Melikhovo.

Anton's youngest and eldest brothers stayed away in spring 1895. Misha was even in April snowbound in Uglich. He was bound in other respects: the death of Sablin, his protector (the brother of the editor 'granddad' Sablin), had blocked hopes of a transfer to the livelier city of Iaroslavl. Anton lobbied for him, first with Bilibin, who told him that Misha was unqualified to be a postmaster, and then with Suvorin. In Petersburg Natalia angled for an invitation: 'You describe your garden and its inhabitants, so that I salivate'. Aleksandr felt put upon: Natalia ('my whore') was showing signs of increasing eccentricity – hoarding food and clothes; his mother-in-law was dying of emaciation (it took four more years); he was up all night indexing *New Times* for a paltry 100 roubles a year; he had stopped drinking again, and his 'loins hurt like an onanist's'.

All Anton's irritation of the previous year, his tangle with Lika and Potapenko and his reading of the German misogynists went into a story called 'Ariadna'. The heroine Ariadna Grigorievna is named after the girl who ruined the life of his Latin teacher, Starov. Her flamboyance was Iavorskaia's; her predicament was Lika's. Like Lika, Ariadna fails to ensnare the introverted narrator, Shamokhin, and takes up instead with a frivolous married man, Lubkov, who abandons her in Europe. Unlike Anton, however, Shamokhin rescues Ariadna and brings her back to Russia, and unlike Lika, Ariadna only seems pregnant. Like Potapenko, Lubkov has the gall to sponge money from his rival. Shamokhin paraphrases Schopenhauer when he describes Ariadna's need to charm and to lie as being an innate as spurting ink is to a cuttlefish. Shamokhin tells the story to Chekhov – for once Chekhov appears in his own story – as they sail from Odessa to Yalta. Shamokhin is after all the ship's bore, and this distances Chekhov from his protagonist. 'Ariadna' explores a conflict – between misogyny and common sense – in Chekhov's own mind.

'Ariadna' had been commissioned for *The Performing Artist*. Its editor, Kumanin, had since incurred Chekhov's disfavour and, as he neared death, his journal folded, Kumanin sold his subscribers and contracts, including Chekhov's 620-rouble advance, to *Russian*

347

Thought, and Lavrov and Goltsev found themselves, at the end of 1895, printing a work offensive to their egalitarianism. Chekhov was able, however, to offset 'Ariadna' with 'Murder', a brooding story of fanatical violence, inspired by what he had seen on Sakhalin and by Misha's stories of Uglich. In May 1895 *The Island of Sakhalin* passed, as Lavrov put it, 'from the belly of the whale' and came out as a book (published by *Russian Thought*) which proved Chekhov's radical credentials. Chekhov had, however, now finished with the penal island. His hope that the work would win him the right to lecture in Moscow university was thwarted; the University was ill-disposed to a man who 'had it in for professors'.

Misogyny permeated another story conceived that summer, printed in *The Russian Gazette* in October – 'Anna Round the Neck'. The phrase is Aleksandr's: he called his dying first wife 'Anna round the neck' – a pun on the civil service award of St Anna. Chekhov's Anna is a girl married off to an elderly civil servant to save her destitute family. Realizing she is sexually attractive, she turns the tables and tyrannizes her husband. Anton was, understandably, in no mood for marriage, the cure that Suvorin proposed for his melancholy. On 23 March 1895 he retorted:

> All right, I'll get married if you want me to. But my conditions are: everything must be as it was before, that is she must live in Moscow, and I in the country, and I shall visit her. I couldn't stand a happiness that went on morning noon and night . . . I promise to be a splendid husband, but give me a wife who, like the moon, does not rise every night in my sky. NB. Marrying won't make me write any better.

348

FORTY-EIGHT

Incubating The Seagull
June–September 1895

IN SUMMER 1895 Anton began to mention his archive. Like his father, Anton scrupulously kept letters and documents. The family always asked Anton if they were looking for a certificate. Anton alarmed Suvorin, who did not want his private thoughts to be widely known, by saying that he had put all his letters in order. This became an annual ritual, which Anton and Masha carried out: letters were sorted into two categories, family and literary, then into boxes, by author, Anton marking the date if the writer had not. Afraid of compromising themselves, people now wrote less spontaneously to Anton, or wrote mainly to provoke a saleable answer. Anton joked at their fears and hopes: he headed a letter to Anna Suvorina 'not for *Russian Antiquity*', but his own tone, as time went on, became more guarded.

The archive shows Chekhov's growing self-esteem. He could see himself as Russia's greatest living writer of fiction. On 21 February Leskov, who had anointed him as 'Samuel anointed David', had died. Nobody mourned the most cantankerous of Russian novelists. Even Anton expressed only indignation that Leskov in his will demanded an autopsy to prove his doctors wrong. A diary entry two years later, however, shows how deeply he felt Leskov's importance: 'Writers like Leskov . . . cannot please our critics, because our critics are almost all Jews who do not know the core of Russian life and are alien to it, its spirit, its forms, its humour . . .' Leskov's idiom – 'you stepped on my favourite corn' – found its way into *The Seagull*.

Melikhovo became all Anton's. After dinner, on 3 June, Misha, Masha and Vania left Melikhovo for the south. They stayed for two days with Georgi in Taganrog. This was Masha's first visit since she was a child: she bathed in the Sea of Azov. From Taganrog Vania returned to Melikhovo three weeks later, but Misha and Masha took Anton's route of 1888, by sea to Batum and then overland to

Kislovodsk. They returned late on 28 June 'thin, tired, exhausted, yet full of the joys of life,' Vania reported to his wife. While Anton enjoyed three weeks' solitude, Pavel ploughed the parched earth, sold the hay, called out the vet[47] to a sick cow, and bought new striking clocks – the elder Chekhovs' main extravagance.

Olga Kundasova began to frequent the house: Pavel recorded her as 'living with us'. To Suvorin Anton complained: 'This person in big doses, no thanks! It's easier hauling water from a deep well.' Olga left to spend the rest of the year with her sister, 1500 miles away in Batum. Anton managed her better, as she acknowledged next April:

> I am struck by many things in your attitude to me that have come to the surface recently, I am struck because I myself am now stony ground, and there was a time when I was good soil. (I ask you when reading this part of my letter not to indulge in the pornographic ideas so typical of you.)

Anton had learnt to say no with yet more determination. He refused to help Olga assemble a library for the psychiatric hospital. He did however defend the peasant arsonist, Epifan Volkov, and after a year, the investigating magistrate, an admirer of Anton's plays, released Volkov. Mitrofan's younger son, Volodia, was expelled from a seminary, and Anton interceded to save him from conscription.

Peace ended on 20 June, when Mitrofan's widow Liudmila came to stay for forty days with her two teenage daughters, Aleksandra and Elena. Anton delighted in their domesticity, and the two girls were exceptionally pretty. Only Pavel counted the days to their departure, despite Liudmila's enthusiasm for Matins and Vespers at Vaskino and the Monastery. Three weeks after these relatives left, Aunt Marfa Loboda, the widow of Ivan Morozov (Evgenia's brother), came for a week. Of all her in-laws Evgenia liked Marfa best: together they prayed at the monastery church.

The gestation of Chekhov's new play, *The Seagull*, was interrupted by a suicidal incident that Anton was to use as the play's crowning touch. Levitan was at Gorki, a remote estate, half way between Moscow and Petersburg, which belonged to his mistress, Anna Turchaninova. Like Sofia Kuvshinnikova, she was married and ten years older than Levitan. She had three daughters, of whom Levitan seduced at least one. He had a row with Anna Turchaninova, and on 21 June he pulled out a revolver and shot himself in the head. The wound was slight, but Levitan's mood was not. On 23 June he wrote to Anton:

> Dear Anton, if at all possible, come to see me, just for a few days. I am horribly unhappy, worse than ever. I would come to see you but I have no strength left. Don't refuse. A big room is at your disposal in a house where I live alone, in the woods, on the shore of a lake.

Neither compassion nor the fishing moved Anton, so Anna Turchaninova wrote:

> I don't know you, Mr Chekhov, but I have an urgent request at the insistence of the doctor treating Isaak. Levitan is suffering very severe depression which is pulling him into the most terrible state. On 21 June, in a minute of despair, he tried to kill himself. Fortunately we managed to save him. The wound is no longer dangerous, but Levitan needs meticulous, loving and friendly care. Knowing from what he has said that you are a close friend, I decided to write and ask you to come and see the patient immediately. A man's life depends on your coming. You, only you, can save him and bring him out of complete indifference to life, and at times a furious determination to kill himself.[48]

On 5 July, telling nobody where he was going, Anton made his way to Gorki and saw Levitan. From Gorki he wrote to Leikin to say he 'was on the shores of a lake 50 miles from Bologoe' for ten days. He told Suvorin that he was with a patient on the Turchaninova estate, 'a marshy place, smelling of Polovtsians and Pechenegs'.

Anton stayed only five days and, instead of turning home, travelled just as secretively from Bologoe to Petersburg. Leikin learnt that Anton was at Suvorin's. He drove straight round to see Anton there 'thin and jaundiced'; Anton claimed Suvorin had telegraphed for him. Leikin's were not the only prying eyes; Kleopatra Karatygina hoped to join Suvorin's new theatre and, like many actresses Anton had known, she named him as a referee.

Anton was back in Melikhovo by 18 July. Tania and Sasha Selivanova, whom he now called the 'enchanting little widow', joined him. Four days later, Anton went back to Moscow to see Suvorin: they spent two days walking and talking. Suvorin came down to Melikhovo to meet Tania and talk about the theatre. On 24 July Pavel's diary records: 'Full moon. The guests went for a walk in the woods.' The walk shaped Tania's future. She charmed Suvorin, who would prepare the way for her in Petersburg. Tania was translating Edmond Rostand's *La Princesse lointaine* – a source for the cult of the 'Beautiful Lady' in Russian symbolist drama. (Tania's enthusiasm for modern French drama made Anton spend several weeks studying French grammar.) In *The Seagull*, the little play that Treplev stages to annoy his mother parodies Russian plays yet unwritten: the Symbolist drama which Tania was adapting and *Hannele's Assumption*, in which the pretty Liudmila Ozerova had made her début, helped Chekhov imagine what such drama might sound like in Russian.

The Seagull is full of cruel parody. The shot bird symbolizing youth destroyed was aimed at Ibsen's *Wild Duck*; the young writer Treplev, jealous of his mother's lover, parodies Hamlet and Gertrude. The middle-aged actress, Arkadina, who holds all the men – her brother Sorin, her son Treplev and her lover Trigorin – in thrall, caricatures every actress that Anton had ever disliked, and echoes Iavorskaia's mannerisms, such as kneeling before Anton, like Vasantasena before Charudatta, calling him 'my only one!' The boring schoolteacher Medvedenko mimics Mikhailov, the teacher in the village of Talezh, near Melikhovo. The medallion that Nina gives Trigorin with the coded reference to his lines 'If you need my life, come and take it', mocks Avilova and her medallion. The lakeside setting of *The Seagull*, the pointless killing of the seagull, and Treplev's first attempt to shoot himself, all commemorate Levitan. The unhappy fate of Nina, adored by Treplev and seduced by Trigorin, reflects – and, as we shall see, anticipates – the story of Lika, Anton and Potapenko.

Chekhov was most cruel to himself. Trigorin, the traditional writer, and Treplev, the innovator, standing for old and new movements, both ineffectual and mediocre, really personify two aspects of Chekhov, one the analytical follower of Turgenev and Tolstoy, the other the visionary prose-poet. Much of Trigorin is Anton – with his fishing rods, his dislike of scented flowers, his self-disparagement. Lines from Chekhov's prose (a description of a broken bottle on a weir) and from his letters (to Lika about obsessive writing) are given to Trigorin in the play. Like Potapenko, however, Trigorin seduces and abandons Nina; like Anton, Treplev is the man to whom she briefly returns, undeterred in her desire for a career on stage. *The Seagull* is nevertheless not primarily a confessional work: Trigorin is only part Potapenko and Anton only part Treplev. The authorial Chekhov is there as Doctor Dorn who looks on with amused compassion, and deflects possessive women.

The Seagull develops to a surreal degree the pattern of Turgenev's *A Month in the Country* of 1849: a country estate, an ironical doctor, a dominant heroine and an absurdly long chain of unrequited love – nobody loves the schoolteacher Medvedenko, who loves Masha, the manager's daughter, who loves Treplev, the young writer, who loves Nina, the neighbour's stepdaughter, who loves Trigorin, the older writer, who is in thrall to Arkadina, the actress. The structure is innovative: four acts flow, not broken into scenes. Act 4 reiterates, like a musical piece, the motifs of Act 1. Never did Chekhov write such a literary play: the text alludes to Maupassant, whom Chekhov admired as much as his heroes do. The opening lines 'Why do you always wear black?' – 'I'm in mourning for my life.' are out of *Bel-Ami*, while the passage Dr Dorn reads in Act 2, on the dangers of writers to society and of women to writers, is from Maupassant's travel book *Sur l'eau*. Shakespeare too, in particular *Hamlet*, is grafted into the play. Traditions are reversed. All the material of comedy – couples in love, youth against age, servants outwitting their masters – is there, but the action resolves uncomically. There are no happy reunions; age is unscathed, youth perishes, and the servants sabotage the household.

On 21 October 1895 Chekhov told Suvorin that his comedy, satirizing his intimates, attacking the theatre and its actresses, was unstageable: 'I am writing it not without pleasure, though I offend stage rules terribly. A comedy, three female parts, six male, four acts, landscape (view of a lake); a lot of talk about literature, not much action, 13 stone of love.' Anton did all he could, from conception in May 1895 until its first performance in October 1896, to stir up the hostility of those who had to watch and act his play. It is as if the author against his own will propelled *The Seagull* into reality.

FORTY-NINE

The Fugitive Returns
September–December 1895

ON 6 AUGUST 1895 Lika Mizinova brought her baby to Moscow. She made her peace with her mother and looked for work. Then she went to Tver province with chocolate for Granny Ioganson's name day. Christina was put, as Lika had been, in Granny Ioganson's care: a nurse was found. On 23 September Masha brought Lika to Melikhovo. In November Lika wrote to Granny:

> Masha Chekhova often stays with me and I with her. She lives with her brother Vania and still works in the Rzhevskaia boarding school. When I'm home, I read, play the piano and sing, and time passes quickly ... I've been twice to the Chekhovs' estate, once when I arrived, before term started, and spent two weeks there and I've also been going down for Saturday and Sunday with Masha, I am loved there as I used to be ...

Lika's mother, Lidia Iurgeneva, doggedly independent, could not afford wood to heat her quarters. Physically and emotionally, the Chekhovs gave Lika warmth that autumn.

Potapenko was still banned from Melikhovo, but, in December 1895, back in Tver, Lika stood up for him against Masha: 'I have and shall have only one thing – my little girl! ... never blame Ignati for anything! Believe me he is the man you and I thought he was.' Ignati Potapenko by November had made an act of contrition, at least to Anton, for he felt the lack of sympathetic company in Petersburg:

> Dear Antonio, ... I did think that our true spiritual bond must not be broken by any external circumstances. And if I were to let myself doubt your friendship, I still should say 'That will pass, that is temporary.' So – everything is bright between us, as before, and I am terribly glad.

Anton devised a suitable penance. Potapenko accepted without demur.

He, the man most ridiculed in *The Seagull*, was to oversee the play's realization. Potapenko was easily supervised: he was one of Suvorin's dependants, and he dined regularly with Aleksandr at the Petersburg monthly writers' dinners. Potapenko found Chekhov a typist in Moscow, a Miss Gobiato, who at snail's pace, for a few kopecks a page, made two copies for transmission to Petersburg. Potapenko had one last laugh: Aleksandr sent Anton a newspaper cutting from Zhitomir (in the Ukraine) which showed that library users preferred Potapenko to Chekhov.

Miss Gobiato was too slow: Anton finally sent a manuscript to Suvorin, who was told to expect it from the hands of 'a tall handsome widow' – Sasha Selivanova. Anton told Suvorin to let Potapenko, and nobody else, read it. Suvorin (who admired Potapenko's wife Maria) was shocked by the play; he told Anton that Trigorin, torn between Nina and Arkadina, was too obviously Potapenko, torn between Lika and his wife. Anton disingenuously replied that if this were so, the play would be unstageable. Suvorin, as Chekhov might have suspected, showed *The Seagull* to his confidante, Sazonova. She was already worried by Suvorin's fondness for decadent drama. On 21 December her diary anticipated public opinion:

> I read *The Seagull*. A thoroughly depressing impression. In literature only Chekhov, in music Chopin make that impression on me, like a stone on your soul, you can't breathe. It is unrelieved gloom.

Iavorskaia still hoped that Chekhov would provide her with a triumphal chariot of a play, that *The Seagull* would be in the same neoromantic vein as Rostand's *La Princesse lointaine*, which she and Tania were taking to Petersburg for the new season. In Moscow, in early December, Chekhov read *The Seagull* to a large company in the blue drawing room at Iavorskaia's hotel. Tania recalls:

> Korsh ... considered Chekhov his author, since he had put on the first production of *Ivanov* ... I remember the impression the play made. It was like Arkadina's reaction to Treplev's play: 'Decadence!' 'New forms?' ... I remember the argument, the noise, Iavorskaia feigning delight, Korsh's amazement: 'Dear boy, that's bad theatre: you have a man shoot himself off-stage and don't even let him speak before he dies!' etc. I remember Chekhov's face, half embarrassed, half stern.

Iavorskaia and Chekhov had no more to say to each other. Anton then took his manuscript to Vladimir Nemirovich-Danchenko, whose suggestions he respected and adopted.

Anton now treated Lika as lightly as his old sweetheart Sasha Selivanova. He was celibate, he told Suvorin on 10 November:

> I am afraid of a wife and family life which will restrict me and as I imagine them won't fit in with my disorderliness, but it is still better than tossing about in the sea of life and going through storms in the frail boat of dissipation. Anyway I don't love my mistresses any more, and with them I gradually become impotent.

Anton visited Sasha Selivanova in Moscow to drink beer and vodka, and invited Lika to sing and walk in the woods. Only the faraway aroused desire. Liudmila Ozerova, the Petersburg actress, intrigued Anton even more after a fiasco in Schiller's *Intrigue of Love*. He wrote to Suvorin on 21 October: 'Reading *The Petersburg Newspaper*, where her acting was called simply absurd, I can imagine the little Jew-girl crying and going cold.'

After searching the attic in Melikhovo, Anton found Elena Shavrova, now Mrs Iust's manuscripts, which he had mislaid. He offered to make up to her for his delinquency and confided that he was writing a story ('My Fiancée', the future 'House with the Mezzanine'), as well as a play, about lost love: 'I used to have a fiancée'. Inviting each other to rendezvous in the Great Moscow hotel, she and Anton began a cautious game. Shavrova's letters become flirtatious. On 11 November she hinted at the relationship – of a young actress with a distinguished older man – that she sought: 'You know, I often recall Katia from "A Dreary Story" and I understand her.' On 3 December she wrote: 'It's nice to know that *cher maître* has loved, which means he could have and understand this earthly feeling . . . I think somehow that you analyse everything and everyone too finely to fall in love . . .'[49] For the New Year Shavrova praised 'Ariadna' as a *vraie femme aux hommes*, and wished Chekhov 'as few boring days, hours and minutes as possible'.

Autumn left Anton no time for love or boredom. The creative impulse that had started in spring 1894 intensified. As soon as *The Seagull* was despatched, he sat down to work on his most nostalgic story, 'The House with the Mezzanine'. The scenery and the secondary characters (an idle landowner and his domineering, weeping mistress) stem from 1891, the summer of the mongoose at Bogimovo. The narrator (an artist, never seen to paint a picture) stumbles on a decaying estate where a mother and her two daughters live, argues with the elder daughter and falls in love with the younger, only to have her snatched away when she responds. The sense of loss lies in the decaying pine needles and lime trees, the half-abandoned house and the narrator's passivity. The secondary theme of the story was to run through Chekhov's later plays and stories: the narrator argues the pointlessness of social activism in the face of the misery of the peasantry's condition. The elder sister is an activist and denounces art and idleness. The puzzle for the critics is that neither the active sister nor the artist is approved. In Chekhov's work the conflict is often between two sides of himself, the active landowner and contemplative artist, or the egalitarian and the misogynist.

As an activist, Chekhov now proposed a new school for the villagers, pooling his resources with the peasants' and whatever Serpukhov council granted towards the 3000 roubles needed. His neighbours were unhelpful. The Chekhovs and Semenkoviches, the new owners of Vaskino, visited each other, but Anton barely spoke to the seedy Varenikovs who lived to the east of Melikhovo. Varenikov offered to exchange a large amount of forest for a small amount of hayfield, but Masha would not agree. Varenikov had behaved badly in August: when the Chekhov cows strayed, he demanded a rouble per head to release them. Anton told him to keep the cattle. Varenikov surrendered: 'Have your cows collected; please forbid your servants to let them into your hayfields.'[50]

Anton in Moscow drank with Sasha Selivanova and chased up Miss Gobiato the typist. Masha taught from Monday to Friday. Pavel managed the estate tyrannically and the servants got drunk, quarrelsome and disobedient. After opening the kitchen windows to freeze the cockroaches to death, Pavel complained to Masha:

> Roman has quarrelled with his wife, and she has turned nasty, she wouldn't milk the cows, I had to ask and beg Aniuta to go and do the milking, and Mashutka to feed the hens and ducks, the old woman [Mariushka] with tears in her eyes put the bread in the oven ... What is happening, can we allow the servants and workmen such freedom that they don't obey those that live in the house? Whom

do they serve? . . . Roman used to be considerate when he wasn't
allowed so much freedom and rope, now he has got above himself,
he has become hypocritical, he has found out Antosha's weak point
. . . All week two strapping lads have failed to get the manure out
of the stables, we've had to hire a daily woman. We are sitting with
no firewood, it's cold in the rooms.[51]

Pavel's despotism irritated Anton. He complained to Aleksandr of
Pavel 'nagging at mother over dinner and lecturing us at length about
medals and awards.'

When Anton was in Melikhovo, harmony reigned, but he restricted
his commands to the garden. He would prune raspberries, manure
asparagus, minister to sick dachshunds, but would not reprimand the
men-of-all-work, Ivan, Roman and his brother Egor. Anton would
wander off to the woods: Pavel's diary, in Anton's hand, for 8 November reads: 'Clear morning: went hunting with the dachshunds, but
didn't find the badger in his den.'

Levitan, still prey to depression, came on a few of these walks –
this time without a gun. He was touchingly grateful for Anton's visit
after his attempted suicide. Anton gave him *The Island of Sakhalin*,
inscribed 'in case he should commit murder in a fit of jealousy' and
end up a prisoner there. At the end of July Levitan wrote:

> I constantly observe myself and see clearly that I am completely
> going to pieces. And I am fed up with myself, and how fed up.
> I don't know why, but the few days you spent with me were the
> most peaceful days this summer.

In October Levitan came back to Melikhovo for two days.

Others needed Anton's support. Misha, downcast at being denied
a tax inspectorate at Iaroslavl, asked Suvorin for help. Suvorin thought
his letter muddled and tactless; Anton had to explain what Misha
wanted. Suvorin went to the Finance Ministry and fixed Misha's posting, sending Chekhov a telegram: 'Say *merci*, my angel.' Misha would
not be leaving Uglich alone. After Mamuna's betrayal, he fell in love
with Olga Vladykina, a governess to Uglich's richest manufacturer.
He drove her home from a party across the dangerous ice of the
Volga. She agreed to marry Misha, but was hurt that Misha would
not announce the engagement until he had received Anton's approval.

Masha had a measure of independence in the form of a monthly allowance of 30 roubles from Misha and 'granddad' Sablin. Misha gave her the 1600 roubles due from the publication of his smallholder's encyclopaedia. Only Aleksandr still grumbled: he could not get his elder sons into school; little Kolia threw a cat from a third-floor window and expressed no remorse. Aleksandr turned to Vania and Sonia, as pedagogues:

> Would you take over the training of my piglets? ... As soon as I leave the house they dash off God knows where, grab their hats and clear off ... better that you should have the money than a stranger. Kolia ... is useful, he can fetch vodka from the pub.[52]

Vania was willing, but it took two years to weaken Sonia's opposition.

By autumn 1895 Chekhov had regained his hold over old acolytes, although Bilibin objected to being exploited for his Post Office connections. When Shcheglov asked after eighteen months' silence why Chekhov could not drop him a few friendly lines, he was won over by the response and opened to Chekhov 'both my heart and my hotel room'. He recorded in his diary (10 October 1895): 'There remain three persons, meeting whom makes my heart race: A. P. Chekhov, A. S. Suvorin and V. P. Gorlenko [*a Kiev critic*].' A planned reunion never happened, however, and Shcheglov left, disappointed, for the provinces.

For years Anton had put off meeting Tolstoy, but in August 1895 he stayed with Tolstoy at Iasnaia Poliana for thirty-six hours, even though a private talk with Tolstoy was now no more feasible than with the Pope. Anton had avoided being brought in, like a trophy, by Sergeenko and other Tolstoyans. Access to Tolstoy, even for intimates, was controlled by his disciple, Chertkov. Anton's visit was arranged by the journalist Mikhail Menshikov.[53] Anton had an audience, not a conversation, with Tolstoy. The following morning, Chertkov and Gorbunov-Posadov, in the master's presence, read extracts from his unpublished novel *Resurrection*. Anton let Tolstoy's vegetarianism and anarchism pass, merely pointing out the heroine's implausibly light sentence for conspiracy to murder.

Tolstoy, compiling readers for the masses, had read Chekhov's prose and praised many of his stories, though not for what Anton liked in them. He deplored Chekhov's lack of a guiding idea: his most perceptive remark was that Chekhov merged with Garshin would make a great writer. Anton's person, however, charmed Tolstoy, in particular his 'young lady's gait'. Chekhov did not return like a Muslim from the *haj*, but he did feel admiration for the man, largely because he saw how much Tolstoy's daughters loved their father, and believed, as he later told Suvorin, that a mistress, wife or mother could be deceived, but a daughter could not.

Anton did not become a Tolstoyan: on 1 December he told Suvorin that he would enter any monastery that took unbelievers. He was, however, inspired to Tolstoyan activity. He pestered Aleksandr, who briefly edited a journal for the blind, until a blind old soldier who was begging at Iasnaia Poliana was housed. That autumn and winter Anton sent hay for the schoolteacher's cow, built a new school for the peasants, found cousins Volodia and Aleksandra places in a seminary and a dressmaking school, nagged Sytin, the Moscow publisher, to honour his agreement to publish *The Surgical Chronicle* run by Professor Diakonov. Innumerable writers – such as a Jew, Gutmakher, from Taganrog, and a derelict bookseller, Sveshnikov – owed publication of their work to Anton.

Anton spent the first two weeks of December in Moscow in the Great Moscow Hotel, working on 'The House with the Mezzanine'. Ivan Bunin, then an unknown writer, later to be a kindred spirit, and his companion, Balmont, the drunken decadent poet, were in the hotel. Balmont reached for an overcoat and was stopped by a porter: 'That is Anton Chekhov's overcoat.' Balmont and Bunin were overjoyed at a pretext for meeting Chekhov, and entered his room in the morning. Anton was out, but Bunin sat down and furtively read the manuscript of 'A Woman's Kingdom'. Years passed before he met Anton and confessed.

After an all-night party at *Russian Thought*, Anton arrived in Melikhovo at 6.00 a.m. on 17 December to what he feared would be 'hellish boredom'. The family gathered. Masha arrived, followed by Vania, accompanied not by his wife, but by Sasha Selivanova. Misha came on Christmas Eve for a parental blessing on his marriage to Olga. Pavel was happy because the samovar had been repaired and he had bought a new washstand:

Matins at 7 a.m. Mass at 10. We dined without the priest [*but with*] the schoolteacher, visitors and family. We spent the day well, the

Boys came then Peasants with Felicitations. The servants received good presents.

Dr Saveliev, fellow Taganrogian and medical student, also came. Anton wanted to write, not to celebrate, but he revealed his resentment only to Suvorin on 29 December: 'All day eating and talking, eating and talking'.

VII

The Flight
of the Seagull

To think, my lord, if you delight not in man, what
lenten entertainment the players shall receive from
you.   Shakespeare, *Hamlet II*, ii

FIFTY

Two Diversions in Petersburg
January–February 1896

WHEN NEW YEAR'S DAY 1896 DAWNED, it was nearly minus 30°C at Melikhovo. Guests dispersed to Moscow while Anton packed his bags for Petersburg. The peasant women and children gathered for New Year gifts from Pavel. The Chekhovs' reactionary neighbour Semenkovich rode over from Vaskino: one of his anecdotes struck a chord in Anton's heart – his uncle, the poet Fet, so loathed the University of Moscow that whenever his carriage passed the building, he stopped his driver, opened the window and spat.

Peasant beggary and sociable gentry were soon out of mind. Anton took the morning train to Moscow with Vania. From Moscow he took the overnight express to Petersburg and the Hotel Angleterre. Ignati Potapenko was less in evidence: his second wife had reined him in. On one quiet evening in a frantic fortnight, with Aleksandr's encouragement Chekhov took the *insortable* Natalia to the theatre. Every other evening Anton moved like a comet through a galaxy of actresses. He took Kleopatra Karatygina to see Ostrovsky's *Poverty is no Vice* at Suvorin's Literary-Artistic Circle. She recalled:

> Chekhov grabbed me behind the wings and dragged me off . . .
> Suvorin in his overcoat and hat, holding a stick, was sitting in the
> front box. He was banging the stick and growling, I felt a savage
> outburst coming and pleaded with Chekhov to let me out, but he
> assured me it would be fun and persuaded me to sit down . . . We
> could hear Suvorin [*cursing one of the actresses*]: 'You bitch, you
> bitch! . . .' Chekhov managed to seize him by his coat sleeve . . . I
> took fright, rushed out of the box and then Chekhov and I laughed
> so loud that he said his spleen would burst.[1]

Kleopatra, like Natalia, was abandoned for more fashionable company. *Schadenfreude* and curiosity drove Chekhov to Lidia Iavorskaia's benefit night on 4 January. She starred in Rostand's *La Princesse lointaine*, in Tania Shchepkina-Kupernik's version. This magnificent translation was the last service that Tania performed for Lidia. Now that Iavorskaia was betrothed to Prince Bariatinsky, she was turning her back on her lesbian past. After an all-male dinner with the cadaverous Grigorovich, Anton went to the theatre with Suvorin. The next evening Anton scandalized Sazonova by calling Iavorskaia, as the 'distant princess', a washerwoman covering herself in garlands. On the subject of Tania's verse he was milder – she had a vocabulary of only twenty-five words, ecstasy, prayer, aquiver, murmur, tears, dreams, but could write entrancing verse. After this sally, Chekhov went off to dine with Potapenko, the critic Amfiteatrov and the novelist Mamin-Sibiriak. Suvorin could not come. 'A pity,' said Anton cruelly, 'You're an excellent companion. You pay for everyone.' Suvorin felt an outsider: some blamed Anton's liberalism for Suvorin's disagreements with his rabid colleagues. The journalist Gei yelled at Chekhov on the steps of the Maly Theatre, accusing him of alienating the magnate from his acolytes. On 8 January, to escape these tensions, Chekhov went to Tsarskoe Selo to drink and dine with a fellow-provincial, the Zola of the Urals, Mamin-Sibiriak.

Mamin was one new friend who put Anton at his ease. Anton's impromptu quips in foyers and restaurants, however, sowed seeds of hostility towards him in the Petersburg theatrical world. Lidia Iavorskaia showed no resentment – she sent affectionate notes to Anton that January and met him for tea at Suvorin's, and in private. She had left Korsh's theatre and his bed. She now needed to please the Petersburg public, but was at loggerheads with Suvorin, who loathed her mendacity – she constantly demanded more money – although her notoriety was a crowd-puller no entrepreneur could dispense with. Matters came to a head on the night of 11 January. Iavorskaia missed the dress rehearsal of Sazonova's play. Suvorin was dragged from his bed. Trembling with rage, he sat down to write to her but was lost for words. Anton then started to dictate a mild note: 'You will hurt the author's and your colleagues' feelings if you don't come.' Sazonova took over: 'The play must run tomorrow. Kindly learn the part and be at the rehearsal at 11.' The next evening the play was performed. Sazonova forgave Anton for his lily-livered tone with Iavorskaia: 'I went to the director's room for a smoke. Chekhov praises my play. I am so touched I could throw my arms round his neck.'[2]

Anton had to leave for Melikhovo: on 22 January 1896 Misha was to marry Olga Vladykina, and Anton's absence would have been an insult. Natalia, said Aleksandr, 'thinks you were running away from women or chasing after women.' Certainly, Anton had taken pains to elude Lidia Avilova, in whom he had suddenly lost interest, but there was no woman waiting for him in Moscow.

Back in Melikhovo the only relative waiting for Anton was cousin Georgi from Taganrog, who had brought Santurini wine and pickled mussels to celebrate Anton's thirty-sixth birthday. The surly Roman had shot a hare for dinner. Pavel reported the usual rows in his son's absence. On 4 January Roman had 'caused a scandal' and on 6 January Ivan the workman had been dismissed for drunkenness. Pavel had hired an Aleksandr Kretov, who proceeded to seduce the maid. The good news was that the red cow had calved and that the post office at Lopasnia had been opened and consecrated: with God's blessing, guests would now herald their arrival. Aunt Marfa's good news was, however, her idea of a joke: 'Darling Antosha, Congratulations on your new happiness and new bride. I've found you a bride, ninety thousand dowry . . .'[3]

Anton spent his birthday – it was minus25°C – helping the piebald cow to calve. The next day he used cousin Georgi's departure to make a day trip to Moscow, and sent apologies to Lidia Avilova, promising to see her shortly in Petersburg. Petersburg missed Anton. Suvorin, wrote Aleksandr, was so moody after Anton's departure that nobody dared come near: he had even rowed with his intimates, the venomous Burenin and the devious Syromiatnikov. Anton had hurt Natalia by eating too little, not taking her out and not giving her the puppy he had promised. Aleksandr was sending Natalia to Moscow to sell books, but, he reassured Anton, his pariah of a wife would not spoil her brother-in-law's marriage to an officer's sister. 'She's a coward and unlikely to dare to undertake the journey from Lopasnia solo.' Potapenko would not attend the wedding either, writing from Moscow:

Dear Antonio, I had intended to come to Melikhovo, but the forth-coming marriage there sticks in my path. I'm sure that the solemn event will bring Misha the maximum happiness . . . As I do not personally have this maximum I try to avoid such spectacles. Come here, Antonio, because I want to see you. Suvorin sent a note to me at the station asking me to bring you to Petersburg. I'm definitely going on Thursday.[4]

Misha married Olga at Vaskino church: of the bride's family only Olga's brother came. After the wedding, which did nothing to dispel Anton's boredom in the snow-bound wastes, he met Potapenko in Moscow, and fled to Petersburg for three weeks.

On this second visit Anton stayed in Suvorin's house on Ertel Lane and was subjected to Suvorin's gloom. On 27 January, a night or two after Anton's arrival, the two men went for a long walk. Suvorin recalled the radical daring of his youthful *Sketches and Tableaux*. Anton asked, 'Why not give me a copy of this book as a present?' but Suvorin had decades ago given away the last copy. The two men went into the next second-hand bookshop they came to, where Suvorin spotted the copy he had given twenty years before to the lawyer who had defended him when the book had been prosecuted. Suvorin inscribed it, and gave it to Anton.

On 2 February Sazonova saw her daughter Liuba act: 'dreary, boring . . . every mistake she makes is a knife in [*Sazonova's husband*] Nikolai's heart.' Anton appeared with Suvorin. To her he seemed damaged and she thought the hero's enslavement to the heroine in 'Ariadna' explained it. 'Not much of a story,' she wrote in her diary. 'Some cruel woman must have given him a hard time and he's described her to vent his feelings.' At a banquet for the ageing actress Zhuleva, Suvorin shocked the company by kissing his former contributor Syromiatnikov. To kiss a man who purloined journalists' copy for the secret police was gross indecency in Russian intellectual circles. Anton was revolted and showed it. He refused Syromiatnikov's hand. The battle for Suvorin's soul intensified. Anton at first hung on: much of 1896 was to be spent together in conversation and communion before the breach between them widened.

Anton's friendship with Potapenko, that had survived such strains, was weakening. Anton avoided seeing him alone. Potapenko was hurt not to be invited to the Zhuleva banquet: Anton did not get him a ticket. Potapenko proposed a journey to Finland; Anton refused. To avoid discussion, he said that he was leaving for Moscow on 10, not 13, February. Potapenko protested: 'As for Finland, that would be really swinish on your part, so you must silence your conscience and come.' Two days later, finding Anton still in Petersburg, Potapenko was indignant: 'Let me tell you you are a swine ... I shan't see you off because I'm expecting a typewriter to be delivered at 8 this evening.' Anton found Potapenko a bore. He neither sang nor fornicated. The typewriter had replaced his flowing pen and symbolized the domesticity that his second wife had wrought. Potapenko was ending his last fling, with Liudmila Ozerova, whose success in Hauptmann's *Hannele's Ascension* and equally spectacular failure in Schiller's *Intrigue and Love* had awoken Anton's interest. This winter Potapenko introduced the two; by the autumn, Potapenko would cede Ozerova to Anton.

Anton preferred the tedium of Leikin to Potapenko's hen-pecked state. Loyalty to his first regular publisher took Anton not only to pancake night – the last feast before the Orthodox lent – but also to two other evenings, listening while Leikin priced each dish and related his dachshunds' utterances. Apart from a late evening being vamped by Lidia Iavorskaia – who still hoped for a Chekhov play of her own – Anton shunned company. Of his relatives he entertained only his older nephews. He took them to a Punch-and-Judy show, stuffed them with food, and bought them clothes. Aleksandr was gruff: 'Both are greedy, over-ate and we shall have to give them castor oil. The gauntlets will be lost in an hour, and the jackets will be outgrown in 1½ months ... In their sloppiness they are their mother's children.'

Elena Shavrova, with whom Anton had maintained a flirtatious tutorial relationship for six years, now lived in Petersburg as Mrs Iust, an official's wife. The story she was writing was appropriately called 'Caesar's Wife' – her virtue had to be above suspicion. Anton, when she met him, seemed 'very unkind'. Kleopatra Karatygina begged Anton to put in a word for her with theatre managements or face 'hellish revenges Nos. One to Five'. As he caught the Moscow train, Anton replied, equally unkindly: 'As I am an absolute zero in the Maly Theatre, all five items of your hellish revenge acted on me more weakly than the bite of a paralysed mosquito.' At Suvorin's masked ball for Shrove-Tide, Lidia Avilova, dressed in a black domino costume, had, she claimed, more luck. She sought a response to the inscribed silver medallion she had anonymously sent Anton a year ago. Anton told her she would get her answer in autumn, on the day that *The Seagull* was performed on stage.[5]

FIFTY-ONE

Lika Rediscovered
February–March 1896

ANTON AND SUVORIN took sleeping compartments with two actresses in the latter's theatre, Aleksandra Nikitina and Zina Kholmskaia. When they arrived in Moscow on 14 February, the men took a room in the best hotel, the Slav Bazaar, and then went to a party, where Anton listened to a couple communicating ardently in code, a device he was to use five years later in *Three Sisters*. The actresses went home, but Anton was invited in two days' time to discuss, as Aleksandra Nikitina put it, 'this and this and this.'

The next day Suvorin and Chekhov joined the throng of pilgrims at Tolstoy's Moscow house. Anton was all tact when Tolstoy began to discuss *Resurrection*. Tolstoy had already formed his opinion of Chekhov as a fine writer corrupted by medicine and free thinking. Chekhov noted in his diary:

> Tolstoy was irritable, made cutting remarks about decadents . . .
> Tolstoy's daughters Tatiana and Maria were . . . both telling fortunes
> and they asked me to pick cards, and I showed each of them an ace
> of spades, and that upset them . . . They are both extraordinarily
> likeable and their relationship with their father is touching.

Suvorin weighed up with the Tolstoys the pros and cons of sudden or slow death; he noted: 'Death has been trying to get into their house. First the Countess was ill, now he is. He has kidney stones and he suffers terribly.' Anton had a happier impression. For Tatiana Tolstaia, however, there were consequences Anton never knew about: his visit generated a passion she soon felt compelled to repress.

After a Saturday in Serpukhov discussing school-building, Anton got back to Melikhovo early on Sunday 18 February and slept. He awoke to find that his father had a new initiative: the Melikhovo schoolteacher had been employed to paper the living room. Life for

Pavel, Evgenia and Masha had been snowbound and lonely. One parental letter to Misha and Olga was pathetic:

> We were deeply touched by your letter. In it are expressed all the feelings of hearts that love from the soul. In the twilight of our years such a letter is a great consolation. We spent Shrove Tide just the three of us, with Masha. We expected visitors from Moscow, but nobody came.[6]

For five days Natasha Lintvariova brought from the Ukraine loud laughter. Masha, back teaching in Moscow, came only for the weekends. Cousin Georgi had left with a consignment of books for Taganrog library. February was severe: two peasants were frozen to death. March gave no respite. The estate was under six feet of snow: no school could be built until spring. *The Seagull* awaited an indulgent censor and a daring director. The great prose work that was to fill Chekhov's mind that year was only germinating and he had not yet disinterred *The Wood Demon* for transformation into a viable play. In the evenings, trying to escape Pavel's ranting, Anton picked through the books he had bought, or had been given, to despatch to Taganrog library and, although his eyes tired by candlelight he became absorbed in fortuitous reading of an extraordinary variety of literature.

His private life was empty. Kleopatra Karatygina gave her manuscript to Aleksandr to post on. Anton's reaction was chilling; on 28 February she concluded: 'We don't need to use X-rays to see that the mysterious thread that bound us has broken . . .'[7] Elena Shavrova was chastely silent until spring; Iavorskaia, too, broke off communication. Lika Mizinova, however, reappeared. For the last weekend of February, as of old, she came down with Masha. Her daughter Christina, of whom nobody spoke, stayed with Granny and the nurse. Although she still suffered from stage fright, Lika wanted to sing. Her love for Anton was rekindled, as if the past two years had never happened. Perhaps the imminent publication of 'The House with the Mezzanine' revived memories of the summer of 1891, of the younger Lika who infused the story. Anton foresaw the searchlight that *The Seagull* would fix on Lika, and felt a guilty affection.

When Anton went to Moscow on 29 February for five days, he left his father alone in the house with just the dachshunds, Brom and Quinine, for company. The new workman Aleksandr slept in the kitchen. Evgenia had gone to Iaroslavl to stay with Misha and Olga. Lika was in Moscow. Anton preserved a pencilled scrawl from her on lined paper. It reads: 'Come, but in 10–15 minutes. I'm *very heppy*.' The next few months were the most intense episode in their long love affair.[8] Neither Potapenko nor Anton's actresses were in evidence, and mutual compassion, shared loneliness and bitter experience seem to have brought Lika and Anton closer than at any time in the last six years.

Intimacy with the girl whom he had taken apart to create the heroine of *The Seagull* inspired Chekhov to revise his play. The author entrusted his own antihero to get the play past the Petersburg censor: Potapenko, sublimely unembarrassed, agreed. On 15 March 1896 the play was posted to Petersburg.

In mid March the pond filled with melted snow; work began on the new school at Talezh; the ewes were shorn. Vania in Moscow was asked to bring for Easter: paint for Easter eggs, ten small candles and two quarter-pound candles, an Easter prayer book in a vermilion leather binding and a wall calendar. Anton spent his energies helping supplicants – Aleksandr, cousin Volodia, Taganrog's citizens, and total strangers.

Visitors ventured to Melikhovo, though melting snow made the roads almost impassable. Mud and ruts held Lika back: 'Tell me about the state of the road, whether there is a chance of coming and going back without risking my life.' All three brothers came on the same train, in separate carriages, Misha and Olga for ten days, Vania without Sonia (ill at ease with her in-laws) for two, Aleksandr with his eldest son, Kolia, for four. Spring brought headaches, pains in the right eye and more ominous symptoms for Anton. He never forgot what a peasant had said when he treated the man for TB: 'It's no use, I'll go with the spring waters.' In Pushkin's words, 'I don't like spring./I find the thaw dreary ... stench, mud – in Spring I'm sick/ My blood ferments; my feelings, mind are strained by anguish.' 'Spring Feelings of an Unbridled Ancient', a poem by Count A. K. Tolstoy, caught Anton's attention: 'All my breast burns,/ And every splinter/ Tries to leap on every splinter.' As he waited for the ice to break, Chekhov wrote, he saw the ice as the splinters of his soul.

The family, too, feared spring and Anton's discreet wads of paper full of blood and phlegm. On 17 March Pavel changed the rooms around: Anton was moved to Masha's, the warmest in the house, and Masha took his study. Easter, the climax of Pavel's and Evgenia's year, coincided with Pavel's name day: 'Vania gave me a white tie, Antosha bought me an Easter prayer book and a pound of wax candles.'[9]

Despite the schisms in Petersburg, Suvorin's need for Anton's company was even more urgent than Anton's need for his. Suvorin's thoughts were Chekhovian, and passionately necropolitan:

> 23 March 1896. Today is Easter Saturday. Gei [*the journalist*] and I went to the Alexander Nevsky monastery and, as is my custom, I went to the graves of my dead. How much that is tragic is buried in these graves, how much grief and horror . . . At Gorbunov's grave we opened the lantern hanging from the cross, took the oil lamp out and lit it. I said, 'Christ has arisen, Ivan . . .' Soon you will lie in the grave where three already lie. All that's easy to imagine – being carried into church, where and how the speeches will be, the coffin being lowered, the earth hitting the coffin lid. How often I have seen it, but never was it so bad for me as at Volodia's funeral. I shall be laid next to him. That's what I told Chekhov. The cemetery is very near the Neva. My soul will come out of the coffin, go down underground into the Neva, meet a fish and enter it.[10]

Next to the graves of his first wife, shot dead in 1873, of his daughter, Aleksandra, who died in 1880, of Volodia who shot himself in 1887 and of Valerian, whom diphtheria took in 1888, Suvorin became morose and distressed: his son-in-law Kolomnin (soon to die) and Anton Chekhov were the two men whom he trusted and loved.

FIFTY-TWO

The Khodynka Spring
April–May 1896

THE FIRST STARLING returned to Melikhovo on 1 April. Two days later Anton invited Lika via Masha: 'The week after Easter you can travel our roads without risk of death.' That evening Pavel noted in the diary: 'Antosha went without supper.' For four days Anton coughed badly. Asking Potapenko to return *The Seagull*, he told him he was suffering from 'the old boredom. I spat a bit of blood for 3 or 4 days, but I'm all right now, I could drag joists about or get married.' He would not admit to TB. When Ezhov, desperate that his new wife was showing the same fatal symptoms as the first, asked for advice, Anton was bland, gulling himself as much as Ezhov:

> All that is clear from your letter so far is that your wife has been prescribed creosote and that she has had pleurisy ... I've had a cough for a long time and coughed up blood, but I'm still fine, putting my faith in God and science, which is now curing the most serious lung diseases. So you have to have hope and try to avoid disaster. The best thing, of course, would be to go and take koumiss [*fermented mares' milk*].

Although Anton gave him letters of recommendation, as he had once given money, Ezhov never forgave Dr Chekhov the deaths of his wives.

In April Melikhovo came to life. Whitebrow, the young dog Pavel had given away to Semenkovich while Anton was away, came running back after six weeks' absence. He was caught up and banished again. The starlings flocked. Evgenia wrote to Misha and Olia:

> The starlings came on Friday 5th and have nested in the two new boxes, one opposite the dining-room window, the other the one you built on to the house so that I could see them from the corridor window. Antosha and I are listening to them singing ... Aniuta

[*Naryshkina, the maid*] has got engaged to a man in Vaskino, there've been two balls, but for us their wild parties are very disturbing and unpleasant.[11]

The late spring; the starlings; the coughing of blood; the rowdy peasants and the neighbouring gentry; endless troubles with labour and materials for the new school; a morning spent with Tolstoy: all was grist to Chekhov's narrative mill. After a winter's inactivity, he had got down to a long work – originally intended to be a novel for the popular monthly, *The Cornfield*. The fee, more than 1000 roubles, was the temptation, the censorship of popular magazines the stumbling block. Known as 'My Life', the work was first called 'My Marriage' as a companion piece to 'The House with the Mezzanine' (which was printed in *Russian Thought* that April and could have been called 'My Non-Marriage'). 'My Life' too is a first-person narrative, 'a provincial's story' instead of 'an artist's story'. As Chekhov worked, its scope broadened.

'My Life' contains everything Chekhovian – a gruesome anonymous provincial town, inconclusive wrangling between activist and quietist philosophers, lyrical landscapes, dialogue of the deaf between man and woman, the lure of the theatre, the peasantry's instinctive values. The story tests intuition against ideas: how 'a little profit' (the hero's nickname) is gained from following instinct and enduring one trial after another. The narrator's loss of status, of wealth, of a wife is outweighed by inner peace, despite the melancholy ending, where we see the hero visiting with his little niece the cemetery where his sister is buried. Chekhov takes another look at Tolstoy's slogans – non-resistance to evil, simplification – and his hero becomes a test-bed on which Tolstoyan principles are tried to breaking point. Chekhov does not debunk Tolstoy, but strips his ideas of sanctimony. The Tolstoyan refrain uttered by one character, 'Lice eat grass, rust eats iron, lies eat the soul' is moral poetry, but not a blinding light. 'My Life' is both an existential story and a classic, using devices of Tolstoy (the railway as an instrument of destruction) and Turgenev (the living consoled at the graveside). The composition of 'My Life' took virtually the entire year; by the end of April less than half was drafted.

The fiction was fed by the events that summer (not least by Anton's many railway journeys); writing such freshly inspired prose reconciled him to the drudgery of revising *The Seagull*, and quarrying *Uncle Vania* out of the ruins of *The Wood Demon*. Confessional though it is, 'My Life' breaks with the parodic mode of *The Seagull* or 'The House with the Mezzanine'. The use of autobiographical material is freer from caricature and vindictiveness. The conflict between a violent father and an introverted son may have been autobiographical for Anton, but the son breaks out, not from the lower classes to the gentry, but downwards. The story has some cruelties: the hero's sister is a failed actress called Kleopatra, and the character's début, dumbstruck and pregnant in an amateur production, was painful reading for both Karatygina and Lika Mizinova. Nevertheless, the reader of 'My Life' is moved to compassion, not mockery. The traits of Misail, hero and narrator of 'My Life', recall Aleksandr (also known as 'a little profit' for his trade in songbirds in Taganrog). Aleksandr's vegetarianism and weakness for alcohol are ascribed to Misail, but so are his open mind and versatility as a craftsman.

While 'My Life' was being written, Aleksandr gave Anton frequent cause for pity, anger or laughter. First Toska caught scarlet fever, and Aleksandr's colleagues shunned him for fear of infection. Then Aleksandr went to Kiev as a freelance reporter on the doctor's conference, only to be robbed, together with seven doctors, in his sleeping compartment. 'Disgracefully robbed in the carriage under anæsthetic,' he claimed. Aleksandr began drinking again in Kiev.

The grimness of country life in 'My Life' reflects reality. At the end of April, Pavel recorded, 'There is no food in the house for the cows. The horses get 2½ measures of oats per day.' In early May life was still hard: 'Assumption. Because of the rain the clock in the dining room has stopped. The herd of horses got into the garden. We tried to stoke the stoves in the rooms, but there was no wood to be found.' Chekhov complained to Elena Shavrova: 'It's devilish cold. A savage northeast wind is blowing. And there's no wine, there's nothing to drink.' In spring a troika sent over half-thawed mud to meet the train from Moscow was a dangerous vehicle, so that Anton had to forgo Lika: 'If Lika comes, she'll squeal all the way.' It needed only a breakdown in communication for the affair to falter again, and although Anton, to judge by the circumstantial evidence, was close to committing himself to Lika, he again began a double game. His tone towards Elena Shavrova, who was staying with her mother and sisters in Moscow, became affectionate. On Iavorskaia's notepaper, he asked her why she wanted to flee: 'Actually, you ought to take a trip to Australia! With me!' – and apologized for seeming 'very unkind':

> This paper was brought on Rue de la Paix, so let it be the paper of peace! ... Let this cutting, bright colour wring tears of forgiveness from your eyes ... Now guess: who gave me this paper?

The banter became mutual; Elena Shavrova pondered a liaison with her *cher maître*. She sent him her 'Indian Summer' (literally: 'A Woman's Summer'), inscribed 'a sign of deep respect, gratitude and other warmer feelings'.

Unknown to Anton, a hundred miles south in Iasnaia Poliana, the story led Tatiana, Tolstoy's daughter, to record in her diary for 19 April 1896:

> Today papa read Chekhov's new story 'The House with the Mezzanine'. And I had an unpleasant feeling, because I sensed the reality in it and because the heroine was a 17-year-old girl. Now Chekhov is a man to whom I could become wildly attached. Nobody has penetrated my soul at the first encounter as he has. On Sunday I walked to the Petrovskys and back to see his portrait. And I've only seen him twice in real life.[12]

Tatiana told her mother; the countess, forgetting that she was a doctor's daughter and a leveller's wife, retorted that Chekhov was too poor and of too low a birth to be considered as a husband. Tatiana questioned common friends about Anton: 'Has he been spoilt by women?' she asked the editor Menshikov[13], and she urged Anton to visit. Faced with her mother's hostility and Anton's unresponsiveness, she fell instead for a married man, Sukhotin, whose wife she eventually became.

Chekhov's lowly birth bothered only aristocrats. Poverty bothered Anton more. He was committed not only to an extended family and to friends fallen on hard times, but also to the peasantry. The council and richer peasants might contribute, but he was liable for 1000 roubles towards the new school at Talezh. Suvorin gave him an advance on his collected plays and stories, but Anton was now wary of debts to Suvorin. He put out feelers to his new publisher, Adolf Marx, the proprietor of *The Cornfield*, who published his authors superbly. Marx would not tell him what Fet had been paid for his

Collected Poems, but equally told Chekhov not to reveal his fee for 'My Life'. The idea of selling his collected works to Marx for a substantial sum was born. For the time being, Anton had a little leeway. The Talezh teacher, Mikhailov, became the foreman for the school building. Anton instructed the carpenters, who were putting on the roof timbers, not to take orders from his father and left for a few days in Moscow.

On his return the roads were still 'vile, mud, deep ruts filled with water', but visitors crowded the house and the annexe. Both younger brothers brought their wives. It became hot. The starlings' eggs hatched and they stopped singing; by 13 May it was over 30°; mosquitoes plagued everyone. Finally Lika came. She had taken a cottage with her baby and the nanny near Podolsk, half way along the line from Moscow to Lopasnia. Meetings and journeys to and from Moscow could now seem casual. Once again a family friend, she came down with Vania, the flautist Ivanenko, or even the postmaster. Pavel occasionally mentioned her sourly in the diary as Mlle Mizinova.

Pavel was preoccupied with Moscow's churches. Tsar Nicolas II, three years after his accession, was to be crowned in Moscow, the old capital; the city had a week of pomp in mid May. Unknown to each other, Pavel and Suvorin (accompanied by Iavorskaia) watched the five-hour coronation in the Uspensky cathedral. Pavel returned to Melikhovo directly and was not among the crowd of some 700,000 people, for whom the authorities had erected on Khodynka field in western Moscow 150 stands, each barred by a narrow gate admitting only two at a time: these stands were to distribute half a million 'presents' – a tin mug and a coronation sausage – with the lure of a special prize, a silver watch, at each stand. On 18 May a stand collapsed in the stampede. The horror was worsened by the callous authorities: the honeymoon of Nicolas II and his people ended. Khodynka precipitated the collapse of the Romanov dynasty. (The dynasty sensed nothing: the ball at the French embassy, even after the ambassador had inspected the corpses, went ahead.) A journalist to the marrow of his bones, Suvorin went to Khodynka:

> Up to 2000 people were crushed to death. Corpses were being carted all day and the crowd went with them. It's a rutted place with pits. The police arrived only at 9, and people had started gathering at 2

... There were a lot of children. They were lifted up and saved over people's heads and shoulders. 'I haven't seen any gentry. It's just workmen and artisans lying there,' said a man about the suffocated ... What bastards these police officials are, every one of them, and these bureaucrats.

Suvorin returned to Moscow three days later, obsessed by Khodynka, meeting more eye-witnesses and public servants. On 30 May he left a third time for Moscow and invited Anton to the Hotel Dresden. Anton spent all day examining the children at Talezh school and joined Suvorin late at night. The next day was one of the most horrible in Anton's life, even for a man who had seen the prisons of Sakhalin. In west Moscow he stood on the site of a massacre. His diary is laconic: 'On 1 June we were at the Vagankovo cemetery and saw the graves of those who perished at Khodynka.' Suvorin's diary gives a more graphic account:

Chekhov and I were at the Vagankovo cemetery a week after the catastrophe. The graves still smelt. The crosses were in rows, like soldiers on parade, mostly six-cornered, pine. A long pit had been dug and the coffins were placed next to each other. A beggar told us that the coffins were put on top of each other in three layers. The crosses are about four feet apart. The inscriptions are in pencil, about who is buried, sometimes with a comment: 'His life was 15 years and 6 months.' Or 'His life was 55 years.' 'Lord, accept his spirit in peace.' 'Those that suffered at Khodynka field.' ... 'Thy grievous path of agony came on thee unawares, The Lord has liberated thee from all thy grief and cares.'

The next day Anton went home to Melikhovo, while Suvorin went north, to his villa on the Volga at Maksatikha. Suvorin had, a fortnight later, nightmares of corpses. Anton said little about it, but Vagankovo cemetery and Khodynka affected him profoundly. He stopped writing for a fortnight after hearing the news of the disaster and did not begin work on 'My Life' again until 6 June. After his walk among the mass graves with Suvorin he did not write a letter for five days.

Khodynka swept Lika from Chekhov's mind. She sent a furious note, outraged that he had passed Podolsk on 30 May and not taken her with him to the Hotel Dresden: 'Very nice of you, Anton, to send a postcard and let me know that you've steamed past! The fact that you stayed in Suvorin's hotel room is of absolutely no interest to me . . .' Anton alleged that he had never received her angry response, though it was neatly filed away in his archive at the end of the year, and pleaded with her 'to leave together for Moscow on the 15th or 16th and have dinner together.' This made Lika relent, and she agreed to meet him once again on the Moscow train. Again, Anton was not there, and she showered him with reproaches. She then received another invitation from Anton, who made it clear that a visit to the optician was the most pressing reason for him to travel to Moscow. Missed trains, like muddy roads, seemed sufficient cause for mutual affection to collapse again into reproaches and irony.

Lika replied angrily, and Chekhov put off his journey to Moscow by a day and arranged to meet Lika for lunch with Viktor Goltsev at *Russian Thought*. Now Viktor Goltsev was to play the same role in Anton's relations with Lika as Potapenko had, becoming a second string, just as Elena Shavrova was to Chekhov. Anton's next letter to Lika ended with a telling remark which applied to his relations with both women: 'I can't tie up and untie my affairs any more easily than I can tie a necktie.' The words 'tie up' and 'untie', *zaviazyvat´* and *razviazyvat´* connect Chekhov's love life to his writing: they also mean 'to devise a plot' and 'to devise the end of the plot'.

FIFTY-THREE

The Consecration of the School
June–August 1896

ANTON SAW LIKA IN MOSCOW and also commissioned a bell tower for Melikhovo church; building was to begin once Talezh school was finished. He saw an optician who cured his headaches: Anton's short-sighted right eye had been strained by the long-sighted left: a pince-nez put the finishing touch to Anton's image. Other prescriptions, electric shocks, arsenic and sea-bathing, were ignored.

In July Elena Shavrova departed south for the summer and autumn, hurling an affectionate letter to Anton out of the Moscow–Kharkov mail train as it steamed through Lopasnia: Anton found her arch catch phrases *Chi lo sà?* and *Fatalité* irritating. He and Lika were for the time being in harmony: she came for five days to Melikhovo. No rival was in sight or in touch.

Summer visitors to Melikhovo spent their time out of doors: Ezhov came on a bicycle; the Konovitsers brought Dunia's brother, Dmitri, another pioneer cyclist. Olga Kundasova, again patient and assistant in Iakovenko's clinic, disturbed the peace. Depression made her look, Chekhov told Suvorin, 'as if she'd been a year in solitary confinement'. At the end of June Masha returned from the Lintvariovs and Evgenia came back from Moscow: the household ran smoothly. Misha and Olga stayed in the annexe where *The Seagull* had been written. There were only routine distractions: a neighbour's cows in Chekhov's woods; dysentery in a nearby village.

To his editor, Lugovoi,[14] Chekhov sent the first third of 'My Life': 'a rough-hewn wooden structure which I'll plaster and paint when I finish the building'. Lugovoi liked the manuscript and tucked it away in Adolf Marx's fireproof safe. As well as Marx's generous fee came more bounty: Suvorin sent Anton a three-month railway pass. Anton paid his mortgage interest and dreamed of journeys. In Petersburg, however, his affairs were going less smoothly. The censors were baulking at *The Seagull*. Sazonova noted (3 June): 'Chekhov is melancholic. Suvorin too. The former is upset because of the play, the other is complaining of weakness and old age.' Potapenko, however, was optimistic, for the censor Litvinov, a crony of Suvorin's, was well disposed towards Chekhov. Unfortunately, Potapenko was not on the spot:

> Hotel Fassman. Dear Antonio! As you can see, I've ended up in Karlsbad, my aim being to rid my liver of stones etc., etc. A little bit of a problem with your *Seagull*. Contrary to all expectation, it has got caught in the nets of the censorship, but not badly, so it can be rescued. The whole trouble is that your decadent has a lax attitude to his mother's love life, which the censor's rules don't allow. You'll have to insert a scene from Hamlet: 'A bloody deed! almost as bad, good mother/As kill a king and marry with his brother.' . . . Actually, we'll get out of it more easily. Litvinov says the whole thing can be put right in 10 minutes.

Potapenko wanted Anton to tour Germany with him and his friend – it would be cheap and, Potapenko swore by his liver, enjoyable – but Anton would never travel with Potapenko again. Potapenko did not get back to Petersburg and the censor until late July. By then Litvinov had returned the play to Chekhov with blue pencil marks where he wanted changes. Reluctantly, Chekhov made Treplev more indignant about his mother's liaison with Trigorin, and deleted a scene where Dr Dorn is revealed to be Masha Shamraeva's father. Potapenko belatedly took up the baton:

> I don't know what's happened to your *Seagull*. Have you done anything about it? Tomorrow I'll go and see Litvinov . . . There are rumours that literature is to be abolished; so we shan't need censors . . . Lavrov will have a stake put up him, Goltsev will have his tongue cut out.

Anton was beginning to be cast down by the antagonism of Petersburg to his work. His mood was worsened by a letter from Isaak Levitan, in the throes of manic depression, staying in the appropriately named resort of Serdobol [*Heartache*] on the Gulf of Finland:

> The rocks here are smoothed by the ice age . . . Ages, the sense of the word is simply tragic . . . Billions of people have drowned and

will drown. We are Don-Quixotes ... tell me in all honesty, it's stupid, isn't it!! Yours – what a senseless word – no, just Levitan.

Anton's reply, if any, is not extant, but his own depression is clear in a letter he wrote to Aleksei Kiseliov:

I live out my years as a bachelor, 'We pluck a day of love like a flower.' I can't drink more than three glasses of vodka. I've stopped smoking.

He became restless. On 20 July, for the fourth time in seven months, Anton left Melikhovo to see Suvorin. He gave no reason for such a hasty trek. Suvorin's country house in Maksatikha, where the Mologa and the Volchina rivers meet, was reached by train to Iaroslavl and then river boat. Did Anton go for the fishing, or for counselling on his personal, theatrical or financial affairs? Had he intended to travel further north, to console Levitan? Petersburg was uninviting, for Aleksandr had become demented after his drunken binge in Kiev, although he was writing articles on the care of the insane. He complained to Anton: 'The old woman Gaga is wasting away ... I have an abscess between my cheek and my gum. We've got a puppy named Saltpetre, it messes.' Natalia's postscript asked why Chekhov had 'forgotten his poor relatives'.

On Anton's return to Melikhovo he found that Lika's behaviour changed. Neither affectionate nor angry, she wrote in a scrawl that betokened emotional disarray, heralding her arrival, hinting that she had found a new lover: 'Viktor Goltsev and I will come on Saturday for the consecration of the school. I'm not yet fully infected; when I kiss you I shan't infect you.'

The consecration of the school galvanized everyone. Anton spent a whole day at council meetings in Serpukhov. He could stand the formalities only because he was leaving next month to see Suvorin in the Crimea. He was besieged by mad patients. One of the Tolokonnikovs, whose factories polluted the village of Ugriumovo [Sullen], kept a female relative on a chain to stop her abusive shrieking: for weeks Anton searched for a hospital to take her.[15] On the eve of the consecration, a peasant showed violent melancholia con delirio.

Aleksandr did not come to the consecration: Dr Iakovenko and Olga Kundasova represented the mentally unstable. The occasion was so alcoholic that guests were immobilized for two days at Melikhovo with hangovers. The servants made merry, except for Roman, whose baby son had died. The consecration was so moving that Chekhov transmuted it into an episode of 'My Life'. Even Pavel's thirst for ceremony was satisfied: 'The village elders offered the school governor bread and salt, an icon of the Redeemer and speeches of thanks. Cherevin the manager offered Masha a bouquet. Girl choristers sang *May you live many years.*' Chekhov himself made a rare diary entry:

> 4 August. The peasants from Talezh, Bershovo, Dubechnia and Shiolkovo offered me four loaves, an icon, two silver salt cellars. The peasant Postnov from Shiolkovo made a speech.

Next came the consecration of the bell tower. (Anton had the church painted orange.)

'My Life' was sent to *The Cornfield* – 'I'll put the sweetening in and polish it up in proof form,' he told Lugovoi. He sent the last draft of *The Seagull* for Potapenko to take over the next hurdle. The Moscow *News of the Day* was advertising the play – 'Chekhov's *Seagull* flies towards us,/ Fly, my darling, fly to us,/ To our deserted shores!' wrote the poetaster Lolo Munshtein. Anton cringed. It was time to leave.

FIFTY-FOUR

Night on a Bare Mountain
August–September 1896

ANTON WANTED to make the best use of the rail pass Suvorin had given him. He decided first to visit Taganrog, and end up in Feodosia with Suvorin, but was vague about the itinerary. He told only his sister that he would go to Kislovodsk, a spa in the north Caucasus. He teased Potapenko: 'I'll be in Feodosia, I'll make a pass at your first wife' – for Potapenko, saddled with alimony, wanted a pretext for divorce. Potapenko could not, however, fathom Anton's motives: 'What mad idea to go to Feodosia? It's utter horror! Do you really want to write a novel about the life of cretins! . . . I hear you have some convict's travel warrant.' On 23 August 1896, a few days after Anton left, Potapenko wrote to him about the *The Seagull*, literary adventures and liver stones. He began: 'And where you've vanished to, nobody knows. You gave me a Feodosia address, but I think you've gone to the Caucasus.' The frankest of men, Potapenko suspected from Anton's evasions that he had abducted Lika.

Three clues might point to a journey with Lika. Firstly, the route that Chekhov took was one that Lika had proposed for a journey four years ago. Secondly, Lika vanished at the same time as Chekhov. Thirdly, Lika's letters that autumn would suggest that Anton had promised her marriage exactly a year after his arrival in the spa of Kislovodsk. Yet would Anton, who valued privacy so much, have provoked gossip by taking a woman as attractive and alluring as Lika to his birthplace and then to a fashionable mountain spa? And does a promise of 'mutual bliss', as Anton had put it, have to be sealed with a preliminary honeymoon? In any case, would Lika have gone to Feodosia? She knew that Suvorin advised Anton not to marry her, and panicked at the thought of meeting him.

Where did Lika vanish to? On 19 August Chekhov left Melikhovo with Lika and her friend Varia Eberle for Moscow, where Anton would catch the express train south. Even Granny Ioganson was non-plussed. She had no news of Lika until 5 September, after which Lika reappeared in Podolsk, between Melikhovo and Moscow:

5 September: They've brought Christina and the nanny.
6 September: How could Lika send [the baby's] things off in such a rush? Now the child has no clean linen, it's terribly annoying.
16 September: Lika still hasn't moved from Podolsk, I am so disappointed, as I expected to see her in Pokrovskoe tomorrow.[16]

Nobody in Kislovodsk or Taganrog saw Lika; Anton spent his time in both places with male friends. If Lika disappeared with any man, it was probably not Anton, but Viktor Goltsev. Maybe the date, 1 September 1897, for 'mutual bliss' was set before Anton's departure south, or after his return.[17]

Anton spent a day or two in Taganrog, seeing cousins and the library, avoiding admirers. He wrote no letters from his birthplace, and almost nothing until his holiday ended. He sent instructions: Masha was to buy timber for a new school at Novosiolki, Potapenko was to act for The Seagull. His diary is terse:

In Rostov I had supper with my old schoolmate, Lev Volkenshtein . . . At General Safonov's funeral in Kislovodsk I met A. I. Chuprov, then A. N. Veselovsky in the park.[18] On the 28th went hunting with Baron Steingel, spending the night on Mt Bermamyt; cold and a very strong wind . . .

To cousin George in Taganrog Chekhov revealed only that he had met friends in Kislovodsk 'as idle as himself.' Kleopatra Karatygina recalls stumbling on Anton in Kislovodsk: hot and irritable, he was cajoled into posing for a photograph. Anton found relief from the heat by going on a boar hunt on Mount Bermamyt with a man who should have known better, his colleague Dr Obolonsky, who was next to appear in Anton's life when catastrophe struck. Mount Bermamyt is a remarkable place for climbers and hunters, but no careful doctor would let a tubercular patient spend a night there. The guide books of the time warned:

8559 ft above sea level, 20 miles from Kislovodsk . . . Bermamyt is a virtually bare rock usually swept by winds blowing off Mt Elbrus. There are ruins of a Tatar village, but no protection from rain and wind ... People travel to Bermamyt to watch the sun rise ... It is always cold on Bermamyt and snow falls even in August and the temperature falls well below zero ... The northeast winds that prevail at this time often strengthen at Bermamyt to hurricane level ... It is especially important not to chill the stomach: it should be wrapped in a woollen cummerbund.[19]

The trip to Mount Bermamyt undoubtedly shortened Anton's life.

A day or two later, Anton made for the warmth of the Black Sea. Reaching Novorossiisk, where his brother Alexandr had been so unhappy, Anton was only a night's sailing from Feodosia. Suvorin had waited for him for eleven days. The ten days that Chekhov spent with Suvorin, regardless of his 'cretinous' sons, he would call the 'one bright spell' in 1895 and 1896. The fact that he wrote no letters is evidence of his bliss, not distress. He and Suvorin were more relaxed than ever in each other's company, even though – or perhaps because – Suvorin now deferred more to Anton, than Anton to Suvorin, and Anton saw clearly the flaws in Suvorin's character. On 22 August at dinner with Shcheglov, Suvorin conceded: 'Chekhov is a man of flint and a cruel talent with his harsh objectivity. He's spoilt, his *amour propre* is enormous.' The same summer Chekhov told Shcheglov: 'I'm very fond of Suvorin, very, but, you know, *Jean*, sometimes at grave moments in life those with no strength of character are worse than evildoers.'[20]

Iavorskaia's marriage to the young Prince Bariatinsky was the topic of the day. Both were already married, and needed the Tsar's consent. The prince's mother was horrified, but the Bariatinsky sons needed Iavorskaia's earnings. Moreover, Bariatinsky, a budding writer, wanted a mascot. Iavorskaia broke with Tania. Suvorin's diary echoes what he told Anton, who still had an interest in both women:

5 August. Shchepkina-Kupernik ... was having lunch with Iavorskaia and her husband Bariatinsky, the conversation touched on these two ladies' past, which there was so much gossip about. 'No smoke without fire,' said Tania ... After lunch Iavorskaia-Bariatinskaia flew at Tania in front of her maid, speaking in French, accused her of gossiping and so on ... 'My husband is in hysterics,' she said ... 'He doesn't want to see you again, and you must leave right now.' – 'But I'm just wearing a blouse, let me change.' – 'You can change, but that's all.' Tania left without even changing. She borrowed 500

roubles from me and is off to attend lectures in Lausanne. She is very upset.

Suvorin noted Anton's sigh at the mention of Iavorskaia, but Anton was not seriously affected by her marriage. He was content to pass the warm Crimean days drinking, chatting in the sun, by the water. Suvorin's chief 'cretin', as Potapenko called him, Aleksei the Dauphin, was elsewhere, usurping his father's power. Moscow and Melikhovo left Anton in peace: he merely read the proofs for the first third of 'My Life'. A few telegrams arrived from Petersburg. Potapenko had done Anton a final favour (in an act of ineffective benevolence or effective revenge), propelling *The Seagull* through the Imperial Theatre Committee. Unfortunately the play was given to the theatre least suited to Chekhov, the Aleksandrinsky theatre with its Sarah Bernhardt techniques, and its repertoire of French farce. *The Seagull* was to be directed by Evtikhi Karpov, who was inexperienced, unimaginative and cocksure. Worse, the first performance was set for Levkeeva's benefit night on 17 October. Levkeeva, a comédienne, would find in the heroine of *The Seagull* only a satire on her own career as an actress, and her followers would be outraged. The one good omen was that Potapenko and Karpov had cast some fine actors, notably Savina and Davydov, and the still unknown Vera Komissarzhevskaia.

Suvorin, now sixty-two years old, was depressed as Anton left Feodosia:

> The earlier you are born the sooner you die. Today Chekhov said: 'Aleksei and I will die in the 20th century.' – 'You may, but for sure I'll die in the 19th,' I said. – 'How do you know?' – 'I'm utterly certain, in the 19th. It's not hard to see, when every year you get worse.'

Unable to shake Suvorin's pessimism, Anton telegraphed Masha to have Roman meet the local train from Serpukhov with a coat and galoshes, and left the Crimea where the weather had turned as bitter as his host's mood. Suvorin accompanied him, and they stayed a day in Kharkov to watch a performance of Griboedov's *Woe from Wit*. On 17 September 1896 Anton stepped out in sunshine at Lopasnia. The burden of running Melikhovo had fallen on Masha and Pavel. She had bought four magnificent beams for the new school. Pavel had the schoolteacher paper the annexe for Antosha's return, and then his own room. Four weeks in charge had restored Pavel's patriarchal confidence. He told Misha:

> We expected you for the Feast of the Exaltation of the Cross, you had two government holidays, you could have come, but you refused to accept our hospitality and see us. Mother baked an excellent pie, sturgeon gristle with mustard oil, which you would have liked . . . For the cattle we made the same 40 tons of hay as last year, that's not enough. Mariushka only bothers Antosha with her ducklings and chickens, he will build a run in the cattle yard for the fowls, but she hatches them in her kitchen and feeds them there, they grow up and get into the garden. Our summer is still magnificent . . . All summer we have been eating mushrooms fried in sour cream. The clock goes well, on time and strikes every five minutes. The weather-cock on the annexe spun nicely, but a storm has shaken it to bits.

Chekhov had handed 'My Life' over to the censor, who baulked at the narrator's disrespect for a provincial governor and at the author having a general's widow take a drunken lover. The editors talked the censor round, and Anton was free of his story and of *The Seagull*; Suvorin had the script for the play and the Imperial Theatre Committee passed it for performance, albeit with condescension:

> the 'symbolism' or 'Ibsenism' . . . has an unpleasant effect . . . If that seagull weren't there the comedy would not change in the slightest . . . We cannot pass . . . quite unnecessary characterization, such as Masha taking snuff and drinking vodka . . . some scenes seem to be thrown onto paper haphazardly with no proper connection to the whole, without dramatic consequentiality.[21]

The Imperial Theatre Committee represented Petersburg attitudes and made it clear how the city would receive the play. Chekhov nevertheless went ahead.

FIFTY-FIVE

Fiasco
October 1896

THE GLOW of Feodosia faded slowly. 'I'm overwhelmed by laziness. I was terribly spoiled in Feodosia,' Anton told Suvorin. He bought tulip bulbs, inspected his schools, treated his patients, agitated for a paved road from the station to the river Liutorka and sent Dr Obolonsky a book 'in memory of the boar we killed on Mount Bermamut'. Lika reappeared the following week. Whatever had happened that August, her attitude to Anton was cooler. Letters stopped, and she came with a male companion (this time, the flautist Ivanenko). The day she arrived death struck Melikhovo: the brightest girl in the village, Dunia, died of a twisted gut. She was buried in the churchyard. Lika always took flight when any tragedy or even tumult struck Anton's household: she left with Ivanenko the next day, not to return, until Anton begged her a month later.

While he was away, Anton had transferred decisions on casting *The Seagull* from Potapenko to Suvorin and Karpov. Now that Lopasnia telegraph office was open, he sent countless messages to Petersburg, booking tickets and lodging for friends and relatives. Chekhov composed the audience as carefully as Suvorin and Karpov did the cast: the drama in the auditorium was to be as tense as the one on stage.

All summer Anton had helped others by stealth and been found out by accident. He paid half the school fees for a Taganrog boy, Veniamin Evtushevsky, the nephew of Anton's aunt Liudmila, and lobbied publishers to subsidize Dr Diakonov's journal *Surgery*. The same systematic organization behind the wings is characteristic of his love life and his new writing. To the two last weeks of August 1896, or the two first weeks of September 1896, we can ascribe one of Chekhov's most furtive achievements: rewriting *The Wood Demon* as *Uncle Vania*. He cut the cast by half, removing confidants and confidantes, merging a drunken Don Juan with the saintly conservationist doctor, 'The Wood Demon', to produce a flawed Doctor Astrov. He took out virtually all the music from Tchaikovsky and cut the melodrama; in the new play the lovesick uncle no longer kills himself. Uncle Vania, unlike Uncle Georges, cannot even hit a target at point-blank range. The last act of *The Wood Demon* with its sentimental reconciliations *al fresco* is thrown out altogether. Chekhov had finally found 'a new ending'. Idyllic comedy (despite the suicide) is transformed into bitter 'scenes from country life': the city dwellers leave their country relatives devastated by their wrecked lives. Anton added just one new character, the nanny Marina, the one religious believer in the household, the keeper of its awful secrets. Why was Chekhov so secretive about his new play, a work of genius that he had created out of a work he had disowned? When publishers or actors appealed to Chekhov to let them have *The Wood Demon*, the very mention of which was painful to him, Anton told nobody that he was revising it. In late autumn he baldly announced to Suvorin the existence of '*Uncle Vania*, which nobody knows about'.[22]

On 1 October Anton set off for Petersburg in an even more cynical frame of mind about the city's theatres after reading the August issue of *The Theatregoer*, where a certain S. T. pointed out that the director's mistress was always a lead actress in productions. 'From this contribution, written frankly and in detail, I learnt that Karpov is living with Kholmskaia,' Chekhov told Suvorin.

First Anton had a week's work in Moscow. A new project, encouraged by Suvorin, preoccupied him. He wanted to take advantage of new press laws to become joint editor, with Viktor Goltsev, of a liberal newspaper. It says much for Goltsev that Anton took this, his last collaboration, so far. Anton's room at the Great Moscow was a rallying point for all his contacts. He had a loyal ally, the young corridor footman Semion Bychkov:

> I'd been a factory worker, a yard man, worked in a puppet theatre, in pantomime and done everything ... Of all the people staying at the hotel only Anton Chekhov spoke to me simply, man-to-man, without pride, with none of that looking down on you. And he gave me his writings, I started reading and that minute a new light illuminated me ... 'Why,' I said, 'Mr Chekhov, do you live alone? You ought to get married.' 'How could I, much as I'd like to,

Semion,' he laughed, 'I never get any time! My public wears me out.' . . . I loved him fervently with all my soul.[23]

Semion Bychkov had his work cut out as Anton's social secretary. A number of women – Tania, Lika, Shavrova, Kundasova – wanted to be sure of seeing Anton alone in his room. Anton begged Kundasova 'meet me on very urgent business' there. Tania, packing her bags for exile, asked to see Anton before she left. There is until mid October no record of Lika's whereabouts.

Arriving in Petersburg, on Wednesday 9 October, after two days, presumably full of discussions of which we know nothing, Anton fell into the arms of the Suvorins. He handed over the manuscript of his *Plays*, including *Uncle Vania*, for Suvorin's printers and, as in January, began a round of theatrical visits. To the cast's dismay, Anton missed their first reading of *The Seagull*, just nine days before the first performance. Neither did Savina, who was to play Nina the 'Seagull', turn up to that reading. The first night was just nine days off. Levkeeva, whose benefit night it would be, came to listen, glad that she would not be acting in so glum a piece. For a while Levkeeva had thought she might play Masha. The cast was horrified and she withdrew. On the 9th Anton missed the first rehearsal (he had gone instead with Suvorin to watch Vera Komissarzhevskaia act).[24] 'Never had there been such a shambles in our ant hill,' recalled Maria Chitau, who now played Masha.[25]

Anton, anxious to prepare the audience, not the cast, contacted Potapenko: 'I need to see you. We have *business* [*Chekhov's code for anything embarrassing*] . . . Would you like to come and see me around midnight? We need to talk in confidence.' The business in hand is clear from Chekhov's note to Masha, due to arrive for the first performance:

> I've been to see Potapenko. He's in a new flat, which he pays 1900 roubles a year for. He has a fine photo of Maria [*his second wife*] on his desk. This person never leaves his side; she is happy, brazenly so. He has aged, he doesn't sing or drink and is boring. He will be at *The Seagull* with his whole family and he may happen to have a box next to our box, and then Lika will have a very bad time . . . The play will not be a sensation, it will be dismal. Generally my mood is bad. I'll send you the money for the journey today or

tomorrow, but I advise you not to come. If you decide to come
alone without Lika, then telegraph *Coming*...

Anton felt as diffident about the play as about Lika, but Lika came
under her own steam, a day before Masha. Anton succeeded in keeping
the Potapenkos away until the second performance, to lower the tension in the Chekhovs' and Suvorins' box, where Lika would have to
endure sitting with Suvorin.

Anton was ill, and confessed to Suvorin that he had coughed blood
again. Nevertheless, he went to examine Grigorovich, for whom he
still felt reverence and gratitude. Grigorovich, the last survivor of the
first 'realists', was mortally ill. Suvorin recorded: 'He is a dying man,
no doubt. Chekhov talked to him about his illness and, to judge by
the medicines he is taking, thinks he has cancer and that he will soon
die ... Actually, I have the same trouble in my mouth.'

As in 1889 after Kolia's death, Anton's sexual desire surged after
contact with the grave. Intriguing fragments from Potapenko to Anton
survive. The first runs: 'Thanks, but alas! I can't [*come?*]! Furious
dictation from home.' The second includes the line: 'I surrender a
certain actress to you in her entirety.' Potapenko was formally trans-
ferring to Anton Liudmila Ozerova; Anton showed interest not only
in Liudmila Ozerova, but in the actress Daria Musina-Pushkina, with
whom he had been close five years before: she responded eagerly. He
attended the second rehearsal of *The Seagull*, distressed after seeing
Grigorovich, uneasy after a dream that he was being forcibly married
to a woman he disliked, a dream natural enough after all the attempts
friends in Petersburg had made over the years to marry him off.

Just six days before the first night, the forty-two-year-old Savina
refused to act the eighteen-year-old 'Seagull'; the next day the role
was given to Vera Komissarzhevskaia, at thirty-two a more plausible
jeune naïve. Actresses argued over whether Savina could now play
Masha. Savina withdrew in a huff. Anton was unhappy with Karpov's
staging, which was using sets meant for bourgeois farces and quite
unsuited to Chekhov's scenes in a dilapidated country estate.

Bad omens did not spoil the rehearsal Anton attended with Potapenko on 14 October in the theatre. Anton began to trust the cast,
and was impressed by Komissarzhevskaia. (Suvorin had thought her
dreadful as Klärchen in *Sodom's End* and neither he nor Chekhov had

at first shared Karpov's infatuation with her genius.) Komissarzhev-skaia hit on a solution to the play's most intractable monologue, Treplev's symbolist play-within-a-play which Karpov feared would make the audience laugh. Her fine voice hypnotized the listener, as she worked from her lowest alto to a climax and then lowered to inaudibility as 'all lives, completing their sad cycle, perish'. She decided (and Anton was won over by her musicality) to render Treplev's piece not as parody, but as poetry.

The next night, the dress rehearsal was dismal. Wrapped in a white sheet, Komissarzhevskaia looked absurd, and, clearly, Karpov had a bad eye for sets and costumes. Maria Chitau as Masha was lost in a dress meant for the ample Savina. Sazonova was indignant at the way her husband Nikolai was made up for Trigorin:

> Rehearsal without an author, sets and one actor missing ... Nikolai protected Komissarzhevskaia from Karpov who is so inexperienced that he is making her do her main final scene from the rear wings, blocking her with a table ... when I told Karpov that the play was under-rehearsed, he left ... Chekhov was invited [*to dinner*] but didn't come.

The next day, 17 October 1896, Lika arrived, but did not join Anton, Suvorin and Potapenko at the full dress rehearsal. The cast were tired by ten days' work. Chekhov sensed that the play was doomed and told Suvorin he wanted to take it off. The morning of the performance Chekhov took Masha to Lika's room in the Angleterre. Forty years later, Masha recalled her reception:

> Sullen and stern, Anton met me at the Moscow station. Walking down the platform, coughing, he said: 'The actors don't know their parts. They understand nothing. Their acting is horrible. Only Komissarzhevskaia is good. The play will flop. You shouldn't have come.'

Chekhov feared that Potapenko might not stay away and that his wife might attack Lika. He watched the dismal last rehearsal, had his hair cut, and steeled himself.

The first night caused a scandal in the auditorium, the worst that anyone could then recall in a Russian theatre. The play had been put on in the wrong city, in the wrong month, at the wrong theatre, with the wrong cast, and above all before the wrong audience. Many had come to applaud Levkeeva, who was performing two hours later in a warhorse of a farce. Others came to vent their dislike of Chekhov and modern drama. Very few at all had any idea at all of what they were going to see. The actors, perturbed, tried to adapt to the audience's mood, but Komissarzhevskaia, the most sensitive of actresses, lost her spirit: her 'Seagull' was earthbound. After Act 1, shuddering, in tears, she ran to Karpov: 'I'm afraid to go on stage . . . I can't act . . . I'll run from the theatre.' Karpov forced her back, but the play was lost. All Anton's friends and all the performers in *The Seagull* that night were shocked in their own ways; all agreed that Petersburg's vindictiveness had killed the play. Suvorin's and Chekhov's diaries have the same understatement: 'The play was not a success.'

Suvorin concluded that: 'The audience was inattentive, they didn't listen, they chatted, they were bored . . .' Masha recalled:

> From the very first minute I sensed the public's indifference and ironic attitude to what was happening on stage. When, later in the act, the curtain rose on the inner stage and Komissarzhevskaia, who was acting very hesitantly that night, appeared wrapped in a sheet and began her monologue: 'People, lions, eagles, grouse', you could hear open laughter, loud conversations, sometimes hissing, in the audience. I felt cold inside . . . Finally a real scandal broke out. At the end of Act 1 thin applause was drowned by hissing, whistles, offensive remarks about the author and the performers . . . I sat it out in my box to the end.

Maria Chitau found Anton sitting in Levkeeva's dressing room. She wrote:

> [*Levkeeva*] was looking at him with her bulging eyes, half apologetically, half pityingly, her hands were still. Chekhov sat, his head a little bowed, a lock of hair falling over his brow, his pince-nez sitting crooked on the bridge of his nose . . . They said nothing. I stood with them in silence. A few seconds passed. Suddenly Chekhov leapt up and rushed out.

Even Sazonova, who had found the play depressing and Anton rude, was appalled:

> The audience was somehow spiteful, they were saying 'The devil knows what this is, boredom, decadence, you wouldn't watch if it were free . . .' Someone in the stalls declared, 'C'est du Maeterlinck!' At dramatic points people laughed out loud, the rest of the time

they coughed in a way that was quite indecent ... That this piece flopped on a stage where any rubbish is a success speaks for the author. He is too talented and original to strive with mediocrities. Chekhov kept disappearing behind the wings, to Levkeeva's dressing room, and disappeared after the end. Suvorin looked for him but couldn't find him; he was trying to calm down Chekhov's sister who was in the box ... Levkeeva's celebrations were as usual, with speeches, gifts, kisses, the audience clapped furiously a mediocre actress after booing our greatest writer after Tolstoy.

Like Suvorin, Leikin was dismayed. He recalled 'Reviewers walked the corridors and the buffet with *Schadenfreude* and exclaimed "The fall of a talent", "He's written himself out." '[26] As Suvorin, lost for words, left his box, Zinaida Gippius's husband, the novelist Dimitri Merezhkovsky, told him that *The Seagull* was not clever, because it lacked clarity. Suvorin retorted rudely, and from that moment Zinaida Gippius took charge of the anti-Chekhovian camp.

Karpov retreated to his office. Chekhov entered, his lips blue, his face frozen in a grimace, and said in a barely audible voice, 'The author has flopped.' Anton then vanished into the freezing streets of Petersburg.[27]

FIFTY-SIX

The Death of Christina
October–November 1896

WHILE THE reviewers scribbled to meet their deadlines, the author wandered the streets. Anton's disappearance caused a commotion. Seven weeks later, he gave vent to his disgust in his diary:

> True, I ran out of the theatre, but not until the play was over. I sat out two or three acts in Levkeeva's dressing room . . . Fat actresses, in the dressing room, talked to officials in respectful buoyant tones, flattering them . . . serfs visited by their masters.

While Levkeeva reclined on her laurels, Chekhov walked to the Peripheral Canal; back in the centre of Petersburg, he found Romanov's restaurant still open and ordered supper. Perturbed, Aleksandr called on the Suvorins in search of his brother. Then Anton walked back to Suvorin's house, spoke to nobody, went to bed and pulled the blanket over his head. Masha waited for two hours in silence with Lika at the Angleterre; then Aleksandr rang. Neither he, Potapenko nor Suvorin had seen Anton since Act 2. At 1.00 a.m. Masha took a cab to the Suvorins:

> It was dark and only miles away, after a whole enfilade of rooms did a light shine through the open doors. I went towards the light. There I saw Anna, Suvorin's wife, sitting alone with her hair down. The whole setting, darkness, an empty flat, depressed my mood still further. 'Anna, where can my brother be?' I asked her. Apparently trying to distract and calm me, she started chatting about trivia, about actors and writers. After a while Suvorin appeared and started to tell me about the changes and reworkings he thought were necessary to make the play a success in the future. But I was in no mood to listen to this and just asked him to find my brother. Then Suvorin went off and quickly came back in a cheerful mood. 'Well, you can calm down. Your brother is back, he's lying under a blanket, but he won't see anybody and refused to talk to me.'

Through the blanket Suvorin and Anton exchanged words. Suvorin reached for the light switch. 'I beg you, don't turn the light on,' Anton shouted. 'I don't want to see anyone. I'll tell you just one thing: you can call me [*a very coarse word, says Anna*] if I ever write anything for the stage again.' 'Where have you been?' – 'Walking the streets, sitting. I couldn't just say to hell with that production. If I live another 700 years, I won't let the theatre have another play.'[28] Anton said he would take the first train out of Petersburg: 'Please don't try and stop me.' Suvorin told Anton that the play did have faults: 'Chekhov is very proud, and when I let him know my impressions, he listened with impatience. He couldn't take this failure without deep upset. I very much regret that I didn't go to the rehearsals.'

Confident of the play's triumph, Suvorin had written his review in advance; now he had to compose new copy. Then he left a letter by Chekhov's bed.

While Anton slept, Lidia Avilova tossed and turned. Unlike Lika, she had had no inkling that her life would be publicly enacted. She watched the Seagull hand Trigorin the same silver medal on a chain that she had inscribed and given to Anton, but the page and the line numbers no longer referred to Chekhov's lines 'If you need my life, come and take it.' At home, she picked up the Chekhov volume from which she had encrypted her message. The new message made no sense. Only in the early hours of the morning did she decide he might have encoded one of her own books of stories. She found the page and line: they now, she claims, gave the message 'Young ladies should not go to balls.'[29] Rebuffed, she went back to bed.

Modest Tchaikovsky had been in the audience: 'It is many years since the stage last gave me such pleasure and the audience gave me such unhappiness as on Levkeeva's benefit night,' he wrote to Suvorin.[30] Elena Shavrova, the youngest of Chekhov's admirers, had also been there; profoundly shaken both by the play and by its reception, she consoled her *cher maître*:

All I know is that it was amazement, ecstasy, intense interest and at times sweet and awesome suffering (the monologue of the World Soul) and pity and compassion for them, the characters in the play – the pity you feel only for real, live people. *The Seagull* is so good, so touching.[31]

398

Shavrova would soon give her *cher maître* a physical token of her compassion.

In mid morning Chekhov got up, not waking Suvorin or his wife, rang Potapenko, wrote a note for Masha, a letter to Suvorin and one to Misha in Iaroslavl and then left the house. Masha's note ran:

> I'm leaving for Melikhovo . . . I shall be there by two p.m. [*tomorrow*]. What happened yesterday has not stricken me or embittered me very much, because the rehearsals prepared me for it – and I don't feel all that bad. When you come to Melikhovo, bring Lika with you.

The letter to Suvorin ended: 'Hold up the printing of the plays. I shan't ever forget last night, but I slept well and am leaving in a very tolerable mood. Write to me.' To Misha, Anton made fewer pretences:

> The play has flopped and failed sensationally. There was a heavy tension of misunderstanding and disgrace in the theatre. The acting was abominable, stupid. The moral is: don't write plays. Nevertheless I'm still alive, healthy and in perfect eupepsia. Your Daddy Chekhov.

Before leaving the Suvorins, and without asking, Anton took from the library the last three issues of *The European Herald*, in which a long essay by Sokolov, 'At Home', presented a shattering picture of the miseries of the Russian peasant. 'At Home' was to be one of the progenitors of Chekhov's harsh post-*Seagull* prose.

Accompanied by Potapenko and Vasili, Suvorin's manservant, who was, like Emilie the governess, as much Anton's follower as his master's, Chekhov went to the station. He would not wait for the overnight sleeper. He showed his rail pass and took the first train to Moscow, the slow noon goods and passenger train. After wandering at night in an icy city, he sat for a day and a night in an ill-heated train. The effect on his lungs would soon be apparent. As the train trundled the 440 miles to Moscow, Chekhov took out Aleksandr's note. It was to be the only time that Aleksandr praised Anton's serious plays: the gesture brought them closer:

> I got to know your *Seagull* tonight in the theatre for the first time; it is a wonderful, excellent play, full of deep psychology, thoughtful and heart-rending. I shake your hand firmly and with delight.

On the back of Aleksandr's note Anton drafted a placatory letter to Anna Suvorina:

> Dear Anna, I left without saying goodbye. Are you angry? The fact is that after the performance my friends were very upset; someone was looking for me in Potapenko's flat after 1 a.m., they searched the Moscow station for me ... It's touching, but unendurable. In fact I'd decided that I'd leave the next day regardless whether it was a success or a failure. The sound of glory overwhelms me: I left the next day even after *Ivanov*. So I felt an irresistible urge to run, and it would have been impossible to get downstairs and say goodbye to you without giving in to your charm and hospitality and staying on. I kiss your hand firmly, in the hope of forgiveness. Remember your motto! I've had my hair cut and now look like Apollo. Imagine, I think I'm in love.

Though the motto on Anna Suvorina's writing paper was 'Comprendre – pardonner', Anton was cautious when he wrote to her, and when he copied out his draft letter, he excised the phrases about being in love. This love was not Lika, but Liudmila Ozerova.

On the train Anton's mind was soon embroiled in the misery of peasants. The journals he had taken from Suvorin led him to write to the author for an offprint. He arrived in Moscow before dawn on 19 October 1896 and got into the last third-class non-smoking carriage of the first train to Melikhovo. At 8 a.m. he stepped out of the train, leaving behind his dressing gown and bed linen. (The station master retrieved them for him the same day.) Melikhovo provided opportunities to forget. On Sunday drunken peasants caroused in the Chekhov kitchen: Aniuta Naryshkina, betrothed by her father against her will in exchange for the vodka the Melikhovo men were drinking, was being married. Sick peasants had gathered in the three weeks that Anton was away. A three-day council meeting in Serpukhov, to thank Chekhov for his school building and to promise him a new road from Lopasnia, took up the end of October. Anton planned a reference library for Taganrog. 'Peasants', the first work for four years purged of personal material, began to obsess him: he tried (for his command of French was inadequate) to have Vignier d'Octon's *Le Paysan dans la littérature française* published in Russian.

Meanwhile Suvorin was taking steps to salvage *The Seagull*. He and Karpov made cuts and changes so that the play would be less provocative. The next night a full house applauded wildly, although of the actors only Komissarzhevskaia was inspired. The intelligentsia, rather than high society, were watching, and *The Seagull* revived, although the older actors still felt half-hearted. In Suvorin's revision it was performed again on the 24th, 28th and on 5 November, to full houses. Then it was dropped from the repertoire.

Anton ignored reviews, but friends kept him informed. Sympathy was hard to endure, especially Suvorin's frank insistence that Anton had to take responsibility and that he lacked stage experience. Leikin (still smarting because Chekhov had not called on him on this visit to Petersburg) blew hot and cold about *The Seagull* in a sketch in *Fragments*, in a letter to Chekhov and in his diary, which runs:

> If Chekhov gave this play to any run-of-the-mill dramatist the latter would pump it full of effective banalities and clichés and make it a pleasing play . . . If the play really is a flop, that's no reason to knock Chekhov off his writer's pedestal. Look at Zola's plays.

Zina Kholmskaia's consort, Kugel, reviewer for *The Petersburg Newspaper* (but two years later the most perceptive Chekhovian critic in the city), was not unbiased. He mocked Chekhov with questions: 'Why is the writer Trigorin living with an ageing actress? Why do they play lotto and drink beer on stage? How can a young girl take snuff and drink vodka?'[32] Kugel (whom Chekhov compared as a writer to 'a pretty woman with bad breath') shrewdly compared Chekhov's use of recurrent images and phrases, *Leitmotive*, to Wagner's; unfortunately, Kugel loathed Wagner and misunderstood Chekhov. Kugel was undermined on his own paper. Avilova forgave Anton for flaunting her medallion and, as the editor's sister-in-law, was allowed to defend *The Seagull* and its author in the same paper: 'They say *The Seagull* is "no play". Then look at a "no play" on the stage. There are plenty of plays.'

Praise for the play grew louder. The second performance attracted Chekhov's admirers. Potapenko sent an exultant telegram and Komissarzhevskaia herself, not easily swayed by applause, wrote ecstatically to Anton:

> I'm just back from the theatre. Anton, darling, we've won! Sheer wholehearted success, as it should have been and had to be. How I

want to see you right now, I want even more for you to be here, hearing the unanimous shout of 'Author!' Your *Seagull*, no, ours, for my soul has fused with her, lives, suffers and believes so ardently that it will make many others believe.[33]

Lavrov and Goltsev begged Anton to let *Russian Thought* publish the play. Chekhov was regaining faith in himself as a dramatist when Leikin, as snide as he was supportive, wrote that he had remonstrated with Kugel and his editor: 'You have a few true friends in Petersburg.' The difference between 'few' and 'a few' in Russian is just an inaudible gap between two words, *ne mnogo* or *nemnogo*.

Masha and Lika took the overnight express and arrived in Melikhovo only a little later than Anton. Without a hint of resentment at what Anton had done to her, Lika stayed for three days and nursed him through what he called flu. She was rewarded by renewed affection. Then, reassured that Anton was not going to hang himself, Lika left with Masha, carrying her reward, a tan dachshund puppy. Anton took up the cudgels, angrily dismissing Suvorin's taunt that he had fled like a coward. To Leikin he complained that he had a cough and fever – but never mentioned *The Seagull*. Tatiana Tolstaia invited him to Iasnaia Poliana, but Lika's invitation of 25 October excited him more:

> Take the express to Moscow, it has a restaurant car and you can eat all the way ... I've seen Goltsev, he has solemnly announced to me that his illegitimate son, Boris, has been born. He is happy, apparently, that he can still father a baby. Though he puts it on a bit, saying he's too old and so on. So 'certain men' could take a lesson from him ... I cross each day out in the calendar, and there are 310 days left before my bliss!

Chekhov read the warning. Goltsev's child by his secretary (as proud as the father) was the talk of Moscow; Anton even envied Goltsev: 'for at his age I shan't be capable', he told his friend, the dramatist Nemirovich-Danchenko. Lika's mention of Goltsev, as of Levitan five years and Potapenko three years before, was not casual. Nor was the reference to 'certain men'. And could 'bliss' be anything except a date for marriage, or at least commitment? The word provoked Anton to retract, in words as cruel as any of his panic responses to Lika's emotional demands:

Darling Lika, You write that the hour of our bliss will come in 310 days. Very glad, but couldn't this bliss be put off for another two or three years? I'm so afraid! I enclose a sketch for a medal which I mean to offer you. If you like it, write and tell me and I'll order it from Khlebnikov [*the jeweller*].

The design for the medal is inscribed: CATALOGUE OF PLAYS BY MEMBERS OF THE SOCIETY OF RUSSIAN DRAMATIC WRITERS 1890 edition, Page 73, line 1. Lika decoded a title: *Ignati the Idiot, or Unexpected Madness*. Ignati Potapenko, the father of her child, was the last name Lika wanted to recall. All hope of bliss crushed, she went to Granny and Christina and answered Anton:

> How bliss frightened you! I so much suspect you think that Sofia [*Kuvshinnikova*] will prove right and I shan't have the patience to wait three years for you, which is why you offer three years. I am stuck for reasons beyond my control in Tver province and have no hope of being in Moscow before the middle of next week. Although it's real winter here, the Hundred Dachshunds haven't frozen and send their greetings.
>
> I like the medal, but I think with your usual meanness you will never give it to me. I like it in all respects, even its edifying content, and above all, I am moved by your fondness and love of 'your friends'. That really is touching ... You don't seem to know that I am collecting your letters to sell and keep me in my old age! And Sapper [*Goltsev's nickname*] is really a very good man! He is better than you and treats people better than you do! ... You can stay with me without fear. I shan't allow myself any liberties, just because I'm afraid of proof that there will never be bliss ... Goodbye. Your [Ariadna *crossed out*] twice rejected, etc. L. Mizinova ... Yes, everyone here says that *The Seagull* is borrowed from my life as well [*as Ariadna*], and, what's more, that you did a good job on someone else [*Potapenko*] too!

Anton was only a little abashed. He told Goltsev on 7 November that he would see him and Lika in Moscow. Elena Shavrova had also moved to Moscow. On the day he wrote to Lika, Anton, grateful 'for the healing balsam on authorial wounds', sent an affectionate letter to Elena: she had sent him a card with a picture of a masked girl. Elena wanted to stage *The Seagull* in Moscow and perform in farces in Serpukhov. Which was aim and which pretext – staging the play, or seducing the author – was hard even for Anton to decide. Anton's distraction affected all Melikhovo; the servants slacked, and the family bickered. 'Nobody fed the cattle this morning,' grumbled Pavel.

Fate had reserved its cruellest twist. The plot of *The Seagull* had reflected Lika's misfortunes: it now foreshadowed them. Lika had left Anton to be seduced and abandoned, pregnant, by Potapenko, just as Nina leaves Treplev to be seduced and abandoned, pregnant, by Trigorin. Chekhov darkened his play by adding one event: Nina's baby dies. 9 November was Christina's second birthday. Granny Ioganson's diary ends the story of an unlucky love-child:

> 9 November, Saturday: Little Christina is very poorly. Wheezing, chest full of phlegm.
>
> 10 November, Sunday: The doctor came, thank God, examined her, and there is hope he can help.
>
> 12 November, Tuesday: Lika took the evening train to Moscow . . . Little Christina still wheezing.
>
> 13 November, Wednesday: Lika has come back from Moscow, Christina is dangerously ill. She has croup. We telegraphed Lika's mother to come. Our doctor came, no hope of recovery. The Lord's Holy will be done.
>
> 14 November, Thursday: Our darling Christina passed away at 4 a.m. Poor Lika, what an angelic little girl she has lost, may the Lord console her and turn her mind to all that is good, to lead a sensible life.

FIFTY-SEVEN

Cold Comfort
November – December 1896

NEWS OF Christina's death took days to reach Melikhovo. Anton had put Lika out of his mind, as he wrote a report on all fifty-nine schools of the district. Petersburg gave him no peace: the 8 November issue of *The Theatregoer* graphically recalled the audience's unruliness at the first performance of *The Seagull*, and though the reviewer sympathized, his list of abuse – 'an inflated entity, the creation of servile friends' – was hurtful. Suvorin, like Anton, was sick of the theatre: 'Iavorskaia tells all sorts of foul stories about me. And I have to die in this bog! ... The theatre is tobacco, alcohol. It's just as hard to wean yourself off it.'

Aleksandr had again surmounted his own particular addiction, and had written *Alcoholism and Possible Ways of Fighting It*, a pamphlet which argued for a colony for alcoholics on a Baltic island, but he had quarrelled with the Dauphin; his children were failing in school and the eldest, Kolia, was torturing the dog. From Petersburg Potapenko sent grim news of Anton's latest devotee: 'Dear Antonio, ... I gave your regards to Komissarzhevskaia. She is in deep sorrow. Enemies, anonymous letters, undermining – in a nutshell, the usual story of any talent that turns up in the actors' milieu.'

While Misha was brewing beer for the Chekhov family on Saturday 16 November, Christina was being buried. Sofia Ioganson recorded: 'They're cleaning the whole house, afraid, as the heartless doctor puts it, of infecting other children ... Lika is with the two nannies. I'm sorry, very sorry for Lika.' The news made Anton put off his journey to Moscow by a day or two. Then he left Melikhovo before dawn and took a room in the Great Moscow.[34] Evgenia was staying in Moscow with Vania's family. Anton sent her a note:

405

Dear Mama, I've arrived today, Sunday at 11. I need to see you, but as I am up to my neck in business and am leaving tomorrow, I shan't get round to visiting you. Please come and see me on Monday morning at nine or ten. You can have coffee with me. I shall get up early.

Lika stayed with Anton all day and he prescribed her a sedative. At 7.00 p.m., when Lika had left, Elena Shavrova arrived with a manuscript, leaving a chaperone in her carriage. She and Anton discussed life in Italy. After a Biblical seven years, the inevitable happened in the hotel room. The *cher maître* became the *intrigant* (as she put it). When Elena came to her senses and asked the time, Anton's watch had stopped. Shavrova regained her carriage and frozen chaperone: it was midnight. All that year broken timepieces – a motif for *Three Sisters* – had put the Chekhovs' lives in disarray. Now an erotic whirlwind swept Anton off his feet. Shavrova's next letter to Chekhov was decorated with a hand-painted devil in a red coat. She wrote that she wanted fame even more than love, and she would be back with a watch that worked.

Evgenia never got her coffee. At dawn Chekhov sent a porter with a note, 'Dear Mama! Have to go home. Halva!! Buy and bring. Off to the station.' Early the same morning Misha had left Melikhovo to take Masha to the station; he brought back Anton, off the first train from Moscow. Like a returning prodigal son and grateful father rolled into one, Anton had the white calf slaughtered; Melikhovo's rhythm resumed. Chekhov wrote the briefest note to Lika: 'Dear Lika, I'm sending you the prescription you were talking about. I'm cold and sad and so there's nothing more to write about. I'll come on Saturday or on Monday with Masha.'

Lika came to Melikhovo instead, a week later with the painter Maria Drozdova and Masha. It is hard to say what distressed Lika more – to have lost Christina or to be superseded by others in Anton's affections. She spent four desolate days in Anton's study, silently playing patience on his desk, while he wrote letters in pencil on his lap. Drozdova painted Pavel's portrait; Evgenia's new crockery arrived from Muir and Mirrielees; old Mariushka moved out to live in the cattleyard, and a new cook took her place. Books were ordered, sorted, and sent to Taganrog library. On Monday, without Lika, Chekhov went to Moscow to settle his accounts: he had missed the small print in Marx's contract and only now discovered that he could not reprint 'My Life' as a book for a year. He took the watch that had compromised Elena to Bouret, the watchmaker, who gently told Anton he had forgotten to wind it up.

When Anton got back, bearing felt slippers he had bought for Pavel, a disconsolate Lika was still in his study. Chekhov read a letter from Vladimir Nemirovich-Danchenko, who lamented, as did other friends, that they never talked properly

> because ... you crush me with your giftedness, or whether because we all, even you, are unbalanced or lack conviction as writers ... But I fear that so much diabolical pride – or, to be exact secretiveness – has accumulated in you, that you will just smile. (I know your smile.)[35]

On 26 November Anton gave Nemirovich-Danchenko, who was soon to be more his interpreter than his friend, the same defence of silence as he had to Lika. He sounded like his own fictional doctors in 'A Dreary Story' or *Uncle Vania*:

> What can we talk about? We have no politics, we have no life on a social, circle or even street level, our town existence is poor, monotonous, oppressive, boring ... Talk about one's personal life? Yes that can sometimes be interesting, and perhaps we might, but we straight away get embarrassed, we are secretive, insincere, held back by an instinct for self-preservation ... I'm afraid of my friend Sergeenko ... in every railway carriage and house loudly discussing why I am intimate with N when Z loves me. I am afraid of our moralizing, afraid of our ladies.

After Anton had posted this letter one of the stoves began to smell of smoke and the whole family developed headaches. Then tongues of flame spurted out between the stove and the wall.[36] As Pavel recorded: 'Tonight we caught fire, the wooden beams above the chimney in Mama's room. The Prince and the Priest took part in extinguishing it and put it out with a fire-hose in ½ an hour.' Even Anton was moved to open his diary: 'After the fire the Prince told us that once when he had a fire in the early hours he lifted a barrel of water weighing four hundredweight.' The Herculean Prince Shakhovskoi was a welcome guest; fortunately Melikhovo was surrounded by ponds and Anton, who had seen every year one house or another nearby burn to the ground, had prudently bought a fire engine – a stirrup-pump with a bell and a long hose mounted on a cart. Moreover, he and Masha had insured everything from the house to the cows.

Prince Shakhovskoi demolishing the stove and smashing the walls with an axe to get at the flames, stoked by the draught from a badly made chimney, was a sight that Chekhov recreated in 'Peasants'. Peasants doused flames in the attic and the corridor; November's mud and slush flooded the floors that Aniuta had scrubbed; the stench of soot was unendurable. Anton's water closet was out of action. Evgenia, her bedroom wrecked, took to another bed and did not get up for a fortnight. Pavel forgot the pose he had adopted for Drozdova's portrait and roared at all whom he held to blame. The bereaved Lika, brought up, however negligently, in a genteel household, could not bear the shambles into which the fire had thrown the Chekhovs and left the next afternoon.

Constables and the insurance agent came. Masha saw the insurers in Moscow and sought builders and a stove-maker. The temperature was dropping to minus20°C, so the need for a stove-maker was pressing, but the first one they found remembered working under Pavel and refused to come. Weeks passed before Melikhovo was habitable, but the insurers paid, and for a long time Aleksandr teased his brother as 'the arsonist'.

Chekhov wanted to see Suvorin again, but fire or Lika, or both, had stopped him inviting Suvorin to Melikhovo. Instead, he wrote:

> In the last 1½–2 years there have been so many different events (a few days ago we even had a fire in the house) that my only way out is to go to war like Vronsky [*in Anna Karenina; war was feared in late 1896*] – only not to fight, but to treat the wounded. The only bright spell in these 1½–2 years has been staying with you in Feodosia.

Small clouds passed between Anton and the Suvorins. Anna Suvorina had forgiven his flight, but had been hurt to find that *The Seagull* was not dedicated to her. Chekhov discovered that, instead of 10 per cent of the takings from five performances of *The Seagull* in the contract that Suvorin had arranged, he was receiving 8 per cent, on the basis that the play had only four acts.[37] In any case, until they received the contract the Society of Dramatists would not pay him, and Anton had left it on Suvorin's desk from which it had vanished. Short though the play's run had been, it had had full houses and the author was owed 1000 roubles. To cap Suvorin's sins, his printers sent proofs of plays and stories haphazardly.

After the fire Lika stayed away. On 1 December Masha warned her brother: 'Viktor Goltsev was at Lika's this morning.' Despite his rival's presence, Anton invited Lika. Chicken pox had stopped classes at the 'Dairy' school so that Masha could bring Lika, but Lika did not come. She threatened not to come for New Year 'so as not to spoil your mood'. If he wrote her a pleasant letter by the 30th she might come. She had endured worse embarrassment, as more people identified her as the prototype of The Seagull: 'Today there was a reading of *The Seagull* . . . and people were raving about it. I even went upstairs . . . so as not to hear it.' Now Lika had for consolation a young landscape painter, Seriogin, whom she proposed to bring with her, as Masha's guest. She knew it would upset Anton: 'You can't bear young people more interesting than yourself.' Anton invited her, affectionately calling her *Cantaloupe*. He mentioned Seriogin only in his diary.

On 20 December Anton went to Moscow to prescribe not for Lika (whom he avoided, despite inviting her to Melikhovo), but for Levitan, whose heart was worn out and whose mind was ravaged by depression that twice brought him to the brink of death. Anton examined Levitan and noted: 'Levitan has widening of the aorta. He wears a patch of clay on his chest. Excellent sketches and a passionate thirst for life.' He pressed Levitan to come to Melikhovo: the artist replied that he couldn't bear trains, and feared upsetting Masha.

The approach of New Year enlivened Melikhovo. The stove-makers and carpenters left; a house painter papered the walls; mice were poisoned. Twenty flagons of beer were delivered. Misha and Olga came; Vania arrived alone. Pavel had the snow swept from the pond, so that the guests could skate. The widowed Sasha Selivanova, Anton's childhood sweetheart, partnered Vania on the pond. Gentry and officials gathered like rooks. Never had Melikhovo seen such a crowd. Those who could not come wrote. Usually they begged: Anton's cousin Evtushevsky wanted a job in Taganrog cemetery; Elena Shavrova wanted a critique of her new story; a neighbour wanted a publisher for his article on roads.

The strain told on Anton. Franz Schechtel had heard that he was ailing. 'You need to get married to a worldly, daredevil girl.'[38] Anton's reply was half serious:

> You obviously have a bride you want to get off your hands as fast as possible; but sorry, I can't marry just now, because, firstly, I have the bacilli in me, very dubious tenants; secondly, I haven't a penny, and thirdly; I still think I'm too young.

When Shcheglov gave the same advice, Chekhov specified as a wife a 'blue-eyed actress singing Tara-ra-boom-de-ay'.

As Lika drew back, Elena Shavrova came forward: 'I've been taking bromide and reading Charles Baudelaire ... When will you be in Moscow? I'd like to see you. – You see, I'm being frank.' On New Year's Eve, she wished him 'love, lots of love: boundless, calm and tender.' Out of the blue, Emilie Bijon, governess to the Suvorins, whom Chekhov had known for ten years, was also emboldened:

> Vous trouvez peut-être étrange de recevoir de mes nouvelles, je n'en disconviens pas, maintes fois je désirais vous écrire mais au fond je sentais trop bien que je suis un rien et même misérable en comparaison de vous par conséquent je n'osais risquer cette demande mais cette fois-ci j'ai pris le courage dans mes deux mains et me voici écrivant quelques mots à mon cher et bon ami et docteur.[39]

Emilie was one of the most self-effacing of the women who pined for Anton.

New Year approached. A sheep lambed. The Chekhov family dressed up as mummers and called on the Semenkoviches. Chekhov dressed his sister-in-law Olga as a beggar, and gave her a note:

> Your Excellency! Being persecuted in life by numerous enemies I have suffered for truth and lost my job and also my wife is ill with ventriloquy, and my children have rashes, therefore I humbly ask you to grant me of your bounty *quelque chose* for a decent person.

Lika came with Seriogin and saw the New Year in. In the kitchen the servant girls, dropping wax onto cold saucers, looked into the future. Vania, in no hurry to get back to his family, took Sasha Selivanova to the Talezh school and put on a magic-lantern show. Whenever his guests let him, Chekhov would creep into his study to 'Peasants' and write, or cross out, a few lines.

FIFTY-EIGHT

A Little Queen in Exile
January–February 1897

PRETTY, SMALL, regal though forlorn, someone else had, like Emilie Bijon, brooded for months before sending Chekhov her New Year wishes for 1897:

> To my dear doctor, A. C.
> I have known ephemeral happiness
> And am plunged by you into an ocean of suffering.
> I am too weak to struggle – I am dying.
> The light of life is barely glimmering in my eyes . . .
> Liudmila Ozerova.[40]

Once Anton's guests had gone the family succumbed to chills, migraine and fever; the district nurse, Zinaida Chesnokova, was on constant call for codeine. Nursing his parents, writing 'Peasants,' planning his rest in the Great Moscow Hotel, Anton took another burden: the 1897 census. He agreed to supervise fifteen census-takers for the district and make returns for his village.[41] It was a task as onerous as his survey of Sakhalin; the gain for 'Peasants' was not worth the drain on his strength. The house was besieged by officials and the piano buried in papers.

Kolomnin, Suvorin's son-in-law, sent them a new table clock to replace the clock that rain had stopped, but the post gave it such a hard ride that it arrived in fragments. Anton made another journey on 14 January to Bouret, who shook his head: the clock was beyond repair. It was a bad time for timepieces: that evening Anton invited Elena Shavrova to room No. 9 in the Great Moscow: he was there just that night, he told her, and could not leave the hotel. 'Despite Mrs Grundy, I shall come and see you,' she replied. Nevertheless, they went for a ride in a cab. In a journey around Moscow as eventful as Madame Bovary's with Léon around Rouen, Elena Shavrova lost the hood of her coat, broke a brooch, and her watch, which, she promised, kept good time, went haywire. After Elena returned to stay with her mother that night, she had, she told Anton, nightmares 'of poisoned men and women, and I blame you for that.'[42]

Anton stayed another night at the hotel. He called on Viktor Goltsev, who held a party every 15 January, although Masha had warned him that he would find Lika there. He actually seemed to be relieved by Lika's liaison with Goltsev. He and Goltsev calmly discussed their plans jointly to edit a newspaper.

After Anton went home, he devoted his energy until mid February to the census, the school for Novosiolki, and to 'Peasants', which he was now finishing. He even joined the Moscow doctors' campaign against corporal punishment. Lika faded from his life, and Elena Shavrova's affection was deflected into useful work. The performances that she was to put on in late February in Serpukhov were to be in aid of the new school. Anton treated Shavrova as he had Lika: he teased her too about other suitors, real or imaginary, as a pretext for his neglect. It needed only a few weeks of intimacy for Anton to feel an irresistible urge to tease, deflect and even repulse a woman.

Winter at Melikhovo was dominated by food: the family gorged, the animals starved – there was abundant livestock and little fodder. Pavel's diary records: 'We ate a goose . . . We ate a roast piglet . . . Half the hay in the barn is gone, God grant it lasts to spring. There's no more wheat straw. We've burnt all the brushwood, we haven't bought wood yet.' A dog was mauled to death by Zalivai, a new hound; Roman shot a cat. This grim tally, like the tedium of the census, was magnified into the horror of 'Peasants'.

Chekhov's thirty-seventh name-day was dismal. None of his brothers came: only the priest and the cantor. The census cast a pall. Chekhov was disturbed by angry demands from a person in Rostov: someone calling himself Anton Chekhov had been borrowing money. Halfway through his expected life span, he began to think religiously. His diary affirms agnosticism as a valid faith:

> Between 'God exists' and 'There is no God' lies a whole enormous field which a true sage has great difficulty in crossing. But a Russian knows only one of these two extremes and the middle between them doesn't interest him, which is why he knows either nothing or very little . . . A good man's indifference is as good as any religion.

On 6 February, the census over, after attending a peasant wedding and helping Quinine give birth to a single puppy, Chekhov fled to Moscow for a very wild fortnight, some of it with Liudmila Ozerova, who had written again on 31 January: 'Dear, very, very good Anton, You've probably forgotten her and she understands that she has no rights, but she begs, begs you not to fail to visit her as soon as you come to Moscow, The very littlest Seagull.' Their first night was not happy. Liudmila wrote on 9 February: 'Perhaps it wasn't my fault, but you recalled some other woman whom you love and that's why you found me so repellent and despicable ... Your little Queen in exile. P.S. Don't fail to come *tomorrow*.' When Anton left Moscow to watch Shavrova performing in Serpukhov, Liudmila took the train with him as far as the outskirts of Moscow. Anton's enchantment with her had faded as soon as she fell into his arms. He wrote to Suvorin two days later:

> Guess who visits me? What would you think? Ozerova, the famous Ozerova-Hannele. She comes, sits with her feet on the sofa and looks sideways; then, when she goes home, she puts on her little jacket and her worn out galoshes with the awkwardness of a little girl ashamed of being poor. She's a little queen in exile.

In his diary, Chekhov now called her 'an actress who fancies she is great, an uneducated and slightly vulgar woman'. Her feelings were very different:

> Dear Anton, I'm back! Moscow is empty and bottomless. And I don't doubt that you despise me deeply. But, amidst the gloom that surrounds me, your kind, simple, tender words have penetrated very very deep into my soul, and for the past eighteen months I couldn't help dreaming how I'd see you and surrender to you all my sick, hurt soul and you would understand everything, sort it out, console and calm it, and instead I met Kolomnin [*Suvorin's son-in-law*] ... The first night, after you left, I got a very bad chill, and I spent the last day of Shrove Tide so ill that I didn't peck at my corn, and I can't wait for my little white birdy to fly to me, I am burning with desire to caress it as soon as possible.

Elena Shavrova saw more of Anton than did Ozerova. The author of 'Caesar's Wife' had her writings and acting as a pretext. She asked her *cher maître* or 'a certain *intrigant*' to meet her. Anton coyly answered: 'A certain young man (a civilian) will be at the Assembly of the Gentry at the Georgian evening.' Olga Kundasova also surfaced. No longer subsidized by Anton and Suvorin, she was rushing around Moscow, giving lessons, engaging distinguished minds in debate. Her relations with Anton relaxed: she agreed to come to Melikhovo. Rumours of Anton's frenetic love life spread. Masha, who had taken Maria Drozdova to Melikhovo, joked, 'Give my regards to all the ladies who are visiting you.' Aleksandr wrote on 24 February: 'I hear you spent a long time in Moscow and led a life of fornication, the buzz of which has even reached Petersburg.'

Chertkov, the grandson of the man who had owned Chekhov's grandfather, was just then being expelled from Russia for his activities on behalf of Tolstoy. (He went to England and began to preach non-resistance to evil there.) Tolstoy went to Petersburg for the first time in twenty years to see Chertkov off. The furore over Chekhov's deportation jolted Chekhov's liberalism to the left. On 19 February, a dinner at the Continental for Moscow's literati to celebrate the supposed emancipation of the peasantry thirty-five years before sickened Anton:

> To dine, drink champagne, roar, make speeches about the people's self-awareness, about the people's conscience and so on, when slaves, the same serfs, in frock coats scurry round the tables, and outside in the freezing cold the coachmen wait – that's like lying to the Holy Ghost.

There were other dinners, just as alcoholic. At a gathering at *Russian Thought*, with the architect Schechtel on 16 February 1897, Anton and Stanislavsky met for the first time though eighteen months would pass before anything came of it. More upsetting were the consultations Levitan asked for:

> I've nearly kicked the bucket again. I'm thinking of arranging a council of physicians at my place, with Ostroumov in charge . . . Shouldn't you drop in on Levitan and just as an ordinary decent person offer some advice on how to arrange it all? Do you hear, you viper? Your Schmul.

After Goltsev's Shrovetide pancake party (which Lika shunned), Anton visited Levitan's studio with an acquaintance and covertly studied the artist. In Levitan's wrecked body he saw his own future. Anton dis-

cussed Levitan's tuberculosis with his old teacher, Professor Ostroumov, who was one day to deliver Anton's sentence. Death, Ostroumov
predicted, was imminent. Levitan, Anton noted, was 'sick and afraid'.

After some unhappy nights, Chekhov left with Ozerova to watch
Shavrova and her company act in Serpukhov. The dresses came from
Paris, the diamonds were real, and the actors were good, but they
made only 101 roubles for the new school. After the show Anton
reached Melikhovo at 2.00 a.m. on 23 February 1897 and slept all
day. In his absence the family had celebrated Shrovetide with pancakes,
coped with shortages of fuel, and dealt with veterinary emergencies,
while Maria Drozdova painted a portrait of Pavel. On Anton's return
Masha and Drozdova gladly fled to Moscow. Masha was too dutiful
to protest at his long absence; Maria Drozdova too much in love
with Anton, though he teased Maria as Udodova (*Hoopoe*), instead of
Drozdova (*Thrush*). Pavel's dislike of Maria Drozdova, who ate more
pancakes than he did, was tempered by her painting him. In Anton's
absence Pavel had asserted himself as usual. He had the servants chop
the ice on the pond and one poor woman load it into the cellar. The
horses fared badly: Pavel's diary for 13 February shows his ruthlessness: 'minus22°C in the morning . . . The horses were worn out, deep
snow, God forbid we take such a cart load of wood again. Why doesn't
the Society for the Protection of Animals do something about it?'

Anton rested. On 1 March he announced to Suvorin that he would
hereafter 'lead a sober chaste life'. Aleksandr and Vania had been taken
aback by Anton's philandering: Vania, seeing the array of potential
sisters-in-law, begged him not to marry. Elena Shavrova planned one
more performance in Serpukhov, to see her *intrigant* again, as she
packed her bags to be a virtuous wife in Petersburg. Liudmila Ozerova,
however, was in Moscow; her passion all the stronger, for Anton
giving reasons, such as the lack of a dowry, not to marry her. On 26
February she wrote:

All my things, to wit: my pink jacket, my slippers, my handkerchief
and so on and also Neglinny Passage, Tverskaia Street, the Moscow
City Duma etc. send their regards, are impatient for your arrival
and miss you very very much. I'll tell you in secret that they are
very jealous not just of you and Petersburg, Serpukhov and Lopasnia
but of the air, and I was indescribably saddened because you love
and want money, but perhaps you need it for some good cause.

Liudmila Ozerova had only seen *The Seagull*. The next day she read the play and was bowled over: she had found her role, and foolishly addressed Anton by Arkadina's extravagant phrase – 'My only one':

> Anton, my only one, to fall at your feet, meekly to caress and kiss your hands, to look endlessly into your eyes. To reincarnate in myself all your great soul!!! Words, looks, thoughts cannot convey the impression that <u>our</u> *Seagull* made on me.

Almost by the same post a more interesting actress approached Anton. Chekhov had sent Vera Komissarzhevskaia his *Plays*. The actress still had Avilova's silver medallion which Anton gave her as a prop. (It interested its owner no more than the stuffed seagull in the play interested Trigorin.) Komissarzhevskaia felt she personified the Seagull and wrote to Anton as if he were Trigorin: 'You will visit me, won't you? Potapenko tells me that you're expected by 1 March. Are you? I doubt if I'll go away for Lent, although I've completely collapsed. Come, Anton, I terribly want to see you.'[43]

Chekhov found this invitation to Petersburg irresistible, and the forthcoming Congress of Theatre Workers in Moscow for the first three weeks of March was a pretext to leave Melikhovo. He wanted to deliver 'Peasants' to Goltsev and Lavrov in Moscow, even if no censor could pass the text as it was.

In 'Peasants' he had beaten the 'realists' at their own genre, drawing on his deep knowledge and understanding of the villages around Melikhovo and the peasants who worked in Moscow hotels as waiters. His plot was minimal: the narrator is a camera. A sick waiter, Nikolai, loses his job and goes back to his village with his wife Olga and their daughter Sasha. Shocked by the squalor of his relatives, he dies, while Olga and Sasha are forced to wander off and beg. (Chekhov intended to take the story further with the girl's entry into prostitution in the city but the censor made it clear that this would be too sensitive and sordid a theme.) Chekhov contrasts a beautiful valley with imagery of smashed crockery, beaten children, in a series of tableaux that cover autumn, a savage winter, and spring – six months which bring tax arrears, the rape of an errant wife, the beating of another wife by her drunken husband, fire, and the death of Nikolai. 'Peasants' shows the gentry as hateful creatures from an alien world. The good that is left is a strange residue of ideals, as the peasants listen to Olga reading the Bible, words unintelligible, but consolatory to them. From 'My Life' Chekhov takes the spectacle of the drunken thieving peasants who are more human than their masters, for they recognize the truth and justice that they have lost. This uncompromising picture was to anger Tolstoy and other self-appointed spokesmen of the peasantry. The school of protest writing welcomed Chekhov to its camp.

FIFTY-NINE

Cutting the Gordian Knot
March 1897

LIUDMILA OZEROVA, Elena Shavrova, Vera Komissarzhevskaia and Lidia Avilova all called for Anton. So did Levitan. He wanted Anton to examine him, and to be painted for the Moscow's leading gallery-owner, Tretiakov, by the Petersburg artist Braz. Anton alerted Elena Shavrova, about to leave for Petersburg:

> Dear Colleague. The *intrigant* will arrive in Moscow 4 March at noon on train No. 14 – in all probability. If you haven't left yet, telegraph me just one word: 'home' . . . But if you also agree to have lunch with me at the Slav Bazaar (at 1 p.m.) then instead of 'home' write 'agree'. The telegraph operator may think that I've offered you my hand and heart, but what do we care what they think!! I shall come for one day, in a rush.

Elena received the letter on 4 March – too late to respond. She searched the Great Moscow and Slav Bazaar, and left notes at *Russian Thought*, but he was 'as elusive as a meteor.' One note 'in deep despair' begged him to see her in Petersburg. But that evening Anton took his stethoscope to Levitan. He calmed the patient, but wrote to Schechtel: 'Things are bad. His heart doesn't beat, it gasps. Instead of a tick-tock you hear "fff-tock". In medicine we call that a systolic murmur.'

In the morning he was back in Melikhovo. Pavel had brought in the priest, to shrive the family and the servants in preparation for Easter. Dung was being tipped onto the greenhouse beds. Anton was short of money because the censor had held up 'Peasants' and Suvorin still had not found the contract for *The Seagull*. Aleksandr broached Suvorin on Anton's behalf and wrote up his adventures as a farce, celebrating a salmon that Natalia had just cooked. It began:

The Missing Contract or the Salmon Tail
A Play in 5 Acts
by Mr Goose

Cast: *Suvorin's Porter; Suvorin's footman, Vasili; A. S. Suvorin; Mr Goose; Mrs Goose*

Act 1. *The spreader of enlightenment and builder of schools.*

Goose (*entering Mr Suvorin's hall, reading a letter*). 'Put on your trousers and go and see Suvorin: ask where the contract and stamps are and why he persists in not answering my letters. I need the money desperately, since I'm building another school...' (*aside*) Bare-arsed educators! No money but building schools like water. Burdening me with things to do. Won't bother even to send me a pound of country butter or a piglet for the New Year ... Governors, indeed, dog turds.[44]

Aleksandr came to stay for a few days with his two elder sons. (It was to be his last visit to Melikhovo.) They stayed in the cottage. Aleksandr was hoping for help: Kolia, expelled from grammar school, seemed doomed by the genes he had inherited, according to Aleksandr, from his mother's 'decaying landowner's family'. All evening the priest and Aleksandr drank beer. (Aleksandr had lapsed again.) In the cold morning sun, Aleksandr was sobered by a talk with Anton:

> My brother was hunched, warming himself in the sun looking mournfully at his surroundings. 'I don't feel like sowing or planting, or like looking into the future,' he broke the silence. – 'Stop, that's nonsense. You're just depressed,' I reassured him, aware I was being banal. – 'Now,' he said firmly, turning his face towards me. 'After my death I leave such-and-such to our sister and mother, and such-and-such for education.'

On 9 March 1897 Aleksandr and his sons left. Kundasova came for two days. Nursing Brom, who had been mauled by a hound, and Quinine, whose puppy had died, Anton was withdrawn. The coming of spring, the ice breaking on the river and the prospect of a hæmorrhage, Levitan's terminal illness, the commission for his portrait, all turned his thoughts to death. At tea his father sickened him: 'going on about the uneducated being better than the educated. I came in and he shut up.' Anton replied to neither Ozerova nor Shavrova. At last, the theatre contract for *The Seagull* had been replaced, and he had 582 roubles, enough to visit Suvorin and the actors in Moscow, and Komis-sarzhevskaia and Avilova in Petersburg.

On 19 March, as the first starlings flew into Lopasnia, Anton was spitting blood. The next day Suvorin came to Moscow and settled in the Slav Bazaar. On 22 March Anton took his room in the Great Moscow, and in the evening he went to dine with Suvorin at the Ermitage. Before they had begun to eat, Anton clutched his napkin to his mouth and pointed at the ice bucket. Blood was gushing up uncontrollably from a lung.

VIII

Flowering Cemeteries

Oh this South! Oh this Nice!
Oh, how their radiance disturbs me!
Life, like a wounded bird,
Tries to arise – and cannot . . .

Fiodor Tiutcher

SIXTY

The Doctor is Sick
March–April 1897

STILL CLUTCHING ice to his blood-stained shirt, Anton Chekhov was taken by cab to Suvorin's suite, No. 40, at the Slav Bazaar. He fell on to a bed, telling Suvorin 'Blood's coming from my right lung; it did with my brother and my mother's sister.' They summoned Dr Obolonsky, but he could not persuade Anton to go to hospital. Anton scrawled a note to Bychkov, his devoted footman at the Great Moscow, to send the proofs of 'Peasants' on his windowsill to the Slav Bazaar. The hæmorrhage did not abate until morning. Anton was calm, though afraid, but his friends panicked. Lidia Avilova, invited to call, could not find him. Bychkov had been ordered to tell only Vania where Anton was.

All day Chekhov and Suvorin stayed indoors. Anton asked Vania to call, as he was 'unwell'. Shcheglov came to see Suvorin. Thrilled to find his two idols together, he left without noticing Anton's perilous state.[1] Anton too seemed to ignore it. Early next morning he told Suvorin that he had letters to answer and people to see back in the Great Moscow. Suvorin remonstrated, but Anton spent Monday there: he sent a touchy teenager a critique of her novel about fairies; he apologized to Avilova. He wrote, talked, and spat blood into the wash basin.

At daybreak on Tuesday 25 March Doctor Obolonsky was handed a note: 'Bleeding, Great Moscow No. 5, Chekhov'. Obolonsky took Anton straight to Professor Ostroumov's clinic by the Novodevichie cemetery, then went to the Slav Bazaar and woke up Suvorin. At 1.00 p.m. Suvorin saw Anton:

Chekhov is in Ward No. 16, 10 above his 'Ward No. 6', as Obolonsky remarked. The patient is laughing and joking as usual, clearing his throat of blood in a big tumbler. But when I said I watched the ice moving on the Moscow river, his face changed and he said, 'Has the river thawed?'

Suvorin telegraphed Vania, revisited Anton and took the night train to Petersburg, where he tried to allay fears. Sazonova wrote in her diary: 'I'm told it's just hæmorrhoidal blood, but they still put him in a clinic.'[2] Aleksandr was alarmed by Suvorin's vagueness.

Professor Ostroumov, who had taught Chekhov, was at Sukhum on the Black Sea. His juniors mapped Chekhov's lungs, showing the top of both, particularly the left, badly damaged by tuberculosis. Wheezing exhalations came from both lungs. Ostroumov was no believer in the curative power of Robert Koch's 'tuberculin'. Treatment was conservative: ice packs, peace and nutrition, until the threat of a fatal hæmorrhage had receded; convalescence with subcutaneous arsenic, exile to a dry climate and a diet of koumiss.[3] Anton was carefully watched – doctors are unruly patients. Visitors were admitted by pass, in twos, and forbidden to ask questions.

Anton wanted his parents kept in the dark. When Masha arrived at the Kursk station on Tuesday morning to start teaching, Vania silently handed her a pass to the Ostroumov clinic. Only next day was she calm enough to visit. Lidia Avilova came twice, once bearing flowers.[4] Dr Korobov, who had known Anton for sixteen years, was turned away. Anton was fed cold broth. He asked Masha for tea and some eau de Cologne; Viktor Goltsev for caviar, four ounces of black, eight of red; Shavrova for a roast turkey. She sent a grouse, which Anton washed down with fine red wine from Franz Schechtel and Dr Radzwicki, Anton's optician. Sablin of *The Russian Gazette* sent a roast chicken and, when this gave Anton erotic dreams, a woodcock. Flowers and letters also poured in, as did unsolicited manuscripts and solicited books. Anton wrote passes for the visitors he wanted. Goltsev and Liudmila Ozerova called. Elena Shavrova, confined in Petersburg with a chill, wired her sister Olia on 29 March for news:

> I found him up properly dressed as always, in a big white, very bright room with a white bed, a big white table, a little cupboard and some chairs. He seems to have lost a little weight and his bones are show-ing, but he was awfully nice, as always, and bantered cheerfully with me ... What do you think I found him doing? He was choosing lenses for a pince-nez.[5]

A more important visitor had come the previous day. On Wednesday 26 March Lidia Avilova left the clinic in distress and walked round the Novodevichie cemetery, where she met Tolstoy. Tolstoy needed no pass: on Friday he appeared at Chekhov's bedside. Weeks later Anton recalled the visit to Mikhail Menshikov:

> We talked about immortality. Tolstoy recognizes it in a Kantian sense; he supposes that we shall all (people and animals) live in a principle (reason, love), whose essence and aims are a mystery to us. But I see this principle or force as something like a shapeless mass of aspic; my ego – my individuality and mind – will merge with this mass. I don't want this immortality.

At four the next morning Anton suffered a severe hæmorrhage. The doctors forbade all pleasure except letter-writing. Anton, wanting to be discharged home, declared Melikhovo healthy, on a watershed and free of fevers, but the doctors exiled him south, to the Mediterranean or the Black Sea, from September to May.

On 3 April the bleeding stopped. Visitors came again, except from 1.00 to 3.00 p.m. when, as Chekhov put it, 'the sick animals are fed and exercised'. A week later he was discharged. His health was a matter of public bulletins. On 7 April, appeasing the censor by hastily replacing page 193, which blamed the state for the peasants' misery, *Russian Thought* published 'Peasants'. Never was Chekhov so fêted by the intelligentsia. A wave of sympathy forced even Burenin to acclaim him. Late in April Sazonova observed: 'It sounds like a funeral knell. He must be very bad and they're holding a requiem. Really, they say that his days are numbered.' The literary world commiserated.

Lika neither wrote nor visited. Elena Shavrova showered her *cher maître* and *intrigant* with letters. She offered him the health of 'the stupid, indifferent and dim'; she promised to kiss Professor Ostroumov all over; she told him of a French play, *L'évasion*, about a married woman's happy adultery, a play where it was said 'doctors have no right to be ill'. He could still be her *intrigant*: 'What do we risk? As long as Tolstoy doesn't find out.' All she requested was that Anton should: 'Tear my letters into little pieces (jealous men are dangerous), I don't want someone else to do it';[6] he never did. On 11 April, Shavrova shook off her husband and came, but Anton had been discharged the night before. Olga Kundasova was running round Moscow for Anton, returning to their owners all the books he had borrowed.

Vania ran messages, while Aleksandr worried. Misha and Olga went to Melikhovo on 6 April to make ready for Anton's return. Anton had left Masha penniless and the cupboards bare; Vania was to bring beer, best beef and to see that Anton brought money. Misha wrote to Vania: 'Desperate famine here, brother . . . we have thin gruel instead of soup. Be a pal and bring parsley (roots), carrots and celery. If you have the money, some onions too. We have to feed Anton up now.'[7] Masha's sinking spirits were restored by Maria Drozdova. Pavel and Evgenia seemed not to know what was happening. They sheared the sheep, and mucked out the cattle. Only Misha's arrival on the 6th alerted them that something had happened to Anton.

On Good Friday, emaciated and weak, Anton was brought by Vania and laid on Masha's divan. Here he injected arsenic into his abdomen, read and wrote letters. The comfort was cold. Dr Sredin, who treated himself and others for TB in Yalta, urged Anton to go to Davos. The radical novelist Aleksandr Ertel revealed that 16 years ago he had been given a month to live, but wondered if Anton's will to live matched his own.[8] Menshikov said that he had wept as he read 'Peasants' and that Petersburg was awash with rumours of Chekhov's illness; he wrote again, advocating a diet of oats and milk and a stay in Algiers, which had done wonders for Alphonse Daudet (who was to die in eight months).[9]

Emilie Bijon sent two touching messages in French.[10] Cousin Georgi in Taganrog urged Chekhov: 'the south is warmer and the ladies are passionate'.[11] Warm comfort came with Lika Mizinova on 12 April, the eve of Easter. She left on the 18th (Vania's birthday), with Sasha Selivanova, who had arrived three days before. Pavel was glad: 'At 9.45, glory to the All Highest, the two fat ladies left.'[12]

On Sunday 13 April forty male and twenty-three female peasants lined up for Easter gifts of money from the Chekhovs. Pavel's diary sounds vigilant:

14 April: . . . Antosha liked the roast beef. Ants got into the house . . .
23 April: . . . The cherries are in leaf. Antosha is busy in the garden.

Importunate visitors – 'the loud-mouth Semenkovich', Shcheglov and the vet – annoyed Pavel. Two students turned up, to be fed and housed. On 19 April, seeing his brothers off, Anton risked a three-mile journey to survey the second school he was building. Dr Korobov, who had come to photograph Anton, not to heal him, then took Anton to Moscow for two days. (The other doctor to visit in April was Dr Radzwicki with a case of Bessarabian wine and lenses to correct Anton's astigmatism.)

Anton was glad to see his visitors go. Shcheglov had pestered him with a play, which, Anton told Suvorin, read as if it had been written by a cat whose tail the author had trodden on. Suvorin was the only man Anton longed to see. He telegraphed that he would be in Petersburg by the end of May. Anton joked 'I'll marry a handsome rich widow. I take 400,000, two steamboats and an iron foundry.' Suvorin replied by wire, 'We consider dowry too small. Ask for bathhouse and two shops more.'[13]

Illness freed Anton's conscience, and he felt free to travel. No woman would, he told Suvorin, 'be stupid enough to marry a man who'd been in a clinic'. From Courmayeur, a tuberculosis resort, Levitan exhorted Anton on 5 May:

> Is this really a lung disease?! Do everything possible, go and drink koumiss, summer is fine in Russia, then let's go south for the winter, even as far as Nervi, together we shan't be bored. Do you need money?

and then from Bad Nauheim, where he was having hydrotherapy, on 29 May:

> No more blood? Don't copulate so often. How good to teach yourself to do without women. Just dreaming of them is far more satisfying ... If Lika is with you, kiss her sugar-sweet lips, but not a whit more.[14]

Given the public acclaim for 'Peasants' – which augured well for the sale of Chekhov's books – and the excuse of illness, Anton could at last live out an idea he had preached periodically, but never practised: that the prerequisite of personal happiness was idleness.

SIXTY-ONE

An Idle Summer
May–August 1897

PHOTOGRAPHS THAT Dr Korobov took of Anton at the end of April 1897 show a man whose body and morale are wrecked. Anton's main symptom, apart from a morning cough, was an evil temper. A three year period of creativity, that had begun with Lika's departure in March 1894, was over. Between April and November 1897 he published nothing and wrote only letters. He pruned roses and supervised tree planting. He gave up medicine and council business and only kept an eye on the school at Novosiolki. While Masha saw to it that plans were drawn, materials bought and workers hired, Anton pondered his future. He could not stand milk diets, and ruled out the barren steppes of Samara where consumptives spent months drinking koumiss. Taganrog's winters and springs were as severe as Moscow's. Yalta and the Crimea had frozen and bored him in 1894. The Caucasian spas were vulgar – Kislovodsk in the north, Borjomi in the south – even if the dry mountain air had Alpine qualities. The idea of Switzerland repelled him. Anton's options were the French seaside, Biarritz on the Atlantic or Nice on the Mediterranean, both refuges for Russians, so he would not be lonely. He considered North Africa, whose climate had rallied so many, but could he afford to travel for eight months, after an idle summer?

Elena Shavrova proposed summer and autumn in Kislovodsk. Kundasova, to judge by her conspiratorial visits, was also willing to travel to the Caucasus. Lika was ready to return to Paris and accompany Anton; so was Masha's friend, the artist Aleksandra Khotiaintseva, who had discreetly fallen in love with Anton. Anton was, however, shedding women friends. A symptom he had hidden at the clinic, he told Suvorin on 1 April, was impotence. Elena Shavrova was put off. On 28 May Chekhov arranged to meet her in Moscow: the letter arrived too late. Anton had arrived with Lika. Elena sent telegrams and spent an evening at the station in Moscow to catch him on his way back. 'Fate is unjust, the post incorrigible, and you elusive,' she lamented, before leaving for the Caucasus and Crimea where she hoped to meet him.

Anton asked Liudmila Ozerova to play her favourite part, little Hannele in Hauptmann's *Hannele's Ascension*, at the annual play staged on 4 June by Dr Iakovenko in his asylum. (The church had *Hannele's Ascension* banned from Imperial theatres; it was now preformed only in private theatres.) Ozerova demanded her own music and props. Anton gave the part instead to Olia, Elena Shavrova's younger sister. The 'little Queen in exile' had lost her lover and her part. On 3 May she hinted that she would take an engagement in Warsaw if Anton did not protect her career. On 14 May she was so shattered by what must have been Anton's rejection of her as a woman and as an actress that she wrote: 'Anton, I don't know how I stayed alive after reading your letter. Now the last thread that held me in this world has been torn. Farewell.'[15]

One old flame, Daria Musina-Pushkina, the 'cicada' whom Chekhov had squired five years ago, came to Melikhovo on 3 May. The next day she visited the monastery with the family. Her husband had been killed hunting, and she was now a rich Mrs Glebova. 'A very nice interesting woman, she sang about thirty romances to me and then left,' Chekhov told Suvorin.

On 25 May Anton stopped injecting arsenic. He masked the smell of medicine with *Vera Violetta*. Any exertion, however, laid him low. After taking examinations at Talezh school on 17 May, he was shattered. He tried quiet pursuits. He studied French. He fished with Ivanenko, catching fifty-seven carp in one session. June was peaceful: Masha, Misha and his wife Olga, and Vania, without his wife, left on a three-week trip to the Crimea. Anton moved out of Masha's room into the guest cottage, away from visitors and the rows between Pavel and the servants. 'Antosha has moved to the hermitage. To acquire sanctity by fasting and labour, as a hermit,' Pavel joked. After two weeks Anton left, via Moscow, to stay with Levitan on the estate of a rich Mæcenas, Savva Morozov. Morozov bored him, and Anton ran back to Melikhovo, with Lika, three days later. Lika told Masha in the Crimea:

21 May 1897: This is the second time in June that I have defiled your virgin bed with my sinful body. How nice to sleep on your bed knowing that it is forbidden fruit to be tasted only by stealth. I didn't go to the Crimea only because I am stuck, penniless; Anton is all right ... His mood is fine, he makes relatively little fuss at dinner ... Have you started an affair with somebody?[16]

Since the birth of Christina, and despite all her travails, Lika had put on weight, and in her new role her tone towards Anton softened. Now that she had become more Anton's nurse than his mistress, Lika would even condone his affair with Elena Shavrova, though she could bring herself only to call her 'the lady writer'. She tacitly acknowledged Dr Astrov's dictum that a woman can be a man's friend only after being first an acquaintance and then a mistress. Lika felt bitter, however, that Masha now preferred her painter friends, Drozdova and Khotiaintseva, to her. She stayed with Anton at Melikhovo for seven periods of three to eight days from May to August. They also met when Anton ventured to Moscow. She became once again chief aspirant:

13 June 1897 ... I know that if my letter is to interest you it has to breathe civic grief or lament on the unwashed Russian peasant. What can I do if I'm not as intellectual as Mme Glebova? By the way, here is an indispensable novelty for you: there is a new face paint which neither water nor kisses can wash off! Pass it on to the appropriate person.

17 June. Do I have to keep looking for you? If you want I can come and see you this evening, at Levitan's [in Moscow].

24 June. Divine Anton, you stop me sleeping. I couldn't get away from you all night. Keep calm, you were cold and proper as ever.[17]

Lika realized that Anton really would go into exile when summer ended. She had no money, and retreated to her family's estate. On 5 July she offered a meeting; a week later, from Moscow, she invited herself to Melikhovo: 'You see how I love you, why don't you stay?' When Anton finally risked a journey to see Suvorin in Petersburg at the end of July, Lika saw him off. The finality of the coming separation sank in. On 1 August Lika sent the longest letter she had written to him:

You frightened me by telling me at the station that you would leave soon. Is it true or not? I must see you before your departure. I must sate my eyes and ears on you for a whole year. What will become of me if you've gone before I get back? ... It is as though the last few years of my life had not existed and the old *Reinheit* [*purity*] you so prize in women, or rather in girls!, had come back ... I'm *hors concours*. If I had two or three thousands, I'd go abroad with you and I'm sure I wouldn't get in your way at all ... Really I deserve a little more consideration from you than that joking-ironic attitude I get. If you knew how little I feel like joking sometimes. Well, goodbye. Tear this letter up and don't show it to Masha.

The letter was filed by Masha. Anton's tone, however, turned tactful and tender.

The Suvorins had gone on holiday to Franzensbad. From there they urged Anton to move abroad. Anna Suvorina opened Anton's letter to her husband. 'But I didn't find out what I most wanted to know, when you're coming to see us.'[18] She wrote again, on paper with a picture of a man eyeing a streetwalker. 'I seem to have a premonition that you will come! and so you and I shall go wild once a month. Don't fear the doctors, they lie.' She proposed a journey to Lake Como with her children: Boria would teach him to bicycle, and Nastia would flirt. Suvorin was heading back to Petersburg: the only fun he had in Franzensbad was talking to Potapenko's daughter. He wished Potapenko's articles were as interesting as the chatter of his seven-year-old child 'who hates people and loves animals'. Anna begged Anton to lure Suvorin out of the city. On 12 July 1897 Sazonova's diary notes: 'Suvorin is stuck in town, waiting for Burenin and Chekhov. Burenin is to take his place in the newspaper, and Chekhov he wants to go abroad with.'

Anton had business in Petersburg. The monopoly on 'My Life' expired in summer 1897; Suvorin could profitably reprint the story with 'Peasants' as one volume. The book, being over ten printer's sheets, was exempt from precensorship: cuts imposed on *Russian Thought* could be restored. 'Peasants' had received a burst of applause, and a backlash of condemnation. The right wing liked the idea that the worst enemy of the Russian peasant was the Russian peasant himself; the Marxists agreed that capitalism had degraded the peasantry further. An evangelical anarchist like Tolstoy, however, thought this work 'a sin before the people', a view shared by adherents of the underground revolutionary movement 'People's Will', for whom the peasantry was the standard-bearer of revolt.

In Petersburg Chekhov was to have sat for a portrait by Iosif Braz. Braz now arrived, with luggage and two nieces, to paint Chekhov at Melikhovo. Braz used Masha's room, with its north-facing windows, and piled her furniture in Anton's study.

Braz's arrival signalled to others that they too could descend on Anton. Kundasova and Lika visited. When Masha came back, Misha and his wife settled for July. Volodia, the Taganrog cousin, also came. On 29 June, on his way to Kiev, Aleksandr dumped Kolia and Toska at Melikhovo, with no linen and no time limit. They ran wild. Pavel had them sent back to their stepmother in Petersburg on the 17th. Semenkovich dropped in from Vaskino to rant and chat, bringing with him holidaymakers and their French governess for Volodia's delectation. Local schoolteachers, doctors, postmaster and priest called on business or recreation: they all depended on Chekhov and Melikhovo for a living or for entertainment. Anton, when Braz was not asking him to pose, hid, reading Maeterlinck's *The Blind*. He wryly commented that he would not be surprised if some relative asked to board a menagerie at Melikhovo.

Braz worked slowly, exasperating himself and his sitter, and after seventeen days the portrait was still unfinished. Few liked Braz's harrowing picture, but Masha fell in love with the painter. When, on 22 July, Braz and his nieces left, Anton and Lika accompanied them as far as Moscow. After an unhappy farewell to Lika in Moscow, Anton went to Petersburg for two nights with Suvorin. They discussed Anton's accounts, which showed that Anton could afford eight months abroad. Before falling asleep. Suvorin wrote in his diary:

> On Saturday, 26 July 1897 I am leaving for Paris. I could not induce Chekhov to come. His excuse is that he will have to leave in autumn to spend the winter abroad; he wants to go to Corfu, Malta, but if he went now, he would have to return. He said he would translate Maupassant. He likes Maupassant a lot. He has learnt French fairly well.[19]

Petersburg, Anton found, 'expected a consumptive, emaciated man barely breathing.' (Doctors were aghast that he had gone there even for two days.) Anton avoided Aleksandr and Potapenko.[20] Leikin wired an invitation to his country estate on the river Tosna and met the first steamboat on Sunday 27 July. He was amazed: 'Chekhov looks cheerful and his complexion is not bad. He has even put on weight.' Anton chose a pair of white Vogul laika puppies from Leikin's kennels, but stayed a mere three hours, sampling milk (which he detested) from Leikin's three cows. The laikas were to be fetched by Suvorin's valet, Vasili Iulov, and delivered by train to Vania in Moscow. In his hurry to get away – Anton claimed an appointment with a professor of medicine in Moscow – he lost the pince-nez with the expensive lenses which Dr Radzwicki had prescribed. In Moscow he spent all day looking round premises for Suvorin's new bookshop, and then had a satisfying night: 'after sinning I always have rising spirits and inspiration,' he told Suvorin. Anton hid from his public, but reporters claimed to have spotted him everywhere from Bad Nauheim to Odessa or Kislovodsk.

August was hot enough to ignite the forests around Melikhovo. It was 45°, the leaves went yellow; there was no grazing. Anton was too exhausted to save forests. He told Tikhonov in Petersburg, 'I am completely out of sorts. I just want to lie down.' As he rested, Khotiaintseva painted him. The new puppies, Nansen and Laika, arrived on 3 August, driving Brom the dachshund to fury. The last relatives left. Volodia was prised from Madeleine the governess and given the fare back to Taganrog. At the Feast of the Dormition, Pavel recorded: 'No guests staying, just the Semenkoviches, the French woman, the priest and the teacher from Talezh . . . doctor Sventsitsky from Moscow and Zinaida Chesnokova staying the night.' The latter two were treating Mariushka, who was sent to a Moscow clinic. Exhausted by the estate, everyone felt ill: Masha took bromide, Pavel drops. Tiresome guests stayed: the flautist Ivanenko had fallen for Maria Drozdova. ('Ivanenko talks without stopping . . . Ivanenko has come again,' Pavel's diary complains in June.) As Anton was too sick to maintain domestic harmony, Roman rebelled against Pavel, who recorded on 15 June: 'Began mowing hay 7.30 a.m. 24 peasants. Roman got 3 roubles. He spent them on vodka for the men and women. They didn't finish mowing.' After the death of their baby, Roman had quarrelled with his wife. All the servants seemed in turmoil. Masha the maid was pregnant by Aleksandr Kretov. Anton promised a dowry if the ex-soldier married her, but Kretov was evasive.

Only Anton, had he been well, would have been sufficiently unflustered to run Melikhovo smoothly, and Pavel, Evgenia and Masha would have to face autumn and winter without him. Evgenia's letters do not mention Anton's health or departure, though she fussed about everything else: buying cloth, harvesting potatoes, Mariushka's cataract. On 22 August Pavel wrote to Vania: 'Anton will go soon. His health is much better, he is more cheerful, he has stopped coughing ... It is lonely for us to be on our own, I and your mother, to live in the country. Masha will go to Moscow each week.'[21] Nobody detained Anton. Aleksandr was absorbed in two new-found missions, bicycling and temperance. He and his doctor, the psychiatrist Olderogge, had chosen an island in the Ålands as a colony for alcoholics. Anton had talked to Suvorin, who spoke to the Finance Minister, Sergei Vitte: a 100,000 rouble grant was in the offing. In Iaroslavl Misha and Olga, expecting their first child, asked little of Anton beyond a loan. Only Masha was unhappy. With Braz's and Maria Drozdova's encouragement, she had decided to train professionally as an artist, but, despite Levitan's protection, she was rejected by the Moscow College of Art. Iosif Braz had left Melikhovo, and Masha, at thirty-four, faced spinsterhood with all the duties and few of the benefits of a wife.

Lika thought of following Anton to France; the painter Aleksandra Khotiaintseva actually arranged to do so. Friends urged him to depart. Levitan kept up a barrage. Loathing all Germans, Levitan still took Bad Nauheim's baths and gymnastics: 'I occasionally copulate (with the muse, of course),' he wrote. For Levitan the Riviera scenery was 'cloying'. He himself was drawn, despite the fatal damp, to the woodlands north and west of Moscow which inspired his paintings, but advised Anton: 'Everyone agrees that the climate of Algiers does wonders for lung diseases. Go there and don't let anything bother you. Stay until summer and if you like it, longer. Very probably I shall come and join you.' To Masha Levitan confided: 'My dear, glorious girl. I terribly want to see you, but am so bad that I am just afraid of the journey, and in this heat as well. I recovered a bit abroad, but I am still horribly weak ... I must have sung my song.'[22]

Anton had pleaded poverty. Levitan and Kundasova believed him. Levitan spoke to Morozov, Kundasova to Barskov, editor of *Children's Leisure*. They told the tycoons their duty: each to advance Chekhov 2000 roubles. Accepting only Suvorin's money, Anton left Melikhovo at 8.00 a.m. on Sunday 31 August. Olga Kundasova saw him off. Masha followed him to Moscow, where Lika intercepted him with a note: 'I'll fetch you by cab between 9 and 9.30 – not too late for supper, I think. I badly want and need to see you. Where are you going? Abroad?' The next day Anton left Moscow for Biarritz, after a last meeting with Lika, to which neither of them ever later referred.

SIXTY-TWO

Promenades

September–October 1897

Two old Taganrog boys met Anton at the Paris Gare du Nord on 4/16 September 1897: Ivan Pavlovsky, a former revolutionary, now Paris correspondent of *New Times*, and an engineer, Professor Beleliubsky. They took Anton to Suvorin's hotel, the Vendôme. Suvorin was now in Biarritz, but his son Mikhail, Anna Suvorina and Emilie Bijon lingered in Paris. After sixty hours in a carriage, choked by the cigars of his German companions, Anton took the air. He had a hæmorrhage: Anna Suvorina found out and wrote to Aleksandr. After four days, Anton followed Suvorin's tracks to Biarritz, but Suvorin had already left for his theatre in Petersburg. He promised to see Anton in France in October.

In Biarritz, too, Chekhov was met by friends (and wind and rain). Vasili Sobolevsky, editor of *The Russian Gazette*, his partner, Varvara Morozova, their three children and a governess, were on holiday there. Chekhov liked their ménage. They offered him a room, but he stayed in the Hotel Victoria. Biarritz, Russians complained, was crowded with Russians. Anton told Suvorin on 11/23 September:

> The plage is interesting; the crowd is good when they are doing nothing on the sands. I stroll, listen to blind musicians; yesterday I went to Bayonne and saw *La belle Hélène* at the Casino . . . For 14 francs I have a room on the first floor, service and everything . . . Poliakov [*the railway magnate*] and his family are here. Help! There are very many Russians. The women are just about tolerable, but the old and young Russian men have little faces like ferrets and are all shorter than average. The old Russian men are pale, obviously exhausted at night by the cocottes; for anyone with impotence can only end up exhausted. The cocottes here are vile, greedy, all out in the open – and it is hard for a respectable family man who has come here to rest from his labours to restrain himself and not be naughty. Poliakov is pale.

The Atlantic gales limited Anton's stay to a fortnight. He too fell for a Biarritz cocotte: Margot, aged nineteen, promised to follow when he moved.

Anton had advances from Suvorin, from Adolf Marx of *The Corn-field*, from Goltsev of *Russian Thought* and from Sobolevsky, Fiodor Batiushkov, the Russian editor of a new international magazine, *Cosmopolis*, had commissioned a story, but Anton did not feel like writing. The President of France had visited Russia in August 1897: a clause in the new Franco-Russian alliance forbade the French post to accept packages printed in Cyrillic, to protect Russia from seditious literature. Anything that Chekhov wrote or proof-read had to be a letter on thin paper. For months his creative outlet was a notebook in which fragments of dialogue, characterization and plot were mingled with addresses and lists of plants for the garden. On its blank pages Tania Shchepkina Kupernik had written 'Darling Antosha, the Great Moscow Hotel is a haven of bliss' and 'Mio caro, io t'amo'.

Letters to Biarritz encouraged Chekhov to idle and rest. Masha wrote: 'Just remember why you went to warm regions and don't let town life tempt you too much, my girlfriends and yours have asked me to tell you. Levitan is, he says, very ill again, tomorrow I mean to see him.' The Suvorins were returning to Russia. Emilie Bijon had gone to Brumath in Alsace to see her son Jean. She wrote to Anton after receiving his letter in French: 'Votre photographie est sur ma table, tout en vous écrivant il me semble vous parler et que vous m'écoutiez attentivement, et parfois un petit sourire. Un mot de vous fera mon bonheur.'

Lika first wrote on 12 September:

> I have been thinking recently about your affair with the lady writer and here is what I have come up with: a man has been eating and eating delicious refined dishes and he was fed up with everything and longed for a radish ... I as usual am thinking about you, so everything is in the old rut. But there is some news: Tania Shchep-kina-Kupernik has come back to Moscow, looking more beautiful and her face has even more of the *Reinheit* which you prize in women and which Mme Iust has so much of ... Anyway I'm not envious of her, she's very nice and interesting.

Anton offered to go to Paris to meet Lika's train if she came. As for insisting on *Reinheit* in women, he protested that he also valued kindness, her virtue. Anton told her that Margot in Biarritz was providing him with French lessons. Lika was seeking money to 'throw herself on Anton's neck' by mortgaging her share of the family land. Olga Kundasova and Lika now strolled the streets of Moscow together. As Olga counted the men who turned to look at them, she, with her six years' extra experience, helped Lika to reach a conclusion on 5 October:

> I hope Margot stirs you up properly and wakes up the qualities which have been dormant so long. Suppose you came back to Russia not a sour-puss but a live human being, a man! What will happen then! Masha's poor girlfriends! . . . you know nothing about cheese and even when you're hungry you like just to look at it from a safe distance, not to eat it . . . If you keep on like this with Margot, then I am very sorry for her, then tell her that her colleague in misfortune sends her regards! I once stupidly played the part of the cheese which you refused to eat.

Once again, Anton was without his pince-nez in Europe. He asked Masha to send Dr Radzwicki's prescription on his desk; she sent the first Latin writing she saw, a chemist's prescription. Anton strolled the beaches, formally dressed, charming Sobolevsky's little girls, while their father, looking like Petronius, bathed. Myopia made it hard to avoid encounters. On Anton's last three days in Biarritz he bumped into Leikin, whose diary for 20 September/2 October notes: 'I see Chekhov coming up to me . . . he is not bathing here, just enjoying the sea air. I think he is completely recovered. He climbed up the steep cliff from the sea with us and there was no sign of his being out of breath.'

On 22 September/4 October Anton and Sobolevsky left together for Nice via Toulouse. On the Côte d'Azur they settled into a hotel Leikin had recommended, La Pension Russe on the Rue Gounod, then a stinking alley that ran from the station to the Promenade des Anglais. Its attraction, apart from cheapness, was its Russian owner (a Mme Vera Kruglopoleva). The Russian cook was a former serf who had stayed in France thirty years ago when her owners returned to Russia, and now occasionally made the *borshch* or *shchi* her guests pined for. She lent the *pension* mystery: she was married to a negro sailor and had a mulatto daughter, Sonia, who was seen at night as she plied her trade on Nice's streets. Anton had told his family that he would spend only October in Nice, but the autumn weather was too fine to leave. The Russian company was much to his liking: the dead as well as the living. At Caucade, in the west of Nice, lay the cemeteries, the Orthodox graveyard being at the very top of the hill, closest to heaven, with the best view of the sea. Here lay exiled revolutionaries, wounded officers, consumptive aristocrats, doctors and priests who had ministered to expatriate Russians, surrounded by hibiscus, palms and bougainvillaea. For the living, there were two churches, a reading room, and Russian lawyers and doctors.

By October, when Sobolevsky left, Anton had been befriended by two men. One was Professor Maxim Kovalevsky, biologist and revolutionary, who lectured at the Sorbonne, but whose base was the marine biology station at Villefranche. Kovalevsky was the widower of the mathematician and dramatist Sofia Kovalevskaia, who had perished of TB six years earlier. Kovalevsky, a life-enhancing companion, was very afraid of further endangering Anton's health. Anton was also looked after by Nikolai Iurasov, the Russian vice-consul at Menton, who lived in Nice: his son worked at the Crédit Lyonnais. (This eased Anton's transfers of money from Moscow to Nice and back.) Iurasov, a man 'of exemplary kindness and inexhaustible energy', so bald that the seams of his skull were visible, offered teas, suppers, New Year and Easter parties to his countrymen. Iurasov, Kovalevsky and Anton were often joined by a decrepit professor of art, Valerian Iakobi, and by Doctor Aleksei Liubimov, dying of lung cancer.

Warmed by male companionship, Anton got over Margot's desertion. She had followed him but vanished, perhaps to a healthier protector. Margot's replacement, to judge by Anton's letters to Masha, was, apart from her physique, a good teacher of French, adept at correcting the mistakes that Russians make in the language. Thanks to her, he read and spoke French far better. She did not visit La Pension Russe, however, and Anton found climbing her stairs too tiring.

Reading Maupassant had prepared Anton for the Riviera: Maupassant's travel book *Sur l'eau*, written when the writer was cruising the Côte d'Azur on his yacht *Bel-Ami*, had provided quotations for *The Seagull* and an appreciation of this 'flowering cemetery of Europe' where so many hoped to elude death. The flowers and trees left Chekhov unmoved, but he valued the politeness and the cleanliness of the French. He played safe: as autumn approached he forbade himself excursions after sunset, so that a fellow guest, N. Maksheev, tempted him in vain to gamble at the casino: 'Dear Doctor! Being of sound mind, I assert that I possess a method of turning 2000 francs into a large sum of money at roulette. If you still have a desire to take part, then we must come to terms and act . . .'[23] Vasili Nemirov-ich-Danchenko (the elder brother of Vladimir) spent his time in Monte Carlo; Anton merely watched him gamble. Ignati Potapenko was, however, more Mephistophelean: 'Antonio! . . . I'll soon find a reliable system of winning in Monte Carlo and then I'll come and enrich you and myself.'[24]

The inmates of La Pension Russe interested Anton little: they used him as a doctor. One Russian resident in Nice prompted Anton to take his first political stand: Rozanov, a Jew who rented apartments, sold Russian journals and published Le Messager franco-russe, fervently stood up for Alfred Dreyfus, the Jewish officer convicted of treason. Anton knew Rozanov not through buying newspapers, but by treating Rozanov's wife. Rozanov's 'enchanting smile' and 'very delicate and sensitive soul' began to turn Anton into a Dreyfusard. Despite this radical transformation, Anton still hoped to see Suvorin. Suvorin recorded that his doctor advised him to go to Nice: 'Chekhov is also calling me. I want to go but I fear the theatre will be even worse in my absence.' Then Aleksandr told Anton that he had seen Suvorin and his servant Vasili on a tram, off to buy a ticket abroad. On 15 October, with his son Mikhail, Suvorin set off for Paris again.

One hundred roubles a month went a long way. Anton bought all the newspapers,[25] had his shirts laundered and drank all the wine and coffee he wanted. He enjoyed piquet with Kovalevsky and going to concerts, when not confined indoors. The Mæcenas Morozov tactfully offered 2000 roubles; Barskov, the children's magazine editor, at Kundasova's prompting, proffered 500 roubles a month. Anton spurned the money and berated Levitan and Kundasova for embarrassing him. Levitan cursed the touchy Anton as 'a striped hyena, pagan crocodile, spineless wood-demon'. Anton had published nothing for six months: his money came from Suvorin's editions and from stagings of Ivanov in Petersburg, and from The Seagull and Uncle Vania which were being staged only in the provinces.

Only news of Melikhovo distressed Anton. Masha's letters showed that she detested the irksome responsibility. She forgot how to collect the monthly payments from Petersburg that Anton had arranged for her. Anton belittled her worries: 'If it's hard, put up with it – what can you do? I shall be sending you rewards for your labours,' he wrote on 6 October. An estate made no sense if the owner was away eight months of the year. Pavel became unbridled, as he told Misha: 'Mama and I will sit alone like recluses in the house, worried, and then arguing to exhaustion about trifles, and we each stick to our opinion.'[26] In the same letter Evgenia complained: 'The authorities [Pavel] are pretty unkind to me ... Masha is pestered for money, she hasn't got any, she is vexed, I have nothing but woe.'

The servants suffered. Aniuta Naryshkina, married off by her relatives in exchange for vodka, and Masha Tsyplakova, pregnant by Aleksandr Kretov, were in hospital. Infected by the midwives, Aniuta died of puerperal fever. When Masha Tsyplakova gave birth, Pavel made her leave the baby in an orphanage. Anton insisted that the baby be taken into the household, ordered the mother to receive seven roubles a month, and paid for her foundling foster-brother, who had no fingers on one hand, to go to school. Until Tsyplakova was back at work, Pavel, Evgenia and Masha were left with the elderly Mariushka and the indefatigable Aniuta Chufarova. Worse nearly happened: Mariushka and Tsyplakova, overcome by fumes in the bathhouse, had to be revived by Masha. Roman still ran the stables, but his wife Olimpiada, in Pavel's view, infected the estate with genteel idleness. The village elder retired. The peasants and authorities could not find a new elder, to settle disputes and govern the village. One had his finger bitten off by a horse, and was barred by the authorities. Another had, like many Melikhovo peasants, typhoid.

The family tried to refurbish the guest cottage so that Anton could live in it all year: again, stove-makers were called to Melikhovo, but, Evgenia reported, 'The stove in the cottage is still unfinished. The stove-maker fell and smashed himself in the stable.' Masha complained: 'All the Melikhovo inhabitants complain of your absence ... build up your health, if not for yourself, then for others, for very many of these others need you. Forgive me for moralizing, but it's true.' After the stove was finished, the Talezh schoolteacher Mikhailov papered the cottage (as well as the drawing room); Semenkovich, who was an engineer, supervised the insulation of the walls with Swedish board and of the doors with double felt and heavy curtains. Now the temperature was much higher inside the cottage than out, which presented a predicament, as Pavel explained to Misha on 5 December 1897:

> God alone knows how much his health has improved, . . . to come here when it is cold is to endanger himself. The cottage is his favourite summer residence, he likes solitude and quiet, but things are not suited for winter, firstly to leave +18 for minus25 degrees and reach our house, you have to wrap up against the cold, breathe and swallow whatever God sends. Secondly: he has to come in the morning for coffee, at 11 for lunch, at 3 for tea, at 7 for supper and above all to go and sit on the throne.

Constant war raged between the farm dogs, the laikas and the dachshunds: the human inhabitants of Melikhovo were kept awake, robbed of food, even bitten, and the flower beds were ravaged. As Pavel put it, the dogs behaved like mongooses. Anna Petrovna, the old mare the Chekhovs had bought with the estate, died ten weeks after she had her last foal. Pavel was pitiless – 'the highest authority was strict today', Evgenia lamented to Misha.[27] He searched high and low for someone to flay the horse and buy the skin for 3 roubles.

Anton's brothers were content. Misha told Masha that Olga had 'arranged his life so that every desire was anticipated'. In September, for 50 roubles a month, Aleksandr persuaded Vania and Sonia to take his son Kolia. Kolia spent a few days' holiday in Melikhovo and then took to Moscow a note from his father:

> The bearer of this letter is the swine that you, Vania and kind Sofia, are so generously taking under your wing . . . If annoyed or angered he begins to whisper something unintelligible (probably threats) . . . He detests books . . . he likes hammering nails, washing up . . . he loves money and getting sweets . . . He can't tell the time . . . he gets into fights.

Anton did not ask after his dachshunds or his nephews. He had settled into La Pension Russe so well that, on the dank evenings which kept him to his room, he began to write again.

SIXTY-THREE

Dreaming of Algiers
November–December 1897

THE PROSPECT of losing his self-respect and his *Reinheit* by living on Morozov's charity, made Anton write. His works that autumn are small scale: they recall boyhood landscapes: stories like 'The Pecheneg' and 'Home' evoke the horror of a visitor stumbling onto a barbarous estate on the Don steppes. Chekhov's block was broken: that autumn 'On the Cart', a picture of a village schoolteacher's despair, owes much to the complaints relayed from Melikhovo. He began 'A Visit to Friends', a story for *Cosmopolis*: the plot anticipates his final play *The Cherry Orchard*. He asked Masha to send the draft of an early story to work on: Masha worked with scissors to make the papers look like a letter rather than a contraband manuscript.

Chekhov's fame was now international. At the end of September, in the *Wiener Rundschau*, Rudolf Strauss proclaimed:

> ...we have before us a mighty, mysterious miracle of Strindberg content in Maupassant form; we see exalted union which seemed almost impossible, which nobody has managed before: we love Strindberg, we love Maupassant, therefore we must love Chekhov and love him twice as much. His fame will soon fill the whole world.

Masha and Potapenko sent Anton cuttings. Translators (some inept, all enthusiastic) pestered Anton to let them put his works into French, Czech, Swedish, German and English. One, Denis Roche, stood out: he paid Chekhov 111 francs, half the fee he received for the French version of 'Peasants.'[28] Anton was learning a daily quota of French phrases, sending hundreds of French classics for Taganrog library, and even confidently correcting Masha's French. He asked for a journalist's card from Sobolevsky to get the best seats to listen to Patti and Sarah Bernhardt and to attend the Algiers festival. He now frequented Monte Carlo, and won, cautiously betting on low numbers and on red and black. Anton was now able to focus on the roulette wheel: the pioneer of Russian ophthalmology, Dr Leonard-Leopold Girshman, lived in Nice with his tubercular son. Anton treated the son; the father prescribed a new pince-nez for Anton. In November Chekhov weighed himself (with his hat, autumn coat and stick) and found 72 kilos adequate for a man of his height, six foot one.

On 18/30 October La Pension Russe said goodbye to Maxim Kovalevsky, who went to lecture at the Sorbonne. Kovalevsky had promised to take Anton to Algiers, and Anton waited anxiously for his return. Meanwhile he expected Suvorin, but although caviar and smoked sturgeon arrived, Suvorin did not. On 7/19 November Suvorin turned back to Russia, to his wife's surprise, for she thought that Anton would dispel his gloom. Professor Iakobi, although even iller than Anton, was wintering in Russia. Anton confessed to Dr Korobov that he was bleeding again: he took potassium bromate and chloral hydrate every two hours. He told Anna Suvorina on 10/22 November:

> ... the last hæmorrhage which is still going on today, began three weeks ago ... I walk slowly, I go nowhere except the street, I don't live, I vegetate. And this irritates me, I am out of spirits ... Only for the Lord's sake, don't tell anyone about the bleeding, that is between us ... if they find out at home that I am still losing blood, they will shriek.

The women in Anton's circle wanted him back in Russia: Evgenia suggested that he come back for Christmas and then leave again. Anna Suvorina lauded Russia's powdery snow and called his illness 'treachery': she blamed it on exertions with Margot and, earlier, with Lidia Iavorskaia. She told him to come to Petersburg. The Suvorins' daughter Nastia was to star in Viktor Krylov's farce *Let's Divorce* on 20 December. Apart from her acting, her fiancés (once the Suvorins gave up the idea of marrying her to Chekhov, Nastia went through several engagements) were the talk of Petersburg.[29] Emilie Bijon, however, reminded Anton of the reality of a Russian winter: 'je n'ai pas vu le soleil depuis mon retour ...'

In La Pension Russe Anton moved downstairs and saved himself the effort of climbing two flights of stairs. Kovalevsky still promised to accompany Anton to Algiers, but by December he was wavering, telling Sobolevsky:

Chekhov was showing blood even before I left Beaulieu. I hear it still happens to him at times. I think he has no idea of the danger of his state, although to my mind he is a typical consumptive. I am frightened of the idea of taking him to Algiers. Suppose he gets even iller? Advise me.[30]

Anton told Kovalevsky that he 'dreamed of Algiers all day and all night'.

Anton was content in Nice. Russia excelled, he decided, only in matches, sugar, cigarettes, footwear and chemists' shops. Had he been tempted to return early, a letter that Sobolevsky wrote on 12 November would have deterred him:

> Crossing the Russian frontier after a quiet life abroad is the return of a patient who has been discharged from fresh air into his unventilated room smelling of sickness and medicines ... Starting with our governess detained on the border for a passport irregularity and ending with the revolting stench and filth of Moscow in autumn, crowded with cursing drunks, etc., all this put me into a state you could call demoralization.[31]

Anton appeased Melikhovo with a stream of presents which returning Russians delivered – ties, purses, scissors, corkscrews, gloves, perfume, coin-holders, playing cards, needles. Pavel and Masha were placated; in return they sent all the newspapers. Masha ran two local schools, mediating between a radical schoolteacher and conservative priest; she taught in Moscow; she helped ewes lamb, caught runaway dogs, nursed sick servants, paid off importunate monks. She moaned loudest to Misha (who summoned Evgenia to help his pregnant wife Olga): 'Papa is rebellious ... I am not going to let mother go to you soon. There is nobody to do the house work ... I am utterly worn out, my head never stops aching. Come for Christmas yourself.'[32]

Pavel wanted full cupboards for an influx of guests: he stocked up on kvas and begged Misha for ham. Misha sent frozen river fish and fresh grouse from the Volga, so tempting that Pavel induced Evgenia to break their strict fast and eat Arctic herring on a Wednesday. Pavel ordered entertainments from Vania:

> Mama asks you to bring your Magic Lantern with you with pictures, gifts will be given to the Boys and Girls in the Talezh school on the 2nd day of Christmas and it is good to show, for greater solem-

nity, the village schoolchildren pictures they have not yet seen, which will bring them in particular indescribable joy . . . Antosha will pay for everything.[33]

Misha and Olga sent a goose, but did not come. Pavel had promised to teach his grandson Volodia to ride, but Vania came alone. The only guest, to Pavel's disgust, was Maria Drozdova. On Christmas Day the family treated the three local midwives to sausages and vodka. New Year's Eve was little merrier, Pavel wrote: 'Vania and the School-teacher came. We had supper at 10. Mlle Drozdova got the lucky coin. Then we started playing cards.'

In Petersburg, Aleksandr reported, at the Suvorins' New Year party, Anna drank to the absent Anton, while Suvorin moodily lurked in his study, telling Aleksandr he would not go to Nice, as Anton was off with Kovalevsky to Algiers. In January 1898, however, Kovalevsky plucked up courage and told Anton that rheumatism and flu prevented him sailing for Africa. This, Anton replied dejectedly, 'depressed me very much for I have been delirious about Algiers.'

Lika Mizinova had mortgaged her land, but the bank withheld funds and she could not come to France. Instead she would open a milliner's shop; physical work would heal her dejected spirits. Masha was scorn-ful: Lika was too disorganized to compete with professionals. On 13 January Lika told Anton she had her old looks and her former self, 'the self that loved you hopelessly for so many years.'[34] Anton told Lika he approved, and would flirt with the prettier milliners, but privately agreed with Masha: 'Lika will hiss at her milliners, she has a terrible temper. And what's more she is very fond of green and yellow ribbons and enormous hats.'

In France Anton celebrated Russian New Year's Eve on 12 January 1898, watching the roulette wheel with a new companion, Aleksandra Khotiaintseva, who had moved to the *pension* on Russian Christmas Day. Khotiaintseva feigned a polite interest in roulette, but proved good company. They did not stay long at the tables: Anton was moni-tored by a Russian doctor, Dr Valter (another Taganrogian staying at the *pension*) and had to be in his room by 4.00 p.m. Khotiaintseva and Anton liked shocking the guests: Aleksandra would stay in his room until the signal for her departure, a donkey that brayed at ten. She painted cutting watercolour caricatures of the women guests. She and Anton called them Fish, the Doll, Red Ribbons, the Clothes Moth and the Slum. She observed Anton with loving sharpness, telling Masha, whose close friend she had become:

> Here it is thought indecent to enter a man's room, and I spend all my time in Anton's. He has a wonderful room, a corner room, two big windows (here the windows always reach the floor), with white curtains.
>
> 11/23 January 1898 ... we have to listen to the stupid talk of the most repulsive ladies here. I tease Anton that he is not recognized here – these fools really have no idea about him ... Anton and I are great friends with Marie the maid and join her cursing the other clients in French.[35]

Brewing tea in his room, Anton spoke with passion on one topic: Alfred Dreyfus.

SIXTY-FOUR

Chekhov Dreyfusard
January–April 1898

IN 1894, AT a travesty of a trial the Jewish officer Alfred Dreyfus had been sentenced to life imprisonment on Devil's Island for betraying French military secrets to Austro-Hungarian intelligence. In autumn 1897 a colonel of the security services and a senator forced the French government to re-open the Dreyfus case. Dreyfus's brother Matthieu named the real traitor, Major Esterhazy, in *Le Figaro*. French and Russian public opinion polarized: anti-Semites and nationalists faced democrats and internationalists. Major Esterhazy was, however, 'cleared'. Anton wondered if 'someone had carried out an evil joke'. Two weeks' study convinced him of Dreyfus's innocence.[36] On 1/13 January Emile Zola's polemical article *J'accuse* came out in 300,000 copies of *L'Aurore*: the storm led to Zola's prosecution. Nothing that Zola had written won such vindictive fury from the French establishment, or such admiration from Chekhov, as his *J'accuse*. Chekhov made his first political stand. He now praised Korolenko, who had gone mad after undergoing the same ordeal as Zola when he stood up for Udmurt villagers accused of human sacrifices. Anton read the Voltaire he had bought for Taganrog library – Voltaire's defence of Calas, the judicially murdered Protestant, was a precedent for Zola's defence of Dreyfus. Chekhov's fondness for Jews was rather like his fondness for women: even though, to his mind, no Jew could ever fully enter into Russian life, and no woman ever equal a male genius, he vigorously defended their rights to equal opportunities.

Aleksandra Khotiaintseva had gone, leaving Anton a portrait of himself. To Kovalevsky (29 January/10 February 1898), Anton denied he would marry her:

> Alas, I am incapable of such a complex, tangled business as marriage.
> And the role of husband frightens me, it has something stern, like

a regimental commander's. With my idleness I prefer a less demanding job.

A new girl had entered his life: on Russian New Year's Day a bouquet of flowers came from Cannes, followed by a letter from an Olga Vasilieva. Khotiaintseva was amused. She told Masha around 9/21 January:

> Two little girls came from Cannes to see Anton, one of them asked permission to translate his works into foreign languages ... Little, fat, bright pink cheeks. She lugged a camera along to photograph Anton, ran round him saying, 'No, he's not posing right.' The first time she came with daddy and noticed Anton cursing French matches, which are very bad. Today she brought two boxes of Swedish matches. Touching?[37]

Like Elena Shavrova, Olga Vasilieva was just fifteen years old when she came under Anton's spell. Unlike Shavrova, she was a sickly, self-sacrificing orphan. Now an heiress, she and her sister had been adopted by a landowner. She spoke English – which, like many Russian girls brought up by an English governess, she knew better than Russian – and set about translating Chekhov. To her he was a god who would dispose of her fortune and her person. She would follow Anton from France to Russia, seeking affection and advice, offering everything. In Nice she found him newspaper cuttings, looked up quotations, sent him photographs she had taken, and asked him the meaning of the most basic Russian words. He treated her with a gentleness rare even for him, and tongues were soon wagging.

Anton was growing to like the women folk of the *pension*. The Fish, the Doll, Red Ribbons, the Clothes Moth and the Slum were more good-natured than he or Aleksandra had allowed. The Fish, Baroness Dershau, became a fanatical Dreyfusarde under Anton's influence, as did many Russians in Nice. When Suvorin's granddaughter, Nadia Kolomnina, came to Nice, Anton used flirtatious banter to convert her too. Only Anton's brothers sat on the fence: Aleksandr and Misha, dependent on Suvorin's patronage, could not afford their own opinion.

Anton now found *New Times* repulsive, and ordered instead the liberal *World Echoes*, which exposed the bias of Suvorin's paper.[38] Suvorin saw Dreyfus as the villain in a war between Christendom and Jewry, on which hung the future of civilization: the question of whether Dreyfus was innocent or guilty was a technicality. Anton argued so vehemently with Suvorin that the latter conceded: 'You've convinced me'. Nevertheless, attacks on Dreyfus and then on Zola – even while *New Times* was pirating Zola's novel *Paris* – were even more virulent in the weeks following Anton's remonstrations. Pavlovsky, the Paris correspondent of *New Times*, and himself a supporter of Dreyfus, found his copy either binned or distorted. The Russian correspondent on the Riviera, Michel Deline (Mikhail Ashkenazi), sent Suvorin a protest:

> It's not my attitude to the Dreyfus case, but yours which is disgrace-ful. I refer you to someone whom you love and respect, if you are capable of loving and respecting anybody: A. P. Chekhov. Ask him what he thinks of your attitude to this case and to the Jewish question as a whole. Neither you nor *New Times* will be unscathed by his opinion.[39]

Deline's rebuke upset Chekhov more than Suvorin: he hated his name being cited in a public airing of what he still considered private differ-ences, and he ostracized Deline. Anton was bewildered because Suvo-rin would not retrieve *New Times*'s honour from the Dauphin and Burenin. Anton told Kovalevsky that Suvorin was the most weak-willed man he knew when it came to reining in his own family.[40] Anton's tone to Suvorin cooled: he joked that a Jewish syndicate had bought him for 100 francs. He told Aleksandr that 'he no longer wanted letters from Suvorin, in which he uses love of the military to justify his paper's lack of tact': he was disgusted by Suvorin's pirating of Zola, while pouring filth on the man. Yet the two friends still wanted to meet in March.

Dreyfus helped Anton forget Algiers, if not illness. He added guai-acol, an exotic creosote, to his medication. He was downcast at the death of Dr Liubimov on 14/26 January and his burial. Nuisances in La Pension Russe, such as Maksheev the gambler, tempted him to move to a French-run hotel. The Fish, the Doll and the Slum joined forces to dissuade Anton from moving. Maksheev was leaving; the newly converted Chekhovians and Dreyfusardes demanded that the manageress let them and Anton dine separately in the drawing room. Baroness Dershau ('Fish', signing herself *Neighbour*) showered Anton with notes. She borrowed glue to mend her fan, and brewed him tea.

Nevertheless Anton was tired of Nice. On 17 January his name day was celebrated very quietly with a visit from Iurasov, the consul. Anton wrote to Suvorin on 27 January:

> The Russian cemetery is splendid. Cosy, green and you can see the sea. I do nothing, I only sleep, eat, and make offerings to the Goddess of Love. My present French woman is a very nice creature, 22, with an amazing figure, but I'm now a bit bored with all this and want to go home.

Chekhov's notebooks spawned ideas, but 'A Visit to Friends', the last story that he wrote in Nice, reworked the woes of the Kiseliovs in Babkino into ironic fiction. It was written very slowly. A dissolute husband and self-deceiving wife are faced with the bankruptcy of their estate: they invite the narrator, an old friend, to advise them. He realizes that his hostess is inveigling him into marrying her sister, and thus bailing them out. Too strong to succumb, too weak to protest, he flees, pleading an appointment. The scenes of false merriment and the evocation of a derelict garden are among Chekhov's finest creations, but the story must have had unhappy associations. 'A Visit to Friends', published in February 1898, went unnoticed by the critics and was never republished, although it would be recycled into *The Cherry Orchard*. Anton's inspiration lapsed into a prolonged hibernation.

In winter Melikhovo was even quieter; Pavel even put up with Roman's idle wife Olimpiada. The livestock lambed and calved, giving milk for Evgenia and delight to old Mariushka who, Pavel reported, 'is beside herself with joy at lambs gambolling and bleating, and kisses them'.[41] Only the dogs gave cause for distress. Village boys fed them broken glass wrapped in bread and killed both the laikas that Leikin had given Anton. (Leikin was later told that the laikas had died of distemper.) The dachshunds, Pavel complained, were attacking everybody, the family, visitors, children. Brom bit Pavel so severely on the hand that all the medical workers of the district were mobilized. Presents, delivered by the Fish, Doll, Slum and Clothes Moth, consoled Pavel. At Shrovetide Pavel watched his guests carefully: 'Everyone ate pancakes . . . Drozdova 10, Kolia 6, Masha 4.'

On 5 February Evgenia had a telegram from Iaroslavl, which gave her an escape. She left to see her newborn granddaughter, whom

Misha and Olga had named Evgenia after her. Misha announced to Masha: 'We've registered Antosha as the godfather . . . I'll ask you to deduct 11 roubles from Antosha's money that you keep . . . Mother wonders if Antosha will be offended that I've arranged such a cheap christening.[42]

Aleksandr had written a farce for Suvorin's theatre. It was taken off after one night because it had no part for the director's mistress. He fulminated to Anton: 'My play is off because of cunt; . . . expect an offprint of my play which depends so disgracefully on the vagina of Mme Domasheva and the penis of Kholeva . . . Our theatre, led by Iavorskaia, is a very mangy cloaca.'[43] Aleksandr took to drink. Family gave him no pleasure. Natalia loved only Misha, shielding him from his delinquent step-brothers, and found her husband repellent. Little Kolia was rebelling at Vania and Sonia's tutelage, spending, while Uncle Anton was in Nice, his holidays at Melikhovo.

At the end of February toothache struck: the dentistry was brutal. Anton needed a powerful distraction. His fervent admirer, the dramatist Sumbatov-Iuzhin, had come to the Côte d'Azur to win 100,000 roubles to build a theatre. Anton went with him to Monte Carlo. Potapenko was heralding his arrival for the same reason:

> (26 December 1897) . . . I've found a way or two of gambling with chances of winning, true, not a lot, but still it's more honourable than writing for *God's World* . . . when I win, I'll build a theatre in Petersburg and give Suvorin a run for his money.
>
> (5 February 1898) Dear Antonio, Don't joke with me. I really am coming to Nice . . . You're wrong to say one can't win at roulette. I'll prove it to you. I'll prove amazing things. Wait for me with bated breath.

On 2/14 March, Potapenko arrived. The next day, Sumbatov lost 7000 francs and Anton 30. Potapenko was winning. Later, he confessed:

> Monte Carlo had a depressing effect on Anton, but it would be wrong to say that he was immune to its toxins. Perhaps I did in part infect him with my confidence . . . that there was in gambling a simple secret which just has to be divined and then . . . Well, then, of course, the writer's greatest dream emerged: to work freely . . . So he, sober, calculating, cautious, gave in to temptation. We bought a whole pile of form books, even a miniature roulette wheel and for

hours sat, pencil in hand, covering paper, with figures. We were working out a system, looking for the secret.

On the back of an old letter Anton scrawled five columns of figures. Five days later, Sumbatov, Potapenko and Chekhov were spotted in Monte Carlo. Sumbatov, 10,000 francs down, went back to Russia. Potapenko, dishevelled, with black bags under his eyes, was 400 up; a week later he won another 110 francs. As Queen Victoria arrived from England, Potapenko left Nice for Russia. Shortly afterwards, Grünberg, the accountant at *The Cornfield*, wrote to Anton saying that Potapenko had informed him that Chekhov needed an advance: he was therefore sending 2000 francs to Anton, assuming that a manuscript was imminent. Anton was tight-lipped; he had lent half this sum to Potapenko. At the end of April, Potapenko, unabashed, wrote: 'I shall send you 1000 francs. About this money, by the way, I've told nobody here. To avoid unwanted exclamations and head-nodding, I innocently lied to everyone and said that you and I had each won 700.'

Nice offered Anton no escape from penury and disease. The unfinished official portrait also caught up with him. Masha had returned to Braz the portrait he had begun at Melikhovo. Anton refused to risk his lungs by going to Paris to pose. Braz was promised by the Tretiakov gallery his expenses to go to Nice and start the portrait anew. On 14/26 March Braz started work in a studio in Nice. Anton was resigned, but severe: he would sit mornings only, and for only ten days. (He loathed the Jeremiah-like expression which Braz had captured so well, but for the time being managed to keep his dislike of the portrait to himself.)

In mid April Anton began his return home. Escorted by Maxim Kovalevsky, with a large bag of sweets, he took the train to Paris to linger there until warm weather set in at Melikhovo, where even now it was freezing. The rooks and starlings had flown back. The frogs croaked. On 24 April a cuckoo called. Pavel pronounced it time for Anton to return.

Anton had reasons to stay in Paris. Suvorin's diary reads: 'I meant to go to Paris, where Chekhov has arrived from Nice, but I fell ill and am staying at home.' A week later, however, Suvorin raced to France on the *Nord Express*. Anton was giving Bernard Lazare, author of *L'affaire Dreyfus*, a two-hour interview in French.[44] Anton met Matthieu Dreyfus (who was studying Russian), and Jacques Merpert, friend of Dreyfus, employee of Louis Dreyfus, the corn trader. (Merpert taught Russian: Anton was to send him one-act Russian plays for his pupils.)

Anton moved from the dingy Hotel Dijon to the splendid Vendôme, to live a floor beneath Suvorin. Dreyfus tainted the air. Suvorin's diary for 27 April/9 May 1898 brands all radicals as a mob:

> Chekhov is here. All the time with me. He told me that Korolenko had persuaded him to stand for election to the Union of Writers . . . these swine become judges of a remarkable writer! There it is, the mob from which contemptible mediocrities jump out and run things. 'I was almost blackballed,' Chekhov said . . . I asked [*de Roberti, a philosopher*] if he'd seen Zola? 'Well, did he say anything about Dreyfus?' 'He said that he's convinced of his innocence.' 'Well, the proof?' 'He hasn't any.'[45]

Nevertheless, Anton recalled the three weeks in Paris as his happiest abroad. Suvorin, a month ago too melancholy to speak, was animated. He and Anton bargained for exhibits for Taganrog museum. Anton and Pavlovsky spoke up for Dreyfus, and believed they had won Suvorin round. 'What a guilty back he has,' thought Anton as Suvorin turned away from them.

Taganrog, relatives reminded Anton, needed his help. Anton was anxious to support the museum, hotels and sanatoria, to counteract the new foundries which choked the city and crippled its workmen. Scouring Paris for trophies for his native city, Anton enlisted sculptors, Antokolsky and Bernshtam, to carve a twenty-foot statue of Peter the Great for Taganrog's 200th anniversary. Anton bought a boater for Pavel, an umbrella for Evgenia, nightshirts for himself, and strolled the streets in a top hat. He thought of seeing Zola, but did not trust his French: Russia's and France's Dreyfusards exchanged just salutations.

May promised to be hot and dry at Melikhovo. The trees were in leaf; Pavel opened all the windows and doors. Laden with gifts, Anton boarded the Nord Express for Petersburg. Suvorin, believing Anton's health had recovered in Paris, saw him off. He had given Anton 1000 francs, a cushion and a pair of gold cuff links. (Anton left the money with Pavlovsky to give back.) Anton wanted to return unnoticed. He wired Aleksandr in Petersburg: 'Meet me no fuss'. Masha was to come to the station in Moscow the next day. Only she and Potapenko were to know of his arrival.

SIXTY-FIVE

The Birth of a Theatre

May–September 1898

SUVORIN HAD warned his wife to send out the carriage for Anton.[46] Anna brought Anton to the Suvorin house. Nastia reported to her father that she found Anton 'awfully unimproved, and his voice struck me as somehow weakened.'[47] Anton's desk was piled with letters when he reached Melikhovo on the evening of 5 May 1898. Nobody congratulated him on his recovery: Evgenia wrote to Misha that he had lost even more weight.[48]

The important letter was from Vladimir Nemirovich-Danchenko, whose elder brother, the novelist Vasili, Anton had kept company at the roulette tables. Since 1890 Anton had trusted Vladimir and respected him for having abandoned a career as a playwright in order to teach and direct actors properly. Nemirovich-Danchenko now dominated the Moscow Philharmonic School, a respected music and drama college. In 1898 Nemirovich had merged his best six actors – one being Olga Knipper[49] – with Konstantin Stanislavsky and his best four actors from the Society for Art and Literature into the Moscow Arts Theatre. This was to be the first private theatre able to rival Russia's officially subsidized state theatres in its repertoire and its acting; it had the advantage of rich patrons and of freedom from the restrictions that the Imperial Theatre Committee placed on the repertoire of the state theatres. Nemirovich-Danchenko's enthusiasm and Stanislavsky's genius – two bears in one den, they admitted – was a heady brew. With the wealth of Stanislavsky (director of a cotton mill) and of Levitan's patron, Savva Morozov, a militant theatre was formed, needing only a new repertoire. The stimulus to relaunch *The Seagull* had come from Vasili Nemirovich-Danchenko. In November 1896 he had written to his brother Vladimir, disparaging *The Seagull*. The brothers' rivalry was such that Vladimir was bound to defend

456

whatever Vasili attacked. Moscow's theatre was born of Petersburg's spite:

> Dear Volodia! You ask about Chekhov's play. I love Anton with all my heart and value him. I don't consider him in the least great or even of major importance ... This is a boring, drawn-out thing that embitters the listener. Where have you seen a 40-year-old woman renouncing a lover of her own free will. This isn't a play. There is nothing theatrical in it. I think Chekhov is dead for the stage. The first performance was so horrible that when Suvorin told me about it tears welled in my eyes. The audience was right, too. The auditorium expected something great and got a bad, boring piece ... You have to be infatuated with yourself to stage such a thing. I'll say more, Chekhov is no playwright. The sooner he forgets the stage, the better ... I nearly left before the end.[50]

Vladimir Nemirovich-Danchenko's letter to Chekhov on 25 April 1898 changed Anton's life:

> Of contemporary Russian authors I have decided to cultivate only the most talented and still poorly understood ... *The Seagull* ... enthrals me and I will stake anything you like that these hidden dramas and tragedies in every character of the play, given a skilful, extremely conscientious production without banalities, can enthral the auditorium too. Perhaps the play won't arouse explosions of applause, but a real production with fresh talents, free of routine, will be a triumph of art, I vouch for that. All we need is your decision ... I guarantee you will never find greater reverence in a director or worshippers in the cast.
>
> I am too poor to pay you a lot. But believe me, I'll do everything to see you are satisfied in this respect. Our theatre is beginning to arouse the strong indignation of the Imperial theatres. They understand we are making war on routine, clichés, recognized geniuses and so on.[51]

Anton had sworn he was finished with the theatre. He merely sent word through Masha that he had read this letter. Nemirovich-Danchenko wrote again on 12 May:

> I need to know right now whether you are letting us have *The Seagull* ... If you don't, you cut my throat, since *The Seagull* is the only contemporary play that enthrals me as a director, and you are the only modern writer of great interest to a theatre with a model reper-

457

toire . . . I shall come down to see you and discuss *The Seagull* and my stage plan.

After Nemirovich-Danchenko posted this letter, he received Anton's refusal. He wrote again:

> But *The Seagull* is on everywhere. Why not put it on in Moscow?
> . . . There were unprecedented reviews in the Kharkov and Odessa papers. What's worrying you? Stay away from first performances, that's all. Can you forbid the play ever to be put on in Moscow, when it can be acted anywhere without your permission? Even in Petersburg . . . Send me a note to say you have no objection to my staging *The Seagull* . . . unless you are hiding the simplest one, that you don't believe I can stage the play well.

Anton answered evasively, and warned Nemirovich-Danchenko he would have to hire his own horses from the station. Vladimir did not go to Melikhovo that summer, but assumed, rightly, that Anton had given in to his logic. On 18 June Anton went to see him in Moscow: the new Moscow Arts Theatre had the play for its first season in autumn 1898.

Anton did not foresee how close he would become to the Moscow Arts Theatre. He enjoyed the warm summer and the rich blossom and fruits it brought, but his spirits were low. Tychinkin, Suvorin's typesetter, reported to his master that Chekhov was 'as sad' as ever.[52] Now that Anton was back, Masha could rest after eight months' slavery. She went first to the Crimea and then with Maria Drozdova to Zvenigorod to paint. Anton lay low, going to Moscow only once. Old guests, 'the Siamese twins of mediocrity', Gruzinsky and Ezhov, visited. Ivanenko again settled into Melikhovo. Anton was more resolute in staving off women guests. Elena Shavrova, denied even a stone when she asked for bread, pleaded for a rendezvous. Lidia Avilova could get out of Anton only a signature 'with a big tail underneath like a hanged rat's.' Lika was now in Paris training to be an opera singer, while Olga Kundasova was in the Crimea. Aleksandra Khotiaintseva was the only girlfriend to arrive in May.

Later, the women flocked. Tania Shchepkina-Kupernik announced her return 'flying to you on wings of love, with starch and olive oil'. Olga Kundasova beat her to it, but Tania arrived on 5 July for three days. After four years' exile she took over the household diary: 'Here

I found everything as before, people, flowers and animals. God grant it goes on. A clear day and fragrant air. [*And in Pavel's hand*] At supper we laughed loud.'

Anton now threatened to marry Tania off to Ezhov, and called her Tatiana Ezhova. Tania reappeared only once, six weeks later, that summer. A fragment of paper that Kundasova passed to Anton, probably while he stayed overnight in Serpukhov on 23 July, hints at an assignation: 'Si vous êtes visible, sortez de votre chambre; je vous attends. Kundasova.'[53] Anton's eighteen-year-old cousin from Taganrog, Elena, came and scandalized Melikhovo by staying up till midnight with the neighbours' French tutor. Two days later Tania reappeared together with Dunia Konovitser. A day later, Natalia Lintvariova left her water mills and came for a week.

From Nice Olga Vasilieva sent money for Anton's new school: she was to appear in Moscow in October to gaze on Braz's portrait of Chekhov in the Tretiakov gallery. Anton's first trip to Moscow was 18–20 June. He stayed with Vania, went to the operetta, where trained apes were performing, and discussed with Nemirovich-Danchenko the revival of *The Seagull*. Only on 1 August did Anton venture far from home, to see Sobolevsky and Varvara Morozova 200 miles away near Tver. By the 5th he was back. Autumn was in the air: he would have to leave Melikhovo. He had now resigned himself to spending the eight cold months of the year in the Crimea: even though it was no cheaper than living in Nice, he could at least feel he was still in his motherland, and medical opinion approved. Anton told almost nobody, so that in September Lika was meeting trains in Paris, assuming that he was returning to Nice. On 9 September Anton left Melikhovo to spend six days in Moscow before taking the train south.

Melikhovo was falling apart. The garden and woodland were neglected. Labour and enthusiasm were short. Vania and Misha came without their family, for only a few days at a time. Evgenia travelled to Taganrog, for the first time in fourteen years. Her two sisters-in-law, Aunt Marfa and Aunt Liudmila, and Evgenia were, Cousin Georgi wrote to Anton,

all three very glad to see each other, they chat until midnight. Today we are setting off together to the town park to listen to the music . . . Tomorrow we are off to the Greek monastery, where there is a bishop from Jerusalem, Auntie [*Evgenia*] wants to have a look at him.

In mid August Pavel went to Iaroslavl for a fortnight to see his granddaughter.

The men of Melikhovo also sensed that the village had lost its centre of gravity. The priest Father Nikolai stirred the peasantry up against the Talezh schoolteacher Mikhailov, and the battle ended, despite Anton's conciliation attempts, in Father Nikolai being sent away. The household lost its best servant when Aniuta Chufarova, so expert with a horse, a mop or a whalebone corset, left to marry. Then Roman, the man of all work, took to drink again: Olimpiada, the wife he had banished a year before, had died. Anton persisted in his efforts, cajoling funds from neighbours and authorities to buy desks, slates and bricks and mortar for a new building, his third school, for the Melikhovo children, who were taught in a leased cottage.

Confined to home, his interest in the estate waning, cut off from close friends, Anton tried to write, even though the process felt, he told Lidia Avilova, like 'eating cabbage soup from which a cockroach has just been removed'. Advances from *The Cornfield* and from *Russian Thought* had to be paid off. In summer 1898 Anton developed ideas born in Nice. Despite his grim mood, the stories of that summer are among his finest work. He offered *The Cornfield* the longest, 'Ionych'. It concerns a provincial doctor who, from humble origins, becomes as proud, sterile and heartless as his bourgeois patients. The narrative has the familiar Chekhovian scene of a nonproposal in a garden. Particularly powerful is the evocation of Anton's boyhood world, Taganrog's moonlit cemetery and steppe landscape. Anton's other work was a trilogy of short stories, published in *Russian Thought* in July and August 1898. Friends roaming the countryside each narrate a life ruined by moral cowardice. 'Gooseberries' is about a man's ruthless determination to acquire an estate on which he can grow his own gooseberries, however sour. 'The Man in the Case' is about a schoolteacher of Gogolian grotesquerie. The last story, 'About Love', is the most moving: a miller tells of his hopeless love for his best friend's wife. The first two stories became classics instantly, for their morality is unambiguous. 'Gooseberries' is against avarice, 'The Man in the Case' is against false witness. 'About Love', however, was problematical to critics and the public, for it implies that moral sacrifice can be sloth or cowardice.[54]

Anton referred to this burst of creativity as visits to the 'muddy spring'. Pavel had heard a sermon which contrasted the 'muddy spring' of vice that foolish travellers prefer to the 'clear spring' of Christ, and irritated Anton at table by constantly harping on the two springs. The 'muddy spring' of inspiration, however, dried up, as the prospect of exile to the Crimea loomed. Anton had his first hæmorrhage of the autumn.

Anton arrived in Moscow on 9 September 1898 for the first rehearsal of *The Seagull*. The rehearsal, although only of two acts, was a revelation. Weeks of hard work had gone into discussions with the cast, most of whom were unknown names. Stanislavsky had spent the summer on his brother's estate near Kharkov working on a *mise-en-scène*. Anton found himself a longed-for oracle, not a nuisance, and his interest in theatre revived once again.

Anton also watched a rehearsal of *Tsar Fiodor* by Aleksei Tolstoy and was bewitched by the actress, Olga Knipper, who played the Tsaritsa Irina. She had also noticed him, at the rehearsals of *The Seagull* a few days before:

> We were all taken by the unusually subtle charm of his personality, of his simplicity, his inability to 'teach', 'show' . . . When Anton was asked a question, he replied in an odd way, as if at a tangent, as if in general, and we didn't know how to take his remarks – seriously or in jest.[55]

Old friends also waited for Anton. They saw that he was no more Avelan leading his squadron into new revels. Even Tania Shchepkina-Kupernik, who greeted him with enthusiastic doggerel, seems to have realized that things were different now.[56]

Suvorin came to Moscow. He and Anton dined at the Ermitage and then went to the circus, with the artist Aleksandra Khotiaintseva. Three weeks later, Anton wrote to Suvorin à propos of the latter's criticism of the Moscow Arts Theatre. He said nothing about *The Seagull* or Olga's interpretation of Arkadina, but he was overwhelmed by the rehearsal of *Tsar Fiodor* on the eve of his departure. In it he singled out, without naming her, Olga Knipper: 'Irina, I think, is splendid. The voice, the nobility, the depth of feeling is so good that

I have a lump in my throat . . . If I had stayed in Moscow I should have fallen in love with this Irina.'

He took the train for the Crimea on 15 September, preoccupied by Nemirovich-Danchenko's and Stanislavsky's troupe and by their liveliest actress, Olga Knipper.

SIXTY-SIX

The Broken Cog
September–October 1898

IN JULY NATALIA rejected Aleksandr. He complained to Anton: 'Veneri cupio, sed "caput dolet", penis stat, nemo venit, nemo dat.'[57] In August 1898, while Natalia was away, Aleksandr bought an exercise book, bound it himself in leather and made indelible blue-black ink out of oak galls. He entitled this diary *The Rubbish Dump*.[58] It catalogues his domestic miseries. On his wife's return, Aleksandr became impotent. On 28 September 1898, he told Anton: 'I am *schwach* and even by the domestic hearth cannot produce enough material for coitus, let alone onanism.' Natalia demanded that he ask Anton for treatment.

On 4 October Vania's wife, Sonia, wrote from Moscow:

> Dear Aleksandr, Kolia [*Natalia's elder stepson*] refuses to work, he behaves so badly that even our patience is exhausted. He won't obey anybody, even the most gentle treatment is useless. I even resorted to Masha's help, but he just turned his back on her and wouldn't even talk to her . . . How do I get him to you?

On 5 October Aleksandr's *Rubbish Dump* expresses complete turmoil: 'I howled like a wolf . . . Natasha is trying to calm me, saying that Sonia wrote and sent the letter in the heat of her wrath.' Aleksandr wrote to Vania: 'Nikolai has written his own death sentence: now he won't be accepted anywhere . . . Put him on a train . . . there is no hope for his correction.'

In Petersburg Suvorin was thinking about Anton. Aleksandr noted:

> There was a conversation between Suvorin and Tychinkin about buying all Anton's work at once, to give Anton the maximum amount of money at once, and then starting to publish 'The Complete Works'.

To consider publishing his 'Complete Works' meant that Anton now feared that he would soon die. He was seeking a capital sum to see him through terminal illness and take care of his family after his death. Most Russian writers towards the end of their creative lives hoped to publish their 'Complete Works'. Tolstoy had advised Chekhov to do his editing now, and not to entrust the work to his heirs. Suvorin's publishing, however, was sloppy: he generously corrected accounting mistakes as soon as Chekhov mentioned them, but could not offer good proof-reading, production or distribution. As the sons took over, their father's empire crumbled; Suvorin could not bring the Dauphin to heel. Tychinkin, the head printer, advised Chekhov against 'Complete Works', arguing that Anton would make more money by reprinting individual volumes. The typesetter, Neupokoev, had mislaid Anton's manuscripts – and begged him not to tell Suvorin. Anton's affection for Suvorin was not enough to stop him leaving. Sytin, the publisher in Moscow, to whom Anton had thought of selling the rights to his works, now angered him by breaking a promise to print a medical journal, *Surgery*.[59] Anton was at a loss. Fellow writers, upset at his plight, took it upon themselves to market Chekhov's 'Complete Works'. They knew that his departure for the Crimea marked the final phase of his life. The novelist Ertel, himself tubercular, wrote to a friend on 26 September 1898:

> What is Chekhov? One of the prides of our literature ... Now once this major young writer is seriously ill – and I believe he has consumption ... money has to be sought, because the works of a writer whom all Russia reads won't cover the costs of rest, nor a journey south, nor the necessary surroundings for a sick man, especially one with a large family on his hands. Judge for yourself, isn't this disgraceful?[60]

Anton showed less distress than his sister. Masha had bad headaches. Anton told her on 19 September to abstain from alcohol, tobacco, fish, to take aspirin, then subcutaneous arsenic, potassium iodate and electric shocks: 'and if that doesn't help, then wait for old age, when all this will pass and new diseases will start.' Masha had endless messages to pass to Moscow and Petersburg, items to be sent on to the Crimea – ties, cuff links, a balaclava to be bought from Muir and Mirrielees, a waistcoat to be repaired. She had to send Anton all his postage stamps from Lopasnia. Anton didn't want the local postmaster, Blagoveshchensky, to lose his job now that his main customer was 800 miles away. She was equipping the third school, for which Anton had donated his 1000 roubles from the Moscow Arts Theatre. Melikhovo had become a millstone. Pavel and Masha had to cope with the autumn work that Anton instructed them to carry out on the estate: fencing the hayrick against the horses, planting an avenue of birches, ploughing the park. Masha had the moral support of Aleksandra Khotiaintseva who frequently came to stay, and they hired a new workman. Masha found relief only in art: she and Aleksandra Khotiaintseva began to paint Tania Shchepkina-Kupernik.

Winter came early: three inches of snow fell on 27 September; the horse and cows went on winter fodder. Four sheep and two calves were slaughtered. On 8 October Pavel made a diary entry: 'The windows are iced up as in winter. A bright sunrise. It is cold in all the rooms. They still haven't brought wood.'

The Crimea, at first bathed in warm sunshine, was not as dreary as Anton had feared. He was in a romantic mood. Stopping at Sevastopol, awaiting the boat to Yalta, he was befriended by a military doctor who took him to the moonlit cemetery. Here Anton overheard a woman telling a monk: 'Go away if you love me.' In Yalta his Romantic mood persisted. Olga Knipper was on his mind. He told Lika that, despite the bacilli, he might flee to Moscow for a few days: 'Or I'll hang myself. Nemirovich and Stanislavsky have a very interesting theatre. Pretty actresses. If I'd stayed a bit longer, I'd have lost my head.'

In Yalta he found women eager to befriend him. Mrs Shavrova was staying there with her third daughter, the frail Anna. So were Suvorin's granddaughters Vera and the flirtatious Nadia Kolomnina. The headmistress of the Yalta girls' school, Varvara Kharkeevich, took Anton under her wing and made him a school governor. Anton had distinguished male company in Yalta: the opera singer Fiodor Chaliapin, the poet Balmont, and a cluster of tubercular doctors around Dr Sredin, but the man who was most useful to him was Isaak Sinani, who ran Yalta's book and tobacco shop. Through Sinani newspapers, telegrams, letters and visitors all found Anton.

For the first weeks Anton migrated from one rented apartment to another in the hilly suburbs of Yalta. Soon he was so resigned to this 'flowering cemetery' that he decided both to buy a country cottage and to build a town house. On 26 September Sinani took Anton seventeen miles west along the precipitous coast road to Küchük-Köy, to look at an estate a Tatar farmer was selling for 2000 roubles. Anton sketched it for Masha: a stone, red-roofed Tatar house with a cottage, cattle shed, a kitchen, pomegranates, a walnut tree and five acres, hospitable Tatar neighbours – the drawback being a terrifying access road. Soon, however, access would be easier, for the government had that year decided to build a coastal railway, and next year there would be a fast coastal boat service. Masha replied that stone was safer than the flammable rotten wood of Melikhovo, and that no road was worse than Melikhovo's tracks (Serpukhov council procrastinated over building an all-weather road from Lopasnia.) Vania, who liked the prospect of holidays in a family dacha, also approved. It was too cheap to miss. A week later Anton decided also on a house in Yalta: a site at Autka, 200 feet above and twenty minutes from the centre, was for sale at 5000 roubles. He would build on it for the whole family.

During this flurry of decisions, on 12 October 1898, Sinani had a telegram: 'Kindly communicate how Anton received news of death of his father.' Sinani did not tell Anton until next day. Bewildered, Anton wired to Masha: 'Kingdom heaven eternal peace father deeply sorry write details healthy completely don't worry look after mother Anton.' Nobody had warned him during the three days that led to Pavel's death.

On the morning of Friday 9 October, when Masha was still in Moscow, Pavel dressed without putting on the truss for his hernia. He went to the stores and lifted a twenty-pound bag of sugar. As he straightened up, a loop of gut was pinched by his abdominal muscles. In agony he crawled back to bed. Evgenia panicked; it was some time before she sent to Ugriumovo for the doctor. After 'fussing around him for four hours' he insisted Pavel be taken to Moscow. Evgenia sent a servant to Lopasnia with a telegram for Masha.[61]

Jolted over frozen ruts, Pavel was driven to Lopasnia. It was dark. The doctor put him on a train for Moscow. Three hours later he delivered Pavel to Professor Liovshin's clinic and vanished. Liovshin administered chloroform to the patient immediately.

Masha was with Vania that evening and still knew nothing. At 10.30 they received a second telegram, and she rushed to the clinic. Next Sunday she wrote to Anton:

After 3 a.m. Professor Liovshin came down and started shouting at me for abandoning an old man – there was nobody with him. He said the operation had been difficult, that he was worn out, that he had cut out two feet of gut, and only a healthy old man could stand such a long operation . . . he took pity on me and started saying that the operation was successful, that I could even hear my father's voice. He took me upstairs, I was surrounded by bloodstained house surgeons and I heard our father's voice, fairly cheerful. Again the professor addressed me and said that so far all was fine but anything could happen and told me to come back at 8 a.m. and to pray.

Masha and Vania returned next morning and waited until 1.00 p.m., when Pavel awoke, his pulse and temperature normal:

In the evening I found father far better, cheerful, amazingly well cared for! He asked me to bring mother, started talking about the doctors, saying that he liked it here, he was worried only by slight pain in his belly and black and red matter he was bringing up.

Vania telegraphed Aleksandr, who caught the overnight Moscow express, bringing with him his camera and glass plates. On the morning of Monday 12 October he went straight to Vania's school house. His *Rubbish Dump* records:

He was alone in the ward, all yellow from the bile . . . but fully conscious. Our appearance gave him much joy. 'Ah, Misha too has come, and Aleksandr is here!' . . . Two or three times in the conversation he said, 'Pray!'

Pavel then began to show symptoms of gangrene, but Misha and Aleksandr repressed their mutual dislike, and the three brothers dined together at one of Moscow's best restaurants, Testov's. A second operation was performed. After dinner Aleksandr called at the clinic. The porter called out, 'It's all over.' Pavel had died on the operating table. Aleksandr wired an obituary to make *New Times* the next day.

Evgenia complained that four days of suffering was too little. Aleksandr felt that she believed 'the longer a man takes to die, the closer he is to the Kingdom of Heaven: he has time to repent his sins.' Aleksandr wanted to photograph the body:

The porter told me that father's body was still in the basement and for 20 kopecks took me there. On a sort of catafalque I saw my father's body, completely naked, with an enormous bloody plaster covering the whole belly, but the light made it impossible to photograph.

The clinic refused to wash the body until Misha brought a new shroud. Misha, furious that Aleksandr had brought his camera, took charge, as the only civil servant. Aleksandr felt 'completely out of place and unwanted' and was taken to the station by Vania. (Misha and Aleksandr barely spoke to each other again.) Pavel was buried in the absence of his two eldest sons, Aleksandr and Anton. The funeral was a shambles. Masha took 300 roubles from her savings bank and borrowed another hundred. Sergei Bychkov, Anton's faithful servant in the Great Moscow hotel, followed the coffin to the cemetery. Misha wrote to Anton that the funeral was 'such a profanation, such a cynical event that the only thing I am pleased about is that you did not come.' Anton confessed that he felt all the more guilty: had he been in Melikhovo, the mishap might not have been fatal.[62]

Pavel, even if more resented than obeyed, had been a pivot on which life at Melikhovo revolved. Anton saw Pavel's death as the end of an era. Ignoring his mother and sister's wishes that they should stay on at Melikhovo, he told Menshikov: 'The main cog has jumped out of the Melikhovo machine, and I think that life in Melikhovo for my mother and sister has now lost all its charm and that I shall now have to make a new nest for them.'

Anton found a young architect, Shapovalov, to design a house at Autka: he hoped it would be completed by April 1899. A week later Masha left Evgenia in the care of the lady teacher at Melikhovo, and took the train south for a fortnight. (Evgenia refused Misha's invitation to Iaroslavl: perhaps she loathed his letters addressing her as 'greatly weeping widow'.[63]) On 27 October Masha was greeted by Anton in Yalta: 'I've bought a building plot, tomorrow we'll go and look at it, amazing views.'

The Russian public felt for Anton. He was deluged with letters, while the papers worried about his own imminent demise. Misha urged Anton on 20 October:

> Buy an estate, marry a good person, but definitely get married, have a baby – that is a happiness one can only dream about . . . Let your

future wife – somehow I'd like it to be Natasha Lintvariova or Aleksandra Khotiaintseva – arrange your life to be just happy.[64]

Misha wrote to Masha of Khotiaintseva: 'such a glorious person and so talented that I'd like Anton to marry her.'[65] Anton thought of Lintvariova and Khotiaintseva as the salt of the earth, but not as potential wives. He was thinking instead of Knipper, annoyed that Petersburg's papers ignored her Irina. He shared Nemirovich-Danchenko's anger when Suvorin accused the Moscow Arts Theatre of plagiarizing others' productions. Nemirovich-Danchenko, recasting *The Seagull*, had told Anton: 'Suvorin, as you foretold, was Suvorin. He sold us in a week. To your face he was delighted with us, once in Petersburg he fired off a vile little article, I can't forgive myself for talking to him about joining his *Company*.'[66]

From Paris Anton received two photographs of a leaner Lika. One was inscribed: 'Don't think I really am such an old witch. Come soon. You see what just a year's separation from you does to a woman.' The other carried the words of a romantic song she used to sing to Anton:

To dear Anton Pavlovich, in kindly memory of eight years' good relations, *Lika*.

Whether my days are clear or mournful,
Whether I perish, destroying my life,
I know only this: to the grave
Thoughts, feelings, songs, strength
All for you!!

(Tchaikovsky, Apukhtin)

If this inscription compromises you, I'm glad.

Paris 11/23 October 1898

I could have written this eight years ago and I write it now and I shall write it in ten years' time.

IX

Three Triumphs

Actresses: The ruin of the son of the family. Of frightful lubriciousness, go in for orgies, get through millions of francs, end up in the workhouse. Though there are some who make good mothers of families.

Flaubert, *Dictionary of Received Ideas*

SIXTY-SEVEN

The Seagull *Resurrected*
November–December 1898

In Yalta Anton moved from dacha to dacha, until Dr Isaak Altshuller took him in for a fortnight. Altshuller, though his surname suggested 'old card-sharp', inspired confidence, for he too had TB and would prescribe only what he took himself. Altshuller urged Anton to accept exile, and shun the fatal cold of Moscow. Then, until his own house was built, Anton settled in Au mur, a villa owned by Kapitolina Ilovaiskaia, a general's widow and ardent fan.[1]

Masha never forgot being taken to see Anton's building site at Autka:

> I was upset and annoyed that he had bought a site so far from the sea. When we reached it, what I saw was hard to credit. An old Tatar vineyard, fenced with wattle, not a tree, not a bush, absolutely no buildings ... beyond the wattle fence was a Tatar cemetery and, naturally, a corpse was being buried while we were watching. It was the most grim impression.

Only later did Masha appreciate the view of the Uchan-Su river tumbling down to the sea and of the steamboats far below arriving and departing. Her reaction upset Anton; back at Au mur, the villa where they were staying, she relented and sketched a plan of the house they would build.

At 4000 roubles, an acre of land was cheap. The promised railway was raising prices. Safe from casual visitors at Autka, Anton could receive 'subversives' and Jews, even though they were banned from Yalta. The Yalta Mutual Credit eagerly lent Chekhov money to build his house. Its director had the Autka mosque divert a pipe to give him the water for cement. Lev Shapovalov, hitherto an art teacher, only twenty-seven, made his name turning Masha's sketches into plans for a house with a half-Moorish, half-German façade. While the architect drew, Anton hired a Tatar contractor, Babakai Kalfa, to dig foundations and cart materials. Babakai had chosen a name for this idiosyncratic house, Buyurnuz, 'As you like it'. Friends – Tolstoy or Sergeenko – were perturbed at Anton's enormous financial commitments, for he was not sure whether 5000 roubles that Suvorin had given him was an advance or overdue payment. The Moscow Arts Theatre raised Anton's hopes of more money, and so did Suvorin with a proposal to publish all Chekhov in a uniform edition at a rouble a volume. Castles in Spain, however, did not pay for a castle in the Crimea; even at 30 kopecks a line, Chekhov, his strength waning, would now earn little from new work.

Yet Anton hung on to Melikhovo as a summer dacha. He reassured those who depended on Melikhovo: the postmaster, schoolteachers, district nurses, craftsmen, servants. He ran Melikhovo from afar: arbitrating between the female teachers at Talezh, who were feuding over firewood. He assured the bumbling Doctor Grigoriev, who had failed to save Pavel, that his reputation was unsullied. He defended the postmaster against anonymous accusations of abusing customers. Melikhovo, without either Pavel or Anton, nevertheless collapsed. While Masha was in Yalta, Evgenia, despite the company of a lady schoolteacher, trembled. 'Grief has overwhelmed me, I cannot live in Melikhovo,' she told Misha.[2] When Masha got back she found her mother fraught: 'whether the samovar hums, or the stove whistles or a dog howls, it all produces fear and worry about the future,' she reported to Anton. Fire broke out nearby. Masha and Evgenia took servant girls to sleep in their rooms. The ground froze, but no snow fell, so that Melikhovo was virtually cut off from the railway.

On 13 November 1898 Anton gave his mother short shrift: 'After youth comes old age; after happiness, unhappiness, and vice versa; nobody can be healthy and cheerful all their lives . . . you have to be ready for anything. You just have to do your duty as best you can.' A week later snow fell. Masha locked up Melikhovo. Roman drove her by sledge, with linen and crockery, to the station. Evgenia and a servant, Masha Shakina, followed two days later. They stayed until spring in Masha's Moscow flat, in four small rooms, with borrowed furniture. Masha went back once a month, if blizzards allowed, to pay old Mariushka, Roman and the maid Pelageia. Melikhovo was doomed. The dachshunds were left to the servants and the yard dogs.

Thieves dug up Varenikov's apple trees. Roman guarded Melikhovo, ringing bells through the night. Varenikov caught two lads and thrashed them.[3] Varenikov then had the teacher Terentieva in tears by telling her he would now close Melikhovo school.

By December Masha wanted to join Anton in the Crimea, for she believed that she too was ill. 'I cough badly in the mornings, I have constant pain in the left chest.' The doctor prescribed quinine, codeine and stout. Anton told her that she had the family's bad lungs. Masha took a lively interest in the new house. Could Anton enlarge the rooms? Would Melikhovo *have* to go, to pay for this palazzo? 'No, and no,' replied Anton, but he prepared Masha and Evgenia for life in the Crimea. As governor of Yalta's girls' school and friend of its headmistress, Varvara Kharkeevich, Anton offered Masha a post as geography mistress there: the present geography teacher 'volunteered' his resignation. Anton told Evgenia that he was installing an American kitchen, a flushing lavatory, electric bells and a telephone; he was planting roses and cypresses; coffee and halva were cheap; stone houses did not catch fire; rheumatism would not trouble her; her Taganrog in-laws, Marfa and Liudmila, were a day's boat ride away; she could bring Mariushka to live with her; Autka church was a minute away. Anton then bought the Tatar house he had seen two months before at Küchük-Köy. Here Evgenia could keep a cow and a kitchen garden, while Masha, if she faced the rock climb, could bathe in the sea. Anton's boldness was astute. Soon he was offered four times the 2000 roubles he had paid.

Anton did not worry about Evgenia. Kundasova told him on 28 November: 'As for her mental condition, it is not gloomy, let alone depressed. In my view, Pavel's death has not affected her too much because she is a loving mother; her children are dearer than a husband to her.' Anton received more consolation for his own state of health than he could absorb. The provincial press alarmed everyone. All Simferopol was told: 'Ominous symptoms inspire serious concern for his life.' Anton sent angry telegrams; the papers retracted, but nobody was misled about his health. One school friend, Vladimir Sirotin, wrote of his own terminal condition. Another, Lev Volkenshtein, offered to do the conveyancing on Anton's property. Kleopatra Kara- tygina wrote in such distress that Anton telegraphed: 'Perfectly well safe sound respects thanks.' Aleksandra Pokhlebina, now a landowner at daggers drawn with her peasants, had seen her old love with Masha in the Tretiakov gallery by his portrait, but had hung back. She broke four years' silence that November 1898: 'My heart is torn to pieces when I think what is happening to you. How happy I would be if I knew you were well ... I feared the news of the loss of your father would finally undermine your health.'⁴ Dunia Konovitser sent chocolate. Natalia Lintvariova came to Yalta: she dithered and roared with laughter about the possibility of buying a plot of land herself.

Elena Shavrova was pregnant in Petersburg, while her ailing sister, Anna, kept Anton company in Yalta. He paid more attention, however, to the eighteen-year old Nadia Ternovskaia, a protégée of his landlady, Ilovaiskaia. Nadia's father, a bullying archpriest, turned a blind eye to his daughter's excursions with Anton. Nadia was singled out, she later told her children, because she never talked of literature.⁵ She loved music passionately and played the piano for Anton, and she was very pretty. Yalta gossiped and Nadia's father made enquiries. Another Nadia – Suvorin's granddaughter, Nadia Kolomnina – flirted with Anton, but soon went back to Petersburg. She warned Anton that Ilovaiskaia's villa, which Nadia Ternovskaia frequented, 'is very damp, everyone knows that. Abandon it as quick as you can, take all your furniture and move to another palazzo.'⁶ Another woman tempted Anton: Olga Soloviova, a Valkyrian wealthy widow who owned the estate of Soğuk-Su, next to Anton's Küchük-Köy.

Male company was all *memento mori*. Dr Vitte, from Serpukhov hospital, was in Yalta recuperating from a heart attack. He looked as if he had been 'run over by a train'. Anton himself was often too weak to walk uphill, sometimes even to leave his room, but Anton rejected radical measures. On 9 October the actress Vera Komissarzhevskaia had begged him: 'There is a Doctor Vasiliev in Rostov. You must go and let him treat you: he will cure you. Do it, do it, do it, do it, do it, I don't know how to ask you ... It's awful if you won't, you'll just cause me pain. Do it. Yes?'⁷ Anton promised – if ever he was in Rostov – to contact this electrotherapist. His 'catarrh of the intestines' gave him constant diarrhœa. In late November a lung hæmorrhage began. On the third day he summoned Altshuller: 'Je garde le lit. Young colleague, bring your stethoscope and laryngoscope.' Once the blood had been staunched, he asked Masha for his stethoscope, percussion hammer and ice-pack. He ordered comforts – a karakol hat, a cassowary blanket, a samovar – from Muir and Mirrielees. Evgenia sewed him nightshirts. Vania sent him the pince-nez which he always forgot on his travels, and a new cork pad to stop it sliding off his nose. Anton wrote to Suvorin: 'Tell nobody, my blood frightens others more than me, so I try to spit it out furtively.'

His spiritual suffering in Yalta was greater – 'I'd like to talk to somebody about literature . . . but here [there is only] irritating swinishness'. Newspapers came late. 'Without papers one would fall into gloomy melancholy and even get married,' he told Sobolevsky on Christmas Eve. Anton befriended the editor of The Crimean Courier, but, unable to improve the paper, gave up. He loved his future house, but hated Yalta's wintry filth. All Yalta was ashamed when the newspapers printed Anton's telegram to Moscow, saying that he felt like Dreyfus on Devil's Island.

He missed Suvorin, despite the fact that New Times was 'splashing about in filth'. The paper had outraged even the government, which banned it for ten days. The poet Balmont declared New Times 'a brothel by appointment to the crown'. Pavlovsky, Suvorin's Paris correspondent, sought Anton's help to switch to a liberal Moscow newspaper. Potapenko abandoned Suvorin. Suvorin was like Zeus the Bolt-thrower and the Dauphin like an angry bull, Aleksandr reported. New Times was printing the specious Le Dessous de l'affaire Dreyfus by the real traitor Esterhazy. Anton told Suvorin that rehabilitating Dreyfus was the 'great cultural victory of the age'. Suvorin replied that pro-Germans were whitewashing Dreyfus.

The taciturn Vania gave Anton brotherly support; on 19 December he came for a fortnight with supplies. Misha was voluble, but unhelpful. He offered his mother asylum, but she suspected he really wanted her as a nurse to his baby daughter. He did not pay for burying Pavel, and held back Masha's allowance. In Petersburg Aleksandr was even less help. He was supporting his sister-in-law Anastasia: her husband Pushkariov had lost his last penny on a bingo machine he had invented. Aleksandr's eldest son Kolia, meanwhile, had been caught robbing passengers at the railway station. Natalia feared that he would corrupt his brothers, in particular her own son, the seven-year-old Misha, so Aleksandr enrolled the fourteen-year-old boy in the merchant navy. Little Anton, now twelve and ineducable, was working for Suvorin as a bookbinder's apprentice. As New Times sank, Aleksandr himself was searching for a new career. On 24 November he told Anton: 'I am thinking of opening a new sort of brothel, like a touring theatre. If my planned institution arrives in Yalta "to enliven the season" you of course will be the first free customer.' To this letter Potapenko added a greeting, and Emilie Bijon 'un gros baiser'.

Anton was now a citizen of Yalta, his movements monitored by the press. He sat on committees for schools, the Red Cross and famine relief. As Babakai's men dug foundations, Anton wrote: two months at Au mur produced four stories. Three – 'An Incident in Practice' for *Russian Thought*, 'The New Dacha' for Sobolevsky's *The Russian Gazette*, and 'On Official Business' for Menshikov's *The Week* – use Melikhovo material, a Satanic factory, or hostile, thieving peasants. 'On Official Business' is the most powerful of this trio: a magistrate and a doctor are called in a blizzard to a remote village to investigate a suicide, and the magistrate is haunted by nightmares of misery. The radical protest in 'Peasants' and 'My Life' strengthens: the oppressed now become threatening to their oppressors. In Yalta, as Anton told Masha, 'there are neither nobles nor commoners, all are equal before the bacilli.' In a brighter tone he wrote 'The Darling' for a weekly called *The Family*. It portrays a woman utterly absorbed by any man – impresario, timber merchant or schoolboy – on whom she dotes. 'The Darling' startled radicals. It enchanted Tolstoy who saw an ideal, not irony, and called it, to Anton's face, the 'work of virgin lace-makers'.

Anton was tense, as Altshuller realized, because of *The Seagull*. His lungs and intestines suffered. The Petersburg première had sickened him; another fiasco could kill him. *The Seagull* and *Uncle Vania* had been performed everywhere but the capital – the latter play had earned Anton 1000 roubles and held the provinces spellbound. In November 1898, from Nizhni Novgorod, Chekhov heard from Maxim Gorky, a thirty-year-old herald of revolution, Russia's first 'proletarian' writer. He said he had wept like a woman when he first saw *Uncle Vania*; it was 'a blunt saw through my heart,' Act 4 'a hammer on the audience's head': the effect was 'a childhood garden dug up by a giant pig'. Gorky's postscript ran: 'I am a very absurd and crude person, but I have an incurably sick soul.' Anton responded warmly. Gorky initiated an unlikely friendship, disarming in January 1899 all Anton's defences: 'I am as stupid as a locomotive . . . but I have no rails under me.'[8]

Enough people had seen a Moscow rehearsal or provincial performance for *The Seagull* to acquire an awesome reputation. Masha was
fêted as Anton's plenipotentiary. She began to relish life. She dined
with actors and actresses and became self-confident, an amusing guest.
She made friends with Anton's school friend Vishnevsky, who played
the part of Dr Dorn, and with Olga Knipper, who, though fifteen
years too young, played Arkadina. Anton's friends clustered round
Masha. Sasha Selivanova vaccinated her against smallpox; Dunia
Konovitser (Efros), Anton's fiancée in 1886, was as close as twelve
years ago; Elena Shavrova and Tania Shchepkina-Kupernik visited.
Masha was invited to Mrs Shavrova's house and, though she disliked
the Shavrova girls' monocled *cavalieri*, she found Elena Shavrova
beautiful and interesting. Olga Shavrova even invited her to become
an actress. Levitan, near death, was too ill to court her – 'I lie breathing
heavily like a fish out of water,' he told Anton – yet Masha felt she
might still find 'personal happiness'. She did not want to teach geography in Yalta. She meant to enjoy the Moscow season and study art.

On 17 December 1898, with carriages jamming the streets, *The
Seagull* opened to a full house. Nemirovich-Danchenko telegraphed
'colossal success mad with happiness'. Anton wired back 'Your telegram has made me healthy and happy'. Nemirovich-Danchenko
requested *Uncle Vania* exclusively for the Moscow Arts. Anton's school
friend Vishnevsky telegraphed, '*Seagull* will be our theatre's battle-
ship.' The Seagull, Nina, was badly interpreted by Roksanova (soon
to be ousted), and Stanislavsky acted Trigorin like 'an impotent
recovering from typhoid', but the audience was ecstatic. Olga Knipper
won special praise. Nemirovich-Danchenko told Anton: 'She is so
involved in her part that you can't tell her apart from [*Arkadina's*]
elegant actress's get-up and vulgar charm, meanness and jealousy.'
Masha encouraged her brother's instincts: 'A very, very nice actress,
Knipper, was playing; she is amazingly talented, it was pure enjoyment
to see and hear her.' Tania Shchepkina-Kupernik wrote to Anton:
'for the first time in three years I have had enjoyment in the theatre
. . . Everything was new, unexpected, enthralling . . . Knipper was very
good.'

Many old friends made contact. Levitan got off his sick bed, paid
double for a ticket and said that he now understood the play; torn
between older and younger women, he felt for Trigorin. Even the

actor Lensky, a sworn enemy since he had been caricatured in 'The Grasshopper', was enchanted by *The Seagull*. By January 1899 Sergei Bychkov, the footman at the Great Moscow Hotel, had seen *The Seagull* four times: he reminded Chekhov 'how passionately Liudmila Ozerova wanted to act your Seagull'.[9] Women clamoured to be Seagulls. Kundasova informed Anton that her sister Zoia was widowed and free: Nemirovich-Danchenko must give her the part.

Knipper fell ill and two performances of *The Seagull* were postponed, a loss for Anton, who was to receive 10 per cent of the gross takings. Yet he now equated his bond with the Moscow Arts theatre with marriage to an actress. To Elena Shavrova and to Dunia and Efim Konovitser he used the same image: 'I have no luck with the theatre, such awful luck that if I married an actress we would probably beget an orang utan or a porcupine.' Anton was paying for a Moscow flat, an estate and school at Melikhovo, buildings in Autka and a farmhouse at Küchük-Köy. He had indigent relatives and not long to live. Rather than beg, as Levitan advised, from rich patrons, he took decisive action.

SIXTY-EIGHT

'I am a Marxist'
January–April 1899

HOW ODD OF ANTON to send Piotr Sergeenko as agent to Petersburg to sell his complete works to Adolf Marx! Sergeenko, Anton's schoolmate, had become a comic writer under the pseudonym 'Navel', and he was one of many who had failed to follow Anton into serious literature. Chekhov derided Sergeenko's *How Tolstoy Lives and Works* and his novel, *Daisy*: he called him a 'hearse on legs'. A Tolstoyan, Sergeenko hid nothing from his family. Anton's lubricious talk embarrassed him, just as his po-faced tone irritated Anton. Only Sergeenko's pedantry qualified him as an agent.

For five years Anton had been impressed with Marx, who published in Russian and did business in German. Marx's *The Cornfield* was Russia's best family weekly, offering a literary supplement, and reference books as bonuses to subscribers. He produced standard writers beautifully, and paid well. Tolstoy had advised Marx to secure Chekhov. All Petersburg knew that Russia's greatest writer (after Tolstoy) was in financial straits. Sergeenko expected that, despite an opening bid of 50,000 roubles, Marx would pay 75,000 roubles for exclusive rights – enough to keep the Chekhovs secure. Anton offered Suvorin first refusal. Suvorin consulted his heirs: the Dauphin objected violently, and Suvorin wired Anton: '. . . can't see why hurry when property rights rising look before you leap is your health really bad.' Sergeenko reported Suvorin demurring:

'Chekhov is worth more. And why should he hurry.'
'So you'll give more?' There was a hiss, nothing more.
'I'm not a banker. Everyone thinks I'm rich. That's rubbish. I've a moral responsibility to my children, and I have one foot in the grave.'[10]

Suvorin offered Chekhov a 20,000 rouble advance: 'Write and tell me what made you do it think all the best dear Anton.' Anton wanted no auction. He was breaking not so much with Suvorin as with shoddy printing and accounting. It was a Biblical moment. 'I am being sold into Egypt,' he told Vania; he told Aleksandr that he was parting from Suvorin 'as Jacob parted from Laban'. At the end of 1899 he confessed to Khudekov: '. . . like Esau I sold my birthright for a mess of pottage'. Sergeenko negotiated for eight hours at a stretch, pushing Marx and his assistant Julius Grünberg, until 75,000 was agreed as a fee for the right to publish all Chekhov's past and present works. By 31 January a contract was drafted. The contract was, everyone agreed, a coup for Marx and a disaster for Anton. Marx made 100,000 roubles in the first year – much of Chekhov's work had already been typeset by Suvorin. Sergeenko erred by not getting 75,000 as a lump sum. Too late, on 12 February, Suvorin wired:

> your deal for two years let alone ten is disadvantageous your repu-
> tation is just starting to soar to giddy heights and you throw your
> hand in . . . I warmly shake your hand Suvorin.[11]

Chekhov received 25,000 on signature of the contract and the rest at two eight-month intervals. Marx received the right to everything Chekhov had written and or would write. Anton's name day passed unmarked as telegrams flew, hammering out the contract. Sergeenko secured increments for new work: 250 roubles per printer's sheet (24 pages), rising by 200 roubles every five years. Anton wired an undertaking to die before he was 80. Marx and Grünberg baulked loudly in German at the thought of what a Chekhov story would cost in 1949: the contract was then set to expire altogether in 1919. Sergeenko won few concessions: Anton could keep fees from periodi- cals or charitable publications, and, fortunately, his theatre takings. Marx inserted Draconian clauses: he could reject 'unfit' work, and Chekhov would pay a penalty of 5000 roubles per printer's sheet published elsewhere. Worst of all, Anton had to send by July 1899 a fair copy of all publications. 'That will force Mr Chekhov to make an effort,' Marx told Sergeenko.

The contract ruined 1899. Anton had destroyed most manuscripts and had few copies of his early work. He despatched all who loved him to the libraries to make copies. Lidia Avilova, as sister-in-law of the editor of *The Petersburg Newspaper*, found two copyists for dozens

46. Anton with the Suvorin family at Feodosia, September 1896. He is sitting second from right with Emilie Bijon on his left; Suvorin is standing second from left, between Anne and Nastia Suvorina

47. The schoolteachers at Talezh and Melikhovo, Aleksandr Mikhailov and Maria Terentieva

48. Lidia Iavorskaia

49. The Seagull being shot down

50. Back from the clinic, April 1897

51. With Quinine the dachshund, May 1897

52. Lika Mizinova with Anton, May 1897

53. TOP LEFT Vera Komissarzhevskaia

54. ABOVE RIGHT Daria Musina-Pushkina with Anton, 31 May 1897

55. ABOVE Aleksandra Khotiaintseva, c. 1898

56. BELOW With Moscow Arts Theatre members, spring 1899; *standing* Vishnevsky, Luzhsky, Vladimir Nemirovich-Danchenko, Olga Knipper, Stanislavsky, Roksanova, Nikolaeva, Andreev; *sitting* Raevskaia, Artiom, Anton, Lilina, Tikhomirov, Meyerhold

57. Vladimir Nemirovich-Danchenko   58. Olga Knipper

59. The Yalta house nearing completion, mid 1899

60. LEFT Dr Altshuller

61. ABOVE Anton in his study at Yalta, 1900

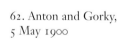

62. Anton and Gorky,
5 May 1900

63. Anton and Olga on honeymoon at Aksionovo, June 1901

64. Anton with the Tolstoys, 12 September 1901

65. Evgenia, Masha, Olga and Anton at Yalta, February 1902

66. In the garden at Yalta with a tame crane, March 1904

of stories from the late 1880s. Nikolai Ezhov traced stories in *The Alarm Clock* and *Amusements*: with his usual incompetence he dropped whole paragraphs as he copied. Aleksandr in Petersburg wrote out the *New Times* stories personally: the Dauphin forbade him to bring in a copyist or to remove volumes from the office. During the winter, spring and summer of 1899, Chekhov revised this material. To Marx's annoyance, he reserved himself extra rights: to reject half of the 400 stories he had retrieved, and radically to rewrite, in proof, those he chose to preserve. From 1899 to 1901 rewriting took more of Anton's energy than new composition. Readers noticed with dismay that each new edition of Chekhov's stories threw out more early pearls. Marx made Suvorin pay 5000 roubles for the right to sell his stock – 16,000 volumes of Chekhov's work. Suvorin nobly offered Anton 70 per cent of the profit from the sales of these. Marx's monopoly made Chekhov's *Plays*, which included *The Seagull* and *Uncle Vania*, unavailable for three years.[12]

Masha, advised by the lawyer Konovitser, feared that Anton had been cheated: Marx was offering 125,000 roubles for the works of far more lowly writers. Masha consoled herself she could be a helpmate, like Countess Sofia to Tolstoy, and collect, copy and edit. Never had her role as sister given her so much fulfilment. Only Dr Obolonsky clouded her horizon: he hinted that she had TB. Anton's brothers, however, wanted their due. Aleksandr begged 1000 roubles for his new dacha, while Misha, who had put two years' work into Melikhovo, lamented to Masha in January 1899 in tones like Uncle Vania's:

> I lived in Melikhovo as you all saw, ate and drank at common cost, and where my 4400 roubles went I don't know; when I went to Uglich, I had, I'm ashamed to say, nothing but a pillow, a frock coat, a suit, three pairs of underpants, four calico shirts and half a dozen socks.[13]

Anton promised Aleksandr money, but ignored Misha's hints. He settled down to review his old work, recalling Pushkin's elegiac line: 'and with revulsion I survey my past'. Relief from debt made the Herculean task seem lighter: he told Nemirovich-Danchenko he 'had been given a divorce by the Holy Synod'. To the Tolstoyan Gorbunov-Posadov, who could no longer reprint Chekhov in his editions for the masses, he declared 'it has fallen on my head like a flower pot from a windowsill'. He joked 'Any moment I'll become a Marxist.'[14] Sergeenko felt he had done his best: even if Suvorin had matched Adolf Marx's offer Anton would 'never have had accounts until the Third Coming'. Sergeenko pocketed 500 roubles for his trouble and wired 19,500 to Anton.

Anton had his first cheque book. He regretted planning his house so thriftily; now he splashed out on furnishings and the garden. He hired a Tatar gardener, Mustafa, who spoke little Russian but shared Anton's love of trees. He gave Evgenia ten roubles (a sum which made her quite content). His wealth, like his health, was public knowledge. Letters poured in. Gavriil Kharchenko, the sole survivor of the brothers who had worked in Pavel's shop, wrote from Kharkov, where he was now a prosperous shop assistant.[15] Kharchenko gladly took up Anton's offer to pay his daughter's school fees. Consumptive writers got in touch. Epifanov, who like Chekhov had written for *Amusement* in the early 1880s, was dying of TB: through Ezhov, Anton paid him 25 roubles a month and considered moving him to Yalta. A Father Undolsky was lent the cost of rebuilding the church school in the Tatar village of Mukhalatka.[16]

Losing Chekhov at the height of his fame was a blow to the finances and morale of *New Times*, and there was more turbulence ahead. In February 1899 the police murderously attacked a student demonstration; even government ministers protested, but Suvorin's editorial supported the police. Public opinion raged against Suvorin. A 'cat's concert' was to be organized under his windows by students and journalists. Clubs and societies cancelled their subscriptions. In a bungling attempt to counter rumours, the Dauphin published circulation figures: *New Times* had, instead of the reputed 70,000, only 34,000 subscribers. Journalists broke away to form a rival newspaper. Contributors boycotted *New Times*. Finally the writer's union summoned Suvorin to a court of honour on charges of dishonourable conduct.[17] Until the 'trial' Suvorin could not sleep.

Anton loathed kangaroo courts. In April 1899 he told Suvorin that to submit was to be in the 'pathetic situation of little wild animals which, when caged, bite off each others' tails'. Suvorin, Anton reported to Aleksandr, was writing letters 'like the liturgy of penitence. Clearly, he is miserable.' For a time Anton softened: on 9 March he told Ezhov (a Suvorin acolyte to the end) 'Of course I'm sorry for Suvorin. But

I'm not at all sorry for those around him.' As over the Dreyfus affair, however, Suvorin's private recantation was belied by public intransigence. Anton despaired: he even told Sergeenko that Suvorin had 'all the marks of criminality.' In vain Anna Suvorina appealed to him on 21 March: 'If you were his friend or just loved him, you would not stand by the wayside at this time ... I imagine if you were in his shoes what he'd have done! ... Forgive me ... I'm just hurt for him, that he has no friend.'[18] Anton felt deviousness in Anna's charm, but agreed, when spring set in, to talk to Suvorin in Moscow. In early April Anna pleaded again. Tychinkin, Suvorin's typesetter, complained in April: 'The atmosphere here is very oppressive, you feel you're in a nightmare.'[19] All literary Petersburg seemed distressed. Shcheglov was miserable. Barantsevich, on his infant son's death from meningitis, wept every day.

Lika Mizinova, who was taking her first faltering steps as a concert singer in Paris, got less response than Suvorin from Anton. He told her in the New Year that he was not writing because she wasn't answering. She was outraged: 'I love you far more than you are worth and treat you better than you treat me. If I were a great singer now I'd buy Melikhovo from you. I can't bear to think I shan't see it again.'[20] Anton teased her: he announced he was marrying ... Adolf Marx. He told her she was just like Aleksandra Pokhlebina who would try to kill herself with a corkscrew; he might see her in Paris in the spring. Lika responded 21 February 1899: 'I promise to be polite to your bride and will even try somehow not scratch her eyes out! Better leave her behind in Russia! No, never get married! It's bad! Better just live with Pokhlebina, but don't wed! She loves you so.' Lika was in touch with Masha: she guessed what kept Anton in Russia. Masha was quite sure. In February 1899 she was invited backstage to meet Nemirovich-Danchenko's cast: 'Knipper started jumping up and down, I gave her your regards. I advise you to woo Knipper. I think she is very interesting.' Anton responded immediately, 'Knipper is very nice and of course I'm stupid not to be living in Moscow.' Soon Olga Knipper was calling on Masha. Their friendship bound the Knippers to the Chekhovs and the Chekhovs to the Moscow Arts Theatre.

Anton longed for a break from exile. At Easter he would go to Moscow to meet his theatre company, Knipper, Lika, Masha, and his mother. Never, however, had Anton liked metropolitan Russia less.

He loathed the authorities, and the radical students. Once students had graduated, he told a colleague, they forgot all ideals and became money-grubbing oppressors. He read the French newspaper *Le Temps* for honest reporting. He did not miss the peasantry, swamped as he was by letters from Melikhovo complaining of deceit and hostility. Masha's school term ended on 12 April, the lease on the Moscow flat a week later, and they would have to live at Melikhovo: the prospect of Easter there was grim. On 10 March Masha told Anton:

> Sell Melikhovo as quickly as possible, that's what I want. Crimea and Moscow! For Russian countryside any province and place will provide beauty, fishing and mushrooms. Melikhovo reminds me too much of father. Constant repairs, bother with servants and peasants.

While Babakai mixed cement, Mustafa planted trees. Vukol Lavrov, an editor of *Russian Thought*, had given Anton Zolotariov's *Flora for Gardeners* and, this Bible in hand, Anton planted an Eden to replace Melikhovo. Odessa's nursery catalogues and the nearby Nikita Gardens inspired him. The Mediterranean flora he had seen in Nice did well in Yalta. Soon twelve cherries, two almonds and four white mulberry trees were planted; bamboos were also on their way. Here, not in Paris, Anton told Lika, they would meet.

Nadia Ternovskaia, the archpriest's pretty daughter, was in Odessa, where her brother taught, for the opera, which she loved fanatically. Anton had got her tickets and she sent violets and flirtatious letters. Tatiana Tolstaia, though she disliked *The Seagull*, was overwhelmed by her father's dramatic readings, interrupted by fits of weeping and laughter, of 'The Darling' to motley audiences of musicians and foreigners. She wrote: 'Father has read it four times in a row and says the piece made him wiser. And I recognize myself in "The Darling" so well that I am ashamed.'[21] The infatuated teenager Olga Vasilieva, struggling to render Chekhov into English, sent notes asking the meaning of every unusual word. Suvorin's granddaughter, Nadia Kolomnina, coyly flirted by letter from Petersburg. She sent Anton waltzes for other women to play him on Ilovaiskaia's piano.[22] Yalta laughed at Anton's followers. Women who patrolled the promenade or the road to Autka were named *Antonovkas*, after a Russian apple, a fruit he was not tempted to pluck. In chastity[23] and isolation, Anton signed himself Antonius, Bishop of Melikhovo, Autka and Küchük-

Köy. By April isolation and the company of sick doctors were wearying Anton: he complained to Suvorin that he was 'like a priest with no parish'. It was still too early, however, to go to Moscow, where April was freezing cold, and Anton's friends were alarmed by his determination to leave. Miroliubov, the singer and editor, tried to cut off his escape by wiring Vania: 'Going north madness disease not cured must guard wants go Monday.'[24]

Gorky, dressed in rough peasant garb, came to Yalta and detained Chekhov. They argued politics and literature; Anton showed Gorky Küchük-Köy. That same April, two other writers appeared in Yalta, the dandified Ivan Bunin and the jovial journalist Aleksandr Kuprin. The next generation of Russian prose-writers was at Chekhov's feet. Bunin and Gorky hid the distrust that broke into warfare, once Bunin became the doyen of émigré literature, and Gorky the Bolsheviks' Minister for Literature. Kuprin, Bunin's friend, lacking Gorky's wild excesses and Bunin's fastidiousness, was the jester. These disciples were no jackals but, as Anton saw, three geniuses in the making. Gorky would prove the Judas, Bunin the Peter of the Chekhovian church. Suvorin was now morally and physically a thousand miles away: Anton directed his affection at Bunin, whom he and Masha called Bouquichon, after a foppish manager on Prince Orlov-Davydov's estate near Melikhovo.

Anton's share of the takings for a dozen performances of *The Seagull* was only 1400 roubles, for the Ermitage theatre had very few seats. The theatre's patron, the rich merchant Savva Morozov, was promising a far larger theatre, to make them and Anton rich. Their repertoire, however, also needed expansion, and they wanted *Uncle Vania*, which Stanislavsky thought greater than *The Seagull*. Chekhov had to be induced to withdraw the play from the Maly theatre. This proved easy, when the professors of the Imperial Theatre Censor committee, who governed the Maly's repertoire, took umbrage at the play's aspersions on a professor and asked for changes. On 10 April, the day that the Committee met, Anton took the boat from Yalta to Sevastopol for the train to Moscow. A doctor met him at the station and took him to the warmth of Masha's flat.

SIXTY-NINE

Last Season in Melikhovo
April–August 1899

ON ARRIVAL IN MOSCOW Anton was summoned to the Theatrical Committee and insulted. He withdrew *Uncle Vania* from state theatres and passed the Moscow rights to the play to the Moscow Arts Theatre. Masha's flat was too cold, so they moved to warmer quarters. No sooner had Anton settled than he started on proofs for Adolf Marx. He grimly told visitors that, as he had not long to live, he had sold his work, to edit it definitively.[25] Friends were dismayed by how much he rejected. In July 1899 a former editor, Menshikov, told Anton that he made Herod seem like an infant by comparison, and that others would disinter the work after his death, but Anton's response was that the public should be spared juvenilia. While Anton's cull disposed of his weaker humorous stories, and his revisions cut the purple passages from many stories, very often he reacted to some fine work with a distaste that is unaccountable, unless the work that he rejected had some private unhappy associations.

Lent ended on Sunday 18 April. Anton went, unannounced, to see the Knippers. Olga Knipper lived with her widowed mother and her mother's two brothers, Sasha Salza, an army officer, and Karl Salza, a doctor. The Knippers and Salzas were second-generation Russian, German-speaking Lutherans. They had not yet intermarried with Slavs. Anton had not known such people before. They were indefatigably robust – the Knippers had been ruined, and were fighting their way back to prosperity. They were also musical. Olga could sing as well as act, and her mother Anna, although nearing fifty, was a soloist as well as Professor of Singing at the Conservatoire. Uncle Sasha, an amateur singer, was a heavy-drinking, sometimes rowdy, rake. The Knippers and the Chekhovs were struck by each other's strangeness. Olga enchanted Anton in life, just as Tsaritsa Irina had on stage. She lacked Lika Mizinova's classical beauty, or the intensity of

Komissarzhevskaia: her eyes were small, her jowls heavy. Her character was spontaneous but organized: she worked and played hard. She could hike across fields, nurse the sick, behave genteelly, or prance uninhibitedly.

From 18 April 1899 on Anton became monogamous. He flirted perfunctorily with Masha's wealthy new friend, Maria Malkiel, but barely bothered with others, even the archpriest's daughter, Nadia Ternovskaia. (Nadia worried, 'the reason you don't want to stay in Yalta is that there won't be any *Antonovkas?*'[26]) Anton took Olga to see Levitan's exhibition and his renowned *Haystacks in Moonlight*. In May Melikhovo would be warm enough to be habitable, despite its neglected state. Anton invited Olga to spend a few days there with him. She agreed, as long as Nemirovich-Danchenko would release her from rehearsals.

Four days after Easter, Tolstoy called. The next day his daughter came and invited Anton and Masha to call. Tolstoy and Anton talked of many things: Tolstoy, who respected those he violently disagreed with, spoke up for Suvorin, who had wired Chekhov a draft of his trial defence. Anton replied that he should deny the union's right to try him. Suvorin wired a new draft. 'Beautifully written, but too many details,' Anton responded with exhortations, then he gave up, realizing that he was 'just a stone splashing into water'. Lidia Avilova was staying with her brother in Moscow, and Anton used her as a conduit to Petersburg's 'judges'. For a while Suvorin regained his equilibrium, bought a new estate, and tried to forget about his forthcoming 'trial'. Anton urged him to write a novel and give up journalism. On 1 May 1899 Anton invited Lidia Avilova to meet him, with her children, for coffee and buns at the station, before she departed for the country. It was a courtesy owed to her, as an attractive, talented woman and a keen researcher retrieving his stories.[27]

After seeing Avilova off, Anton went to see *The Seagull*. It was the first time that Anton had seen a play he had written performed to his specifications. *The Seagull* was put on specially, with no sets and few props, in a theatre so freezing that Anton gave Stanislavsky advice only on Trigorin's shoes and trousers, and the tempo of the final act. Although Stanislavsky had comic experience – he had been a fine Nanky Poo in *The Mikado* – he played his heroes as neurotics, and slowed Chekhov's allegro to an adagio: Anton was unhappy with him as an actor, and dubious of him as a director.

'With no resident status', as Anton put it, he could write nothing new, although his mind seethed with new ideas, as his notebooks show. His new friend Gorky was banned by both police and doctors from visiting Moscow. They exchanged presents: Chekhov sent an engraved gold watch; Gorky promised a rifle. In mid July, after emerging from three weeks in prison, Gorky made Anton a very original present, too late for Anton to make any use of it: 'a fallen woman, Klavdia Gross, will bring you her life story, which she has written. She is decent, speaks languages, a proper miss – a fine woman even if a prostitute. I think she is more use to you than to me.'[28]

The family home, it was agreed, was in Yalta: on 2 May Anton asked Vania, who was off to the Crimea on holiday, to keep an eye on the builders, and take with him the family treasures, notably Pavel's icon of St John the Divine. Valuables went for safety to Yalta; Melikhovo was a fire risk, neglected and underinsured. Vania could live for free in Autka, attended by Mustafa: the roof was on, the kitchen nearly ready. Vania was grateful for Anton's lobbying to secure him pensionable rank, and was content to spend his school holidays as site manager in the Crimea.

On 5 May Anton gave Olga Knipper a signed photograph of the cottage at Melikhovo where he had written the play that brought them together. Three days later he joined his sister and mother there, after eight months' absence, to be met by two berserk, half-feral dachshunds. There, the next day, he greeted Olga; her short visit gave her a misleading, rosy impression of Melikhovo. Masha invited her to return: 'We long to see you, dear Olga; the horses will wait for you on Saturday'.[29]

After Olga had left, Melikhovo lapsed into chaos. A month passed in the search for stove-makers, and haggling to finish the third school. Melikhovo was like Arkadina's and Sorin's estate in *The Seagull.* 'I constantly shout loud abuse, I tear my vocal cords, but neither I nor the guests are given horses,' Anton complained. Made to feel unwelcome at Melikhovo, Misha told Masha on 16 May:

All the hints in my letters to Antosha have been left unanswered, worse, his letters to me are full of anxiety that I might bring my family down to Melikhovo . . . I am sad that circumstances prevent me meeting our mother and showing her our little Evgenia. In secret from you two (I was afraid you'd be offended) I got in touch with the Semenkoviches and asked them to put me up just for a month from 20 June . . . at the end of June Antosha will send you round his houses in Yalta to deal with building. Is that your job? Are you a builder, a manager? Don't you have enough to do in Moscow and Melikhovo? People go to the Crimea to rest.

Anton did not feign any liking for Misha's company. On 21 May 1899, without the blessing he coveted from his mother, Misha took his wife and child to the Crimea: they stayed at Alupka, forty miles from Gurzuf and Vania's family. The house at Autka was not yet habitable and Küchük-Köy was too remote for either Vania or Misha, even had Anton consented. Vania moved in with Misha at Alupka.

June began warm. Anton returned to Melikhovo, to sell it. The whole district was in shambles. The bridge over the river had collapsed and the district head of schools had been charged with embezzlement. Masha no longer saw any prospect of staying there, as she told Maria Drozdova in mid June.

> I feel like a tram that's left the rails and can't get back on them and is jumping all over the place. I have no idea where we shall live . . . Anton is ripping everything off the walls, sending it to the Crimea, now the comfortable wicker armchair has vanished from the balcony.[30]

The estate was advertised for 25,000 roubles with a 5000-rouble mortgage. Brom, the dachshund dog, foamed at the mouth and was shot as a rabies suspect. Anton ordered ropes, matting, packing cases and stripped the house. He mobilized Sinani in Yalta to store his possessions in the outbuildings already nearing completion. Cousin Georgi in Taganrog counted Anton's railway wagons, as they rolled in from Melikhovo via Moscow, and oversaw the transfer of books, wardrobes, desks, divans and the 'archive' on to the boat to Yalta. Ironwork, plumbing, door fittings and wallpaper were ordered from Moscow for Shapovalov to install in Autka.

In Moscow Nemirovich-Danchenko made a start on *Uncle Vania*, to astound the 1899–1900 season. Anton asked his colleague Dr Kurkin for a cartogram of Serpukhov district that Stanislavsky could use as Astrov. In a postscript to Masha's letter he began his correspondence with Olga, addressing her 'Hello, last page of my life' and, as he had Kleopatra Karatygina and Tania Shchepkina-Kupernik, 'Great artist of the Russian land'. Olga was off to Georgia, to stay with her brother Konstantin in the cathedral city of Mtskheta. She and Anton arranged to meet in late summer.

Anton took time away from Melikhovo to visit Petersburg. He arrived on the morning of 11 June, met Adolf Marx and asked him to print the plays with diagrams of Stanislavsky's staging.[31] He had his photograph taken in two studios. He did not go to see Suvorin. The dank cold sent him back the same day to Moscow.

All summer Masha was stranded in Melikhovo, fighting cockroaches and showing buyers round. Anton lived in Moscow with Masha the servant, whose lover haunted the kitchen. He strolled the boulevards and chatted to 'fallen' women at the Aquarium. He visited Pavel's grave, which was overgrown with brambles, and found an estate agent. Now that he had built his last school, he wrote to Suvorin, he had no sentiment for the estate: it was 'mined out' as literary material. By July two potential buyers had appeared. The first, Ianov, was a burnt-cork manufacturer who strung the Chekhovs along week by week. By the time Ianov dropped out, the other buyer, the young Boris Zaitsev, eventually a fine emigré prose writer, had bought another estate. Anton descended on Melikhovo to dig up any shrub that could be replanted at Autka. On 5 July 1899 he abandoned for ever his dachs-hund bitch Quinine and the estate into which he had poured so much time and energy.

Anton's mind was on Olga Knipper. He said he would meet her in the Caucasus, 'on condition you do not make me lose my head.' He told Masha to rely on the estate agent. She protested that there were no horses to fetch buyers from the station. She begged Anton to come to Melikhovo and 'rest' until autumn frosts drove him to the Crimea. Aghast at coping alone with the sale of an estate – 'To hell with buyers. I'm sad and lonely' – she would rather take the 21,000 roubles that Ianov seemed to be offering, than ruin her health, and Anton's, seeking better offers.

Anton had his way. On 8 July 1899 he wired Olga and arranged to meet her in the Black Sea port of Novorossiisk. From there they would take the overnight boat to Yalta together. Four days later he took the train south to Taganrog. Misha, back from the Crimea, went to the station to intercept him before he left Moscow, but there were so many friends seeing Anton off that Misha could not get a word in. (He took his wife and child, in Anton's absence, to Melikhovo, and lived there, beset by bittersweet memories, for a week.) In Taganrog Anton stayed not with his cousins but at the Hotel Europe. He visited the brothel, which was now run by a Jew. He saw a body covered with flies in the market, and started an appeal for a mortuary. From a Tatar vendor he had his first (but not his last) taste of koumiss, fermented mares' milk. He told the town's councillors what trees to plant. He felt ill and he let an old school friend, Dr Shamkovich, examine him at the hotel. On 17 July he took a boat to Novorossiisk.

Misha and his family returned desolate to Iaroslavl. An escaped convict was prowling Melikhovo, so Masha spent the nights shaking in her bed. Meanwhile Anton led Olga Knipper off the boat at Yalta. To the dismay of the *Antonovkas*, their arrival together was noted in the *Crimean Courier*. Anton stayed in the Hotel Mariino, while Olga found lodgings with the ailing Dr Sredin. For twelve days they strolled Yalta, took a carriage up to the viewing point at Oreanda and watched Babakai build the house and Mustafa the garden at Autka. The trees that had been planted in spring were growing rapidly. Olga and Anton were not altogether happy, for travel and travails had shattered Anton's precarious summer health. Anton reported to Masha, 'she was having tea with me; she just sits and says nothing.' The next day he wrote, 'Knipper is here, very nice, but she is depressed.' He lost interest in everything else. He told Masha to sell Melikhovo for half price.

Sazonova, who had recorded Anton's moods in 1896, was in Yalta; her husband had inherited an estate nearby. Her diary from 24 to 31 July 1899 notes:

> Chekhov took to Massandra the Moscow actress who acted in his *Seagull*. We dined in the town park . . . We met Chekhov there, he came and sat at our table. He wears grey trousers and a desperately short blue jacket. He complains that in winter he is worn down by visitors in Yalta. He has settled out of town on purpose . . . Chekhov is not a conversational man . . . He either replies reluctantly or starts to pontificate like Suvorin, 'Ermolova is a bad actress . . . Gorky is a good writer . . .'
>
> I saw Chekhov on the promenade. He sits all alone on a little bench.[32]

On 2 August 1899 Olga and Anton took a carriage across the mountain towards the ancient Tatar capital of Bakhchisarai. Through sultry heat they crossed the beautiful Kök-Köz [*Blue Eye*] valley, wondering who was waving frantically at them: it was a group of doctors who had recognized Chekhov. They took the train together to Moscow, and parted more than friends. For a fortnight Anton had written nothing.

The agent had found a new buyer for Melikhovo, a timber merchant called Mikhail Konshin, who would buy the estate in his wife's name, but was interested only in felling and selling Chekhov's forests. Konshin was to pay 23,000 roubles and 5000 for fittings. He had not sold his last estate, so the agreement was that he would pay 1000 roubles cash, give an IOU for 4000, and find the rest over the years. In their hurry, the Chekhovs ceded everything, but Konshin, like Marx, had fleeced Anton. The 10,000 roubles that Anton promised Masha as her share melted away. Anton banked the 5000 that Konshin eventually put down and let her draw 25 roubles a month interest – no more than her salary from the 'Dairy' school, or the allowance that Misha secretly made her.

Konshin moved into Melikhovo on 14 August and Masha went to join Anton in Moscow. Evgenia lived with Konshin until 20 August. In Masha's absence, Quinine, the dachshund bitch, had her eye ripped out by a farm dog and ran into Varenikov's yard, where she died in agony. Masha had gone back to pack the crockery. Breaking the news of Quinine's end, she told Anton: 'Not a lot of fun, darling! God grant we get out of here quickly. It has been raining ever since we came. The road is sheer horror. We are wet to the bone . . . Give my regards to your Knipper woman.' When the sale was over, Masha made her feelings plain to Misha:

> On Monday 6 September I am taking mother and the old Mariushka to the Crimea on the mail train . . . We sold Melikhovo, but how! . . . I am so fed up with Melikhovo that I agreed to anything . . . Anton didn't want to accept these terms. Perhaps Konshin is a crook, what can we do! . . . I don't think I shall have any money for a long time, which is why I turn to you. *Merci* I received the cheque, Anton forbade me to stop teaching, hinting that I shall have no private life, but I don't care. I shall spend a winter in Moscow and then see what happens . . . Anton was very ill when he came back from the Crimea – he had bad bronchitis, a high temperature and even some bleeding.[33]

On 25 August Anton finished the proofs of his collected *Plays* for Marx. He called his symptoms 'flu'. He was seen off from Moscow to Yalta by Olga Knipper, who was led away in tears and then comforted by Masha. Anton had gone to make the Yalta house habitable for his womenfolk.

SEVENTY

Uncle Vania *Triumphant*

September–November 1899

ANTON SPENT THE NIGHT of 27 August 1899 at his new house. Only the servant's quarters and kitchen wing were ready: walled in by packing cases, attended by Mustafa, he camped with a paraffin stove and two candlesticks. He brewed tea with water from his own well. He dined at the girls' school. Mustafa lugged trunks and boxes from cellars all round Yalta. Anton checked linen, chose wallpaper, urged the builders to sand the floors and install the water closet. He planted out Olga's gift, a 'Queen of the Night' cactus, which he called the 'Green Reptile'. He joined a consumers' union for groceries and claimed a 20 per cent discount on baths for members of the writers' union. He ordered grass seed for Küchük-Köy and hundreds of flowerpots. All the Marx money was spent: no more was payable until December. Konshin had not paid up. Anton borrowed 5000 roubles from Efim Konovitser, his lawyer. *Russian Thought* advanced 3000. 'We Chekhovs,' Misha told Masha, 'are bad savers.'

Nadia, the loveliest *Antonovka*, did not visit. Nadia's father, the archpriest, had quarrelled with Varvara Kharkeevich, the headmistress who was providing Anton's dinners, and Anton, in sympathy, ostracized both father and daughter. Anton's social conscience cost him much. When he found a bed for a sick teacher, *News of the Day* printed '*Chekhov's Colony*: in his new estate the writer is setting up a colony for village teachers of Serpukhov district, a cheap hotel for intellectual toilers.' Anton was flooded with appeals and, once the telephone was put in, he knew no peace. Although it linked him only to Yalta, telegrams often came just before dawn, when Moscow actors stopped celebrating. Anton ran, coughing, barefoot across unfinished floors, to answer the telephone.

On September 1899 Anton met the boat bringing Evgenia, Masha, Dr Kurkin and old Mariushka from Sevastopol, all prostrate with seasickness, Evgenia terrified of drowning. Mustafa climbed to the first-class deck to collect their luggage. A ship's officer, seeing a Tatar among the first-class passengers, struck him in the face. Mustafa bore the blow, then pointed to Anton, whose face was distorted with rage, and said: 'You haven't hit me, you've hit him.' The *Crimean Courier* reported the incident. Shortly afterwards Mustafa left Chekhov's service – either because of this outrage or because Evgenia did not want a Moslem in her house – and the Chekhovs hired Arseni Shcherbakov, who had worked in the Nikita Botanical Gardens and whose hobby was reading the *Lives of the Saints*. With Arseni, the house acquired its first pets, two tame cranes who danced after the gardener, and to whom old Mariushka became devoted.

The house was hardly fit to live in. Until October there were no internal doors: newspapers hung over the doorways. Visitors still gathered: the Chekhovs' old neighbour at Melikhovo, Prince Shakhovskoi, his marriage broken, clung to Anton, asking why families fell apart. Vania announced that he was coming for Christmas. Elena Shavrova, devastated by the death of her baby, sent her translation of Strindberg's *The Father* and came to Yalta.[34] In Moscow Ezhov insisted that Epifanov should die in Yalta, and that Chekhov should pay the sick man's fare.

Masha, on leave from teaching, toiled hard. She told Olga on 12 September:

> The house is charming, amazing views, but alas, far from finished. My room is not ready, nor is the lavatory, of course, there's dust, shavings, flies and a mass of workers banging away constantly. But the telephone works. Yalta ladies invite my brother to eat, but he is inexorable and prefers to dine at home. By evening people gather and carriages stand in a long line on our street, just like outside a theatre. We give visitors tea and jam, that's all. I'm quite good at being chambermaid. At 7 in the morning mother and I go to market for food. I don't get tired at all, the weather is enchanting, the air ravishing, my suitors delightful! Yesterday Prince Shakhovskoi sent me an enormous basket of fruit and roses.

Shakhovskoi took back to Moscow a pair of cuff links depicting two birds, one melancholy, one coquettish, for Olga Knipper, and Anton's cassowary blanket, which had moulted: this he handed to Anton's in-law Petrov at Muir and Mirrielees.

In the country Stanislavsky devised the staging of *Uncle Vania*, while in Moscow Nemirovich-Danchenko struggled to interpret the text; privately, he expressed to friends the same reservations as the Imperial Theatre Committee. Nemirovich-Danchenko spent days drilling Olga Knipper, who dithered: was the Professor's wife Elena wanton or idle? As Nemirovich-Danchenko, fearless of Suvorin's critics, wanted to take *Uncle Vania* to Petersburg, too, into enemy territory, Anton withdrew the permission he had given for *Uncle Vania* to be staged by others there.

Just as Nemirovich-Danchenko wanted a monopoly of Anton's plays, so Olga was seeking a monopoly of Anton's love life. One by one, she got to know his women friends. She met Lika the day after parting with Anton. Kundasova could be ignored. On 21 September Olga Knipper told Anton:

> She [*Kundasova*] stood in the living room, saying she was paralysed, that she had forgotten where she was. Then she recovered; we chatted, had tea and lemon, and rye porridge. She was so elegant, sheer charm. But, you know, it was painful to look at her – she has been so knocked about by life she needs peace and affection so badly.[35]

On 29 September 1899 the Moscow Arts Theatre opened its new season with *Uncle Vania*, A. K. Tolstoy's *The Death of Ivan the Terrible* and Gerhart Hauptmann's *Lonely People*. Anton sent the company a telegram: 'we shall work mindfully, cheerfully, tirelessly, unanimously.' The theatre appointed him 'inspector of actresses'. Clouds were gathering, however, over Nemirovich-Danchenko and Stanislavsky. Their patron Morozov was charged with fraud. *Ivan the Terrible* was coolly received. Olga wrote to Anton: 'Nobody is delighted by the Terrible's acting. You rightly distrusted Stanislavsky playing Ivan . . . What a night poor Stanislavsky is having today. The trouble is that audiences don't like him as an actor . . .'[36] Chekhov and Hauptmann, in his most Chekhovian play, *Lonely People*, were the last hope. Nemirovich-Danchenko and Olga both urged Anton to write them a third play.

Anton sent a jewel box instead. His mind plotted a garden, not a play, and his creativity was still dissipated revising early work for Adolf Marx. Never had he felt so detached from writing, or so absorbed in horticulture. He tore himself away from the garden only once in

October, to show Evgenia Küchük-Köy. The mountain road shook her and Anton resolved that this summer residence would have to be sold. The Autka house was becoming habitable, Anton's study now had a desk and a door, and the Chekhovs had hired a maid, Marfa Motsnaia, for 8 roubles a month. Masha told Misha:

> Everyone now has their own room, we are sorting ourselves out, there is very little furniture. Anton's study and bedroom have turned out pretty well, we now have an upright piano. There is masses of cleaning – lime everywhere, impossible to wash off, everything covered in dust ... I have to leave my Moscow flat and look for a little one, cheaper, of course – those are my orders. To move to Yalta for good, before I have a job in the Yalta school, is something Anton finds unsuitable for me, and that's it.

Masha rebelliously dreamed 'of getting some money and living as freely as I can'. Konshin, however, still failed to pay what he owed for Melikhovo.

Anton's health succumbed to an exceptionally wet autumn. He talked again of surgery for hæmorrhoids; his intestines lost in a day's diarrhœa a month's painstakingly gained weight. He feared loneliness, telling a colleague, Dr Rossolimo, 'without letters one could hang oneself, learn to drink bad Crimean wine and couple with an ugly, stupid woman'. Rumours that Anton was about to marry had fed Petersburg and Moscow gossip for years. Now the gossip became warmer. Aleksandr asked first, on 11 October 1899, 'Petersburg is persistently marrying you off to two actresses, what shall I tell them?' (The second, Olga Knipper's 'shadow', was the stunningly beautiful Maria Andreeva.) Rumours even reached Nizhni Novgorod. Gorky, still a happily married man, told Anton: 'It's said you are marrying an actress with a foreign surname ... if it's true, I'm glad.'

After four dress rehearsals, *Uncle Vania* was performed for the first time in Moscow on 26 October 1899, two years after it had been published. Masha arrived in Moscow from Yalta too late for the triumph. Only Nemirovich-Danchenko and Olga were at first unhappy with the play: Nemirovich-Danchenko had removed forty of the fifty pauses Chekhov had specified; Olga blamed Stanislavsky for making her act Elena as highly sexed. Nemirovich-Danchenko had made Stanislavsky 'go through [his] part literally like a pupil in drama school'.

(Having seen Stanislavsky act Trigorin, Anton could not believe he could be lecherous enough as Dr Astrov: 'Inject some testosterone into him,' he had advised Nemirovich-Danchenko.) The second performance on 29 October, at which Masha accepted the author's acclaim by proxy, was even more triumphant: the theatre and Chekhov's fame were safe. There were to be twenty-five performances of *Uncle Vania* this season, and *The Seagull* would be played once a fortnight: Anton's share of the earnings, with full houses, would be some 3000 roubles. The theatre, Nemirovich-Danchenko announced, stood, like the world in Russian folk myth, on three whales: A. K. Tolstoy, Hauptmann and Chekhov.

The Knippers and Chekhovs drew closer. Masha reported on 5 November: 'Knipper and I meet very often, I've dined several times at her home and now know her Mama, i.e. your mother-in-law, and a drinking aunt.' Olga befriended Masha, as the gateway to intimacy with Anton. Masha praised her: 'What a fine person she is, I am more sure every day. A very hard worker and, I think, extremely talented.' Olga spent nights with Masha, who lived near the theatre, though the flat was in chaos. (The servant girl had given birth to a baby daughter.) In the same letter, Masha revelled in her new life, telling Anton: 'With the girls we have a servant, a French teacher, the German teacher often calls, the class assistants keep visiting, the headmistress, Masha and her baby which squeals and Olga Knipper's laughter – just imagine!'

Both Anton and Masha touched on an impediment to the Knipper-Chekhov alliance: Olga's relations with Vladimir Nemirovich-Danchenko were more than professional. A charismatic teacher, he held her in thrall, despite her mother's opposition. In Russian theatres a leading actress tended to be the director's mistress. There was no break in the liaison between Knipper and Nemirovich-Danchenko, even when Olga and Anton behaved as if they were betrothed (not that Nemirovich-Danchenko showed any jealousy).[37] Conversely, Anton and Nemirovich's wife 'Kitten', whom Olga detested, were old friends.[38] On 5 November Masha offered to help Anton: 'Nemirovich . . . came to see me, stayed for a long time, we chatted a lot, and it occurred to me that I might lure him away from Knipper.'

Unlike Olga, Anton had no other irons in the fire. Although Lika Mizinova was back in Moscow and lonely, Anton did not write to her, and Masha repelled Lika's attempts to join the theatrical throng. Anton thought only of Olga Knipper and he told Masha forlornly on 11 November, 'I envy Nemirovich, I have no doubt that he enjoys success with a certain person.' Anton felt, he said, like the piano: neither it nor he was played on. At Autka he planted cypresses, and put up barbed wire between himself and the Tatar cemetery. In the Indian summer, his self-esteem boosted, he felt well. He decided to sell Küchük–Köy and buy a cottage and a few acres of rocky coast at Gurzuf nearby, for swimming. Nemirovich-Danchenko talked of bringing the Moscow Arts Theatre to Yalta so that Anton might see *Uncle Vania* performed.

Anton had given Marx copies of his works: now only proofs would arrive to plague him. That autumn inspiration came back. For *Russian Thought* he wrote his archetypical Yalta work, 'The Lady with the Little Dog': a cynical adulterer, Gurov, on holiday in Yalta, seduces the unhappily married Anna, only to find her image so haunting that he travels to the provincial town where she is stifling and turns an affair into an intractable involvement. Just as the reader wonders how it can end, the author talks of new beginnings and ends the narrative. 'The Lady with the Little Dog' seems to defend adultery and to explode Tolstoy's *Anna Karenina*: of all Chekhov's works it upset Tolstoy most. Gurov is a very ambiguous hero: he is Don Juan in love. We first meet him classifying women as predators or victims or, with Nietzschean scorn, as a lower race: has he in the end fallen in love, or have his first grey hairs frightened him? The only unambiguous elements are the mountains and sea, against which what 'we do or think when we forget the higher purpose of existence' is ephemeral. The story's empathy with adulterers awoke Chekhov's readers. 'The Lady with the Little Dog' showed them that, despite the rumours of Chekhov's moribund state, he had something new to say.

On 24 November 1899 Anton finally confirmed to Nemirovich-Danchenko that he was mulling over a new play. 'I have a plot for *Three Sisters*,' he wrote, but would not start it until he had finished 'The Lady with a Little Dog' and another story. Before winter set in, he planted a lemon tree from Sukhum, oleanders and camellias. A stray puppy slept under the olive tree and was adopted by the Chekhovs. Stray cats in search of a home, however, were mercilessly shot – even though Aleksandr in Petersburg now edited the *Journal of the*

Society for the Protection of Animals. November's winds ripped the leaves off the magnolias and kept Anton indoors. He watched flames fan across the mountain scrub, towards his uninsured property. It was cold: he slept in a hat and slippers under two eiderdowns, with the shutters closed. He struggled with a new story, and made notes for *Three Sisters,* his most complex and subtle play to date. He wrote few letters; even Olga Knipper received none that November. Anton's brothers were resentful. Misha complained to Masha:

> Mother is somewhere at the edge of the world, way over the mountains, I am in the far north, you are neither here nor there . . . Anton has become proud . . . This year he gave me just one minute of his time, in an express railway carriage . . . How has the money been spent this year: 25,000 from Marx, 5000 from Konshin, 3000 from *The Seagull* and *Uncle Vania?* If the house and estate cost 25,000, then, by my reckoning, 8000 has gone missing.

Anton had over 9000 roubles in his Yalta Mutual Credit passbook.

His spirits fell when he left the house on 20 November. Epifanov, a colleague from his freelance days, was in a hospice in Yalta. Anton found him lying in filth on a straw mattress. Epifanov asked for apple fudge. Anton brought him a piece. The dying man's face lit up; he hissed, 'That's the real thing!' In a day or two Epifanov was dead. Anton's notebooks brood on mortality and Yalta: 'aristocrats, commoners, the same revolting death'. He told Gorky: 'I am overwhelmed by consumptive paupers . . . they upset my sated and warm peace. We've decided to build a sanatorium.' He began an appeal for the penniless incurable intellectuals who were flocking to Yalta. Undoubtedly the example set by Chekhov was as great a lure for the sick as the reputedly therapeutic climate of the Crimean coast.

SEVENTY-ONE

'In the Ravine'

November 1899–February 1900

IN NOVEMBER 1899 Anton was composing 'In the Ravine'. It opens with an anecdote that Bunin had told him, of a deacon who ate all the caviare at a funeral. It then moves to sombre memories of Meli-kovo, and especially the Tolokonnikovs, the ruthless peasant-manufacturers. A novel in miniature, giving the lie to any criticism that Chekhov's plots lack action, 'In the Ravine' maps the collapse of the Khriumin family: a woman scalds to death her sister-in-law's baby, and drives her father-in-law into beggary. The 'ravine' is both a moral and a physical abyss: only the hills overlooking the ravine, where the victims wander and keep their faith, rise above the gloom. (At this time Anton was himself literally in a ravine, for the engineers were raising the Autka road by fifteen feet, so that 'every Amazon riding past can see what is happening in our yard'.)

He was distressed by death all round. On 27 December he told Prince Shakhovskoi: 'I am terribly bored and lonely because of an involuntarily virtuous life. I just drink a bit of wine.' A damp cold winter worsened his health. The Dutch stoves that the architect had installed worked badly: he asked Masha to send paraffin stoves. Evgenia and Mariushka found cooking an invalid's diet beyond them. Anton's 'catarrh' grew so recalcitrant, meanwhile, that he gave himself strong enemas. He had pleurisy and wore a compress over his left collarbone. His exercise was catching the mice that plagued the house (for cats now avoided his territory) in a humane trap on a bookcase and carrying them by the tail for release in the Tatar cemetery. The stray dog now sheltered on shavings in a shed and was named Kashtanka.

Yalta speculated about the source of 'The Lady with the Little Dog'. When the weather cleared, women, originals or copies, appeared on the promenade with Pomeranians on leads. In Moscow Anton was talked of even more. *Uncle Vania* was seen by members of the Tsar's family and by the Procurator of the Holy Synod, Konstantin Pobedonostsev, the Savonarola of Tsarism. Tolstoy noted in his diary: 'outraged'. He told Nemirovich-Danchenko that Telegin's guitar and the cricket chirruping (which the actor Vishnevsky had spent a month learning from a cricket in the Sandunov public baths) were the only good things. He told the actors that Astrov and Vania should marry peasant girls and leave the Professor's wife alone.

Masha was again in a whirl, enjoying the success of *Uncle Vania* and studying three times a week at an art school set up by Khotiaintseva. She treated the exhaustion and headaches of her new life with injections of arsenic in her back. She taught at school; she sued Konshin, the purchaser of Melikhovo. She dined with Olga Knipper, Prince Shakhovskoi and his new love. 'Alas, the poor Princess! I have learnt to chat a lot and therefore feel fine in society . . . something like a *salon* has come of it,' she told Anton. She was also friendly with Olga's rival, Maria Andreeva, whom Anton found attractive. Aleksandra Khotiaintseva, Lika Mizinova, Dunia Konovitser and Maria Drozdova all gathered around Masha and Olga. Their pretext was that they were collecting money, by raffles and subscriptions, for Anton's projected sanatorium; they hoped, in vain, to be invited to Yalta.

There were violent winter storms. Neither the telegraph nor the mail boat could reach Yalta, and Olga's letters petered out. Anton felt isolated. Some of the *Antonovkas* reappeared, including Nadia Ternovskaia, who had been previously out of favour: Evgenia approved of her as a bride for Anton, even if she had no dowry. News of Nadia reached Knipper: on 19 January 1900 she wrote: 'Masha tells me that you're marrying a priest's daughter. I could come and admire your conjugal happiness and, while I'm there, disturb it a bit. We had an agreement – remember the Kök–Köz valley.' A month later Knipper was still joking: 'Tell your priest's daughter that she can hold you in her embrace since "that nasty woman" won't be coming until early spring.'

Exhausted by her roles in the Hauptmann play and in *Uncle Vania*, Olga bore her separation from Anton calmly. Anton was less calm about her liaison with Nemirovich-Danchenko. Masha hinted on the eve of his fortieth birthday: 'I want you to marry quickly, to take a clever, sensible girl, even without a dowry . . . I saw Nemirovich . . . wearing a coat with moiré silk lapels.' Anton's next letter to Olga asked: 'Have you been carried away by the moiré silk lapels? It's all the fault of the moiré silk coat lapels.' Nemirovich-Danchenko told Olga, when she urged him to show Anton the theatre in Yalta, 'To the director you are valuable, to the author invaluable.' Maria Drozdova, still Masha's closest friend, met Olga, and a fortnight later wrote to Anton:

> Olga Knipper loves Nemirovich very much and doesn't love me at all . . . the great actress to judge by these photographs has put on weight and is better looking. I envy Nemirovich . . . You are seriously in love with Knipper and want to go abroad, I think that's what you mustn't do.

Anton joked that Olga's photo made her look like 'a Jewess . . . secretly studying dentistry, with a fiancé in Mogiliov' and talked of summer abroad on his own. Olga rose to the bait on 5 February: 'That's unbelievably cruel . . . we shall be together in summer. Yes, yes, won't we, won't we?' Masha saw through Anton's stratagem: 'You try to scare us with your departures . . . some people get desperate when they hear you mean to go away.'

The beauty and the ministrations of the *Antonovkas* left Anton unmoved. In February 1900 Masha took Lika to *The Seagull*. Masha told Anton: 'She wept in the theatre, I suppose [*in Pushkin's words*] "memories unrolled before her their long scroll".' At the Moscow Arts Theatre, Lika fell for Aleksandr Sanin-Schoenberg, an officer turned stage director. She and Anton never spoke or wrote to each other again, even though Lika continued to meet Masha, Vania and Misha.

Melikhovo would not fade away. Three quarrelsome women teachers used Anton as their arbiter; he implored Serpukhov to relieve him of all civic duties. When Misha wondered if Masha missed the estate, as Evgenia missed her chickens and calves, Masha responded:

> The buyer came, I handed the lot to him and we left for Moscow . . . To this day I have been carefree and cheerful because I haven't got Melikhovo and God grant I shouldn't have, nor any unpleasant worries. I live surrounded by respect – thanks to our brother. I have lots of friends.

Masha reached Yalta on 20 December and ended Anton's isolation. She took a cab to the house, for Anton was too ill to meet her, and forbade Evgenia to wait in the rain. After Masha came Levitan. Anton remarked how he missed Russian countryside, so Levitan asked Masha for cardboard and painted haystacks in the moonlight for Anton's fireplace. Anton's New Year festivities were muted. That Christmas Grigorovich died. Although they had drifted apart, Grigorovich still seemed to Anton to be the most influential of the Grand Old Men to have recognized his genius. Khudekov of *The Petersburg Newspaper* reported to Anton: 'He talked a lot about you; how deeply he felt for the "involuntary exile" doomed to live far from friends in boring, boring Yalta.' Anton had also drifted away from the Petersburg circles to which Grigorovich's notice had first given him access. After signing his contract with Marx and receiving Suvorin's last payments, Anton barely wrote to the Suvorin household, even though Emilie Bijon reproached him,[39] and Nastia Suvorina, on the verge of engagement, sent outrageously flirting letters.[40] Suvorin had lost Anton, but was gaining Misha, who, bored in Iaroslavl, on bad terms with his superiors, dreamed of writing for *New Times*. Suvorin tried to use the younger brother to lure the elder back. Misha wrote to Anton on 22 January 1900:

> Both, he and she, greeted me like a relative, poured out their souls to me for two whole evenings . . . The old man with tears in his eyes, Anna with burning cheeks, assured me how upset they were that relations between you and them had broken down. They love you very much. 'Misha, dear boy, I know why it's happened. Antosha would not forgive my paper its policies, that's it . . .' They are deeply aggrieved that you sold your works to Marx, not Suvorin. Anna blames her husband entirely . . . 'Aliosha, you know Anton. He's a gifted, decisive, bold man. One day he's here, the next he's off to Sakhalin.' . . . Suvorin has asked me to persuade you to buy your works back from Marx . . . Suvorin went on, 'I loved Anton terribly much, and still do. You know, he made me younger. I have never been so frank to anyone in my life as I have with Anton . . . I'd gladly marry Nastia to him.'[41]

Anton refuted Suvorin's version. 'I write for your eyes alone,' he replied to Misha, 'since you've been bewitched.' Suvorin's efforts nevertheless won over Misha, who became, a year later, his employee.

In the New Year Anton was awarded the Order of Stanislav 3rd grade 'for services to education'. (It was awarded to half the teachers in Taganrog *gimnazia*.) Anton was also elected to the writer's section of the Academy. Honorary academicians had no salary, but they were exempt from arrest, censorship and customs inspections (and also from Academy prizes). Chekhov nominated a man he disliked, the critic Mikhailovsky, and a man he pitied, Kazimir Barantsevich, to be fellow academicians. Becoming *Academicus* made him the butt of his friends and the object of begging letters. His maid's uncle called him 'your excellency'.

Levitan, close to death, was struck by Anton's gloom. 'Your fever is a fever of self-infatuation – your chronic disease . . . your Achilles heel,' he wrote on 7 February. When he saw *Uncle Vania* in December, he liked best the bit 'where the doctor kisses Knipper'. On 16 February he revived old amorous rivalries: 'I went to see Masha and saw my darling Knipper. I begin to fancy her more and more: I notice an inevitable cooling towards the honorary academician.'

'In the Ravine', published in *Life*, allied Chekhov with men whom Suvorin thought criminal: radical Marxists like Gorky and Posse, the editor of *Life*, who were often under arrest or police supervision. Karl Marx, as much as Adolf Marx, cut Anton off from Suvorin. Though their affection never died, Chekhov warned Misha, and others, against Suvorin as the owner of *New Times*. Posse had printed 'In the Ravine' 'in an orgy of misprints', but Anton joined the radicals nevertheless. The story's originals were, Anton asserted, even worse than his characters, but in his view: 'drunken syphilitic children are not material for art'.

Dr Altshuller examined Anton at the end of February 1900 and reported that his left lung was worse, though his right lung was clear. Spring came early in Yalta. Some mornings Anton did not cough. The old women, Evgenia and Mariushka, frightened of responsibility when Masha was away, forgot their giddiness and pains. Chekhov's new prose, ending a year of silence, was widely lauded. Anton rested. *Three Sisters* was still only an idea.

In mid February the camellias blossomed after ten degrees of frost. Anton proudly announced: 'I could have been a gardener'. He longed for the coming of the mountain to Mahomet, when Nemirovich-Danchenko, Olga and the theatre's elite would arrive to perform in the Crimea. Ever since Christmas he had asked Masha to persuade Olga to spend the summer in Yalta. They had eaten pancakes together at Shrovetide, first at Masha's and then at Vania's, and were now on *ty* terms. Masha evidently felt equal to the sophisticated Olga and able to befriend and manage her, as she had done with Dunia Efros, Olga Kundasova and Lika Mizinova, on her brother's behalf. Masha and Olga declared themselves inseparable. Anton could be sure that if one came to Yalta, the other would too.

SEVENTY-TWO

Olga in Yalta
March–July 1900

FOR ANTON, Andrei Vishnevsky was the first herald of spring in Yalta. He arrived to check the ramshackle theatre and the electric lighting that would be its undoing. Vishnevsky maddened Anton by harking back to school days and by making him read the cues for his Dr Dorn and Uncle Vania. Chekhov's revenge was gentle: he created the good-natured fool in *Three Sisters*, Kulygin, not just for, but out of, Vishnevsky himself. All five performances (a Hauptmann play, as well as their Chekhov repertoire) planned by the Moscow Arts theatre for Yalta were sold out: even the Crimean Karaims (an indigenous Judaic sect) were coming. At Anton's request, there would be no cast list and no individual curtain calls. Rarely had he anticipated so intensely a public event, but all he had to do in practical terms was to meet the government electrician at the theatre and persuade the Yalta magistrate that Hauptmann's *Lonely People* had been passed by the censor.

The Chekhovs had money, for the Society of Dramatists and Composers sent royalties of 1159 roubles for the quarter. A migration to the Crimea began. Cousin Georgi was coming from Taganrog. Gorky bought thirty tickets for the Yalta performances. Masha was to come in the sixth week of Lent and bring Olga: she sent ahead pillows, crockery and bedsteads. Evgenia expected a flood of visitors. On 12 March Georgi arrived to stay with Anton; Gorky (followed by a police spy) came to Yalta on the 16th; on the 25th a party of Moscow doctors arrived to witness their colleague's apotheosis.

Anton put his foot down. He asked Olga not to bring Vishnevsky when she came: 'or he'll always be under our feet and won't let us say a word, and he'll give us no peace, since he'll be reciting *Uncle Vania* all the time.' Anton told Sergeenko that he could not have him to stay, and recommended a distant resort. At the end of March an express train reached Sevastopol with three wagons full of theatre sets. This cost 1300 roubles, to be defrayed, as Nemirovich-Danchenko reminded Anton, by putting on, with Anton's permission, *Uncle Vania* in Petersburg. On 2 April Masha and Knipper arrived.[42] Olga had a room next to Masha's, downstairs. Anton slept upstairs. The stairs creaked loudly and Evgenia slept lightly, so night-time visits between Olga and Anton were difficult. Sheltering an actress, let alone one who visited her son's bedroom, was enough to stretch Evgenia's tolerance.

On 7 April the theatre company arrived in Sevastopol for the start of their Crimean tour. They brought a new Nina for *The Seagull*: Maria Andreeva. The next day Anton's hæmorrhoids bled: he and Olga put off joining the actors until Easter Sunday, the 9th. In Sevastopol Anton, for the first time, saw *Uncle Vania* performed and endured the roar when the audience spotted the author. He walked next day over the ruins of ancient Chersonesus and then returned to see Olga as a high-minded seductress in Hauptmann's *Lonely People*. Not Olga's best role, it moved Lazarevsky, a young poet who had begun to pester Anton, to behave very tactlessly: 'I found the actress Knipper so loathsome that if I'd met her in real life she'd have been just as loathsome. I shared this opinion with Chekhov.'[43]

On 13 April, a day ahead of the theatre, Olga and Chekhov left Vitzel's hotel in Sevastopol for Yalta. When Stanislavsky arrived there, he found Anton warming himself in the sun, watching the sets being unloaded. For ten days the Chekhovs were besieged by actors and writers. Anton saw both his plays performed, a medley from his stories, and scenes from other productions. He withstood ovations. Gorky's *Song of the Hawk* also roused the audience. Anton bore fame politely, and gave Nemirovich-Danchenko a gold medallion shaped like a book. It was inscribed 'You gave my Seagull life'. On 24 April there was a farewell lunch, and the company, with Olga, sailed over rough seas back to Sevastopol, leaving behind in Anton's study three palm branches wrapped in red moiré ribbon 'to A. P. Chekhov, the profound interpreter of Russian reality', and in Anton's garden the swing and the bench on which Olga had lounged as Elena in Act 1 of *Uncle Vania*. Despite her commitment at Mrs Rzhevskaia's school, Masha stayed on a week in Yalta. She went back to Moscow for the school examinations, but promised to return by mid May.

Olga also promised to return, if Anton did not run away to Paris.

She smoothed her path with Evgenia: 'We brought such disorder into your home that we really are ashamed to think of it. You are probably resting now and getting back to normal after our invasion. Thank you for everything, everything.' Olga and Anton were open about their intimacy. In Iaroslavl Misha sounded out Masha: 'Here there are rumours are that Anton is getting married. I nearly believed them. Especially when there was talk of a young lady with a German surname. I remembered you once mentioning a Knipper.' Masha accepted Knipper as a friend and as Anton's mistress, but the prospect of a sister-in-law, of a power in the household, disturbed her profoundly. In her letters to Olga 'darling Olechka' alternates with 'vile German' and 'how piggish of you'. (Half jocular abuse was part of Masha's epistolary style – a tone which Lika also adopted but which Olga, either frankly angry or unequivocally intimate, could never catch or get used to.)

Despite Evgenia's horror of being alone, Anton left for Moscow four days after his sister. He would not stay in his sister's apartment, but chose the Hotel Dresden which had a lift and a room by a W.C. In that hotel room he and Olga met, unobserved by anyone who mattered. On arriving Anton wired Suvorin, who with the Dauphin took the night train to Moscow. On 13 May, Masha left Moscow to be with her mother. Chekhov told Suvorin how Stanislavsky bored him. Suvorin added:

> I talked about the sale of his works to Marx. He had only 25,000 roubles left. 'Isn't it bad for you to have sold your works?' – 'Of course it is. I don't feel like writing.' – 'You ought to buy them back,' I told him. 'I've got to wait two years or so,' he said, 'I don't care much about property.' We took a cab to the cemetery. We went to see his father's grave. We searched for a long time. In the end I found it . . . He saw me off to the train. He is better. He had just one bleed, a small one, in winter . . . I feel fine with Chekhov. I am 26 years older than him. We met in 1886. 'I was young then,' I said. 'But you were still 26 years older.'

Anton called on the dying Levitan. Again, despite his affair with her daughters, Levitan was being nursed by Anna Turchaninova. His temperature climbed to 41°C. Turchaninova wrote: 'Horror is creeping in. I can't believe I shan't get him through.'[44] When Anton left for Yalta after just nine days in Moscow, Olga asked in her next letter:

'You left yesterday horribly upset, dear writer. Why?' Anton told her that he had been tormented by a headache and fever which had forced him to leave Moscow.

In his absence Evgenia had grumbled: her teeth needed attention; Anton had not left enough money; she was afraid. For Misha his abandoned mother was reason enough to come to Yalta. Within a week Anton, despite ill health, was travelling again. On 29 May Masha explained to Olga, with a touch of *Schadenfreude* towards the latter:

> Gather your things and come and see us and don't argue! . . . yesterday we saw Antosha off to the Caucasus. He went off in the company of Dr Sredin, Gorky, Dr Aleksin and Vasnetsov [*an artist*]. They devised this journey quickly and got moving quickly. Their route is: Novorossiisk, Vladikavkaz, the Georgian Military Highway, Tiflis, Batum and back to Yalta. The main reason Anton left was because relatives – Misha, his wife, the child and a nanny – descended, quite unexpectedly, without warning. Noisy and boring. Any day Vania is coming, also with family . . . The writer is back on 8 June. You probably won't meet.

Gorky had got together this party: two doctors, three consumptives and a painter. Perhaps Anton and Olga nevertheless intended to meet on this tour of the Caucasus, for, as Anton's party set out, Olga and her mother were in Vladikavkaz and meant to cross the Caucasus over the Military Highway before they rested in the mountain resort of Borjomi. Rain washed the roads away and made a rendezvous at this point impossible. At Tiflis a newspaper reported that Chekhov, Gorky and Vasnetsov were staying a week in the Northern Furnished Rooms. Anton did not know that Olga was also in Tiflis, but Olga's sister-in-law read the papers and telephoned Anton, who at first snubbed her as an intrusive fan.[45] Anton and Olga met when his party and hers left Tiflis across central Georgia by train, separating after a few hours; Olga and her mother took the branch line up to Borjomi.

Masha knew nothing of this: on 12 June she was writing to Knipper: 'If you don't come in four days then everything is finished between us and we don't know each other any more. Today we are seeing off Misha and his family. It was sad, I had got used to them.' Anton contrived to miss his brother and niece by one day. Gorky and his family left a few days later. Olga arrived on 23 June.

Six happy weeks followed, though little is known of them. Chekhov did little but work slowly at *Three Sisters*. There were a few clouds: Maria Andreeva had arrived before Olga, and was staying in a Yalta hotel. Anton had not yet shaken off the poet Lazarevsky, who spotted Anton having tea with Masha and Olga:

> Chekhov sat behind Knipper and peered out from there. He was dressed, unlike Gorky, very fastidiously. Gold cuff links, yellow shoes, a jacket, coat, all most elegant. I went over to Andreeva. Chekhov has a more than ordinary liking for her.

Evgenia and Masha left Autka for the cottage by the sea at Gurzuf. Anton and Olga were alone in the house, recalling Chekhov's entry at that time in the notebooks which he sporadically kept, that to keep visitors away he should keep a French woman in his house and pretend she was his concubine. They no longer feared the creaking stairs that disturbed Evgenia or Masha, when Olga crept with pillow and candle to Anton's room, or when she visited him at dawn after a swim in the sea. (She called herself an 'otter'.)

Supplicants and visitors were ignored, except for the teenager, Olga Vasilieva, whom Anton had taken pity on in Nice and who had embarked on the translation of his works into English. Iurasov, the consul at Menton, begged Anton to humour her: 'Olga Vasilieva loves you very much and your word is law to her ... She doesn't know what to do with her fortune – and she has nobody to lean on. She is an unhappy creature, pathetic and worthy of compassion.'[46]

Vasilieva sent Anton an Oriental rug and asked which English journals might print her translations.[47] Anton replied 'I am of so little interest to the English public that I don't care in the least.'

On 22 July Levitan died. Everyone Levitan had known received a scrap of paper with the line: 'Burn all letters when you hear of my death.'[48] Masha lovingly did as Levitan asked; Anton did not.

A different perturbation spoilt the end of Olga's stay. Early in August a letter arrived from the first Seagull, Vera Komissarzhevskaia: 'I've come to Yalta for a few days, I'm at Massandra and should be very sad not to see you, if only for a minute.'[49] Olga felt that it was the author, not his new play, that Komissarzhevskaia sought. On 3 August Chekhov took his original Seagull to his coastal cottage at Gurzuf, but she won neither the right to stage the new play, nor the author's love – just a photograph inscribed 'on a stormy day when the sea roared, from quiet Anton Chekhov.' Two days later, Anton sailed with Olga to Sevastopol, where they stayed at a hotel. We can only guess why Olga wept on the train about 'all that I went through in your house'. Was it Evgenia's disapproval or Komissarzhevskaia's arrival? Back in Yalta, Anton saw nobody. Komissarzhevskaia wired from Gurzuf: 'I've waited two days. Coming by boat to Yalta tomorrow. Upset by your lack of intuition.' They met. Komissarzhev-skaia, after a rough sea voyage, complained a week later:

> I thought that when I saw you I'd flood you with questions and say something to you in exchange . . . You know it's awfully strange but I felt sorry for you for a time . . . sorry, sorry to the point of sadness. And there was something elusive in you all the time, which I don't trust.

Despite an affectionate letter from Anton, Olga still felt 'thrown overboard', but told Masha: 'We parted tenderly. He was very emotional; I was too, I howled.'[50] Their future seemed uncertain. Vania assured Olga that Anton would winter in Moscow. Olga, however, told Masha: 'Odd of you to ask what your brother and I have decided? As if one could decide anything with him. I don't know myself and it makes me suffer.'

Stanislavsky and Nemirovich-Danchenko hoped to see Olga and Anton more closely united. They wanted Anton Chekhov bound to their theatre. Stanislavsky wrote to Nemirovich-Danchenko on 8 August:

> Yesterday I wrung it out of Chekhov: he's off tomorrow to Gurzuf to write, and a week later will come to Alupka to read what he has written . . . A play set among the military with four young female roles. top secret.[51]

Nemirovich-Danchenko knew something more binding, apparently before Olga, let alone Anton, told anybody else. He told Stanislavsky, 'The business of Knipper's marriage to Anton is settled.'[52] As he worked on *Three Sisters*, Chekhov was unwittingly writing his marriage contract to both a theatre and an actress.

SEVENTY-THREE

Three Sisters

August–November 1900

In fine August sunshine Anton stayed behind in Yalta while Olga went to Moscow. Anton had to get *Three Sisters* onto paper, even though the play had already been worked out in his mind. The subject had deep personal reverberations for Anton: after the Golden, Markova, Ianova, Lintvariova and Shavrova sisters, Chekhov must have felt 'three sisters' to be the fairy-tale motif of his life.

There was also an English inspiration. In 1896 Anton had sent to Taganrog library a biography of the Brontë sisters: three talented, unhappy girls, stranded in Yorkshire; a despotic father; a mother they do not recall; a brother, once their idol, now a drunken ne'er-do-well. Chekhov's Prozorova sisters have much in common with the Brontës. *The Geisha*, a Sidney Jones operetta popular in Moscow in 1899, in which three English officers woo three geishas, also underlies *Three Sisters*. Memories, too, shaped the play: the officers with whom Anton was friendly at Voskresensk in 1884; a wait in Perm in the Urals, on the way to Sakhalin. Like 'The Lady with the Little Dog', the play shows marriage as tyranny: the tensions between the real Olga and Masha are anticipated in the fate of the gentle sisters, forced by their sister-in-law's pregnancies, room by room, out of their house. In this cruellest of Chekhov plays the sisters do not deserve their fate: comedy is incidental. Only the Moscow Arts Theatre could realize the polyphony of *Three Sisters*, where two or three conversations are heard simultaneously, or where nonverbal effects – the clock and the camera, the fire, the trees in the garden and the songs and music – mark the progression of time as strongly as the words of the text.

It was hard to write a play. Vania's wife and son were staying. Varvara Kharkeevich brought two girls, and 'Kitten' Nemirovich-Danchenko, bored without her husband, called to talk nonsense. Anton fled to his bedroom, then moved out to Gurzuf, but it was all in vain, for 'some snout crawls in', he complained to Olga. He compiled hate lists: 'a playful Jew, a learned Ukrainian and a drunken German'; ladies who asked for a summary of Herbert Spencer. The Stanislavskys came and would not go; Anton led them off to Varvara Kharkeevich to hear a Hungarian playing the harp.

Stanislavsky was, he admitted, 'raping creativity'. Anton had to be made to finish *Three Sisters* before the autumn. Anton procrastinated: would next year not be soon enough? Olga wanted the author as well as the play in Moscow. Could he not write it in the Hotel Dresden? It would be, Olga lamented, 'too cruel to separate all winter' and not spend the autumn together. Like Komissarzhevskaia, she wanted intimate discussion: 'we have talked so little and so vaguely', but Anton loathed 'a conversation with serious faces'. She cajoled him: 'Do you remember seeing me onto the stairs and the stairs squeaking so treacherously? I loved all that so awfully.' She fussed over him. Who was cleaning his study and ironing his shirts? 'You're not quarrelling with your mother? And you're being kind to Masha?' she wrote on 16 August. She sent him another 'Green Reptile'. She and other actors kept up pressure on their author: they were midwives to *Three Sisters* as much as Nemirovich-Danchenko and Stanislavsky, but the midwives could not make the birth of the play any less painful.

Stanislavsky and Nemirovich-Danchenko, meanwhile, held gruelling rehearsals for Ostrovsky's *Snow Maiden*. Moscow swallowed Olga's time. *Lonely People* opened on 25 September. Uncle Sasha confided in his niece: alcohol, debauchery and loneliness had brought him to the verge of suicide: he wanted her to consult Anton about him. On 19 August 1900 Masha left for Moscow, to sell Küchük-Köy for cash. (Konshin had defaulted altogether on Melikhovo and was secretly trying to sell the estate.) Olga was to help Masha find new quarters; they spent their spare time together and slept at each other's apartments, attended assiduously by Vishnevsky. Round them gathered Anton's friends: Lika, Kundasova ('turned into a shadow,' said Masha), Bunin, Gorky, and a new acolyte, the Tolstoyan sailor-turned-gardener Sulerzhitsky. Anton was the magnet that held these disparate people together.

As summer ended, one tame crane flew away and the other, now blind in one eye, hopped dejectedly after the gardener. The maid Marfa Motsnaia was recalled to Livadia by her uncle. Even so Anton was not as isolated as he wanted to be. He asked Masha to have Evgenia with her in Moscow in the autumn. Masha resisted:

> If you only knew what a hard time I had getting her back to the Crimea [*from Moscow*]! The household I have in Moscow is in student style, there isn't a bed, there's too little crockery, I sent it all in spring to Yalta. The rains will pour down, her legs will start aching, it's cold, damp.

Where was Anton off to, she asked, and for how long? Masha wanted to enjoy the theatre season: she would have Evgenia only from January until Easter 1901. Anton overruled her. On 23 September he put Evgenia on the boat for Sevastopol, where a friend of the Chekhovs offered her dinner (she declined because of her false teeth) and put her on the Moscow express.

'I am very grateful, thank you very much for giving me the pleasure,' Evgenia wrote to Anton.[53] Masha was too angry to write. Olga took Evgenia to the theatre when A. K. Tolstoy's magnificent costume drama *Tsar Fiodor* opened on 3 October. Evgenia even asked to be taken to *The Snow Maiden*, but never to her son's plays. (She, like Pavel, seemed to be convinced that Anton's plays and stories were a source of income too shameful to be spoken of.) Olga told Anton 11 October: 'Poor woman, she keeps imagining I'll get my claws into her Antosha and make him unhappy.' Evgenia accepted Olga's hospitality but kept her guard up. Anton relished his solitude and resisted Olga's cajoling: 'Do you really not want to see your actress, to kiss her, to caress her, to fondle her? She is yours.'[54] *Three Sisters* took shape, even though, Anton complained, one sister had 'gone lame'. Adolf Marx's editor, Julius Grünberg, wrote: they had heard that Chekhov was writing '*Two Sisters*' and could hold up volume VII of *The Complete Works* to include it. (Anton replied that Marx would have *Three Sisters* only after it had been staged and after it had been published in a periodical.)

Visitors to Autka were kept at bay, except for the irrepressible Sergeenko[55] and for Olga Vasilieva. Eighteen and independent, she came to Yalta from Nice, bringing with her a nanny and a little girl of three, Marusia, whom she had adopted, she said, from an orphanage in Smolensk. Anton took to the child. Aleksandr Kuprin was bemused to see Marusia clamber onto Anton's knee, and, babbling, run her fingers through his hair. Anton had never been seen to fondle any creature except a dachshund in public. Gossip would have spread like wildfire, had others seen Anton's letters to Vasilieva, where he play-fully called himself Marusia's 'daddy'.

On 9 September the Yalta theatre burnt down, not that Anton cared: 'It was quite superfluous here, by the way.'[56] Life at Autka with old Mariushka as cook was rough. Anton wrote *Three Sisters* on a diet of soup and fish. He stopped work only to recover from bouts of 'flu', catch mice or attend to Kashtanka's broken paw. He ignored his siblings. Vania and Masha sulked: 'I can't imagine why,' he told Olga. Olga begged Anton to come to Moscow, but he insisted that they lived apart not by choice, but because 'of the demon that put the bacilli into me and love of art into you'. Anton would not come until he had finished the play and could attend rehearsals: he would not, he said, leave four heroines to Stanislavsky's mercy. Olga, however, needed a shoulder to cry on. She was hurt by poor reviews of *The Snow Maiden*, by being out-performed by Stanislavsky's wife in Haupt-mann's *Lonely People*, and by anti-Semitic outbursts from spectators in Chekhov's *Ivanov*.

After many telegrams, Anton arrived in Moscow on 23 October 1900 with a manuscript of *Three Sisters*. The next day he read the whole play out to the assembled theatre. There was a dismayed silence afterwards – nobody expected anything so complex or sad. Then Anton went to watch Ibsen's *Dr Stockmann*. He returned to the Hotel Dres-den, where a note from Olga was waiting to seduce him: 'Stay at the Dresden and copy [*out the play*], I'll come, I'll bring perfume and sweets. Do you want me? Answer yes or no.'

On 29 October Anton attended a reading of *Three Sisters*. Stanislav-sky was thrown by Anton's diffidence. Those around him were becom-ing more and more excited. Misha wrote that he had been asked by a lady in a train when Anton was getting married, and that an actress saw Nemirovich-Danchenko raise his glass to the union of Knipper and Chekhov: '. . . it would be very nice if these rumours turned out true.'[57] Yalta speculated: Lazarevsky's diary for 12 November reads: 'I've heard Chekhov has got married. I don't believe it.'

Masha and Anton had promised to keep an eye on Isaak Sinani's son, Abram, a student in Moscow. On 28 October Abram killed him-self. Anton summoned Sinani to Moscow and took him to the funeral, telling him his son had died of 'melancholy'. He warned Masha not to utter the word suicide in Yalta. That night he watched the hero in Hauptmann's *Lonely People* kill himself; the following week Anton's editor at Marx's, Julius Grünberg, died. Anton revised *Three Sisters* in a very gloomy mood. Komissarzhevskaia was still asking for the play. Anton disabused her, yet appealed for her sympathy: 'I'm on the treadmill, i.e. I run round visiting and at night I sleep like the dead. I came here perfectly well, now I'm coughing again and am evil-tempered and, I'm told, jaundiced.' By day Anton lived with Olga and Masha; he slept at the hotel. It was high time he was away. November in Moscow would be fatal. *News of the Day* reported that he was off to Africa and America and that *Three Sisters* was postponed.

In fact *Three Sisters* detained him. So did Suvorin. Anton was taken aback that Nastia had married and that he had not been told. He reproached Suvorin: 'I am almost as fond of your family as of my own,' and asked Suvorin to Moscow. Suvorin, though busy with his theatre, came within days, with Burenin. He noted:

> Chekhov was leaving for the south, for Algiers, he asked me to come and see him. I wanted to be back on the 22nd for the dress rehearsal of *Sons of Israel* or *The Smugglers* as we christened the play. Chekhov talked me out of it. I stayed. On Wednesday I could have met Tolstoy. I had a telegram from Petersburg that there had been a scandal in the Maly Theatre. I took the express at 12 a.m.

The play that Suvorin was staging in Petersburg was a melodrama about smugglers, written by a farce-writer, Viktor Krylov, and a renegade Jew, Saveli Litvin. Its anti-Semitic ranting revolted even a Petersburg audience. Orchestrated by Lidia Iavorskaia, the auditorium threw binoculars, galoshes and apples at the cast. Suvorin's beloved son-in-law, Aleksei Kolomnin, backstage, died of a massive heart attack. In this bereavement too, Anton was unable to console Suvorin.

In late November Anton saw Ibsen's *When We Dead Awaken* and annoyed Stanislavsky and Olga by his 'subtle smile, making fun of what we respect'. (Chekhov always claimed to be unable to see any merit in Ibsen.) Two acts of *Three Sisters* were in rehearsal. Anton would revise acts 3 and 4 in France. He had withdrawn 2000 roubles from his account in Yalta; Adolf Marx sent 10,000 to Moscow (he owed a final 15,000). Anton had money to travel and Olga reluctantly concurred that he had to leave for warmer climes. On 11 December Anton took the train to Vienna. In Nice Suvorin's granddaughter Nadia Kolomnina, as well as Olga Vasilieva with little Marusia, were waiting.

SEVENTY-FOUR

Nice Revisited

December 1900–February 1901

As the Vienna train steamed off, Olga Knipper walked to the end of the platform. Anton's new friend, the Tolstoyan Sulerzhitsky, escorted her home in distress, and Masha attended her until she recovered her buoyancy. Masha, too, was miserable, but would not say why. 'The poor thing didn't sleep all night: something has been happening all this time,' Olga wrote to Anton. Masha's distress may have had something to do with a new friendship. Ivan Bunin had taken upon himself to be, in Anton's absence, attentive to Masha and helpful to Olga.

Europe was now thirteen days ahead of Russia: Anton had forgotten that in Vienna shops would be shut and theatres full for Christmas Day. In his hotel room he looked 'with concupiscence at the two beds'. The next day he took a first-class train for Nice, and on 14/27 December 1900 was back in La Pension Russe, in two rooms with a wide soft bed. In four days Anton made fair copies of the last two acts of *Three Sisters*, expanding Act 4. He devised Chebutykin's ominous lines 'Balzac got married in Berdichev' and cut Andrei's speech in defence of the ghastly Natasha to 'A wife is a wife'. The play that had haunted Anton for two years was now off his hands. Anton was upset that Olga was apparently not writing to him, until he found that another Russian in Nice was being handed all the letters addressed to Chekhov.

On New Year's Day Anton made a pilgrimage to the Beau Rivage where he had first stayed in Nice with Suvorin nearly ten years ago, and only then sent Suvorin belated condolences on the death of Aleksei Kolomnin. To Suvorin Chekhov mused that 'life here is not like ours, it is rich, healthy, young, smiling'. Nice brought out francophilia in him. The Russians, he told Knipper, were all 'squashed-down, as if oppressed ... outrageous idleness'. Despite an unseasonal frost, he told Dr Sredin in Yalta, Nice was paradise and Yalta was Siberia: people here were happy, with no magistrate and no 'puffy-faced Marxists'. A week later Anton saw Nemirovich-Danchenko's mortally ill sister Varvara in Menton, stopping on the way in Monte Carlo. Anton gambled with his friend Franz Schechtel for two weeks, won 500 francs and exclaimed to Olga 'How much Russian money is being lost here'.

The Nemirovich-Danchenkos joined Anton on the Côte d'Azur. To please Olga, perhaps, Anton belittled Nemirovich-Danchenko's wife 'Kitten', whom he had once liked: 'Nemirovich is under house arrest: Katichka won't let him a step from her side, so that I don't see him ... she's just like a merchant's wife ...' Nemirovich-Danchenko had been unwilling to talk about *Three Sisters* at first, but he came to love and understand it as the weeks went by. Stanislavsky did not write about it until mid January. He was puzzled about the death of Tuzenbakh: should the body not be carried across the stage, could Anton insert a crowd scene to explain the sisters' calm? These queries did not distress Anton so much as Stanislavsky's delusion that the play ends with 'the author's uplifting thought which will redeem the play's many depressing minutes'. Nemirovich-Danchenko was practical: he demanded cuts in the sisters' monologues. So did Olga, who found Masha – the one passionate sister, the challenging role Anton had written for her – difficult to act.

Olga was worked to exhaustion by Nemirovich-Danchenko. He wanted her to feel 'the tone' of her part in the new play. When Masha and Evgenia left for Yalta on 19 December, Olga collapsed with a bad cold. She went deaf, took morphine and went to bed. Performances were cancelled, but she did not mope. Had Anton met 'beaucoup de jolies femmes ... Ecrivez-moi si vous y trouvez de bien intéressantes'. She made him write to his mother – 'Why upset the old woman? She'll think I made you change towards her.' Obediently he sent Evgenia 10 roubles and a card every three days. Masha, however, angered Anton. She had delayed banking 15,000 roubles received from Marx: 'not careless, simply swinish'. Masha cried at the injustice of his fury. When he sent instructions to Yalta on repairing the stoves and digging round the fruit trees, she would not reply. He had to ask Dr Sredin if Autka and its inhabitants were safe. 'My family, darling, don't spoil me,' Anton commented to Olga.

Masha and Evgenia had caught the servants Arseni and Mariushka unawares: the house was unheated, moths had eaten a bedside rug and the divan had collapsed under the weight of old newspapers. Masha looked at the garden and told Anton it was bare. He replied tersely that everything was planted to plan and in five years' time she would see that he was right. The crane that had flown away came back, but it injured itself when it began to dance with the one-eyed crane that had stayed behind: it lay dying in the kitchen.

Yalta was cold and Masha was lonely. Olga wrote to Anton:

> Bunin has been with me today, his nerves all shattered, he doesn't know what to do with himself; I am sending him to Yalta; he's angry at Masha for letting him down and keeping her departure quiet, but she was delayed here and did not know what to do, afraid of tying him down. He is talking about Nice.

On Christmas Eve Bunin left for Yalta. He was a godsend. He lived downstairs next to Masha and worked in Anton's sunny study. She called him Bouquichon; he called her Amarantha. Masha's letters to Anton began to sparkle and, while Arseni dug the garden, Bunin appended verses in her name:

> Snow falleth, blizzard bloweth:
> I have fled down to the south.
> Here the cold is not a joke,
> Bunin and I look at the views.
> All day with wood the stoves we stoke
> And go for walks like little ewes.[58]

Masha did not want to teach any more, or cope with Anton's ungrateful finances. She told Olga on 3 January 1901:

> Bunin escorts me . . . I have no time to visit [the sick]. I saw the New Year in at the Elpatievskys' with Bunin and yesterday I went to another fancy dress ball in the Kursaal – pretty good . . . In Yalta people are dying like flies, several friends died after the holidays – it's loathsome.[59]

Ever a dutiful sister, however, Masha left the balls and returned to Moscow on 12 January. Thanks to Bunin, at least she could leave Evgenia behind in Autka. Evgenia was happy: Bunin showed her more affection than her children. She told Anton: 'I've stopped being afraid,

I've calmed down, as if I've arrived in paradise.' Bunin explained to Anton that his country estate was as cold as the North Pole, whereas in Chekhov's sunny study, while the Tatars hammered paving stones into the driveway, he scribbled and read. For a whole month Bunin deputed for Anton and Masha. Anton approved and Masha wrote Bunin affectionate notes.

Misha had a different view of life at Autka and wrote to Vania: 'Mother has been left on her own in Yalta . . . It is a sin, a bad sin. If the old woman gets ill, there's nobody to give her water. Poor Mama!' Misha had a newborn son and wanted Evgenia in Iaroslavl to help, but she stayed in Yalta. On 15 February 1901, the day Anton was due back, she wrote:

> Misha, you write strange things about our life, especially to Masha, why she isn't staying in Yalta, but what would she do here, you ought to ask, and also you mention my going to Moscow and back to Yalta, even now I'm embarrassed at burdening Antosha with the expense, but what can you do, I was so unhappy, I couldn't live, Antosha saw that and he suggested it . . . Please tear up this letter. Why do you imagine Antosha has thousands? He never did, Melikhovo was 23,000, 5 for the bank, 8 owed, we've got only 5 thousand. The Yalta land cost 5000 and the house, outsiders built it and ran up a big sum, Gurzuf, he's taken a lot of money from Marx too, there's not much left, he can't hold on to money.

Once she had found a new place to live in Moscow Masha went to see Misha in Petersburg. He had sent four letters begging her to come: he was burning his boats, planning a new life working for Suvorin. When she got back to Moscow, Masha wrote firmly to Misha that Anton and she had no spare money.

Olga Vasilieva had busied herself in Nice searching the newspapers for news of deserving poor that she could help. She now wanted to sell a house she owned in Odessa and put the proceeds towards a clinic. In Moscow that summer Anton had been approached by Dr Chlenov, who, despite the puns (his name meant 'penis'), wanted to found a clinic for Moscow's syphilitics. Anton decided to direct Olga Vasilieva towards this venture and became embroiled in the sale of her property and the making of Dr Chlenov's clinic, a project which never came to fruition.

In mid January Anton felt that he had exhausted the human material

524

in the *pension*. He told Kovalevsky that he had exhausted Yalta too, and that leaving Melikhovo, where he knew about life in forty villages, had been a creative disaster. Once again he wanted to go to Algiers. Kovalevsky prevaricated: he saw that Anton was even iller than three years ago. He told him the sea was too rough, and then refused outright. With Kovalevsky and Professor Korotniov, Anton took instead the coast road to Italy. Olga Vasilieva begged him not to forget her, and left for Geneva. Anton and his companions stopped in Pisa, then went to Florence. On 30 January 1901 they went to Rome. Anton's mood grew grim: he told Kovalevsky he was writing nothing long, because he would soon die. Anton stayed four more days in Rome and watched a penitential procession in St Peter's. Asked how he would describe it, he replied, 'A stupid procession dragged past.'[60] Feeling deserted by his friends, Anton took trains from Rome to Odessa and, despite his status as an academician, was harassed by the Russian customs. In Odessa he had an estate agent value Vasilieva's house. On 15 February 1901, across terrible seas, he arrived in a freezing Yalta.

Anton had been travelling for three weeks. He had missed the furore surrounding *Three Sisters*. Olga had wired the news of the play's triumph to Nice: 'Grand succès, embrasse mon bien aimé', but news took a long time to reach Anton. Rehearsals had been troubled: the ex-colonel the theatre had hired to make the military dress and behaviour authentic had dared to overrule Stanislavsky. Olga had argued against the heavy red wig that Stanislavsky wanted Masha to wear. The opening night of *Three Sisters* on 31 January 1901 confirmed Chekhov as Russia's greatest dramatist and Moscow Arts Theatre as its leading theatre. The public saw their lives enacted: the three sisters stood for all educated women marooned in the provinces. Olga as Masha had every unfaithful wife in the audience in tears. So moved was the audience that the curtain fell to total silence.

In the audience was Ezhov. He saw the cuckolded schoolteacher Kulygin as a caricature of himself, and reported to Suvorin on 1 February 1901:

All the heroes whine, none is satisfied. There is a drunken old doctor who has read nothing ... There is adultery (Chekhov's favourite theme) ... The content: three sisters, daughters of a brigadier-general, their brother studying to be a professor, all passionately desire to move to live in Moscow ... The play is acted splendidly ... I shall not be writing about this play in *New Times*.[61]

Suvorin thoroughly disliked the play when he saw it a year later in Moscow.

SEVENTY-FIVE

The Secret Marriage
February–May 1901

WHEN ANTON ARRIVED, Bunin moved out to sleep at the Hotel Yalta, where there was a corpse in the next room. Bunin's humour and tact endeared him to Anton, who pressed him to stay. Masha in Moscow was propitiated by a parcel of gifts from her brother: a tartan rug, lace handkerchiefs, scissors and a blotter.

Olga Knipper was still further away. In Moscow the theatres closed for Lent, so Nemirovich-Danchenko and Stanislavsky took their company to Petersburg, where the theatres closed only for the first, fourth and last weeks of Lent. The public enthused in Petersburg as they had in Moscow. Unadvertised, all seats were sold; people queued for tickets until midnight. The press, however, was brutal. Burenin denounced a 'press claque puffing Chekhov'. *New Times* derided Olga in *Lonely People*. Kugel in *The Petersburg Newspaper* reviewed the first night of *Uncle Vania* on 19 February 1901: Knipper is 'a very phlegmatic lady . . . praise of this actress is for me an utter mystery.' Amfiteatrov's *Courier* declared: 'Knipper is a very bad actress.' Critics praised Maria Andreeva, whose Kätchen, the dowdy wife in Hauptmann's play, was more beautiful than Olga's siren Anna Mahr. Olga and Andreeva became enemies. *Three Sisters* changed a few minds: Amfiteatrov, for one, decided that Knipper was a great actress.

When the curtain fell the audiences called out the wording of congratulatory telegrams to Chekhov, but Suvorin's critics accused the Moscow Arts Theatre of destroying him. Nikolai Sazonov told his wife he would never have passed the play when he was censor. The Ministry of Education banned it from 'people's theatres'. Finally, on 20 March, Burenin published a vicious skit: *Nine Sisters and Not a Single Groom*. Burenin's sisters, Hysteria, Cretina and Idiota, utter Chekhovian gibberish, *Tra-ta-tam* and *Tsip, tsip, tsip* and his cast includes trained cockroaches. *Nine Sisters* ends with the sisters sucking their blankets and the theatre collapsing to thunderous applause. Burenin's parody upset Chekhov – all the more so because it was published in Suvorin's paper.[62]

Olga was distraught about her bad reviews: she loved Petersburg and wanted her love reciprocated. Stanislavsky explained to the cast that every critic was the husband or lover of an actress whose nose had been put out of joint by their performance of Chekhov. Petersburg actors queued to apologize and Lidia Iavorskaia showed her support. She took a red carnation from between her breasts and threw it to Stanislavsky, then came backstage and invited the cast to stay as her guests for the fourth week of Lent. Nemirovich-Danchenko and Stanislavsky, to Olga's disgust, accepted. Iavorskaia, Anton's notorious old love, repelled her:

> 24 February . . . Iavorskaia crept into my dressing room again, she pushes in, flattering and keeps inviting me to see her. The brazen woman.
>
> 3 March . . . Iavorskaia has invited me on 5 March, but I certainly shan't go. I can't bear the sight of that coarse woman and have given orders for her not to be allowed in my dressing rooms in the interval.[63]

Another old flame of Anton's approached Olga. She wrote to him on 2 March to say: 'I just had a letter from L. Avilova, you seem to know her. She wishes . . . to get a ticket to the *Sisters*. I replied politely. I cannot get a ticket.' She was angry with 'Kitten', Nemirovich-Danchenko's wife, as well.[64]

Anton was upset by the ordeal the company had endured, but reproached Olga for quarrelling with Iavorskaia (who had sent him a telegram of praise). Anton even renounced writing plays in a country where actresses were abused. Suvorin was punished: for the twenty-fifth anniversary of *New Times* students organized a 'cat's concert' under the windows of his offices; police had to drive demonstrators away. Another student demonstration was attacked by Cossacks and police; news came that the Church's Holy Synod had excommunicated Tolstoy. In a tense and excited Petersburg theatre audiences became even more emotional. Sazonova took a friend, Evgenia, to see *Three Sisters* on 1 March 1901: 'She left the theatre in tears. Masha's affair with an artillery colonel is her own story.' One persona found Anton's drama and personal life amusing. Anna Suvorina wrote to Anton at Easter: 'We all went to see *Uncle Vania*, six times in a row . . . it makes me laugh since I can see and hear many of my kith and kin . . . I'd like to say hello to your "wife" [*Olga Knipper*], but how can I?'[65]

In the middle of all the turmoil Misha Chekhov turned up in Petersburg to take up Suvorin's offer of employment: Suvorin 'could not think what you're fit for', and forgot to assign Misha a salary. Masha supported her youngest brother: 'it's the fate of the boys in our family to be writers, not officials'. Misha declared that he was doing what Anton had advised him to do ten years ago. Now Anton reminded him that Suvorin published *New Times* and was 'an awful liar, especially in his so-called frank moments'; also that Anna Suvorina was petty. The only honest employment with Suvorin would be with Tychinkin in the print shop. Despondent at Suvorin's offhandedness and Anton's disapproval, Misha went back to Iaroslavl to rehabilitate himself. Suvorin wired him. Misha returned to Petersburg, apologizing to Suvorin on 17 March: 'I was always being terrified in my childhood that God would punish me and the Devil lead me astray . . . [*My parents*] made me a weak character.'[66] Misha was employed with Suvorin first as an editor, then in his advertising agency, for 350 roubles a month. Suvorin had won another Chekhov.

Alone with his mother in the Crimea, Anton was reaching a decision. To Bunin he joked: 'marrying a German is better: they are tidier'. Gorky, keeping Olga company in Petersburg, wrote to Anton: 'Why have people everywhere been saying that you are married?' Meanwhile the almonds blossomed and Anton gardened. He was reading proofs for volume IV of *The Complete Works*, but not writing. He had promised another story to the journal *Life*: that journal was now banned. His old editor, Mikhail Menshikov, left *The Week* to work for Suvorin, and another outlet vanished. Anton grew iller. Nikolai Sazonov reported back to his wife that Chekhov would share the fate of the poet Nadson: 'he will be wiped out by consumption and Burenin's parodies'. Masha picked up the ominous adverb in a letter from Bunin: 'Anton is *relatively* well', and asked for his support in Yalta, when she came for Easter.[67] Anton was expecting Olga to come for four whole months. On 5 March, she made him an ultimatum:

I shan't come to Yalta; think and you'll realize why. It's impossible. You have such a sensitive soul and yet you invite me! Can you really not understand?

Anton made a joke of her refusal: she had a lover in Petersburg; he did have a wife, but would divorce her; he had brought expensive perfume for her to fetch from Yalta. On 7 March, he gave in: 'Let me make you a proposal.' Olga held out:

How can I come? . . . How long must we stay hidden? And what's the point? Because of people? People are more likely to shut up and leave us in peace once they see it's an accomplished fact.

Although he loathed trains and hotels, Anton announced he would come to Moscow. To Bunin (who, himself seeking a divorce, had to repress his horror) he made his first unambiguous written declaration: 'By the way, I intend to marry.' He told Olga he was coming to Moscow, but stressed that she would 'get a grandfather, not a spouse.' He would let her act for five more years. A week after this letter Olga told members of the theatre that she had resolved: 'to unite my life to that of Anton Chekhov.' But she still did not have from Anton the firm offer on which she was insisting:

We cannot live just as though we were good friends . . . to see your mother's suffering, Masha's puzzled face – it's awful! In your house I'm between two fires. Say something about this. You never say anything. I have to have a bit of peace now. I am terribly tired.

She dared not drag Anton to Moscow's frozen air, but, faced with her conditions for coming down to Yalta, Anton was now backing off. He wrote to Bunin on 25 March: 'I've changed my mind about marrying, I don't want to but all the same . . . then if I must I shall.' Shortly after Masha had left for Yalta, it was Olga who gave in. She telegraphed: 'Leaving tomorrow Yalta' and got the reply, 'Expect arrival'. On Good Friday, 30 March 1901, she was there.

Bunin was also there for the two weeks that Masha and Olga stayed. They went to the seaside cottage at Gurzuf, where they picnicked, and Anton wrote Bunin a joke bill for his share. When Masha left for Moscow and Bunin for Odessa, Olga left with them. She cried bitterly all the way to Moscow – Masha believed it was from a tooth abscess. Olga's letter to Anton suggests otherwise:

There was no need to separate ... It was for decency, was it? ...
You stayed silent. I decided that you did not want me to be with
you once Masha had left. *Que dira le monde?* There is a sediment of
things left unsaid. I was so looking forward to spring, and now I've
just been on a visit ... everyone in Moscow was amazed to see me
... Come soon; let's get married and clear off, do you want to?

The next day Olga wrote, 'You have already cooled towards me, you
don't look at me as somebody close ... you don't like all this woman's
chatter.'

While Olga Knipper was in Yalta, Olga Vasilieva let Anton know
that she had come to Gurzuf for two months with her foster-child
Marusia: 'Will you curse me very much for my desire to have one
more look at you? Your Marusia is a wonderful child, but I get very
spiteful with her.' At the beginning of April she sent her photograph
to Anton's mother and wrote that she was bequeathing Marusia to
Anton, as thanks

> for all the happiness and joy you brought me with your visits in
> Nice – after Mama's death I was never so happy and shan't be.
> Marusia is a good, kind child – I am not worthy of her. I often envy
> her that I cannot, as she can, count on an affectionate word from
> you.

A week later she wired: 'Voudrais venir Gourzouff être plus près vous,
puis-je, ne vous fâchez pas.' Anton replied that there was a hotel in
Gurzuf and sent regards to 'our daughter Marusia', telling her to
behave 'or else daddy will get angry and pick up the cane'. A week
after Easter Anton arranged to see them. Vasilieva had moved to
Autka, to the house next door. She sent Anton coins, ostensibly as a
pledge for a loan to pay her landlady. The day that Bunin, Masha
and Olga left, Anton wrote to Vasilieva. He told her that he did not
mind her living next door with no chaperone.[68]

Anton's reply to Olga Knipper, however, was as intimate a letter
as she would ever receive from him:

> I didn't keep you because I hate being in Yalta and I also had the
> idea that we would soon meet anyway in freedom ... you had no
> reason to be angry ... I had no secret thoughts.

He appealed to her pity and theatrical ambitions:

531

My cough takes all my energy and I think languidly about the future and am reluctant to write . . . Occasionally I have a very strong desire to write a 4-act farce or comedy for the Arts Theatre. And if I do, if nothing gets in the way, I shan't give it to the theatre before the end of 1903

They would marry and honeymoon anywhere, the Black Sea or the Arctic Ocean. Anton undertook to bring his passport to Moscow for the ceremony: she was now 'Olia', his 'little Lutheran', his 'dog', as henceforth she signed her letters to him. He would marry her the day he arrived 'so long as you promise nobody will know in Moscow': he loathed congratulations, champagne and having to maintain a fixed smile. Waiting for health and warm weather, he chatted every day with Kuprin, a fascinating companion who, as he later boasted, had done everything in life except get pregnant. Anton's notebooks reflect a darker mood:

> a feeling of non-love, a peaceful state, long, peaceful thoughts . . . love is either the remains of something degenerating or part of something that will develop in the future into something enormous, but in the present it doesn't satisfy, it gives far less than you expect.

Olga's next letter to Anton contained an inauspicious joke: 'The revolting Vishnevsky swears by God and crosses his heart that in a year or two I'll be his wife – how about that!' A Grand Duchess, Olga said, had accosted her mother and asked, 'When is her marriage, and how is *his* health?' Thus Anna Knipper learnt of the betrothal.[69] Anton said he would write a will forbidding Olga to remarry after his death. For a fortnight he pleaded illness: he was locked in his study, thinking and coughing. He worried about Vania, who was, although never complaining, barely communicating, in fact, overworked and losing weight; about Gorky and Posse, the editor of *Life*, in prison; about his sick dog; about Olga Vasilieva leaving for France. On 6 May he had a talk with Vasilieva. He deterred his Taganrog cousins from visiting Yalta: Evgenia might be in Petersburg, Masha in Moscow and he in the Arctic or on the Volga.

When Anton came to Moscow a week later, he had his first breakfast with Olga Vasilieva, not Olga Knipper, so that he could introduce Dr Chlenov the venereologist to Vasilieva the potential patron for his clinic. On 16 May Masha left for Yalta to care for Evgenia. On

17 May Anton went, under duress, to see Dr Shchurovsky, who after a thorough examination and interrogation took a full history. Anton gave wild guesses when asked how long his relatives had lived. He admitted that coughing and diarrhœa had plagued him since infancy and hæmorrhages for the past seventeen years. Shchurovsky noted[70] that Anton drank moderately, had given up smoking, that he had not had syphilis, but had been treated for, and cured of, gonorrhœa. Shchurovsky suspected that Anton's childhood 'peritonitis' might be due to a hernia. He found Anton's mental state good and his nerves 'tolerable'. (Anton assured Shchurovsky that his depression was 'auto-intoxication' due to constipation and lifted after a dose of castor oil.) The lungs, however, were bad, with irreversible necrosis, and his gut was badly affected. Severe pulmonary damage and chronic colitis, Shchurovsky hoped, might respond to koumiss, a treatment Anton had not tried. Anton was referred to Dr Varavka at the Andreev sanatorium, in the wilds of Bashkiria, 1200 miles east of Moscow. Olga wrote to Masha the next day:

There is not much comfort – the process has not stopped. He prescribed him a course of koumiss drinking and if he can't, then it's Switzerland. I am cooking up a medicine for Anton, I pound it in the mortar, I let it stand and I boil it, it's for the intestines. God grant that the koumiss does him good! As soon as I sort everything out, we are off. I am awfully sad. Masha, why did you go away! I am sad and afraid.[71]

Olga told Masha everything, except that she and Anton were about to marry. Anton wrote to Masha two days later to say that both lungs now had lesions, that he had the choice of fermented mares' milk in the Urals or Switzerland for two months. As for the wedding and the journey with Olga to the Urals, he even now denied it: 'It's boring to go on one's own, it's boring to be on the koumiss, but taking somebody with me would be selfish ... I would get married but I don't have the papers on me, everything is in the desk in Yalta.' He asked for a few blank cheques. Masha wanted him back in Yalta.

On Thursday 24 May 1901 Anton took Vania on an errand, near the clinic where their father had died. He sent his last proofs to Marx and had his mail directed to Aksionovo, a village half way between the Volga and the Urals. He received a telegram from Dr Varavka:

'Welcome. Have place.' Anton then wired Olga: 'I have everything ready. Need meet before 1 to talk. We definitely leave Friday.' That day Masha could contain her jealousy no more and, despite her close friendship with Olga, told Anton:

Now let me express my opinion about your marriage. Personally I find the wedding procedure awful. And you don't need these extra worries, if you are loved you won't be abandoned and there is no sacrifice involved . . . It's never too late to get tied. Tell that to your [sweetheart *erased*] Knipper woman. The first thing to think about is getting you well. For God's sake don't think I'm guided by selfishness. You've always been the person closest and dearest to me . . . You yourself brought me up to be without prejudices. My God, how difficult it will be to live two whole months without you, what's more in Yalta . . . If you don't answer this letter quickly I shall be hurt. My regards to 'her'.[72]

The day of his marriage Anton left instructions for Vania and 50 roubles which he insisted Vania spend on a first-class boat journey down the Volga. He telegraphed his mother, 'Dear Mama, bless me, I am getting married. All will stay the same.[73] I am off to drink koumiss. Address Aksionovo. Health better.' Evgenia was, Masha later reported, mute with shock, but Anton received a telegram from her, 'I bless, be happy, healthy.'

On the morning of 25 May Olga wrote to Masha:

Today we are getting married and leaving for Aksionovo, Ufa province, on the koumiss. Anton feels well, is nice and gentle. Only Volodia [*her brother*] and uncle Sasha (at Anton's request) and two student witnesses will be in the church. I had a tragedy and rows with mama yesterday because of all this I don't sleep at night, my head is splitting . . . I am awfully sad and hurt, Masha, that you are not here with me these days, I would feel different. I am utterly alone, I have nobody to speak to. Don't forget me, Mashechka, love me, we must, you and I must always be together . . . My regards to your mother. Tell her I shall be very hurt if she cries or is upset because of Anton's marriage.

Three days later, waiting for a boat, Olga described to Masha Anton's best farce:

At 8.30 I set off to the dentist to have my tooth finished . . . at 2 I had lunch, put on a white dress and went to Anton's. I had it all out

534

with my mother . . . I myself did not know to the last day when we would get married. The wedding was very queer . . . There wasn't a soul in the church, there were guards at the gates. Towards 5 p.m. I arrived with Anton, the bride's men were sitting on a bench in the garden . . . I could hardly stand with my headache and at one moment I felt I should burst out either crying or laughing. You know, I felt awfully odd when the priest came up to me and Anton and led us away . . . We were married on the Pliushchikha by the same priest as buried your father. I was asked only for a certificate that I was a spinster, which I fetched from our church . . .[74] I was terribly upset that Vania wasn't there . . . Vania knew we were getting married, Anton had gone to see the priest with him . . . When I got back from the church our servants couldn't control themselves, they lined up to congratulate me and raised a howling and weeping, but I nobly controlled myself. They packed my things, and Natasha that pig let me down . . . she didn't bring the silk bra and the batiste embroidered blouse. At 8 p.m. we went to the station, only our family saw us off, quietly, modestly.[75]

Elsewhere in Moscow, at a reception which Anton had asked Vishnevsky to organize, a bemused crowd wondered what had happened to the newlyweds.

X

Love and Death

The best protection against dragons is to have one
of your own.   Evgeni Shvarts, *The Dragon*

The bedroom smelt of fever, infusions, ether, tar,
that indescribable heavy smell of an apartment
where a consumptive is breathing.
                              Maupassant, *Bel-Ami*

SEVENTY-SIX

Honeymoon
June–September 1901

ANNA KNIPPER offered the couple a quick meal before they caught the train to Nizhni Novgorod. Anton and Olga were met at Nizhni by Dr Dolgopolov, who had tickets for the thousand-mile river journey to Ufa, from where they would get a train to the village of Aksionovo and the sanatorium. Dr Dolgopolov had just certified Gorky as too consumptive for prison, and took Anton and Olga to see him. One policeman opened the door; another sat in the kitchen. Gorky's wife was in hospital giving birth. Gorky talked volubly and, when Anton and Olga finally blurted out that they had just got married, thumped Olga on the back.

Dolgopolov put Anton and Olga on a boat that took them down the Volga and up the river Kama towards the Urals, dropping them at a quay called Piany Bor, 'Drunken Grove'. Here they had a long wait for the connecting boat. They should have changed boats in Kazan. There was no hotel; they camped on the ground, in the rain, while a consumptive spat. 'I shall never forgive Dolgopolov. In "Drunken Grove" and sober. The setting is horrible,' Anton wrote. Olga found a hut and made a bed on the floor. They ate salted sturgeon and tried to sleep. At 5 a.m. a tiny, crowded boat for Ufa picked them up; they slept in separate cabins. Anton was lent a rug, but pestered by admirers. They chugged up the river Belaia through wooded hills; the sun tanned Anton's face and bleached the pink blouse Masha had sewn for Olga. After two nights on the Belaia, at dawn on 31 May 1901, they docked at Ufa. They rushed to catch the 6.00 a.m. train, but there had been a derailment and the train did not leave until two in the afternoon. The windows were jammed and the station carpenter could not budge them. They endured five hours of stifling heat. From Aksionovo wickerwork carts took them over a rough hilly track six miles to the sanatorium.

It was dark when they arrived. They were met by dozens of telegrams and letters and by the news that an Anna Chokhova was there.
She was the wife of Mikhail Chokhov, a vulgar cousin whom Anton
had avoided for fifteen years.[1] Morning showed the beauty of
Aksionovo – an outcrop of hilly forest in the dreary steppes between
the Volga and the Urals, it could have been a resort in lower Austria.
Olga regaled Masha with her first impressions:

> The air was saturated, the fragrance amazing, and it was remarkably
> warm. Here we were met by Dr Varavka (a great name [*it sounds
> like vorovka, thieving woman* D.R.]) . . . Anton travels like a student;
> I had told him that he would have to bring everything with him.
> He assured me we could buy everything locally. It turns out there
> are no sheets or pillows here. The doctor sent over his own . . . The
> sanatorium has 40 little chalets . . . and a house with ten rooms, a
> dining room, a drawing room, billiard room, a library and a piano.
> From a distance the chalets look like big privies. Each has two rooms
> connected only by a narrow verandah, the rooms are middling, all
> white. You get a table, three chairs, a rather hard bed and a cupboard,
> the washstand is on three legs with a jug instead of a sink. Spartan,
> you can see. They will send over some softer beds and I have been
> given a mirror. Our chalet is the end one, so that we get an excellent
> view of the open country; there is a birch wood right by. We get
> morning coffee brought to us, at 1 we go to lunch, two hot courses,
> at 6 a three-course dinner, and at 9 tea, milk, bread and butter.
> Anton was weighed and he began to drink koumiss, so far he takes
> it well, eats very well and sleeps a lot.[2]

Dr Varavka fawned on his new patients: a famous colleague and a
distinguished actress. Anton studied the twenty house rules and named
the place 'a corrective labour camp'. There was no running water, no
bathhouse; the 'park' was scrub, the flowerbeds full of weeds. The
Bashkirs farmed horses and sheep, but no fruit or vegetables. Anton
laughed hysterically and would have fled, but for a landowner who
offered him his sauna, and for the river Dioma, where, with Dr
Varavka and a young patient, Anton sat trout-fishing. Olga lazed with
a book, bathed in the stream, made herself a silk bra, or gathered
strawberries and flowers in the woods. Olga's only ordeal was a trip
to buy bed-linen, which meant travelling to Ufa, which she cursed –
a 'pit: hell, suffocation and dust!'

For the first time since childhood, Anton put on weight. Four bottles of koumiss daily made him twelve pounds heavier by mid-June. Fermented mares' milk was easily digestible. It was also thought to raise the body's defences against tuberculosis, encouraging the growth of benign flora at the expense of tubercular bacilli in the gut. Olga, although she found her own ten stone excessive, tried it herself. Koumiss made them drowsy, drunk and lascivious.

Letters were Anton's lifeline, but they soon became disagreeable. After she had been informed of her brother's marriage Masha, feeling deceived and jealous, turned on Olga:

> You managed to trap my brother! Suppose you're like Natasha in *Three Sisters*! I'll strangle you with my own hands. I shan't bite your throat, just strangle you. You know I love you and must have got strongly attached to you in the last two years. How odd that you're a Chekhov.[3]

The whole family was in turmoil. Vania went to Petersburg to tell Misha of the marriage, and Misha closed ranks with Masha against the intruder. By 8 June Vania was in Yalta, trying to reconcile Masha and Evgenia to what had happened. On 6 June Masha wrote bitterly to Bunin:

> Dear Ivan, My mood is suicidal, I sense the pointlessness of my existence. The reason is my brother's marriage ... why did Olga need all this disturbance for a sick man ... I'm afraid my relations with Knipschitz will change ... dear Bouquichon, find me a rich generous groom.[4]

It took Olga a week to seek a reconciliation: she invited Masha to join their honeymoon. Masha dithered, then declined. She doubted if she and Olga could live together even in Moscow, as they planned: she would sell her flat and live with a family. 'Anton keeps writing everything will stay the same,' Masha wrote to Bunin, 'like hell it will, I want the reality, not a pretence.' Masha feared, as did Dr Altshuller, that Olga would lure Anton to live in Moscow and wreck his health. Evgenia, Masha told Misha, 'dislikes Antosha's spouse and Olga knows that.' On 20 June Olga wrote to Evgenia: 'I thought I'd explain everything ... when we met ... I know how you love Anton, so we've tried to make everything good and friendly at home [*the Moscow flat*], so that Anton will feel good among his womenfolk.'[5] Others were disturbed by

Anton's marriage. Maria Drozdova wrote from Yalta to tell him of her feelings at the news:

> I was painting at the time and all my brushes and palette flew to hell. Right to the last minute I didn't lose hope of marrying you myself. I thought the others were just jokes, while God would give me happiness for my modesty. How I hate Olga, my jealousy is frantic, I can't bear to see you, I hate *her* and you too, always and for ever.[6]

Suvorin, hurt not to have been even informed of the marriage, wrote to Misha:

> Anton has astounded me. Where is he now? I mean, what is his address? His getting married was the last thing I thought would happen after last November when I met him . . . It's fine if he knows what he needs. But suppose he doesn't! It's a lottery.[7]

Others' congratulations were lukewarm: Professor Korotniov talked of the Rubicon; Sobolevsky of 'the other shore so rarely attainable to people like me and you'. Bunin expressed polite amazement.

Anton could not bear to remain at Aksionovo for the two months prescribed. After one month he was determined to leave. Worry about what was happening at Yalta and irritation with his tedious fellow patients drove him away. In vain Dr Varavka promised health and offered improvements; on 1 July 1901 Anton signed the towel that Dr Varavka kept for distinguished patients, to have the signatures embroidered later, and abandoned Aksionovo. He was in such a hurry that he left his passport behind. On 6 July the Chekhovs arrived back in Yalta. 'I'm now asking for a divorce,' Anton wrote to Bunin, inviting him to join them at Autka.

Masha felt depressed by the new status quo. She complained to Misha:

> I am a nothing. I'm neither an artist nor a teacher, but I think I am working hard to build someone else's nest . . . My relations with my sister-in-law are still pretty bad . . . Mother has turned out better, she is being handled well and has calmed down. My mood is nasty, I can't adapt to this new life at all, I pine, I cry a lot and I have to hide it all, and I don't always succeed . . . In Moscow there is a lot of gossip about me, everybody is sorry for me and there are rumours

that I've run away ... Anton is poorly, the koumiss didn't do him much good.[8]

Anton coughed, bled and fretted. Dr Varavka asked him to send a portrait of himself for the chalet where he had stayed. A student doctor at Aksionovo promised good cuisine, fountains, running water, a conservatory and fresh vegetables for next year,[9] but Anton had finished with koumiss. On 3 August 1901, he drew up a will and had it witnessed. Addressed to Masha, it was entrusted to Olga:

> I leave you for your lifespan my Yalta house, the money and the income from my plays; my wife is to have the cottage in Gurzuf and 5000 roubles. You can sell the real estate if you wish.

A few thousand roubles went to his brothers, the residue to Taganrog's schools. The will ended: 'Help the poor. Look after mother. All of you live in peace.'

Anton's inspiration had run dry; now his only income came from the theatres. His plight worried Gorky and his editor Piatnitsky, who asked to see Adolf Marx's contract. By suing or shaming Marx they thought they might be able to break the contract that offered Anton next to nothing for a life's work, but made Marx a fortune. Anton, horrified at the thought of reneging on his agreement, demurred, but sent copies of the contract for Gorky's lawyers. Gorky boasted:

> How I'd love to tear Sergeenko's famous block off for dragging you into this mess. And I'd bash Marx on his bald patch too ... We'll pawn our wives and children, but we'll tear Chekhov out of Marx's thrall.[10]

Anton read the proofs for Marx's final volumes: revising later work was easier than the earlier work in which he found so many imperfections. He busied himself with the problems of others. His cousin Aleksei Dolzhenko asked for 800 roubles to build a cottage: Anton arranged for Olga to hand the money over in Moscow, warning her twice to be polite and gentle to her poor relation. In Taganrog Gavriil Selivanov, after twenty years' silence, was again causing trouble: he threatened to pull down Uncle Mitrofan's sheds unless the Chekhovs ceded terrain. Georgi sought Anton's advice. Olga Vasilieva still wanted help to convert her wealth into a clinic. A Jewish boy needed a letter of support to get into school at Yalta.

Olga felt unwanted. On 20 August 1901, after just six weeks, she left Autka, alone, for Moscow and the theatre. Evgenia refused to bless her as she stepped into the carriage. Anton sailed with her to the railhead. Weeping in the train, Olga wrote to Masha. She posted the letter in Kharkov:

> Do you feel better now I'm gone? You know, I want to shake off all our misunderstandings in the summer months like a vile nightmare . . . We do love each other.

Nobody met Olga in Moscow. She sought out a five-room apartment, a wooden house in a courtyard, for herself and – she hoped – Masha. Her unease persisted. She asked Anton:

> In your house nobody ever mentions me, do they? I shall always stand between you and her. And I fancy that she will never get used to me as your wife, and will thus turn you off me. I am avoided like a sore.[11]

Anton deplored her jealousy: 'What rubbish! Just be silent for a year . . . all life's comforts are to be found in nonresistance for the time being.' In Yalta Masha resigned herself to her new situation, telling Misha on 30 August:

> Recently Antosha has been so gentle and kind that I wouldn't have the strength to abandon him, anyway his health is no better. The sister-in-law has rented a flat in Moscow where I shall live and Antosha will come for a time . . . bad though I feel, I still want to stay with him.

The young poet Lazarevsky, who had become a 'Person from Porlock' in the Autka house, recorded Masha as 'the first and last of old maids, more likeable than the most beautiful ladies . . . a charming, suffering face'. On 31 August 1901 Masha left for Moscow; she stayed first with the Knippers and then with the Konovitsers until the new quarters were ready. Sharing was bearable, for Masha spent days at school, Olga evenings at the theatre, and servants, notably Masha Shakina who became pregnant every year, ran the household. Olga's passport listed her as the wife of a Yalta doctor. She bore her colleagues' teasing that Chekhov's latest play was *Two Sisters*, as the author had taken one (Masha, played by Olga) away for himself.

The day he was left alone with his mother, Anton took the draft of a new story, 'The Bishop', out of his suitcase and wrote. He would join Olga while Moscow was still warm, in mid September. Now that he was married, few *Antonovkas* bothered to call. Anton renounced old dalliances and gave Lazarevsky a rude message for Avilova.[12] A Polish girl, another Masha, was hired to cook; Arseni the gardener resumed work; the tame crane trumpeted with delight. Finally Ivan Bunin arrived on 5 September. Finding Anton 'ill and lonely', he visited daily; his tact and wit restored Anton's spirits. Nearby, at Gaspra, Tolstoy was recuperating from a nearly fatal attack of pneumonia. Anton's concern at this time was for Tolstoy's health, not his own. (The government forbad bulletins, and stationed a priest outside the house in Gaspra, to announce his deathbed recantation of heresy.) If Tolstoy died, Anton believed, Russian literature would lose its moral bulwark. His attendants, when Anton visited, found Chekhov 'aged, coughing all the time, talking little', but apparently happy to be without his sister and his wife.

Anton still had Vladimir Nemirovich-Danchenko as a rival, but Anton's and Olga's marriage made it possible to ignore his role in Olga's life. Anna Knipper, Olga's mother, now lifted her ban on the Moscow Arts Theatre director's visits. 'Your mama has made up with Nemirovich-Danchenko? So she no longer fears for her daughter?' Anton asked. Olga, for her part, dismissed Anton's former girlfriends as ruthlessly as she had once courted them.[13] Lika Mizinova was a marked woman. On 25 August 1901 she presented herself at the Moscow Arts Theatre for public entrance tests. Lika was told to read Elena in *Uncle Vania*, a role which Olga had made her own. Unabashed, Olga told Anton how she and Nemirovich-Danchenko had humiliated Lika:

> Lika Mizinova tried to imitate me, a dirty trick, but everything she read was complete rubbish (just between ourselves) and I was sorry for her, frankly. We rejected her unanimously. Sanin suggested she open a hat shop. Tell Masha about Lika. Perhaps she can have a non-speaking part.

After this rebuff Masha, Vania and Misha made a point of befriending Lika, while the theatre company found her a role as an unofficial, unpaid social secretary.

When Olga wanted to install her cat Martin in the new flat, Anton forbade her: 'I am afraid of cats ... Get a dog instead.' He was furious with Olga's refusal to give her new address when she moved apartments – she preferred to receive her letters at the theatre – and stopped replying to her, but he had met a woman with willpower to match his own. She remonstrated with telegrams. To build up his health for renewed conjugal life, he drank bottles of kefir (Tatar fermented milk); Dr Altshuller also made him massage himself with eucalyptus oil and turpentine.

On 17 September, after ignoring Olga's birthday on the 9th, Anton arrived in Moscow for the Arts Theatre's new season.

SEVENTY-SEVEN

When Doctors Disagree

October 1901–February 1902

FOR THREE SEASONS in a row the Moscow Arts Theatre had put on a Chekhov play that was new to the Moscow public. For October 1901 Anton had given them nothing. *Three Sisters* was still a magnet; it had played for only half of last season. They also had Gorky's first play, *The Petty Bourgeois*, which promised to cause a scandal. They opened with Ibsen's *Wild Duck*, but the public and critics agreed with Chekhov: 'tired, boring and weak'. Stanislavsky was shattered by a fire that had burnt down a family factory, and then he was struck down with tonsillitis: his performances let the theatre down. Then Nemirovich-Danchenko made the mistake of staging his own introspective play *In Dreams*. The reviewers slated the play, Olga had no confidence in her part in it, and she was worried by Nemirovich-Danchenko's depression.[14] After three rehearsals, Stanislavsky cancelled a revised production of *Ivanov*. Anton was pressed for a new play. At rehearsals of *Three Sisters*, he hindered more than he helped, but the author's presence at performances of this play and of *Uncle Vania* filled the house: Anton earned some 8000 roubles that season (and another 1000 roubles from productions all over Russia).

Moscow was still warm enough for his lungs. Petersburg, where he planned to go, was not. Aleksandr came to Moscow to talk to Masha and Anton. Though he stayed the night, he never met Olga. He told Misha that Anton looked 'pretty bad'. Aleksandr, on his way to the Caucasus for *New Times*, was sober. He hid his drinking until he was far away. Suvorin sent Ezhov to Moscow. Ezhov twice met the man who had, he felt, libelled him in *Three Sisters*; 'a shadow of the old Chekhov,' he told Suvorin. The weather grew colder. Olga used friends as sitters while Anton was confined indoors. Anton left the house only to help Olga Vasilieva. At nineteen she was adopting a second orphan girl, and asked Anton to come to her solicitor's to witness her will.

Masha was rarely at home. She taught at a school for 40 roubles a month.[15] She went with Aleksandr Khotiaintseva to an art studio, where they were painting Abram Sinani for his bereaved parents. She sold a painting. In the evenings she received girlfriends whom Anton no longer met, while Olga's relatives kept Anton company. Anton liked Olga's Uncle Sasha, another Aleksandr in name and character, with his womanizing, drinking, and public outrages. Uncle Karl the doctor and Olga's brothers, the lawyer Volodia and the engineer Konstantin, left Anton cold. Masha told Misha: 'The worst thing about Antosha's marriage is his wife's numerous bourgeois relatives who have to be taken into account.'[16]

In Yalta, Evgenia moaned, begging to be fetched to Moscow. Anna told her she must wait until he got back, and Masha placated her by saying that the apartment Olga had chosen had a smelly lavatory, rats decomposing beneath the floorboards and walls too thin for privacy. If Evgenia agreed to stay, Masha would bring her to Moscow in the New Year. Anton guaranteed this journey and Evgenia calmed down.

It was cold, and by mid October Anton knew he had to leave Moscow. To Miroliubov, the editor of *Everybody's Magazine*, Anton confided: 'My wife is crying, and I forbid her to leave the theatre. In a word, commotion.' Vania told a friend that Anton would not let Olga quit, telling her that life 'without work was impossible.' In the end Olga let him go alone. She sent Evgenia a complicated and patronizing list of instructions which confused and insulted her, even though Olga's intention was to provide Anton with a diet that was easily digested as well as nourishing:

> Here he has been eating grouse, turkey, partridge, poussin; he eats salt beef, pork chops, but not often. He likes tongue, cook him kidney, liver, fry mushrooms in sour cream. Make fish soup, but give him rissoles very sparingly. And please give him a sweet or fruit pastille, or get chocolate from Vernet's. Find fresh eggs for his breakfast.

On 28 October Anton travelled from the railhead to Yalta, frozen from the six-hour coach ride over the mountain. He brought with him an ox tongue that had gone off in the heat of the railway carriage and yet another clock, broken on the journey. Intact were dried and salted mushrooms, slippers for Evgenia and felt boots for the ancient Mariushka. A passionate letter from Olga was following him: 'Antonka, how much I want to have a little half-German, to use your phrase "a half German which would distract you and fill your life". There is confusion and struggle inside me.' Olga reproached Anton for not begetting a child as soon as they married; yet the longing for a child was his. A fortnight later she reported the arrival of her period: 'Once again we shan't have a little half-German . . . why do you think that this little half German will fill my life?' Masha and Olga moved again to a bright new flat, in the same building as Vishnevsky, close to the Sandunov baths, with central heating and electric lighting. (The servant girl's baby daughter, Anna, was sent to a baby farm in the country and was not heard of again.) Olga's letters regaled Chekhov with what she had eaten and drunk; Masha's with the absurdities of theatre life.

Until the New Year Anton led a monotonous life in Autka, working desultorily at 'The Bishop'. His health deteriorated. After Dr Altshuller examined him on 8 December 1901 he suffered a hæmorrhage and began to take creosote. Diarrhœa and hæmorrhoids followed. Altshuller decided to abandon his trip in the New Year to the Pirogov congress in Moscow. At Christmas Dr Shchurovsky came to the Crimea to Tolstoy's bedside. Dr Altshuller and he compared notes. Shchurovsky found Anton's state 'serious'.[17] Altshuller used more drastic remedies: large compresses, some with cantharides (Spanish fly) to irritate the tissues and disperse pleurisy. There were few diversions. The pianist Samuelson came and played Chopin's C-major nocturne for Anton. Gorky, after illegally stopping in Moscow for an ovation at the Moscow Arts Theatre, kept Anton company. (When he visited, a gendarme patrolled outside.) A wild crane broke off its flight south to join the surviving tame crane in Anton's garden and kitchen. Visitors filled Anton's study with smoke and made him miss meals. Masha did not come until 18 December, followed by Bunin. Anton begged Olga to secure leave from the theatre for Christmas. How else could they conceive a child? She offered a few days, perhaps in Sevastopol to save travelling, but she did not come, blaming her director for keeping her in Moscow. Anton's colleagues, Dr Chlenov and Dr Korobov, she said, claimed that Moscow could do him no harm. On

549

Christmas Day 1901 Olga begged Masha for affection; she felt 'very lonely and utterly abandoned'. The next day she had Masha's report that Anton was 'iller than we thought' and promised to rush to Yalta, with or without leave: 'I know I must give up my personal life . . . but it's hard to do it straight away.' Still she did not come. In Moscow, as winter deepened, Olga's thoughts turned to babies. On Anton's forty-second name-day, 17 January 1902, she told Anton: 'I began to squawk like a baby, I can. Everyone was alarmed and began telling people that a baby Chekhov has been born and congratulating me. God grant they are prophetic.' A week later there was a wild party in the theatre from midnight until morning. The actors slid down waxed boards; the actor Kachalov fought a boxing match in drag – pink tricot and high heels; Chaliapin sent for beer and sang gypsy songs; Masha laughed hysterically; everyone exchanged joke presents. 'I had a baby in nappies: Dr Grinevsky broke its head off,' Olga reported. This was horribly prophetic.

Winter was cold in Yalta. Dr Altshuller confined Anton to the house for the whole of January 1902. Olga persisted in inviting Anton to Moscow; she reported a Dr Bobrov at the Pirogov medical congress of January 1902 saying that consumptive southerners, like Anton, were best treated by northern air. Dr Altshuller insisted that Yalta was the only haven in a Russian winter. The medical congress had Dr Chekhov in mind: on January 11 the Moscow Arts Theatre gave them a matinee performance of *Uncle Vania* and they responded with telegrams to the author and the gift of a large reproduction of the Braz portrait that Anton loathed.

Anton wrote to Olga of the weather, which, as she told him, she could find out from the newspapers. To Masha Anton spoke of finance: they had failed again to sell an estate. The purchaser of Küchük-Köy did not like what she had bought, and had to be repaid. (The Chekhovs had no prospect now of being paid for Melikhovo.) There were consolations in January 1902. *Three Sisters* was awarded the Griboedov prize; after injections of arsenic, Tolstoy recovered his health.

Evgenia and Mariushka were too set in their ways to heed diet sheets. They fed Anton the rich food they had always cooked and, unable to digest fat, he lost all the weight that koumiss had put on. By 9 January it was −10° in Yalta. Anton felt that he had been 'in Kamchatka for twenty-four years'. He had nowhere warm to wash.

Masha left for Moscow on 12 January and broke her promise to take Evgenia: Anton could not be left on his own. He complained of boredom and loneliness, not breathlessness and emaciation. He despaired of writing the comedy he had half-promised the theatre. If he deserted literature for gardening, he wrote, he might live ten years longer, but he had to sit down after pruning one rose bush.[18]

Misery worked its way into 'The Bishop', which was completed by 20 February 1902. In Bunin's opinion the finest Russian story, a short work which took fifteen years to pupate, 'The Bishop' is Chekhov's last analogy between the cleric and the artist. On Palm Sunday a provincial bishop, taken ill, wonders why he reduces the congregation to tears. By Easter he is dying, attended only by a grumbling old monk. His awed mother talks to him as a bishop, not a son. Only his niece shows no fear. Harassed by visitors and typhoid, he dies with a vision of himself striding the fields: a phantom resurrection after the crucifixion of disease. Years later not everyone believes that his mother had a bishop for a son. The bishop's life is eerily like Anton's, as are his intimations of early death and doubts about his renown; the similarities would make painful reading for those who knew Anton and his mother. 'The Bishop' was Chekhov's swan song, and a pro-genitor of modern prose about loneliness and death, such as Thomas Mann's *Death in Venice*.

Anton had given up Misha to Suvorin's clutches. Aleksandr, mean-while, felt lonely and cold, and broke the ice with a letter to Anton: *New Times*, he said, was to him 'a latrine', and hostility to Chekhov in Petersburg might lose him his job. He lived all year, sometimes alone, in a freezing dacha he had built, with fancy poultry in runs he had designed, writing pot-boiler novels during his sober spells. This year Anton's affection for his elder brother was rekindled as he himself deteriorated. In January 1902 Altshuller warned Olga:

> The process has taken a step further . . . he has been very badly nourished . . . his irresponsible excursions north are harmful and dangerous to his health . . . loneliness cannot fail to have a bad effect.[19]

In Moscow Dr Dolgopolov, Olga complained: 'simply swore at me for not giving up the theatre.' The Chekhovs' new friend, Sulerzhitsky, who was in Yalta, getting over pleurisy, reproached Olga:

Anton is more depressed than anyone. Yesterday he had another small bleed, he is suffocating confined to the house. You must come, he is not just your husband but a great writer whose well-being is vital to everyone, to all Russian literature. The Arts Theatre must ... despatch you here.[20]

In letters all that winter Olga bewailed her own egotism, but her flattery of Anton sounds like Arkadina's from *The Seagull*: 'You are the Russian Maupassant!' She made sentimental journeys, taking tea in Room No. 35 in the Hotel Dresden from which Anton had 'abducted' her. She promised erotic delights – 'I kiss you hard, tastily, long and penetratingly, so all your sinews feel it', 'I shall bite off your ear', 'I shall hug you till your ribs crack' – and demanded: 'be rough to me and I'll like it, then you'll kiss and caress me.'[21] She talked of loneliness in letters that told with relish of excursions and parties until dawn. She asserted 'I must build you a life that is good, pleasant, peaceful,' and added the rider 'that's my dream for old age.'

The sisters-in-law got on harmoniously in Moscow until March 1902: living together, they could enjoy a private life without gossip. Olga had Nemirovich-Danchenko to lean on; Masha had Bunin. Masha's letters to Anton depict Olga on Anton's name day, carousing past dawn with a crowd of men. The Stanislavskys also hinted to Anton at her *joie de vivre* – Maria that she flirted with Konstantin, Stanislavsky that her neckline shocked even the roué Aumont, at whose theatre they were rehearsing.[22]

Now *Antonovkas* visited Olga in Moscow, not Anton in Yalta. Curiosity about Olga drove Tania Shchepkina-Kupernik and Nina Korsh to risk rebuff; Maria Drozdova shocked Olga by flirting with her brother and talking of her sexual adventures. Olga could not endure either Lika Mizinova or Maria Andreeva, both of whom Masha persisted in cultivating. At Christmas Olga told Anton: 'Lika was drunk and kept pestering me to drink with her, but I evaded her, I don't like it.' To Masha she portrayed Lika (whom many in the company now adored) as a man-crazed, drunken harridan. Ousting Olga's rival, the beautiful Maria Andreeva, from the theatre was harder. To Anton Olga accused Andreeva of acting so badly as to destroy Nemirovich-Danchenko's reputation as a playwright.'[23] Olga saw him as one writer facing three merchants – Stanislavsky, Morozov and the actor Luzhsky; Nemirovich-Danchenko was a David among

Philistines, 'plucked and gnawed at on all sides'. If he left the Moscow Arts Theatre, she said, she would go too. Anton was aware that Olga was loyal to the director, not to the theatre.

Back in Moscow, Masha set out Olga's dilemma to Misha: 'I can't understand her – she's sorry for her husband and she is lonely, at the same time she cannot bear to be away from her roles, probably she's afraid someone might act them better.'[24] Olga meanwhile signed a three-year contract. Savva Morozov, the patron, made the theatre into a shareholders' company. The three 'merchants' invited twelve trusted actors to take 3000 rouble shares in the theatre. Morozov offered a subsidy of 30,000 and a building refurbished by Franz Schechtel at a nominal lease. The shareholders' overall profit in the first year, Vishnevsky reckoned, would be 50,000 roubles. Olga Knipper took a share. The talented actor-director Vsevolod Meyerhold and the producer Sanin-Schoenberg were cut out. Within a year both left.[25] Olga Knipper was as tied to the theatre as to Chekhov. Suvorin visited Moscow in early February 1902, to stage his play *The Question*. He visited Olga and praised her, to her face and by letter to Anton. Possibly this was Suvorin's ploy to win back Anton's friendship, but Olga never forgave the vilification of Suvorin's reviewers.

In fact Anton prized Olga's independence. She earned more than 3000 roubles a year, and only once asked him to cover a mysterious debt. He would not ask her to break a contract. He would rather be with her in Moscow's political ferment, than drag her to the tedious tensions of 'this mangy Yalta'. 'You need not weep,' he told Olga, 'you live in Moscow not because you want, but because we both want that.' He complained nevertheless about her masters' ruthlessness in depriving him of her company. Stanislavsky assured him it was more fun to be married to an absent actress than an ever-present nonactress. Nemirovich-Danchenko, however, finally succumbed to Masha's appeals and Anton's hints. At the end of January 1902, returning from his sister's death bed in Nice, he promised 'I shall definitely let Olga come and see you for a short time ... I am very frightened (as a director) by her extraordinary pining for you.' He then telegraphed, 'I guarantee Olga will be free 21 February to 2 March.'[26] Anton called this 'a teaspoonful of milk after forty years' famine'.

SEVENTY-EIGHT

Conjugal Ills
February–June 1902

On Friday 22 February 1902, Olga and Anton embraced after four months apart. They spent five days in seclusion. 'The Bishop' was sent to Petersburg. No visitors came; correspondence stopped. Masha was in Moscow. Their week together was clouded twice. On Tuesday Olga bled: she presumed she would not conceive. Parting on Thursday was muted: Anton did not kiss her goodbye as she left for the dash over the mountains. 'You were coming outside,' she wrote to him, 'but the wind stopped you, and I . . . only realized what had happened when the driver had moved off.' Olga had a roast duck and a bottle of wine to fortify her until she reached Simferopol.

At the station there were no Pullman cars, so Olga took an ordinary train. She suddenly fell ill: 'I couldn't get to the door of the ladies', I collapsed and couldn't get up, my arms and legs wouldn't obey me, I broke out in a cold sweat. I thought I had food poisoning.' On the train Olga confided in a sympathetic fellow-traveller, who told her she must be pregnant. She doubted it. In Moscow she felt little better. She changed trains and proceeded straight to Petersburg, where the theatre performed in Lent. She had lost weight, her head ached and she dosed herself with quinine. Another actress gave her stimulants. She took painkillers and bandaged her head. By 9 March she was more her old self, eating grouse. Anton stopped worrying. He was cross with her: she would not give him an address.

During their reunion, Anton had received a telegram: Gorky, barely out of prison, had been elected to the Academy of Sciences, whose president was a cousin of the Tsar. In a final round he had won the necessary majority, nine white to three black balls. Gorky was unexpectedly pleased. Then the government and Tsar annulled the election. The radical Korolenko immediately announced his resignation, and pressed Chekhov to resign. Anton pondered. His sympathies were radical, but like Tolstoy he distrusted political gestures.[27]

Marital life left Anton with a coughing fit that went on for days and nights, but pleasant memories. The day that Olga left, four *Antonovkas* re-emerged – the headmistress Varvara Kharkeevich, her sister-in-law Manefa, Sophie Beaunier and Dr Sredin's wife, Sofia. Anton told Olga: 'They all have an identical little smile: "we didn't want to disturb you!" As if we'd spent five days sitting naked and doing nothing but make love.'

In Petersburg that March Olga acted almost every night. *New Times* now praised her, but the reviewer was Misha Chekhov, her brother-in-law, and she was embarrassed. *The Petersburg Newspaper* attacked Nemirovich-Danchenko's play mercilessly as 'a waste of effort, dead meat'. The author leant on Olga for moral support, while she too needed comfort. Suvorin came to tempt Olga: 1000 roubles a month to join his theatre. There were also painful encounters. Lika Mizinova was in Petersburg, following the director Sanin-Schoenberg who, driven out of the Moscow Arts Theatre, now worked for the Aleksandrinsky theatre; Lika and he were betrothed. Their happiness upset Olga. Anton calmed her down:

> Why so sour? I've known Lika for a long time and, whatever else, she's a good, clever and decent girl. She'll be unhappy with Sanin, she won't love him and above all won't get on with his sister and probably in a year will have a big fat baby and in eighteen months start being unfaithful.

Anton's prophecy, wrong on all counts, did not reconcile Olga to her rival.

Olga also disliked Misha and his wife, her namesake – 'Where did he get a wife like that from?'[28] She dined with them, but could not stop his fawning reviews. Anton washed his hands: 'He loves Suvorin and rates Burenin highly. Let him write what he likes.' Masha lied to Olga. 'You made a good impression on him, he liked you.'[29] In fact Misha had let his sister know of his true feelings:

> I saw *In Dreams* on the office ticket and our sister-in-law arranged *Three Sisters* ... Every time we met, the sister-in-law asked if I'd seen one thing or another? I answer no. She knew full well that I had no ticket, but I simply can't ask her to get me one ... One evening O. visited me! She brought the children sweets ... as though

she were duty-bound to visit us, because we are damned relatives who'll take offence if not . . . [*Late one evening*] I went to see Lika (for the fifth time) and of course she was out. I passed by O.'s lodgings, knocked. 'Come in!' I did. And, it seemed, at a bad time. Nemirovich-Danchenko was with her, they were having tea and jam. I had interrupted a conversation. I didn't know what to do with myself. O. apparently did not know what to do with me.[30]

On this occasion Nemirovich-Danchenko and Olga had attacked Misha as Suvorin's hack (even though they were off to see the old man themselves). Offended, Misha left.[31]

On 31 March 1902, Olga acted Gorky's *Petty Bourgeois*, a play in which she had to run up and down stairs. Back in the wings she collapsed in agony, and surgeons were sent for. Professor Jakobson and Dr Ott chloroformed their patient and operated at midnight. Olga woke in the morning, badly shocked; in pencil she scrawled a note to Anton, but did not post it for four days:

> I left Yalta hoping to present you with a little Pamfil, but I didn't realize, I kept thinking it was gut trouble, I didn't realize I was pregnant, much though I wanted to be . . . Ott and the other one decided on a curettage and confirmed that it was an embryo of 1½ months. You can imagine how upset I was. I've never been in the hands of gynæcologists before.[32]

Nobody telegraphed Anton, for fear that the news would bring him to Petersburg in spite of the winter cold, but, because Olga's daily letters had stopped, Anton began to worry. Olga wrote on 2 April from the obstetrical clinic: she said she was sitting up and Stanislavsky was taking her back to her lodgings; the season was over, and she hoped to come to Yalta on Easter Saturday.

If this had been just an early miscarriage, Olga could have travelled. Anton, a good gynæcologist and obstetrician, must have been perplexed: how could Olga have been six weeks pregnant, when she had only spent seven nights with him, five weeks previously, at the end of her cycle? Why did two of Petersburg's most distinguished surgeons operate in the middle of the night for an early miscarriage? Nemirovich-Danchenko and his wife set off for Yalta on 6 April to put Anton's mind at rest. Stanislavsky's telegrams swore that there was no danger. Olga gave other clues: 'pains in the left side of my belly, bad pains from an inflamed ovary and maybe that's why I miscarried . . . I still have an inflamed left ovary. My poor belly is swollen and hurts all over.'[33] She told Masha: 'Don't tell Anton! the pains are horrible and I am still suffering.'[34] On Easter Sunday she sat up; she began daily enemas and was allowed to Yalta only with a midwife. She grudged the 3 roubles a day. She told Anton she would sleep in the drawing room, 'I do have various female instruments and need my own room. It's embarrassing to keep these vile things where a great writer can see them.' On 14 April, a week after Easter, Olga was carried on a stretcher from the boat and taken straight to bed in Autka. Nilus, who was painting Anton's portrait, packed up his equipment and fled. Anton and Masha became Olga's doctor and nurse.

Anton never talked of his doubts about the diagnosis and operation on Olga. His behaviour was caring, but distant. Three months later he wrote to Wilhelm Jakobson and received a telegram from the surgeon in reply: 'No suspicions, remains of egg removed, inflammation of lining.' Bleeding in February, illness throughout March, Olga's collapse and unspeakable ovarian pain, the midnight operation, the swollen belly, followed by peritonitis, indicated, however, not so much miscarriage and curettage as an ectopic pregnancy, laparotomy and infection.[35] Only recently had Petersburg surgeons first dared remove an embryo in a fallopian tube: abdominal surgery was risky in 1902 and ectopic pregnancies were fatal. Anton would have known that an ectopic pregnancy erupts between eight and twelve weeks from conception. If this was what had happened to Olga, conception must have taken place when she and Anton had been 800 miles apart.

A season of illness followed, but Olga's physical vitality and Anton's discretion pulled them through. Their distress lay in suspecting that, despite Ott's airy assurance that Olga could conceive 'triplets right away', Olga's fertility must be lowered, if she now had a ruptured Fallopian tube and a damaged ovary. Anton had little time to beget a child.

Anton, depressed by Olga's and his own ills, grew restless and decided that Yalta was too far from Moscow and Autka was too hilly for walking. Two properties nearby had burnt down because the fire brigade had no water. He wanted Masha to inspect property in Sevastopol instead. By 24 April he was alone with Olga. Masha had returned to Moscow to examine her pupils, to have an abscess treated by a lady doctor, to flirt (openly) with Stanislavsky and (secretly) with Bunin, and to celebrate Lika's wedding. From Moscow she boisterously berated Olga: 'Still full of fat, what are you raging about, you lay-about of a sister-in-law? Get up and earn some money for your husband and his crippled sister.' She did not joke with Misha: 'Olga behaves rather oddly towards me, so does Antosha and I am suffering.' By mid May Olga seemed stronger than her husband. They waited to hand over the household to Masha. On 24 May Anton and Olga left for Moscow, the second and last time they would take this journey together. In Moscow Dr Varnek, an obstetrician, found Olga's ovaries inflamed. He put her to bed for three weeks, prescribing summer at a Bohemian spa, Franzensbad, and rest for a year. Olga howled in distress. Anton would not go to Franzensbad.[36] His diagnosis was peritonitis: she should convalesce for two years, and eat only cream.

In Moscow Olga's abdominal pains grew worse. Anton was too ill to nurse her. Vishnevsky, a tireless *cavaliere servente*, came to the rescue. At midnight on 1 June 1902 he drove round Moscow to find a doctor who had not yet left for a weekend in the country. In the morning he found one. Olga was now skeletal; she was given morphine. When she could be moved, she would be taken to the gynæcologist Maxim Strauch's clinic. On 6 June 1902 Olga told Masha:

> All the Yalta suffering is nothing compared to one night in Moscow. I raved with pain, I tore my hair and if I could have, I'd have done myself in. I roared all night in an alien voice. The doctor says no man has any concept of this pain . . . Everyone is lighting a candle in church for me.

Vishnevsky exhausted himself nursing both Chekhovs. Nemirovich-Danchenko came every day and stayed from noon till six in the evening. Stanislavsky, meanwhile, took practical action. He opened negotiations with Olga's rival, in love and in the theatre. After visiting Olga, he wrote to his wife: 'Komissarzhevskaia will lead the conversation around to transfer to our theatre. That wouldn't be bad! Especially now that there is little hope of Knipper for next season . . . I'm very sorry for her and Chekhov.'[37]

In Olga's absence, Lika and her new husband, staying in Yalta at a villa where Anton had once rented rooms, were visiting Masha. Evgenia and the servants went on a three-day pilgrimage to a monastery. Anton hated the vigil in Moscow and dreamt of sailing down the Volga, as his brother Aleksandr was doing. Olga made a super-human effort to rally. Maxim Strauch decided that she could go straight to Franzensbad, but she lapsed again with terrible nausea. Dr Strauch brought a Dr Taube to see her. He, like Anton, diagnosed peritonitis, an often fatal inflammation of the whole belly. Olga rallied again. Anton took to Taube; 'a popular and very sensible German,' he told Nemirovich-Danchenko. After four days Anton felt that Olga might be able to avoid a second operation, but he still refused to contact Olga's mother so as 'not to start a flood of tears'.

As she improved, Anton began to go out. He met Vera Komissar-zhevskaia, with her lover and manager Karpov. He watched a boxing match. He left town to fish. One old flame – Olga Kundasova – was bold enough to sit for hours with Chekhov's wife (who asked her to leave). Feeling affection for both Anton and for Suvorin, Kundasova strove to keep their friendship alive. As Anton's physical health declined, her mental health improved. For all Kundasova's radicalism, she was beholden to Suvorin, as a man who supported her and was not afraid of sparring with her, and she reported to him on Anton's health. She appealed to Anton to heal the rift. Suvorin longed to see Anton. He had told Konstantin Nabokov, uncle to the future novelist, 'There are only two interesting younger men in the whole of Russia, Chekhov and Orlenev [an actor], and I have lost both of them.'[38] On 11 June 1902 Kundasova wrote to Anton from Petersburg:

> To me Aleksei looked none too good and very irritable psychologi-cally. *As you wished, there was no discussion of you except for the matter of your health.* I beg you with all my heart, write him a few words, perhaps he has not long to live and, clearly, your silence weighs heavily on him. Remember how wretched it is to love somebody and have no response.[39]

Kundasova pumped Olga for information, and told Suvorin that Anton was in no state to go to Petersburg: Suvorin would have to come to the Crimea in August.

On 14 June Anton slipped the leash. He had decided, after Easter, 'to be a hermit' and mull over a play for their Theatre. Olga could sit up, take chicken soup, and even walk, though she was still too swollen to put on her corset. The selfless Vishnevsky would watch over her and nurse her. Anton told Nemirovich-Danchenko: 'The main thing is that I may leave, and tomorrow, the 17th, I set off with Savva Morozov for Perm [*in the Urals*]. I'll be home by 5 July.' The day Anton left, Olga's mother came to take his place with the patient.

SEVENTY-NINE

Liubimovka
June–September 1902

Accompanied by Savva Morozov and two Germans, and equipped, despite the heat, with a new overcoat and Swedish padded jacket, Anton retraced his honeymoon route of a year before. This time, however, he sailed past 'Drunken Grove' in the dark and headed northeast up the Kama to Perm, to the country of *Three Sisters*. Boats and trains slowly took Anton and his party to the Urals where Morozov owned an estate and a chemical plant. Morozov may have been one of Russia's 'Rockefellers', subsidizing the arts and revolutionaries such as Gorky, but his workers lived in squalor with a drunken paramedic and an empty pharmacy to treat them. On discovering conditions at the plant, Anton made forcible protests, to which Morozov responded magnificently: the working day was cut from twelve to eight hours. Morozov then abandoned Anton and toured his lands. Anton wandered in the sultry heat 'tormented by having nothing to do, by isolation and his cough', noted a student engineer at the plant.[40] It was all, Anton told Nemirovich-Danchenko, 'too grey and depressing to write a play about.' On 28 June 1902, seen off by the workers, whose school was now named after him, Anton took the train back to Moscow.

The object of Anton's trip had been not to discover new horizons so much as to escape from a tedious bedside. Nevertheless, he and Olga had exchanged telegrams and letters daily. 'I'm not worried about you, since I know my little dog is well,' Anton wrote on his first day away. He now called her 'stick' as well as 'dog'. She colluded with him, declaring herself in the hands of decent doctors. To others Olga revealed her nausea, boredom and despair. She was allowed only to read and play patience, forbidden to start guitar lessons. 'How foul, grey and boring everything is,' was her lament to Masha. Her hair was falling out and her intestines needed enemas of olive oil. She was 'indifferent to everything or morbidly irritable'. She told her mother-in-law: 'I sit like a sad widow, I mostly lie down . . . If Vishnevsky comes, we sit and read in silence . . . I am a complete cripple. I keep thinking I shall never get better. And what use am I without health?'[41]

On 2 July Anton returned to Moscow and the sun shone. The Stanislavskys were themselves off to Franzensbad and invited Anton and Olga to stay in their country house at Liubimovka during their absence. The house stood on the river Kliazma, northeast of Moscow, surrounded by forests and meadows. Here Stanislavsky's servants Egor and Duniasha attended them. Olga lay and later swam and rowed. Anton fished and handed each catch over to Egor to be cooked. Visitors were turned away, and church bells were muted. Olga lived downstairs, Anton and Vishnevsky upstairs, all 'sleeping like bishops'. Dr Strauch checked on his patient. The neighbours, the Smirnovs, were considerate. Their two teenage daughters courted Anton. So did their eccentric English governess, Lily Glassby, who spoke pigeon Russian. Olga was too taken aback to interfere as Lily fed Anton ice cream, addressed him in the intimate form, and wrote him affectionate notes: 'Christ be with you, brother Antony, I love you.'[42]

Anton wrote almost no letters, and did no work on the play which the theatre was waiting for: he was absorbing material. Nemirovich-Danchenko and Stanislavsky invested their hope for the following season in Gorky's *Lower Depths*. Anton read the proofs and told Gorky he had 'almost hopped with pleasure' at the play. Confident that Gorky would fill the Moscow Arts Theatre for the autumn, he could take his time germinating his new comedy. Liubimovka's household and suburban trains imbue the setting for *The Cherry Orchard*. Anton encouraged Egor's ambition to be literate and independent, offering him Vania's services as a teacher. Egor's clumsiness and precious language were absorbed into the character of Epikhodov, while Lily Glassby's pathos infuses Charlotta. Duniasha gave her name to the fictional servant.

The river fish, mushrooms and fresh milk of Liubimovka delighted Anton. He told Masha that it was paradise after Yalta: he longed to own a dacha near Moscow. By August Olga was out of danger. Strauch said she could start rehearsals in two weeks. Even in paradise, however, Anton was restless. He had hidden two hæmorrhages from Olga, wanted to escape scrutiny and decided to visit Yalta alone. The theatre and Dr Strauch, he knew, would forbid Olga to risk a rough railway ride. She felt deserted, though the Stanislavskys returned home just as Anton left, and Anton implied that he would soon be back. Although she put a brave face on Anton's departure from Liubimovka, Olga was very angry.

Left in Yalta to cope alone with a drought-stricken garden, Masha had not had a happy summer. Her letters to Olga also hint at an unhappy love affair with Bunin. Bunin, between leaving his first wife and finding his second, had a succession of affairs, abroad and in Russia. Masha wrote to him: 'Dear Bouquichon, I was very sad when you left . . . Of course it'd be nice to be one woman in ten, but nicer still to be the only one, to combine the Yakut girl, the Temir girl, the Sinhalese girl. etc . . .'[43] Anton's arrival would have raised Masha's spirits, had it not coincided with a letter from Olga so hurtful that Masha destroyed it – too late, for Anton had casually read it. Olga sensed a plot: she accused Masha and Evgenia of luring Anton from her when they knew she was confined to bed. Masha replied in distress:

> For the first time in our lives mother and I have been called cruel for, as you put it, expecting Anton all the time. Even though we took such loving care of you when you were ill in Yalta and in Moscow!! What are we to do – I can't rub myself off the face of the earth. I'll tell you frankly that it is quite enough for me just to hear about my brother that he is happy and healthy and occasionally to see him.[44]

Olga could not bear brother and sister to be in concert. She told Masha:

> Why entangle Anton in our relationship? . . . I was hurt because your stubborn waiting seemed to imply that you didn't want Anton to be in the Moscow dust fussing around me, his sick wife . . . If you'd trusted me as you used to and tried to understand me just a bit, you'd never have shown that letter to Anton . . . You're chasing me out of your heart as hard as you can . . . *This* letter at least you *won't* show him, I beg you.[45]

To Anton she wrote on 28 August 1902:

> Why didn't you tell me straight out that you were going for good? . . . How it hurts me that you treat me like a stranger or a doll that

mustn't be disturbed. You are going to hate my letters. But I cannot be silent. You and I have to face a long separation. I'd have understood if you'd spent September in Liubimovka. Our life just doesn't make sense any more. If only I knew you needed me, and not just as an enjoyable woman ... How horrible, Anton, if everything I write should arouse no more than a smile, or perhaps you show this letter to Masha as she did [*mine to you*].[46]

Olga attacked Anton for misleading her into expecting him back at Liubimovka. Anton's replies are a disconcerting mix of resentment, fair-mindedness and manipulation.

I can't think why you're angry with me, I wouldn't have left but for business and hæmhorrhages ... I won't write a play this year, I don't feel like it ... Masha did not show me your letter, I found it on mother's desk and realized why Masha was upset. It was a horrible rude letter, and above all, unfair ... naturally I understood your mood. But you must not, must not do that, darling, you must fear unfairness ... Don't tell Masha I have read your letter to her. Or, anyway, do as you like. Your letters chill me ... Don't let's separate so early before we've had a proper life, before you give birth to a boy or girl for me. And when you do, then you can act as you wish.

Only in September 1902 did Olga, Anton and Masha declare a truce. Anton forced himself to make extravagant protestations of affection to Olga:

I take my little dog by the tail, swing her round several times and then stroke and caress her ... I do a *salto mortale* on your bed, stand on my head, grab you, turn over several times and throw you to the ceiling before catching you and kissing you.

The Stanislavskys had returned, cursing Europe. Liubimovka came to life. They took Olga on expeditions to buy honey, to fish and to explore Moscow's dosshouses before starting work on Gorky's *Lower Depths*.

Moscow injected Olga with new spirit. Franz Schechtel's *Art Nouveau* conversion gave the Moscow Arts Theatre a permanent home: a large theatre with fine dressing rooms and electricity. Olga could go to the baths. She enjoyed an uninhibited evening with her mother and uncles – '*Bohème* in full swing ... I love the spirit of our house ... we all sincerely love each other.' After a vigil by his sister's deathbed,

Nemirovich-Danchenko was back: Olga talked to him at length. She was, on Dr Strauch's advice, looking for a new apartment. She felt secure by September and wrote, in her sole response to Anton's chilling offer of her freedom: 'I shall present you with a good son for next year. You write that if we have a child I can do as I like.' Olga tried to put her conflicts with Masha in a good light: 'I am not a beast, and Masha is not an underdog. She is stronger than me. I just seem stronger because I talk loudly and boil over.' A long chat with Masha, Anton thought, got rid of festering 'little splinters', but relations between Anton and Olga were cool. Anton forgot her thirty-fourth birthday on 9 September, though he had asked for the date months before. She nagged him to answer his translators' queries. Olga's and Anton's letters exchange medical details: her enemas and his creosote.

In Yalta Anton's health was so bad that he forbade Altshuller to examine him. On 4 September Masha left Yalta to join her sister-in-law and resume teaching in Moscow. Coughing uncontrollably and unable to eat what the new cook, Polia, prepared, Anton was buoyed up only when the actor-manager Orlenev, a likeable rogue, engineered a visit from Suvorin. The day Masha left, Suvorin and Orlenev came to lunch and stayed. Suvorin's diary is terse: 'I spent two days there, almost all the time with Chekhov, in his house.' Of this encounter Anton revealed only that Suvorin 'talked about all sorts of things, and much that was new and interesting.'

Anton's interest in the outside world revived. He belatedly resigned from the Academy over Gorky's disqualification.[47] He took up his share in the theatre. He lamented Zola's mysterious death from carbon monoxide poisoning, possibly murder. He wanted to travel. Inspired by Suvorin, cautioned by Altshuller, he decided to visit Moscow when the first frosts dried the air, then winter in Italy. Anton warned Olga that Altshuller had allowed him only a few days in Moscow on his way abroad – which augured badly for begetting a child. Masha assured him that Olga was 'quite healthy and very cheerful, she can climb to the third floor.' Dr Strauch came to the Crimea and called, formally dressed, on Anton. He pronounced Olga cured. Anton asked her:

Has Strauch said you can have children? Now, or later? Oh my darling, time is passing! When our baby is 18 months old I shall probably be bald, grey and toothless.

Anton wrote more intimately: 'The longer I lived with you, the deeper and broader my love would be.' He asked her where Nemirovich-Danchenko's wife was, and Olga dismayed him by telling him that she, Olga, not 'Kitten', was nursing Nemirovich-Danchenko, who was prostrate with an ear abscess.

Anton totally rewrote his farcical monologue *On the Harm of Tobacco* and sent it to Adolf Marx. Anton told Stanislavsky that this was all he had the energy for. Evgenia and Polia, the kitchen maid, set off for Moscow ahead of him. From Sevastopol Evgenia took the fourth-class freight and passenger train; she felt trapped in an express, and preferred trains that lingered at every town on the route. Evgenia stayed in Moscow for four days, then set off for Petersburg, travelling third-class in order to sit with Polia (servants were banned from first-class compartments). At long last she would see her four Petersburg grandchildren.

In Yalta the dogs and the cranes were sated, but Anton starved, revolted by the dead flies floating in old Mariushka's borshch and coffee. Anton sent instructions for his own reception in Moscow. Olga was to buy cod liver oil, beech creosote, export beer. She promised to meet him with a fur coat, 'a warm bed and a few other things too.' On 14 October he arrived at the 'convent' where Olga, Masha and their tenant, a piano teacher, lived. He brought with him the first sketches of his valedictory story, 'The Bride'.

'The Bride'
October 1902–April 1903

ON ARRIVAL Anton wrote a note to summon Ivan Bunin, who visited. What transpired, we do not know, but almost certainly Anton was again intervening in Masha's personal life, perhaps at her request. She was seven years older than Bunin, not a noblewoman, and Bunin was unlikely to offer her marriage. Masha was shocked by the outcome of this meeting. The next day she left to stay with their mother in Aleksandr's freezing quarters in Petersburg. She returned too ill to receive anyone. Anton made a joke of his intervention: he sent Bunin a photograph of a man inscribed with a notorious decadent verse 'Cover your pale legs'. Bunin packed to go abroad. Masha's letters to him in November 1902 are downcast: 'Darling Bouquichon, What's happened? Are you well? You've vanished and God knows what I'm to think! I've been very ill . . . Is it a new love affair? Your Amarantha.' They would, however, meet again in December, when Anton withdrew to Yalta, and their involvement would flicker on and off for some years.

Chekhov summoned a masseur to ease the pains that were plaguing his limbs: TB was entering his spine. Suvorin came from Petersburg to supervise the Moscow staging of *The Question*, his play on sex before marriage. He called on Anton, but neither enjoyed the meeting. Adolf Marx dashed Anton's hopes of renegotiating the agreement. He brought out a cheap reprint of all Chekhov's works as a bonus for subscribers to *The Cornfield*, so the market was flooded. No publisher would now help Anton break free. Gorky and Piatnitsky's efforts had been in vain. Even so Anton was to tell Olga a year later that he did not feel cheated by Marx:

> I hadn't a brass penny then, I owed Suvorin, I was being published in a really vile way, too, and above all, I was about to die and wanted to put my affairs in some sort of order.

Meanwhile Anton's main source of income was under threat, for deep splits rent the Moscow Arts Theatre. The theatre could survive Vsevolod Meyerhold, too magnetic a rival for Nemirovich-Danchenko and Stanislavsky, going to Kherson on the Black Sea,[48] but Sanin's departure did harm. He took Stanislavsky's methods to Petersburg, where *The Seagull* was a success in the Aleksandrinsky theatre. Sazonova's diary on 15 November conceded, 'If they meant to show how boring rural life is, they succeeded fully'.

Anton announced to Miroliubov, the editor of *Everybody's Magazine*, that his new story was 'The Bride'. Submitting to Olga's regime, he tinkered with the work, and wrote a few letters. He complained: 'I'm not allowed out anywhere, I'm kept at home, they fear my catching a chill.' In six weeks, however, he and Olga had repaired their relationship: 'We had no unpleasant minutes,' Anton recalled. On 27 November, driven out of Moscow by his incessant cough, he left for Yalta with the faint hope of a child. Olga saw him off at the station, and took home his fur coat and boots. At the flat a dachshund was waiting for her. Brom's and Quinine's offspring lived in Petersburg; this dog came from another line. Olga called him Schnap.

Anton returned to five months of solitude. Snow was falling in Italy and, because of an outbreak of plague in the Mediterranean, Odessa was a quarantine port, and travel to and from Europe by sea was restricted. Anton despaired of wintering abroad, even though the new season promised an income of 3000 roubles from Petersburg performances alone. He now had assistance from cousin Georgi, who ran the Russian Steamship Company offices in Yalta. Anton liked Georgi, but feared the influx of Georgi's kin from Taganrog. In Autka, for conversation, he had the pious cant of Arseni, the cranes, who lived with Mariushka in the kitchen, and two mongrel dogs, one-eyed Tuzik and stupid Kashtanka. By early December he was begging Suvorin to visit him.[49] On 9 December Olga wrote to tell him:

> Unwanted visitors [*menstruation*] have arrived and hopes for a little otter cub have collapsed. My darling Anton, will I really not have children?! This is awful. The doctors must have been lying to console me.[50]

Anton immediately consoled her:

Dog, you'll definitely have children, that's what the doctors say. All you need is to be fully recovered. Everything is intact and in working order, rest assured, all you lack is a husband living with you all year round.

A week later, he insisted that he was not hiding from her anything about her health. Olga revived and *The Lower Depths* triumphed, despite Stanislavsky's disdain for its sordid setting and crude socialist rhetoric. Dr Chlenov, the venereologist, took Olga to see Moscow's whores and give her role authenticity. Olga's brother Volodia married and at the wedding she ate, drank, danced and sang, while the bride's mother danced a cancan. She had apparently stopped pining for the 'little half-German who would rake through your wardrobe and smear my ink over the desk'.

Passions ran high in the theatre. Hardly had they toasted the new season with dinner at Testov's and a telegram to Yalta, hardly had Vishnevsky declared that they needed a *noisy* success, than they celebrated the triumphant première of *The Lower Depths* with supper, cognac and gypsy songs at the Ermitage. Gorky, who had regaled everyone with accounts of his lovelife, and brought a bedraggled example, left early. For no reason that anyone could recall a drunken row burst out, and Savva Morozov was beaten up.

After Berlin Gorky's play took Moscow by storm. It moved the theatre's political profile sharply to the left: some supporters were repelled. *The Lower Depths* made money: Vishnevsky, the theatre's accountant, reported 75,000 roubles banked by the New Year, and actors were given a pay rise. Olga would now receive 3600 a year, and was disappointed only because her enemy Maria Andreeva was paid the same. Olga was less annoyed by disorder in the theatre than by the bedbugs and mice that infested their flat whose lease would expire in March 1903. She was feeling well now and longed for quarters well away from Vishnevsky, whom she found a bore and a noisy eater.

A week before Christmas 1902, Masha arrived in Yalta to look after Anton. His mood was lachrymose. He expressed a fondness for a poem by his acolyte Fiodorov: it ends 'A barrel-organ sings outside. My window is open . . . I thought of you and was sad. And you, you are so far.' Masha told Olga on 20 December:

Altshuller said that he has listened to Anton's chest and found a
deterioration which he blames on his long stay in Moscow. He had
a temperature, hæmorrhage and constant coughing. Altshuller points
out that one of us must be with him because he plays up with mother
... Altshuller is serious and does not mince his words.

Gorky, freed from police surveillance, had been sent by his wife and
doctor to rest in Yalta: he too was coughing blood. The next day he
and three doctors turned up at Anton's house. One was Dr Sredin,
who claimed (prematurely, for nephritis was to fell him) to be
recovering from TB even more advanced than Anton's. Anton
removed the compress that Altshuller had put on his chest. He felt
so much better, he assured Olga, that he was going to the dentist.
The dentist, Ostrovsky, was a barbarian – 'dirty hands, instruments
not sterilized' – and deserted Anton in mid operation for his duties
in the Jewish cemetery. In any case, by Christmas Anton had fever,
aching limbs, insomnia, coughing and pleurisy. Altshuller diagnosed
flu. Masha nursed him, constantly cooking, providing a breakfast of
five soft-boiled eggs, two glasses of cod-liver oil and two tumblers of
milk. She left Yalta for Moscow on 12 January. Anton relapsed. *The
Odessa News* announced that 'Chekhov has fully recovered from his
chest disease.'

Olga demanded bulletins by telegram, accusing Anton of hiding his
illness. She was fed up with living apart, and embarrassed to be an
absent wife. She did not, however, come to see him as the doctor asked.
'I can't believe Altshuller on his own,' she told Anton 11 February, 'he
is not that expert.' She sketched out a life: they would buy a properly
heated dacha near Moscow where Anton could see her often. From
mid January, she went on expeditions with colleagues, inspecting
country houses where a consumptive might survive a Moscow winter.

For his forty-third name-day Olga gave Anton mints, a large leather
wallet, a tie, a case of beer, and sweets. Travellers brought these
presents to Yalta. Anton became irritable. The beer had frozen in the
freight car and exploded; the mints were from the wrong shop and
had no taste; the wallet was too big for banknotes; the tie was too
long. He complained to Masha that nobody came to his name day
and that all her presents were useless too. (He was delighted, however,
with bronze piglets from Olga's Uncle Sasha and ivory elephants from
Kuprin.) Olga treated him like a petulant child. She sent Shapovalov,

the architect, with new mints. On 1 February Anton listed what he really wanted: chocolates, herrings, bismuth, toothpicks and English creosote. Suvorin, equally depressed, wanted contact again, but Anton was too wan to maintain the friendship, even though it had sparked into life the previous autumn. Olga Kundasova begged Anton, in five close-written pages, to forgive the old man his political crimes: 'Don't be so imperturbably calm and write to him ... there are many things it is best to forget.' Anton wrote, but brusquely. Suvorin, now that the Dauphin 'was ruining his life', was no longer a stimulating correspondent.

Flotsam from Anton's past surfaced in Moscow. The actor Arbenin, who had married Glafira Panova, told Olga that Anton had pursued Glafira in Odessa fourteen years before. Anton vehemently denied seducing her. Vera Komissarzhevskaia confronted Olga in Moscow. She wanted to have the rights to stage Anton's new play, and warned him, 'You seem to have forgotten my existence, I exist all right, and how.' 'If the actress bothers you,' Olga told Anton on 3 February, 'be sure I shall wallop her. I think she's mentally ill.'[51] A crone, the sister of the dramatist and inventor Pushkariov, whom Anton had known in his student days, called on Olga with her comedy set in Bulgaria: Pushkariova wanted the Chekhovs to have it staged. As she was, through Aleksandr and Natalia, a remote sister-in-law, Olga was polite. To Anton she was sarcastic:

> She has eyes like olives, poetic curls and a single tooth which hangs on her soft lip, crimson and tasty. You have good taste ... You propose when you come to Moscow to sleep three in a bed, so I'll invite her.

Lika Mizinova, with her husband Sanin and her old friend Viktor Goltsev, also braved Olga, who disabused Anton of any fantasies he might have had: 'Lika has got horribly stout – she is colossal, gaudy, rustling. I feel so scrawny by comparison.'

Altshuller's compresses of Spanish fly pulled Anton through pleurisy. By his forty-third birthday, 16 January, he could sit at his desk. Altshuller warned Olga a week later: 'The stay in Moscow has had a far worse effect on his lungs than any previous journey.'[52] Evgenia was worried: she wrote to Masha and to Vania's wife in Moscow: 'For several days I was in floods of bitter tears in case you found out he

571

was ill. I asked Georgi to write that Anton was well, but thank God he is now.'[53] At the end of January Altshuller allowed Anton to ride into Yalta for a haircut, but henceforth forbade him to walk or to wash. Surely, Olga demanded, he could stroll on the covered veranda and wash with buckets of hot water, or eau de cologne? Anton had no illusions: 'You and I have little time left to live.' He relented about his presents and made the wallet a portfolio for drafts of his story. A better present arrived: Olga was bored with Schnap, the dachshund which had been given to her, and Shapovalov brought the dog down from Moscow.

Anton never let Olga read his manuscripts. She was hurt to be almost the last of his intimates to read 'The Bride'. What had taken him a day in 1883, and a week in 1893, took a year in 1903, a slowing down which marked not just the decline in Anton's vitality, but the extreme care with which, in his final period, every phrase was chosen. When it was published in autumn 1903, all who knew Chekhov read it as a farewell. As with all the work he treasured, he grudged the censor the slightest change. 'The Bride', like *Three Sisters*, portrays three women trapped in a remote northern town, but this time they are ordered vertically: grandmother, mother, and Nadia the heroine. Nadia deserts her fiancé and her windswept garden for university. Her liberation at the end of the story from provincial boredom would be a triumph, but for the narrator's sly interpolation of the phrase: 'or so it seemed to her'. 'The Bride' shows inspiration, perfectionism and thrift. It recycles material from *Three Sisters*. In the speeches of Nadia's mentor, Sasha, who dies while taking a koumiss cure, Chekhov adumbrates the ragged-trousered philanthropist Trofimov of *The Cherry Orchard*.

The Cherry Orchard, through superhuman effort on the part of Anton, was now crystallizing too. The image of cherry blossom had recurred in Chekhov's prose for fifteen years. In autumn 1901 he first mentioned it to Stanislavsky as a setting for a future play. The title *The Cherry Orchard* was first mentioned to Masha in 1902, shortly after the news came that the cherry trees at Melikhovo had been chopped down by Konshin, the purchaser. Not until 1903, however, did Anton confirm to Olga that this play would be the 'vaudeville or comedy' he had vaguely promised to the theatre.[54] He weighed each of its four female roles as a vehicle for Olga. She saw the play as hers and was furious when he thought of letting Komissarzhevskaia stage it in Petersburg. She told him that Nemirovich-Danchenko needed a monopoly, and that Anton, as a shareholder, could not let the company down. Nemirovich-Danchenko backed her that February: 'Your wife is pining manfully. Really, can't you live near Moscow? What doctor do you *really* trust? We awfully need your play.' The degree to which Anton was still spellbound by his first Seagull is shown by his frankness when he wrote to Komissarzhevskaia and disassociated himself from Olga's intransigence: 'My wife is either sick or travelling, so we never make a proper go of it.' To nobody else would he confess so unambiguously his unhappiness with his marriage.

While he struggled to write, Olga went skiing. Shrovetide came and she had a pancake party. In April she took her first automobile ride with the actors, delighted that Nemirovich-Danchenko's wife was left behind. The company was seriously split at this time: Savva Morozov and Olga's *bête noire* Maria Andreeva wanted revolutionary plays that filled the house; Olga, the Stanislavskys and Nemirovich-Danchenko wanted to stage drama of literary value. On 17 February the Moscow season ended with a triumphant *Three Sisters*.

A row erupted in the theatre on 3 March. Morozov backed the left wing who would one day destroy capitalists like himself; he blamed Nemirovich-Danchenko's conservatism for the theatre's ups and downs. Nemirovich-Danchenko walked out, Olga shouted, Andreeva wept. The split was hard to mend: Olga apologized to Morozov and persuaded him that the theatre needed both Nemirovich-Danchenko and Stanislavsky. Nemirovich-Danchenko then left for Petersburg to prepare for the company's tour there.

Olga's brother Kostia was in Moscow and she bought her four-year-old nephew birthday toys. 'I hellishly wanted a son like that for you and me,' she wrote to Anton. She urged him to take second opinions: her doctor Strauch would prescribe life near Moscow. Next winter she would adopt a different, but unspecified, plan for their conjugal life 'about which I have not spoken to Masha, so as not to upset her for no good reason'. Anton's friend from his Nice days, Prince Sumbatov, also rejected Altshuller's prescription of Yalta and compresses: a friend had 'definitely and radically recovered after two years in Switzerland on a special mountain air cure . . . I can't help thinking that you're not fighting the illness forcefully enough'.[55]

Anton agreed to go to Switzerland at Easter with Olga, on one passport 'so that you can't run away from me', but would not talk of the future. In March life improved. Cubat, the Petersburg delicatessen, opened in Yalta: now Anton could buy caviare, smoked meats and other northern delights he had missed. The only visitor he wanted was Bunin, but Bunin let him down by travelling past the Crimea without stopping off on his way to see his sister in Novocherkassk. In Moscow Olga and Masha had now moved to yet another apartment. Despite Anton's veto, Olga allowed a smoky tomcat to move in with her. She was pleased with her bright bedroom next to Anton's study, high ceilings and room for her mother's grand piano. Olga made light of Anton's shortness of breath: 'Don't fear the stairs. There's nowhere to hurry to, you can rest on the landings, and Schnap [*which Anton was to bring with him*] will console you. I shall say silly things to you.'

During Lent Mariushka cooked nothing edible for a consumptive. Anton grew testy. After booking a Pullman compartment from Sevastopol to Moscow, he stopped his almost daily letters to Olga. Stairs were bad news, and she had again withheld her exact addresses in Petersburg and Moscow. Anton raged. On 17 March 1903 he asked Vishnevsky where his wife and sister lived. Olga retaliated by demanding he take her mother's portrait down and send it: 'nobody needs it in Yalta, and I'm never there'. Under threat of divorce proceedings, she finally wired the new address. (After this spat, jokes spread around Moscow that Olga would divorce Anton and marry Vishnevsky.) Anton sent her no Easter greetings. Marriage seemed very unalluring.[56] Olga relented. In mid March the Stanislavskys took her to spend a few days at St Sergei monastery. The monks had read Chekhov and told Olga that she should 'dine, drink tea with her husband and not live apart'. Protestant by confession and nature, she was nevertheless subdued by their admonitions.

Anton disliked the theatre's bargain with Suvorin: in exchange for the right to stage Gorky's *Lower Depths* in Petersburg, Suvorin would lease the Moscow Arts Theatre his own building for their Petersburg season. (Suvorin had by now stopped vilifying Stanislavsky.) Gorky was outraged: 'Between me and Suvorin there can be no agreements.'[57] The man who had staged the anti-Semitic *Smugglers, or Sons of Israel* two years before should not have *The Lower Depths*. Despite these ructions, the season was sensational. Anton earned 3000 roubles, as well as 2000 for performances in other cities and theatres. *Uncle Vania* received ovations. At the première of *The Lower Depths* in Petersburg secret policemen replaced the ushers.

Two weeks before Easter, Masha came down to Yalta to soothe her disgruntled brother. Anton had checked the proofs of 'The Bride': the censor had left it untouched. He left the house just once, for the funeral of his colleague Dr Bogdanovich. On 10 April Olga summoned him to Petersburg. She had a large room to herself and the weather was warm. 'You and I could flirt.' He wired back 'Don't want go Petersburg. Well.' and left, with Schnap, for Moscow. He arrived on 24 April 1903, the day before Olga returned from Petersburg. He felt very ill, but went to the baths and had five months' worth of dirt steamed and beaten out of his skin.

EIGHTY-ONE

The Cherry Orchard
May 1903–January 1904

THE FIVE FLIGHTS of stairs up to the new Moscow flat were 'martyr-dom' for Anton. It was very cold outside. For a week he sequestered himself with Olga, Schnap and proofs for Marx and Miroliubov, and wrote letters. Friends and old colleagues descended, diagnosing and commiserating. He emerged in the second week of May to buy Evgenia spectacles for church and for the garden. He summoned Suvorin, who came and talked for two days. Anton urged him to publish his old friend Belousov, a crippled tailor who made trousers by day and translated Robert Burns by night.

Anton followed Suvorin to Petersburg, to see not him, but Adolf Marx, who was now willing to re-negotiate the contract if Chekhov came in person. Marx offered Anton 5000 roubles 'for medical treat-ment' – which Anton hastily refused – and a trunk of Marx editions, which he accepted. He and Marx put off discussions until August. Although the weather was warm and Anton had not seen Aleksandr, he would not stay. Anton avoided Lika too. Sanin, her husband, on military training, was worried and wrote to her: 'I can't wait for you to come to Moscow – I can't bear life without you . . . Chekhov is in Petersburg now. Are you sure he won't be looking in on you?'[58]

Masha had gone to Yalta to care for Evgenia and the garden. All at the Moscow apartment would have been peaceful, had Schnap not run under a cab. Schnap survived, his neck awry, but Anton was summoned for losing control of him; it took ten days to secure an acquittal. In May, Anton spoke to other doctor friends: none would countenance his plan to travel to Switzerland. Finally, on 24 May, he allowed Professor Ostroumov, who had taught both him and Dr Obolonsky, to examine him. Anton disliked Ostroumov, who used the *ty* form and called him 'a cripple'. Ostroumov found both Anton's lungs to be heavily damaged by emphysema and his intestines ruined by TB. He prescribed five medicines, and countermanded his pupils' recommendations. Anton had wasted four winters in Yalta: he needed dry air. Olga could renew the search for a house near Moscow. To Olga's relief, Ostroumov told Anton to bathe.

Masha was distraught at the implications of Ostroumov's new recommendations. Just as she was about to repaper Anton's study, she feared that the Yalta house might be sold, for Anton had already put the cottages at Gurzuf and Küchük-Köy back on the market. If so, she could not take up the post of headmistress of Yalta girls' school, which, rumour had it, was hers for the taking. Suddenly her home and her career were threatened. She could not sleep, she told Misha, for anguish. Misha encouraged defiance – 'If I'd obeyed the man who opposed my marriage and my move to Petersburg, I wouldn't have what I have now'[59] – and travelled 1300 miles to see her. He had hidden plans: he coveted the Gurzuf estate for himself. When he found that Masha wanted 15,000 roubles for a house that had cost 2000 – for the planned coastal railway had inflated prices – he turned on her: 'You high-principled people of rare purity of soul have been infected by the general tightfisted Yalta mood. It's a sin. I'm sad, sad, sad.'[60]

Anton assured Masha he would spend Moscow's treacherous spring and autumn in Yalta, when the Crimea, Ostroumov agreed, was safer for consumptives. The day after he saw Ostroumov, Anton left with Olga for the country: an admirer, Iakunchikova, had lent them her dacha on the Nara river southwest of Moscow. He fished the Nara, and invited his brother Vania to come and join him. He wanted silent company and told Vishnevsky that excitement might be bad for him. Did Vishnevsky not recall a performance where 'three workmen in make-up had to tie down your genitals with string to stop your trousers bursting on stage and causing a scandal?' Safe from voluble visitors, Anton wrote by the large window of the cottage or ranged the countryside west of Moscow, with Olga, in search of a house.

Anton accompanied Olga north to his haunts of the early 1880s, when, a novice doctor, he worked in Zvenigorod and Voskresensk. On 12 June, after sending off 'The Bride', rewritten in proof, he visited the dilapidated grave of Dr Uspensky of Zvenigorod, then stayed with Savva Morozov at New Jerusalem. Old friends, like Eduard Tyshko, were as crippled as Anton. No property suited Anton and after a fortnight he was back at Nara. He had not visited Babkino where he had spent three summers with the Kiseliovs, but memories merged with summer impressions into *The Cherry Orchard*. Kiseliov was bankrupt and Babkino under the hammer: when all failed, Kiseliov found, despite his gross incompetence, like Gaev in the play, a post in a bank.

Masha waited for the couple, tempting them with enormous peaches and plums and a lush green garden at Yalta. On 6 July Anton and Olga set out to join her and Evgenia, for two months. Olga put up with her sister-in-law and mother-in-law to ensure that Anton could work at *The Cherry Orchard* undisturbed. A third season with no new Chekhov play would doom the theatre. Anton had begun the play at Nara, but the search for a house had broken his train of creative thought and several pages had been lost when they blew out onto the rain-soaked grass. On 17 July 1903, resting on his wife's estate, Nemirovich-Danchenko wrote to Olga: 'I am very pleased you are in Yalta.' To Stanislavsky he wrote a week later, 'Olga writes that he sat down to his play again once they arrived in the Crimea.'[61] Anton blamed 'idleness, the wonderful weather and the difficult plot' for his sluggish progress. Stanislavsky wrote to Olga at the end of July 1903:

> What upsets us most is that Anton does not feel very well and is sometimes down in the mouth. We have often cursed Ostroumov. He talked rubbish and spoiled Anton's good mood ... we think about the play at other times, when we worry about the fate of the theatre.[62]

Olga drove visitors away. Only Tikhomirov, her colleague, could sit in the house for six hours at a time. The poet Lazarevsky's visit was cut short. His diary reads: 'once Knipper comes everyone is tense in the house ... he is in love with his wife'.[63] Masha told him that even she had limited access to Anton. The theatre was in rehearsal, but gave Olga leave until mid September to be Anton's 'Cerberus', as she put it. She felt strong: 'I am round and tanned. I get up at 6 a.m., run to bathe and swim a lot and pretty far. I eat, sleep and read and nothing else,' she reassured Stanislavsky. She made Anton work every day when he was physically able. She was now getting ready for *The Cherry Orchard* and 'drowning her new part with tears'. Vishnevsky was preparing for his new part too: Anton put him on a diet.

Others doubted Anton's stamina. Sanin wrote to Lika on 14 August 1903:

> I hardly recognized the old Chekhov. It was very painful to look at the photo ... But Knipper puts a brave face on it ... then asked with embarrassment, 'Do you see anything wrong?' She's afraid to admit it to herself.

Olga had the company of her brother Kostia: she had used her influence to get him transferred from the fever-ridden Persian border to Yalta, where he would assist the writer and engineer Garin-Mikhailovsky in building a grandiose coastal railway.

The absence of visitors was both a comfort and an exasperation, and Anton resumed his banter with Aleksandr. He wrote to him in a language Olga did not understand: 'Quousque tandem taces? Quousque tandem, frater, abutere patientia nostra? ... Scribendum est. [*How long are you going to be silent? How long, brother, are you going to try our patience ... You must write.*]' On 22 August 1903 Aleksandr responded with a warmth and robustness (in Latin and Greek) that seemed to have faded from their relationship fifteen years ago. Aleksandr pleaded for Masha and Olga's maid, the pregnant Masha Shakina:

> she could be expelled by Olga for abusing her 'cactus' with a married man whom I do not know ... please intercede with my dear *belle-sœur*: would she not forgive the guilty girl? ... Don't forget that a woman's shift is a curtain to the entrance into a public assembly where only members are allowed entry on condition that they remain standing.[64]

He was content with his sons, though Kolia had killed a dachshund, and Anton was too backward to chase the servant girls. Misha, his pride, was at twelve years old chatting in French and German, reading, despite Natalia's ban, his uncle's works, acting in amateur theatricals and chasing girls. As for Aleksandr's own potency:

> My life is pretty celibate,
> But I don't curse my luck.
> I fuck, although not well, but
> All the same, I fuck.

By September, despite his painfully slow pace, Anton was sure of his plan for *The Cherry Orchard*. He warned Stanislavsky's wife: 'At places it is even a farce; I fear I shall get it in the neck from Nemirovich-Danchenko.' Stanislavsky feared worse, telling his sister Zinaida on 7 September: 'I imagine it will be something impossible on the weirdness and vulgarity of life. I only fear that instead of a farce again we shall have a great big tragedy. Even now he thinks *Three Sisters* a very merry little piece.'[65]

Like *The Seagull, The Cherry Orchard* is subtitled 'comedy', even though it focuses on the destruction of a family and their illusions. The new play is crowded with reminiscences of earlier work and of personal traumas. The cherry trees that blossom in Act 1 recall those of his boyhood in Taganrog; the cherry trees axed in Act 4 recall the trees of Melikhovo, bought ten years earlier and now felled by Konshin. As in Anton's first play, feckless owners face an auction. The merchant Lopakhin, who urges them to sell land for cottages and then betrays them at the auction, has overtones of Gavriil Selivanov in Taganrog twenty-seven years before. The breaking string that punctuates Act 2 and Act 4 was first heard in the steppe stories of 1887. The seedy student Trofimov reminds us of the mentor, Sasha, in 'The Bride'; the feckless heroine marrying off her children to save the estate uses the tricks and phrases of the heroine in 'A Visit to Friends'. Anton's friends furnish the plot: Gaev and Ranevskaia lose the estate, as the Kiseliovs lost Babkino; Charlotta and the servants recall the motley entourage at Stanislavsky's Liubimovka.

An elegy for a lost world, estate and class, *The Cherry Orchard* nevertheless displays Anton's farcical invention at its richest. As in all Chekhovian comedy, however, the ending is grim, for the old retain power while the young are scattered to the winds. One factor alone is missing from the play: passion. Only the mistress of the house, Ranevskaia, who comes to Russia from her lover in France and then leaves again, is a sexual being. Nobody else expresses ardour, any more than Charlotta's rifle or Epikhodov's revolver ever fire. The doctor, increasingly inert in Chekhov's plays, fails to call. Death, in an ending which heralds Samuel Beckett, is banal: a senile servant is forgotten in a locked house. Black humour, menace, wistfulness, the characters' doll-like quadrilles, the dominance of landscape over inhabitants; all these qualities make *The Cherry Orchard* the progenitor of modern drama from Artaud to Pinter. The engineer Garin-

Mikhailovsky saw the same incongruity between Anton's creative imagination and his doom as we see in the owners of *The Cherry Orchard*. He noted: 'Chekhov could hardly walk, noises came from his chest. But he seemed not to notice. He was interested in anything but illness: . . . Why are such precious contents locked up in such a frail vessel?'[66]

Olga was happy. Her compliant husband even let her cat into the house. They slept in separate rooms, but she came to Anton each morning after her dawn swim. On 19 September 1903 Olga left, with Schnap but without the cat, for Moscow, for the opening of the theatre season. She was hoping that she had conceived, and was confident that the play would follow her shortly. Anton bathed in the afterglow of her affection: he wrote to his 'little horse': 'I stroke you, groom you and feed you the best oats.' He was finishing *The Cherry Orchard* with pleasure – for once ending a play not with a gun, but an axe – but he was tormented by his cough and pains in his muscles. Altshuller forbade him to wash, applied Spanish fly and beseeched him not to go to Moscow. Anton would ignore this advice.

Masha returned to Moscow on 8 October and reported on Anton's progress under her care. The same day Olga exploded with jealousy to Anton:

> You are doing something about your health at last?! Why is that so difficult when I am there? . . . Probably Altshuller thinks I am wearing you out. He avoids talking to you about health when I am there. And when I leave, you begin to eat twice as much and Masha can do anything.

Anton retorted that in Moscow he would live apart from her in furnished rooms. All he wanted was somewhere to sit in the theatre and a large lavatory; she could take a lover if she wanted. Diarrhœa, coughing and Altshuller's Spanish fly compress were making Anton's life unbearable. He complained to Olga: 'Once Masha left, the dinners naturally got worse; today for example I was served mutton which I am forbidden now, so I missed the main course . . . I eat eggs. Darling how hard it is to write a play.' Olga barely sympathized: her constipation was a match for Anton's diarrhœa. Masha had left a diet sheet in Yalta and Anton had written instructions for Mariushka and the cook. One of them even jotted down an invalid's menu. They were to provide chicken and rice, cherry compôte and blancmange; they blithely served beef, salt fish and potatoes. Anton went on hunger strike: on 15 October he was at last fed his diet.

The theatre rehearsed *Julius Cæsar* with a heavy heart: Shakespeare was not their territory and Stanislavsky was a weak Brutus. When it opened, *Julius Cæsar* was an unexpected success, but Anton still felt Stanislavsky's pressure to deliver *The Cherry Orchard* forthwith. On 14 October Anton packed up the new play and posted it to Moscow. He did what he said was absurd in Ibsen's *Hedda Gabler*: he sent the only copy. In Moscow Olga's visitors queued for permission to copy it or merely to glance. Gorky offered 4500 roubles to print it in his annual, *Knowledge*. Anton was dubious. Did his contract with Marx permit this? Was an annual a periodical? To get round the stipulations of Marx's contract with Anton, Gorky then promised 10 per cent of the proceeds to charity. (Despite his proletarian affiliations Gorky could behave like an aristocratic patron, for he was both Russia's best paid author and her most lavish commissioning editor.)

Anton wanted the play kept secret, but Nemirovich-Danchenko recounted the plot to Efros, the company's most sympathetic critic, on *The Courier*. Efros garbled the résumé and his garbled version was reprinted in the provincial papers. Anton berated Nemirovich-Danchenko for this breach of confidence, in a telegram too violent to show to Olga; he broke off all relations with Efros. Never had he been so touchy about a play and its production. He dictated the casting, the scenery and the mood. Altshuller could not stop him planning a journey to Moscow to supervise everything.

Nemirovich-Danchenko came round to *The Cherry Orchard* slowly: he felt it was 'more of a play' than Anton's previous drama, that it was 'harmonious and had new characters', but he found the tears excessive, which exasperated Anton, given that Varia was the only character who wept at all. Stanislavsky's own floods of tears at Act 4, and his claim 'This is not a comedy nor a farce, as you wrote: it's a tragedy,' dismayed Chekhov. Stanislavsky's wife hit the right note: 'Many cried, even the men; I thought it full of the joy of life and I find it fun just travelling to rehearsals . . . *The Cherry Orchard* somehow seemed not a play but a musical production, a symphony, to me.'[67]

Gorky was printing the play, but told his editor Piatnitsky, 'Read aloud, it doesn't impress one as a powerful piece. And what the [*characters*] are all moping about I don't know.'[68]

The day the play arrived in Moscow, Olga's period came. After five months together, she and Anton would still have no baby. Quarrels broke out. The whole family was in a crisis whose nature we can only guess at. Bunin, now frequenting Masha and Olga, may have been involved. Olga's close collaboration with Nemirovich-Danchenko undoubtedly unsettled Anton. Evgenia's letter from Yalta to Vania in Moscow suggests that Anton had had enough of his wife, his sister and his mother:

> Antosha told me that Masha had to find her own flat, while Olga could go and live with her mother ... poor Masha does not want to leave them, please don't talk to her about my letter I only ask you to let me come and live with you until we find somewhere ... Olga has got her own way, she has persuaded Antosha to get rid of us, she can do as she wants, but he is sorry for us and never sees anything through. E. Chekhova.[69]

Olga seemed disturbed that her enemy Maria Andreeva (who was thirty-one) was favoured by Anton for the part of the seventeen-year-old ingénue, Ania. (Anton next proposed Andreeva for Ania's pious foster-sister Varia, but Olga was not appeased.) In a letter to Nemirovich-Danchenko Anton accused him of ignoring him for years: 'I've been asking you to get an actress for Ranevskaia.' On 5 November Nemirovich-Danchenko wired a cast list, letting Anton choose actresses for only the minor roles. Olga put forward Schnap, despite his snoring and farting, to be Charlotta's nut-eating dog: Anton said no – he specified a 'small, shaggy, sour-eyed dog'.

One of the pet cranes died. Anton moaned that Olga wrote either like Arkadina in *The Seagull*: 'Do you know you are a superman?' or like a nurse and courtesan: 'Are you spraying your throat? You're not making rude gestures in the morning? Would you like your Hungarian [i.e. *herself*] to come in at night with pillow and candle and then vanish grumbling?'[70] She heeded neither his angry entreaties not to keep valuables at home, nor his demands for a parcel of lavatory paper. Instead she gave him instructions to buy a Bukhara quilt in Yalta.

By 9 November the play was copied and the actors began work. Anton strained at the leash but Olga would send for him only when dry frosty weather began. In the meantime she ordered a fur coat of young Arctic fox, warm enough for a Moscow winter, but light enough for a frail body. Anton stipulated that it had to have eiderdown padding, a fur collar and a matching hat.

The story of *The Cherry Orchard* took on a life of its own. After selling the timber from the Melikhovo plantations, Konshin declared himself insolvent, and the estate was put up for auction. Masha negotiated a sale to her Moscow neighbour Baron Stuart. Not a kopeck came of it. Baron Stuart took out a private mortgage, for five years and at 5 per cent, with Masha who at last now had funds.

Evgenia abandoned Anton to Mariushka's cooking and Arseni's caretaking and took Nastia the servant to Moscow on 18 November. She descended on Olga, who put her up in Anton's study. (Evgenia soon moved to Petersburg to spend Christmas with Misha, his children and Lika Mizinova.) Alone, Anton vented his bile. Stanislavsky was stopped from inserting spring noises – frogs and corncrakes – into a summer act. Nemirovich-Danchenko's questions revealed, Anton grumbled, that '[he] has not read my play. It began with misunderstandings and will end with them.' Anton feared that the première would be used as a pretext to mark his twenty-fifth year as a writer. In vain, for he hated the prospect of Jubilee celebrations, he protested that this would not be due until 1905. Olga hinted that she might soon call Anton to Moscow. 'Have you dreamt of your Hungarian? Will you be making rude signs in the morning? Although we shall sleep together here and I shan't be coming in the morning straight from the sea.' On 29 November she telegraphed: 'Frosts. Talk Altshuller and come.'

Many years had passed since Anton had last celebrated Christmas, New Year and his name day in Moscow. He experienced a surge of energy and attended rehearsals almost daily, disconcerting Stanislavsky: 'The author has come and confused us all. The flowers have fallen and now we only have new buds.' Anton was upset too. The censor had removed two of Trofimov's tirades and new words had to be spliced in, while Stanislavsky cut two magically evocative episodes from Act 2. Anton, only half in jest, offered the play outright to Nemirovich-Danchenko for 3000 roubles. At home, once he had his breath back after climbing the stairs, he received friends. They were perturbed. Bunin often stayed with Anton until Olga returned:

> Usually she left for the theatre, sometimes a charity concert. Nemirovich-Danchenko would fetch her; he wore a dress coat and smelt of cigars and expensive eau-de-Cologne. She wore evening dress, was perfumed, beautiful and young, and went up to her husband saying: 'Don't be bored while I'm out, darling, anyway you always feel fine with Bouquichon...' Sometimes he would wash his hair. I tried to amuse him ... About 4 a.m., sometimes at daylight, Olga would come back, smelling of wine and perfume. 'Why aren't you asleep, darling? It's bad for you.'[71]

Before Christmas Bunin went abroad, never to see Anton again. Lika did not venture from Petersburg, but her husband gave her a view of Anton's condition:

> Potapenko says that he is finished as a writer and a man. 'It is simply pitiful to read him, to see him now, in life or a photograph ... No, I put a cross on Chekhov. The man has got in an impasse and is finished. Why did that Knipper marry him? I saw them in Moscow, saw Masha [*who said*] "What horror! What a misfortune!"'[72]

Olga knew that her behaviour towards Anton was attracting unflattering comment, and told Evgenia:

> I can't tell you how much Anton's illness has upset me all this time. You must think very badly of me when you look at your life ... It's awfully hard for me suddenly to abandon my vocation ... I know you have different views and understand all too well if in your heart you condemn me.[73]

Consul Iurasov and Professor Korotniov invited Chekhov to winter once again in Nice, but *The Cherry Orchard* detained him. In any case, he was barely well enough to venture into the street, let alone cross Europe. Just before the New Year, Gorky, Leonid Andreev, and their lawyers drafted a letter to Adolf Marx, urging him to give Chekhov a new contract for his forthcoming twenty-fifth jubilee. Anton told them to desist.

In Petersburg Evgenia was forgetting her worries with Misha's family, but on 7 January Anton ordered her back: 'You've outstayed your welcome, it's time you came to Moscow. Firstly we all miss you, and secondly we need to discuss Yalta.' There appeared to be nothing to discuss, but a crucial day was approaching, 17 January, Anton's forty-fourth name day, the day set for *The Cherry Orchard*'s first performance.

EIGHTY-TWO

Last Farewells
January–July 1904

'THINGS WERE RESTLESS, something ominous hung in the air. It was no time of joy, that evening of 17 January 1904,' Olga recalled in 1929. Few plays had been so well rehearsed as *The Cherry Orchard*. The theatre was packed, and behind many seats sickly looking spectators stood. These 'angels' were said to be consumptives from Yalta, a *memento mori* to the celebrities in the stalls and boxes: Rachmaninov, Andrei Bely, Gorky, Chaliapin and almost all Chekhov's Moscow friends. Anton was not in the theatre for the first three acts. He was recovering after a night at the opera, listening to Chaliapin sing. *The Cherry Orchard* was having a muted reception. Nemirovich-Danchenko sent a carriage with a disingenuous message: 'Couldn't you come for the third interval, though you probably won't get curtain calls now?'

During the third interval Anton was duly brought on to the stage. Into the centre of a half-circle of distinguished academics, journalists and actors, to loud applause, walked a living corpse, hunched, pale and emaciated. Stanislavsky was aghast. A voice from the stalls cried out, 'Sit down!' There was no chair. Speeches began. Professor Veselovsky spoke: Anton recalled his hero Gaev addressing a bookcase on its 100th anniversary. He muttered 'Bookcase!' and everyone sniggered. Speeches and telegrams were read until Anton, his eyes like a hunted animal's, was led off to lie on a dressing-room divan. Gorky chased out everyone except the young actor Kachalov who, made up as Trofimov, looked as moribund as Anton. Half an hour later, the play over, the audience too subdued by the third interval to applaud loudly, Anton went to sup with the actors. He was showered with speeches and given presents of antique furniture: he detested it. What he really wanted, he told Stanislavsky, was a new mouse trap. The police charged the theatre for holding an 'unauthorized public gathering'.

Tickets were readily available for the next performances of *The Cherry Orchard*. A black comedy was ill attuned to the public's mood of Jingoism on the eve of the Russo-Japanese war, which was declared on 24 January 1904. Three days later, the Japanese sank the Russian Pacific fleet at Port Arthur. In a mournful, even apocalyptic mood, reviewers tended to dismiss the play as a political allegory about gentry overthrown by commoners. In Petersburg by the end of Lent, *The Cherry Orchard* was playing to half-empty houses. Gorky set up the text, but his almanac *Knowledge* ran into the sands of censorship. Time was needed for Russia's mood to turn elegiac and for Nemirovich-Danchenko to find the necessary 'lace-like' touch to make the play a success in the even more turbulent year that was to come.

Anton wanted to flee to the Riviera or the Crimea. The stairs to the Moscow apartment were 'real agony'. Jubilee celebrations for his writing career had brought many a past acquaintance out of the woodwork. Demands on his sympathy were unbearable. Olga's nephew, Liova, had tuberculosis of the spine: the prognosis was paralysis or death. The eldest Golden sister, Anastasia, married to the dramatist Pushkariov, her beauty, wealth and health all gone, begged for a pension. Lidia Avilova wanted advice on charity for wounded soldiers. The Gurzuf schoolteacher asked Anton to make the church remarry him to his late wife's sister. Kleopatra Karatygina wanted money to send her consumptive brother to a sanatorium.

Anton needed an undemanding occupation. Goltsev made him *Russian Thought*'s literary editor and fed him manuscripts to sort out. Anton abandoned the brilliant opening pages of two stories he would never finish, 'The Cripple' and 'Disturbing the Balance', and set willingly to skimming over, and even annotating, beginners' prose. On 14 February 1904, as Evgenia headed for the Crimea, Olga took Anton to Tsaritsyno, fifteen miles south of Moscow, to look at a dacha. The area had an unhealthy reputation, but the house was built for winter living. At Tsaritsyno there had been a derailment and Anton had to return in a freezing cab. Altshuller was appalled when he heard that this had happened.

The next day Anton and Schnap took the Crimean express. At Sevastopol he was met by Evgenia's maid Nastia – Evgenia had gone ahead overland – and they sailed to Yalta. Playing with the yard dogs and sleeping with Evgenia, the dog settled back into Yalta life better than his master. The house was so cold that visitors kept their fur coats on. Anton found undressing laborious; the bed was hard and cold; Nastia's soup was 'like dishwater, the pancakes as cold as ice'. He was too ill to travel abroad and it was too expensive to travel anyway – war had hit the Russian rouble.. The solitary tame crane had belatedly migrated south. There was no congenial company: Bunin, now 'all parchment and sourness', as Anton described him, was in Moscow with Masha and Olga. *The Cherry Orchard* had followed Anton into the provinces: it was being performed in Rostov-on-Don, then in Taganrog (to frenzied acclaim) and on 10 April in Yalta, but so badly that Anton walked out.

Olga, with Vania's help, went on inspecting houses near Moscow, though winter was nearly over and she knew it was pointless. The local climate, the vendor's price, or the cost of installing a lavatory aborted every sale. Olga had more success in provoking Maria Andreeva to resign from the company. Stanislavsky accepted her resignation,[74] much to Andreeva's distress and Olga's delight:

> She swore at everybody, including me . . . Nobody regrets her departure, in the management, that is, I don't know about the actors. What will come of it! I hope there is no split in the theatre. I still don't know what to do, Gorky is involved, there is no argument about that.[75]

Now Olga had only one enemy in the theatre, Nemirovich-Danchenko's wife, who, as Baroness Korf by birth, was unshakeable. Olga had, however, rivals outside. In Moscow Komissarzhevskaia was wildly acclaimed as Nora in *The Doll's House* at the Ermitage theatre. Olga declared that she ought to be ashamed of herself, her repertoire and her company. Worse, after Komissarzhevskaia's company came one led by Lidia Iavorskaia whose person, Olga claimed, 'gave everyone the horrors'. Olga was seriously frightened when her uncles, Karl the doctor, Sasha the captain, were despatched to the Manchurian front, and her brother Kostia was sent to extend the Trans-Siberian railway to the war zone. In Moscow, Dr Strauch died of a liver disease: Olga lost her gynæcologist and ally in her fight to keep Anton in Moscow.

Anton was less affected by the war. His nephew Nikolai was conscripted and Lazarevsky, his most persistent visitor, was drafted to Vladivostok. Olga sent Anton soap, despite Altshuller's ban on washing (for fear of Anton chilling his lungs). Although Altshuller visited frequently, offering company rather than treatment, Anton felt lonely, in need of something to do, but too weak to do much. He advised Olga's distraught sister-in-law Lulu about her son's tuberculosis, collected for the Yavuzlar sanatorium and posted manuscripts to Goltsev and even their authors. Aleksandr, who sensed a last chance, came to stay for March, with Natalia (whom Anton had not met for seven years), the twelve-year-old Misha and their dachshund. Anton told Olga: 'Aleksandr is sober, kind, interesting. Generally promising. And there is hope that he won't be a drunk again, though there is no guarantee.' Masha arrived on 19 March, followed by Vania at Easter, for a family reunion which they suspected might be their last. Only Misha was missing, opening station bookstalls for Suvorin in the Caucasus.

When her lease expired, Olga moved to a flat with an electric lift, electric light and two lavatories, one of them working. Again she tantalized Anton with her vagueness about the address. Anton doubted that the lift would work. He had plans for the summer: he would go to Manchuria as a doctor and war correspondent. Nobody believed him, but he repeated his plan. He wrote to Uncle Sasha at the front, and supplied him with pipe tobacco.[76] Olga dismissed Anton's plans as a childish whim. 'Where will you put me? Let's do some fishing instead.' She still hoped for a child. If Moskvin, who played the clumsy Epikhodov, could beget a son, 'When are you and I going to?' On 27 March 1904, Easter Saturday, she asked, 'Do you want a baby? Darling, I do too. I shall do my best.'

Anton had been sent proofs of *The Cherry Orchard* to check for Adolf Marx's edition. He lingered as long as he could, waiting for *Knowledge* to clear the censorship. When he returned the proofs to Marx in April, Marx published so fast that the *Knowledge* almanac was unsaleable, and Anton was badly embarrassed.

The Cherry Orchard opened in Petersburg on 2 April. Suvorin unleashed his curs again. Burenin in *New Times* declared: 'Chekhov is not just a weak playwright, but an almost weird one, rather banal and monotonous.' The company was nervous and Nemirovich-Danchenko's wife, Olga reported, put on a white dress and a green hat and went to church to light candles for luck, but the Petersburg audience, despite the hostile reviews, was very responsive. Olga had, however, uncomfortable encounters. Dr Jakobson, who had operated on her two years before, visited: 'he was a hellish bore'. She had already clashed with Lidia Iavorskaia: now was confronted with another Lesbian alliance between two of Anton's old loves:

> Maria Krestovskaia confessed to me, told me all her love for and disillusionment in Tania Shchepkina-Kupernik, who by the way has married a barrister, Polynov. Krestovskaia's voice shakes when she says that this Tanichka is an infinitely vicious creature.[77]

By mid April Aleksandr, Vania and Masha had left Anton in Yalta. The tame crane flew back for spring. Anton took bismuth for his guts and opium for the pains in his chest. (Altshuller issued heroin in case the pain became worse.) Nothing relieved his emphysema: 'How short of breath I am,' he groaned to Olga. His teeth were crumbling but Ostrovsky, the grubby Yalta dentist, was away. Anton was upset by the casualties on the Manchurian front: there would be no news of Uncle Sasha until May. Once spring had set in, Anton fled to Moscow. Olga's doctor Taube would examine him and send him abroad for treatment. He arrived on 3 May, so ill from the journey that he went straight to bed from the lift. He would never get up again for more than a few hours at a time. 'The Germans are coming to pay their respects,' Masha wrote to Evgenia, as Taube and his colleagues gathered. Their diagnosis was pleurisy and emaciation, their prescription enemas and yet another special diet. Anton was to consume brains, fish soup, rice, butter and cocoa with cream. Coffee was forbidden. Taube stopped Altshuller's boiled eggs and Spanish fly compresses. Too weak to sit, irritable and dejected, Anton conceded that he was in good hands: 'My advice, let Germans treat you ... I have been tortured for twenty years!!!' he told his Yalta colleague Dr Sredin.

When Masha found out that Olga was planning to take Anton to Germany, she bitterly opposed her sister-in-law. She feared he would die there. In any case, Olga kept even Anton's kith and kin away from his bedside. Masha told Evgenia: 'I don't see him often – I am very afraid of Olga.'[78] Olga and Masha had a violent quarrel and on 14 May Masha took leave of her brother and left Moscow for Yalta. Vania called daily and found out from the servants how Anton was. The only close friend to break through the cordon that Olga had erected around Anton was the indomitable Olga Kundasova; she had what she later told Suvorin was 'one of the most upsetting encounters [*with Anton*] a mortal could endure', so upsetting that she refused to reveal what had passed between them.

Anton's letters to Yalta calmed his mother and sister, but privately he colluded with Olga and Dr Taube. Three opiates set his mind at rest: morphine controlled his pain; opium, as a side effect, had finally staunched his diarrhœa; the heroin would ease anything worse. He knew that he could hope for a merciful death, like Levitan's, from heart failure, rather than from a hæmorrhage. To die in Germany, far from a distraught family, in the arms of a skilled nurse like Olga, was his most attractive option. To one visitor Anton said, 'I am going away to croak'. Maddened by idleness, he tried to read Goltsev's manuscripts. He longed for coffee. 20 May brought a severe attack of pleurisy, but Dr Taube saved him. On 22 May Olga bought railway tickets for 2 June to Berlin and Badenweiler, a spa in the Black Forest, where Taube's colleague, Dr Schwörer, practised. Hail and snow fell. In Yalta Masha was struggling with the cesspit. Olga begged her to write to Anton:

> he sat several times in the dining room and had supper there. Taube came. He says that the pleurisy is definitely better and that it is lack of air and motion that makes him so difficult. Tomorrow we'll let him have morning coffee. His guts are strong, so enemas can be given.[79]

On 25 May Anton asked for his 4500 roubles from *Knowledge* for *The Cherry Orchard*, even though Gorky and Piatnitsky faced insolvency, because Adolf Marx had ignored Anton's pleas and pre-empted their publication of the play. The 4500 roubles arrived. Olga and Anton were ready to depart, when new agony struck, despite morphine. On 30 May, at dawn, Anton sent a note to Vishnevsky: 'Get me at once Wilson the masseur. I haven't slept all night, in agony from rheumatic pains; tell nobody, not even Taube.' Wilson came round immediately. The next day Anton went for a last carriage ride through Moscow's streets. He told Masha that he feared spinal tuberculosis. Olga also wrote to Masha: she now doubted that Anton would be able to travel. To relieve the muscle pain Taube administered aspirin and quinine and Olga injected arsenic. She could spare only a few minutes a day for the theatre. In Yalta Masha despaired and confided in Misha: 'My heart aches. Something is going to happen to him. The Yalta doctors say he would be better off staying in Yalta. Olga was very harsh to me and I could hardly see Antosha at all, I didn't dare go into his room.'[80] Misha offered Masha clichés: 'Where there is hope, even a weak ray of it, not all is lost.' He hoped to bring his family to Yalta, while Anton was away, for a holiday.

Olga was impatient to leave: she was now injecting Anton with morphine. She blamed their new flat, where the heating boiler had broken down, for his rheumatic pains. On 3 June, as Gorky prepared to sue Adolf Marx for publishing Chekhov's *The Cherry Orchard* too early (the litigation would prove abortive), the Chekhovs left for Berlin.

In Berlin Olga's brother Volodia, now a singer, was waiting for them. So was Gorky's rejected wife, Ekaterina, with her children. Anton wrote to Masha, more gently than before, and thanked Altshuller. Here, at the Savoy, he could enjoy coffee. On 6/19 June Anton was treated to a carriage drive to the Zoo; he was introduced to Iollos, the correspondent for Sobolevsky's *Russian Gazette* – 'interesting, agreeable and infinitely obliging,' Anton reported to Masha. Iollos was to be the Chekhovs' guardian angel in Germany. On 7/20 June a leading Berlin specialist, Professor Ewald, forewarned by Taube, visited the hotel. Ewald examined Anton, shrugged his shoulders and left the room without a word. 'I cannot forget Anton's smile, gentle, cooperative, somehow embarrassed and dismayed,' Olga recalled. Ewald was appalled at the idea of a dying man being shunted across Europe.

Iollos wrote to Sobolevsky 'Chekhov's days are numbered, he is terribly emaciated ... cough, breathlessness, a high temperature, he cannot climb stairs.' The Chekhovs crossed Germany by train to Badenweiler. Here they settled in the best hotel, the Römerbaden. Anton seemed to improve. After two days, however, the hotel asked the Chekhovs to move: Anton's cough distressed the other guests. They settled in a small pension, the Villa Frederika. Anton wrote to Dr Kurkin that he was now bothered only by emphysema and thinness, and was desperate to escape the tedium of his life in Badenweiler and flee to Italy.

Dr Schwörer, who attended Anton, was married to a Russian, a

Zhivago, whom Olga had known in her school days. He was a considerate doctor, but to Anton's dismay offered the same advice as Dr Taube. Again, coffee was forbidden. Anton sunned himself on a chaise longue and had massages. To his mother he wrote that he would be well in a week. Masha wrote to him of her distress: 'Vania came down on his own. We wept when he said . . . that he couldn't sleep at night, because he kept seeing your sickly image.' Olga dutifully sent Masha regular bulletins and on 13/26 June hinted at the likelihood of Anton's dying:

> I beg you, Masha, don't lose control, don't cry, there is nothing dangerous, but it is very grave. Both of us knew we could hardly expect complete recovery. Take it like a man, not a woman. As soon as Anton feels a little better I shall do everything I can to come home quickly. Yesterday he was so out of breath that I didn't know what to do, I galloped for the doctor. The doctor says that because his lungs are in such a bad way, his heart is doing double the work it should, and his heart is by no means strong. He gave him oxygen, injected camphor, we have drops to give him and ice to put on his heart. At night he dozed upright and I made him a mountain of pillows, then injected morphine twice and he went to sleep properly lying down . . . Of course don't let Anton sense from your letters that I have been writing to you, or that will torment him . . . I don't think your mama should be told that he is not getting well, or put it gently, don't upset her . . . Anton has been dreaming of coming home by sea, but that is impossible . . . I have just been to Freiburg, he ordered me to get him a light-coloured flannel suit . . . If Taube had hinted that something could happen to his heart, or that the process was not stopping, I'd never have decided to go abroad.

To Evgenia Olga praised the food, the beds, the landlord, the weather, so cheerfully that cousin Georgi congratulated Anton on his full recovery, even though Dr Altshuller had just told Georgi: 'They've taken a year off his life. They'll have destroyed Chekhov.'[81] Once more Anton appeared to pick up. While Olga went thirty miles to Basle to have her teeth crowned, Anton proudly came down to the dining room. To a young colleague, Dr Rossolimo, Anton wrote ironically: 'I just have shortness of breath and serious, probably incurable, idleness.'

Olga told Nemirovich-Danchenko the bald truth:

Anton is sun-tanned, but feels bad. His temp. all time, today even in the morning it was 38.1°. Nights are agony. He can't breathe or sleep . . . You can imagine his mood . . . He never complains.[82]

Sometimes Anton forgot about death. He devised a subject for a play: passengers on an ice-bound ship. Olga took him on carriage rides around Badenweiler. He envied on behalf of the Russian peasant the German peasant's prosperity. In the evenings Olga translated the newspapers: he was pained by the *Schadenfreude* of the German press at Russia's defeats in the war with Japan.

Villa Frederika was boring and dark, with monotonous food. The Chekhovs moved to the Hotel Sommer, where Anton watched people coming and going to the post office from a sun-drenched balcony. Two Russian students staying in Badenweiler offered to help. Anton discussed summoning a dentist and sent Masha instructions on writing cheques and gardening. Masha could no longer bear the wait. On 28 June she and Vania, using cousin Georgi's 50 per cent discount, took a Black Sea boat to Batum, for ten days in the Georgian spa of Borjomi. A Yalta seamstress kept Evgenia company.

On 27 June/10 July 1904 Olga wrote to Nemirovich-Danchenko: 'He is losing weight. He lies down all day. He feels very miserable. A change is taking place in him.' Schwörer let him drink coffee and administered oxygen and digitalis, while Olga injected morphine. Anton warned Masha 'the only treatment for breathlessness is not to move', but still made Olga fetch his new suit from Freiburg.

A letter came from Potapenko in San Moritz: 'I stretch out my hand and squeeze yours.' Anton, however, was locked in his own racing mind. He improvised a story. Diners in a hotel wait for dinner, not knowing that the cook has vanished. At 2.00 a.m. on 2/15 July, he awoke delirious, despite a dose of chloral hydrate. He raved of a sailor in danger: his nephew Kolia. Olga sent one of the Russian students to fetch the doctor and ordered ice from the porter. She chopped up a block of ice and placed it on Anton's heart. Dr Schwörer came and sent the two students for oxygen. Anton protested that an empty heart needed no ice and that he would die before the oxygen came. Schwörer gave him an injection of camphor.

German and Russian medical etiquette dictated that a doctor at a colleague's deathbed, when all hope was gone, should offer champagne.[83] Schwörer felt Anton's pulse and ordered a bottle. Anton sat up and loudly proclaimed 'Ich sterbe' [*I'm dying*]. He drank, murmured 'I haven't had champagne for a long time,' lay down on his left side, as he always had with Olga, and died without a murmur, before she could reach the other side of the bed.

EIGHTY-THREE

Aftermath
July 1904

DR SCHWÖRER, his wife and the Russian students did all they could to help Olga. The consul came down from Baden-Baden. Olga's sister-in-law Elli and Sobolevsky's correspondent Iollos took the train from Berlin. Anton's body lay all day in the hotel room. Telegrams were sent to every close relative, except Anton's aunt Aleksandra. Olga wrote about Anton's last hours to her mother. The first letter of condolence came. Dunia Efros, Chekhov's first fiancée, staying by the Vierwaldstättersee, opened a French newspaper: 'What horror, what grief,' she wrote. Olga's telegram to Vania was forwarded to the Caucasian resort of Borjomi. It read, 'Anton quietly passed away from weakness of heart. Tell mother and Masha carefully.' Vania and Masha were 500 miles from Yalta. Masha wired the boat at Batum. The captain delayed sailing until the bug-ridden overnight train from Borjomi had brought Chekhov's brother and sister. The same day, 3 July 1904, Misha and Aleksandr, independently, instructed by Suvorin, left Petersburg. In Yalta the telegrams were no secret. Bells tolled; posters went up all over town announcing a requiem mass in Autka, by the Chekhov house. Evgenia alone was kept in the dark until her family had gathered. On the boat from Batum a woman came up to Masha and gave her an icon of the Virgin.

Olga presumed that she would bury Anton in Germany and return to Russia alone, but a flurry of telegrams from Russia, few of which expressed any sympathy for her bereavement, forced her to change her mind.

When and where will Anton be buried reply prepaid Suvorin.

Communicate *New Times* details my brother's death Aleksandr Tschechoff

Bury Anton Moscow Novodevichie convent Vania and Masha in Caucasus Misha with mother Mikhail Tschechoff.[84]

Repatriating a body required the services of a *Leichenführer* on special trains, and a petition from the Russian embassy in Berlin to fourteen German railway regions, to allow a refrigerated car carrying a sealed coffin to be coupled to a passenger express. Olga waited and wrote to her mother. Then she went to Berlin, and waited in the Savoy hotel for Anton's body. At the Potsdamer station the embassy chaplain held a service on a siding, while diplomats continued to lobby the railway.

Russia was flooded with memoirs. In Yalta the bereaved assembled. On 7 July Misha broke the news to Evgenia: with Vania and Masha, they took the train to Moscow. That morning a train carrying Anton's body (in a red luggage van) and Olga in a first-class carriage pulled into Petersburg. Kleopatra Karatygina was one of a dozen people waiting for it. So was Natalia Golden, who told a student who accompanied her how close a friend and collaborator she had been to Anton twenty years before. A government minister also met the train, but he was there to pay respects not to Chekhov but to a General Obruchiov, whose corpse was also being repatriated. Suvorin was the only representative of the state. The philosopher Vasili Rozanov watched Suvorin run to sit and talk to Olga:

> He almost ran with his stick (he walked terribly fast), cursing the inefficiency of the railways, their clumsiness in shunting the carriage . . . Looking at his face and hearing his half-swallowed words, I felt I was watching a father meet the corpse of his child or the corpse of a promising youth, dead before his time. Suvorin could see nothing and nobody, he paid attention to nobody and nothing, he was just waiting, waiting, wanting, wanting the coffin.[85]

On leaving Olga's compartment, Suvorin collapsed to his knees. A chair was brought and he sat alone and motionless. Suvorin arranged a requiem, a refuge for Olga, and a refrigerated carriage for the journey to Moscow. A priest and a few choristers held a brief service on the platform.

Suvorin had other concerns: he immediately sent Aleksandr to Yalta to retrieve his frank letters to Chekhov. Unable to get a reply out of Misha, Aleksandr turned back halfway and wired him again from Moscow: 'Bring without fail from archive old man's letters. My instructions not to leave without them, am buying grave, at Vania's flat.'[86] In Moscow Aleksandr was told to meet the coffin in Petersburg, and on 8 July he headed back. His brother's body sped past him, from Petersburg to Moscow. He missed Anton's funeral as he had his father's.

On 9 July a procession of 4000 began a four-mile walk across Moscow, from the station to the Novodevichie cemetery. Olga leant on Nemirovich-Danchenko's arm. The family arrived from Yalta when the procession was midway. Evgenia, Vania, Misha and Masha broke through to the catafalque, with great difficulty, for Evgenia's legs were weak, and the students guarding the cortege did not recognize them. Masha and Olga embraced; months of hostility were set aside. At the graveside Nikolai Ezhov placed a silver wreath on Suvorin's behalf. Gorky wrote to his wife:

> I am so depressed by this funeral . . . as if I were smeared with sticky, foul-smelling filth . . . Anton who squirmed at anything vile and vulgar was brought in a car 'for transporting fresh oysters' and buried next to the grave of a Cossack widow called Olga Kukaretkina . . . People climbed trees and laughed, broke crosses and swore as they fought for a place. They asked loudly, 'Which is the wife? And the sister? Look, they're crying . . . You know he hasn't left them a penny, Marx gets the lot . . . Poor Knipper . . . Don't worry about her, she gets 10,000 a year in the theatre,' and so on. Chaliapin burst into tears and cursed: 'And he lived for these bastards, he worked, taught, argued for them.'[87]

At the apartment, Lika Mizinova joined the family. She stood in black, silently staring through the window for two hours.

EIGHTY-FOUR

Epilogue
1904–1959

IMMEDIATELY AFTER the funeral Olga left with Evgenia, Masha, Misha and Vania for Yalta. Aleksandr in Petersburg wept alone. Suvorin sent him back to the Crimea in pursuit. After the distress of the funeral, whatever Suvorin felt privately, publicly he disowned Anton.[88] On 22 July he told Ivan Shcheglov, 'Chekhov was the bard of the middle classes. He never was and never will be a great writer.' Suvorin transferred his protection and even his affection to a new figure, the fifty-year-old philosopher Vasili Rozanov.

At the forty-day requiem in Moscow on 10 August the church was crowded. By the graveside a choir of nuns sang. Olga Kundasova and the Chekhovs' old landlord, Dr Korneev, appeared. Korneev gave a communion loaf for Evgenia. On it were written the names of her dead: father-in-law, brother, husband, sister and two sons: 'For the peace of the souls of Georgi, Iakov, Pavel, Feodosia, Nikolai, Anton.' On 18 August Olga left Yalta. Her brother Kostia and Olga Kundasova came to stay with her in Moscow. She was beginning rehearsals for *Ivanov* in which her performance as the doomed wife, Anna, would be especially moving.[89]

Olga won Masha a few weeks' leave until the Chekhov inheritance could be clarified. Anton's 'will' of 1901, leaving everything to Masha, informally drawn up and improperly witnessed, was declared invalid, but Olga, to the family's relief and even gratitude, renounced all claim on the estate and gave to Masha the substantial sum in her and Anton's joint account. She would live on her earnings as an actress and shareholder in the theatre. All the survivors agreed that Anton's intentions should be honoured and that all his estate should pass to Masha, who would look after Evgenia and the Yalta house. The lawyers pondered the next step. As Anton had died effectively intestate, Russian law gave the inheritance to all his siblings. A year passed before Olga and the Chekhov brothers had signed a legal deed, giving Masha 'all the income and profit as heirs from literary works, theatrical plays and estate'. The houses and money in the bank were worth 80,000 roubles. This and Chekhov's plays now made Masha a rich woman.[90]

Trusting only Masha to keep her in comfort, Evgenia was relieved. Her sister-in-law Liudmila, and Irinushka, who had nursed Anton as a baby, came from Taganrog to live with her in Yalta. Aleksandr visited her and wrote to Vania:

Old Mariushka is alive, toothless, and has no intention of dying. Mother has got two worthless mongrels to replace Tuzik, who was poisoned. She's very afraid, seriously, that her children may steal her inheritance and send her packing. She doesn't believe in her children's decency.[91]

To Misha, Aleksandr wrote:

She fixedly thought I was the main crook, able to lead you astray into a conspiracy. When she heard I had written a renunciation at Vania's, she bowed down almost to my feet ... She won't give me Suvorin's letters: 'Masha told me not to.' The old ladies are not that unhappy, they laugh loud all the time.[92]

Evgenia enjoyed the garden, prosperity, and rides in the automobiles that came to ply the route from Yalta to the railhead. She died aged 84 in 1919.

Masha gave up schoolteaching and assumed responsibility for the home at Yalta as a temple to her brother. Once memoirs and letters were published, it was her life's task to manage the enormous archive. Through revolution, civil war, Stalin's terror and German occupation she never relaxed her grip on the Chekhov heritage. Her private life was set aside.[93] She bought a dacha, which she sold to a Yalta dentist for diamonds just before revolution made real estate and money valueless. She died, aged 94, in 1957.

Aleksandr plunged back into alcoholism. In 1908, Natalia forced him out, despite his pleas.[94] He lived with a servant, a dog and his chickens outside town. In 1906 he published vivid recollections of his and Anton's childhood. Masha and Misha, indignant at what they saw as Aleksandr's slurs on their father, ostracized him.[95] Aleksandr's obituary ran:

For a whole year he endured [*throat cancer*], the knowledge that it was incurable oppressed him horribly and he had many hours of severe physical and moral torment. He found peace at 9 a.m. on 17 May 1913.

Masha told Olga that none of the family would go to the funeral.[96] Misha worked for Suvorin's agencies until revolution destroyed them. Until his death in 1936, he was, like Masha, his brother's biographer. His son Sergei gathered an archive of all his kin except Masha and Anton. Vania remained a teacher. In December 1917 Vania's son Volodia, who knew he was incurably ill, stole his cousin Mikhail's revolver from a desk drawer and shot himself. Broken by this tragedy and by hunger, Vania died in 1922, aged sixty-one.

Aleksandr's son Kolia, discharged from the navy, appeared in Yalta, 'pathetic, ragged'. Masha gave him money to go to Siberia. In 1911 he reappeared: 'I wept, because I was sorry for him,' Masha told Olga. In the revolution Kolia returned to the Crimea, married a woman twenty-four years older, and ran a smallholding with chickens and even a cow. Always a sailor, he kept a logbook.[97] He welcomed the Bolsheviks and may have been shot in 1921 by the White Army as it fled the Reds. Kolia's brother Anton, the typesetter, was conscripted in 1908 and was dead by 1921.[98]

Mikhail, Aleksandr's youngest son, suffered nervous breakdowns and alcoholism. He told friends that he had been seduced by his mother, Natalia. In 1919 she died: Mikhail forgot where he buried her. Mikhail's theatrical talent made him a star in the Moscow Arts Theatre. In 1915 he eloped with another Olga Knipper, the niece of Anton's widow. The marriage broke up, just after a child, Olga Chekhova, was born. In the 1920s, Mikhail, his wife and daughter all ended up in Germany. Mikhail Chekhov eventually taught Stanislavskian acting to Hollywood. His ex-wife, now Olga Tschechowa, became an actress, was photographed with Adolf Hitler, and, allegedly, spied for Stalin. Thanks to her, the Nazis protected Chekhov's Yalta house.[99]

Olga Knipper-Chekhova, like Masha, died in her nineties. She was the linchpin of the Moscow Arts Theatre. Even when Stalin in 1935 made it his official theatre, Olga adapted.

Suvorin had power wrenched from him by the Dauphin, who was irascible to the point of madness. In 1912 he died of throat cancer, with the same stoicism as Aleksandr Chekhov. The letters Suvorin had written to Anton have not been seen since 1919. Suvorin's sons fled Russia and lived in Yugoslavia and France, where in 1937 the Dauphin, following his mother's and younger brother's example, gassed himself.

Dunia Efros, Anton's first fiancée, left Russia for France. In 1943, aged eighty-two, she was seized by the Vichy police and gassed by the Germans. Olga Kundasova stayed in Russia, living until 1947: she burnt her archive. Lika Mizinova remained faithful to Sanin-Schoenberg: when he became psychotic, she nursed him to sanity. Lika died in Paris of cancer in 1937. Elena Shavrova-Iust, destitute after her husband was executed, sold her Chekhoviana to live. Lidia Iavorskaia divorced Prince Bariatinsky in 1915; in 1919 she escaped arrest in revolutionary Petrograd and fled to England, dying in 1921.[100] Tania Shchepkina-Kupernik obliterated her Bohemian image and became a Soviet children's writer. Lidia Avilova, first abroad and then in Russia, persuaded herself that she had been Anton's only love. Just before dying in 1942, she met Aleksandr Smagin, Masha's faithful admirer. The two victims of unrequited passion commiserated. Lidia Avilova was just one of a scattered congregation who mourned Anton Chekhov all their lives.

NOTES

PART I *Father to the Man*

1 However, it is interesting how often Chekhov uses the name Egor (the native Russian form of George) for characters in his work who are associated, however ironically, with the warrior St George.

2 £3000 at today's prices, a rouble being ²/₃ ounce of silver.

3 Anton never mentioned Aleksandra, his last surviving aunt by blood. Among Pavel's papers (331 33 1v, 54a) is a scrap with the names of her children and sons-in-law.

4 Efrosinia was influential: in 1902 Chekhov claimed to have spoken Ukrainian in his infancy.

5 To Olga Knipper 2 Feb. 1903.

6 See *OR*, 331 81 1: Egor's letters to Pavel 1859–78.

7 Pavel Chekhov's first placement had been with the late Iakov Morozov, who would have been his father-in-law, in Rostov in 1841. The link between the Morozovs and Chekhovs was renewed in Rostov six years later: Ivan Morozov and Pavel Chekhov found they both had siblings in Taganrog.

8 See *Zhizn' P. E. Chekhova* in *Krasnyi Arkhiv*, 1939, 6.

9 Family letters to Mitrofan up to 1860 were stitched together into a book: *OR*, 331 34 1.

10 His name day, St Antony's, was the 17th.

11 See *LN68*, 531–7.

12 See Aleksandr's letter to Anton 17 Jan. 1886 in *Pis'ma*, 1939, 131–2.

13 The Jewish boys called him 'Sashinkoch'. He acquired a smattering of Yiddish and never forgot the Jewish boys' panic call: *Ferkatse di huzen, loif aheim*, Roll up your trousers, run home.

14 See *RGALI*, 2540 53 1: Aleksandr's memoirs (extracts in *Vokrug Chekhova*, 1990).

15 See I. Bondarenko, *Biografia eshchio ne okonchena* in I. M. Sel'vaniuk, V. D. Sedegov, *Sbornik statei i materialov 3*, Rostov, 1963, 309–30.

16 See *OR*, 331 82 4: Aleksandr's letters to Masha, 1890–8.

17 Our main source for information about Chekhov's teachers is P. P. Filevskii, *Ocherki iz proshlogo Taganrogskoi Gimnazii*, Taganrog, 1906.

18 See *RGALI*, 540 1 382: Zelenenko, *Vospominaniia o Taganrogskoi gimnazii*, typescript.

19 Many teachers recalled Chekhov, but Aleksei Markevich, a history teacher, proudly proclaimed at the end of the century, 'I am not in the habit of reading stories like Chekhov's.'

20 A third boy, Misha Cheremis, remembered as the Pederast, also worked for a time in the Chekhov shop: the children remembered only his phrase, 'Let's not be sensible.'

21 Chekhov drank Santurini most of his life, though he admitted it tasted like 'bad Marsala'.

22 As the knout was soaked in tar and fish oil, the effect on the boys' clothes was devastating. The one occasion when the knout struck him, Anton desperately soaked his trousers in chemicals, only to find

that he had destroyed the fabric. A school friend's mother took pity and bought him a new pair, so that the damage was never discovered by Pavel.

23 See memoir by A. A. Dolzhenko (Anton's cousin) in *Iz shkol'nykh let...*, 1962, 14–19.

24 See M. Semanova, *Teatral'nye vpechatleniia ...* in *Sbornik materialov*, Rostov, 1960, 157–84.

25 See *OR*, 331 31 1: Aleksandr's letters to his parents, 1874–96.

26 See her memoirs in *LN68*, 538–41.

27 To Pavel 10 Aug. 1875. See *OR*, 331 31 1.

28 See *OR*, 331 82 14; Nikolai Chekhov's letters to his parents, 1875–89.

29 See *OR*, 331 33 12a: Evgenia's letters to Aleksandr and Nikolai include this note (2 Jan. 1875).

30 See *OR*, 331 33 12a: Evgenia's letter to Aleksandr and Nikolai Chekhov.

31 Vrondy in his old age remembered Anton as an adept and favourite pupil with whom he would often play *loto*, a demure form of bingo, after class.

32 See *OR*, 331 81 11: Pavel's letters to his wife and children, 1876–90.

33 See *OR*, 331 33 125: Evgenia's letters to Pavel Chekhov, 1876–90.

34 See *OR*, 331 81 12: Pavel's letters to Evgenia, 1876, 1884 and 1891.

35 See *OR*, 331 81 38: Pavel Chekhov to G. P. Selivanov.

36 Mitrofan deferred to his 'spiritual adviser', the elderly Father Vasili Bandakov, whose volumes of 'Short Teachings for the Simple Folk' were used by the lazier priests of southern Russia. One of Bandakov's sermons is subtitled 'composed in the house of the Chekhovs'. In 1890, at Mitrofan's request, Anton wrote an obituary: 'He preached at every opportunity, never bothered about time or place ... Bad harvests, epidemics, conscription ... he was passionate, bold and often cutting.'

37 See *RGALI*, 860 1 576: M. I. Il'kov, typescript memoir.

38 See *OR*, 331 58 29: G. P. Selivanov's letters to Anton.

39 To Aleksei Suvorin junior. See 331 59 71a: A. A. Suvorin's letter to Anton 8 Nov. 1888.

40 Anton was to encounter old Taganrogians all his life: Drs Eremeev, Saveliev, Shamkovich, Tarabrin, Valter, Zembulatov; lawyers (Kolomnin, Konovitser, Kramariov, the Volkenshteins, one of whom Anton saved from expulsion from school after an anti-Semitic incident); performing artists (Vishnev[ets]ky); writers (Sergeenko); academics, civil servants, even revolutionaries.

41 To V. A. Tikhonov in February 1892. The brothel was run by N. Pototsky, who left Taganrog *gimnazia* with a silver medal in 1862. Years later Aleksandr Chekhov still asked after Pototsky.

42 See *OR*, 331 32 3, Aleksandr's letters to Anton, 1876: 27 Sept. 1876, printed in *Pis'ma*, 1939, 33–5.

43 See *OR*, 331 33 126: Evgenia's 20 letters to Anton, 1876–1904.

44 In Russia this title has been reassigned to the Chekhov play once known as *Platonov*, but *Platonov* has nothing to do with 'fatherlessness' and has references that point to the 1880s.

45 Chekhov's books were plundered by family and 'friends', lost in peregrinations, or given away to school, prison and city libraries. See Balukhaty and Khanilo in bibliography.

46 See *OR*, 331 81 19: Pavel's letters to Anton, 1878.

47 See *RGALI*, 331 81 25: Pavel's letters to Mitrofan and Liudmila Chekhov, 1876–93: 2 Feb. 1878.

48 See *OR*, 331 82 15: Nikolai's letters to Pavel Chekhov, 1879–84.

49 See *RGALI*, 2540 1 158: Pavel's letters to Ivan Chekhov, 1879–98.

50 See *OR*, 331 81 20: Pavel's letters to Anton, 1879.

PART II *Doctor Chekhov*

1 See M. P. Chekhov's memoirs in *Vokrug Chekhova*, 184–5.

2 See *OR*, 331 58 29: Gavriil Parfentievich Selivanov's letters to Anton, 1879–80: 5 Sept. 1879.

3 *The Dragonfly* had chequered prospects; not until 1906, when Russian censorship collapsed, was it transformed into *Satirikon*, one of Europe's sharpest humorous weeklies.

4 See *OR*, 331 81 20: Pavel's letters to Anton, 1879–85: 18 June 1880.

5 See *OR*, 331 81 16: Pavel's letter to Nikolai, 23 Aug. 1880.

6 See *OR*, 331 35 9: O. and P. Agali's letters to Anton, 1880–1.

7 See *OR*, 331 55 21: Anisim [Onisim] Petrov's letters to Anton. Chekhov used the name Anisim once, for a corrupt, demented and semiliterate policeman in a story, 'In the Ravine' (1899).

8 See *OR*, 331 48 49: Solomon Kramariov's letters to Anton, 1881, 1904.

9 Anastasia's husband, Putiata shared the editorship of *Chiaroscuro* with Pushkariov.

10 Despite the marital links that bound the Goldens to the Chekhovs, Anton's younger brothers and his sister obliterated the Golden name from history.

11 Many an Anna Ivanovna pined for a Chekhov: we shall call her Anna Sokolnikova.

12 See *OR*, 331 82 12: A. I. Khrushchiova-Sokolnikova, née Aleksandrova, documents.

13 Chekhov's opinions coincided with those of two men whom he venerated, Turgenev and his future publisher Aleksei Suvorin, but he would not know this until five years later.

14 *The Unnecessary Victory* has generated four screenplays this century.

15 'Slough' from *Continual Dew* (1937).

16 The first page of Chekhov's case notes is given in I. Geizer, *Chekhov i meditsina*, 1960, 12.

17 Pelageia's entry each afternoon with the question, 'Isn't it time you had your beer?' was used much later by Chekhov for Dr Ragin's servant in 'Ward No. 6.'

18 See *OR*, 331 50 1 a–m, for Leikin's 205 letters to Anton, 1882–1900.

19 See *RGALI*, 2540 1 149: Aleksandr's letters to Ivan Chekhov, 1882–97.

20 Cut from *Pis'ma*, 1939: see *OR*, 331 32 8: Aleksandr's letters to Anton, 1882.

21 See *OR*, 331 81 16: Pavel's letter to Anton and Nikolai, 2 Jan. 1883.

22 A little of Anton's studies can be gleaned from E. Meve, *Meditsina v tvorchestve* . . . Kiev, 1989.

23 See *OR*, 331 81 13: Pavel's letters to Aleksandr Chekhov, 1874–94: 22 Mar. 1883.

24 This passage (13 May 1883) was cut from *PSSP*: see *Kuranty*, 8 Sept. 1993, 9.

25 See *OR*, 331 33 126: Evgenia's letter to Anton, 2 July 1883.

26 Sabaneev, brother of Chekhov's chemistry lecturer, edited *Nature and Field Sports*. He paid Chekhov nothing.

27 See *PSSP*, XVIII, 82–3.

28 See *OR*, 331 81 15: Pavel to Nikolai Chekhov, 2 Dec. 1883.

29 Unfortunately, Popudoglo's books were unusable and, except for an antiquarian compendium of naval terms which Chekhov found useful for comic purposes, were given to a junk dealer.

30 See *OR*, 331 55 8: Liodor Palmin's letters to Anton, 1883–6.

31 See *RGALI*, 549 1 10: Chekhov's case notes, with a commentary (*c.* 1920) by Dr Rossolimo.

32 See A. B. Derman, ed., *A. P. Chekhov: Sbornik dokumentov . . .*, 1947, 20–3.

33 Quote in *PSSP*, 2, 473.

34 See *OR*, 331 82 15: Nikolai's letters to Pavel Chekhov, 1879–87.

35 There was a much younger fourth Markova sister, Nina. See *RGALI*, 549 1 352 and 549 3 1 for Elizaveta Markova-Sakharova's and Nina Markova's recollections of the Chekhov brothers.

36 See *OR*, 331 82 21: Nikolai's letters to Anton, 1883–9, and *OR*, 331 47 45b: A. S. Kiseliov's letters to Anton, 1886.

37 See *OR*, 331 42 7: Liubov Dankovskaia's letters to Anton, 1884: October.

38 *Pakosti* for *Novosti*; *News of the Day* was delivered to the Chekhovs in the mid 1880s: Evgenia read it and, to Pavel's annoyance, then mislaid it.

39 In Chekhov's circles Plevako was notorious: with the editor of *The Alarm Clock*, the homicidal Kicheev, he once found a provincial theatre closed: Plevako paid the cashier 500 roubles – a full

house takings – and had the actors brought from their hotel to perform, while he and Kicheev lurked invisible in the gallery. Plevako acted for the Chekhovs in 1905.

40 Dr Ilarion Dubrovo's death from diphtheria on 20 May 1883, after sucking out a child's infected membranes, inspired stories by both Leskov and Chekhov.

41 See *OR*, 331 42 54: M. M. Diukovsky's letters to Anton, 1884–93.

42 See *OR*, 331 64 46a: Maria Ianova's letters to Anton, 1885–6.

43 An organization set up in St Petersburg in 1859 to help writers and their families.

44 See *OR*, 331 50 iv, g: Leikin's letters to Anton, 1885 and 1886.

45 See *OR*, 331 62 27: Natalia to Anton, a sheet from a notebook, marked 1885 by Chekhov.

46 See *OR*, 331 73 10: Pavel's letter to Misha, 11 Aug. 1885.

47 See *OR*, 331 31 1: Anna's postscript to Aleksandr's letter to Pavel, 13 Aug. 1885.

48 See *OR*, 331 82 2: Aleksandr's letters to Maria Chekhova, 1883–7.

49 Chekhov was at a loss for a title: he talked to Leikin's second-in-command, Bilibin: they came up with Leikin-like titles: *Cats and Carp*, *Flowers and Dogs*. Leikin himself suggested *In the Maelstrom* or *Dolls and Masks*. Chekhov in despair pondered *Buy the book or I smash your face*.

50 See *OR*, 331 47 45b: A. S. Kiseliov's letters to Anton, 1886.

51 Mlle Sirout [*in Russian* 'I shit'] is almost certainly, like Masha's girlfriend Josephina Pavlovna [pronounced colloquially *Zhopa*, 'arse'], Anton's invention.

52 See *OR*, 331 64 20: Evdokia Efros's

three letters to Anton, 1886: 27
June.
53 See *OR*, 331 36 75b: Viktor
Bilibin's letters to Anton, 1886.
54 This passage (28 Dec. 1885) was cut
from the *PSSP*: see *Kuranty*, 8 Sept.
1993, 9.
55 See *OR*, 331 63 25a: Franz
Schechtel's letters to Anton, 1885–
6. The joint effort of hauling Kolia
over the coals made Schechtel a
family friend of the Chekhovs. Aunt
Fenichka even urged him to
convert from Catholicism to
Orthodoxy. When Schechtel was
late with sketches for the cover for
Motley Stories, Anton gave him, as
punishment, a choice of 'Egyptian
plagues'; Schechtel chose No. 10
'A pair of circus girls, alive and
fresh, delivered to your house'.
'When,' Anton asked Schechtel
that Easter, 'are we going to screw
the circus girls?'

PART III *My Brothers' Keeper*

1 Anna Suvorina's memoir is in M. D.
Beliaev, A. S. Dolinin, *A. P.
Chekhov. Zateriannye proizvedneiia,
Neizdannye pis'ma, Novye
vospominaiia.* Leningrad: Atenei,
1925, 185–95.
2 See *Pis'ma A. S. Suvorina k V. V.
Rozanovu*, Spb, 1913, 10; see also
V. V. Rozanov, *Mimoliotnoe 1994*,
133–4.
3 See *OR*, 331 63 25e: Franz
Schechtel's two letters to Nikolai
Chekhov, 1886.
4 Cut from *Levitan: Pis'ma*, 1956; see
OR, 331 49 25a, Levitan's letters to
Anton, 1885–6.
5 Cut from *Pis'ma k A. P. Chekhova*
1939: see *OR*, 331 32 12.
6 In fact the author was
Skabichevsky, a critic as scabious as
his name.

7 See *OR*, 331 33 5b: Georgi
Chekhov's letters to Anton, 1888:
30 Apr.
8 See *OR*, 331 47 45b: A. S. Kiseliov's
twenty letters to Anton, 1886.
9 See Masha's account, *Vokrug
Chekhova*, 231.
10 See *OR*, 331 58 31: A. L.
Selivanova-Krause's letters to
Anton, 1887–95.
11 See *OR*, 331 50 1d: Leikin's letters
to Anton, 1887.
12 See *OR*, 331 47 48: Maria
Kiseliova's letters to Anton, 1886–
1900.
13 Cut from A. S. Suvorin, *Dnevnik*:
quoted in V. Lakshin, *Proval* in
Teatr, 1987, 4, 83–91; more
extensively in *Novoe literaturnoe
obozrenie*, 1995, No. 15, 147–51.
14 See *OR*, 331 82 2: Aleksandr's
letters to Masha, 1883–7: 28 Apr.
1887.
15 See *OR*, 331 82 17: Nikolai's letter
to Masha, 1887.
16 In Taganrog cousin George was
working for a third Tchaikovsky
brother, Ippolit (the fat,
heterosexual Tchaikovsky who told
jokes), director of the shipping
company there.
17 See N. M. Ezhov *Aleksei Sergeevich
Suvorin, Moi vospominaniia o niom,
dumy i soobrazhenia* in *Istoricheskii
vestnik*, SPb, 1915, 1, 110–38.
18 Cut from *PSSP*: see *OR*, 331 22 14:
Anton's letters to Schechtel,
1886–1902; 4 June 1887. The
passage was inked out by Schechtel.
19 From a draft of a letter in 1904 to
the writer Doroshevich, quoted in
PSSP, 2, 401–2.
20 From Suvorin's letter of the late
1880s to his leader-writer Diakov,
quoted in *PSSP*, 2, 401.
21 See M. P. Chekhov's memoirs; also
P. A. Sergeenko, *O. Chekhove*, in
Niva, 1904, 10, 217–18.

22 See *RGALI*, 189 1 2: Ezhov's draft *Humorists of the 1880s*; quoted in *PSSP*, XI, 412–13.

23 See Davydov's *Koe-chto o Chekhove*, quoted in *PSSP*, XI, 414.

24 See *OR*, 331 82 9: Anna Sokolnikova's letter to Evgenia Chekhova, 20 Jan. 1888.

25 The two writers had exchanged only a few words at an evening gathering a few days previously; Chekhov and Garshin's mother had taken to each other, when Chekhov visited the bookshop belonging to Evgeni Garshin, the writer's brother – a critic who became very hostile to Chekhov.

26 See *OR*, 331 49 42a: A. Lazarev-Gruzinsky's letters to Anton, 1887–8.

27 That same autumn the *Dir* was wrecked on the shores of the Crimea.

28 See *OR*, 331 48 27: Korneev's letters to Anton, 1886–94.

29 See *OR*, 331 33 14: Natalia Golden's letter to Anton, 18 Nov. 1888.

30 See *OR*, 331 59 71a: A. A. Suvorin's letters to Anton, 1888.

31 This letter (24 Nov. 1888) is cut in the *PSSP*: see A. P. Chudakov, ' "Neprilichnye slova" i oblik klassika' in *Literaturnoe Obozrenie* 1991, 11, 54.

32 Pleshcheev notes 14 v 1891, see *Pis'ma russkikh pisatelei k Suvorina*, Leningrad 1927, 130.

33 Bowdlerized in the *PSSP*: see *RGALI*, 594 1 269.

34 She was still writing Anton from Kharkov, inviting him there to help her husband.

35 See S. I. Smirnova-Sazonova's diary, *LN*87, 305.

36 Shcheglov reconstructed the play, a poor piece, in 1911 as *The Power of Hypnotism*.

37 See *OR*, 331 59 75: Anastasia Suvorina's letters to Anton, 1889–1900.

38 See Vladimir Nemirovich-Danchenko's letter to Anton in *Ezhegodnik MKhaTa*, 1944, 1, 93.

39 See *RGALI*, 189 1 19: Lazarev-Gruzinsky to Ezhov, 1884–91: letters of 10 Dec. 1888, 21 Jan. 1889.

40 See N. M. Ezhov, *A. P. Chekhov* in *Istoricheskii vestnik*, 1909, 11, 595–607.

41 See *OR*, 331 59 46: Anna Suvorina's letters to Anton, 1887–1901.

42 At Obock Ashinov was joined by Father Paisi, who had once dug Mitrofan Chekhov's cellar, and Dr Tsvetaev, whom Chekhov had met at Voskresensk. When the French fired on the Cossacks, some of the invaders crossed the Danikil desert to serve the Negus of Abyssinia.

43 See *OR*, 331 82 16: Kolia's postcard to Evgenia.

44 See *OR*, 331 82 25: Kolia's letter to an unidentified Aleksandr Viktorovich (May? 1889).

45 See *OR*, 331 32 15: this passage is cut from *Pis'ma*, 1939.

46 See *OR*, 331 82 25: Kolia's letter to an unidentified Aleksandr Viktorovich (May? 1889).

47 See *RGALI*, 459 1 4617: Aleksandr Chekhov's letters to A. S. Suvorin, 1888–96.

48 See *OR*, 331 31 1: Aleksandr's letters to Pavel Chekhov, 1874–96.

49 See *RGALI*, 2540 1 43: Misha's letters to his parents, 1888–1901.

50 See *OR*, 331 31 1: Aleksandr's letters to Pavel Chekhov, 1874–96. Another mourner held her grief back: in 1953 Tatiana Ivchenko aged 103, dying in Kharkov, insisted on being buried next to Kolia Chekhov.

She had brought Kolia milk in his last weeks of life.

51 See *OR*, 331 63 25b: Franz Schechtel's letters to Anton, 1887–9.

52 See *RGALI*, 189 1 19: Lazarev-Gruzinsky's letters to Nikolai Ezhov, 1884–91: 24 June 1889.

53 See *OR*, 331 81 21: Pavel Chekhov's letters to Anton, 1886–96.

54 Kleopatra Karatygina had acquired by marriage the Karatygin surname which had a generation before belonged to one of the finest actors in the Russian theatre. See *LN68*, 575–86: Karatygina, *Vospominaniia o Chekhove*.

55 See *Pis'ma russkikh pisatelei k Suvorinu*, Leningrad, 1927, 38 (misdated 1897).

56 See *OR*, 331 81 32: written on the back of Pavel Chekhov's letter to Anna Ipatieva-Golden.

57 See *OR*, 331 58 27v: P. Svobodin's letters to Anton, 1889; partly in *Zapiski OR*, 16, 1954.

58 See *OR*, 331 50 1zh: Leikin's letters to Anton, 1889: 26 Aug. 1889.

59 The story eventually had an echo in the Chekhovs' life: in 1917 Anton's nephew Volodia shot himself.

60 Professor Storozhenko avenged the insult in 1899: as theatre censor, he blocked *Uncle Vania*.

PART IV *Années de Pèlerinage*

1 See *OR*, 331 47 13a: K. A. Karatygina's letters to Anton Chekhov, 1889.

2 See *OR*, 331 63 3a: E. K. Shavrova's letters to Anton Chekhov, 1889.

3 See *RGALI*, 189 1 19: A. Lazarev-Gruzinsky's letters to Ezhov, 1884–91: 21 Oct. 1889.

4 See *OR*, 331 59 46: Anna Suvorina's letters to Anton: 12 Nov. 1889.

5 See *RGALI*, 640 1 189: Svobodin's letters to Lavrov: 11 Oct. 89.

6 See G. Shaliugin, 'Uchitel slovesnosti', in *Chekhoviana* 1990, 124–9.

7 See *OR*, 331 46 33: A. Ipatieva-Golden's letters to Anton, 1889–91.

8 This passage is to be found in Vl. I. Nemirovich-Danchenko, *Rozhdenie teatra*, 1989, 60–1.

9 See *OR*, 331 47 13b: Kleopatra Karatygina's letters to Anton Chekhov, 1890.

10 See *OR*, 331 49 25b: this phrase is cut from *Levitan*, 1956.

11 Quoted from Vl. Rynkevich, *Puteshestvie k domu s mezoninom*, Rostov, 1990, 54–7: the Ioganson diary is in *GPB*, SPb, and in *MXaT*.

12 Lieutenant Schmidt wrote his recollections in *Nasha Gazeta*, Tallinn, 1927, XI: see G. Shaliugin, 'Ia i moi voennye sputniki', *Oktiabr'*, 1987, 5, 195–201.

13 See *OR*, 331 46 1a: Aleksandr Ivanenko's letters to Anton, 1889–91: 28 May 1890.

14 See *RGALI*, 2540 1 161: Masha's letters to Ivan Chekhov, 1890–1908: 8 May 1890.

15 This letter is cut from the *PSSP*: see A. P. Chudakov, '"Neprilichnye slova" i oblik klassika' in *Literaturnoe Obozrenie*, 1991, 11, 54.

16 P. Kononovich is recorded as a pupil of Taganrog *gimnazia* in the 1850s: if General Kononovich is a relative, this might explain his affability to Anton.

17 See *OR*, 331 33 126: Evgenia's letters to Anton, 1875–1904.

18 See *LN87*, 294–300: *Plavanie A. P. Chekhova* (from the log of the *Petersburg*).

19 See *OR*, 331 33 125: Evgenia's

letters to Pavel Chekhov, 1875–90.

20 See *RGALI*, 2540 1 160: Evgenia's letters to Ivan, 1888–1905.

21 See *OR*, 331 31 1: the letter to Masha 8 Oct. 1890 is filed with Aleksandr's letters to his parents.

22 See *RGALI*, 2540 1 483: Masha's letters to Mikhail Chekhov, 1884–1904: 15 Oct. 1890. A year later Suvorin offered Vania a career in his Moscow bookshop, see *RGALI*, 2540 1 143.

23 See *LN68*, 496.

24 See N. M. Ezhov, *A. P. Chekhov* in *Istoricheskii vestnik* 1909, 11, 595–607.

25 See *RGALI*, 2540 1 158: Pavel's letters to Ivan, 1879–98: 29 Nov. 1890.

26 See *Vokrug Chekhova*, 278–80; *OR*, 331 83 25: Misha's *Chekhov i mangusy*.

27 May the gods serve you, the nymphs love you and the doctors not treat you. Yours A. See *OR*, 331 59 71b: A. A. Suvorin's letters to Anton, 1889–92.

28 See *OR*, 331 43 11b: N. Ezhov's letters to Anton, 1890–1: 20 Oct. 1890.

29 See *OR*, 331 46 1a: Ivanenko's letters to Anton, 1889–91.

30 See *LN68*, 479–92: Leontiev-Shcheglov's diary.

31 See *OR*, 331 52 46: Daria Musina-Pushkina's letters to Anton, 1891, 1896–8.

32 See *OR*, 331 63 4a: Elena Shavrova's letters to Anton, 1889–91: 14 Jan. 1891.

33 See *OR*, 331 52 2a: Lika Mizinova's letters to Anton, 1891–2; in *Perepiska* 1984, II, 16–59.

34 See *Novoe vremia*, No. 1017, 4 July 1904.

35 See *RGALI*, 2540 1 158: Pavel's letters to Ivan, 1879–98: 7 Apr. 1891.

36 Both Misha and Masha in their memoirs imply that the palmcat was given to Moscow Zoo; the Zoo's records do not mention it.

37 See *OR*, 331 81 8: Pavel's notebooks, 1880–97.

38 See *RGALI*, 2540 1 158: Pavel's letters to Ivan, 1879–98: 3 May 1891.

39 Grillparzer's play *Sappho* was performed in Moscow that year; the nicknames were topical.

40 See Chaleeva's memoirs (in Soligalich local museum), quoted in A. V. Kandidov, *A. P. Chekhov v Bogimove*, Kaluga, 1991, 32.

41 See *OR*, 331 36 38: Bezdetnov's letter to Anton Chekhov.

42 Cut in *PSSP*: see A. P. Chudakov, ' "Neprilichnye slova" i oblik klassika' in *Literaturnoe Obozrenie*, 1991, 11, 54.

43 See *OR*, 331 52 2a: Lika Mizinova's letters to Anton, 1891–2; in *Perepiska*, 1984, II, 16–59.

44 See Sazonova's diary, 15 Mar. 1895, *LN87*, 307.

45 See *OR*, 331 81 83: Fenichka Dolzhenko's letter to Evgenia, 9 July 1891.

46 Quoted by Aleksandr in *Pis'ma*, 1939, 246. Anton used Pavel's prayer in 'The Duel'.

47 See *OR*, 331 46 33: Anna Ipatieva-Golden's letter to Anton, 25 Sept. 1891.

48 See *OR*, 331 81 25: Pavel's letters to Mitrofan and Liudmila, 1876–93: 27 Oct. 1891.

49 See *OR*, 331 63 4a: Elena Shavrova's letters to Anton, 1889–91: 17 Nov. 1891.

50 See *MXaT*, (Sanin) 5323/ 1933–73: L. S. Mizinova's letters to Sofia Ioganson, 1877–99.

51 See *OR*, 331 46 1a: Ivanenko's letters to Anton, 1889–91.

52 See *OR*, 331 49 12b:

NOTES

Lazarev–Gruzinsky's letters to Anton, 1889–92: 4 Nov. 1891.

53 See *OR*, 331 39 25: Volter's letter to Anton, 15 Jan. 1892.

54 See *OR*, 331 58 27g: P. Svobodin's letters to Anton, 1891; partly printed in *Zapiski OR GBL*, 16, 1954.

55 See *OR*, 331 43 9: Lt Evgraf Egorov's letters to Anton Chekhov, 1882–92.

56 This story, the first Chekhov set in western Europe, is told by a terrorist who, assigned to spy on a minister, elopes with the mistress of the minister's son. Revised, it was published in 1893.

57 Chekhov had also written 'A Great Man', now known as 'The Grasshopper', showing a saintly doctor destroyed by his wife's treachery: this bombshell (for the main characters were recognizable as the Levitan *ménage*) exploded in spring 1892.

58 See *OR*, 331 96 37: Aleksandr Smagin's thirty-four letters to Masha, 1888–92.

59 See E. M. Shavrova-Iust's memoirs in I. M. Sel'vaniuk, V. D. Sedegov, *Sbornik statei i materialov 3ii*, Rostov, 1963, 267–308.

60 See *OR*, 331 81 21: Pavel's letters to Anton, 1886–96: 3 Jan. 1892.

PART V *Cincinnatus*

1 Nikolai Ezhov teased Anton in a skit, *Certified Authentic*: a Mr Mongoose buys 600 acres, but the forest is not his and the piano is unplayable.

2 See *OR*, 331 96 37: Aleksandr Smagin's letters to Masha, 1888–May 1892.

3 See *OR*, 331 96 38: Aleksandr Smagin's 34 letters to Masha, June 1892–1929.

4 See *O semie*, 1970, 203.

5 Cockroaches were believed to leave a house only before a fire.

6 See *MXaT*, (Sanin) 5323/ 1933–1973: L. S. Mizinova's letters to Sofia Ioganson, 1877–99.

7 See *OR*, 331 52 2a: Lika's letters to Anton, 1891–2; some in *Perepiska*, 1984, II, 16–59.

8 Leskov had written 'The Unmercenary Engineers': an officer resists corruption and is committed to a psychiatrist, who declares death the ultimate medicine. Leskov's late 'Hare Park' pays homage to 'Ward No. 6': a secret policeman, nursed by the radical he persecuted, dies in a madhouse.

9 See *OR*, 331 63 25v: Franz Schechtel's letters to Anton, 1891–3.

10 See *OR*, 331 48 79a: O. P. Kundasova's letters to Anton, 1892–1904: 25 May 1892.

11 In remoter areas peasants believed that doctors were deliberately spreading cholera: in Samara, on the Volga, they killed one doctor and drove the others out.

12 Petrov was a shop assistant in Muir and Mirrielees, the Moscow store where the Chekhovs ordered everything from crockery to rifles. Sixteen years earlier, at Petrov's wedding in Kaluga, Aleksandr, Kolia and Masha had been poor relatives: now the scales had tipped the other way.

13 See *OR*, 331 93 78: Lika Mizinova's letters to Masha Chekhova, 1891–3.

14 Pavel began a diary on arrival in Melikhovo: it records comings and goings, the weather, and incidents, odd and banal. See A. P. Kuzicheva, E. M. Sakharova *Melikhovskii letopisets*, 1995.

15 See *OR*, 331 56 38: A. A. Pokhlebina's letters to Anton, 1892–8: 10 July 1892.

16 See *OR*, 331 51 12: Klara Mamuna's letter to Anton.

17 See *LN68*, 855–870: E. Z. Balabanovich, *Chekhov v pis'makh brata* . . . : letter of 26 June 1892.

18 See *OR*, 331 81 21: Pavel Chekhov's letters to Anton, 1886–96.

19 See *RGALI*, 459 1 4617: Aleksandr's letters to A. S. Suvorin, 1888–96: 13 July 1892.

20 See *OR*, 331 59 46: Anna Suvorina's letters to Anton: undated, filed as sheets 36–7.

21 Dr Obolonsky, a 'vulture' for a lucrative patient, showed his concern: 'I've heard . . . your stay depends on the degree of Suvorin's illness. They say he's seriously ill . . . he believes you and in you unconditionally. Arrange for him to invite me to examine him.' See *OR*, 331 54 7: N. N. Obolonsky's letters to Anton, 1889–1901.

22 Anton also examined Leskov, who feared his doctors were lying about his terminal heart condition. He reassured Leskov, but told others that the novelist had at most a year to live.

23 See Zankovetskaia's memoirs, *LN68*, 592–3.

24 See *LN68*, 493–510 for V. A. Tikhonov's and Leikin's diaries.

25 See *OR*, 331 81 13: Pavel's letters to Aleksandr, 1874–94.

26 See *OR*, 331, 52 2b: Lika's letters to Anton, 1893–4.

27 See *LN68*, 570–2.

28 See *LN68*, 484.

29 The same journalist also attacked Chekhov as 'a writer without support or goal' and hoped 'he gets closer to human sufferings . . .', but now Chekhov overlooked abuse from *Russian Thought*.

30 The Suvorins and Chekhov were all relieved they had not gone: the Russian contribution was just a party of bureaucrats, who were the butt of the American President's sarcasm.

31 Anton's letter to Gorbunov-Posadov, Chertkov's editor, 26 Apr. 1893.

32 Potapenko's memoirs are in *V vospominaniiakh*.

33 Suvorin was not intentionally cheating Anton, but *New Times* had notoriously bad bookkeeping.

34 See *RGALI*, 459 1 2161: O. P. Kundasova's letters to A. S. Suvorin, 1891–1908.

35 See *OR*, 331 43 11g: N. Ezhov's letters to Anton, 1893: 16 Apr.

36 That Athenian night was beautiful. The beautiful is unforgettable. Dear poet, if you only knew what a headache . . ./I await the supreme vice and send you your dowry./My little Sappho. Come at once, urgent. See *RGALI*, 571 1 1204: Lidia Iavorskaia's fifty-one letters to Shchepkina-Kupernik, 1893.

37 See *OR*, 331 64 2: T. L. Shchepkina-Kupernik's letters to Anton, 1893–1900.

38 See *OR*, 331 64 34: Lidia Iavorskaia's letters to Anton, 1893–6.

39 See *PSSP*, 5, 506: see *RGALI*, 459 3 12.

40 See *LN68*, 479–92; Leontiev-Shcheglov's diary.

41 See *OR*, 331 56 36a: Potapenko's letters to Anton, 1893–5. See *Perepiska II*, 1984, 62–76.

42 See *OR*, 331 46 1b: Ivanenko's letters to Anton, 1892–4.

43 See *OR*, 331 93 79: Lika Mizinova's letters to Masha, 1894.

PART VI *Lika disparue*

1 See *OR*, 331 52 2b: Lika's letters to Anton 1893–4; some in *Perepiska* II, 1984, 16–59.
2 Miroliubov was soon to leave the opera and become Chekhov's last editor.
3 See *OR*, 331 93 79: Lika Mizinova's letters to Masha Chekhova, 1894.
4 See *OR*, 331 64 34: Lidia Iavorskaia's letters to Anton Chekhov, 1893–6.
5 See *OR*, 331 56 36a: Potapenko's letters to Anton, 1893–5. See *Perepiska* II, 1984, 62–76.
6 See *OR*, 331 95 2: Potapenko's letters to Masha, 1894–5.
7 See *OR*, 331 64 2: T. L. Shchepkina-Kupernik's letters to Anton Chekhov, 1893–1900.
8 Quoted in *PSSP*, 5, 611.
9 See *OR*, 331 50 11: Aleksandra Liosova's three letters to Anton, 1894.
10 Quoted from E. M. Sakharova, *A. I. Ivanenko – vechnyi drug* in *Chekhoviana: Melikhovskie trudy i dni*, 1995, 327–334.
11 See *OR*, 331 46 1b: Ivanenko's letters to Anton, 1892–4.
12 See *LN68*, 479–92; Leontiev-Shcheglov's diary.
13 See *OR*, 331 81 13: Pavel's letters to Aleksandr Chekhov, 1874–94: Aug. 1894.
14 See *MXaT*, (Sanin), 5323: L. S. Mizinova-Sanina's letters to Lidia Iurgeneva.
15 See *MXaT*, (Sanin), 5323/ 1933– 1973: L. S. Mizinova's letters to Sofia Ioganson, 1877–99.
16 See *IRLI*, fond 285, S. I. Smirnova-Sazonova papers.
17 Sablin's brother, a tax inspector (died in 1895), protected Misha; Mikhail Sablin, a theatre manager, edited *The Russian Gazette*. The Sablins and Misha made Masha a monthly allowance, which Anton pretended not to know about.
18 Chekhov's library had two books on syphilis, and none on TB, yet Potapenko remembers him telling a consumptive passenger on a train to abandon work and family and live in Algiers.
19 See *RGALI*, 2540 1 483: Masha's letters to Misha, 1884–1904: 7 Aug. 1894.
20 See *OR*, 331 81 21: Pavel's letters to Anton, 1886–96.
21 See *OR*, 331 33 1v: Pavel Chekhov, various documents.
22 See *O semie*, 1970, 179.
23 See A. P. Kuzicheva, E. M. Sakharova, *Melikhovskii letopisets*, 1995.
24 See *RGALI*, 571 1 1137: Masha's letters to Shchepkina-Kupernik, 1894–1951.
25 See *OR*, 331 33 14: Natalia Golden-Chekhova's letters to Anton, 1888, 1894.
26 See L. Z. Abramenkova, 'Sosed Chekhovykh V. N. Semenkovich' in *Chekhoviana: Melikhovskie trudy i dni*, 1995, 264–72.
27 Mikhailov became Medvedenko in *The Seagull*. In 1895 the peasants called for his dismissal.
28 Quoted in *PSSP*, 5, 587.
29 See *OR*, 331 43 11d: Nikolai Ezhov's letters to Anton, 1894–7.
30 See *OR*, 331 93 80: Lika's letters to Masha Chekhova, 1895.
31 See A. Ia. Al'tshuller, *A. P. Chekhov i L. B. Iavorskaia*, in *Chekhoviana*, 1990, 140–51.
32 See *OR*, 331 64 34: Lidia Iavorskaia's letters to Anton Chekhov, 1893–6.
33 See *OR*, 331 52 2v: Lika's letters to Anton, 1895–6; some in *Perepiska* II, 1984, 16–59.
34 See *OR*, 331 48 79a: O. P. Kundasova's letters to Anton, 1892– 1904.

35 See *OR*, 331 48 83a: Dr P. I. Kurkin's letters to Anton, 1892–5.
36 Quoted in *PSSP*, 6, 381.
37 See *OR*, 331 59 46: Anna Suvorina's letters to Anton, 1889–1901.
38 See *LN68*, 484.
39 See *LN68*, 502.
40 Misha said that the story was based on the Iaroslavl tax inspector Sablin's unhappy marriage.
41 See *OR*, 331 82 59: Misha's letters to Masha, 1890–6: 12 Jan. 1895.
42 See *MXaT*, 5323/19: S. M. Ioganson's diary, book 5, 1895–7.
43 See M. A. Sheikina, 'Iz pisem I. V. Chekhova k S. V. Chekhovoi' in *Chekhoviana: Melikhovskie trudy i dni*, 1995, 315–27; *RGALI*, 2540 1 238–43.
44 See *RGALI*, 289 1 16: N. Ezhov's letters to Leikin, 1894–1903.
45 In August 1895 Ezhov asked Leikin for an advance of 200 roubles for the marriage. Leikin replied that he was glad Ezhov had found the love of his life, and sent him 50.
46 Chekhov asked Korobov to translate a passage from Nietzsche for his new play.
47 Glukhovskoi, the vet, had, as an insurance agent too, a double interest in the Chekhov cows.
48 See *OR*, 331 60 62: Anna Turchaninova's letters to Anton Chekhov, 1895, 1900.
49 See *OR*, 331 63 4v: Elena Shavrova-Iust's letters to Anton Chekhov, 1895.
50 See Ilia Sats, *Iz zapisnoi knizhki*, Moscow-Petrograd, 1923, 53–4.
51 See *OR*, 331 81 24: Pavel's letters to Maria Chekhova, 1885–98: 15 Dec. 1895.
52 See *RGALI*, 2540 1 149: Aleksandr's letters to Ivan Chekhov, 1882–97: 31 July 1895.
53 Menshikov's articles upset all Serpukhov district, proving that Prince Viazemsky was not a precursor of Tolstoy, emancipating peasants and giving away property, but a dissolute drunkard. The meeting with Tolstoy was marred for Anton by neuralgia which struck the whole of his right face. He took painkillers, quinine, ointment, and had a tooth pulled, but the pain persisted for two weeks; a year later an optician would diagnose the cause.

PART VII *The Flight of the Seagull*

1 See Kleopatra Karatygina's memoirs, *LN68*, 575–86.
2 See Sazonova's diary, *LN87*, 307–8.
3 See *OR*, 331 52 29: Marfa Ivanovna Loboda's letters to Anton, 1881–1902; 4 Jan. 1896.
4 See *OR*, 331 56 36b: Potapenko's letters to Anton 1896. See *Perepiska* II, 1984, 62–76.
5 A flirtatious conversation is reconstructed in unChekhovian detail in Avilova's memoirs (*V vospominaniiakh* 121–208), but her account is partly corroborated by other records. She recalls being surprised by Anton's visit to Petersburg, first catching sight of him that year in a theatre box: 'How ridiculous and weird it was: papa Suvorin and maman Suvorin and Chekhov, their baby, in the middle.'
6 See *OR* 331 73 10: Pavel Chekhov's letters to Misha, 1885–98: 5 Feb. 1896.
7 See *OR*, 331 47 13v: Kleopatra Karatygina's letters to Anton, 1892–1904.
8 This view is Vl. Rynkevich's, in *Puteshestvie k domu s mezoninom*, Rostov, 1990. See *OR*, 331 52 2v:

Lika's letters to Anton, 1895–6; some printed in *Perepiska* II, 1984, 16–59.

9 See A. P. Kuzicheva, E. M. Sakharova, *Melikhovskii letopisets*, 1995.

10 In the printed versions of Suvorin's diary Gei is misread as Chekhov (Suvorin's hand was appalling) and it was therefore thought that Chekhov had fled Melikhovo at Easter 1896 to be with Suvorin. A close reading of Suvorin's manuscript confirms, however, that he strolled the cemetery with Gei, not Chekhov.

11 See *OR*, 331 73 11: Evgenia's letters to Mikhail Chekhov, 1885–1903.

12 See T. L. Sukhotina-Tolstaia, *Dnevniki*, 1979, 372.

13 See Menshikov's letter to Chekhov, 20 Aug. 1896, quoted in *PSSP*, 500–1.

14 Lugovoi was Aleksei Tikhonov, the brother of V. A. Tikhonov, editor of *The North*.

15 Iakovenko refused beds to the insane whom Chekhov wanted interned; relatives had to apply for a council grant of 5 roubles a month to pay for a chain, a guard and sedatives. Tolokonnikov gave Anton a violin as a mark of his gratitude for the bromide he prescribed.

16 See *MXaT*, 5323/19: S. M. Ioganson's diary, book 5, 1895–7.

17 This is not the view in Rynkevich's *Puteshestvie k domu s mezoninom*, Rostov, 1990.

18 Volkenshtein was the Jewish boy Chekhov had saved from expulsion in 1877; Chuprov taught Chekhov statistics at Moscow University; Professor Veselovsky was an academician.

19 See Grigori Moskvich, *Putevoditel' po Kavkazu*, SPb, 1911, 83.

20 See *LN68*, 479–92; Leontiev-Shcheglov's diary.

21 See *PSSP*, XIII, 364–5.

22 The revision was done after *The Seagull* had been completed. Firstly, *Uncle Vania*, like *The Seagull*, has no scene divisions. Secondly, August and September 1896 are the only months between two works ('My Life', 'Peasants') when Anton could have found time to rewrite the play. Thirdly, details added to *Uncle Vania* reflect Melikhovo in summer 1896: Mariushka, the cook's tame chicks (the Konovitsers refused to eat them), and Marina's speckled hen on-stage in *Uncle Vania*; in June Chekhov's visit to Mal´tsy for dysentery, and Dr Astrov's to 'Malitskoe' for typhus; on 15 August a visitor Menshikov 'in dry weather wears galoshes, carries an umbrella, so as not to perish of sunstroke', and Vania mocks Serebriakov: 'An oppressively hot day, and our great scholar goes out with an umbrella, in his overcoat, gloves and galoshes.'

23 Bychkov's memoirs, told to V. E. Ermilov, are in *Kavkazskii krai* Krasnodar?, 1913, No. 145.

24 Sazonova wrote: 'We were all at *Sodom's End*. We saw Chekhov. He came to see our actors.'

25 See *V vospominaniiakh . . .*, 350–5.

26 See *LN68*, 499–510 for Leikin's diary.

27 Karpov's memoirs (dubious) are in *V. F. Komissarzhevskaia . . . Materialy*, 1964, 214–5.

28 Anna Suvorina's memoir, in M. D. Beliaev, A. S. Dolinin, *A. P. Chekhov. Zaterrianyne proizvedneiia, Neizdannye pis'ma, Novye vospominaiia . . .* Leningrad: Atenei, 1925, 185–95.

29 I have not been able to trace this line in Avilova's printed works.

30 *PSSP*, 6, 523.
31 See *OR*, 331 63 4g: Elena Shavrova's letters to Anton, 1896.
32 Kugel had not met Lika, who drank, or her friend Varia Eberle, who took snuff.
33 Quoted in *PSSP*, 6, 532; written 21 Oct. 1896.
34 See E. M. Shavrova-Iust's memoirs in I. M. Sel'vaniuk, V. D. Sedegov, *Sbornik statei i materialov 3ii*, Rostov, 1963, 267–308.
35 See *Perepiska*, 1984, II, 150–1.
36 See K. A. Chaikovskaia, 'Melikhovskie pozhary' in *Chekhoviana*, 1995, 272–7.
37 Russian dramatists usually received two per cent of the gross takings for each act of their play.
38 See *OR*, 331 63 25g: Franz Schechtel's letters to Anton, 1894–1900: 17 Dec. 1896.
39 See *OR*, 331 36 72: Emilie Bijon's letters to Anton, 1896–1900.
40 See *OR*, 331 54 50: Liudmila Groupillon-Ozerova's eight letters to Anton, 1896–7.
41 Meanwhile Nikolai Ezhov was enrolled as census taker for the dosshouses of Moscow.
42 See *OR*, 331 63 4d: Elena Shavrova's letters to Anton, 1897.
43 See *OR*, 331 48 7: Vera Komissarzhevskaia's letters to Anton, 1897–1903.
44 See *Pis'ma*, 1939, 331–3.

PART VIII *Flowering Cemeteries*

1. See *LN68*, 479–92; Leontiev-Shcheglov's diary.
2 See Sazonova's diary, *LN87*, 309.
3 Koumiss is fermented mares' milk; it tastes like a mixture of champagne, chalk and rancid butter. It is easily digested and its bacteria are thought to be beneficial.
4 According to her memoirs she elicited from Anton a confession of undying love; at the time, however, she told Leikin (see his diary *LN68*, 499–510) that Chekhov was forbidden to speak.
5 See *PSSP*, 6, 616–7: Olga Shavrova's account is hard to believe.
6 See *OR*, 331, 63 4d: Elena Shavrova's letters to Anton, 1897.
7 See S. M. Chekhov, *O semie*, Iaroslavl, 1970, 118.
8 See *PSSP*, 6, 631–2.
9 See *Zapiski GBL VIII* 1941, 49.
10 See *OR*, 331 36 72: Emilie Bijon's letters to Anton, 1896–1900.
11 See *OR*, 331 33 51: Georgi Chekhov's letters to Anton, 1897: 13 Apr.
12 See A. P. Kuzicheva, E. M. Sakharova, *Melikhovskii letopisets*, 1995.
13 See Sazonova's diary, *LN87*, 310.
14 Cut from *Levitan: Pis'ma*, 1956; see *OR*, 331 49 25.
15 See *OR*, 331 54 50: Liudmila Groupillon-Ozerova's eight letters to Anton Chekhov, 1896–7. Anton's letters to her are lost.
16 See *OR*, 331 93 80: Lika's letters to Masha, 1895–7.
17 See *OR*, 331 52 2g: Lika's letters to Anton, 1897; some printed in *Perepiska* II, 1984, 16–59.
18 See *OR*, 331 59 46: Anna Suvorina's letters to Anton, 1889–1901.
19 *Dnevnik*, 1923/1992: this passage is followed in published versions by a series of morbid reflections attributed to Chekhov. A closer look at Suvorin's manuscript suggests they are Suvorin's own thoughts. Roskina's transcription of Suvorin's diaries (in *RGALI*) may soon be published by the author of this book.
20 The Potapenkos were now *non*

gratæ at the Suvorins, viz. Emilie Bijon (Dec. 1897); 'M. Potapenko . . . s'est permis d'écrire un sale feuilleton concernant les malheureuses governantes, qu'ils méprisent et sa femme qu'était elle?'

21 See *RGALI*, 2450 1 59 [a fragment also used by Vania to write to Aleksandr].

22 Quoted in A. Fiodorov-Davydov, A. Ia. Shapiro *Levitan: Dokumenty*, 1966: letter 29 July 1897.

23 See *OR*, 331 51 18: N. Maksheev's letters to Anton, 1897–8.

24 See *OR*, 331 56 36v: Potapenko's letters to Anton, 1897–9.

25 He refolded *New Times* for the Russian reading room in Menton; he resold *World Echoes* to State Counsellor Kulakov, a resident of the *pension*, for 2 francs a month.

26 See *OR*, 331 73 10: Pavel's letters to Misha, 1885–98: 17 Sept. 1897.

27 See *OR*, 331 73 11: Evgenia's letters to Misha, 1888–1903: 3 Nov. 1897.

28 Russia had refused to sign the international convention on copyright, so Russian authors had no right to be paid for foreign editions of their work.

29 Grigorovich still hoped: he wrote to Suvorin (29 Oct. 1898): 'As for your Nastenka, I've always dreamt of Chekhov . . . he is himself so nice and talented that nothing better can be desired. But how does Nastenka feel?' See *Pis'ma russkikh pisatelei k Suvorinu*, 1927, 42–3.

30 18 Dec. 1897: quoted in *PSSP*, 7, 517.

31 See *OR*, 331 59 25: Vasili Sobolevsky's letters to Anton, 1892–1904.

32 See *OR*, 331 73 11: Masha's postscript to Evgenia's letter to Misha, 3 Nov. 1897.

33 See *OR*, 331 81 23: Pavel's letter to Vania, 22 Dec. 1897.

34 See *OR*, 331 52 2d: Lika's letters to Anton 1898; some printed in *Perepiska* II, 1984, 16–59.

35 Quoted in *PSSP*, 7, 493.

36 Tolstoy wavered; Alphonse Daudet believed that twelve officers could not be wrong. Lidia Iavorskaia was, however, a fiery *Dreyfusarde*.

37 Quoted in *PSSP*, 7, 516.

38 Suvorin had won his own Dreyfus affair. In 1892 *New Times* exposed fraud by the Odessa branch of Parisian grain traders, Louis Dreyfus & Co., who sued Suvorin for libel and lost. Moreover, Suvorin was convinced that Zola had abused him and his wife by calling the anarchist in *Germinal* Souvarine and his partner Anna.

39 Quoted in *PSSP*, 7, 528.

40 Kovalevsky's memoirs of Anton Chekhov are in *Vokrug Chekhova*, 361–6.

41 See *OR*, 331 73 10: Pavel's letters to Misha, 1885–98: 8 Jan. 1898.

42 Quoted in S. M. Chekhov, *O semie*, Iaroslavl, 1970, 135–7.

43 Cut in *Pis'ma*, 1939; see *OR*, 331 32 24: Aleksandr's letters to Anton, 1898.

44 The interview was so heavily edited that Chekhov refused permission to publish.

45 See N. A. Roskina, 'Ob odnoi staroi publikatsii' in *Voprosy literatury*, 1968, 6, 250–3.

46 See *RGALI*, 459 2 14: A. S. Suvorin's letters to Anna Suvorina; quoted *PSSP*, 7, 567.

47 See *RGALI*, 459 1 4172, May 1898: Nastia Suvorina seldom mentioned Chekhov in her letters.

48 See *OR*, 331 73 11: Evgenia's letters to Misha, 1888–1903: 8 May 1898.

49 Married to Ekaterina ('Kitten', formerly Baroness Korf), Nemirovich-Danchenko was both teacher and lover of the twenty-eight-year-old Olga

Knipper. (Anton's familiarity with Nemirovich-Danchenko's wife 'Kitten' once aroused Lika Mizinova's jealousy.) Knipper, after an affair with a student Dmitri Goncharov (an aristocrat with a hereditary disease), forced her mother, a singer, to let her study for the stage.

50 Quoted in V. Lakshin, *Proval* in *Teatr*, 1987, 4, 86.

51 See *Perepiska*, 1984, II, 153–4.

52 Tychinkin set type by night and taught in school by day; reputed to be Petersburg's most absent-minded man, he was the only employee of *New Times* widely trusted by the writers whom Suvorin published.

53 See *OR*, 331 48 79a: Olga Kundasova's letters to Anton, 1892–1904.

54 Lidia Avilova was convinced that 'About Love' told of Chekhov's renunciation of love for her. She angered Anton, by accusing him of exploiting intimate secrets for literary gain.

55 See Olga Knipper's memoirs in *Vokrug Chekhova*, 381–2.

56 See *Perepiska*, 1984, II, 82; *OR*, 331 64 2; T. Shchepkina-Kupernik's letters to Anton, 1893–1900: minuscule script on mauve and white card, 8 Sept. 1898.

57 'I want sex, but "I've got a headache", my penis stands, nobody comes, nobody gives.' Cut in *Pis'ma*, 1939; see *OR*, 331 32 24: Aleksandr's letters to Anton, 1898.

58 *RGALI*, 2316 2 35.

59 The journal was saved when Suvorin wheedled a subsidy from Vitte, the Minister of Finances.

60 Ertel to Vostriakov, quoted in N. Gitovich, *Letopis'*, 522–3.

61 See *OR*, 331 81 66: Evgenia's letters to Masha, 1891–1914.

62 It was Vania whom Anton rewarded for his management of the catastrophe. He asked Anatoli Iakovlev, his former pupil, the son of a senior civil servant, to exchange favours. Anton would get Iakovlev's stories published for securing Vania's promotion to pensionable civil service rank.

63 See *RGALI*, 2540 1 49: Misha's letters to Evgenia, 1888–1904, end Oct. 1898.

64 See *PSSP*, 7, 648 and S. M. Chekhov, *O semie*, Iaroslavl, 1970, 151.

65 See *OR*, 331 82 60: Misha's letters to Masha, 1897–8: 25 Oct. 1898.

66 See *PSSP*, 7, 632: see Vl. I. Nemirovich-Danchenko, *Teatral'noe nasledie*, 1954, II, 144.

PART IX *Three Triumphs*

1 Anton had met the Ilovaiskys in Voronezh in the famine of 1892.

2 See *OR*, 331 73 11: Evgenia's letters to Mikhail Chekhov, 1888–1903: 7 Nov. 1898.

3 For this Varenikov was summoned by the magistrates, but the authorities dropped the case.

4 See *OR*, 331 56 38: Aleksandra Pokhlebina's letters to Anton, 1893–8.

5 See E. A. Polotskaia, 'Ialtinskaia redaktsia "Shutochki"' in *Chekhoviana*, 1993, 101–16.

6 See *OR*, 331 48 4: Nadia Kolomnina's letters to Anton, 1896–1900.

7 See *OR*, 331 48 7: Vera Komissarzhevskaia's letters to Anton, 1896–1900.

8 Many of Gorky's letters to Chekhov are printed in *Perepiska*, 1984, II, 297–365.

9 See *OR*, 331 37 64: Semion Bychkov's letters to Anton, 1898–9: 3 Jan. 1899.

10 Sergeenko's letters and diaries are quoted in *PSSP*, 9, 282.

11 See *LN87*, 261.

12 In 1900 Rainer Maria Rilke wrote to Chekhov (331 57 24): 'J'ai l'intention de traduire aussi *Oncle Vania* ... toutes mes démarches pour me procurer l'édition imprimée de vos œuvres dramatiques ont été en vain.' Unable to find Chekhov's *Plays*, Rilke turned back to lyrical poetry.

13 See *OR*, 331 82 61: Misha's letters to Masha, 1899–1901: 24 Jan. 1899.

14 The jest had its serious side. Adolf Marx was a very bourgeois publisher, but Karl-Marxists now acclaimed Chekhov as a champion of the working classes against their exploiters, and Chekhov promised his next major story to *Life*, a staunchly left-wing journal.

15 See *OR*, 331 61 52: Gavriil Kharchenko's letters to Anton, 1899–1901.

16 See A. M. Melkova, *Novye materialy* ..., in *Chekhovskie chteniia v Ialte*, 1987, 110–22.

17 The Russian institution of 'court of honour' is thought to have hounded Tchaikovsky to suicide. Suvorin was eventually condemned, but 'sentenced' merely to a reprimand. Anton then told a Taganrog journalist: 'When hounds can't catch game, they torture cats.'

18 See *OR*, 331 59 46: Anna Suvorina's letters to Anton, 1889–1901; quoted in *PSSP*, 9, 282.

19 See *OR*, 331 60 64: Konstantin Tychinkin's forty-six letters to Anton, 1896–1902.

20 See *OR*, 331 52 2e: Lika's letters to Anton 1899; some are in *Perepiska*, II, 1984, 16–59.

21 See *OR*, 331 60 43: T. Sukhotina-Tolstaia's letters to Anton, 1896–9.

22 The banter hid some mysteries: a letter from Nina Korsh (the daughter of the Moscow theatre owner) had, in a male hand, a note, perhaps not a joke: 'Listen, Chekhov, I must talk seriously. If you invited me only to hear a humiliating refusal, and one transmitted to a girl who has been intriguing against me, then that is vile.' Around 1899 Nina Korsh conceived a child: the father is unknown. In the 1950s Nina Korsh's daughter told the scholar Iu. K. Avdeev that she believed Chekhov was her father, but I have found no written corroboration and Anton's casual references to Nina Korsh and her daughter belie the claim.

23 Levitan had wished him (8 Feb. 1899, *OR*, 331 49 25g): 'The Lord send you everything except sluts with gonorrhœa.'

24 See *PSSP*, 8, 472.

25 See the memoirs of Anatoli Iakovlev, whom Anton had tutored as a boy, *LN68*, 597–604.

26 See *OR*, 331 60 24: Nadezhda Ternovskaia's letters to Anton, 1899; E. A. Polotskaia, 'Ialtinskaia redaktsia "Shutochki"' in *Chekhoviana*, 1993, 101–16.

27 Given Anton's absorption in Olga Knipper, it is unlikely that he came to this brief encounter laden with the erotic angst in which Avilova's memoirs steep this meeting.

28 Quoted in *PSSP*, 8, 517.

29 See *OR*, 331 105 1: Masha's letters to Olga, 1899. Some are in *Knipper-Chekhova*, 1972, II.

30 See *RGALI*, 549 1 408: Masha's letters to Maria Drozdova, 1898–1905; see *PSSP*, 8, 516.

31 Marx would break the agreement and print just Chekhov's texts, without the Stanislavsky *mis-en-scène*, which have only

recently been published – as though Brahms's symphonies were printed without dynamics.

32 See Smirnova-Sazonova's diary, *LN87*, 310.

33 See *RGALI*, 2540 1 483: Masha's letters to Misha, 1884–1904: 3 Sept. 1899.

34 See *OR*, 331 63 4z: Elena Shavrova-Iust's letters to Anton, 1899. Anton left unanswered Shavrova's next letter on 13 Dec. 1899: 'There is in the world a person who has some points of contact with your soul, who loves you hopelessly, from afar, and wants nothing.'

35 See *Perepiska*, 1934, and *OR*, 331 76 1: Olga Knipper's letters to Anton, June–Sept. 1899.

36 Cut from *Perepiska*, 1934. See *OR*, 331 76 1: Olga Knipper's letters to Anton, June–Sept. 1899.

37 Forty years late, Olga Knipper the *grande dame* was heard, in a penetrating *sotto voce*, saying to Nemirovich-Danchenko, 'Volodia, do you remember when you used to call me your vaulting horse?'

38 Masha wrote to Anton 31 Oct. 1899: 'I completely share your liking for Katichka Nemirovich.'

39 See *OR*, 331 36 72: Emilie Bijon's letters to Anton, 1896–1900.

40 See *OR*, 331 59 75: Anastasia Suvorina-Miasoedova's letters to Anton, 1889–1900.

41 See S. M. Chekhov, *O semie*, Iaroslavl, 1970, 179–82.

42 That day, Anton told Sobolevsky, he wanted to be in Monte Carlo, betting on *quatre premiers*.

43 See Lazarevsky's diary, *LN87*, 319–56.

44 See *OR*, 331 60 62: Anna Turchaninova's letters to Anton, 1895, 1900: 20 May 1900.

45 See *OR*, 331 77 14: Olga's letters to Masha, 1900: 7 June.

46 See *OR*, 331 64 28: Nikolai Iurasov's letters to Anton, 1898–1904.

47 See *OR*, 331 38 14: Olga Vasilieva's ninety-seven letters to Anton, 1898–1904.

48 See *OR*, 331 92 56: Adolf Levitan's letter, enclosing the request, to Masha.

49 See *OR*, 331 48 7: Vera Komissarzhevskaia's letters to Anton, 1896–1904: 1 Aug. 1900.

50 See *OR*, 331 77 14: Olga Knipper's letters to Masha, 1900: 9 Aug.

51 See *PSSP*, 9, 365.

52 See *PSSP*, 9, 381: Nemirovich-Danchenko, after Olga's mother, was in the second week of August 1900, the first to be told.

53 See *OR*, 331 33 126: Evgenia's letters to Anton, 1875–1904: 26 Sept. 1900.

54 Cut from *Perepiska*, 1934: see *OR*, 331 76 5: Olga's letters to Anton, Sept. 1900.

55 See *LN68*, 621–8, memoirs of Sergeenko's son.

56 Two months later the department store Muir and Mirrielees burnt down in Moscow. (Anton remarked to Tania Shchepkina-Kupernik in 1899 that to get rid of women playwrights one should invite them to Muir and Mirrielees and burn it down.) Fires in Yalta and Moscow inspired the fire in *Three Sisters*.

57 See S. M. Chekhov, *O semie*, Iaroslavl, 1970, 196–8.

58 See *Vokrug Chekhova*, 357 (Maria Chekhova's memoirs).

59 See *OR*, 331 105 3: Masha's letters to Olga Knipper, 1901: 3 Jan.

60 Kovalevsky's memoirs of Anton Chekhov are in *Vokrug Chekhova*, 361–6.

61 See *RGALI*, 459 2 1233: Nikolai Ezhov's four letters to Suvorin, 1897–1901.
62 See Smirnova-Sazonova's diary, *LN87*, 311–12.
63 Partially cut from *Perepiska* 1934; see *OR*, 331 76 9: Olga's letters to Anton, Feb. 1901.
64 Cut from *Perepiska*, 1934; see *OR*, 331 76 10: Olga's letters to Anton, Mar. 1901.
65 See *OR*, 331 59 46: Anna Suvorina's letters to Anton, 1889–1901: Apr. 1901.
66 See S. M. Chekhov, *O semie*, 1970, 212–13.
67 See *OR*, 429 3 12: Masha's letters to Bunin, 1901–3: 8 Mar. 1901.
68 When this poor little rich girl is mentioned in Anton's correspondence with Olga Knipper, his tone is so casual that it would seem that Vasilieva was not the shadow between them. Had Marusia been Anton's child – and I believe she was not – it would be unlikely for a man of Anton's circle not to acknowledge the fact.
69 Olga's account conflicts with what Nemirovich-Danchenko told Stanislavsky, see fn. 52.
70 See *RGALI*, 549 1 49: Shchurovsky's scribbled notes, a mix of abbreviated Russian, Latin and German, on two sides of a sheet of paper, will need further deciphering.
71 Not in *Knipper-Chekhova*, 1972, II; see *OR*, 331 77 15: Olga's letters to Masha, 1901: 18 May.
72 See *OR*, 331 79 25: Masha's letters to Anton, 1901: the *Pis'ma*, 1954 text is almost complete.
73 Maria Sergeenko claimed that before the wedding Anton, drinking with friends, deplored men who married actresses, and left saying that he had 'a little business to attend to'. (See *LN87*, 348.) On that day Anton had a demented plea for a meeting from a teenager Olga L. (See *OR*, 331 49 3.)
74 Olga, as a Lutheran marrying an Orthodox, risked expulsion from her community. 'At Mama's concert our Ober-pastor twice told me off for marrying, so that I was quite frightened. He said that their church cannot leave the matter unpunished ... I shall threaten to convert to Orthodoxy.' Cut from *Perepiska*, 1934; see *OR*, 331 76 15: Olga's letters to Anton, Nov. 1901: 30 Nov.
75 Cut in *Knipper-Chekhova*, 1972, II, 20–4: see *OR*, 331 77 15: Olga's letters to Masha, 1901.

PART X *Love and Death*

1 Anna Chokhova, of whom Olga knew only dimly, had brought her consumptive son.
2 See *OR*, 331 77 15: Olga's letters to Masha, 1901: 2 June 1901.
3 Partly cut in *Knipper-Chekhova*, 1972; see *OR*, 331 105 3: Masha's letters to Olga, 1901.
4 See *OR*, 429 3 12: Masha's letters to Bunin, 1901–3: 6 June 1901.
5 See *OR*, 331 77 10: Olga's letters to Evgenia Chekhova, 1900–2.
6 See *OR*, 331 42 46b: Maria Drozdova's letters to Anton, 1900–4.
7 See *OR*, 331 73: A. S. Suvorin's letters to Misha, 1890–1902: 10 June 1901.
8 See *RGALI*, 2540 1 483: Masha's letters to Misha, 1884–1904: 11 Aug. 1901.
9 See *OR*, 331 38 8: Dr Varavka's letters to Anton, 1901; 331 36 54: A. Bernshtein's, 1901–3.
10 Quoted in *PSSP*, 10, 322.

11 Cut in *Perepiska*, 1934; see *OR*, 331 76 12: Olga's letters to Masha, August 1901: 30 Aug.

12 If Lazarevsky is telling the truth, this belies the love letter that Avilova claims Anton wrote her on his wedding day.

13 Olga Vasilieva seemed to offer no threat: Knipper's mother was giving her singing lessons.

14 Maria Andreeva complained to Stanislavsky of Nemirovich-Danchenko and Knipper's 'close relationship'.

15 She and Evgenia each had a secret monthly 35 roubles from Suvorin, paid via Misha.

16 See *RGALI*, 2540 1 483: Masha's letters to Misha, 1884–1904: 6 Oct. 1901.

17 See A. Goldenveizer, *Vstrecha s Chekhovym* in *Teatral'naia zhizn'*, 1960, 2, 18.

18 Illness was all around. Anton was a governor of Yalta's sanatorium, gruesomely named Yavuzlar (*The Inexorable Ones*) for indigent consumptives.

19 See *V vospominaniiakh*, 698.

20 See *PSSP*, 10, 452.

21 Cut from *Perepiska*, 1934: see *OR*, 331 76 16–18: Olga's letters to Anton, Dec. 1901–Jan. 1902.

22 See *PSSP*, 10, 447, 459.

23 Cut from *Perepiska*, 1934: see *OR*, 331 76 17: Olga's letters to Anton, 1–16 Jan. 1902.

24 See *RGALI*, 2540 1 483: Masha's letters to Misha, 1884–1904: 21 Jan. 1902.

25 Morozov begged Anton to take a share too; he secured Anton's consent by undertaking to recover as investment the 5000 roubles that was owed by Konshin for Melikhovo.

26 See *PSSP*, 10, 454, 462.

27 He distrusted radicals, too, after placing in the Yavuzlar sanatorium a 'medical student' called Grinevich, who had died of a twisted gut before the inmates could lynch him as a police spy.

28 Cut from *Perepiska*, 1934; see *OR*, 331 76 20: Olga's letters to Anton, 1–15 Mar. 1902: 8 Mar.

29 See *OR*, 331 105 4: Masha's letters to Olga, 1902.

30 See *OR*, 331 82 62: Misha's letters to Masha, 1902: 30 Mar. 1902.

31 In contrast, Lika Mizinova visited Misha's family and they had a 'most amusing excellent evening'. Misha ended this letter by asking Masha to extract 5 or 6000 roubles from Anton to build a dacha, where Anton could spend the summer fishing and Misha eventually retire.

32 Cut from *Perepiska*, 1934; see *OR*, 331 76 21: Olga's letters to Anton, 16–31 Mar. 1902: 31 Mar.

33 Cut from *Perepiska*, 1934; see *OR*, 331 76 22: Olga's letters to Anton, Apr. 1902: 4 Apr.

34 See *OR*, 331 77 16: Olga's letters to Masha, 1902: 6 Apr. 1902.

35 For this tentative diagnosis I am grateful to Dr Pavel Houris of Corfu and Sister Jane Kondou.

36 Franzensbad was the Suvorins' favourite watering hole.

37 See *PSSP*, 10, 522.

38 See *PSSP*, 11, 361.

39 See *OR*, 331 48 79a: Olga Kundasova's letters to Anton 1892–1904.

40 See *V vospominaniiakh*, 583–96.

41 See *OR*, 331 77 10: Olga's letters to Evgenia Chekhova, 1900–2: 24 June 1902.

42 See Harvey Pitcher, *Lily: An Anglo-Russian Romance*, Cromer, 1987; see *OR*, 331 59 2: Lily Glassby's letters to Anton, 1902.

43 See *OR*, 429 3 12: Masha's letters to Bunin, 1901–3: 5 Aug. 1902.

44 See *OR*, 331 105 4: Masha's letters to Olga, 1902: 17 Aug.

45 See *OR*, 331 77 16: Olga's letters to Masha, 1902: 24 Aug. 1902.

46 See *Perepiska*, 1936, 369–71.

47 Only Chekhov, Korolenko and a mathematician, Markov, resigned over Gorky.

48 Meyerhold blamed Knipper for alienating him from Chekhov.

49 Suvorin did not come, but began sending Chekhov copies of the forbidden revolutionary newspaper *Liberation*, which Suvorin coded as 'works of Ezhov'.

50 Cut from *Knipper-Chekhova*, 1972; see *OR*, 331 76 27: Olga's letters to Anton, Dec. 1902.

51 Cut from *Knipper-Chekhova*, 1972; see *OR*, 331 76 31: Olga's letters to Anton ii 1903.

52 See *PSSP*, 11, 442.

53 See *OR*, 331 81 66: Evgenia's letters to Masha, 1891–1914: 20 Jan. 1903.

54 For a fuller account of the genesis of *The Cherry Orchard* see the author's *The Cherry Orchard: Catastrophe and Comedy*, New York, Twayne, 1994.

55 See *OR*, 331 59 80: Aleksandr Sumbatov's letters to Anton, 1889–1903: 12 Feb. 1903.

56 At this juncture Anton was receiving many confessions from unhappily married friends: he had a desperate letter from his old admirer Shcheglov, whose wife had betrayed him for years. See *OR*, 331 50 6i: Ivan Leontiev-Shcheglov's letters to Anton, 1900–4.

57 See *PSSP*, 11, 470.

58 See *MXaT*, 5323/44–62: Sanin's letters to Lika, 1903: 16 May.

59 See *OR*, 331 82 62: Misha's letters to Masha, 1902–4: 6 June 1903.

60 See *OR*, 331 82 62: Misha's letters to Masha, 1902–4: 8 June 1903.

61 See *PSSP*, 11, 542, and Gitovich, *Letopis'*, 758.

62 See Gitovich, *Letopis'*, 758–9.

63 See *LN87*, 319–56.

64 Cut from *Pis'ma*, 1939: see *OR*, 331 32 27: Aleksandr's letters to Anton, 1903.

65 See *PSSP*, 11, 562.

66 See *V vospominaniiakh*, 597–9.

67 See *PSSP*, XIII, 497.

68 See *PSSP*, 11, 598.

69 See *RGALI*, 2540 1 160: Evgenia's letters to Vania, 1888–1905: 27 Oct. 1903.

70 Cut from *Knipper-Chekhova*, 1972: see *OR*, 331 77 4: Olga's letters to Anton, 1–16 Nov. 1903.

71 Tania Shchepkina-Kupernik's memoirs record an almost identical scene.

72 See *MXaT*, 5323/44–62: Sanin's letters to Lika, 1903: 14 Dec.

73 See *OR*, 331 77 11: Olga's letters to Evgenia, 1903–4: 29 Dec. 1903.

74 There was reason to let Andreeva go: she had been denouncing Knipper and Nemirovich-Danchenko to Stanislavsky; she was fainting on stage; Gorky had fallen in love with her (while everyone felt for Gorky's wife, who had TB); Andreeva's husband was accused of embezzling. (In 1905 Andreeva was reinstated. Her career as a Bolshevik and as Gorky's consort was assured.)

75 Cut from *Knipper-Chekhova*, 1972: see *OR*, 331 77 6: Olga's letters to Anton, 15–29 Feb. 1904.

76 This mad desire to cross Siberia again was stimulated by new grounds for jealousy. Olga casually mentioned on 16 March that she had met her first love, the mill-owner Dimitri Goncharov, and that, despite his illness, he

wanted to act with her in the
Moscow Arts Theatre.

77 Cut from *Knipper-Chekova*, 1972:
see *OR*, 331 77 8: Olga's letters to
Anton, Apr. 1904: 15 Apr. Anton
hints at relations with Krestovskaia
in his letter to Suvorin from a
Blagoveshchensk brothel.

78 See *OR*, 331 79 31: Masha's letters
to Evgenia, 1903–14: 9 May 1904.

79 See *OR*, 331 77 18: Olga's letters
to Masha, 1904: 22 May.

80 See *RGALI*, 2540 1 483: Masha's
letters to Misha, 1884–1904: 27
May 1904.

81 See *PSSP*, 12, 353.

82 See *PSSP*, 367, 374, 377.

83 I am grateful to M. A. Sheikina for
this information.

84 See *OR*, 331 66 78–124: telegrams
to Olga Knipper-Chekhova, July
1904.

85 See *Pis'ma A. S. Suvorina k V. V.
Rozanovu*, SPb, 1913, 10. For a
fuller account of that morning, see
A. Rostovtsev, 'Pamiati Chekhova'
in *Obozrenie teatra*, 2–7 July 1914.

86 See *RGALI*, 2540 1 478:
Aleksandr's letters to Misha,
1883–1904: 4 July 1904.

87 See *LN68*, 618–9.

88 In 1909 Suvorin's *Istoricheskii
vestnik* published a scandalous and
venomous exposé by Ezhov which
portrayed Chekhov as a conceited
mediocrity.

89 See Shcheglov's diary, which,
however, found her *Cherry Orchard*
'could have been more
entertaining' (*LN68*, 486).

90 See *OR*, 331 79 13: documents on
the Chekhov inheritance.

91 See *RGALI*, 2540 1 150:
Aleksandr's letters to Vania,
1898–1905: 9 Sept. 1904.

92 See *RGALI*, 2540 1 478:
Aleksandr's letters to Misha,
1883–1904: 9 Sept. 1904.

93 After Bunin left, Masha had a
flirtation, which ended in 1912, with
Baron Stuart, the purchaser of
Melikhovo; Aleksandr Smagin pined
all his life for her.

94 See *RGALI*, 5459 1 402:
Aleksandr's letters to Natalia,
1908: 5 Nov.

95 In 1939, with uncharacteristic
liberalism, the Soviet state
published Aleksandr's letters to
Anton, and his wayward genius was
recognized. See his son's memoirs
in M. A. Chekhov, 1986.

96 See *OR*, 331 77 18+ and 331 105
7+: Masha's and Olga's fifty-year
correspondence after Anton's death
is a little known mine of
biographical and historical
material.

97 See *OR*, 331 84 38: Nikolai
Aleksandrovich Chekhov's
notebooks.

98 In the mid 1930s a woman,
apparently his wife, wrote to Masha
from a prison camp. Masha hid the
letter behind a stove; in the 1940s,
when it was found by a secretary,
Masha destroyed it.

99 See Vladimir Knipper, *Pora
galliutsinatsii*, 1995. Olga
Tschechowa's daughter 'proved'
her Aryan blood by sending to
Sumy, under German occupation,
for her grandmother, Natalia
Golden's, wedding certificate,
where Jewishness was not
mentioned.

100 Her obituary, as Princess
Bariatinsky, is in *The Times*, 5 Sept.
1921.

SELECT BIBLIOGRAPHY

Works I have found particularly useful are asterisked. All quotations are translated from the standard edition of complete works and letters. Place of publication is Moscow unless indicated.

Chekhov's writings

IN RUSSIAN

*A. P. Chekhov, *Polnoe sobranie sochinenii i pisem* (*PSSP*): 1–18, works [referred to as *I–XVIII*]; 1–12 (+ indices), letters [referred to as *1–12*], 1973–83.

Some items missing from *PSSP* can be found in:

A. B. Derman, ed., *A. P. Chekhov Sbornik dokumentov* . . . , 1947 [inc. student post-mortem report].

A. P. Chudakov, ' "Neprilichnye slova" i oblik klassika' in *Literaturnoe Obozrenie*, 1991, 11, 54.

'Podtsenzurnyi Chekhov' in *Kuranty*, 8 Sept., 1993, 9 [lists some cuts in *PSSP* 1–4].

L. Shcheglov [allegedly after Chekhov], *Sila gipnotizma* in *Zhizn' vverkh nogami*, SPb, 1911.

IN ENGLISH

Michael Frayn (tr.), *Chekhov: Plays*, London, 1993 [actable versions of the mature plays].

Constance Garnett (tr.), (revised D. Rayfield) *The Chekhov Omnibus*, London, 1994 [classic selection of prose fiction].

Ronald Hingley (tr.), *The Oxford Chekhov* (complete mature works) 9 vols, 1972.

Gordon McVay (tr.), *Chekhov: A Life in Letters*, Folio Society, London, 1974 [best selection].

Donald Rayfield, 'Sanitising the Classics' in *Comparative Criticism* 16, Cambridge, 1994, 19–32.

Brian Reeves (tr.), *The Island of Sakhalin*, London, 1993.

Bibliographical and reference works

*N. I. Gitovich, *Letopis' zhizni i tvorchestva A. P. Chekhova*, 1955
[fundamental; much is unique, some inaccurate: a new chronicle is imminent].
*E. E. Leitnekker, *Arkhiv A. P. Chekhov*, 1939 [a full catalogue of letters
to Anton in the *Otdel rukopisei* archive as of 1939. Excludes family
correspondence: now outdated].
*I. F. Masanov, *Chekhoviana: sistematicheski ukazatel'*, 1930 [a list of 2766
publications on Chekhov, nearly complete up to, 1929; supplements
Gitovich].
I. Iu. Tverdokhliobov, 'Novye daty' in *Chekhoviana*, 1990, 213–25.
*P. A. Nikolaev, *Russkie pisateli 1800–1917*, A–M 3 vols, 1992–5 [standard
reference to Chekhov's contemporaries].
A. P. Chekhov Dokumenty, fotografii, 1984 [best pictorial record].
A. P. Chekhov: Materialy . . . pushkinskogo doma, Leningrad, 1982 [mostly
pictorial].
A. P. Chekhov: rukopisi, pis'ma, biograficheskie dokumenty: opisanie materialov,
TsGALI, 1960.

Letters to Anton

ALEKSANDR CHEKHOV
*I. S. Ezhov, *Pis'ma A. P. Chekhovu ego brata Aleksandra Pavlovicha*, 1939
[nearly complete, but Rabelaisian passages and Tsarist sentiments cut].

MASHA CHEKHOVA
*M. P. Chekhova, *Pis'ma k bratu A. P. Chekhovu*, 1954 (*Pis'ma*, 1954) [fairly
complete, well annotated].

OLGA KNIPPER-CHEKHOVA
*A. P. Derman, *Perepiska A. P. Chekhova i O. L. Knipper*, 1934, 1936 [2 vols,
up to 10 Oct., 1902. 90 per cent complete, cut by Olga Knipper].
A. V. Khanilo, 'Iz pisem M. P. Chekhovoi k O. L. Knipper-Chekhovoi' in
Chekhovskie chteniia v Ialte, 1993 [extracts 1904–45].
V. Ia. Vilenkin, *Olga Leonardovna Knipper-Chekhova*, 1972 [2 vols. Vol. 1:
correspondence 1896–1959; vol. 2: letters to Anton Nov., 1902–4; very
selective and heavily cut].

ISAAK LEVITAN
*A. Fiodorov-Davydov, A. Shapiro, *I. I. Levitan: Pis'ma, dokumenty,
vospominaniia*, 1956 [full, but bowdlerized: 1966 edition has more
information].

MENSHIKOV
Zapiski GBL VIII, 1941.

VL. I. NEMIROVICH-DANCHENKO
Ezhegodnik MKhaTa, 1944, vol. 1.
Vl. I. Nemirovich-Danchenko, *Teatral'noe nasledie*, 1954, II, 144.

PAVEL SVOBODIN
Zapiski Otdela rukopisei Gosudarstvennoi Bibliotèki Lenina, 16, 1954 [about 50 per cent complete].

FATHER UNDOLSKY
A. M. Melkova, 'Novye materialy . . .', in *Chekhovskie chteniia v Ialte*, 1987, 108–25.

COMPILATIONS
Chekhovskie chteniia v Ialte, 1973, 154–78 [Masha and Misha Chekhov, Sergeenko: in articles by A. M. Melkova, S. M. Chekhov].
Slovo: sbornik vtoroi, 1914, 199–289 [Grigorovich, Mikhailovsky, Tchaikovsky, Soloviov, Polonsky, Pleshcheev, Urusov].

Zapiski OR GBL 8, 1941 [letters to Masha from Evgenia, Aleksandr].
*M. P. Gromova et al., *Perepiska Chekhova*, 1996, 3 vols. (expanded from *Perepiska* I, II, 1984) [Leikin, Grigorovich, Pleshcheev, Svobodin, Lavrov, Mizinova, Potapenko, Shchepkina-Kupernik, Komissarzhevskaia, V. Nemirovich-Danchenko, Stanislavsky, Gorky, Bunin, Knipper].
E. N. Konshina, *Iz arkhiva Chekhova, Otdel ruk.*, 1960 [inc. duller letters from various Drs (Valter, Diakonov), Diagilev etc.].
M. V. Teplinskii, '. . . o sakhalinskom puteshestvii . . .' in *A. P. Chekhov: sbornik statei Iuzhno-Sakhalinsk*, 1959 [includes letters from Bulgarevich and Feldman].

Writings of Chekhov's relatives and contemporaries

IVAN BUNIN
I. A. Bunin, *O Chekhove*, New York, 1955 [memoir, biography, and critique: trusts Avilova].

PAVEL CHEKHOV
*A. P. Kuzicheva, E. M. Sakharova, *Melikhovskii letopisets: Dnevnik P. E. Chekhova*, 1995 [Pavel's Melikhovo diary, complete, well illustrated and indexed].
Vstrechi s proshlym 4, 1987, 43–80 [Pavel's letters to Vania, 4 Oct. 1890–3 May 1891].

VANIA (IVAN) CHEKHOV
M. A. Sheikina, 'Teper' . . . (Iz pisem I. P. Chekhova k S. V. Ch-oi)', in *Chekhoviana*, 1995, 315–27.

MASHA CHEKHOVA
Iz daliokogo proshlogo (recorded by N. A. Sysoev), 1960 [the fullest text of Masha's memoirs].

MISHA CHEKHOV
Sergei Mikhailovich Chekhov, *O semie*, Iaroslavl, 1970 [a turgid but thorough documentation of Mikhail's years in Iaroslavl 1894–1901].

MIKHAIL ALEKSANDROVICH CHEKHOV
Literaturnoe nasledie, 1986, 2 vols [vol. 1 includes memoirs and letters].

COMPILATIONS
Solntse Rossii, SPb, 1914, 25 June [a selection of minor memoirs, some never reprinted].
*Vokrug Chekhova (comp. E. M. Sakharova), 1990 [siblings', widow's, nephews' and niece's memoirs; well annotated].
Khoziaika chekhovskogo doma, Simferopol, 1969 [Masha's memories recorded by S. M. Chekhov; memoirs of Masha by Marinetta Shaginian, M. A. Sofiiskaia; Masha's letters to and from Bunin, A. V. Sredin].
*Chekhov v vospominaniiakh sovremennikov (comp. N. I. Gitovich), 1986 [non-family memoirs; authoritative and well annotated; previous editions, 1947, 1954 and 1960 are inferior, but have some different material].
Iz shkol'nykh let Anton Chekhova, 1962 [inc. many Taganrog memoirs: Dolzhenko, Volkenshtein, Tan, Drossi, Vishnevsky].
*Literaturnoe nasledstvo 68: Chekhov (ed. V. V. Vinogradov), 1960 [vast compendium of diaries, letters etc.].
*Literaturnoe nasledstvo 87: Iz istorii russkoi literatury . . . (ed V. R. Shcherbina), 1977 [Sakhalin material, log of Peterburg, diaries of Smirnova-Sazonova and Lazarevsky].
M. D. Beliaev . . . *A. P. Chekhov: Novye vospominaiia*, Leningrad, 1925 [inc. Anna Suvorina's memoirs].
I. M. Sel'vaniuk, *Sbornik statei i materialov 3*, Rostov, 1963 [inc. Elena Shavrova's memoirs].

Biographies and biographical material

BOOKS AND BOOK-LENGTH ARTICLES IN RUSSIAN

E. Balabanovich Dom, *A. P. Chekhova v Moskve*, 1958 [a study of the Korneev house].

E. Balabanovich, *Chekhov i Chaikovskii*, 1973.

*S. Balukhatyi, 'Bibliotèka Chekhova' in *Chekhov i ego sreda*, Leningrad, 1930, 210–418 [a primary but incomplete source on what Chekhov read].

G. Berdnikov, *Chekhov*, 1974 [the best of the Soviet biographies].

Iu. A. Bychkov, *Techenie Melikhovskoi zhizni*, 1989 [illustrations of Melikhovo better than text].

Maria i Mikhail Chekhovy, *Dom-muzei A. P. Chekhova*, 1937 [an inventory of the Yalta house].

A. P. Chudakov, *Anton Pavlovich Chekhov*, 1987 [for children; excellent on early years].

E. A. Dinershtein, *Chekhov i ego izdateli*, 1990 [good on Leikin and Marx, poor on Suvorin].

*P. P. Filevskii, *Ocherki iz proshlogo Taganrogskoi Gimnazii*, Taganrog, 1906.

I. Geizer, *Chekhov i meditsina*, 1960 [uninformative, except for frontispiece].

M. Gromov, *Chekhov*, 1993 [integrated critical and biographical study].

A. V. Kandidov, *A. P. Chekhov v Bogimove*, Kaluga, 1991.

A. V. Khanilo, *Pometki na knigakh Chekhova*, Berlin, 1994 [supplements Balukhaty, inc. forensic study of Chekhov's underlinings].

*Vladimir Knipper, *Pora galliutsinatsii*, 1995 [a biography of the Knipper-Chekhov descendants].

V. F. Komissarzhevskaia [. . .] Materialy, Leningrad-Moscow, 1964.

*A. P. Kuzicheva, *Vash Chekhov*, 1994 [chronicle of last Melikhovo years, 1895–8].

L. Maliugin, I. Gitovich, *Chekhov: povest'-khronika*, 1983 [told as fiction].

E. Meve, *Meditsina v tvorchestve A. P. Chekhova*, Kiev, 1989 [uninformative].

Grigori Moskvich, *Putevoditel' po Kavkazu*, SPb, 1911.

Vl. I. Nemirovich-Danchenko, *Rozhdenie teatra*, 1989 [unexpurgated version of memoirs].

A. Roskin, *Antosha Chekhonte*, 1940 [for children, but new archival material on young Chekhov].

*Vl. Rynkevich, *Puteshestvie k domu s mezoninom*, Rostov, 1990 [a study of Lika Mizinova].

P. A. Sapukhin, *A. P. Chekhov na Sumshchine*, Sumy, 1993 [despite errors, unique material].

Ilia Sats, *Iz zapisnoi knizhki*, Moscow-Petrograd, 1923.
M. Semanova, *Chekhov v shkole*. Leningrad, 1954.
Iu. Sobolev, *Chekhov*, 1934.
T. L. Sukhotina-Tolstaia, *Dnevniki*, 1979.
A. S. Suvorin, *Pis'ma A. S. Suvorina k V. V. Rozanovu*, SPb, 1913, 10.
*A. S. Suvorin, *Dnevnik*, 1992 [reprint of 1923 edition, despite Roskina transcription in RGALI].
A. S. [Suvorin], *Pis'ma russkikh pisatelei k Suvorinu*, Leningrad, 1927 [inc. Grigorovich, Leskov, Pleshcheev].
M. Turovskaia, *O. L. Knipper-Chekhova*, 1959 [sparse on early years].
I. P. Viduètskaia, *A. P. Chekhov i ego izdatel' A. F. Marks*, 1977.
Boris Zaitsev, *Chekhov*, New York, 1954.

ARTICLES

L. Z. Abramenkova, 'Sosed Chekhovykh V. N. Semenkovich' in *Chekhoviana*, 1995, 255–64.
A. Ia. Al'tshuller, 'A. P. Chekhov i L. B. Iavorskaia' in *Chekhoviana*, 1990, 140–51.
[Semion Bychkov] *Kavkazskii krai*, Krasnodar, 1913, No. 145.
K. A. Chaikovskaia, 'Melikhovskie pozhary' in *Chekhoviana*, 1995, 264–77.
G. V. Chermenskaia, 'Ia iskusil ... (Chekhov i N. M. Ezhov)' in *Chekhoviana*, 1995, 278–314.
D. M. Evseev, 'Progulki po chekhovskoi Moskve' in *Chekhoviana*, 1993, 244–55 [guide to Moscow buildings associated with Chekhov].
*N. M. Ezhov, 'A. P. Chekhov' in *Istoricheskii vestnik*, 1909, 11, 595–607.
N. M. Ezhov, 'Aleksei Sergeevich Suvorin, Moi vospominaniia o niom, dumy i soobrazhenia' in *Istoricheskii vestnik*, SPb, 1915, 1, 110–38.
A. Goldenveizer, 'Vstrecha s Chekhovym' in *Teatral'naia zhizn'*, 1960, 2, 18.
*V. Lakshin, 'Proval' in *Teatr*, 1987, 4, 83–91 [on suicide of Suvorin's son].
Z. G. Livitskaia, 'Iz ialtinskogo okruzheniia' in *Chekhovskie chteniia v Ialte*, 1993, 129–36 [Kharkeevich, Shapovalov].
A. S. Melkova, 'Vesna 1899' in *Chekhovskie chteniia v Ialte*, 1993, 121–8 [Ternovskaia, Beaunier].
E. A. Polotskaia, 'Ialtinskaia redaktsia "Shutochki"' in *Chekhoviana*, 1993.
N. V. Reformatskaia, 'Rasskazhi pro Diaiu Sashu ...' in *Chekhoviana*, 1993, 90–8.
O. Ia. Remez, 'Vizitnaia kartochka Epikhodova' in *Chekhoviana*, 1990, 167–81 [Liubimovka setting].
*N. A. Roskina, 'Ob odnoi staroi publikatsii' in *Voprosy literatury*, 1968, 6,

250–3; *'Dnevnik Suvorina . . .' in *Novoe literaturnoe obozrenie*, 15 (1995), 130–73 [on cuts in Suvorin diary].
*L. M. Sadygi, 'Chernil'nitsa . . . Avilova' in *Chekhoviana*, 1993, 190–237 [merciless to Avilova].
*E. M. Sakharova, 'A. I. Ivanenko' in *Chekhoviana*, 1995, 327–34.
E. M. Sakharova, 'Vash A. Chekhov . . .' in *Chekhoviana*, 1993, 76–90 [on 'Uncle' Sasha Salz].
*M. Semanova, 'Teatral'nye vpechatleniia' in *Sbornik statei i materialov*, Rostov, 1960, 157–84.
G. Shaliugin, 'Ia i moi voennye sputniki' in *Oktiabr'*, 1987, 5, 195–201 [on Lt. I. Ia. Schmidt].
G. Shaliugin, 'Uchitel' slovesnosti' in *Chekhoviana*, 1990, 124–9 [on Suvorin link with story].

BOOKS IN ENGLISH

Ronald Hingley, *A New Life of Anton Chekhov*, London, 1976.
Virginia Llewellyn-Smith, *Chekhov and the Lady with the Little Dog*, Oxford, 1973.
*Carolina de Maegd-Soëp, *Chekhov and Women*, Ohio, 1987 [archival research in 1960s].
Harvey Pitcher, *Chekhov's Leading Lady, Olga Knipper*, London, 1979.
Harvey Pitcher, *Lily: An Anglo-Russian Romance*, Cromer, 1987.
*V. S. Pritchett, *Chekhov. A Spirit Set Free*, London, 1988 [a very perceptive biography].

OTHER MATERIAL
Krym: Putevoditel', Simferopol, 1914.
N. M. Kulagin, N. V. Petrov, *Moskovskii zoologicheskii sad*, 1895 [full catalogue of Moscow zoo].
R.-D. Kluge, ed., *Anton P. Čechov: Werk und Wirkung*, Wiesbaden, 1990 (2 vols) [some biography among critiques, in various languages].
Grigori Moskvich, *Putevoditel' po Kavkazu*, SPb, 1911.
F. S. Stulli, *Moia zhenit'ba* in *Vestnik Evropy*, 1885, 10, 571–620; 11, 104–44 [fiction on Taganrog material].

ARCHIVE MATERIAL (this is a list of only the most fruitful sources)

MKhaT	Moscow Arts Theatre Museum Archive
OR	Manuscript section of Russian State Library
RGALI	Russian State Archive for Literature and Art

JNPUBLISHED DOCUMENTS BY ANTON

OR

331 70 49	Full text of Anton's letter to Nikolai March 1886.

RGALI

549 1 10	Chekhov's case notes on Bulychiov, with a commentary (c. 1920) by Dr Rossolimo.
594 1 269	Full text of Anton's letter to Aleksandr 2 Jan. 1889.

MEMOIRS OF ANTON

RGALI

189 1 2	Ezhov's draft Iumoristy 1880ykh godov.
540 1 382	Zelenenko, Vospominaniia o Taganrogskoi gimnazii typescript.
549 1 49	Dr Shchurovsky's notes after examining Chekhov 17 May 1901.
549 1 329	A. Lazarev-Gruzinsky [full ms].
549 1 350	Dr P. G. Rozanov, Chekhov v 8okh godakh.
549 1 352	El. (Lily) K. Markova-Sakharova.
549 1 354	N. G. Serpovskii [Babkino].
549 3 1	Nina Markova.
860 1 576	M. I. Il'kov, typescript.
860 1 580	P. I. Messarosh [Taganrog 1870s].

LETTERS TO ANTON FROM FAMILY (all in Otdel rukopisei, Russian State Library)

331 32 1–32	Aleksandr's letters to Anton, 1874–1904.
331 33 50	Georgi Chekhov's letters to Anton, 1888.
331 33 51	Georgi Chekhov's letters to Anton, 1897.
331 33 14	Natalia Golden's letters to Anton, 18 Nov. 1888– 1904.
331 33 126	Evgenia's 20 letters to Anton, 1876–1904.
331 46 33	Anna Ipatieva-Golden's letter to Anton, 25 Sept. 1891.
331 52 29	Marfa Ivanovna Loboda-Morozova's letters to Anton, 1881–1902.
331 62 27	Natalia to Anton, 1885.
331 81 18	Pavel's letters to Anton, 1876–8.
331 81 20	Pavel's letters to Anton, 1879.
331 81 21	Pavel's letters to Anton, 1886–95.
331 81 32	Pavel Chekhov's letter to Anna Ipatieva-Golden.
331 81 80	Mitrofan's letters to Anton, 1879–94.
331 82 2	Aleksandr's letters to Masha, 1883–7.
331 82 10	Anna Sokolnikova's letters to Aleksandr.

331 82 12	A. I. Khrushchiova-Sokolnikova, *née* Aleksandrova, documents.
331 82 20	Nikolai Chekhov's letters to Anton, 1876–9.
331 82 21	Nikolai's letters to Anton, 1883–9.

OTHER CHEKHOV FAMILY CORRESPONDENCE
OR

331 31 1	Aleksandr's letters to his parents from 1874–96.
331 33 IV	Pavel Chekhov, various documents.
331 33 12a	Evgenia's letter to Aleksandr and Nikolai Chekhov.
331 33 125	Evgenia's letters to Pavel Chekhov, 1876–90.
331 34 1	Family letters to Mitrofan Egorovich Chekhov.
331 73 10	Pavel's letter to Misha, 11 Aug. 1885.
331 77 10	Olga's letters to Evgenia Chekhova, 1900–2.
331 77 13+	Olga's letters to Masha, 1899+.
331 81 8	Pavel's notebooks, 1880–97.
331 81 11	Pavel's letters to his wife and children, 1876–90.
331 81 12	Pavel's letters to Evgenia, 1876, –84, –91.
331 81 13	Pavel's letters to Aleksandr Chekhov, 1874–94.
331 81 15–6	Pavel to Nikolai Chekhov, 1880–3.
331 81 24	Pavel's letters to Maria Chekhova, 1885–98.
331 81 25	Pavel's letters to Mitrofan and Liudmila, 1876–93.
331 81 66	Evgenia's letters to Masha, 1891–1914.
331 81 71	Mitrofan's letters to Pavel Chekhov, 1876–80.
331 81 83	Fenichka Dolzhenko's letter to Evgenia, 9 July 1891.
331 82 2	Aleksandr's letters to Maria Chekhova, 1883–7.
331 82 4	Aleksandr's letters to Masha, 1890–8.
331 82 9	Anna Sokolnikova's letter to Evgenia Chekhova, 20 Jan. 1888.
331 82 14	Nikolai Chekhov's letters to his parents, 1875–90.
331 82 15	Nikolai's letters to Pavel Chekhov, 1879–84.
331 82 16	Nikolai Chekhov's postcard to Evgenia.
331 82 17	Nikolai's letter to Masha, 1887.
331 82 59–62	Mikhail Chekhov's letters to Masha, 1890–1904.
331 83 25	Misha's 'Chekhov i mangusy'.
331 84 38	Nikolai Aleksandrovich Chekhov's notebooks.
331 105 1+	Masha's letters to Olga.

RGALI

2316 2 35	Aleksandr's *The Rubbish Dump* [*Svalka nechistot*].
2540 1 43	Misha's letters to his parents, 1888–1901.
2540 1 47	Aleksandr's letters to Evgenia, 1892–1906.

2540 1 49	Mikhail's letters to Evgenia, 1888–1904.
2540 1 150	Aleksandr's letters to Ivan Chekhov, 1898–1905.
2540 1 158	Pavel's letters to Ivan Chekhov, 1879–1898.
2540 1 160	Evgenia's letters to Ivan, 1888–1905.
2540 1 161	Masha's letters to Ivan Chekhov, 1890–1908.
2540 1 238–43	[Vania to Sonia].
2540 1 478	Aleksandr's letters to Mikhail Chekhov, 1883–1904.
2540 1 483	Masha's letters to Mikhail Chekhov, 1884–1904.
2540 53 1	Aleksandr's memoirs.
5459 1 402	Aleksandr's letters to Natalia, 1908: 5 Nov.

LETTERS TO ANTON CHEKHOV FROM FRIENDS (*Otdel rukopisei*)

331 35 9	O. and P. Agali's letters to Anton, 1880–1.
331 36 20	Barantsevich's letters to Anton, 1888–1900.
331 36 54	A. Bernshtein, 1901–3.
331 36 72	Emilie Bijon's letters to Anton, 1896–1900.
331 36 75b	Viktor Bilibin's letters to Anton, 1886.
331 37 64	Semion Bychkov's letters to Anton, 1898–9: 3 Jan. 1899.
331 38 8	Dr Varavka's letters to Anton, 1901.
331 38 14	Olga Vasilieva's 97 letters to Anton, 1898–1904.
331 42 54	M. M. Diukovsky's letters to Anton, 1884–93.
331 43 9	Lt Evgraf Egorov's letters to Anton Chekhov, 1882–92.
331 43 11	N. Ezhov's letters to Anton, 1890–1904.
331 46 1a	Aleksandr Ivanenko's letters to Anton, 1889–91: 28 May 1890.
331 47 13	K. A. Karatygina's letters to Anton Chekhov, 1889–1904.
331 47 45	A S. Kiseliov's letters to Anton, 1884–1904.
331 47 48	Maria Kiseliova's letters to Anton, 1886–1900.
331 48 4	Nadia Kolomnina's letters to Anton, 1896–1900.
331 48 79a	O. P. Kundasova's letters to Anton, 1892–1904.
331 48 83	Dr P. I. Kurkin's letters to Anton, 1892–1904.
331 49 42a	A. Lazarev-Gruzinsky's letters to Anton, 1887–8.
331 48 7	Vera Komissarzhevskaia's letters to Anton Chekhov, 1897–1903.
331 48 27	Korneev's letters to Anton, 1886–1894.
331 48 47	Piotr Gavriilovich Kravtsov's letters to Anton, 1879–96.
331 48 49	Solomon Kramariov's letters to Anton, 1881, 1904.
331 49 25	Levitan's letters to Anton, 1885–1900.
331 49 42a	A. Lazarev-Gruzinsky's letters to Anton, 1887–8.
331 50 1a–m	Leikin's letters to Anton, 1882–1900.
331 50 6g	Leontiev-Shcheglov's letters to Anton, 1890.

331 50 11	Aleksandra Liosova's three letters to Anton, 1894.
331 51 12	Klara Mamuna's letter to Anton.
331 51 18	N. Maksheev's letters to Anton, 1897–8.
331 52 2	Lika Mizinova's letters to Anton, 1891–1900.
331 52 46	Daria Musina-Pushkina's letters to Anton, 1891, 1896–8.
331 54 50	Liudmila Groupillon-Ozerova's 8 letters to Anton Chekhov, 1896–7.
331 55 6	Ivan Pavlovsky's letters to Anton, 1894–1904.
331 55 8	Palmin's letters to Anton, 1883–6.
331 55 21	Anisim [Onisim] Petrov's letters to Anton.
331 56 36	Potapenko's letters to Anton, 1893–1903.
331 56 38	A. A. Pokhlebina's letters to Anton, 1892–8.
331 57 24	Rainer Maria Rilke's letter to Anton.
331 58 20	Elizaveta (Lily): Markova-Sakharova's letters to Anton, 1885–90.
331 58 27	P. Svobodin's letters to Anton, 1887–92.
331 58 29	G. P. Selivanov's letters to Anton.
331 58 31	A. L. Selivanova-Krause's letters to Anton, 1887–95.
331 59 2	Lily Glassby's letters to Anton, 1902.
331 59 25	Vasili Sobolevsky's letters to Anton, 1892–1904.
331 59 46	Anna Suvorina's letters to Anton, 1887–1901.
331 59 71	A. A. Suvorin's letter to Anton, 1887–92.
331 59 75	Anastasia Suvorina's letters to Anton, 1889–1900.
331 59 77b	Evgenia Suvorina's letter to Anton.
331 60 24	Nadezhda Ternovskaia's letters to Anton, 1899.
331 60 43	T. Sukhotina-Tolstaia's letters to Anton, 1896–9.
331 60 62	Anna Turchaninova's letters to Anton Chekhov, 1895 and 1900.
331 60 64	Konstantin Tychinkin's 46 letters to Anton, 1896–1902.
331 61 52	Gavriil Kharchenko's letters to Anton, 1899–1901.
331 63 3	E. K. Shavrova's letters to Anton Chekhov, 1889–1900.
331 63 25a	Franz Schechtel's letters to Anton, 1885–6.
331 63 25e	Franz Schechtel's two letters to Nikolai Chekhov.
331 64 2	T. L. Shchepkina-Kupernik's letters to Anton Chekhov, 1893–1900.
331 64 20	Evdokia Efros's three letters to Anton, 1886.
331 60 62	Anna Turchaninova's letters to Anton, 1895, 1900: 20 May, 1900.
331 64 34	Lidia Iavorskaia's letters to Anton Chekhov, 1893–6.
331 64 46a	Maria Ianova's letters to Anton of 1885–6.

331 66 78–124   Telegrams to Olga Knipper, July 1904.
331 92 56   Adolf Levitan's letter to Masha.

OTHER CORRESPONDENCE
MKhaT
(Sanin) 5323   L. S. Mizinova-Sanina's letters to Lidia Iurgeneva.
5323/19   S. M. Ioganson's diary, book 5, 1895–7.
5323/44–62   Sanin's letters to Lika, 1903: 16 May.
5323/, 1933–   L. S. Mizinova's letters to Lidia Iurgeneva and Sofia
1973   Ioganson, 1877–99.
OR
331 73 3   A. S. Suvorin's letters to Misha, 1890–1902.
331 81 38   Pavel Chekhov to G. P. Selivanov.
331 82 25   Nikolai Chekhov's letter to an unidentified Aleksandr
   Viktorovich.
331 93 78–80   Lika Mizinova's letters to Masha Chekhova, 1891–8.
331 96 37–8   Aleksandr Smagin's 34 letters to Masha, 1888–1929.
331 95 2   Potapenko's letters to Masha, 1894–5.
429 3 12   Masha's letters to Bunin, 1901–3.
RGALI
189 1 7, 19   Lazarev-Gruzinsky to Ezhov, 1884–91.
189 1 21   Leikin's letters to Ezhov, 1884–99.
191 1 2400   A. P. Kolomnin obituaries.
289 1 16   N. Ezhov's letters to Leikin, 1894–1903.
289 2 5   N. Ezhov's letters to Leikin, 1889–95.
459 1 1343   N. Ezhov's letters to Suvorin, 1888–1912.
459 1 2161   O. P. Kundasova's letters to A. S. Suvorin, 1891–1908.
459 1 4156   B. A. Suvorin's letters to his father, Suvorin, 1893–1911.
459 1 4172   Nastia Suvorina's letters to her father, Suvorin, 1888–
   1912.
459 1 4850   T. Shchepkina-Kupernik's letters to Suvorin.
459 1 4617   Aleksandr Chekhov's letters to A. S. Suvorin, 1888–96.
459 2 14   A. S. Suvorin's letters to Anna Suvorina.
459 2 138   A. S. Suvorin, drafts of autobiography.
459 2 140 (1–7)   A. S. Suvorin's diaries [part].
459 2 356   A. S. Suvorin's letters to Anna Ivanovna, 1879–1911.
459 2 1233   N. Ezhov's letters to Suvorin, 1897–1901.
459 3 12   Suvorin's drafts of letters.
549 1 408   Masha's letters to Maria Drozdova, 1898–1905.
571 1 344–5   T. Shchepkina-Kupernik's letters to her father, L.
   Kupernik.

571 1 401	T. Shchepkina-Kupernik's letters to Lidia Iavorskaia, 1915.
571 1 1137	Masha's letters to Shchepkina-Kupernik, 1894–1951.
571 1 1204	Lidia Iavorskaia's letters to Shchepkina-Kupernik, 1893.
640 1 189	Svobodin's letters to Lavrov.
675 2 328	Nina Korsh's application to join Drama Union, 1924.
2540 1 143	A. S. Suvorin's letters to Ivan Chekhov, 1891–2.

INDEX

This index includes all persons, places, periodicals and works of literature which are relevant to Anton Chekhov's life and which are mentioned in the main body of the text or the footnotes. Minimal biographical information is given wherever ascertainable. I have also included a number of headings for topics and institutions which recur in the work. Persons are listed under the surname most commonly used for them; in square brackets I list pseudonyms, real, maiden or married names less widely used, and many of these are cross-referenced.

To make it easier for the reader to reconstruct the Cyrillic, the transliteration of Russian names is somewhat fussier than in the main body of the text (´ indicates the 'soft sign', è the 'e oborotnoe') and, to facilitate pronunciation I indicate the stressed syllable of Russian names with an acute accent over the relevant vowel. Russian entries nevertheless follow the English alphabetical order. Works of literature are entered under the heading of the author; Russian names of periodicals and literary works are cross-referenced if not nearly identical with, or in immediate proximity to, the English entry.

Psaltí, Mikhaíl Nikoláevich (journalist) 325, 327
Psiol river 167–8, 172, 174–5, 190, 194, 209–10,323
Pushkarióv, Nikolái Lukích (1842–1906) 68, 83, 90, 107, 253, 477, 571
Pushkarióva, Nadézhda Lukínichna 571
Púshkin, Aleksándr Sergéevich (1799–1837) 18, 149, 155, 372, 483, 505
Putiáta, Nikolái Apollónovich (1851–90) 165, 179, 186–7, 607
Quinine (drug) 196, 475, 554, 592
Quinine [Khína] Márkovna (1892–9, dachshund bitch) 293–4, 307, 319, 345, 358, 371, 413, 419, 474, 490, 492, 494

Rachmáninov, Sergéi Vasílievich (1873–1943) 182
Racine, Jean (1639–99) 218, 311
  Phèdre 217, 311
Radzwícki [Radzvítsky], Dr Piotr Ignátievich (1860–1931, ophthalmologist) 424, 426, 433, 438
Ragózina Gully [Bálka] 59, 65, 69, 153
Razvlechenie, see Amusement
Red Cross 478
Renan, Joseph Ernest (1864–1910) 337
  L'Abbesse de Jouarre 337
Répin, Iliá Efímovich (1844–1930, painter) 182, 187, 286
Reutlinger [Réitlinger], Èdmund Rudól'fovich 28–9, 32, 68
Riazán' 292
Ried [Knípper], Luíza (Olga Knipper's sister-in-law) 512
Riga 292
Rilke, Rainer Maria (1875–1926) 621
Riviera, *see* Côte d'Azur
Robérti, Evgéni Valentínovich [de] (1843–1915, philosopher) 454
Roche, Denis (French translator) 443
Roksánova [Petróvskaia], María Liudomírovna (1874–1958, actress) 479
Román, *see* Postnikov
Románov dynasty 378
Románova, Grand Duchess Ól'ga 532
Románov's restaurant (Petersburg) 397
Rome 203, 244, 265, 525

Rossolímo, Dr Grigóri Ivánovich (1860–1928) 499, 594
Rostand, Edmond (1868–1918, dramatist) 316, 334, 352, 355, 365
  La Princesse lointaine [The Distant Princess] 301, 316, 352, 355, 365–6
  Les Romanesques 334
Rostóv-on-the-Don 6, 66, 412, 476, 589, 605
Rothschild 80
Rózanov, I. (editor of *Le Messager franco-russe*) 440
Rózanov, Dr Pável Grigórievich (1853–after 1934) 106, 108, 121, 123
Rózanov, Vasíli Vasílievich (1856–1919, philosopher) 139, 598, 600, 609, 626
  Ephemera [Mimoliotnoe] 609
Rózanova, Varvára Ivánovna (died after 1934) 123
Rozhdéstvenka 73
Rubins[h]téin, [?] 38
Rubins[h]tein, Antón Grigórievich (1829–94, composer) 164
Rumiántsev Museum (Lenin Library, Russian State Library) xix, 218–19
Russia, hotel in Petersbury 303
Russian Antiquity [Russkaia starina] 349
The Russian Gazette [Russkie vedomosti] 98, 305, 335, 348, 436, 478, 593, 615
The Russian Review [Russkoe obozrenie] 270
Russian Shipping [Russkoe sudokhodstvo] 147
Russian Society of Dramatists and Operatic Composers 159, 193, 408, 509
Russian Thought [Russkaia mysl'] 220, 270, 280, 282, 284, 290, 296, 299, 304–6, 335, 341, 347–8, 360, 375, 380, 402, 414, 418, 425, 431, 437, 460, 478, 486, 501, 588
Russkoe literaturnoe obshchestvo, *see* Society of Russian Writers
Rýkov, Iván Gavrílovich (1829–after 1885, banker) 86, 110–11
Rzhev (town in Tver province) 274
Rzhévskaia, Liubóv' Fiódorovna (head of Rzhevskaia ['Dairy'] school) 142, 207, 254, 272, 300, 409, 494, 510

Sabanéev brothers (chemistry lecturer, and journal editor) 608